Donald Winnicott Today

What in Winnicott's theoretical matrix was truly revolutionary for psychoanalysis? In this book, the editor and contributors provide a rare in-depth analysis of his original work, highlighting the prominence he gave to early psychic development, and how this revolutionised the theory and practice of psychoanalysis.

Including re-publications of selected Winnicott papers to set the scene for the themes and explorations in subsequent chapters, the book examines how he expanded on Freud's work, and how his discourse with Melanie Klein sharpened his thought and clinical innovations. Divided into three sections, it covers:

- Introductory overviews of the development of Winnicott's theoretical matrix
- Personal perspectives from eminent psychoanalysts of the influence of Winnicott on their own work
- The extensions of Winnicott's late work on contemporary psychoanalysis

Drawing on her own extensive knowledge of Winnicott and the expertise of the distinguished contributors, Jan Abram shows us how Winnicott's influence is fundamental in understanding how psychoanalytic practice and theory is continuing to develop. As such, it will be an inspiration to experienced psychoanalysts, psychotherapists and students alike.

Jan Abram is a psychoanalyst in full time private practice in London and Fellow of the Institute of Psychoanalysis. She is currently Visiting Professor, Centre for Psychoanalytic Studies, University of Essex and a member of the 'Paris Group' – a Working Party of the European Psychoanalytic Federation.

Contributors: Jan Abram, Haydée Faimberg, Lisa Farley, Dodi Goldman, André Green, Zeljko Loparic, Marion Milner, Thomas Ogden, Christopher Reeves, René Roussillon, Nellie L. Thompson, Daniel Widlöcher, Donald W. Winnicott, Kenneth Wright.

THE NEW LIBRARY OF PSYCHOANALYSIS
General Editor: Alessandra Lemma

The New Library of Psychoanalysis was launched in 1987 in association with the Institute of Psychoanalysis, London. It took over from the International Psychoanalytical Library which published many of the early translations of the works of Freud and the writings of most of the leading British and Continental psychoanalysts.

The purpose of the New Library of Psychoanalysis is to facilitate a greater and more widespread appreciation of psychoanalysis and to provide a forum for increasing mutual understanding between psychoanalysts and those working in other disciplines such as the social sciences, medicine, philosophy, history, linguistics, literature and the arts. It aims to represent different trends both in British psychoanalysis and in psychoanalysis generally. The New Library of Psychoanalysis is well placed to make available to the English-speaking world psychoanalytic writings from other European countries and to increase the interchange of ideas between British and American psychoanalysts. Through the *Teaching Series*, the New Library of Psychoanalysis now also publishes books that provide comprehensive, yet accessible, overviews of selected subject areas aimed at those studying psychoanalysis and related fields such as the social sciences, philosophy, literature and the arts.

The Institute, together with the British Psychoanalytical Society, runs a low-fee psychoanalytic clinic, organizes lectures and scientific events concerned with psychoanalysis and publishes the *International Journal of Psychoanalysis*. It runs the a training course in psychoanalysis which leads to membership of the International Psychoanalytical Association – the body which preserves internationally agreed standards of training, of professional entry, and of professional ethics and practice for psychoanalysis as initiated and developed by Sigmund Freud. Distinguished members of the Institute have included Michael Balint, Wilfred Bion, Ronald Fairbairn, Anna Freud, Ernest Jones, Melanie Klein, John Rickman and Donald Winnicott.

Previous general editors have included David Tuckett, who played a very active role in the establishment of the New Library. He was followed as general editor by Elizabeth Bott Spillius, who was in turn followed by Susan Budd and then by Dana Birksted-Breen.

Current members of the Advisory Board include Liz Allison, Giovanna di Ceglie, Rosemary Davies and Richard Rusbridger.

Previous Members of the Advisory Board include Christopher Bollas, Ronald Britton, Catalina Bronstein, Donald Campbell, Sara Flanders, Stephen Grosz, John Keene, Eglé Laufer, Alessandra Lemma, Juliet Mitchell, Michael Parsons, Rosine Jozef Perelberg, Mary Target and David Taylor.

ALSO IN THIS SERIES

TITLES IN THE NEW LIBRARY OF PSYCHOANALYSIS TEACHING SERIES

THE NEW LIBRARY OF PSYCHOANALYSIS

General Editor Alessandra Lemma

Donald Winnicott Today

Edited by
Jan Abram

LONDON AND NEW YORK

First published 2013 by Routledge
27 Church Road, Hove, East Sussex, BN3 2FA

Simultaneously published in the USA and Canada
by Routledge
711 Third Avenue, New York NY 10017

Routledge is an imprint of the Taylor & Francis Group, an informa business

British Library Cataloguing in Publication Data

A catalogue record for this book is available from the British Library

Library of Congress Cataloging in Publication Data

Donald Winnicott today / edited by Jan Abram.
    p. cm. — (The new library of psychoanalysis)
Includes bibliographical references and index.
1. Psychoanalysis. 2. Winnicott, D. W. (Donald Woods), 1896–1971.
I. Abram, Jan.
BF173.D556 2012
150.19'5092—dc23   2012001911

ISBN: 978–0–415–56487–8 (hbk)
ISBN: 978–0–415–56488–5 (pbk)
ISBN: 978–0–203–10570–2 (ebk)

Typeset in Bembo
by Swales & Willis Ltd, Exeter, Devon

MIX
Paper from
responsible sources
FSC® C004839

Printed and bound in Great Britain by
TJ International Ltd, Padstow, Cornwall

For JvR

Contents

Figures and tables

Figures

Tables

Contributors (in order of
chapter appearance)

Thomas H. Ogden (Chapters 2 and 7)
Thomas Ogden MD is a Supervising and Personal Analyst at the
Psychoanalytic Institute of Northern California and a member of
the International Psychoanalytical Association. He has published
nine books, the most recent of which are *Creative Readings: Essays
on Seminal Analytic Works; Rediscovering Psychoanalysis: Thinking and
Dreaming, Learning and Forgetting; This Art of Psychoanalysis: Dreaming
Undreamt Dreams and Interrupted Cries; Conversations at the Frontier of
Dreaming*; and *Reverie and Interpretation: Sensing Something Human*. His
forthcoming book, *The Analyst's Ear and the Critics Eye: Rethinking
Psychoanalysis and Literature* (co-authored with Benjamin Ogden) will
be published later this year. He was awarded the 2004 International
Journal of Psychoanalysis Award for the Most Important Paper of the
Year and the 2010 Haskell Norman Prize for 'outstanding achieve-
ment as a psychoanalytic clinician, teacher and theoretician.'

Jan Abram (Editor – Preface, Introduction, Chapters 3 and 14)
Jan Abram PhD is a psychoanalyst in full time private practice in
London. She is a Fellow of the Institute of Psychoanalysis, London
where she currently teaches the work of Winnicott, is deputy Chair
of the Foundation Course in Psychoanalysis and Honorary Secretary of the Scientific Committee. She is a Training Therapist for
the Lincoln Institute of Psychotherapy and the London Centre for
Psychotherapy. Presently she is Visiting Professor for the Centre for
Psychoanalytic Studies, University of Essex and Honorary Senior

Lecturer for the Psychoanalysis Unit at University College London and Honorary Research Fellow the Anna Freud Centre. She was director of the Squiggle Foundation (1996–2000) and Honorary Archivist of the Winnicott Trust (2002–2011). Amongst her publications, *The Language of Winnicott: A Dictionary of Winnicott's Use of Words* (1996 1st edition; 2007 2nd edition) was awarded Outstanding Academic Book of the Year in 1997. She is currently a member of the 'Paris Group' – the Working Party for the Specificity of Psychoanalytic Treatment Today of the European Psychoanalytic Federation. Her current research, linked with the 'Paris Group,' involves a continuation of the themes related to psychic survival in clinical psychoanalysis (see Chapter 14).

Zeljko Loparic (Chapter 4)
Zeljko Loparic has a PhD in Philosophy from the University of Louvain (1982), and a post-doc from the University of Konstanz. He is full professor at the Department of Philosophy at UNICAMP. He was Director of the Center for Logic, Epistemology and History of Science (CLE) of the same University (1983–1985), and founder and first president (1989–94) of the Brazilian Kant Society. In 1999, he founded a journal for philosophy and psychoanalysis *Natureza Humana*. In 2004–2008 he presided over the Brazilian Society for Phenomenology. In collaboration with Elsa Oliveira Dias, he founded the Brazilian Winnicott Society (2005), which offers a professional training course on Winnicottian psychoanalysis. He authored *Heidegger Defendant* (1990); *Ethics and Finitude* (1995, 2nd ed. 2004); *Heuristic Descartes* (1997); *Kant's Transcendental Semantics* (2000, 3rd ed. 2005); *On Responsibility* (2003) and *Heidegger* (2004), as well as numerous papers published in national and international journals on the general philosophy of science (Mach, Carnap, Kuhn), history of philosophy (Descartes, Kant, Heidegger), and philosophy and history of psychoanalysis (Freud, Klein, Lacan, Winnicott).

Marion Milner (Chapter 6)
Marion Milner (1900–1998) was a distinguished British psychoanalyst whose work in the cultural and educational field preceded her becoming a psychoanalyst. Her well-known early books explored the nature of art, leisure and education. In 1950, she published 'On not being able to paint,' which is an autobiographical account of her voyage into the unconscious in her effort to reach the 'prelogical'

area of the mind. In 1969 she published 'The hands of the living god' which is a painstaking account of her analysis of a severely disturbed patient. She was a well-respected Training Analyst of the Institute of Psychoanalysis and a contemporary of Donald Winnicott. Her own distinctive contribution to psychoanalysis, clinically and theoretically, can be seen in her major works – *The Suppressed Madness of Sane Men* and *The Hands of the Living God*.

André Green (Chapter 7)

André Green was a psychoanalyst who lived and worked in Paris. He is Past-President of the Paris Psychoanalytical Society and was Vice-President of the International Psychoanalytic Association. He was co-editor of the *Nouvelle Revue de Psychanalyse*. He also wrote numerous books, including *On Private Madness; The Work of the Negative; The Fabric of Affect in the Psychoanalytical Discourse; The Chains of Eros; Life Narcissis; Death Narcissism* and *Key Ideas for a Contemporary Psychoanalysis*. His most recent publication is *Illusions and Disillusions of the Psychoanalytic Work* published by Karnac Books.

Haydée Faimberg (Chapter 8)

Haydée Faimberg MD is a Training and Supervising Analyst, Paris Psychoanalytical Society (SPP) and Argentine Psychoanalytical Association (APA). She is a former Vice-President of the International Psychoanalytical Association (IPA). She currently works in private practice in Paris.

She created what came to be called 'the Haydée Faimberg "listening to listening" method for clinical discussions' – using a concept she coined initially in the context of psychoanalytical listening during sessions. This method is used in the ongoing Forum of the European Federation, International Psychoanalytical Congress (IPA), Latino American Federation (FEPAL), NAPsac (North America) and in some psychoanalytic institutes. Since 1993 she has been co-chair, with Anne Marie Sandler, of the ongoing Annual Clinical Meeting of British-French psychoanalysts. She also created and chaired a Conference on Intra-cultural and Inter-cultural Psychoanalytical Dialogue (IPA) (Paris, 1998), where the essay included in this book was presented.

Transmission of the narcissistic mode of solving conflicts between three generations is a main focus of her research, for which she coined the concept of 'Oedipal configuration and its narcissistic dimension'; identified the functions of 'appropriation and intrusion' which regulate narcissistic object relations; developed the concept of 'telescoping of generations' and the alienating narcissistic unconscious identifications where three generations are condensed; and defined the function of 'listening to [the patient's] listening'. She has conducted research on the 'psychic consequences of Nazism in psychoanalytic patients' (her first study on the telescoping of generations was presented at the first congress of the IPA held after the war in Germany). She has written papers on Lewis Carroll and Italo Calvino and is a contributing author to 15 books (18 chapters). She received the 'Haskell Norman International Award 2005' and delivered the 44th Annual Freud Lecture, at the Psychoanalytic Association of New York (PANY) in 2009. Her main book is *The Telescoping of Generations: Listening to the Narcissistic Links between Generations,* 2005.

René Roussillon (Chapter 9)
René Roussillon is a psychoanalyst and Training Analyst and Supervisor of the Societé de Psychoanalyse de Paris. He is a Professor at the University of Lyon and was awarded a PhD in clinical psychology in 1988. In 1989, he was appointed Professor of Clinical and Pathological Psychology in the University of Lyon-II. From that point onwards, he has been the head of the clinical psychology department in Lyon University and of the research team focusing on 'the subjectivation process in borderline states.' He is also the director of the clinical 'psycho-hub' of the Rhône-Alpes region in France, a facility that he founded in 2007. In 1991, he became a Full Member of the Paris Psychoanalytical Society and of the Lyon/Rhône-Alpes Psychoanalytical Group; he is a former president of that association. He has published several books in French on psychoanalysis, as well as a significant number of articles (which have been translated into English, German, Italian, French, Portuguese, Russian, Turkish, Greek, Romanian and Bulgarian). In 1991, he was the recipient of the prestigious 'Maurice Bouvet Award' for his book *Paradoxes et Situations Limites de la Psychanalyse* [*Paradoxes and Borderline Situations in Psychoanalysis*]. The main topics of his research work in psychoanalysis have to do with psychical trauma, the analysing situation, and the various forms of transference that may prove problematic within that setting.

Daniel Widlöcher (Chapter 10)
Daniel Widlöcher is Honorary Professor of the Pierre et Marie Curie University, Paris. He is a Member and Training Analyst of the French

Psychoanalytical Association and its past President. He is also a past President of the International Psychoanalytic Association.

Kenneth Wright (Chapter 11)

Kenneth Wright is a psychoanalyst in private practice in Suffolk, a Member of the British Psychoanalytical Society and a patron of the Squiggle Foundation. A well-known commentator on Winnicott, he lectures nationally and internationally and has published papers on psychoanalysis, the creative arts and religion. His book *Vision and Separation: Between Mother and Baby* (1991) was awarded the Margaret S. Mahler Literature Prize (1992) and his recent book *Mirroring and Attunement: Self Realization in Psychoanalysis and Art* was published in 2009 by Routledge.

Dodi Goldman (Chapter 15)

Dodi Goldman is a Training and Supervising Analyst and on the faculty of the William Alanson White Institute, New York. He is the author of *In Search of the Real: The Origins and Originality of D.W. Winnicott*. He serves on the International Board of the Israel Winnicott Center and is in private practice in New York.

Christopher Reeves (Chapter 16)

Christopher Reeves PhD is a retired child psychotherapist and former Principal of the Mulberry Bush School. After studying psychology and philosophy at Oxford he trained at the Tavistock Clinic in the course of which he attended seminars run by Donald Winnicott. He completed his doctorate in Philosophy at London University in 1979 with a thesis on models of the mind in the early writings of Freud. He is a former President of the Medical Section of the British Psychological Society and a former editor of the *Journal of Child Psychotherapy*. He was Director of the Squiggle Foundation (2009–2011), an organization dedicated to promoting the knowledge and application of Winnicott's ideas.

Nellie Thompson (Chapter 17)

Nellie Thompson PhD is an historian and member of the New York Psychoanalytic Society and Institute, where she serves as the Curator of the Brill Library's Archives and Special Collections. Her research interests include the role of women psychoanalysts in the psychoanalytic movement, both as institutional actors and contributors to psychoanalytic theory and clinical work. Among her publications are: 'Early Women Psychoanalysts', 'Helene Deutsch: A Life in Theory,' 'Early American Women Psychoanalysts, 1911–1941,' 'A Measure of Agreement: An Exploration of the Relationship of D.W. Winnicott and Phyllis Greenacre,' and 'Karl Abraham in New York: The Contributions of Bertram D. Lewin'. She is co-editor, with Peter Loewenberg, of *100 Years of the IPA:Centenary of the International Psychoanalytical Association, 1910–2010, Evolution and Change* (2011), London: IPA Publishing, and is currently working on a study of Phyllis Greenacre.

Lisa Farley (Chapter 18)
Lisa Farley is Assistant Professor of Education at York University in Toronto, Canada. Her research investigates the place of affect in encountering and representing historical knowledge and the implications of psychoanalytic thought for thinking about theories of childhood history and education.

Anne Patterson (Glossary)
Anne Patterson is a psychoanalyst practising in London and a Member of the Institute of Psychoanalysis. She is Assistant Editor for the New Library of Psychoanalysis. She also works as consultant psychiatrist in psychotherapy in the NHS. Her special interests include psychoanalysis and literature, French psychoanalysis and, within the NHS, teaching and training.

Preface

Winnicott's writings amount to well over 600 published papers as can be seen in Knud Hjulmand's *Complete Bibliography* 2007. In addition there is an uncalculated amount of unpublished material in the Winnicott archives in London and New York (see the Appendix for more information on the publications and archives). In the past few years there have been many interesting findings in the Winnicott archives as will be seen in this volume (see Chapters 14, 17 and 18).

My aim for this volume is to focus on the revolutionary nature of Winnicott's theoretical matrix. Each paper presents a rare in-depth analysis of Winnicott's conceptualizations. The core themes in each chapter, including Winnicott's own, highlight the prominence of early psychic development, both internal – *intra-psychic,* and interpersonally – *inter-psychic.* It is this prominence that constitutes a revolution in the theory and practice of psychoanalysis and thus advances the Freudian project.

In the Introduction the main arguments of each paper are woven together to show how each author examines Winnicott's writings in original and generative ways. The chapters are grouped into three sections and each part begins with a re-publication of a selected Winnicott paper to set the scene for the themes and explorations of the subsequent chapters:

1 Introductory overviews

These four complementary introductions illuminate the evolution of Winnicott's work and together offer a comprehensive panorama of the theoretical matrix.

2 Personal perspectives

The seven chapters in this second section are written by analysts who have made significant contributions to psychoanalysis. While each author's perspective is grounded in Freud's work, many of their own original developments, as seen here, have been inspired by Winnicott's innovations.

3 Late Winnicott studies

This section begins with one of Winnicott's final formulations written just before he died. The subsequent chapters were written for this collection by colleagues I have been corresponding with for many years.

This book has been gestating for many years. I have learnt an enormous amount from the process of selecting and editing the papers and working with all the authors. This volume fills a gap in the Winnicott secondary literature and I hope the reader will find the collection as illuminating and as inspiring as I do.

Jan Abram, London 2012

Acknowledgements

Firstly a warm thank you to Dana Birksted-Breen who, when Editor of the New Library series, encouraged me to produce this book; and to Alessandra Lemma, the present Editor of the New Library series, who offered further encouragement and helpful editorial suggestions. I am grateful to the Editorial Board of the New Library and the anonymous reviewers who offered suggestions and recommended the publication of this book.

Naturally, I am very grateful to all the authors of the chapters in this volume who agreed to have their papers either re-published or published for the first time – Haydée Faimberg, Lisa Farley, André Green, Dodi Goldman, Zjelko Loparic, René Roussillon, Thomas Ogden, Christopher Reeves, Nellie Thompson, Daniel Widlöcher, and Kenneth Wright. There has been a lively 'two way' exchange over many years concerning our mutual passion for Winnicott's innovations. Thanks also go to Anne Patterson, who towards the end of the book's development assisted in the research for the footnotes and references for Chapter 1 and prepared the Glossary. I am also grateful to Anne for her careful reading through and checking of the final manuscript.

Thank you to Steph Ebdon of The Marsh Agency for her sustained support and sound advice. My thanks also goes to the Winnicott Trust for their past sponsorship of my work on Winnicott since the early 1990s. For this volume I am grateful for their permission to re-publish Winnicott's papers for Chapters 1, 5 and 13.

A warm thank you to Peter Fonagy, Mary Target and David Tuckett for their positive reception of my proposal for this book and for facilitating the Donald Winnicott Today Conference at University College London in 2006.

I am indebted to scores of colleagues and students, at home and abroad, all of whom help to illuminate my appreciation of clinical psychoanalysis and have thus made significant contributions to my evolution. My special thanks go to the Fellowship Group 2003, the Contemporary Freudian Study Group and the 'Paris Group'.

My gratitude goes to many more colleagues, especially: Gérard Bayle, Leo Bleger, Cathy Bronstein, Donald Campbell, Laura Dethiville, Serge Frisch, Knud Hjolmand, Marcel Hudon, François Lévy, Sylvain Missonnier, Michael Parsons, Joan Raphael–Leff, Denys Ribas, Evelyne Sechaud, Jonathan Sklar and François Villa.

As ever, a very special thank you goes to Rosine Jozef Perelberg.

Finally my deep indebtedness goes to my husband and family for their unstinting support.

Special permissions have been granted for the following:

Chapter 1 'D.W.W. on D.W.W.', originally published 1989 as Postscript: D.W.W. on D.W.W in *Psychoanalytic Explorations* Karnac Books; Chapter 5 'A Personal View of the Kleinian Contribution', originally published in *The Maturational Processes and the Facilitating Environment* 1965 London: Hogarth; Chapter 13 originally published 1989 as 'Comments on My Paper "The Use of an Object" and "The Use of an Object in the Context of *Moses and Monotheism*"' in *Psychoanalytic Explorations* 1989 with kind permission of The Marsh Agency Ltd on behalf of The Winnicott Trust.

Chapter 2 is published with kind permission from the journal *Contemporary Psychoanalysis* in which it was originally published in 1985 as 'The Mother, the Infant and the Matrix: Interpretations of Aspects of the Work of Donald Winnicott' 21: 346–371.

Chapter 3, first published as 'Donald Woods Winnicott: A Brief Introduction' by Jan Abram, *The International Journal of Psychoanalysis* (2008) 89: 1189–1217, is re-published with kind permission of Wiley Publishers.

Chapter 6 was originally published as 'Winnicott and the Two Way Journey' by Marion Milner in *Between Reality and Fantasy* edited by Simon Grolnick and L. Barkin (1978, pp. 37–42) and is published with kind permission of Jason Aronson Publishers Inc., an imprint of Rowman & Littlefield Publishers, Inc.

Chapter 7 was originally published as 'Potential Space in Psychoanalysis' in *Between Reality and Fantasy* edited by Simon Grolnick and L. Barkin (1978, pp. 169–189) and is published with kind permission of Jason Aronson Publishers Inc., an imprint of Rowman & Littlefield Publishers, Inc.

Chapter 9 was first published in *The Psychoanalytic Quarterly*, Chapter LXX No. 2: 299–323 and is re-published here with kind permission of *The Psychoanalytic Quarterly*.

Chapter 11 'The Search for Form: A Winnicottian Theory of Artistic Creation' by Kenneth Wright was originally published in *Mirroring and Attunement*, pp. 141–155, 2009, and is reproduced with kind permission of Routledge.

Chapter 12, first published as 'The Deconstruction of Narcissism' by René Roussillon, *The International Journal of Psychoanalysis* (2010) 91: 821–837, is re-published with kind permission of Wiley Publishers.

Chapter 14 contains materials sent by D.W. Winnicott to the New York Psychoanalytic Society prior to his 1968 lecture 'The Use of an Object.' This has been published with kind permission of The Archives, A.A. Brill Library, New York Psychoanalytic Society and Institute.

Chapter 14 also contains hitherto unpublished material published for the first time with kind permission of The Winnicott Trust.

The Epigraph quotes in Chapter 16 first published in *Therapy and Consultation in Child Care* (1993) by Barbara Dockar-Drysdale Free Association Books is re-produced with kind permission of Mrs. Sally Cooper.

Chapter 18 'Squiggle evidence: the child, the canvas and the "negative labour" of history' by Lisa Farley first published in 2011 in History and Memory is reproduced with kind permission of Indiana University Press.

Epigraph quotes of Winnicott (1968a) for Chapter 3 first published in *Babies and Their Mothers* (1988) Free Association Books and Chapter 17 (1987) first published in *The Spontaneous Gesture* with kind permission of The Marsh Agency Ltd.

Figures 18.1–4 are reproduced with kind permission and thanks to the archive and Wellcome Library, London (The Wellcome Trust).

Figures 18.5–8 are reproduced with kind permission of The Marsh Agency Ltd on behalf of The Winnicott Trust.

The hitherto unpublished sentences on the front cover in D.W. Winnicott's hand-writing, and used as the epigraph for the Introduction, are published for the first time with kind permission of The Winnicott Trust.

Donald Woods Winnicott
(1896–1971)

Donald Woods Winnicott was a paediatrician and psychoanalyst for both adults and children. He was a Training Analyst of the Institute of Psychoanalysis and its President on two separate occasions (1956–1959 and 1965–1968). His contribution to child development has been internationally acknowledged since the 1960s when his most popular book was published by Penguin Books *The Child, the Family and the Outside World*. The full realization of his radical contribution to the development of psychoanalysis is increasingly receiving acknowledgement.

D.W. Winnicott chronology

The following chronological information on Winnicott's life and work is presented according to the evolutionary phases of Winnicott's work as seen in Chapter 3. This chapter was first published for the Education Section of the *International Journal of Psychoanalysis* (Abram 2008) and adapted from the following chronologies: Davis and Wallbridge 1981; Kahr 1996; Phillips 1988; Rodman 2003.

Birth and education

1896 – Born on 7 April, third child and only son of John Frederick Winnicott and Elizabeth Martha Woods, in Plymouth, Devon
1910 – Leaves home to board at The Leys School in Cambridge

1914 – Pre-medical course University of Cambridge, Jesus College

1917 – Surgeon-probationer in the Royal Navy – medical officer on a destroyer at the end of World War I

Foundations (1919–1934)

1919 – Looking for a book on dreams, because he became aware that he was not remembering his dreams on returning from the war, he discovers Freud's *The Interpretation of Dreams* (1900) and Pfister's *ThePsychoanalytic Method* (1915)

1920–1922 – Qualifies in medicine and becomes a full member of the Royal College of Physicians and begins to specialize in paediatrics

1923 – Two hospital appointments: Assistant Physician at the Queen's Hospital for Children in Hackney where he also works as Physician in Charge of the London County Council Rheumatism Supervisory Centre until 1933; Consultant Paediatrician at Paddington Green Children's Hospital until retirement in 1963

1923 July – Marries Alice Buxton Taylor

1923 – Begins analysis with James Strachey

1924 – Sets up in private practice and his father receives a knighthood

1925 – His mother dies

1926 – Melanie Klein moves to London and becomes a member of BPaS

1927 – Registers as a candidate at the Institute of Psychoanalysis (IPaL)

1929 – Begins to attend Scientific Meetings of the BPaS

1931 – First publication *Clinical Notes on Disorders of Childhood*

1932 – Reads Klein's *The Psychoanalysis of Children* (1932) and chooses her to supervise one of his training cases

1933 – Finishes analysis with James Strachey

1934 – Qualifies as a psychoanalyst

Phase One: The environment-individual set-up (1935–1944)

1935 – Qualifies as a child psychoanalyst and becomes the first male child analyst.

Becomes a full member of the BPaS with his reading in paper 'The manic defence' (1958)

1935–1941 – In consultation with Melanie Klein on his analytic child cases

Around this time he starts analysis with Joan Riviere (which will last for five years). Treats Melanie Klein's son Erich but refuses her wish to supervise the work

1939–1962 – Begins broadcasting talks on the radio to mothers at home with their newborn babies

1940 – Appointed as Psychiatric Consultant to the Government Evacuation Scheme in Oxford where he meets Clare Britton (later to be his wife)

1941 – The beginning of the 'Controversial Discussions'. Named by Melanie Klein as one of the five Kleinian Training Analysts (King and Steiner 1991)

1942 – 'Dropped' by Melanie Klein due to not preparing for meetings enough in advance

1944 – At the conclusions of the 'Controversial Discussion' chooses, with the majority of psychoanalysts, not to align with either Mrs Klein or Miss Freud.

Appointed Fellow of the Royal College of Physicians

Phase Two: Transitional phenomena (1945–1960)

1945 – Presentation of first seminal paper 'Primitive emotional development' to the BPaS. Publishes his second book *Getting to Know Your Baby*, a collection of six radio talks

1947 – Presents his second seminal paper 'Hate in the countertransference' to the BPaS

1948 – Father dies and he has his first coronary shortly afterwards. Presents 'Reparation in respect of mother's organised defence against depression' to the BPaS

1949 – Separates from his first wife. Suffers a second coronary. Presents 'Mind and its relation to the psyche-soma'

1951 – Marries Clare Britton. Presents 'Transitional objects and transitional phenomena' to the BPaS

1954 – Presents 'Metapsychological and clinical aspects of regression within the psychoanalytic set-up' to the BPaS

1956 – Becomes President of BPaS for three years and is involved with the negotiations concerning the Paris split. Presents 'The anti-social tendency' and 'Primary maternal preoccupation' to the BPaS

1957 – Two new publications: *The Child and the Family: First Relationships* and *The Child and the Outside World: Studies in Developing Relationships*. Presents 'The capacity to be alone'

1958 – Publication of first collection of psychoanalytic papers, *Collected Papers: Through Paediatrics To Psychoanalysis*

Phase Three: The use of an object (1960–1971)

1960 – Publishes 'Theory of the parent–infant relationship' and writes 'Ego distortion in terms of true and false self'. Melanie Klein dies

1962 – Presents 'The development of the capacity for concern' and 'Morals and education'to the BPaS

1963 – Retires from Paddington Green after 40 years. Presents 'Communicating and not communicating leading to a study of certain opposites' to the BPaS. Probably writes 'Fear of breakdown'

1964 – Publishes *The Child, the Family and the Outside World* for Penguin Books

1965 – Becomes President of BPaS for a second time. Publishes *The Family and Individual Development*, and prepares an Introduction for a book on 16 psychoanalytic sessions with a small child. *The Piggle* is eventually published posthumously in 1977

1967 – Publishes 'Mirror-role of mother and family in child development'

1968 – Awarded the James Spence Medal for Paediatrics. Presents 'The use of an object' to the New York Psychoanalytic Society. Is subsequently seriously ill and hospitalized in New York (see Chapters 3, 14 and 16)

1969 – Writes on and around 'The use of an object' paper and prepares for the publication of *Playing and Reality* and *Therapeutic Consultations*

1970 – After five years of heavy campaigning as Chair of the Freud Statue Committee, the statue is unveiled on 2 October. Writes more on the themes of creativity

1971 – Prepares for the 27th IPA congress to be held in Vienna – 'The psychoanalytical concept of aggression: theoretical, clinical and applied aspects' – where he is invited to present on a panel for child analysis. In January he makes a reservation at the Hotel

Sacher Vienna for a week in July (see Chapter 14) but dies on 25 January. Later that year *Playing and Reality* and *Therapeutic Consultations* are published

References

Abram, J. (2008) Donald Woods Winnicott: a brief introduction *Int J of Psychoanal* 89: 1189–1217.

Davis, M. and Wallbridge, D. (1981) *Boundary and Space: An introduction to the work of D.W. Winnicott.* New York: Brunner/Mazel.

Kahr, B. (1996) *D.W. Winnicott: A biographical portrait.* London: Karnac.

King, P. and Steiner, R. eds (1991) *The Freud–Klein Controversies 1941–45.* London: Routledge.

Pfister, O. (1915) *The Psychoanalytic Method.* Payne, C.R., translator. London: Kegan Paul, Trench, Trubner.

Phillips, A. (1988) *Winnicott.* Cambridge, MA: Harvard UP.

Rodman, F.R. (2003) *Winnicott: Life and work.* Cambridge, MA: Perseus.

Winnicott, D.W. (1958) The manic defence [1935]. In: *Collected Papers: Through Paediatrics to Psychoanalysis* 1958, 129–44.

Introduction

Jan Abram

I am asking for a kind of revolution in our work. Let us re-examine what we do.

(Winnicott 1971: Chapter 14: 321)[1]

The principal aim of this volume is to demonstrate that Winnicott's contribution constitutes a major revolution in psychoanalysis.[2] A sense of self rooted in the newborn's primary relationship is at the heart of his theoretical matrix.[3] Subjectivity, therefore, is inscribed with the m/Other – the primacy of the 'environment-individual set-up' (1958).

Close examination of his theoretical advances reveal that the foundations reside firmly with Sigmund Freud. For Winnicott, psychoanalysis is a theory of emotional development and human nature which can only be examined through the lens of Freud's scientific clinical methodology with its therapeutic aims (1945).

Winnicott's formulations on early psychic development – 'creating the object' and the 'essential paradox of the conception-perception gap' – are inextricably linked with an articulation of the transference-counter transference matrix. This forges an expansion of the analytic setting and creates fertile ground for the recognition of the 'analyzing situation',[4] in which the analyst and analysand engage in 'co-thinking' and 'co-creativity'[5] in the context of the après coup.[6]

Winnicott's psychoanalytic clinical investigations led to his view that aggression is a benign force in the newborn infant. These formulations extend Freud's concept of *hilflosigkeit* through a concept that recognizes different stages of dependency in the infant related to the early holding

1

environment (1965d).[7] While Winnicott's final theory on aggression – the survival of the object – links with the concept of helplessness as well as the *idea* of a self-preservative instinct, at the same time it constitutes a divergence from Freud's late tentative concept of the death instinct.[8] The outcome of these new psychoanalytic extensions on Freud's work, as seen across the whole of Winnicott's work, results in a distinctive psychoanalytic approach that today is understood as a continuation and deepening of the Freudian project (Green 1996).

The consensus of this volume, in the final analysis, argues that Winnicott's canon presents an original psychoanalytic theoretical matrix which creates a major advance in the concept of subjectivity (Ogden 1992).

Part One: Introductory overviews

Freud's development of psychoanalysis as a 'method of investigation' was Winnicott's true starting point.

> . . . as soon as I found Freud and the method he gave us for investigating and for treatment, I was in line with it. This was just like when I was at school and was reading Darwin and suddenly I knew that Darwin was my cup of tea.
>
> (Chapter 1: 33)

In this informal talk, re-published here as **Chapter 1**, Winnicott offers an autobiographical account of his own view on the evolution of his ideas. The 'methodology of investigation' refers to the analyst's position *on* the couch, as well as the analyst's experience *behind* the couch and Winnicott relates how he was 'tremendously helped' by his experience of analysis – first with James Strachey and secondly with Joan Riviere. The insights he gained from analysis initiated his conceptual advances '. . . it was only through analysis that I became gradually able to see a baby as a human being.' (p. 48). This revelation is due to the mobilizing of unconscious infantile states of mind through psychic regression (cf. Chapter 3: 89). This early insight was a defining moment for Winnicott; from then on his focus was on how to understand the earliest stage of development in relation to the psychic environment. At that time this was an area of the mind that psychoanalysis had not yet addressed.

Chapter 1 – D.W.W. on D.W.W[9] – is the transcript of a talk Winnicott gave to the 1952 Club[10] in January 1967 – nearly fifty years after he had discovered psychoanalysis,[11] and four years before he died. The awareness that the baby is a human being led to a further realization that 'there's no such thing as a baby.' These interconnected discoveries of the human condition were psychoanalytically radical in those early days of psychoanalysis and led to Winnicott's formulations on the determining role of the environment.[12] In this way Winnicott was in the process of extending Freud's incorporation of the environment's impact on the ego in the structural model (Freud 1923) (Sandler et al. 1997: 170), although Winnicott laid a stress on the primacy of the environment-individual set-up related to the infant's complex journey of becoming a person (1970). Conversely, while Melanie Klein did not ignore the mother's part in human development, her formulations do not emphasize its power to the same extent (see Chapter 3: 83).[13] The impact of the psychic environment on the infant's states of mind is a formulation that is tied in with the argument against the Kleinian development of the death instinct. Briefly – for Klein the death instinct was innate in the newborn and a manifestation of hate, sadism and envy. For Winnicott the biological life force was akin to primary creativity and he saw the affects of hate, sadism and envy as developmental achievements. He thought that the idea of an innate death instinct was equivalent to the religious notion of original sin. These themes are explored in more detail especially in Chapters 1, 13, 14, 15.

The evolution of Winnicott's formulations on the early environment, alongside his experience of analysis, was amplified by his observations during the Second World War, when he was posted to Oxford to attend children 'difficult to billet' during the evacuation. He became preoccupied with the causes of the antisocial act and the roots of delinquency. Much later, in his paper – 'Providing for the child in health and crisis'– he classifies the environment with an emphasis on the infant's changing needs at each stage of dependency (Winnicott 1965d). The parental environment's responsibility for the individual's mental health never ceases to be important in Winnicott's theories, but, at the beginning, for the infant's future mental health, its 'good enough handling and holding' is absolutely paramount (cf. Winnicott 1965c).

This early discovery led, amongst others, to his concept of 'subjective objects.' This term relates to a category of internal objects that originate from the baby's merger with the mother at the beginning of life. The concepts of 'transitional phenomena' and the 'essential paradox' are overlapping formulations that are intrinsically part of the infant's journey from absolute dependence to relative dependence to 'towards independence'. These formulations account for a distinctive theory of symbolic thinking (Chapters 6, 11) and the 'fate of aggression' (Chapters 13, 14).

Winnicott completes Chapter 1 with his view on psychoanalytic technique and the value of Freud's method of 'free association'. Here, as two years later in his paper 'The use of an object,' Winnicott stresses the value of silence and waiting in the analytic setting. This focus on technique reverberates with his concept of 'object presenting', i.e. facilitation, which in turn reinforces the classical Freudian technique of free association. Although not spoken about directly in this chapter, Winnicott's thesis carries a critique of what he deemed 'over interpretation' of the transference (Chapter 3: 95–96). This should not be misconstrued as a stance that is anti–interpretation, on the contrary, it is a perspective that views interpretation as something that should arise in the 'ripeness of time' in the analytic process – otherwise, he once wrote, it was no more than indoctrination (1971: 51).[14] Chapter 1 is an important autobiographical statement that highlights the inseparability of Winnicott the man and his thought.

That Winnicott's work constitutes a psychoanalytic revolution is matched by the argument that Melanie Klein's contribution also resulted in radically 'reshaping the psychoanalytic domain' (Hughes 1989). While it is important to recognize that the basic assumptions of Melanie Klein and Donald Winnicott are significantly different there are, nevertheless, areas of agreement. Thomas Ogden's analysis, in **Chapter 2**, focuses on the context of the intellectual debates of the BPaS – commonly known as the 'controversial discussions' (King and Steiner 1991). Throughout this paper Ogden argues that 'Although Winnicott's thinking developed in a direction different from that of Klein, he never denounced Kleinian thinking . . .' (p. 46). To some extent this view is confirmed in Chapter 5 by Winnicott himself in which he writes an appreciation of Melanie Klein's contribution highlighting his respect for her innovations. While Ogden's focus is on how Winnicott's contributions '. . . thrived in the medium of intense debate between the classical Freudian and the Kleinian groups,' he argues that '. . . it was not until Winnicott that psychoanalysis developed a conception of the mother as the infant's psychological matrix'. This chapter emphasizes the dialogical in Winnicott's theories and how the scientific developments in the BPaS, in particular his discourse with the Kleinian development, sharpened Winnicott's thinking and led to a significant and different psycho-analytic development.

Chapter 3 offers a linear evolutionary outline and distils the seminal conceptions. This survey proposes that there are three spe-cific chronological phases in which major theoretical advances were established: 1. 1934–1944 The environment-individual set-up. 2. 1945–1959 Transitional phenomena. 3. 1960–1971 The use of an object. The paper traces the development of the two complementary parallel lines of Winnicott's work: psychoanalysis and paediatrics that both illuminate the evolution of his formulations. The key publica-tions are indicated for each phase.[15]

The claim that Winnicott's work constitutes a scientific revolution is substantiated by Zjelko Loparic in **Chapter 4.** Drawing on Thomas Kuhn's theory of the 'structure of scientific revolutions' this perspec-tive offers a clear and convincing argument that shows how Winnicott adds to Freud's oedipal paradigm with the 'baby-on-the-mother's-lap paradigm'. Loparic suggests that this was a solution to Winni-cott's scientific 'crisis' when he realized that babies really could be ill (see Chapter 1: 34, Chapter 3: 80). Loparic demonstrates that Win-nicott's different theoretical outcome from Freud's is related to their different starting points. While Freud's oedipal paradigm emerged from his work with the hysteric, Winnicott the paediatrician and child analyst was faced with the problem of the ill baby on the mother's lap:

> This is, in essence, the paradigm change which accounts for the difference between the Freudian Oedipal, triangular or three-body psychoanalysis and Winnicott's mother-baby, dual or two-body psychoanalysis.
>
> (Chapter 4: 146)

To amplify the different basic assumptions between Freud and Win-nicott, Loparic argues that Freud's philosophical underpinning was essentially Kantian, which meant that he allowed himself '. . . a number of speculative auxiliary suppositions to formulate his metapsychol-ogy . . . '(ibid.). Winnicott built on Freud's clinical methodology, and focused on the subjective experience of his countertransference as will be developed in some of the chapters in Part Two (see Chapters 8 and 10 especially). This emphasis on clinical experience concurs especially with Winnicott's later arguments as seen in Chapter 13 (and explored in Chapter 14), and highlights the reasons for his particular disagreement with Freud's 'speculative' notion of the 'death instinct'.

Loparic comprehensively addresses the distinctiveness of Winnicott's revolutionary investigations and completes his critical survey with an address to the critics of Winnicott (as well as those who romanticize his work). He stresses that, following both Darwin and Freud, Winnicott was foremost a scientist who was loyal to the scientific method. To illustrate this point Loparic cites the invaluable methodology of Winnicott's therapeutic consultations which exemplify his dedication to scientific investigation.

Part Two: Personal perspectives

Winnicott always valued travelling abroad to discuss his ideas and when he was 66 he gave a talk to the candidates of the Los Angeles Psychoanalytic Society in 1962. A transcript of this talk was selected by Winnicott himself to be included in his second volume of collected papers – *The Maturational Processes and the Facilitating Environment* (1965a).[16] This same paper – A personal view of the Kleinian contribution (1965b) – is selected to start Part Two and **Chapter 5** (similar to Chapter 1), is an autobiographical commentary with a focus on his perspective of the psychoanalytic innovations of Melanie Klein. Winnicott comments on the 'Melanie Klein-Anna Freud controversy' and, with little elaboration, he conveys his view that the 'Melanie Klein-Anna Freud controversy . . . hampers free thought' in the BPaS. In 1954 Winnicott had written to both Anna Freud and Melanie Klein to request that they initiate a dismantling of the group system for the 'health of the British Psychoanalytical Society' (Rodman 1987: 71). This is another example of Winnicott's desire for analytic openness and neutrality in the interest of scientific endeavour.

Winnicott's use of the squiggle game in his diagnostic consultations resonated strongly with Marion Milner, whose own original contribution to psychoanalysis was contemporaneous with Winnicott's. They were close colleagues and after his death Milner wrote two tributes – the first was given at a memorial meeting of the BPaS in 1972, and the second was commissioned by the French journal *L'Arc* for an

Introduction

edition dedicated to Winnicott's work in 1977. The two papers, like the title, are thematic 'overlapping circles' and presented together in **Chapter 6.** Milner pays tribute to Winnicott the man, to his ideas and to the ways in which he influenced her – personally, professionally and theoretically.

These tributes were written when Milner was in her seventies and had known Winnicott since the 1930s when she writes how she was 'captivated' by a lecture he gave on the spatula game '. . . by the mixture in him of deep seriousness and his love of little jokes . . . the play aspect of his character, if one thinks of true play as transcending the opposites of serious and non-serious' (Chapter 6: 170).

Marion Milner, who was a child analyst and a 'weekend painter,' discusses how she thinks in pictures and was interested in the 'interplay of edges'. One of her most important books *On Not Being Able to Paint* explores the nature of boundaries and space in painting paralleled with a subjective experience of the inner self (Milner 1950). Her natural disposition to observe and self-reflect, linked with the experience of the 'other', corresponded deeply with Winnicott's approach especially the concept of 'potential space' and the theory of 'playing.' Her appreciation of Winnicott's conceptualizations is manifest throughout this chapter as she evocatively links his ideas with her own original thinking on the prelogical area of experience (see Glossary). However, there is also an area of divergence, posed as a question, related to Winnicott's notion of the core self.

> I can understand him when he claims that the sense of self comes on the basis of the unintegrated state, but when he adds that this state is by definition not observable or communicable, I begin to wonder. Not communicable, yes. Not observable, I am not so sure. I think of the dark still centre of the whirling Catherine wheel and feel fairly certain that it can, in the right setting, be related to by the conscious ego discovering that it can turn in upon itself, make contact with the core of its own being, and find there a renewal, a rebirth . . .
>
> (Chapter 6: 172)

Milner's critique relates specifically to Winnicott's 1963 concept of communication in which he states that the core self must never be communicated with otherwise it will amount to a violation of the self (1963: 187 in 1965a). This divergence between Milner and Winnicott has potential for further exploration.

Winnicott's work is acknowledged by a wide variety of psycho-analytic cultures and many of his books have been translated into 24 languages to date. Arguably, however, it is the French reception of Winnicott's contribution to psychoanalysis that has been the most successful. Initiated in the early 1960s, when his papers were translated and published by *La Revue Française*, today, along with Freud and Lacan, Winnicott's thought is established as fundamental to psychoanalytic development and discourse in France (Birksted-Breen et al. 2010: 16). Four of the subsequent chapters in **Part Two** come from France. Each paper selects a specific concept of Winnicott's that resonates with the French development of psychoanalysis with its philosophical underpinning – potential space, the après coup, a freedom of thought and primary narcissism. As is characteristic of French psychoanalysis the role of the father is as crucial a component to the early psychic environment as is the mother's. This is not a contradiction of Winnicott's schema but does indicate an interesting controversy related to the notion of a 'dual relationship' in early psychic processes.

André Green had Winnicott in mind when, in 1975, he wrote 'Potential space in psychoanalysis: the object in the setting', re-published here as **Chapter 7.** Green addresses the way in which the term 'object' has been used and misused in the psychoanalytic literature since its inception with Freud, and analyzes the evolution of Winnicott's 'object'. Green concludes that Winnicott defines not so much an object as a space in which objects will be created. Winnicott's thought, observes Green, emerges from clinical work and Green's appreciation is especially for Winnicott's late work as seen in *Playing and Reality*. He stresses that Winnicott's observations were a result of the close examination of his countertransference in the clinical situation rather than 'infant observation' or paediatric work. This is an argument that relates to Green's debate with Daniel Stern in which he, Green, argues that infant observation cannot make a contribution to the development of psychoanalysis because it is only within the context of the analytic setting that psychoanalysis as theory and technique can evolve (Green 2000b: 21–6; 2000c: 41–72). Winnicott may well have concurred with this view since, towards the end of his life, he stated that he had learnt much more about early psychic phenomena from the adult patient who had regressed in analysis than he had from his work with children and/or mothers and babies.

With an exploration of the French psychoanalytic concept of the 'double' Green stakes a claim for his addition to Winnicott's notion of 'there's no such thing as a baby' and maintains that '. . . there is no such entity as a baby with his mother. No mother-child couple exists without a father somewhere . . . the child nevertheless is the product of the union of the father and mother. Of this union he is the *material, living, irrefutable* proof' (Chapter 7: 201)

Green argues that a mother who negates the father imago in her mind will cause psychosis in her infant. This reinforces Green's argument that '. . . ultimately *there is no dual relationship*' (p. 201) Here we encounter an area of divergence and potential controversy amongst Winnicott commentators. For instance, in Chapter 4 Loparic argues and emphasizes that Winnicott's work *does* indicate an original dual relationship (see p. 138–145). Green's contrasting position is explored elsewhere in his paper 'On thirdness' (Green 1991 in Abram 2000). The question arises – what constitutes a 'dual relationship' in the context of Winnicott's formulations? Does the core of the theoretical matrix significantly shift the Freudian oedipal structure as Loparic maintains or, with the notion of the father in mother's mind, could it maintain and even enhance it? There is no doubt that the father takes on a different meaning, and therefore a different role in Winnicott's new paradigm. But perhaps the question should stand as an irresolvable paradox concerning the beginning of life (cf. Chapter 16).

Haydée Faimberg's well-known conception of the 'telescoping of generations' (1981/85 in 2005) enlarges on Freud's concept of *Nachträglichkeit* and in **Chapter 8**, her original presentation of 1998 is published for the first time. Faimberg considers the link between Freud's early concept and her own implicit use of it which, she subsequently discovers, is also implicit in Winnicott's concept the 'fear of breakdown'. Faimberg poignantly illustrates that, while never explicitly using the term *Nachträglichkeit*, Winnicott's concept of the 'fear of breakdown' has a continuity with Freud's original concept of *Nachträglichkeit*.

In the context of an intercultural dialogue Faimberg goes to the 'heart of the matter' and proposes, for the first time in 1998, that Winnicott's 'fear of breakdown' offers psychoanalysis an 'excellent example of *Nachträglichkeit*' (p. 206). In order to illustrate her point Faimberg highlights how Winnicott proposes a construction. When the 'fear of breakdown' is felt by the patient in the *present* time of the session, the analyst should interpret that the fear of the future breakdown is based on the breakdown that has *already happened*. This, Faimberg asserts, constitutes a construction as Freud had originally suggested in his paper of 1937 – 'Constructions in analysis'.

Winnicott makes it possible to give – from the present moment of the experience of helplessness in the transference – *a retroactive meaning (to the patient's fear of breakdown in the future) by means of a construction:*

The breakdown he is now experiencing for the *first* time, already took place at a moment when the patient was not yet there to have the experience.

(Chapter 8: 207)

The past, therefore, can only be constructed in the present time of analysis.

This observation links with the concept of early psychic deficiency of the environment and the psychic trauma that occurs as a result. In Winnicott's theory, if there is not a self capable of dealing with the 'thing' (event or lack of holding) then the psyche can only 'catalogue' rather than 'process' the experience (Winnicott 1954). It indicates that the infant was unprotected at a crucial moment of development and therefore, as Faimberg rightly points out, is at the mercy of a 'primitive agony' a 'falling forever.' This is what constitutes break-down in Winnicott's language.

Haydée Faimberg's appreciation of Winnicott's formulation of the 'fear of breakdown' and its implicit reference to the operation of *Nachträglichkeit* is more complex than it may appear. Faimberg wants to emphasize that in the broader conceptualization she pro-poses, following Freud, there are always two phases. Paradoxically, it is the second phase that gives meaning to the first phase, because, as indicated above, there is a Self in the present time more able to experience what had happened. The new awareness that emerges in the context of the transference in the analytic setting means the patient is able to receive the analyst's construction – if offered at the right time – and the 'catalogued' event is brought into conscious-ness. The process from then on enables the early psychic trauma to be put into the past.

Faimberg's 1998 conceptualization was developed from her study with Corel in their paper 'Repetition and surprise: construction and its validation' (Faimberg and Corel 1989 in 2005) in which they emphasize the 'fertile paradox' of construction that it is both retroac-tive and anticipatory (2005: 31). Faimberg terms the first phase – the phase of anticipation – because it anticipates a meaning that is not yet there, due to the fact that nobody was there to register meaning as such. It is the second phase, the construction in the context of the analysis, that the past can be constructed for the first time.

> . . . *Nachträglichkeit,* in its broader conceptualization, is an operation that intervenes in the clinical situation, in the psychoanalytic process, and gives us a conceptual frame of unconscious psychic temporality with which to explore and understand how psychoanalysis produces psychic change. The effectiveness of psychoanalysis thereby comes to the fore.
>
> (Faimberg 2007: 1223)

Faimberg's important contribution retroactively illuminates the originality of Winnicott's formulation 'fear of breakdown,' and at the same time articulates her own original extension of Freud's conception of *Nachträglichkeit.*

'Fear of breakdown' is an evocative example of Winnicott's particular use of words as can be detected in his earliest publications.[17] From his first seminal paper in 1945 he had made a deliberate attempt to stay alive in his writing (by using 'plain English') – matched with his desire to stay alive in his thinking.[18] His allegiance, he wanted to make clear, was to scientific freedom which clearly related to the idea of a 'freedom of thought' (Chapter 10). This is a crucial element of his scientific approach, as Loparic has already shown in Chapter 4. Despite the fact that Winnicott in his later years understood that people had to work hard at understanding where he was coming from, the value of his innovative use of language, as we see throughout this volume, resulted in fresh formulations that in turn led to a new psychoanalytic theoretical matrix.

Ogden celebrates Winnicott's use of language in 'Reading Winnicott' – published in 2001 (sixteen years after his preliminary discussion of Winnicott's theories [re-published in Chapter 2]) and re-published here as **Chapter 9.** Ogden's observations on Winnicott's use of the English vernacular emerged out of teaching Winnicott. The paper under scrutiny is Winnicott's 1945 paper, 'Primitive Emotional Development'. Ogden observes that the writing is '. . . a piece of non-fiction literature in which the meeting of reader and writing generates an imaginative experience in the medium of language' (Chapter 9: 214). Through a dissection of the text Ogden illustrates '. . . the life of the writing . . . as inseparable from, the life of the ideas' (ibid.).

11

An independence of mind was crucial for Winnicott in his thinking and he felt it was crucial to psychoanalytic treatment – non compliance. This sentiment comes through in his theories and his clinical work. As Daniel Widlöcher argues in **Chapter 10**, Winnicott amplifies the notion of the [sense of] freedom and in particular a 'freedom of thought'. Widlöcher explains that since the 1960s French analysts had been interested in Winnicott's work because they were interested in his developmental model with its focus on relationship (cf. Birksted-Breen et al. 2010: 16). Widlöcher explores four levels of freedom and creativity: communication, metapsychological structure, paradox and therapeutic goals. Widlöcher, like Green, celebrates Winnicott's focus on the countertransference and shows how it offers psychoanalysis a new dimension.

> But Winnicott went further than counter transference theorists, pointing out that it is not simply in response to the analysand's transference that an empathic understanding of his or her unconscious can develop – the origins of that kind of mutual communication lie in the interaction between mother and baby. Co-associativeness or co-creativity makes for shared reverie, the infant's capacity to be alone in the mother's presence. She helps her child to play, just as the analyst helps his or her patient to play – in other words, and somewhat paradoxically, to work at the combinatorial associations between representations and affects.
>
> (Chapter 10: 237)

Widlöcher highlights that the notion of 'freedom' functions in a particular way related to Winnicott's notion of 'potential space'. He suggests the term 'co-thinking' to describe how unconscious associations play a role in the analyst's listening. Widlöcher's view is that the self creates the link between the transformations involved in the inter-psychic communication. He examines the concept of paradox in Winnicott's work and concludes that freedom of thought is an integral part of the potential space between the subject and the object and plays a fundamental part in illusion.[19] This notion powerfully resonates with Milner's concept of 'the necessity of illusion' (cf. Milner 1950: 26–34).

The concept of illusion and primary creativity in Winnicott's work relates to the notion of creative living associated with staying alive. This is inextricably linked with Winnicott's notions of the 'spontaneous gesture' and 'recognition'. If the spontaneous gesture is not met in an alive and creative way, then the infant has to withdraw. Extending Winnicott's concept of primary creativity Kenneth Wright, in **Chapter 11**, sets out to formulate a theory of artistic endeavour making use of what he feels is implicit in Winnicott's formulations. In this chapter, resonant with Milner's work, Wright explores the distinction between the notions of interpsychic and self-communication – an examination which reverberates with Winnicott's exploration of the 'place where we live' (Winnicott 1971) – as he moves towards formulating a theory of artistic creation. Wright is not writing from a position of artist, in the way Marion Milner wrote *On Not Being Able to Paint,* but from his position as a psychoanalyst. As such, although this paper is not a clinical paper, it contains a depth of insight that can only emerge from long experience of analytic clinical work. Building on his previous writings, and on Winnicott's original concept of primary creativity, Wright examines the artist's 'search for form' linked with his source of inspiration concerning Winnicott's theory of the mirror-role of mother with its focus on the role of reflection (Wright 1991 and 2009). Here he brings his personal review of how Winnicott extends Freudian principles:

> As Winnicott puts it, the infant has the experience of 'creating the breast' ('primary creativity') but only when the mother is attuned enough to give it in a way that corresponds to the baby's anticipation (Winnicott 1953). It is important to note that this way of thinking subtly transforms the classical concept of wish-fulfillment by stressing its object-relational aspect: primary creativity is more than libidinal satisfaction – *it involves the finding by the baby, and provision by the mother, of an external form (the breast) that corresponds to the baby's inner, subjective state.*
>
> (Chapter 11: 250–251 [italics in original])

Wright quotes from the work of Susanne Langer who simply states that 'Art is the creation of forms symbolic of human feeling,' in order to apply Winnicott's theory of primary creativity to the artist's quest:

> . . . we could say that in creating his work, *the artist, like the baby, creates (or finds) external forms for inner feeling states.* Seen in this way, artistic creation echoes the transaction of 'primary creativity' in

which an inner 'something' is realized through the mother's provision of a matching form.

(Ibid., [italics in original])

Comparing the artist's aims with the baby's spontaneous gesture Wright suggests that the artist makes a *self*-created form which relates to the 'answering form' of the original mother. A review of Winnicott's theory of transitional phenomena aids Wright's desire to create a bridge between Winnicott's theory of the mother–infant relationship and an understanding of the psychic roots of the artist's motivation. But, as Wright the analyst knows, creative endeavour is not necessarily a pleasurable reaching out – and an examination of Natkin's work offers evidence that the artist's skill and motivation may arise from an original deficiency as well as trauma. The canvas thus becomes the artist's *self* provision due to a lack of an 'answering form' from the original mother.

Wright explores his different perspective from two other psychoanalytic theories of the artist's activity – Bollas's 'maternal aesthetic' with its focus on the 'transformational object', and Hannah Segal's emphasis on the reparation of the object. He maintains that both theories, whilst emerging from different basic assumptions, do not account enough for the continual self evolving that Winnicott emphasizes (Chapter 11: 260–261).

In his conclusions Wright returns to the clinical situation and, paradoxically, shows how his exploration of the artist's quest actually illuminates the analytic relationship as an '. . . *affective matrix* in which 'forms for human feeling' (Langer) . . . like the artist's forms . . . must resonate with experience if they are to serve a containing function' (Chapter 11: 264–265).

Self-reflection, as Wright has shown, has a healthy dimension. This is compatible with René Roussillon's recent examination of Winnicott's notion of merger between mother and infant in **Chapter 12**. Roussillon argues that Winnicott expands Freud's concept of primary narcissism and transforms it into a clinical concept.

For Winnicott, primary narcissism cannot be conceived of in any solipsistic way. How it develops should be thought of within the context of the primary psychic relationship . . .

(Chapter 12: 270)

Roussillon suggests that a 'kind of illusion' erases the individual's thought that the relationship with the primary object has impacted on her [sense of] self. This therefore has a clinical implication – to analyze primary narcissism reintroduces '. . . what the primary narcissistic illusion has erased, i.e. the role played by the primary object in its foundation because narcissism involves two and perhaps three people'.

(Ibid.)

This '. . . and perhaps three people' rejoins us to the aforementioned divergence between Green and Loparic on the early psychic predicament. Are there two or three people involved in primary narcissism? The role of the father, in French psychoanalysis, is never far away in conceptualizing early states of mind; but Roussillon with his 'perhaps' seems more equivocal than Green concerning the issue of the 'dual relationship.'

However, his main emphasis in Chapter 12 is that Winnicott's extensions make Freud's concept clinical rather than metapsychological. To initiate this examination Roussillon reviews Freud's paper, 'Mourning and Melancholia' to demonstrate how the 'ego assimilates'. He concludes thus:

Narcissism assimilates the object and takes in the shadow of the object that has fallen on the ego. At the same time, it erases the fact that there is a shadow that has fallen on the ego and is henceforth mixed up with it.

(Chapter 12: 271)

It is important to note that Roussillon's idea of 'illusion' in this chapter is different from the 'illusion' referred to by Winnicott when the baby has the illusion that he is God [as the result of his needs being met]. But it is interlinked in as much as the unconscious memory of 'needs being met' becomes assimilated in the mind in the same way that Roussillon shows that the 'shadow' (of the object) is assimilated. The different quality of 'illusions', therefore, refers to different stages of development. Winnicott's illusion (of omnipotence) refers to the phase of absolute dependence whereas Roussillon's 'illusion' refers to the phase of 'relative dependence' when the baby has to deal with loss and separation (Abram 2007: 130–45).

Part Three: Late Winnicott studies

One of Winnicott's last papers – 'The use of an object' – was given to the New York Psychoanalytic Society in 1968, followed by three discussion papers. Due to a variety of reasons, the discussants seemed to misunderstand Winnicott's thesis (see Chapters 13, 14 and 17). Despite each discussant's appreciation of Winnicott's work the two main areas of criticism concerned his interpretation of the term 'object relating' and the lack of Freudian instinct theory in his argument. After the presentation of his paper Winnicott fell seriously ill and had to be hospitalized in New York for several weeks. Remarkably, from his hospital bed, he wrote his response to the discussion papers which is re-published here as **Chapter 13.** Written two years before he died this paper addresses the points made by Bernard Fine, one of the American discussants, concerning Freud's instinct theory. Winnicott clarifies his disagreement with Freud's concept of the death instinct in this chapter but his main aim is to convey that the newborn baby is not yet able to distinguish whether a sensation is inner or outer: this is why, he argued, instincts were not relevant – *from the baby's point of view.* 'The behaviour of the environment is part and parcel of the child's development, . . . this cannot be omitted' (Chapter 13: 299).

> . . . The crux of my argument is that the first drive is itself *one* thing, something that I call 'destruction,' but I could have called it a combined love-strife drive. *This unity is primary* . . . The fate of this unity of drive cannot be stated without reference to the environment.
>
> (Chapter 13: 299 [my italics])

It will be clear in the light of the papers in Parts One and Two that Winnicott had been leading up to this formulation since the 1940s related to his research on classifying the environment. This paper shows an advance on instinct theory because it expands his concept of primary maternal preoccupation. Linked with this and stimulated by the finding of some unpublished notes in the Winnicott archives, **Chapter 14** offers an interpretation and discussion of Winnicott's final theory of aggression. An examination of the unpublished notes compared to the late writings, including Chapter 13, shows that the notes (which constitute a plan for a paper that was never written), confirm a consolidation of Winnicott's concept of 'survival of the object'. Following on from an exposition of the themes related to 'the use of an object' Chapter 14 aims to demonstrate that Winnicott's critique of instinct theory led to the notion of psychic survival. The author sets out her interpretation of the clinical implications in Winnicott's thesis:

> I propose that the clinical implications in Winnicott's formulations suggest the notion of an intra-psychic surviving and non-surviving object. These intra-psychic objects arise through an admixture of the primary object's oscillations between psychic survival and non-survival of the newborn's needs. I conclude that this specific inter-psychic dynamic between object and subject is at the heart of human development which is naturally revivified in the transference-countertransference matrix. Consequently, the notion of psychic survival constitutes the specificity of clinical psychoanalysis as a therapeutic treatment.
>
> (Chapter 14: 302–303)

Dissociation as a defence is entirely relevant to the above themes of life and death, survival and non survival, and Goldman, in **Chapter 15**, explores another of Winnicott's final preoccupations on the meaning of dissociation. Goldman reminds us of Winnicott's prayer, 'Oh God may I be alive when I die,' and surmises that this expressed desire suggests that:

> . . . Winnicott yearns for a psychic space in which he can simultaneously hold both life and death. His desire, in other words, is not simply to survive omnipotently but to find a way to bridge the ultimate dissociation *between* life and death. Winnicott is recognizing that aliveness and death have meaning only to the extent that a link can be retained between the two.
>
> (Chapter 15: 331 [italics in original])

Goldman discusses how Winnicott shows that psychological aliveness cannot be taken for granted and, as we have seen in the preceding chapters, he confirms the infant's need for a responsive environment, adding that this is the location – between infant and environment – of the *capacity* to feel alive.

For Winnicott, aliveness originates in an undifferentiated field which, *only from an external point of view,* appears as a newborn needing to be met by a responsive environment. Rather than a quality located *within* a distinct individual, aliveness has its roots in a *psychic field* as mother shields infant from premature awareness of 'complications' and 'coincidences' beyond its ken.

(Chapter 15: 332)

Goldman makes the point that Winnicott wanted to concentrate on the life force rather than debate the death instinct and, related to the title of his chapter, quotes Winnicott's observation that:

In each baby . . . is *a vital spark*, and this urge towards life and growth and development is a part of the baby, something the child is born with and which is carried forward in a way that we do not have to understand.

(Winnicott 1964: 27)
(quoted in Chapter 15: 333, italics added)

Goldman makes an important link between Jones's 'aphanisis' and Winnicott's annihilation anxiety and interprets that Winnicott wants to emphasize 'aliveness and being' rather than the Freudian focus on infantile sexuality. The author cites Winnicott's clinical example of the man whose dissociated part was female (Winnicott 1971: 72–5). Goldman concludes that Winnicott's final words, as seen in the unpublished Notes re-published here in Chapter 14, offer further evidence that it was the 'vital spark' in human life that Winnicott noted required facilitation.

An oft repeated misperception is that the father has no role to play in Winnicott's theoretical matrix. The student of Winnicott's writings, however, will see that the father is ever present and the environment will most definitely fail if the father is not actively engaged in the task of parenting from the beginning. But, as we have seen above (Chapters 4, 7, 12), it is a question of emphasis and there is a divergence amongst authors concerning the role of the father and the meaning of a 'dual relationship' in Winnicott's psychoanalytic model. To add to this dialogue Christopher Reeves, in **Chapter 16**, makes a philological examination and tracks the role of the father in Winnicott's writings. He argues and confirms that, although not always directly addressed, the father is integrated in Winnicott's theories.

Reeves offers his interpretation that, without ever naming the roles, Winnicott theorized two distinct fathers and that the two different functions of the father mean that, for the baby, there are effectively two different fathers.[20] After demonstrating that the father was '. . . at once *important, intrinsic* and *implicit* for Winnicott . . .' Chapter 16 proposes that the first distinct role of the father should be termed the co-nurturant father (p. 360). Subsequently, as the baby develops, a different father emerges in Winnicott's writings – one who has to contain the growing child's negative feelings and, crucially (in relation to his later concept 'the use of an object'), one who has to survive them. This father is proposed to be the 'sire father' – loving first, but also 'strict and strong'. However, Reeves comes across a problem in Winnicott's implicit description of the two fathers:

> Underlying the problem is Winnicott's desire to retain both options, to insist on the father's distinctiveness of role and differentiation from mother where the family unit is being viewed as a threesome, while laying stress on the essential continuity of the father's role with that of the mother, when the focus is on the dyadic 'core' of the family – the mother and the baby. It is a characteristic of Winnicott's theorizing not to seek to resolve paradoxes by precise conceptual differentiation.
>
> (Chapter 16: 367)

This observation goes some way towards addressing the divergence between Loparic and Green concerning the existence of a 'dual relationship', at the beginning of the infant's life. Paradox is intrinsic to the human condition from the beginning and its resolution infers a false self solution.

The important question of influence and transmission of psychoanalytic ideas (Chapter 8) and the inevitability of a 'zeitgeist' in psychoanalysis is addressed by Nellie Thompson in **Chapter 17** who analyzes the reciprocal influence of American psychoanalysts on Winnicott's thought. This paper is a sequel to Thompson's earlier paper of 2008 in which she compared and contrasted the work of Phyllis Greenacre with Winnicott's ideas – in particular the earliest relationship (Thompson 2008). In Chapter 17 Thompson extends her focus and uses data from an examination of Winnicott's correspondence that shows how familiar he was with the work of several American analysts. Thompson argues that Winnicott's focus on early object relations relates to the work of Kris, an émigré originally from Vienna, who had written in 1956 that, '. . . we now think that the development of ego functions and object relations are of equal and intrinsic importance' (Kris 1956: 67). This is amplified by Thompson's observation of the collaborative work between Hartmann, Anna Freud, Kris and Loewenstein concerning the development of ego functioning which corresponds to Winnicott's perspective in his paper – 'Ego integration in child development' (1962) – and correlates with the previous themes concerning instinct theory and its relevance at the beginning of life (Chapters 13, 14).

> Their depiction of the mother–infant relationship deeply resonated with Winnicott's view of the importance of the maternal environment in the infant's life. Their writings emphasize that the ego and id are undifferentiated at birth . . .
>
> (Chapter 17: 393)

These American authors, as Thompson points out, stress that the 'ego and id are undifferentiated at birth' and that the mother is the most important environment. This is really no different from Winnicott's view although the language is different, i.e. when these authors refer to the ego and the id Winnicott refers to the merger between infant and mother. In tracing the writings and presentations of papers that focused on the themes of ego functioning and regression, Chapter 17 argues that while it is true that Winnicott's work impacted (and still does) on the work of American analysts, it was equally true that Winnicott was integrating, from reviews and meetings, the opinions and perspectives of several key American analysts, many of whom originated from Vienna (cf. Thompson 2010).

The squiggle game by now is one of the most well-known leitmotivs of Winnicott's work associated with his theory of playing and the discovery of the self. In **Chapter 18** Farley offers an examination of the squiggle game that complements Loparic's view in Chapter 4 and Milner's observation in Chapter 6, i.e. that the legacy of the squiggle game has become much more than a therapeutic intervention. Farley reads the squiggle game as evidence for a psychoanalytic conception of history. Linking Winnicott's observations related to 'discrepancy' and Bollas's 'unthought known' Chapter 18 indicates how important the act of witnessing relates to the concept of history.

Chapter 18 argues that the mother, as 'subjective object,' is the baby's first witness, and in that capacity she is called on to engage the negative labour of attending to experiences that cannot be known or seen directly, even as their unconscious force requires a response.

In this chapter we are reminded of the outside world and global history – the Second World War – as the context in which Winnicott was making history in his application of psychoanalysis with evacuees in Oxford. From her work in the Winnicott Archives in London[21] Farley researches in Winnicott's wartime hostel scheme books and comes across some children's drawings (Chapter 18: 424). There, Farley finds that Winnicott was making use of the squiggle game much earlier than has hitherto been published, i.e. in the early 1940s rather than, as previously thought, from the mid 1950s. This tallies with Marion Milner's observation in Chapter 6 that Winnicott's language medium of pictures and doodles was intrinsically part of his way of relating to himself and others.

The need to articulate trauma in the presence of a witness – as long as the witness is a receptive, reflecting and surviving Other – offers a chance for process and digestion of a 'catalogued' trauma – a wound. Tracing two case histories with the squiggles as evidence, Chapter 18 concludes with a thought that reverberates with Wright's extensions of Winnicott's notion of primary creativity (Chapter 11).

> The squiggle may be evidence of how we make from the stray fragments of the past a meaningful historical narrative. But this history in pictures may also testify to the labour of letting go, or leaving something behind so that the past may become, 'memorable rather than spellbinding' (Phillips 2004: 143) – which is, perhaps, the ultimate act of creativity, the art of history.
>
> (Chapter 18: 445)

Chapter 18, written from the perspective of a new Winnicott researcher, and thus representative for the hope of future Winnicott studies, completes this collection on Donald Winnicott Today. The illustrations, in Chapter 18, which depict Winnicott's clinical work in vivo, are a moving reminder of Winnicott's dedication to Freud's 'methodology of investigation' and his distinctive expansion of theory and methodology. While the evidence of Winnicott's immense contribution to psychoanalysis is collectively demonstrated by the authors in this volume, perhaps it would be true to say that should

Winnicott himself see this volume he would, to begin with at least, go directly to these extraordinary pictures drawn by the traumatized children to whom he offered his help in the 1940s.

Notes

1 This is Winnicott's first sentence for the plan of a paper to be presented at the I.P.A. 1971 Congress in Vienna. The notes are examined and explored in Chapter 14.
2 The word 'revolution' references the work of Thomas Kuhn in his *Structure of Scientific Revolutions* (1970 2nd edition). In Chapter 4 Loparic sets out to examine the evolution of Winnicott's discoveries and applies Kuhn's theory of scientific revolutions. Loparic demonstrates the extent to which Freud's psychoanalytic symbolic matrix was changed by Winnicott. This notion is echoed in Chapter 14. Judith Hughes, in her important study on three British Object Relations psychoanalysts also makes use of Kuhn's notions (although more implicitly), in her 1989 publication *Reshaping the Psychoanalytic Domain*. Hughes argues that the major revolutions in British psychoanalysis emerge from W.R.D. Fairbairn, Melanie Klein and D.W. Winnicott. In France, it is argued that the work of Jacques Lacan represents an equivalent revolution.
3 Editor's note: I follow Ogden by using the term 'matrix.' For me it invokes the quality of holding and fecundity that emerges from the intricate and interweaving concepts in Winnicott's work. His theory, as Ogden has shown in Chapter 9, is inseparable from his use of language. Thus, 'theoretical matrix' seems to describe evocatively the result of Winnicott's contribution. Ogden, in Chapter 2, states that the infant's first psychological matrix is the mother which all the authors in this volume concur with.
4 Donnet's work utilizes and develops Winnicott's notion of 'creating the object' which the French term 'found-created'. Donnet's term 'analyzing situation' emphasizes the nature of the analytic relationship in a way that resonates with Winnicott's emphasis, i.e. that both patient and analyst are equally engaged in a continuous psychic restructuring in the context of the après coup.
5 See Chapter 10 in which Widlöcher discusses his view that Winnicott's contribution promotes a freedom of thought.
6 See Chapter 8 in which Haydée Faimberg illustrates a 'broader concept' of *Nachträglichkeit* and its link with Winnicott's 'fear of breakdown'.
7 Winnicott made a distinction between needs and wishes (Abram 2007: 84, 288, 290–2). I have recently explored this emphasis related to the capacity for desire (Abram 2010).
8 The Kleinian interpretation and development of the 'death instinct', which has a very different emphasis to Freud's concept, fuelled Winnicott's disagreement with Freud (see Chapter 14).

9 This talk was originally entitled 'The Relation of Dr Winnicott's Theory to Other Formulations of Early Development'. This is a significant title related to Winnicott's late examination of comparing his work with other analysts (see Chapter 17). The editors of *Psychoanalytic Explorations* re-named it 'D.W.W. on D.W.W.' The editor's research in the archives of the BPaS included a study of the 'signing in books' for scientific meetings to see those attended by Winnicott. This is where it was noticed that Winnicott used to sign himself in to Scientific Meetings of the BPaS as D.W.W., written forcefully with a thick dark pencil. His wife, close friends and colleagues frequently referred to him as D.W.W.

10 See note 10 of Chapter 3.

11 See Letter to Violet (his sister) of 1919 in the *Selected Letters* (Rodman 1987: 1).

12 Winnicott refers to the 'environment' which refers specifically to the mother's emotions towards her infant. The environment is internalized and includes all aspects of the psychic environment. His emphasis is on the psychic elements of the environment – unconscious to unconscious (See Abram 2007: 164–81).

13 Following Bion (whose work in Second Thoughts suggests that he must have been influenced by Winnicott's work [cf. Winnicott's Primary Maternal Preoccupation 1956 with Bion's 1962 Theory of Thinking]), the post Kleinian development certainly factors in the psychic environment. This has led to some post Kleinian thinkers who place a greater emphasis on the psychic environment than the death instinct as discussed in Roth and Lemma 2008.

14 The issue of timing is a crucial element in analytic technique which offers the patient an opportunity to 'become an analysand' (Donnet 2009: 33). This relates to Winnicott's notion of creating the object (cf. note 4 above).

15 Winnicott's conceptions, as seen in the author's lexicon, *The Language of Winnicott,* are enumerated and linked with the seminal papers written during that phase.

16 Editor's note: It is not clear why Winnicott decided to include this paper and I suggest that it was because he wanted to set the record straight concerning his appreciation of Klein's work. Perhaps it's noteworthy that he gave this talk two years after the death of Melanie Klein.

17 Editor's note: Winnicott's earliest writings were published in The Leys School magazine which can be found in the Archives of the school where he boarded between 14 and 18. The three short essays show Winnicott's capacities as an astute observer of personalities as well as his sense of humour.

18 Post Controversial Discussions it was very difficult to present a piece of clinical work or publish a psychoanalytic paper without conveying one's allegiance to either the Klein group or the Freud group. Winnicott felt this pressure 'hampered free thought'.

19 For a guide to the notion of 'illusion' in Winnicott's work see Chapter 3 and Abram 2007: 200–16.
20 Editor's note: Reeves's postulation of two fathers parallels the distinctions between the 'environment mother' and the 'object mother' as seen in Winnicott's 1963 paper – 'The development of the capacity for concern'.
21 The Wellcome Library London – http://library.wellcome.ac.uk. The search code is PP/DWW (see Appendix).

References

Abram, J. ed. (2000) *André Green at the Squiggle Foundation*. London: Karnac.
Abram J (2007) *The Language of Winnicott: A Dictionary of Winnicott's Use of Words*. 2nd edn. London: Karnac.
Abram, J. (2010) On desire and female sexuality: some tentative reflections. *EPF Bulletin* 64: 155–65.
Birksted-Breen, D. Flanders, S. and Gibeault, A. (2010) *Reading French Psychoanalysis*. The New Library of Psychoanalysis. Teaching Series. London: Routledge.
Donnet, J.-L. (2009) *The Analyzing Situation*. International Psychoanalytical Association. London: Karnac.
Faimberg, H. (1981/85) The telescoping of generations: a genealogy of alienated identifications. In: Faimberg 2005, Chapter 1.
Faimberg, H. (2005) *The Telescoping of Generations: Listening to the Narcissistic Links between Generations*. New Library of Psychoanalysis. London: Routledge and The Institute of Psychoanalysis.
Faimberg, H. (2007) A plea for a broader concept of *Nachträglichkeit*. *The Psychoanalytic Quarterly* 76: 1221–40.
Faimberg, H. and Corel, A. (1989) Repetition and surprise: construction and its validation. Presented at the Congress of the International Psychoanalytical Association Chapter 3 in Faimberg 2005.
Freud, S. (1923) The ego and the id. SE 19, 3–63.
Green, A. [1991] On thirdness. In: Abram 2000, 39–68.
Green, A. [1996](2000) The posthumous Winnicott: on *Human Nature*. In: Abram 2000, 69–83.
Green, A. (2000b) What kind of research for psychoanalysis? In: Sandler et al. 2000a.
Green, A. (2000c) Science and science fiction in infant research. In: Sandler et al. 2000a.
Hughes, Judith M. (1989) *Reshaping Psychoanalytic Domain. The Work of Melanie Klein, W.R.D. Fairbairn, and D. W. Winnicott*. Berkeley: University of California Press.
King, P. and Steiner, R. eds (1991) *The Freud–Klein Controversies 1941–45*. London: Routledge.

Kuhn, Thomas S. (1970) *The Structure of Scientific Revolutions*. 2nd edition. Chicago: University of Chicago Press.

Milner, M. (1950) *On Not Being Able to Paint*. London: Heinemann Educational.

Ogden, T.H. (1992) The dialectically constituted/decentred subject of psychoanalysis. II. The contributions of Klein and Winnicott. *Int J Psychoanal* 73: 613–26.

Ogden, T.H. (2001) Reading Winnicott. *Psychoanal Q.* 70: 299–323.

Rodman F.R. ed. (1987) *The Spontaneous Gesture: Selected Letters of D.W. Winnicott*. Cambridge, MA: Harvard University Press.

Roth, P. and Lemma, A. (eds) (2008) *Envy and Gratitude Revisited*. International Psychoanalytical Association. London: Karnac.

Sandler, J., Holder, A., Dare, C. and Dreher, A. (1997) *Freud's Models of the Mind: An Introduction*. London: Karnac.

Sandler, J., Sandler, A.-M. and Davies, R. eds (2000a) *Clinical and Observational Psychoanalytic Research: The Roots of a Controversy: André Green and Daniel Stern*. The Psychoanalysis Unit U.C.L. London: Karnac.

Thompson, N.L. (2008) A Measure of Agreement: An Exploration of the Relationship of D.W. Winnicott and Phyllis Greenacre. *Psychoanalytic Quarterly* 77: 251–81.

Winnicott, D.W. (1945a) Towards an objective study of human nature. *New Era in Home and School*, Postscript: 179–82.

Winnicott, D.W. (1954) Mind and its relation to the psyche-soma. *Br J Med Psychol* 27: 201–9.

Winnicott, D.W. (1958) Anxiety associated with insecurity [1952]. In: *Collected Papers: Through Paediatrics to Psycho-analysis*. 1st edition 1958. London: Tavistock, 97–100.

Winnicott, D.W. (1962) Ego integration in child development. In: 1965a.

Winnicott, D.W. (1963) The development of the capacity for concern. In: 1965a.

Winnicott, D.W. (1964) The baby as a going concern. In: *The Child, the Family, and the Outside World*. Harmondsworth: Penguin Books.

Winnicott, D.W. (1965a) *The Maturational Processes and the Facilitating Environment: Studies in the Theory of Emotional Development*. London: Hogarth (International Psycho-analytical Library, No. 64).

Winnicott, D.W. (1965b) A personal view of the Kleinian contribution. In: 1965a, 171–8.

Winnicott, D.W. (1965c) Providing for the child in health and crisis [1962]. In: 1965a, 64–72.

Winnicott, D.W. (1965d) From dependence towards independence in the development of the individual [1963]. In: 1965a, 83–92.

Winnicott, D.W. (1971) *Playing and Reality*. London: Tavistock.

Wright, K. (1991) *Vision and Separation: Between Mother and Baby*. London: Free Association Books.

Wright, K. (2009) *Mirroring and Attunement: Self Realization in Psychoanalysis and Art*. London: Routledge.

PART ONE

Introductory overviews

1

D.W.W. on D.W.W.[1]

D.W. Winnicott

Winnicott's notes for his talk to the 1952 Club[2]
January 1967

The method of investigation. P-A.	Freud
Protest against reference to universal	A. Balint
regression from Id satisfaction-frustration in	Ribble
Oedipal triangle	Suttie
	Lowenfeld
Positive-examination of *actual* infant-parent	Freud
relationship	Klein
Diagnosis Theory of psycho-neurosis	
Freud	
Klein for depression and paranoia	
Schizophrenia and schizoid phases	
1940 Delinquency	
Hope Antisocial Tendency Stealing Aggression	
Till secondary gains	
Delinquency Object relating Controls	
Classification of Environment (postponed)	Greenacre
became facilitating environment	
Primary Maternal Preoccupation	
Adaptation, de-adaptation	

Dependence	Bowlby
Individual maturational processes	
Heredity	
Conflict-free sphere in Ego	Hartmann
Primitive Emotional Development	
Study of Individual without loss of interest in environment	
Early is not Deep	
Add Delusional Transference	Little
Real ME FEELINGS	Fairbairn
Aggression movement – object in the way = NOT-ME found by aggression	
(becoming complex)	Erikson
	Laing

Object Seeking   Transitional Phenomena
Essential Paradox

I AM   A paranoid
position
Alone, in the presence of second paradox
Environment as experienced
Added up as memories integrated into belief in
environment
= self control

Add root of paranoia in I AM + introjected
environment
Mania: return of repressed
i.e. deprivation of environmental controls
identification with environment
price: loss of identity creative spontaneity
(Practical applications)
Meanwhile: exploiting Klein contribution
compare dissociation (splitting) with repression
Hence I AM stage   integration to a unit
Capacity for concern
Depressive mood
'value of depression'

In terms of management: the teaching of skills
– vis à vis reparation
In Social Work
The holding technique
Feed-back to P-A

Psyche-soma – relative to intellect
Intellect exploited
Psycho-somatic disorder: a call back to the
body ego from flight to the intellectual
Psychosomatic patient splits medical care

Two categories of people
    A. Carry around 'having been mad'
    B. Not so
    Mad means breakdown of ego-defences
    (as existed at the time, including mother's
    ego-support) with clinical appearance of
    archaic or unthinkable anxiety: Fordham
    Falling forever
    De-integration
    Disorientation
    Depersonalization etc.
    Panic as a defence against unthinkable anxiety
    Winnicott axiom
    A. Fear of madness, madness that was
    B. Drive to remember by experiencing

Aetiology
Surprise
Psychosis Privation
AST   Deprivation
Psycho-neurosis   Internal strains and
stresses in 'not too bad' environment
Concept of good-enough mother   Hartmann
Mother's adaptation Primary Maternal
Preoccupation
Not mechanical
Not primarily via contraptions cf. in autism

Contribution to concept of sublimation   Freud
Three areas for living
   A. Psychic personal reality (inside)
   B. Relationships to objects
   Behaviour in the actual world
   C. Cultural
   Located in potential space between child
   playing alone and 'mother' whose presence
   is necessary
   Implications for Ego theory
   Ego area (not conflict-free sphere)
   Based on actual living experiences that may
   or may not have reality in a child's life
   Theory of actuality as a projection
   But dependence, especially at stage of
   subjective object
   Example: survival of actual after aggressive
   outburst leads to (or re-inforces) the capacity
   for fantasy, hate instead of annihilation.   Freud

Add: Excitement (non-orgiastic) at the junction
of the subjective and what is objectively
perceived – between continuity and contiguity
Additional Notes
Application of these ideas to
Practice of midwifery
Theory of separation
Talking to parents and those with care of children
Social work theory
Psychotherapy, exploitation of first interview
Concept of health   richness of potential
adulthood sex maturity wisdom
Regression
Adolescent doldrums
Family functioning
Democracy as a development of the functioning
family

                                        Anna Freud
                                        Kris

I've realized more and more as time went on what a tremendous lot I've lost from not properly correlating my work with the work of others. It's not only annoying to other people but it's also rude and it has meant that what I've said has been isolated and people have to do a lot of work to get at it. It happens to be my temperament, and it's a big fault.

Let me interrupt myself for a moment, to say that I made some notes. These notes are a little bit along the lines of what I'm going to say. They're not even properly corrected, let alone having vital signif- icance for hanging on walls; but I thought that if you had a pencil you might feel like writing down Hartmann[3] and Hoffer,[4] you know, in the corner at the edge. At the right-hand edge I left room for you to write all sorts of names in so that you can help me, because I'm now getting to the stage where I really would like to be more correlated.

The other side of the thing is that, with me just as with other peo- ple, the development of thought has been along the line of something that has to do with growth, and if I happen to be like somebody else, it just turns up because we're all dealing with the same material. In fact, the series of papers which have meant anything to me have been a continuation of something that happened in my long ten-year analysis with Mr Strachey[5] in which I had a series of dreams. I don't remember any of them, but the point is that I knew that other people had written on this same subject. I also knew that these dreams were different from the others. They were not for analysis; they were con- solidations of work done. And I always said that if I'd started at the beginning I'd have written down these dreams so as to collect them one day, but I never did of course. If you started doing this, you'd never dream them. So then after the end of analysis, these things take the form of papers we feel we must write and the amazing thing is that people can be found to listen. I'm really tracing a sort of compulsion; and if only I could do it well it would be a wonderful opportunity.

At the beginning I do know that – like everybody, I suppose, in this room – as soon as I found Freud and the method that he gave us for investigating and for treatment, I was in line with it. This was just like when I was at school and was reading Darwin and suddenly I knew that Darwin was my cup of tea. I felt this tremendously, and I suppose that if there's anything I do that isn't Freudian, this is what I want to know. I don't mind if it isn't, but I just feel that Freud gave us this method which we can use, and it doesn't matter what it, leads us to. The point is, it does lead us to things; it's an objective way of looking at things and it's for people who can go to something without preconceived notions, which, in a sense, is science.

At the beginning there was myself learning to do analysis as a paediatrician having had a tremendous experience of listening to people talking about babies and children of all ages and having had great difficulty in seeing a baby as human at all. It was only through analysis that I became gradually able to see a baby as a human being. This was really the chief result of my first five years of analysis, so that I've been extremely sympathetic with any paediatricians or anybody who can't see babies as human, because I absolutely couldn't, however I used to try. So this thing happened and then I became very interested in it all.

When I came to try and learn what there was to be learned about psycho-analysis, I found that in those days we were being taught about everything in terms of the 2, 3 and 4 year-old Oedipus complex and regression from it. It was very distressing to me as someone who had been looking at babies – at mothers and babies – for a long time (already ten to fifteen years) to find that this was so, because I knew that I'd watched a lot of babies start off ill and a lot of them become ill early. For instance, I've had a lot of experience like the one I had this week of two very intelligent and normal parents who brought to me the problem of their little baby of 22 months. This baby, at the age of 16 months, had developed a very well organized obsessional neurosis. The parents said, 'Well, what do we do?' and I was able to take the psychoanalytic theory and say to them, 'Do this.' And they did it and the child dropped the obsessional organization and went forward. It was an absolutely direct application. It seems to me that to have said this now is just simply ordinary experience, but saying it in 1935 in this country would have met with the objection, 'But it can't happen.' There wasn't an audience for that, because of the fact that to have an obsessional neurosis one would have had a regression from difficulties at the Oedipal stage at 3. I know that I overdo this point, but it was something that gave me a line. I thought to myself, I'm going to show that infants are ill very early, and if the theory doesn't fit it, it's just got to adjust itself. So that was that.

Now, there were people talking about these things before I came on the scene. I'm abysmally ignorant of what Miss Freud was doing until she came to this country. After then I'm able to catch up because she herself grew and I watched her growing through the experiences in the War Nurseries[6] and she changed, I think, tremendously. She found in a practical job which people were doing and which she was supervising that things were happening which really influenced her, and it was a great pleasure to watch her. I think that she made a terrific contribution, but I didn't know at the time the work that she was doing before this. I also know that Alice Balint[7] was interested in the things that I'm talking about. There were other people who weren't analysts who were talking about these things: there was Suttie[8], and Margaret Lowenfeld[9] who had a tremendous experience of teaching from the very early twenties about mothers and babies; and Merrill Middlemore[10] too.

Now, as regards the psycho-neuroses, I felt that Freud's theory and his developing scheme for things, as far as I could gradually come to learn them, covered the subject; and as far as I know I made no contribution at all in that area. As you know, I came very much in 1930 – 1940 into the learning area of Mrs Klein, and she took the trouble to try to help me with cases and tell me about her own work. I took over from her, without always understanding the patterning, a very great deal which I think was original from her point of view. It really comes down to the localization of fantasy by the patient or the child in the inside. Mrs Klein didn't like that way of putting it: I talked to her about it and she said that wasn't right. But from my point of view, people knew about inner psychic reality through Freud and they knew about fantasy and dream, but it was she who pointed out the importance of the localizations of all that goes on between eating and defaecation and that it had to do with the inside of the body. And I felt that she taught me all this, without which I couldn't do psychoanalysis of children at all, and I couldn't have stopped that child from becoming seriously neuroticized by telling the mother what to do.

Now where did I begin to wake up a bit? I got completely lost in the long controversy that went on during the war and ruined all our scientific meetings, when people were fighting for the rights of Mrs Klein.[11] It had to be done, but it left me completely cold; I didn't know anything about it and I kept out of the way entirely. I find it difficult, even now, to understand. But what happened to me was that I began to be interested in the environment, and this has led to something in me. Now who else was doing this? I don't think I know at the moment. The point is that I was at that time having analysis with Mrs Riviere[12] who was a great friend of Mrs Klein's, and I said that I was writing a paper on the classification of the environment, and she just wouldn't have it. This was a pity really because I'd got a tremendous amount from my five years with Mrs Riviere, but I had to wait a long time before I could recover from her reaction.

I'd just been through a ten-year period in which I did practically nothing but child analysis, but it was wasted really because the fact is that Miss Freud didn't want it because she said that if I gave a case, even if it was a straightforward clinical case, I would give it with a Kleinian slant; and Mrs Klein didn't want it because I wasn't a Kleinian. So I just had to drop the immediate application to teaching and for a little while do work of other kinds.

There was a war on, and there were hostels for difficult children, and working there in Oxfordshire I at last came into touch with maladjusted children whom I'd always avoided having in my clinic because they disrupt any clinic. If you've got three maladjusted children you're preparing reports for the courts, and all the interesting cases you can do something for immediately are wiped out. You're just doing this useless thing, and I'd always sent on my antisocial children to other clinics; and I'm very glad I did in all of the twenty years from 1923 onwards because I was able to have a very large number of children that I could do something for in a very short time. I said to Mrs Riviere one day, 'There's only just a line like that between me and the theory of delinquency, and one day that's going to be something and then I'm going to be separate. And I feel it coming up, you know.' Only I couldn't do it while I was in analysis with her because – I don't say Mrs Klein minded it, but – the psychoanalysts were the only people for about ten or fifteen years who knew there was anything but environment. Everybody was screaming out that everything was due to somebody's father being drunk. So the thing was, how to get back to the environment without losing all that was gained by studying the inner factors.

I think it was a very important contribution from my point of view when suddenly in a lecture I found myself saying that the antisocial act of the delinquent belongs to the moment of hope. So then I had to invent the term 'antisocial tendency' to join it up with your child who steals a penny out of somebody's purse or goes and steals some buns from the larder which he has a perfect right to. I wanted to join that up with the tendencies that can lead to delinquency. In delinquency, which doesn't mean anything definite, the secondary gains have become more important than the original cause, which is lost. But my clinical material brought me to the fact that the thing behind the antisocial tendency in any family, normal or not, is deprivation;

and the result of deprivation is the doldrums, or hopelessness, or depression of some kind, or any other major defence. But as hope begins to turn up then the child reaches out, trying to reach back over the deprivation area to the lost object. This is an important thing, and life was different for me after this because I now knew what to do with my friends who were bringing their children to me because they had an antisocial tendency in a perfectly good home. I found that before the secondary gains turn up this was something not difficult to treat but easy – though not in every case. I think that was a contribution. I don't know anybody who was actually doing this then, and if there was I'd like to know.

Fortunately I've always had to give lectures – like everybody here, I think – but I've found the most valuable thing has been having to lecture to people who aren't analysts. Susan Isaacs[13] in 1936 gave me the job of giving ten lectures a year at the Institute of Education, which I did for about fifteen years, and that was very important to me. I was supposed to be lecturing on rheumatic fever at the beginning, and the early diagnosis of pain so that people didn't get heart disease; but fortunately before long rheumatic fever died out. Anyhow it was found that half the people sent as rheumatic were depressed and half the people sent as choreic weren't choreic at all – they were cases of common anxious fidgetiness; so we got down to looking at all that. But having to lecture to social workers and teachers and parents and all sorts of people is tremendously important. Somebody, perhaps a parent or a social worker, said, 'Look here, I understand this about reaching back over the gap for the object, but you haven't described why another kind of antisocial tendency is destructive.' And it took me three or four years to come round to the very simple thing, which is of course that there are two kinds of deprivation. One is in terms of loss of object and the other is in terms of loss of frames, loss of controls. In a sense you could say loss of mother and loss of father – the paternal father, not the standing-in-for-mother father. The thing is the frame, the strength – the deprivation in terms of that. Then a very complicated thing happens when the child becomes all right and begins to feel confidence in a man or a structure or an institution. He begins to break things up to make quite sure that the framework can hold. This showed me that the antisocial tendency has two aspects to it.

The other thing arising out of this is that when a child is deprived of an environmental control what he does is to become a controlling

37

system identified with the parental situation or with the environment and completely loses his identity. This is the reason why when the controls begin to be re-imposed and these children begin to get confidence and to hand over the controls to someone else, and to establish themselves again, the first thing they have to do is to prove that the controls will be sufficient. When this works, the children will be very aggressive. You could say that they have maniacal attacks sometimes – but the point is that they are beginning to exist. You get an idea here of the extreme importance of the situation for seeing the difference between fact and fantasy, because these children come to know that they have destroyed the world ever so many times just like a baby does with the parents, normally, and yet the world is still there. So they begin to see that there's a fantasy of destruction which is different from reality, and this is the lesson they have got to learn because they didn't learn it when they were babies.

It's quite possible for me to have got this original idea of mine about the antisocial tendency and hope, which has been extremely important to me in my clinical practice, from somewhere. I never know what I've got out of glancing at Ferenczi, for instance, or glancing at a footnote to Freud.

Now we get to the facilitating environment and the maturational process. There's something from Greenacre[14] here that I've culled without acknowledgement, particularly in developing the theories around the maturational processes, heredity and the tendencies that go on to make a human being; and the interaction of this with the environment. Here we have to bring in Hartmann's 'conflict-free sphere' which really, I think I'm right in saying (he didn't mind when I said it to him), has to do with the inherited tendencies. Then I found I had to formulate a sort of theoretical basis of environmental provision starting at the beginning with 100 percent adaptation and quickly lessening according to the ability of the child to make use of failure of adaptation. This has been said in other terms. Mrs Riviere has stressed the mother's failures as being as important for object-relating as the successes, and there is other work in which you can trace these ideas. But I'm not sold on just taking over the concept of 'symbiosis' because this word for me is too easy. It's as if, as in biology, it just happens that two things are living together. I believe it leaves out the extremely variable thing which is the ability of the mother to identify with the infant, which I think is the living thing in this which I've called 'primary maternal preoccupation.' Her ability varies with different children not with her temperament but with her experiences, and with the way that she is at the time, and this seems to me to be a more fruitful line of enquiry.

This brings me to dependence and adaptation theories. It's interesting to me that Mrs Klein's digging further and further back into the conflicts and processes in the individual infant I found more and more difficult. Then one evening Fairbairn came down to talk to us, and this was the sort of evening that goes right beyond my comprehension, and yet it undoubtedly had tremendous importance. The question was whether the first introjection is of a good or a bad object – the sort of thing I'm no good at. At that time I couldn't see anything in Fairbairn[15] I saw later that he'd got an extremely important thing to say which had to do with going beyond instinctual satisfactions and frustrations to the idea of object-seeking. He and Mrs Klein had several things in common. I couldn't see that for years and years. But I didn't get involved in Mrs Klein's theories which are based on the concept of the death instinct and of the hereditary factors that seemed to me to be stressed in her 'Envy' paper.[16] This didn't matter, because by that time she'd contributed such a tremendous amount. That's something that the future has to talk about, not me. But you can see how by this time I was thoroughly sunk in the word 'dependence' and couldn't talk about the infant without taking into account dependence and adaptation; and without seeing that the mother's ability to de-adapt at the pace that her particular infant at the moment could make use of was an extremely subtle thing which belongs to life, and that health and ill-health have sometimes to be thought of in these terms. Therefore I could never quite get into proper communication with Melanie Klein again, but it didn't matter because she and I agreed to differ. She had a terrific brain, and she said, quite rightly, 'I've always acknowledged the importance of the environment in all my writing but I'm talking about the individual.' Well, that was fair enough. I was trying to say something she didn't like and I don't know yet whether she's right or not; but it had to do with the fact that at the beginning it seems impossible to talk about the individual without talking about the mother, because to my mind, the mother or the person in that place is a subjective object – in other words has not been objectively perceived – and therefore how the mother behaves is really part of the infant. And I find it's almost like trying to count the number of fairies on the end of a pin to see how far you can go back talking about what's happening in an infant leaving out the fact that the environment is, at the beginning, part of the infant. I think that the difficulty is that there's a paradox, and it's the same paradox that turns up in transitional phenomena, which I tried to work out to deal with it. The paradox is that the environment is part of the infant and at the same time it isn't. The infant has to accept this eventually in order to become a grown-up at all. It comes out in the transitional phenomena theory because if we take the simple case where there's a transitional object we know that we won't ask the baby, 'Did you create that object or did you find it?' because we know that the two things are true and that he wouldn't have created it if it hadn't been there, but that he did create it; and this is an extremely difficult concept unless one just says there's a paradox and we've got to accept it. It seems to me to have quite a lot of philosophical importance, only I don't happen to be a philosopher.[17] It has importance to the whole of object-relating where objects can be seen creatively.

Now there was one thing that I needed and I couldn't get at myself, which was the full use of the delusional transference concept. This is one of the most difficult things we have to deal with in analysis, and from my point of view I really took this bit from someone. If Margaret Little[18] hadn't been able to make this clear, I was hung up in a way I think a lot of analysts are hung up. I think you can still hear people unable to take a delusional transference, which is one of the most difficult things we have to do. So that's one little bit of my life where I really did get something from somebody else, almost as if I stole it out of my mother's handbag.

Then an important thing that happened to me was recognizing that early is not deep, and this helped me a lot in my attempt to make full use of Klein without getting bogged down. I suddenly realized— in Paris or somewhere – that early isn't deep: that it takes an infant time and development before depth comes in, so that when you're going back to the deepest things you won't get to the beginning. You get to something like 3 or 2 or 1½, and this was very important for me because some mechanisms that have to do with the schizoid groupings seem to belong to early and not to deep, and depression belongs to deep and not to early. And I think this has an effect on our theory of the origin of aggression, because I really believe there's something to be said for talking about aggression (in terms of development in the infant) as being the child's movement – that is, muscle erotism – and something happens to be in the way. It seems to me that this is the beginning of aggression. If you're going to talk about hate, that's a long way further on, and a maniacal episode is also a long way from somebody just happening to kick something because it was in the way when he liked kicking. So I got a glimpse of how I might understand a bit better about the origins of aggression, looking at these two different ways of getting at the beginning of it in the individual.

You can see that there is, incidentally, a corollary to this. I was getting away from the necessity of a verbal interpretation in its fullest form. I've been through the long process of interpreting everything I could possibly see that could be interpreted, you know, feeling awful if I couldn't find anything, and pouncing on something because I found I could put it into words. I've been through all that and realised that in certain cases it was no good at all, along with other people who I know had done the same things. Balint[19] had written on this and others have written since, and many things have been said in the last forty years on the subject of silent hours and of long periods of dependence. Since realising this I've had to deal with a lot of silent phases in analysis that lasted a long time, and it's very difficult to know when it's wasted time and when it's extremely productive, but nevertheless all this is now something I love to study. Today, this afternoon, a patient brought me a dream – a patient who's getting near the end of analysis – and suddenly I saw ahead to a solution of where he was getting to, so I let him have my idea of where he was, and he was so dissatisfied that the dream he'd brought with his own meanings to it had been treated in this way. He was absolutely angry with me and absolutely hopeless and he said, 'When will you ever learn?' If I was right, I'd taken away his opportunity to be creative, to bring it next time and the time after; and if I was wrong I'd interrupted his reaching an important bit of understanding through this dream. It was as much as he could take at the time. We got through it in the end because I've done it before. He said, 'As a matter of fact I've had a very satisfactory day today, but there's only one thing marring it. This evening I shall be worrying about you because you'll be thinking what a rotten analyst you were.' At any rate, there's so much that goes on in analysis if it isn't just a straightforward psycho-neurotic case.

I now became aware that Fairbairn had made a tremendous contribution, even if we only take two things. One is object-seeking, which comes into the area of transitional phenomena and so on, and the other is this thing of feeling real instead of feeling unreal. Our patients, more and more, turn out to be needing to feel real, and if they don't then understanding is of extremely secondary importance. The awkward thing is if they're going to be analysts: they want a bit of understanding then. But the vast majority of my patients haven't been analysts, and I've had to be contented if they went away feeling more real than when they came. No doubt a lot of people have been on to this – Erikson,[20] and I expect many more.

I can't cover all that I want to. I will just say that I don't know whether you'd like to discuss any of this or would like to help me in a letter to try and make amends and join up with the various people all over the world who are doing work which either I've stolen or else I'm just ignoring. I don't promise to follow it all up because I know I'm just going to go on having an idea which belongs to where I am at the moment, and I can't help it.

Notes

1 First published in 1989 under the title 'Postscript: D.W.W. on D.W.W' – this was the transcript of a talk given to the 1952 Club four years before he died (Winnicott 1989). The original talk was entitled, 'The Relation of Dr. Winnicott's Theory to Other Formulations of Early Development'. This re-publication is extended through the inclusion of notes and references by the editor assisted by Anne Patterson.

2 See note 10 of Chapter 3.

3 Heinz Hartmann (1894–1970) was a Viennese analyst who emigrated to the U.S.A. in 1941. Together with Ernst Kris and Anna Freud he founded *The Psychoanalytic Study of the Child* in 1945. He wrote numerous papers on ego psychology and is well known for his concept of the 'conflict-free sphere' described in 1939 (Hartmann 1958) and referred to by D.W.W. at the beginning of this paper.

4 Wilhelm Hoffer (1897–1967) was a Viennese analyst who moved to London in 1938. He worked at the Hampstead Nursery, founded by Anna Freud and Dorothy Burlingham, that was later re-named the Anna Freud Centre. He was elected editor of the *International Journal of Psychoanalysis* in 1949 and in 1957 became president of the British Psychoanalytical Society for three years. He was a prolific writer, perhaps best known for his paper: 'Mouth, Hand and Ego Integration' (Hoffer 1950: 49).

5 James Strachey (1887–1967) was one of the principal translators of Freud's work who, in 1948, started editing the *Standard Edition of the Complete Psychological Works of Sigmund Freud* and became General Editor. He was analyzed by Sigmund Freud and analyzed Winnicott from 1923 to 1933. He was married to Alix Strachey who was analyzed by Karl Abraham in Berlin, the second analyst of Melanie Klein's (see Miesel and Kendrick

1986). Apart from his great achievement of editing Freud's works he is also remembered for his seminal paper on the mutative interpretation (Strachey 1934).

6 In 1941, Anna Freud and Dorothy Burlingham opened the first War Nursery in response to a need for a more permanent residence for traumatized children who were difficult to place in foster care or who could not be evacuated without their mothers. Soon there were three such houses – 'The Hampstead Nurseries' – that provided care for nearly 200 children throughout the course of the Second World War (see Burlingham and Freud 1949; Midgely 2007).

7 Alice Balint-Székely-Kovács (1898–1939) came to the U.K. in 1939 with her husband Michael Balint (1896–1971), but died suddenly in the same year. Both she and her husband were contemporaries of D.W.W.

8 Ian Suttie (1898–1935) was a psychiatrist who worked as a psychotherapist at the Tavistock Clinic during the 1920s. Although never becoming a psychoanalyst he made use of psychoanalytic theory in his work and is best known for a particular perspective on love and hate expressed in his book: *The Origins of Love and Hate* (Suttie 1935).

9 Margaret Lowenfeld (1890–1973) was a British child psychotherapist who is well known for her pioneering development of play in child psychotherapy e.g. the use of sand trays, toys and models.

10 Merril Middlemore (1898–1938) published her work on baby observation in her best-known book *The Nursing Couple* (Middlemore 1941).

11 Melanie Klein (1882–1960) was originally analyzed by Sandor Ferenczi in Budapest and later by Karl Abraham in Berlin. She immigrated to London in 1926 and supervised Winnicott for one of his child cases as he completed his training in child psychoanalysis. She referred her son to Winnicott for treatment while supervising his work on other cases. Between 1941 and 1945 the British Psychoanalytical Society had a series of 'controversial discussions' related to the interpretation of Freud's work. (see Chapter 3 and Introduction.

12 Joan Riviere (1883–1962) was a founder member of the British Psychoanalytical Society and one of Freud's translators in the early years. She was initially a close colleague of Melanie Klein's but later they parted ways (see Hughes 1991). She made a significant contribution to psychoanalysis and her paper on the negative therapeutic reaction is still frequently cited (Riviere 1936).

13 Susan Isaacs (1885–1948) was a British psychoanalyst who made significant contributions to child education. She was influenced by Melanie Klein and perhaps some of her best-known theoretical contributions were made in the context of the Controversial Discussions – in particular her paper presented to the Society in 1943 and later published as 'On the Nature and Function of Phantasy' (Isaacs 1948).

14 Phyllis Greenacre (1894–1989) was a training analyst of the New York Psychoanalytic Institute who was influenced by Hartman and Kris. She wrote

clinical papers on development, psychoanalytic training and creativity. She introduced the idea of 'the imposter' (Greenacre 1958) which is sometimes compared with Winnicott's 'false self' (Winnicott 1963) and Deutsch's 'as-if' personality (Deutsch 1955). (cf. Thompson 2008).

15 Ronald Fairbairn (1889–1964) was a member of the British Psychoanalytical Society who lived and worked in Edinburgh. He is best known for his concepts of 'the schizoid condition' and the 'endopsychic structure' both to be found in his book *Psychoanalytic Studies of the Personality* (Fairbairn 1952). Here Winnicott is referring to a critical review of Fairbairn's book that he'd written with Masud Khan (Winnicott and Khan 1953).

16 Melanie Klein presented her paper 'Envy and Gratitude' at the 1957 International Psychoanalytic Congress but it was not published until 1975 (Klein 1975).

17 Cf. Winnicott 1949.

18 Margaret Little (1901–1994) was in analysis with D.W.W. from 1949 to 1955 (cf. Little 1985).

19 Presumably D.W.W. was referring to Michael Balint's book *The Basic Fault* which was about to be published (Balint 1968).

20 Eric Erikson (1902–1994) was born in Germany and analyzed by Anna Freud in Vienna. He moved to the U.S.A. in 1933 and his best-known books are: *Childhood and Society* (Erikson 1950) and *Identity and the Life Cycle* (Erikson 1959).

References

Balint, M. (1968) *The Basic Fault*. London: Tavistock Publications.

Burlingham, D. and Freud, A. (1949) *Kriegskinder* (War Children) London: Imago.

Deutsch, H. (1955) The Impostor: Contribution to Ego Psychology of a Type of Psychopath, *Psychoanalytic Quarterly*, 24: 483–505.

Erikson, E. (1950) *Childhood and Society*. New York: W.W. Norton.

Erikson, E. (1959) *Identity and the Life Cycle*. New York: W.W. Norton.

Greenacre, P. (1958) Early Physical Determinants in the Development of the Sense of Identity, *Journal of the American Psychoanalytic Association,* 6: 612–627.

Hartmann, H. (1958) *Ego Psychology and the Problem of Adaptation*. Trans. D. Rapaport. New York: International Universities Press.

Hoffer, W. (1950) Mouth, Hand and Ego Integration. In: *Psychoanalytic Study of the Child,* 3–4: 49–56.

Isaacs, S. (1948) On the Nature and Function of Phantasy. *Int J of Psychoanal*, 29: 73–97.

Klein, M. (1957) *Envy and Gratitude and Other Works 1946–1963*. Ed. M. Masud R. Khan. London and Vienna: International Psycho-Analytical Library, 104: 1–346.

Little, M. (1985) Winnicott Working in Areas where Psychotic Anxieties Predominate: A Personal Record, *Free Associations*, 1D: 9–42.

Meisel, P. and Kendrick, W. (eds) (1986) *Bloomsbury/Freud: The Letters of James and Alix Strachey 1924–25*. London: Chatto & Windus.

Midgley, N. (2007) Anna Freud: The Hampstead War Nurseries and the Role of the Direct Observation. *Int J of Psychoanal*, 88: 939–959.

Riviere, J. (1936) A Contribution to the Analysis of a Negative Therapeutic Reaction. *Int J of Psychoanal*, 17: 304–320.

Middlemore, M.P. (1941) *The Nursing Couple*. London: Hamish Hamilton.

Strachey, J. (1934) The Nature of the Therapeutic Action of Psycho-analysis. *Int J of Psychoanal*, 15, 127–159.

Suttie, I.D. (1935) *The Origins of Love and Hate*. Kegan Paul, reprinted 1999, 2001, 2005, London: Routledge.

Thompson, N.L. (2008) A Measure of Agreement: An Exploration of the Relationship of D.W. Winnicott and Phyllis Greenacre. *Psychoanalytic Quarterly*, 77: 251–281.

Winnicott, D.W. ([1966] 1987) The Ordinary Devoted Mother. In: *Babies and Their Mothers* (51–58). Eds. Clare Winnicott, Ray Shepherd and Madeleine Davis. Reading, MA: Addison-Wesley, 1987.

Winnicott, D.W. and M. Masud R. Khan. Book review of W.R.D. Fairbairn, *Psychoanalytic Studies of the Personality* (London: Tavistock, 1952) *Int J Psychoanal*, 1953, 34.

The mother, the infant and the matrix

Interpretations of aspects of the work of Donald Winnicott

Thomas H. Ogden

Donald Winnicott developed his contribution to the psychoanalytic dialogue in the intellectual and social climate of the British Psychoanalytical Society of the 1920's through the early 70's. The British Society during much of this period was sharply and often bitterly divided between the ideas and personalities of Anna Freud and Melanie Klein. Winnicott was analyzed first by James Strachey and then by Joan Rivière, one of the early Kleinian 'inner circle'; he was supervised by Melanie Klein in his psychoanalytic work with children. Although Winnicott's thinking developed in a direction different from that of Klein, he never denounced Kleinian thinking as did many analysts who had been at one point open to Klein's ideas (e.g. Glover [1945] and Schmideberg [1935]).

Winnicott was a dialectician. His thinking thrived in the medium of the intense debate between the classical Freudian and the Kleinian groups. He understood that once we feel that we have finally resolved a basic psychoanalytic issue (either in our theory or in our understanding of patients), it is at that point that our thinking has reached an impasse. Winnicott (1968) states, I think without false humility, that he offered his patients interpretations to let them know the limits of his understanding. Many of Winnicott's most valuable clinical and theoretical contributions are in the form of paradoxes that he asks us to accept without resolving, for the truth of the paradox lies in neither of its poles, but in the space between them.

Object relations theory is not comprised of a discrete collection of principles; rather, it represents a diverse collection of contributions that, in my opinion, have been developed in the context of one of the most intense and fruitful of psychoanalytic dialogues. The facet of the interchange on which I will focus in this paper is the conception of the nature of the dependence of the infant on the mother emerging from the work of Donald Winnicott. I believe that Winnicott's understanding of the role of the mother in early development becomes fully accessible only when it is approached from the vantage point of the dialogue with Klein within which his ideas were developed. The Winnicottian ideas that will be discussed are not simply refutations of Klein, nor revisions of Klein, nor extensions of Klein. These contributions are ideas generated in response to a rich epistemologic dilemma created in large part by the Kleinian contribution. The following three sections of this paper represent attempts at exploring three different forms of Winnicott's conception of the infant's evolving dependence on the mother. There will be an attempt, through the clarification, interpretation and extension of Winnicott's ideas, to make more fully accessible for analytic consideration important meanings implicit in these facets of Winnicott's work.

I The period of the subjective object

Although Klein did not ignore the role of the mother, Winnicott did not feel that Klein understood the nature of the mother–infant relationship.

> . . . she [Klein] paid lip-service to environmental provision, but would never fully acknowledge that along with the dependence of early infancy is truly a period in which it is not possible to describe an infant without describing the mother whom the infant has not yet become able to separate from a self. Klein claimed to have paid full attention to the environmental factor, but it is my opinion that she was temperamentally incapable of this.
>
> (Winnicott 1962a: 177)

The specific qualities of the interpersonal relationship between mother and infant plays a role secondary to that of phantasy in Kleinian thinking despite the fact that for Klein, phantasy is always object

47

related in content. The mother as she actually exists is seen by Klein as eclipsed by the phantasied mother who is constructed by the infant on the basis of the infant's projections: 'The child's earliest reality is wholly-phantastic' (Klein 1930: 238). The idea that the infant is isolated from what an observer would consider reality is not what Winnicott objects to in Kleinian theory. Rather, Winnicott's objection is to what he views as Klein's failure to examine the nature of the influence on psychological development of the infant's dependence on the mother. Klein's focus was almost exclusively on psychological contents: their origins in biology (instinctual deep structure [Ogden 1984]), their intrapsychic elaboration (e.g., by means of splitting, projection, introjection, omnipotent thought, idealization, denial, and so on), and their interpersonal transformations (by means of projective and introjective identification). Winnicott was not unaware of the potential for an interpersonal dimension to Klein's concept of projective identification. However, projective identification was for Klein primarily a process by which psychological contents are modified; it was not intended to address the basic unity of maternal and infantile psychology.

Klein (1946), (1948), (1957) viewed the infant as a distinct psychological entity from the beginning. Psychological development was understood by her as a series of biologically determined defensive transformations engaged in by the infant to take care of himself in the face of internal and external danger. In contrast, Winnicott's theory of development is not a depiction of defensive adjustments made by an infant in the face of danger. On the contrary, it is an exploration of the mother's provision of protective postponement and dosed stimulation. The mother's role, when the infant is in the womb, is to provide an environment that will buy the infant the time that he needs to mature before he will have to face the inevitable task of physical separation at birth. In precisely the same way, the mother's role in the first months of life (prior to the infant's entry into the period of the transitional phenomena at 'about four to six to eight to twelve months' (Winnicott 1951: 4) is to provide an environment in which the postponement of psychological separateness can occur while the infant develops as a result of the interplay of biological maturation and actual experience. (As will be discussed, a crucial part of this interplay involves dosed stimulation including frustration). The fact that the infant can develop only in the protective, postponing[1] envelope of the maternal environment constitutes one level of the meaning of

Winnicott's notion that 'there is no such thing as an infant' (Winnicott 1960a: 39 ftn.).

A new psychological entity is created by mother and infant that is not the outcome of a process of simple summation of parts. The situation is more akin to the interaction of two elements reacting with one another to generate a new entity, a compound. It is the 'compound,' – the mother-infant, that is the unit of psychological development for Winnicott: 'the behaviour of the environment is part of the individual's own personal development' (Winnicott 1971b: 53).

Since the mother-infant is a psychological entity contributed to by (what an outside observer would designate as) the mother and the infant, the unit of psychological development is always both a primitive psychological organization and a relatively mature one. In this sense, all levels of psychological development are represented in the psyche of the mother-infant. (This accounts for the presence of the implicit synchronic developmental axis in Winnicott's thinking that will be described below). The study of psychological development is not simply the study of the growth of the infantile psyche from primitivity to maturity; it is also the study of the development of the mother-infant into a mother and infant.

An aspect of the mother is mixed up with the infant in a state that Winnicott refers to as 'primary maternal preoccupation'. This experience of losing oneself in another ('feeling herself into her infant's place') is the mother's experience of becoming a part of the mother-infant (Winnicott 1956: 304). If there is no aspect of the mother that is at one with the infant, the infant is experienced as a foreign object. One such mother referred to her baby as 'the thing that lives in my house.' (Of course, there is an element of this feeling of alienation in the spectrum of emotions experienced by most mothers). If there is no aspect of the mother outside of the experience of primary maternal preoccupation, the mother has in fact become psychotic. Under such circumstances, separation from the baby is concretely experienced as a form of amputation.

For Winnicott (1951), (1962b), psychological development does not begin with the unfolding of a biologically predetermined set of psychological functions by which the infant takes care of himself in the face of anxiety; rather, early development centres around the mother's initial provision of the illusion of the 'subjective object,' i.e. the creation of the illusion that internal and external reality are one and the same. The mother is able, in her state of primary maternal preoccupation, to provide the infant with what he needs, in the way that he needs it, when he needs it, as if he had 'created' the object.

Winnicott's (1951) use of the idea of the illusion of 'creating the breast' is somewhat confusing if the notion of creating the breast is thought of as involving an awareness of otherness. In the beginning, the illusion created by the mother is not an illusion of the infant's omnipotent power to create what is needed; rather, the illusion is that need does not exist. I believe that the idea of 'invisible oneness' (Ogden 1985) of mother and infant is perhaps more expressive of the form of experience that Winnicott is proposing than the idea of the infant's creating the breast. The creation of the breast is an observable phenomenon only from a point of view outside of the mother–infant unit. Within the mother–infant unit, the creation of the breast is not noticed since the infant in this state does not yet have a point of view from which to notice anything. In a homogeneous field, there are no vantage points; there is no foreground or background. Without difference, there can be no perspective. The mother's caretaking is good enough when it is so unobtrusive as to be unnoticed. Even the stimulation needed by the infant and provided by the mother is unnoticed at first. The infant's ability to be sensorially alive and to make complex discriminations (see Stern 1977) is not the same as awareness of self or of other. The delaying of the infant's awareness of separateness is achieved in large part by means of the mother's meeting of the infant's need before need becomes desire. The infant without desire is neither a subject nor an object: there is not yet an infant.

Because Winnicott's thinking involves a subtle mixture of explicit diachronic[2] conceptions of development and implicit synchronic notions, the idea that the mother must at the outset protect the infant from awareness of desire is an incomplete representation of Winnicott's thinking. It is true that Winnicott (1945), (1971a) repeatedly states that in the beginning the mother must meet the infant's needs and in so doing protect the baby from premature awareness of separateness. In this conception of things, separateness follows oneness in a sequential, chronological way. However, at other times, Winnicott (1954–5), (1963) states that mothering, even at the beginning, must not be too good. The infant is robbed of the experience of desire if his every need is anticipated and met before it is experienced, for example, as appetite. Even under normal circumstances, the meeting of the infant's needs forecloses important possibilities at the same time as it satisfies and protects the infant:

The baby is fobbed off by the feed itself; instinct tension disappears, and the baby is both satisfied and cheated. It is too easily assumed that a feed is followed by satisfaction and sleep. Often distress follows this fobbing off, especially if physical satisfaction too quickly robs the infant of zest. The infant is then left with: aggression undischarged – because not enough muscle erotism or primitive impulse (or motility), was used in the feeding process; or a sense of 'flop' – since the source of zest for life has gone suddenly, and the infant does not know it will return.

(Winnicott 1954–5: 268)

So it is not sufficient to say that the mother must in the beginning meet the infant's needs in order to protect the infant from premature knowledge of separateness (a diachronic statement). Neither is it sufficient to say that the mother from the beginning must meet the infant's need for 'zest' in allowing the infant the opportunity to develop desire through the experience of partially unfulfilled needs. Only a paradoxical statement in which both the synchronic and diachronic axes are represented, can approach completeness: the mother must shield the infant from awareness of desire and separateness, and the mother must safeguard the infant's opportunity to experience desire (and its accompanying knowledge of separateness).

Instinct, defense and individuality

Central to Winnicottian (1971c) developmental theory is the idea that there is a potential individuality at birth and that the mother (both as environment and as object) facilitates the development of that unfolding individuality. In large part, the task of the mother is not to interfere with the infant's spontaneous development that begins as a state of 'formless' (1971e: 64) going on being. The development of the psychological system is not predominantly propelled by the need to find channels for the discharge of instinctual tension (as in Freud's energy model) nor by the need to defend against danger posed by the death instinct (as in Kleinian theory).

This is not to say that Winnicott rejected either instinct theory or the notion of the central role of anxiety in the normal structuring of the psyche in general, and of the ego in particular. For Winnicott, it is all a matter of the timing of the handing over of caretaking (including

51

defensive operations) from the mother (more accurately, the mother-infant) to the infant. If there is a premature rupture of the holding environment, the infant too early becomes a reactive creature, and develops hypertrophied, rigid defensive structures. Under such circumstances, the infant must attempt to deal with psychological tasks that he is not yet maturationally equipped to manage. On the other hand, if the holding environment is 'too good' for too long, the infant is prevented from experiencing dosed frustration, tolerable anxiety, desire, and conflict, and as a result will not develop ways of caring for himself (including defending himself psychologically). All of these qualities of experience – frustration, anxiety, desire, conflicted desire – introduce difference and lead to internal differentiation. The creation of the unconscious mind (and therefore, the conscious mind) become possible and necessary only in the face of conflicted desire leading to the need to disown and yet preserve aspects of experience, i.e. the need to maintain two different modes of experiencing the same psychological event simultaneously. In other words, the very existence of the differentiation of the conscious and unconscious mind stems from a conflict between a desire to feel/think/be in specific ways, and the desire not to feel/think/be in those ways.

For Winnicott, the ability of the infant to make use of the integrating and structuring effects of instinctual experience (including instinctual conflict) depends upon the mother's success in postponing (and yet preserving) the infant's awareness of desire, and therefore of conflicted desire, until, and not beyond, the point where the infant experiences his feelings as his own. Prior to that point, 'the instincts can be as external as a clap of thunder or a hit' (Winnicott 1960b: 141), and therefore disruptive of the infant's developing sense of internally generated desire. Once a sense of self has begun to consolidate (in the way that will be described below), instinctual experience serves to focus and organize the infant's sense of himself as author of his experience (Winnicott 1967). One's being takes specific form in the process of feeling and acting upon one's desires.

The defensive preservation of the self

When there is a prolonged and serious failure to provide a good enough holding environment,[3] the infant is thrown into a state of chaos and disruption of his sense of 'going on being.' (Winnicott

1963: 183) The outcome is childhood psychosis or the nucleus of adult psychotic or borderline states. When the failure of the holding environment is less severe, the infant may be able to develop a defensive personality organization that takes over the caretaking function of the mother. This organization is developed in a state of perceived danger. Instead of the mutually enriching interplay that optimally results from the differentiation of the conscious and unconscious minds and the establishment of a 'semipermeable' repression barrier, there develops an alienation of one aspect of self from another (Winnicott 1960b), (1963). The defensive, caretaking self (the False Self) is established almost exclusively for the purpose of securing the protective isolation of the infant's potential for psychological individuality (the True Self). This isolation of the True Self inevitably leads to feelings of emptiness, futility and deadness. The walling-off of a protected self stands in contrast to the dual role of censorship and selective, disguised expression performed by the unconscious ego in normal development. The difference between normally developing defenses and a psychological split leading to the development of a False Self defensive organization lies in the fact that normally developing defenses enable the individual not only to organize and disavow experience, but also to unconsciously preserve disavowed desires that are nonetheless one's own. In contrast, the formation of a False Self personality organization involves the foreclosure of the development of significant aspects of what might have become oneself.

II The period of transitional phenomena

Although the paradox of oneness and separateness of mother and infant has its origin in the earliest period of development, there is a shift in the quality of this dialectical relationship in the period of development in which transitional phenomena occur. It is to this period that I would now like to turn. Here again, Winnicott's thinking is in part a response to the Kleinian contribution.

The infant's psychological matrix

In both the Kleinian and Winnicottian conceptions of development there is a notion that the infant in the beginning requires insulation from external reality. For Winnicott, the insulation is generated by the maternal provision of the illusion of the subjective object. The infant as conceived of by Klein (1930) is insulated by his 'wholly phantastic' reality. The Kleinian infant sees the world through the lens of his phylogenetically determined preconceptions and in this sense 'creates' his internal and external object world which are at first indistinguishable from one another. This is the Kleinian version of the infant's 'protective shield' (Freud 1920: 30).

The following question then arises in Winnicottian, Freudian and Kleinian developmental theory: Given that the infant is initially insulated from external reality in the ways described, how is the infant able to utilize actual experience in the process of emerging from his initial state of isolation?[4] Here again, Winnicott's contribution to the psychoanalytic understanding of the developmental process involves a shift in perspective (a restatement of the epistemologic problem) from an attempt to understand the development of the infant to an attempt to understand the development of the mother–infant. Neither Klein nor Freud was oblivious to the role of the mother (as object), but it was not until Winnicott that psychoanalysis developed a conception of the mother as the infant's psychological matrix.[5] From a Winnicottian perspective, the infant's psychological contents can only be understood in relation to the psychological matrix within which those contents exist. That psychological matrix is at first provided by the mother. This is a second level of meaning (to be added to the inseparability of the infant from the protective, postponing function of the maternal holding environment) of Winnicott's notion that there is no such thing as an infant. Since the internal holding environment of the infant, his own psychological matrix, takes time to develop, the infant's mental contents initially exist within the matrix of the maternal mental and physical activity. In other words, in the beginning, the environmental mother provides the mental space in which the infant begins to generate experience. It is in this sense that I feel that a new psychological entity is created by the mother and (what is becoming) the infant.[6]

Even though aspects of the infant's psychological contents may be experienced as things in themselves (Ogden 1982) and thus may in themselves be quite impervious to new experience, the infant's psychological matrix (the maternal holding environment) is steadily changing and is highly sensitive to modification by new experience. The holding environment (psychological matrix) shifts not only in relation to the infant's changing emotional needs (e.g., a need to be held, to be calmed, to be entertained, to show off, etc.), but also changes in relation to the infant's shifting maturational and developmental needs (e.g. maturing motor and cognitive capacities).

The period of the transitional phenomenon could be understood as the phase of internalization by the infant (perhaps more accurately described as the appropriation to the infant) of the psychological matrix. The maternally provided psychological matrix is in a state of continual erosion from the beginning, but it is not for several months that the infant begins to consolidate his capacity to generate and maintain his own psychological matrix. In this period of the transitional phenomenon, the role of the mother is one of gradual disillusionment, i.e. a gradual weaning of the infant from maternal provision of the holding environment that had served as the infant's psychological matrix. In the course of this weaning process, the infant develops the capacity to be alone (Winnicott 1958a).

The presence of the absent mother

An important distinction must be made at this point in order to understand Winnicott's thinking about the development of the capacity to be alone: What is internalized in this process is not the mother as object, but the mother as environment. The premature 'objectification' (discovery of the mother as object), and internalization of the object-mother leads to the establishment of an omnipotent internal-object-mother. This internalization of mother as omnipotent object is quite different from the establishment of the capacity to be alone. (The former process is often a defensive substitute for the latter).

In the development of the capacity to be alone, the infant develops the ability to generate the 'space' (state of being) in which he lives, a state referred to by Winnicott (1971a) as 'potential space.' (For a discussion of the concept of potential space, see Ogden 1985). Until the point in development being focused upon, the mother and infant together have created this space intersubjectively. This space is not coextensive with the universe; rather, it is a personal space. It is not exactly limited by our skin, and it is not exactly the same as our mind. In addition to these (inexact) dimensions of body and mind, this experience of a containing space includes the experience of the space in which we work creatively, the space in which we relax 'formlessly,' the space in which we dream,[7] the space in which we play, and so on.

A paradoxical statement must be made about the process of the development of the individual's capacity to generate this space: the child must have the opportunity to play alone in the presence of the absent mother, and in the absence of the present mother. This paradox can be understood in the following way: the mother is absent as object, but is there as the unnoticed, but present containing space in which the child is playing. The mother must not make her presence as object too important, for this would lead the child to become addicted to her as omnipotent object. The development of the capacity to be alone is a process in which the mother's role as invisible co-author of potential space is taken over by (what is becoming) the child. In this sense, when the healthy individual is alone, he is always in the presence of (the self-generated environmental) mother.

Impending annihilation and the disruption of the matrix

Although the maternal contribution to the creation of potential space is unnoticed by the infant, the disruption of this invisible provision is a highly visible event that is experienced by the infant as impending annihilation. At such times, a discrete, separate infant is precipitously (defensively) brought into existence in order to attempt to manage the catastrophe.

Using Balint's (1968) imagery, the infant's relationship to the environmental mother is very much like the adult's relationship to air: we ordinarily take the air we breathe absolutely for granted, taking from it what we need and expelling into it what we do not need. However, if we are deprived of it, even for a few moments, we become acutely and terrifyingly aware of the way in which we are utterly dependent upon it for our lives. Psychologically this corresponds to the failure of the relationship with the environmental mother leading to the calamitous intrusion of awareness of dependency on an absent mother-as-object.

The incompleteness of the process of appropriation to the infant of the psychological matrix was evidenced by a successful engineer who, having married a woman 20 years his senior, could only feel alive when he was working on his car in the garage while his wife was in the house. If she was not at home, he could not work in this engrossed state and would impatiently await her return. On the other hand, he would become enraged if she were to come into the garage while he was working. Her actual physical presence was experienced as a violent, unwelcome, intrusion and made it impossible for him to work.

Many chronic sleep disturbances reflect inadequacy of the development of an internal psychological matrix. Falling asleep involves an act of faith in our capacity to hold our existence over time while giving up almost all forms of conscious control. In sleep, we give ourselves over to our internal holding environment.[8]

Addiction to the mother as object

Fain (1971), (quoted by McDougall 1974) has described forms of infantile insomnia that seem to be related to difficulties in the infant's use of the mother as environment. Some of the infants studied by Fain seem to have become addicted to the actual physical presence of the mother and could not sleep unless they were being held. These infants were unable to provide themselves an internal environment for sleep. Fain has observed that the mothers of many of these infants interfered with the attempts of their infants to provide themselves substitutes for her physical presence (for example, in auto-erotic activities such as thumb sucking), thus rendering the infant fully dependent upon the actual mother as object.

In my experience as a consultant to clinicians working with severely disturbed patients, I have found that therapists doing what they feel to be 'supportive therapy' with borderline and schizophrenic patients are frequently engaged in the process of addicting the patient to the therapist as object. As the following example illustrates, this potential danger exists even in well conducted analytic work with disturbed patients.

A severely disturbed borderline patient had been seen three times per week in psychotherapy for six years and had made significant progress in the course of this work. Due to a countertransference problem arising from an interplay of feelings induced by the patient by means of projective identification and feelings arising from the therapist's own childhood experience, the therapist for a period of time was finding it difficult to tolerate the patient's growing independence. When the patient, S, became anxious about his plan to enroll in a vocational program, he became pleadingly demanding that the therapist phone the agency to get information about enrollment requirements and procedures. Despite the fact that S's associations and dream material made it clear in retrospect that he was unconsciously asking for permission to do this for himself, the therapist acquiesced to his manifest demand. Having made the phone call, the therapist in the next meeting handed the patient a sheet of paper on which he had recorded the information that he had received from the organization. S immediately exploded with rage yelling obscenities at the therapist. He then stormed out of the office terrified that he would hurt the therapist. The patient did not return to therapy for three weeks.

In the course of supervision, it was possible for the therapist to both understand what had happened in the therapy and to predict that the patient would return to the therapy in a pathetic, anxious state that would be designed to reassure the therapist that the patient was utterly dependent upon him. When S did in fact return in this way, the therapist told him that he thought that S must feel that the therapist wanted to turn him into a baby. In the course of the meeting, the therapist also said that it seemed that the patient had decided that falling apart (and thus demonstrating his need for the therapist) was a price worth paying if the alternatives were killing the therapist, leaving him or having the therapist leave S.

The patient seemed relieved that the therapist understood something of what he had been feeling. Before the next meeting, the patient and a friend went to the rehabilitation center where the patient picked up a copy of the enrollment procedures. On the way home he became extremely anxious and began to fear that the meeting with the therapist might have been a figment of his imagination. He called the therapist in a panic asking for an extra meeting immediately. The therapist said that he thought that S could wait until their next scheduled meeting the following day. With that the patient's anxiety subsided.

In the case just described, the therapist had abandoned his role as provider of a therapeutic environment (an analytic space) and had instead begun to insert himself into the patient's life as an omnipotent object. The patient craved such an object relationship (a primitive maternal transference), but was sufficiently healthy to struggle against the enslaving addiction that such a relationship inevitably generates.

Traumatic and non-traumatic discovery of separateness

In the period of the transitional phenomenon, the infant (or patient) must not be abruptly confronted with the experiential fact that he has his own mind, that he has his own area of experiencing within which he thinks his thoughts, feels his feelings, dreams his dreams, and does his playing. The infant requires time to make this experiential discovery for himself. If the infant has this opportunity, the discovery can at least in part be a welcome one (see Mahler's [1968] description of the exhilaration of the practicing subphase of separation-individuation).

The crucial psychological-interpersonal phenomenon that makes possible the weaning of the infant from the maternally provided psychological matrix is the maintenance of a series of paradoxes: the infant and mother are one, and the infant and mother are two; the infant has created the object and the object was there to be discovered; the infant must learn to be alone in the presence of the mother, and so on. It is essential that the infant or child never be asked which is the truth (Winnicott 1951). Both are true. The simultaneous maintenance of the emotional truth of oneness with the mother and separateness from her makes it possible for the infant to play in the potential space between mother and infant.

The experience of the absence of the mother as object is a phenomenon of the depressive position (that is, the period of development in which whole object relatedness is being consolidated). Loss of the mother-as-object is reacted to with feelings of sadness, loneliness, guilt and sometimes desolation. If the capacity to be alone has been achieved (that is, if the environmental mother has been internalized), this loss can be survived. The loss of the mother-as-environment is a far more catastrophic event to which one responds with a feeling of impending loss of oneself. The person experiences himself as on the edge of dissolving. Sometimes, if the situation has not reached a point where the patient has entered a state of panic or has instituted massive defensive withdrawal, the patient may report being unable to think or not knowing who he is.

Once when working with a hospitalized adolescent patient in this state, I addressed the patient (Todd) by name. He looked at me with a combination of bewilderment, fear and despair and said in a monotone, "Todd is lost and gone forever." The patient told me he did not know what his name was but he did not think it was Todd. He then entered a state of utter panic and fled from the office. He screamed in the hallway without words and hurled himself at the walls. It was only in the course of being held tightly in the arms of three of the ward staff that he was able to stop flailing and begin to be calmed.

As the panic mounts for a patient experiencing this form of dissolution of self, there is a powerful need to reconstruct a holding environment. It is often at this point (as in the case just described) that the patient feels compelled to create such havoc (an externalization of the internal catastrophe) that it becomes necessary for police or ward staff, physically and sometimes violently to restrain the patient. It is essential that the containing activity be a human interaction, i.e. that a person be present with the patient in sheets, in restraints, or in a 'seclusion room.' Otherwise, the patient's terror is magnified, leaving him only suicide, profound autistic withdrawal, or self-mutilation as methods of managing his state of psychological catastrophe. In one instance where interpersonal containment was not provided, it was reported to me that a patient who had been locked in a seclusion room enucleated an eye with his fingers in what was later inferred to have been an attempt to shut out unbearable experience.

With this conception of the psychological matrix in mind, it is now possible to reconsider aspects of Kleinian thinking from a slightly altered perspective. For Klein there is an implicit notion that the matrix for the infant's psychological life is ultimately a biological one. The life and death instincts as vehicles for phylogenetically inherited preconceptions are together the organizer and container of psychological life (Bion 1962a), (1962b). Instinctual deep structure (see Ogden 1984) is a biological entity (that organizes psychology) and is never directly experienced, just as one never directly experiences one's brain or one's linguistic deep structure. The experiential manifestation of the structuring function of the instincts is the organizing and containing effect of the attribution of meaning (along biologically predetermined lines) to chaotic barrages of raw sensory data. It goes without saying that psychology is embedded in biology, (i.e. that mental phenomena have physiologic substrates), but Kleinian (and Freudian) instinct theory go farther than that to implicitly offer a conception of biology (perhaps, more accurately termed psychobiology) as a matrix for a system of psychological meanings.

For Winnicott, the infant's biological matrix interpenetrates the maternally provided matrix: both are unobtrusively present unless there is a disruption of the interpersonal matrix. When such disruptions occur, as they inevitably do, the infant must utilize his own biologically-determined psychological defenses, including very primitive forms of splitting, projection, introjection, denial and idealization. From a Winnicottian perspective, these psychological operations are viewed not as defenses against the derivatives of the death instinct, but as facets of the infant's constitutionally given capacity to contain and order his own experience in the face of an emergency arising from the (inevitable) failure of the maternal facet of his psychological matrix.

III The period of whole object relatedness

Thus far, I have addressed the Winnicottian conception of the role of the mother as a holding, postponing environment and the role of the mother as overseer of the weaning process through which the 'internalization' (or appropriation by the infant) of the psychological matrix occurs. I will now turn the focus of the discussion to the role of the mother in the period of development where the infant has achieved 'unit status,' i.e. whole object relatedness in the depressive position.

The survival of the object and the discovery of externality

In the depressive position, the infant is no longer as dependent on the mother as matrix for his psychological contents. He is able to provide much of that for himself. However, his dependence on the mother has by no means ended; it has taken on a new form. The infant is now dependent on the mother-as-object who he is in the process of discovering (as opposed to creating). His continued emotional development including the development of the capacity to 'use objects' (Winnicott 1968) and the development of psychic reality, depends upon her performing her role as external object over time. If in the earliest stage of development, dominant among the functions of the mother is that of holding, and in the period of the transitional phenomenon: the mother's dominant function is that of weaning, in the depressive position,[9] the critical task of the mother could be conceived of as that of surviving over time.

Here again, it is not possible to understand this aspect of Winnicott's contribution to the psychoanalytic dialogue in isolation from an understanding of the Kleinian contribution. What is being developed in this facet of Winnicott's thinking is a theory of the relationship of the infant to his internal objects, the relationship of internal objects to actual objects, and the relationship of internal objects to mental representations of external objects. There is no equivalent concept in classical theory to the Kleinian conception of internal objects. For Klein, the internal object originates in the inherited preconceptions associated with the instincts (which I have referred to as psychological deep structure) (Ogden 1984). The mental representation of the object is not inherited, but the structure for the idea is inherited and is given form as a mental representation when the infant encounters actual objects. The actual breast, for example, is merely a shape that is given to the 'preconception' (Bion 1962a), (1962b) of the breast. It must be emphasized that the 'preconception' is not yet a conception (an idea), it is the potential for a conception that becomes an idea when the preconception meets its 'realization' (Bion 1962a), (1962b) in the actual encounter with the breast. The infant does not anticipate the actual breast in the sense of having a mental picture of it prior to encountering it; on the other hand, he 'recognizes' it when he encounters it, because it is part of his biologically structured internal order that was silently available to be given representational form.

From a Kleinian perspective, the formation of an internal object is only secondarily an internalization process. More fundamentally, this form of mental object has its origins in the infant's psychological deep structure which is given shape through the infant's experience in the world, and is then (re)-internalized with the representational qualities it has accrued. Only those qualities of the actual external object that have correspondence to the structurally preconceived object are utilized ('seen') in creating the internal object representation. Representations of internal objects formed in this way stand in contrast to external object representations which are later developments. The formation of external object representations is predominantly an internalization process and depends upon the capacity of the infant to learn from experience, i.e. to notice and utilize the difference between the actual and the anticipated object. Early on, the actual object is eclipsed by the anticipated object.[10] Because internal objects are the infant's first creations, they operate almost entirely under the aegis of omnipotent thinking.

For Bion (1962a), in his extension of Klein's concept of projective identification, the principal method by which internal objects formed in the way just described, are modified. The mother's containment of a projective identification is a process of modifying an infantile preconception. Through this process, internal objects are gradually 'cleansed' (Grotstein 1980a), (1980b) of projective distortion leading to the formation of external object representations. No mental representation ever entirely loses its connection with its origins as an internal object, but with adequate maternal containment of the infant's projective identifications, mental representations acquire increasing autonomy from these origins and from the omnipotent thinking associated with relations between internal objects. This consolidation of the 'externality' of the object representation is reflected in the degree to which the individual is capable of entering into relationships with actual objects in a manner that involves more than a simple transference projection of his internal object world. The schizoid patient is far more the prisoner of his omnipotent internal object world (which is projected onto his current objects) than is the healthy individual, for whom transference provides only a background for relations with real objects whose qualities are perceived and responded to even when these qualities differ from the subject's transference expectations.

From the perspective developed thus far, the theoretical problem for psychoanalysis is not simply that of accounting for the creation of phantasy objects (internal objects), but also that of accounting for the creation of external objects. In other words, psychoanalysis requires a theory that addresses the way in which the infant develops the capacity to see beyond the world he has created through the projection of his internal objects.

Despite the fact that Winnicott was not satisfied with the Kleinian/Bionian resolution to this theoretical problem (i.e. the notion of cleansing of internal objects through maturation and successive projective identifications), he did accept many of the basic premises out of which this theoretical problem was formulated. Specifically, he adopted the Kleinians' implicit conception of the origin of internal objects in biologically determined preconceptions, although Winnicott's conception of the specificity and nature of these preconceptions differed markedly from Klein's. For Winnicott, the infant is born with only a vague structural readiness for need-fulfilling objects. I infer that this structural readiness accounts for the way in which the infant is not surprised or excited by the object (e.g. the breast) that is empathically provided by the mother, since the breast corresponds to the world the infant anticipates. Unless the object were fully 'expected,' i.e. fully congruent with the infant's internal order of things that pre-exists actual experience, the infant would 'notice' the object, which would result in premature awareness of separateness. It is because the infant is structurally (not motivationally) anticipating the object, that the object can be perceived without being noticed as separate or different from himself.

In Winnicott's conception of development, room has to be made psychologically for the discovery of the external object. Winnicott (1968) states in his enigmatic way, that it is the infant's destruction of the object (while the mother survives the destruction), that allows the infant to discover externality. What I infer he means by this, is that the infant's renunciation of the omnipotence of the internal object entails a crucial act of faith. The infant allows himself to drop out of the arms of the omnipotent internal object[11] into the arms of a (potential) object whom he has not yet met, since until that point the external mother has been eclipsed by the omnipotent internal object mother. From the point of view of an outside observer, the external-object–mother always has been there and has created (with the infant) the illusion of the subjective object. However, the very fact that this illusion has been successfully created and maintained, has allowed the infant not to be aware of the existence of the external–object–mother, who exists outside the realm of his omnipotence. He has, of course, met her but he has not 'noticed' her; he has mistaken her for himself (i.e. his creation). The act of faith that takes place in giving up ('destroying') the internal object is an act of trust in the (as yet invisible) presence of the external–object–mother. It is therefore crucial that the real and separate mother be there (to catch the infant) when the infant is in the process of making room for her and recognizing her, through his act of renunciation (destruction) of the omnipotent internal object mother:

> The subject says to the object [the internal object]: 'I have destroyed you,' and the object [the external object mother] is there to receive the communication. From now on the subject says, 'Hullo, object!

'I've destroyed you.' 'I love you.' 'You have value for me because of your survival of my destruction of you. While I am loving you [the real-mother-in-the-world, outside of the infant's omnipotence], I am all the time destroying you [the omnipotent internal-object-mother] in (unconscious *fantasy*) . . . The subject can now use the [external] object that has survived.

(Winnicott 1968: 90)

The external object at this juncture can be made use of for the first time in development, because the object that is being recognized and interacted with, is an object-in-the-world, outside of oneself. Up to that point, the actual qualities of the object, and the rootedness of the object-in-the-world outside oneself, were not perceptible, and therefore unutilizable. The infant had paid for his (necessary) insulation in the illusion of the subjective object, through postponement of the discovery of a world of utilizable objects, i.e. people with whom he can enter into a realm of shared experience in-the-world outside of himself.

The survival of the object is a form of holding the situation over time in such a way that the object-mother (or therapist) remains consistently emotionally present while the infant (or patient) attempts to carry out the act of trust involved in loosening his grip on the omnipotent internal object.

An inability to renounce the internal object arises either when the external object fails to be there to catch the infant when he allows himself to fall into her arms, or when the infant's experience with the illusion of the subjective object has not instilled in him a faith in the world sufficient to allow him to drop into the arms of an object he has not yet seen. When the external object fails to survive, (i.e. fails to be physically or emotionally present when needed), the infant must tighten his hold on the omnipotent internal object which then becomes the only form of safety available to the infant. The individual becomes imprisoned in his magical internal object world, to which he then rigidly clings. As a result, he develops very little ability to recognize or make use of the externality of his object world.

A later version of this same process occurs when the child allows himself or herself to leave the 'orbit' of the pre-Oedipal mother and move into the 'gravitational pull' of the Oedipal love object. The actual parental object of Oedipal love must be there to 'catch the child' once he has taken the risk of that act of falling in love. When the Oedipal love object is not emotionally or physically there to recognize, accept and (to a degree) reciprocate the child's Oedipal love, the child retreats into the orbit of the powerful pre-Oedipal mother from whose domination he or she may then never be able to escape.

Ruth, guilt and the benign circle

In the same psychological-interpersonal process through which the infant discovers the externality of objects, he also develops a dawning awareness of his impact on the newly discovered external-object-mother. Up to this point he has treated his mother 'ruthlessly' (Winnicott 1954–5), i.e. without ruth (concern). He has done so, not because in his omnipotence he has wished to harm the object, but because he has not yet developed awareness of the object as a subject, and therefore has had no empathy for the object.

The infant, in discovering the externality of objects, begins to develop a sense of how fierce he can be both in his efforts to get what he wants and in his attempts to get rid of what gets in his way. The infant unconsciously fears that he does serious damage to his mother in the course of demanding and taking what he does from her. The function of the mother at this point is to 'hold the situation over time' (Winnicott 1954–5), (1968) so that the infant while damaging the mother in (unconscious) fantasy is at the same time discovering on a moment to moment basis that she is alive and present in a way that differs from his unconscious fantasy experience. It is in the simultaneous experiencing of the fantasied destruction of the internal object mother and the experiencing of a relationship to a mother as object who continues to be present and unretaliative that the infant has the opportunity to juxtapose two forms of experience both of which are real (internal and external reality). It is from this juxtaposition over time that the infant constructs the state of mind which we term psychic reality.

If, for example, the mother is able to bear with (over a period of time) the aggression involved in a vigorous feed and its sequelae, she is there, not only to survive the experience, but also to recognize the meaning of a reparative gift from the infant, and to accept the gift from him (e.g. a bowel movement or a 'coo'). In this way, the mother allows the infant opportunity to make up for the fantasied harm that he has done and continues to do in fantasy, and for the strain that he has, in fact, caused.

Although Klein (1935), (1940) introduced the idea of the development in the depressive position of the wish to make reparation, she did not explore in any depth the nature of the interpersonal interaction mediating either this development or the discovery of the externality of the object. Klein was, of course, aware that the infant's feelings of guilt and his wish to make reparation are object-related phenomena. What she did not focus sufficient attention upon is the nature of the relationship with the real external object: someone must be there to recognize the infant's feelings of guilt and to accept the infant's reparative gift if the infant's psychological act is to be brought to completion. For the completion of this 'benign circle' (Winnicott 1958b: 24) the infant is utterly dependent on the mother as object and cannot grow without her act of surviving his phantasied destruction of her and through her unconscious recognition of the meaning of his gift and her acceptance of it.

In sum, Winnicott's conception of this third form of dependence of the infant on the mother (i.e. the dependence on the mother as object) was developed in the context of Klein's conception of internal objects and her concept of the depressive position. Winnicott differed from Klein in making central the role of the infant's experience with the mother as object. The infant's experience with an object surviving over time in conjunction with his unconscious renunciation of the omnipotent internal object, creates the conditions necessary for the discovery of the external object. This interplay of fantasy and experience with objects also generates the conditions for the creation of psychic reality, which achievement is built upon the differentiation of internal and external reality. Externality is not created once and for all by a single act of 'destruction' (renunciation) of the internal object. The pull of the primitive tie to the internal object must be consistently resisted. In psychological terms, the internal object must be constantly destroyed in unconscious fantasy, thus continually making room for the re-discovery of the external object.

Notes

1 I am aware that I am reversing the usual way of viewing a developmental sequence. Ordinarily, an earlier developmental phase is thought of as preparatory for the succeeding one. I am suggesting that an earlier developmental phase also forestalls the next one. Clearly, no intentionality is being attributed to the biological function of postponement. Psychology

is not merely an epiphenomenon of biology: biology and psychology are inseparable facets of a single developmental/maturational process. Early stages of psychological maturation and development serve to help the organism manage in a state of biological immaturity and in this sense secure the organism time to mature. Freud's (1895), (1896b), (1918) concept of 'deferred action' (*nachtraglich*) addresses the same point: for example, 'The retardation of puberty makes possible posthumous primary processes' (1895: 359).

2 A diachronic developmental axis involves a linear, sequential conception of development in which one phase of development builds upon the previous one through processes that include structural differentiation, integration, and epigenetic unfolding of maturational potentials. Freud's (1905) sequence of psychosexual phases, Anna Freud's (1965) conception of developmental lines, Piaget's (1946) notion of step-wise development of cognitive structures through assimilation and accommodation, and Erikson's (1950) conception of an epigenetic unfolding of psychosocial stages, are all examples of diachronic conceptions of development. A synchronic developmental axis involves a conception of coexisting hierarchically inter-related levels of development. Freud's (1896), (1918) conception of 'stratification,' Klein's (1932) notion of the spreading of libidinal excitation between levels of development, and Lacan's (1957) conception of the Imaginary and Symbolic orderings of experience, represent synchronic developmental conceptions.

3 It is important to emphasize that inadequacy of mothering is only one of the possible causes of failure of the holding environment. Other important causes include prematurity of birth, physical illness of the infant, unusual sensitivity on the part of the infant, 'lack of fit' between the temperaments of a particular mother and a particular infant, and so on.

4 Freud (1900), (1911) understood early psychological development as involving a move from an initial solipsistic world of hallucinatory wish fulfillment. This is viewed as the outcome of the interplay of the biological maturation of the organism and actual experience with objects. The infant at first utilizes hallucinatory wish fulfillment to insulate himself from frustrating external reality. However, as the infant matures biologically, he shifts from his efforts to create gratifying 'reality' hallucinatorily (magically) to an effort to utilize actual experience of frustration to find other (more effective, adaptive and indirect) ways of gratifying his instinctual needs.

5 The word 'matrix' is derived from the Latin word for 'womb.' Although Winnicott (1958) only once used the word matrix in his written work (when he referred to ego-relatedness as the 'matrix of transference'), it seems to me that matrix is a particularly apt word to describe the silently active containing space in which psychological and bodily experience occur.

6 Lacan's (1956) concept of 'the Other' similarly refers to a third psychological entity (an intersubjective entity) generated in the analytic setting that is distinct from the patient and from the analyst: 'The Other is therefore the locus in which is constituted the I who speaks with him who hears . . .' (p. 141).

7 Lewin (1950) refers to this 'backdrop' (p. 83) upon which dreaming occurs as the 'dream screen;' Khan (1972) uses the term dream space for this area of experiencing; Grotstein (1981) refers to this and other backgrounds of experience as the background object of primary identification.

8 Nursery rhymes (often symbolically about sleeping and told at bedtime) are replete with references to the child's fear of falling.

> Rock-a-bye baby
> On the tree-top –
> When the wind blows,
> The cradle will rock.
> When the bough breaks
> The cradle will fall,
> And down will come baby,
> Cradle and all.

The danger here is not simply that of bodily injury, or even that of separation anxiety; it is the danger of the disruption of the container of sleep, the infant's partially internal and partially external psychological matrix.

9 The gradual attainment of the depressive position for Winnicott (1954–5), occurs approximately in the second half of the first year of life. This development is marked by the infant's becoming able to 'play at dropping things,' (p. 263) an ability the infant usually develops to 'a fine art,' (p. 263) by about nine months.

10 When classical analytic thinkers (e.g. Jacobson [1964] and Mahler [1968]) refer to object relations, they are predominantly referring to the real interaction with actual external objects, and the internalization that follows from this interaction. The early object is not predominantly created by the infant; it is responded to, influences, and is influenced by the infant, and modifies the infant's psychological structure through an internalization process. British object relations theory (under the influence of ideas developed by Klein, Isaacs, Riviere and others) places more emphasis on the role of phantasy, projection and deep structural 'anticipation' of objects.

11 For Winnicott, it seems that unconscious omnipotent internal objects are defensively created in response to painful, but inevitable disruptions of the maternal holding environment. The infant deals with the anxiety and feelings of helplessness arising from a premature awareness of separateness by constructing a world of internal objects operating according to rules reflecting his own omnipotence.

References

Balint, M. 1968 *The Basic Fault* London: Tavistock.
Bion, W. R. 1962a *Learning from Experience* New York: Basic Books.

Bion, W. R. 1962b A theory of thinking In: *Second Thoughts* pp. 110–119 New York: Jason Aronson, 1967.

Erikson, E. 1950 *Childhood and Society* New York: W. W. Norton.

Fain, M. 1971 Prélude à la vie fantasmatique *Revue Française de Psychanalyse* 35: 291–364.

Freud, A. 1965 *Normality and Pathology in Childhood: Assessments of Development* New York: International Universities Press.

Freud, S. 1895 Project for a scientific psychology Standard Edition 1.

Freud, S. 1896 Letter to Fliess, December 6, 1896 In: *Origins of Psycho-Analysis* M. Bonaparte, A. Freud, E. Kris (Eds.) New York: Basic Books, 1954.

Freud, S. 1900 *The Interpretation of Dreams* Standard Edition 4: 1–626.

Freud, S. 1905 Three essays on the theory of sexuality Standard Edition 7.

Freud, S. 1911 Formulations on the two principles of mental Functioning Standard Edition 12.

Freud, S. 1918 From the history of an infantile neurosis Standard Edition 17.

Freud, S. 1920 Beyond the Pleasure principle Standard Edition 18.

Glover, E. 1945 Examination of the Klein system of child psychology *Psychoanal. Study Child* 1: 75–118.

Grotstein, J. 1980a The significance of Kleinian contributions to psychoanalysis I. Kleinian instinct theory *Int. J. Psychoanal.* 8: 375–392.

Grotstein, J. 1980b The significance of Kleinian contributions to Psychoanalysis II. Freudian and Kleinian conceptions of early mental development *Int. J. Psychoanal.* 8: 393–428.

Grotstein, J. 1981 *Splitting and Projective Identification* New York: Jason Aronson.

Jacobson, E. 1964 *The Self and the Object World* New York: International Universities Press.

Khan, M. M. R. 1972 The use and abuse of dream in psychic experience In: *The Privacy of the Self* pp. 306–315 New York: International Universities Press, 1974.

Klein, M. 1932 *The Psycho-Analysis of Children* London: Hogarth Press, 1969.

Klein, M. 1935 A contribution to the psychogenesis of manic-depressive states In: *Contributions to Psycho-Analysis 1921–1945* pp. 282–311 London: Hogarth Press, 1968.

Klein, M. 1940 Mourning and its relation to manic-depressive states In: *Contributions to Psycho-Analysis, 1921–1945* pp. 311–338 London: Hogarth Press, 1968.

Klein, M. 1946 Notes on some schizoid mechanisms In: *Envy and Gratitude and Other Works, 1946–1963* pp. 1–24 New York: Delacorte, 1975.

Klein, M. 1948 On the theory of anxiety and guilt In: *Envy and Gratitude and Other Works, 1946–1963* pp. 25–42 New York: Delacorte, 1975.

Klein, M. 1957 Envy and gratitude In: *Envy and Gratitude and Other Works, 1946–1963* New York: Delacorte, 1975.

Lacan, J. 1956 The Freudian thing or the meaning of the return to Freud in psychoanalysis In: *Écrits* pp. 114–145 New York: W. W. Norton, 1977.

Lacan, J. 1957 On a question preliminary to any possible treatment of psychosis In: *Écrits* pp. 179–225 New York: W. W. Norton, 1977.

Lewin, B. 1950 *The Psychoanalysis of Elation* New York: W. W. Norton.

Mahler, M. 1968 *On Human Symbiosis and the Vicissitudes of Individuation* Volume I New York: International Universities Press.

McDougall, J. 1974 The Psychosoma and the Psycho-Analytic Process *Int. Rev. Psychoanal.* 1: 437–459.

Ogden, T. 1982 *Projective Identification and Psychotherapeutic Technique* New York: Jason Aronson.

Ogden, T. 1984 Instinct, phantasy and psychological deep structure: A reinterpretation of aspects of the work of Melanie Klein *Contemp. Psychoanal.* 20: 500–525.

Ogden, T. 1985 On potential space *Int. J. Psychoanal.* 66 Part 2 in press.

Piaget, J. 1946 *Play, Dreams and Imitation in Childhood* New York: W. W. Norton, 1962.

Schmideberg, M. 1935 Discussion, British Psychoanalytical Society, October 16, 1935 Quoted by E. Glover, *Psychoanal. Study Child* 1: 75–118.

Stern, D. 1977 *The First Relationship: Infant and Mother* Cambridge: Harvard University Press.

Winnicott, D. W. 1945 Primitive emotional development In: *Through Paediatrics to Psycho-Analysis* pp. 145–156 New York: Basic Books, 1975.

Winnicott, D. W. 1951 Transitional objects and transitional phenomena In: *Playing and Reality* pp. 1–25 New York: Basic Books, 1971.

Winnicott, D. W. 1954–5 The depressive position in normal development In: *Through Paediatrics to Psycho-Analysis* pp. 262–277 New York: Basic Books, 1975.

Winnicott, D. W. 1956 Primary maternal preoccupation In: *Through Paediatrics to Psycho-Analysis* pp. 300–305 New York: Basic Books, 1975.

Winnicott, D. W. 1958a The capacity to be alone In: *The Maturational Processes and the Facilitating Environment* pp. 29–36 New York: International Universities Press, 1965.

Winnicott, D. W. 1958b Psycho-analysis and the sense of guilt In: *The Maturational Processes and the Facilitating Environment* pp. 15–28 New York: International Universities Press, 1965.

Winnicott, D. W. 1960a The theory of the parent-infant relationship In: *The Maturational Processes and the Facilitating Environment* pp. 37–55 New York: International Universities Press, 1965.

Winnicott, D. W. 1960b Ego distortion in terms of true and false self In: *The Maturational Processes and the Facilitating Environment* pp. 140–152 New York: International Universities Press, 1965.

Winnicott, D. W. 1962a A personal view of the Kleinian contribution In: *The Maturational Processes and the Facilitating Environment* pp. 171–178 New York: International Universities Press, 1965.

Winnicott, D. W. 1962b Ego integration in child development In: *The Matu-*

rational Processes and the Facilitating Environment pp. 56–63 New York: International Universities Press, 1965.

Winnicott, D. W. 1963 Communicating and not communicating leading to a study of certain opposites In: *The Maturational Processes and the Facilitating Environment* pp. 179–192 New York: International Universities Press, 1965.

Winnicott, D. W. 1967 The location of cultural experience In: *Playing and Reality* pp. 95–103 New York: Basic Books, 1971.

Winnicott, D. W. 1968 The use of an object and relating through cross identifications In: *Playing and Reality* pp. 86–94 New York: Basic Books, 1971.

Winnicott, D. W. 1971a *Playing and Reality* New York: Basic Books.

Winnicott, D. W. 1971b Playing: creative activity and the search for the self In: *Playing and Reality* pp. 53–64 New York: Basic Books.

Winnicott, D. W. 1971c Creativity and its origins In: *Playing and Reality* pp. 65–85 New York: Basic Books.

The evolution of Winnicott's theoretical matrix

A brief outline[1]

Jan Abram

Come at the world creatively, create the world; it is only what you create that has meaning for you.

(Winnicott 1968a: 101)

Winnicott's theoretical matrix evolved during the course of three chronological phases in which major theoretical discoveries occurred. Founded on the dialectics within and between the Freudian and Kleinian developments, Winnicott's thought offers 'a major advance in the psychoanalytic conception of the subject' (Ogden 1992: 619).

In essence, from his early days as a psychoanalyst, Winnicott's quest is to address the stage of human development that *precedes* object relations. One of the last pieces he writes offers a succinct conclusion to this focus:

I am proposing that there is a stage in the development of human beings that comes before objectivity and perceptibility. At the theoretical beginning a baby can be said to live in a subjective or conceptual world. The change from the primary state to one in which objective perception is possible is not only a matter of inherent or inherited growth process; it needs in addition an environmental minimum. It belongs to the whole vast theme of the individual travelling from dependence towards independence.

This conception–perception gap provides rich material for study. I postulate an essential paradox, one that we must accept and that is not for resolution. This paradox, which is central to the concept, needs to be allowed and allowed for over a period of time in the care of each baby.

(Winnicott 1971a: 151)

And, if there is any one concept that can be placed at the core of Winnicott's re-vision of psychoanalysis, it is this 'essential paradox' at the very beginning of life. Without the 'environmental minimum' the subject will never be able to live in the world of real objects. (Abram 2007: 352; Ogden 1986: 209; Parsons 2000; Roussillon 1991).

Increasingly, there is wide recognition that Winnicott's thought offers a substantial advance in psychoanalytic theory and practice. This has certainly been assisted by the work of the Winnicott Publications Committee, led by his widow Clare Winnicott who, after Winnicott's death in 1971, edited and published almost all of the unpublished writings (see Publications). These posthumous publications enhanced the appreciation of Winnicott's diverse writings and have inspired generations of clinicians since the 1970s through to the present day. But it was not always like this. For almost thirty years previously, Winnicott was a 'lone voice' in the emphasis he placed on the crucial role of the mother in early infant care and its impact on infantile narcissistic trauma (James 1962: 69). This focus, as we shall see, partly emerged out of Winnicott's response to the conflicts in the British Psychoanalytical Society (BPaS) that led to the controversial discussions between 1941–45 (King and Steiner 1992). As he stated much later, this period in the BPaS '. . . ruined all our scientific meetings . . . but left me completely cold' (1989a: 576). Simultaneously, it led to his resolve to start to concentrate on his own psychoanalytic formulations rooted in his clinical observations and based on Freud's methodology (see Chapter 1).

In autumn 1945, in the wake of the conclusion to the controversial discussions and the 'gentlemen's agreement', Winnicott presents his first seminal paper, 'Primitive emotional development' (1945b). At the very start of that paper, presented a few months before his 50th birthday, he shows how he intends, henceforth, to concentrate on his own formulations and to 'settle down to clinical experience' (p. 137). Ultimately, this intention, takes Winnicott to new psychoanalytic formulations concerning primary psychic creativity and the concept of self (Bollas 1987). Paradoxically though, especially at this moment, the author states that he does not wish to reformulate psychoanalytic theory, rather, the declaration at the start of Winnicott (1945b) suggests more a strong drive to find his own identity as a psychoanalyst who would not be associated with either the Anna Freud or the Melanie Klein groupings. The wish to be true to his own thinking will later become an important aspect of his theory of the true self, i.e. 'non-compliance'. For Winnicott, the capacity to live from the true self constitutes a developmental achievement and depends on a facilitating environment (see Phase Three).

Post controversial discussions, in the atmosphere of the BPaS, Winnicott is determined to keep his thinking alive and thus he finds himself deconstructing the technical language of psychoanalysis. This is a major strength in his writing because his spontaneous, conversational style in the English vernacular means that in the process of reading his texts a powerful intuitive response is evoked (Ogden 2001 [Chapter 9 this Volume]).

One of the pitfalls of Winnicott's use of language, however, is that it can obfuscate the originality of what is being stated, and it has been pointed out that his writing resists fitting in to a clear discernible theory (Modell 1985). This partly came about because of the way much of his work has been published to date, (see Appendix) and partly because Winnicott did not systematically correlate his writings. He regretted this later saying '. . . what I've said has been isolated and people have to do a lot of work to get at it' (1989b: 573 and Chapter 1).

Notwithstanding Winnicott's apology, Ogden has recently suggested that the 'paradoxical nature of Winnicott's thinking requires for its expression [a quality of] language that is continually in movement, continually elaborating new and often contradictory possibilities'[2] (Ogden, in Abram 2007: xxvi). This aptly captures the essence of Winnicott's style which is inextricably linked with his formulations.

The aim of this essay is to illustrate that there is indeed a *discernible theory* in Winnicott's writings but, perhaps because it is dialectically constituted, it has to be continually 'found and used' (1968a: 25) (see Wallbridge and Davis 1982; Abram 2007).

Theoretical phases

Following Sandler et al. (1997) [who followed Rapaport 1959], the author divides Winnicott's work into one Foundation phase – 1919–1934; followed by three major theoretical phases; Phase 1 – The environment-individual set-up – (1935–44); Phase 2 – Transitional phenomena – (1945–59); Phase 3 – The use of an object (1960–1971). The publications and key papers of each phase are tabulated at the end of each section.

Foundations (1919–1934)

Psychoanalysis is superior to hypnosis and must supersede it . . . Only yesterday I saw a man suffering from shell shock put under hypnosis by the man who looks after mental diseases at Barts. This man could never do psychoanalysis because it needs patience and sympathy and other properties which he does not possess.

(1987b: 1)

During the course of these 15 years Winnicott becomes a consultant paediatrician. Alongside his paediatric work he is one of the first candidates to train at the Institute of Psychoanalysis, in both adult and child psychoanalysis, and he qualifies at the end of this first phase in 1934.

Paediatrics

In 1914, at the age of 18, Winnicott chooses to join the pre-medical course at Cambridge University. This means that he is exempt from the World War I call-up, but by 1917 he volunteers and enlists for the Royal Navy as a Medical Officer. For the last 9 months of WWI he is a surgeon probationer on a destroyer and it proves to be a formative experience (Winnicott C. 1978). In 1918, he returns to complete his medical training at St. Bartholomew's Hospital. At some point in 1919, instigated by a concern that he is not remembering his dreams and recognising that this was a kind of symptom (Rodman 2003: 39), he reads Freud's Interpretation of dreams (possibly as the Brill 1913 or 1915, versions). Soon he is writing to his sister Violet about his new 'hobby' – psychoanalysis – telling her why it is 'superior to hypnotism' (Winnicott 1919). Psychoanalysis seems to remain a 'hobby', as he calls it, while Winnicott completes his medical training and qualifies a year later. By 1922 he becomes a full member of the Royal College of Physicians and chooses to specialize in paediatrics.

Major life events occur in 1923 when Winnicott marries Alice Buxton and is appointed Assistant Physician at the Queen's Hospital for Children, Hackney, where he also works as Physician in Charge for London County Council Rheumatism Supervisory Centre until 1933. In addition he is appointed as Consultant Paediatrician at Paddington Green Children's Hospital, where he will remain for 40 years. By 1931, Winnicott has also set up in private practice.

Psychoanalysis

Coincidentally, as Winnicott discovers Freud's writings in 1919, Ernest Jones is in the process of setting up the BPaS. In 1923, The Institute of Psycho-Analysis, London (IPaL) is formed and preparations begin for setting up the first British training in psychoanalysis. In this same year, Winnicott, not yet 30, has his first psychoanalytic consultation with Ernest Jones. He is referred to James Strachey, who has recently set up in private practice as a psychoanalyst. In 1926, the first IPaL Training Committee is established, which is also the year Melanie Klein arrives from Berlin. At that time the BPaS membership consists of 54 members, and includes Marjorie Brierley, Edward Glover, James Glover, Susan Isaacs, Ernest Jones, Melanie Klein, Sylvia Payne, John Rickman, Joan Riviere, Ella Sharpe, Melitta Schmideberg, Nina Searl, Adrian Stephen, Karin Stephen, Alix Strachey, and James Strachey (Rayner 1990: 11).

When he registers as a candidate in 1927, Winnicott is amongst the first group of candidates to follow the formal training in psychoanalysis, and begins to attend BPaS scientific meetings from 1929. His supervisors are Nina Searl and Ella Sharpe for his adult training cases and Melanie Klein, Melitta Schmideberg and Nina Searl for his three child patients. He qualifies in adult psychoanalysis in 1934 and a year later becomes the first BPaS qualified male child psychoanalyst.

Table 3.1 Publications and key papers, 1919–1934

Date of writing	Title and date of publication	Notes
1926	Varicella encephalitis and vaccinia encephalitis (1926)	First scientific paper, co-authored with Nancy Gibbs.
1928	The only child (1928)	A chapter in *The mind of the growing child* (ed) Erleigh, E.V.
1930	Pathological sleeping (1930a)	Case history for the Proceedings of the Royal Society of Medicine.
1930	Short communication on enuresis (1930b)	St Bartholomew's Hospital Journal, where Winnicott is Consultant Paediatrician.
1931	Clinical notes on disorders of childhood (1931a)	The first in a Practitioner's aid series 'designed for the busy GP' by William Heinemann (Medical Books) Ltd. It consists of 20 short papers.
1931	Arthritis associated with emotional disturbance (1931b)	Chapter X in 1931a Masud Khan writes that Winnicott made a 'revolutionary stand' (1975: p. xiii) as a paediatrician particularly concerning his view of arthritis in children citing the case of Eleanor (1931a: 82).
1931	Fidgetiness (1931c)	Chapter X1 in 1931a and selected by DWW for his first Collected Papers (1958a).
1931	A note on normality and anxiety (1931d)	Chapter X11 in 1931a and also selected by DWW for 1958a where he states in the Preface:'. . . in these chapters is represented my attitude as a paediatrician prior to my training in psychoanalysis. I wrote as a paediatrician to paediatricians' (p. ix).
1934	The difficult child (1934a)	Only published in the Journal of State Medicine. Commentary on two previous papers by G.A. Auden and R.D. Gillespie given at the Norwich congress.
1934	Papular urticaria and the dynamics of skin sensation (1934b)	First published in the British Journal of Children's Diseases, and later in 1996a.

Phase 1 – The environment–individual set–up
(1935–1944)

There's no such thing as a baby . . . if you show me a baby you certainly show me also someone caring for the baby, or at least a pram with someone's eyes and ears glued to it. One sees a 'nursing couple.'

(1958c: 99)

This decade can be considered as the first major theoretical stage in that two related and crucial discoveries are made which inform and shape the conceptualizations of the next two phases – the baby is a human being (1989b: 574) and 'there's no such thing as a baby' (1958c: 99).

The first discovery comes about as Winnicott begins his training in psychoanalysis around 1929 when later he reports: 'It was only through analysis that I became gradually able to see a baby as a human being. This was really the chief result of my first five years of analysis . . .' (1989b: 574).[3] André Green adds that his experience of analysis – '. . . enabled him to see the child with the eyes of the analyzed adult who has rediscovered the child in himself, with all his vulnerability and creativity' (Clancier and Kalmonovitch 1984: 120). However, it cannot be ignored that alongside his daily analytic sessions as alternating patient and analyst, Winnicott is confronted with the infant or young child on the mother's lap in his paediatric work. This unique combination inevitably has a profound impact on his understanding and shows that, despite the (later) disappointments of his personal experience of analysis, he also felt 'tremendously helped' (1989b: 575). It is not until 1942, or thereabouts, that he comes to the realization that 'there's no such thing as an infant' (1958c). This thought gradually builds up to into his theory of the parent-infant relationship (1960) (see Phase Three).

This first decade of Winnicott's development as a psychoanalyst is dominated by his work with children as his working week is divided between private practice and the paediatric consultancy posts – mostly at Paddington Green. In addition, from 1939–46, Winnicott is appointed as psychiatric consultant to the Government Evacuation Scheme in Oxford, where hundreds of children are evacuated during World War II.

Paediatrics

As he begins his psychoanalytic education Winnicott finds himself 'astounded' by the verification of psychoanalytic theory in his work as a paediatrician. Gradually though, he begins to notice a 'certain deficiency' in the theory and feels that 'something is wrong some-where' (1965c: 172). Based on his detailed history taking of each case, it becomes clear to him that the origins of oedipal conflict in the personality start much earlier than postulated by Freud's classical Oedipus complex. As he begins treating children in psychoanalysis he is able to confirm his hypothesis, i.e. that oedipal conflict begins much earlier than 3, 4 or 5, and that babies really can be emotionally ill. This observation correlates with the theories that Melanie Klein had been developing since 1920 (Klein 1927, 1928). Winnicott finds that Melanie Klein's approach enables him to reflect on infantile conflicts, anxieties and primitive defences. In 1936 these ideas 'boil up into a paper' he calls 'Appetite and emotional disorder', which can be seen as his proto theory of the earliest parent–infant relationship. In this early psychoanalytic paper Winnicott aims to demonstrate a. how the inner world could be observable in a baby and b. how oedipal conflicts start in babies as young as 5 or 6 months. The way in which Winnicott demonstrates this radical clinical data, is through the ingenious invention of a game with a spatula. The 'spatula game' takes place in the 'set situation' which comprises of Dr. Winnicott sitting opposite mother and baby, aged between 5 and 13 months, sitting on her lap. They are at either side of the corner of a table where a shiny spatula[4] is placed within easy reach of baby. The oedipal dynamic is immediately clear. Winnicott observes that, for the majority of babies, a normal sequence of three stages occur as baby reaches out for the spatula. The way in which mother and infant respond to this 'set-situation' will illuminate a picture of the infant's inner world. And, although at this early stage, Winnicott has not yet fully appreciated the impact of mother's attention on the infant's internal world, the traces of this dawning awareness are evident (see Table 3.2).

These results not only provide evidence for some of Klein's theories, i.e. early anxieties and conflicts of the baby's inner world, but also show the interrelationship between family constellations and their impact on early psychic development – interpsychic and intra-psychic. Winnicott's paediatric clinic became, what he later described as his 'psychiatric snack bar' (Winnicott C. 1978: 28). An evocative description of the clinic is related in Winnicott (1941b).

In his position as Psychiatric Consultant to the Government Evacuation Scheme, Winnicott travels once a week to Oxford to work with the team of social workers. There he meets Clare Britton, a senior psychiatric social worker, and a constructive collaboration begins as Winnicott introduces psychoanalytic ideas to her and the team of residential workers who are in daily contact with the children.[5] Winnicott is responsible for five hostels of children who 'were difficult to billet' and between 1939 and 1946 his weekly visits involve listening to the details of 285 children (1948). The experience of working with the evacuees '. . . had a profound effect on Winnicott because he had to meet in a condensed way the confusion brought about by the wholesale break-up of family life . . .' (Winnicott C. 1984: 1). The experience also leads to further psychoanalytic conceptions such as the antisocial tendency (as sign of hope) and holding (Abram 2007: 47–66; 193–199) (See Phase Two).

40 papers on child health and development are published during this decade, most of which are addressed to those working with families and children.

Psychoanalysis

In 1933, as Winnicott completes his 10 year analysis, James Strachey tells him that he 'would not get what Klein taught from his analysis with him' (Winnicott 1965c: 173). Between 1935 and 1940 as a newly qualified analyst, Winnicott consults Mrs. Klein for his child psychoanalytic cases. During this period, Melanie Klein asks Winnicott to treat her son Erich, which he agrees to, although refuses her wish to supervise the work[6] (Grosskurth, 1986: 233; Phillips 1988: 47). Winnicott also begins a second analysis with one of Klein's strong supporters, Joan Riviere.[7]

On the 21st October 1936 he is elected a Full Member of BPaS, with his reading in paper 'The Manic Defence' (1958b). Like his earlier paper, 'Appetite and Emotional Disorder', written in 1936, this paper demonstrates an allegiance to many of Klein's theories and in the first paragraph he pays tribute to both Klein and Riviere (1958e). However, there are signs of an emerging divergence. In 1958e Winnicott emphasizes the mother's contribution to the baby's emotional development, while in 1958b he begins to make an important distinction regarding the function of fantasy (Khan p.xiv in Winnicott 1965b). As will be seen, Winnicott's stress on the environment's contribution to the individual's mental health will become increasingly central to his formulations as well as the function of fantasy which Winnicott sees as being 'part of the individual's effort to deal with inner reality . . . day dreams are omnipotent manipulations of external reality' (1958e: 130).

It is also important to note, that while Winnicott concurred with Klein's theories of early oedipal anxieties during the thirties, he did not agree that this was evidence of an Oedipus complex. In the early fifties he writes: 'I think something is lost if the term "Oedipus complex" is applied to the earlier stages, in which there are only two persons involved and the third person or part object is internalized, a phenomenon of inner reality' (1988: 49).

Alongside clinical work, Winnicott is invited to broadcast a series of talks for the BBC radio aimed at mothers who are at home with their babies and young children. In addition, he starts teaching Child Development seminars for candidates following the analytic training, and is invited by Susan Isaacs,[8] to lecture on growth and human development for the University of London. Winnicott will continue to present these latter lectures annually for another 20 years or so and in the early 1950s he starts to prepare a book from his lecture notes – Human Nature – which will be published posthumously (1988) (see Phase Two).

Up to 1940, as is evident, Winnicott benefits from his collaboration with Melanie Klein, so much so that in the lead up to the Controversial Discussions, he is designated by her to be one of the named five Kleinian training analysts. The other three were Susan Isaacs, Joan Riviere and John Rickman (King, P. and Steiner, R. 1991: 32). However, by 1942, Mrs. Klein, disappointed that Winnicott does not prepare his contributions to the meetings well enough in advance for her to read them, feels she has to exclude him as one of her collaborators (King and Steiner: xxiv). There are other indicators that suggest further reasons for his shift away from Melanie Klein and her circle.

By 1940–41, Winnicott is completing his analysis with Joan Riviere, and according to his account some time later, he is upset at the end of his second analysis and it will take him some time to recover (1989b: 576). One reason for his disappointment he reports, is because Joan Riviere does not acknowledge his evolving ideas to classify the environment. A relevant reminder here is that Joan Riviere was the analyst who, in 1927, came out in strong support of

Melanie Klein's views that opposed some of Anna Freud's techniques and theories about child analysis. In Riviere's contribution to the Symposium on Child Analysis she states:

> . . . psychoanalysis . . . is not concerned with the real world, nor with the child's or the adult's adaptation to the real world, nor with sickness or health, nor virtue or vice. It is concerned simply and solely with the imaginings of the childish mind, the phantasied pleasures and the dreaded retributions.
>
> (Riviere 1927 in Hughes 1991: 87)

This statement illustrates one of the main arguments at the crux of the disagreement between the two different approaches to child analysis at that time. It was a direct rejoinder to Anna Freud's way of working with children and could be seen to contradict Freud's own writings beginning in 1923, that the ego is subject to equal stress by demands of both the external and inner worlds (Freud 1923; Sandler et al 1997). But, more importantly, Winnicott is realizing that his views are beginning to seriously differ from those of Klein and Riviere.

Winnicott's theoretical divergences, especially with the Kleinian development, towards the end of this first phase, begin to take shape and Winnicott is on the point of articulating his open disagreement with some aspects of Klein's developing theories. But, he finds himself in a difficult position in relation to the principal analysts of the 'controversies', as he tells the '1952 group' in 1967, because by having aligned himself earlier with Klein's thinking on the primacy of the internal world and early oedipal conflicts, he had already demonstrated something of his disagreement with Anna Freud. Thus, his experience, as he saw it, is that for some time to come Miss Freud does not want his contribution perceiving him a Kleinian, and by 1942, neither does Mrs. Klein because as the controversial discussions begin, she no longer deems him a Kleinian (1989b: 576).

For a while, up until 1945, the solution to Winnicott's predicament is defined by the many tasks already in hand – the evacuation scheme, teaching and lecturing, radio broadcasts, committee work, writing and publishing, not to mention a busy psychoanalytic practice. Despite his discomfort about the controversial discussions, Winnicott is nevertheless a very active member of the BPaS and contributes a great deal to the meetings concerning the controversies, and attends all but one of the meetings. He is the assistant director for the Child Department of the London Clinic of Psychoanalysis and in 1942, presents his report to the BpaS (1942).

In 1944 as the controversial discussions conclude, Winnicott, along with the majority of psychoanalysts at that time, chooses non-alignment as the training course divides in two. Meanwhile, in the world outside the heat of the BPaS, he is appointed Fellow of the Royal College of Physicians.

Table 3.2 Key publications, 1935–1944

Date of writing	Title and date of publication	Notes
1935	The manic defence (1958b)	Winnicott's first psychoanalytic paper written for Full Membership of the BPaS. Published for the first time in 1958a.
1936	Appetite and emotional disorder (1958e)	According to DWW this was the first paper where he felt confident to point out his findings on the baby's early oedipal conflicts (1965c p. 172). Moreover, this is the first time he makes a statement on the 'mother's contribution.' This will become one of the major divergences between his own view and Melanie Klein's.
1939	Aggression (1957c)	In 1958a this is the first paper on the development of his theory of aggression which will lead to his disagreement with Freud's concept of the death instinct (see Phase Three).
1941	Observation of infants in a set situation (1941)	This paper follows on from the above 1936 paper and anticipates Winnicott's theoretical discovery 'there's no such thing as a baby.' It was one of the papers selected by DWW for his first Collected Papers (1958a).
1942	Child department consultations (1942)	A report given from his position as assistant director of the Child Department of the London Clinic of Psycho-Analysis. It describes 14 consultations and was selected by DWW for his first Collected Papers (1958a).
1944	Ocular psychoneuroses of childhood (1944)	Originally written for 'The transactions of the Opthalmological Society' and later selected by DWW for his second volume of Collected Papers 1965b.

Phase 2 – Transitional phenomena (1945–1959)

It is an area which is not challenged, because no claim is made on its behalf except that it shall exist as a resting-place for the individual engaged in the perpetual human task of keeping inner and outer reality separate yet inter-related.

(1953a: 90)

Transitional phenomena is the major theoretical achievement during this phase, a concept that develops from the notion of primary unintegration, and naturally evolves from the discoveries of the first major theoretical phase i.e: that 'there's no such thing as a baby' and that the baby is a human being. The psychology of the early infant, therefore, must be taken into account concerning his psychic care.

The themes related to transitional phenomena concern Winnicott's focus on how the baby's undeveloped ego is reinforced by the mother's ego-protection through her unconscious identification with his state of absolute dependence. In this way she facilitates his ability to move from an unintegrated state of mind to one that is integrated. Inner reality is initiated by three processes – 'integration, personalization, and, following these, the appreciation of time and space and other properties of reality – in short realization' (1945b: 149). Unintegration, as distinct from disintegration, is an internal resource and latterly in Winnicott's work associated with the 'illusion of omnipotence,' 'location of culture,' and the 'sense of self' (Winnicott 1967a) (see Phase Three). Transitional phenomena is a concept that accounts for the interpsychic/intrapsychic dynamics of the subject's journey towards the capacity to symbolize i.e. to distinguish Me from Not-me.

Paediatrics

During this second phase Winnicott continues to be in demand to broadcast and lecture to non-analytic groups, and his work at 'the Green' provides him with ample material for the many talks and papers. Later he will say that he finds it the most valuable thing to lecture to people who aren't analysts because their questions force further exploration (1989b: 578). Thus it is, as ever, the combination of applied psychoanalysis in his hospital work and 'pure' psychoanalysis with private patients that enriches his thought. These talks and lectures are published in two separate publications (1945a, 1949a). Later in 1957 the two books are combined into one publication with a new companion volume (see Table 3.3). During these 15 years, Winnicott produces more than 60 articles on child development.

In the middle of this phase, Winnicott starts to prepare a book based on his lecture series on human growth and development that he had been giving annually for almost 20 years to social workers at the Institute of Education (see Phase 1). The book is almost complete in 1954 but he continues to make additions and amendments up to 1967. *Human Nature*, not published in his lifetime, offers a condensed, comprehensive outline of the theoretical matrix and is considered the primer of his oeuvre (1988).

Psychoanalysis

While in the first phase Winnicott finds that his focus on infantile anxieties correlates with the work of Melanie Klein and her discoveries, during this second phase of his work many of his new formulations emerge out of his critical discourse with the new Kleinian developments. We will see how clear it becomes that Winnicott's developments result in a fundamental difference of approach in psychoanalysis, however, it is noteworthy that, overall, this does *not* amount to Winnicott's repudiation of all Kleinian theory (Ogden 1985; 1992). An emphasis on the internal world as well as the '. . . strict application of Freudian principles of technique,' remain a given for Winnicott (1965c: 175).

As we have seen, 1945 marks the beginning of a new era for the BPaS as analysts begin to recover from the 'controversial discussions' – disagreements that had almost split the Society. Winnicott is an active member of the Society and as a Training Analyst and Supervisor he is, at different times in this period, a member of Board and Council, Chair of the committee of the Membership Panel, a member of the Admissions Committee, and is elected President in 1956 (see Chronology). While the 'gentleman's agreement' represents a respect for difference in the interpretation of Freudian texts post controversial discussions, and ensures an equal share of certain positions in the Society, the psychoanalytic developments between the Kleinians and the Anna Freudians gradually become more and more distinct. By the early 1960s the majority of the non aligned analysts, hitherto known as the 'middle group', come together to form the 'independent group'[9] (Tuckett 1996: 739–740). Winnicott is likely to have retained his non–aligned status[10] although his work tends to be associated with the psychoanalysts who chose not to align. It is significant to note that, despite the setting up of an organized group there were many others like Winnicott who felt that 'independence' meant non–aligned to any group (Kohon 1988: 49).

From 1945 to 1957 there are at least 15 seminal papers that introduce original conceptualizations evolving out of the ideas on early infantile processes. Winnicott's increasing emphasis is to scrutinize the elements that constitute good enough mothering and to apply these observations to the analytic setting. In other words what are the essential ingredients of the good enough analyst? Each paper explores how the infant's subjective states of mind in the developing child depend on the mother's emotional attitude to her infant. This theory of primary psychic creativity does not abrogate the responsibility of the patient in analysis for his difficulties, but rather, aims at the recognition of deficiencies in the early interpersonal/ interpsychic environment. The acknowledgement of specific kinds of deficiencies, clarified through the transference-countertransference matrix, assists the analyst's understanding of the analysand's psychic predicament. As will be seen, this links up with Winnicott's theory of regression.

The following is a condensed summary of Winnicott's formulations during this second phase of his work – 1945 to 1960. This list of concepts is presented here chronologically and corresponds to the entries compiled by the author in *The Language of Winnicott*[11] (Abram 2007). Here, each concept is briefly defined, whereas a description of the relevant papers[12] is given in Table 3.3.

Hate (1949c)

The capacity to be aware of one's own hate occurs at the time of relative dependence and the stage of concern and is thus a developmental achievement. The ability to organize one's hate, alongside loving, means that ambivalence has been reached. For Winnicott, therefore, to hate is a capacity related to ego development and object relations, rather than a manifestation of the death instinct[13] (Freud 1921; Klein 1932) (see Phase Three).

Depression (1958f; 1965d)

Winnicott's view on depression focuses on the need for the subject to distinguish between a personal depression and his mother's internalized depressed mood and/or depression. There is also an exploration of a type of depression which is normal and related to the reality principle and disillusionment. This is in contrast to a pathological depression that is an affective disorder, and associated with a blockage in emotional development, based on Freud's formulations of melancholia (Freud 1915). The way depression and depressed feelings are negotiated in each individual is rooted in the early parent–infant relationship, particularly during the time of weaning, when the infant starts to differentiate between Me and Not-me, and when it is a normal part of development to feel sad and to be able to recognize a sense of loss.

Psyche-soma (1954; 1966; 1971g)

The psyche-in-dwelling-in-the-soma describes the successful outcome of the process of 'personalization' that occurs as a result of the mother's handling of her infant during the holding phase. This is the time of absolute dependence, when the (healthy) mother is in a state of primary maternal preoccupation. The use of the word 'psyche' denotes 'imaginative elaboration of somatic parts, feelings, and functions' and is often synonymous with 'fantasy', 'inner reality', and 'self' (1988: 52).

Aggression (1958g)

Winnicott's theory of aggression begins in 1939 (1957c) and evolves through to the third phase by which time his views are radically different from both Freud and Klein (see Phase 3 The use of an object). In the early 1950s he postulates a 'primary aggression' that is synonymous with activity and mobility which is originally part of appetite. Aggression changes its quality as the infant grows and absolutely depends on the kind of psychic environment in which the infant finds himself. With good enough mothering and a facilitating environment, aggression in the growing child becomes integrated. If the environment is not good enough, aggression may manifest itself in a (self)-destructive and/or antisocial way (see Antisocial Tendency).

Transitional phenomena (1953a; 1971a)

This concept refers to a dimension of living that belongs neither to internal nor to external reality; a space that both connects and separates inner and outer. This concept evolves from the notion of unintegration. Winnicott uses many terms to refer to this dimension – the third area, the intermediate area, the potential space, a resting place, and the location of cultural experience. Developmentally, transitional phenomena occur from the beginning, even before birth, in relation to the mother-infant dyad. As the infant begins to separate Me from Not-me, going from absolute dependence through to the stage of relative dependence, he makes use of the transitional object. This necessary developmental journey leads to the use of illusion, the use of symbols, and the use of an object. Transitional phenomena are inextricably linked with playing, creativity and paradox.

Illusion (of omnipotence) (1931e; 1953a)

Through his observations of early disillusionment in children, during the 1930s, Winnicott started to formulate the notion of transitional phenomena and the 'substance of illusion.' He sees that the infant's 'illusion of omnipotence,' comes about as a result of the mother's capacity to adapt to early needs. This adaptation occurs cumulatively from the very beginning and lays the foundations for the infant's subsequent healthy emotional development. Thus a healthy sense of self emerges out of the newborn infant's illusion of having 'created the object' through his need and this makes him feel all powerful, but without being aware of the need for power. The capacity to play is predicated on the experience of the illusion of this type of 'omnipotence,' and is vital to 'living creatively' and 'feeling real.'

Regression (1955a; 1955c)

During this 2nd phase Winnicott sees that Freud 'took for granted' the successful outcome of the early stages of development (1955a:

20), and he illustrates that there are two distinct and different patterns of relating that correlate with either a good enough or a not good enough holding at the start. Regression to dependence may occur in the analytic setting as a way of re-living the not-yet-experienced trauma that happened at the time of early environmental failure. The analytic setting offers an opportunity for the patient to experience a good-enough holding environment (probably) for the first time. Winnicott differentiates between 'regression to dependence' in the analytic set-up from the 'regressed' patient.

Holding (1971h; 1986a)

This was a concept Winnicott began to formulate from his experience with evacuees during World War 2. During this 2nd phase he focuses on the analytic set-up and illustrates, through verbatim reports of sessions, the meaning of 'regression to dependence' and the distinctions between his notions of holding and interpretation.

Antisocial tendency (1958d)

This is another concept that stems from the experience of working with evacuees. The antisocial tendency is associated with deprivation and the antisocial act signifies an environmental failure at the time of relative dependence. In Winnicott's thesis, the antisocial tendency indicates that the infant had experienced a good–enough environment during the time of absolute dependence but it was subsequently lost due to environmental failure. Therefore the antisocial act is a sign of hope that the subject's communication will be received by the environment so that the individual will re-discover the good experience of the time before the loss occurred.

Primary maternal preoccupation (1958h)

The healthy pregnant woman becomes mentally 'ill' just before giving birth and for a few weeks after birth. The emotional and physical health of the baby, according to this thesis, depends on whether the mother is able to go into and, in time, come out of this special state of mind. This concept is not related to whether a woman is a good or bad mother but is simply to do with an intuitive capacity to unconsciously identify with her baby's predicament. If the mother comes to recognize that she was not able to do this and 'missed the boat' with her infant, at a later stage she is likely to try to compensate for this by 'doing therapy' (1958h: 302).

Alone (1958i)

This is a capacity based on the paradox of 'being alone in the presence of another' and signifies health and the peak of emotional maturity. The capacity to be alone should not be confused with the withdrawn state. The sense of loneliness indicates a lack of the experience of having been alone in the presence of the primary m/other.

Table 3.3 Publications and key papers, 1945–1959

Date of writing	Title of books and date of publication	Notes
1945	*Getting to Know your Baby* (1945a)	A pamphlet of six radio broadcasts addressed to mothers and their newborn babies.
1949	*The Ordinary Devoted Mother and her Baby* (1949a)	A pamphlet of nine radio broadcasts.
1954	*Human Nature* (1988)	Based on lectures in Growth and Development for the Institute of Education.
1955	*Holding and Interpretation* (1986a)	An exploration of technique with verbatim reports of a psychoanalysis.
1957	*The Child and the Family* (1957a)	Includes the papers from 1945a & 1949a.
1957	*The Child and the Outside World: Studies in Developing Relationships* (1957b)	Intended as a companion volume to 1957a.
1958	*Collected Papers: Through Paediatrics to Psycho-Analysis* (1958a)	The first collected papers illustrating writings on child development and psychoanalysis.

Date of writing	Title of key papers and date of publication	Notes
1945	Towards an objective study of human nature (1945c)	Psychoanalysis as an objective study of human nature.
1945	Primitive emotional development (1945b)	First seminal paper introducing several original ideas with an emphasis on very early development.
1946	Children's hostels in war and peace (1948)	Based on a lecture given to the Medical Section of the British Psychological Society in 1946.
1947	Hate in the countertransference (1949c)	Developing the concept of hate as first introduced in 1945b.
1947	Babies are persons (1947)	Unusual for that time, focuses on the baby at birth.
1948	Reparation in respect of mother's organized defence against depression (1958f)	Theory of mother's depression as an alien factor in the child compared with group processes in the BPaS.
1948	Environmental needs: The early stages: total dependence and essential independence (1996b)	Introducing a theory of dependence.
1949	Birth memories, birth trauma, and anxiety (1958j)	Exploring Freud's texts on the correlation between birth and anxieties using clinical examples.
1949	Mind and its relation to the psyche-soma (1954)	Introducing a theory of the psyche-in-dwelling-in-the-soma and the body as self.
1949	The innate morality of the baby (1949b)	Innate morality as opposed to innate hate.
1950–54	Aggression in relation to emotional development (1958g)	Towards a radical theory of aggression.
1951	Transitional objects and transitional phenomena (1953a)	Elaboration of the Freudian oral stage and the process of reaching symbolic thinking.
1952	Anxiety associated with insecurity (1958c)	'There's no such thing as a baby.'
1952	Psychoses and child care (1953b)	Two distinct patterns of the early environment.

1954	Metapsychological and clinical aspects of regression in the psychoanalytic set up (1955a)	Developing the notion of regression in the analytic setting.
1954	The depressive position in normal development (1955b)	An appraisal of Klein's theory.
1954	Withdrawal and regression (1955c)	Focusing on modes of regression.
1956	What do we know about babies as cloth suckers? (1993b)	Theory of the transitional object.
1956	The anti-social tendency (1958d)	Conceptualizing the real deprivation at the root of the anti-social act.
1956	Primary maternal preoccupation (1958h)	The mother's particular illness in order to adapt to baby's needs.
1957	The capacity to be alone (1958i)	Based on the paradox of being alone in the presence of m/other.
1958	The family affected by depressive illness in one or both parents (1965d)	The impact on the subject's sense of self.
1959	The fate of the transitional object (1989c)	And its relegation to limbo.

The above psychoanalytic conceptualizations of this 2nd phase emerge as a consequence of Winnicott's approach to psychoanalysis, from 1945, as a study of human nature. Winnicott's observations in paediatrics and psychoanalysis led to his formulations on early psychic processes, particularly unintegration, and evolved into a theory of transitional phenomena. Central to his theory of transitional phenomena is that of primary psychic creativity in the subject and the 'illusion of omnipotence.' The m/other in her state of primary maternal preoccupation is able to adapt to her baby's needs and thus facilitates the 'illusion' that he is all powerful. It is this experience that is at the core of the sense of self. These are the themes that continue to preoccupy Winnicott in the 3rd and final phase of his work.

Phase 3 – The use of an object (1960–1971)

From now on the subject says: 'Hullo object!' 'I destroyed you.' 'I love you.' 'You have value for me because of your survival of my destruction of you.' 'While I am loving you I am all the time destroying you in (unconscious) fantasy.' Here fantasy begins for the individual. The subject can now use the object that has survived.

(1969: 713)

In his last years, Winnicott's discourse seems to be more with Freud than with Klein. The 'use of an object' is the major theoretical achievement of this final phase, and takes Winnicott to the peak of his clinical discoveries. Moreover, it is the concept, if there is any one concept, that brings him into direct disagreement, not with Klein this time, but with Freud. In his final years, as he approaches the certainty of his own death, he seems to feel closer and even identified with Freud to feel able to come to a different conclusion. The major theoretical disagreement alluded to in 'the use of an object' thesis, but not yet spelled out, is Winnicott's conviction that Freud's later theory of the death instinct was a mistake (1989d: 242). He is not alone in this disagreement. There are many analysts of the past and present who disagree with this particular concept of Freud's metapsychology (see Klein G. 1969; 1970; Diatkine in Perelberg 2005). Others go further and argue that Winnicott's psychoanalysis constitutes a Kuhnian paradigm shift (see Chapter 4) (Loparic 2002; 2006; Fulgencio 2007).

Paediatrics

In 1963, after 40 years' service, Winnicott retires from his post as consultant paediatrician at Paddington Green. Meanwhile, he continues to address those working with children and young families. These talks are published in a variety of journals and amount to over 100 articles (see Table 3.4). Every article contains new nuggets of illuminating insight, and, as in the previous phase, serve as an index to Winnicott's evolving thought on the theory and practice of psychoanalysis.

In 1964, *The Child, the Family and the Outside World* (1964a) is published by Penguin Books and brings together most of the articles from the earlier publications (1957a; 1957b). This book has been the most popular of all the Winnicott publications reaching a massive audience outside psychoanalytic circles (1993a: xiv).

At about the same time Winnicott treats a young child of 27 months, he names the 'piggle', who is probably the last child patient he takes into treatment. He writes up the 16 sessions that take place over the course of 2½ years. This is never published in his lifetime, but becomes the first of Clare Winnicott's projects for the WPC (1977).

In the last 2 years of his life, Winnicott also works on a volume to illustrate his later work as a child psychiatrist. 1971b illustrates Winnicott's use of the squiggle game – a diagnostic tool that evolved out of the earlier spatula game – for children and adolescents (1971b).

Psychoanalysis

Winnicott's primary questions during his final eleven years, are associated with a philosophical inquiry. He asks fundamental questions related to what it is that makes life worth living, and what it is that gives the human being a sense of feeling real. There is a powerful sense of increasing freedom and honesty in his thought. He is in continuous demand to speak to the international psychoanalytic world where he addresses these questions and in addition to the 100 articles he writes on child development during this phase, a further 70 papers are addressed to the psychoanalytic community. As a consequence of this sense of freedom in his thought new conceptualizations emerge as he extends the Freudian project. For example, he writes that 'psychoanalysis has been developed as a highly specialized form of playing in the service of communication with oneself and others' (1968d: 593).

In the consulting room he emphasizes the principal technique of waiting – like the facilitating and good enough mother – for the analysand to discover his true sense of self. This plea, linked with his concept of playing as a psychoanalytic concept, clearly builds on Freud's technique of free association. But, it is not so much a return to Freud as a re-vision of free association as the methodology in the analytic setting that truly facilitates contact with the self. In line with Winnicott's argument of 1969, Bollas argues that the technique of free association has been undermined in contemporary clinical psychoanalysis through an over use of 'here and now' transference interventions (Bollas 2002; 2007).

1960 marks a new significant phase in the BPaS when Melanie Klein dies. In this decade Winnicott writes only three essays on his continued disagreement with Klein's theory of envy, one of which is presented at a scientific meeting in 1969.[14] The other two are published posthumously as unfinished writings by the WPC (1989e,f). Despite certain members of the Kleinian group continuing to dismiss the value of his formulations, Winnicott continues to stay very engaged with the work of the BPaS and in 1965 he is elected President for a second time. During this second presidency one of the tasks he chooses is to raise funds for the completion of Oscar Nemon's statue of Freud, which is finally erected three months before he dies[15] (Rodman 2003: 413).

As before, to illustrate Phase 2, the following is a condensed summary of Winnicott's formulations during this third phase of his work – 1960 – 1971, often linked to a seminal paper. This list of concepts is presented here chronologically and relates to the entries compiled by the author in *The Language of Winnicott* (Abram 2007). Here each concept is briefly defined, whereas a description of the relevant paper is given in Table 3.4.

Self (1965e)

Essentially, the term 'self' in Winnicott's theory, is a phenomenological description of subjectivity, and it is the sense of 'feeling real' that Winnicott places at the centre of the sense of self. In this last decade Winnicott distinguishes between the true and false self. The false self, in his theory, is set up to protect the true self. Five versions of a false self are postulated traversing a line from the pathological to the ordinary and healthy false self.

Concern (1963a)

Winnicott postulated a 'stage of concern' related to Klein's 'depressive position' but with a different emphasis on the positive aspects of a sense of guilt. The infant's capacity to feel concern for his mother marks the developmental achievement of the journey from pre-ruth to ruth. The overlapping features of the stage of concern are ambivalence, the benign circle, contributing-in, and innate morality. Winnicott elaborates further his emphasis on the importance of early infant development by stating how 'most of the processes that start up in early infancy are never fully established, and continue to be strengthened by the growth that continues in later childhood, and indeed in adult life, even in old age' (1965b: 74).

Fear of breakdown [1963?] (1974)

The fear of breaking down in the future is based on the breakdown that has already occurred in the past. When this fear becomes the predominant feature in the analysis, Winnicott recommends interpreting this to the patient. This concept is also linked with the fear of emptiness and the fear of death.

Communication (1965g)

With the focus on the mutuality between mothers and their babies Winnicott began to formulate a theory of communication. This relates to the corollary of a pathological split in the personality that was first explored in 'Psychoses and child care' (1953b). Communication constitutes the transmission of feeling states between mother and infant. At the heart of Winnicott's theory of communication is the paradoxical notion of an incommunicado/isolate self that is non-communicating. It must never be communicated with because if communication 'seeps through' it causes a 'violation of the self' and the subject must set up a defence system to seal and protect the true/core self. Another paradoxical question emerges out of this theory – 'how to be isolated without being insulated?' (1965g: 187).

Dependence (1965h)

Winnicott defines three sequential phases of dependency – absolute dependence, relative dependence and towards independence. The infant's successful negotiation of the first two stages of dependence relies on a good enough environmental provision from the very beginning. The successful negotiation of these stages facilitate the stage of maturity he names 'towards independence.' There is no such thing as 'independence' but only 'towards independence.'

Mirror-role of mother (1967b)

Winnicott's main concept is that for the individual to really be able to distinguish between Me and Not-me, he first of all must have internalized the experience of being seen by mother i.e. the mother in her state of primary maternal preoccupation. First the subject apperceives and subsequent to this, if all goes well, apperception moves on to perception as a result of mother's affective mirroring. This concept emerges out of the earlier notion of unintegration related to early psychic processes.

Creativity [1971c]

Following on from the 'mirror-role of mother' Winnicott develops his notions of primary creativity by emphasizing the need for the infant to experience the 'illusion of omnipotence' – that he is God and creates the world. This theory emerges from his notion of primary psychic creativity and how the mother's primary maternal preoccupation facilitates the baby's illusion of omnipotence. This is inextricably linked with the 'theoretical first feed' (1988: 106). However, the mother also has to 'fail' at a later date, in response to the baby's readiness for her to fail; so that the baby can experience disillusion. But, he emphasizes, there can be no disillusion, and an appreciation of the reality principle, without first of all the experience of the illusion of omnipotence. The creative act is not the same as 'creative living.' The latter is associated with the themes explored in relation to the 'location of culture' (1967a) and the 'place where we live' (1971g).

This concept incorporates Winnicott's late conceptions of male and female elements which builds on Freud's theory of bisexuality. The female element is associated with being while the male element is associated with doing (Abram 2007: 125).

Playing (1968d; 1971f)

The capacity to play indicates developmental achievement and maturity and Winnicott emphasises that it is only through playing that the individual can discover a sense of self over and over again. Through playing the subject bridges the inner world with the outer world, within and through transitional space. The capacity to play is synonymous with creative living and constitutes the matrix of self-experience throughout life. Transposed to the analytic relationship, playing is the ultimate achievement of psychoanalysis, because only through playing can the self be continually discovered and thus strengthened. This extends Freud's technique of free association. But Winnicott alerts us to appreciate whether the analysand is able to play or not because 'interpretation outside the ripeness of the material is indoctrination and produces compliance' (1968d: 597).

The use of an object (1969; 1989d)

Here, in the final statement that succinctly [almost] covers the whole of his work, Winnicott explores the meaning of object relating and illustrates how the infant moves from object relating to object usage. Crucial to this journey is the external object's capacity to *receive* the subject's communication and to survive. It is only through the internalization of the experience of the object having psychically survived that the subject can move from object relating to object usage.

The story of Winnicott giving this paper to the New York Psychoanalytical Society in 1968 has been documented (Goldman 1993b: 207; Rodman 2003: 323; Baudry 2009). A paper he wrote after presenting it, (1989d), plus archival material, shows that this concept may well be Winnicott's attempt to replace Freud's 'death instinct' (see Abram [2008] Chapter 14). Winnicott had long disagreed with the Kleinian development of Freud's theory of the death instinct but, in preparation for the Vienna Congress in the early days of 1971, where he was due to present on a panel for Child Psychoanalysis, his notes clearly indicate that this unwritten paper[16] was likely to consolidate his different, and firmly argued views on aggression and dissociation. The 'use of an object' concept epitomizes Winnicott's work and his emphasis is on the interpsychic survival of the object. The notion of an intrapsychic surviving object and a non-surviving object as its corollary, is the author's interpretation of the main argument in the use of an object (Abram 2005; 2007 and Chapter 14).

Table 3.4 Publications and key papers, 1960–1971

Date of writing	Title of books and date of publication	Notes
1945–57	*The Child, the Family and the Outside World* (1964)	A new compilation of the papers from 1945a and 1949a, plus most from 1957a and 1957b.
1950–64	*The Family and Individual Development* (1965a)	A collection of previously published papers aimed at practitioners working with young families.
1958–65	*The Maturational Processes and the Facilitating Environment* (1965b)	Winnicott's second collection of psychoanalytic papers.
1967–70	*Playing and Reality* (1971a)	Final collection of papers written in his last three years.
1962–70	*Therapeutic Consultations in Child Psychiatry* (1971b)	Incorporates illustrations of the squiggle game taken from his last years as a paediatrician.
Date of writing	Title of key papers and date of publication	Notes
1960	The theory of the parent-infant relationship (1960)	Cf. 1945b.
1960	Aggression, guilt and reparation (1984b)	Further developments on theory of aggression.
1960	Ego distortion in terms of true and false self (1965e)	Suggests 5 distinct degrees of the false self.
1961	Adolescence (1962)	First paper on adolescence based on a lecture given in 1961. The adolescent's depressed mood needs, above all, tolerance (Cf. 1965g p. 189–192).
1962	Morals and education (1963b)	Linked with the innate morality of the infant and the impossibility of teaching morals.

1962	Providing for the child in health and crisis (1965f)	Suggesting six stages of developments and the outcome of a failed environment.
1962	The development of the capacity for concern (1963a)	An alternative theory to the 'depressive position' which emphasises the positive elements of that stage of development.
1963	Communicating and Not Communicating Leading to as Study of Certain Opposites (1965g)	A theory of communication that includes the notion of an 'incommunicado' self with whom no communication should occur.
1963	From dependence towards independence in the development of the individual (1965h)	Taking further the notion of dependency at different developmental stages.
1963–65?	Fear of breakdown (1974)	The fear of a future breakdown is based on the past breakdown.
1967	The location of cultural experience (1967a)	An exploration of the earliest culture in the human psyche.
1967	Mirror-role of mother and family in child development (1967b)	Apperception leads to perception only if the infant has the experience of feeling affectively mirrored through mother's primary maternal preoccupation.
1967	The aetiology of infantile schizophrenia in terms of adaptive failure (1968b)	Linked with 1965f and the outcome of early environmental failure.
1967	Environmental health in infancy (1968c).	The mother's health at the early stages is paramount.
1968	The use of an object and relating through identifications (1969)	Reaching a radical theory of aggression.
1969	The use of an object in the context of Moses and Monotheism (1989)	Re-construction of 1969. Reaching a positive divergence from the 'death instinct' and replacing it.
1970	Creativity and its origins (1971c)	A theory of creativity founded on earlier thinking on primary psychic creativity. Incorporating the notion of male and female elements and their dissociation in some patients.

1970	Dreaming, fantasying and living: a case history describing a primary dissociation (1971e)	Distinguishing between dream work and fantasying as a defence.
1970	Playing: creative activity and the search for the self (1971f)	Illustrating a theory of playing.
1970	Basis for self in body (1971h)	D.W.W.'s final description of the 'self.'
1970	Living creatively (1986c)	Living from the true self.

The final Table shows the posthumous publications.

Table 3.5 Posthumous publications and key papers, 1977–2002

Date of writing	Title of books and date of publication	Notes
1963	*The Piggle: An account of the psychoanalytic treatment of a little girl* (1977)	Probably the last child treatment conducted by D.W.W. The book covers 16 verbatim sessions over the course of two and a half years. The first book edited by the WPC.
1939–70	*Deprivation and Delinquency* (1984a)	This volume contains papers written between 1939 to 1970 that focus on the themes of the antisocial tendency and the development of a capacity for concern.
1958–65?	*Holding and Interpretation: Fragment of an analysis.* (1986a)	Winnicott explores the notions of holding and interpretation with a focus on 'regression to dependence'. These concepts are illustrated by verbatim sessions from an analysis conducted in the early 1950s.
1938–68?	*Home Is Where we Start From* (1986b)	A selection of talks to non-analytic audiences.
1949–68	*Babies and their Mothers* (1987a)	A selection of papers inspired by 'the ordinary devoted mother'.
1919–68	*The Spontaneous Gesture: Selected letters of D.W. Winnicott* (1987b)	Selected by F.R. Rodman.
1953–65	*Human Nature* (1988)	Began as D.W.W.'s notes on his lectures to the LSE students in

		human development and growth. Has now become a primer of his work compared to Freud's 'Outline' (Green 2000 in Abram 2000).
1930–70	*Psychoanalytic Explorations* (1989)	This was the last volume worked on by Clare Winnicott before she died in 1984. It is a large volume which includes many illuminating notes and fragments of D.W.W.'s ideas.
1955–69	*Talking to Parents* (1993a)	D.W.W.'s broadcasts.
1930–68	*Thinking about Children* (1996a)	Most recent volume edited by the W. T.
1949–68	*Winnicott on the Child* (2002)	A volume that incorporates both 1987 and 1993.

Date of writing	Title of paper and date of publication	Notes
1960	What irks? (1993c)	Commentary on how much a mother has to tolerate from her infant.
1962	The beginnings of a formulation of an appreciation and criticism of Klein's envy statement (1989e)	Explores his fundamental disagreement with Klein's notion of envy as innate.
1967	Postscript: D.W.W. on D.W.W. (1989b)	Based on a talk given to the 1952 club where D.W.W. correlates his work with others (Chapter 1 this Volume).
1969	Contribution to a symposium on envy and jealousy (1989f)	Continuing the argument in 1989e. Read by Enid Balint at a scientific meeting of the BPaS.

Summary

This brief introduction is intended as a structure to track the evolution of Winnicott's conceptualizations in the context of his professional life in both paediatrics and psychoanalysis. While Winnicott's theoretical matrix clearly emerges out of his ongoing discourse with Freud and Klein, it can be seen how it constitutes a distinct and discernible theory that advances psychoanalysis.

Here, the evolution of the formulations is divided into four sections to illustrate four phases. The Foundation phase is followed by three distinct phases in which a major theoretical discovery is achieved. At the end of these four sections a Table is added to highlight the publications and key papers, with brief notes. The final Table lists the posthumous publications.

From 1945 onwards, 'settling down to clinical work', Winnicott viewed psychoanalysis as a study of human nature. With an emphasis on the concept of health and the baby's dependency as a matter of fact, he observed that the key to the success or failure of the infant's negotia-tion of psychic and physical development, depended on the emotional interpsychic environment – a m/other in a state of primary maternal pre-occupation. By the end of his life Winnicott's quest was to understand what constituted the sense of 'feeling real' and he placed an emphasis on the nature of paradox in human relationships. Thus the matrix of his theory can be seen to constitute one overarching theory – the sense of self. The three principal conceptions that structure the matrix are – the parent-infant relationship, transitional phenomena and the use of an object – as seen in the major theoretical phases of his oeuvre.

That all psychoanalytic theories contain an autobiographical narrative is a convincing argument – 'the theory of the theoretician describes his own self' (Wright 1991: 329). Phillips suggests that the theorist 'organ-izes his or her theory around . . . the catastrophe' and that for 'Freud it was castration, for Klein the triumph of the death instinct, and for Winnicott . . . the annihilation of the core self by intrusion, a failure of the holding environment' (Phillips 1988: 149). We could add that for Bion it was the 'nameless dread', which also comes about as the result of a failing interpsychic environment (Bion 1962: 309). Winnicott's thesis the 'violation of the self', in his theory of communication, is, I have suggested, at the heart of his oeuvre (Abram 2007: 96), in which he presents us with the poignant paradox that 'it is a joy to be hidden and disaster not to be found' (1965g: 186).

Notes

1 This essay is a slightly amended version of Part Two of Donald Woods Winnicott: a brief introduction *Int J Psychoanal* (2008) 89: 1189–1217.
2 Loparic has commented that the nature of human subjectivity itself is paradoxical and that it was this that Winnicott observed and used (personal communication 2008).

3 Cf. Chapter 1.
4 A spatula is a tongue-depressor and in the 1920s it was a shiny metallic L shape made in different sizes to match the age or size of the child.
5 In 1951 Winnicott marries Clare Britton (see Chronology).
6 At this time Winnicott is also treating the daughter of Ernest Jones.
7 It is unclear when this analysis actually began. Some sources state 1936 and others 1940, but it was definitely during this first phase.
8 Susan Isaacs trained and qualified in the same year group as Winnicott. She became Head of the Department of Child Development at the Institute of Education at the University of London.
9 Re-named the Association of Independent Psychoanalysts in 2007.
10 DWW did not join the 1952 club when invited [personal communication Pearl King 2003]. The group was set up in 1952 by 'middle group' analysts. The 1952 club still meets regularly and is [mostly] made up of BpaS analysts who are members of the Association of Independent Psychoanalysts. Membership of the 1952 club is by invitation only.
11 Each entry includes several sub sections that introduce diverging or converging nodal points intrinsic to the main concept.
12 The references are the key papers and/or books concerning the concept. The concepts are, however, present in many other papers and correspondence.
13 Cf. Chapters 4 and 14.
14 Due to illness Winnicott was not able to personally present the paper. Enid Balint, the second wife of Michael Balint, presented it on his behalf. Enid Balint had had a training analysis with Winnicott between 1951 and 1954. She was also responsible for setting up the Marriage Guidance Clinic at the Tavistock Clinic.
15 This statue is now on the corner of Fitzjohn's Avenue and Belsize Lane by the Tavistock Clinic in London, UK.
16 Winnicott died on January 25th 1971 (see Chronology).

References

Abram, J. (2000) (ed.) *André Green at the Squiggle Foundation*, London: Karnac Books.
Abram, J. (2005) L'objet qui survit trad. Fr. D. Alcorn, *Journal de la psychanalyse de l'enfant*, 36: 139–174. Paris: Bayard.
Abram J. (2007a) *The language of Winnicott: a dictionary of Winnicott's use of words*, 2nd edition London: Karnac Books.
Abram, J. (2007b) L'objet qui ne survit pas: quelques reflexions sur les racines de la terreur, trad. Fr. Didier Houzel, *Journal de la psychanalyse de l'enfant*, 39: 247–270. Paris: Bayard.
Baudry, F. (2009). Winnicott's 1968 visit to the New York Psychoanalytic Society and Institute: A Contextual view *Psychoanal Q* 78: 1059–1090.

Brill, A.A. translator (1913) *The interpretation of dreams*, translation of 3rd German edition. London: George Allen.

Brill, A.A. translator (1915) *The interpretation of dreams*, translation of 3rd German edition, 2nd English edition. London: George Allen.

Bollas, C. (1987) *The shadow of the object: Psychoanalysis of the unthought known*, London: Free Association Books.

Bollas, C. (2002) *Free association*, London: Icon.

Bollas, C. (2007) *The Freudian Moment*, London: Karnac Books.

Clancier, A. and Kalmanovitch, J. (1987) *Winnicott and paradox: From birth to creation*, Sheridan A, translator. London: Tavistock. 174 p. [(1984). Le paradoxe de Winnicott: De la naissance à la création. Paris: Payot. (Science de l'Homme series.)].

Davis, M. (1987) The writing of DW Winnicott. *Int Rev Psychoanal* 14: 491–502.

Davis, M. and Wallbridge, D. (1981) *Boundary and space: An introduction to the work of DW Winnicott*,. New York, NY: Brunner/Mazel.

Diatkine, G. (2005) Beyond the pleasure principle. In: Perelberg, R. *Freud a modern reader*, 142–161 London: Whurr Publishers Ltd.

Fulgencio, L. (2007) Winnicott's rejection of the basic concepts of Freud's metapsychology *Int J Psychoanal* 88: 443–61.

Freud, E.L. (ed.) (1970) *The letters of Sigmund Freud and Arnold Zweig*, Robson-Scott, E. and Robson-Scott, W. and translators. New York, NY: Harcourt, Brace and World.

Freud, S. (1900) The Interpretation of Dreams SE 4, 1–626.

Freud, S. (1917) Mourning and Melancholia SE 14, 243–259.

Freud, S. (1921) Beyond the pleasure principle SE 18, 7–64.

Freud, S. (1923) The ego and the id SE 19, 3–63.

Gillespie, W.H. (1971) Donald W. Winnicott. *Int J Psychoanal* 52: 227–8.

Goldman, D. (ed.) (1993a) *In one's bones: The clinical genius of Winnicott*, Northvale, NJ: Aronson.

Goldman, D. (1993b) *In search of the real: The origins and originality of D.W. Winnicott*, Northvale, NJ: Aronson.

Green, A. (2000) The posthumous Winnicott: on Human Nature In: Abram, J. (ed.) *André Green at the Squiggle Foundation*, 69–83. London: Karnac Books.

Grosskurth, P. (1986) *Melanie Klein: Her world and her work*, New York, NY: Jason Aronson.

Guntrip, H. (1975) My experience of analysis with Fairbairn and Winnicott *Int Rev Psychoanal.* 2: 145–156.

Hjulmand, K. (2007) D.W. Winnicott Bibliography: Chronological and alphabetical lists. In: Abram, J. *The language of Winnicott: A dictionary of Winnicott's use of words*, 2nd edition 363–435. London: Karnac Books.

Holmes, R. (1985) *Footsteps: Adventures of a romantic biographer*, London: Hodder & Stoughton.

Holmes, R. (1992) Biographer's footsteps. *Int Rev Psychoanal* 19: 1–8.

Hughes, A. (ed) (1991) *Joan Riviere: The inner world and Joan Riviere*, London: Karnac Books.

Issroff, J. (2005) *Donald Winnicott and John Bowlby personal and professional perspectives*, London: Karnac Books.

James, M. (1962) Infantile narcissistic trauma – Observations on Winnicott's work in infant care and child development *Int J PsychoAnal* 43: 69–79.

Kahr, B. (1996) *D.W. Winnicott: A biographical portrait*, London: Karnac Books.

Kermode, F. (2004) Clutching at insanity – Rodman FR. *Winnicott: Life and work* [Review]. London Rev Books 4 Mar, 26(5): 1–8.

Khan, M. (1975) Introduction. In: Winnicott, D.W. *Through paediatrics to psycho-analysis*, 2nd edition, xi–xviii. London: Hogarth. (International Psycho-analytical Library, No 100.)

King, P. (1972) Tribute to Donald Winnicott. *Bull Br Psychoanal Soc* 57: 26–8.

King, P. and Steiner, R. (eds) (1991) *The Freud-Klein controversies 1941–45*, London: Routledge.

Klein, G. (1976) *Psychoanalytic theory: An exploration of essentials.* Madison, CT: International Universities Press, Inc.

Klein, M. (1927) Symposium on child-analysis. *Int J Psychoanal* 8: 339–70.

Klein, M. (1928) Early stages of the Oedipus complex. *Int J Psychoanal* 9: 167–180.

Klein, M. (1932) *The psychoanalysis of children*, London: Hogarth.

Kohon, G. (ed.) (1988) *The British School of Psychoanalysis: The independent tradition*, London: Free Association Books.

Kuhn, T. (1962) *The structure of scientific revolutions*, Chicago: The University of Chicago Press

Layland, W.R. (1996) Kahr, B. *D.W. Winnicott: A biographical portrait* [Review]. *Int J Psychoanal* 77: 1269–71.

Little, M. (1985) Winnicott working in areas where psychotic anxieties predominate: A personal record. *Free Associations* 3: 9–42.

Loparic, Z. (2002) Winnicott's paradigm outlined. *Rev. Latinoam. Psicopat. Fund.* V, 1, 61–98 (available on line at www.centrowinnicott.com.br)

Loparic, Z. (2006) *De Freud a Winnicott: aspectos de uma mudanca paradigmatica* [From Freud to Winnicott: Aspects of a paradigmatic change] Winnicott e-Prints 5 (2): 1–29.

Milner, M.B. (1978) D.W. Winnicott and the two-way journey. In: Grolnink S.A. and Barkin L. (eds). *Between reality and fantasy: Transitional objects and phenomena*, 37–42. New York: Aronson.

Modell, A.H. (1985) The works of Winnicott and the evolution of his thought. *J Am Psychoanal Assoc* 33(Suppl): 113–37.

Neve, M. (1991) Interview with Clare Winnicott, June 1983 [Appendix B]: In: Rudnytsky, P.L. *The psychoanalytic vocation: Rank, Winnicott and the legacy of Freud*, 180–93. New Haven, CT: Yale University Press

Newman, A. (1995) *Non-compliance in Winnicott's words: A companion to the writings and work of D.W. Winnicott.* London: Free Association Books.

Ogden, T.H. (1985) The mother, the infant and the matrix: Interpretations of aspects of the work of Donald Winnicott. *Contemp. Psychoanal.*, 21: 346–371.

Ogden, T.H. (1986) *The matrix of the mind: Object relations and the psychoanalytic dialogue*, Northvale, NJ: Aronson.

Ogden, T.H. (1992) The dialectically constituted/decentred subject of psychoanalysis. II. The contributions of Klein and Winnicott. *Int J Psychoanal* 73: 613–26.

Ogden, T.H. (2001b) Reading Winnicott, *Psychoanal Q* 70: 299–323.

Parsons, M. (2000) *The dove that returns, the dove that vanishes: Paradox and creativity in psychoanalysis*, London: Routledge.

Perelberg, R.J. (ed.) (2005) *Freud: a modern reader*, London: Whurr Publishers Ltd.

Phillips, A. (1988) *Winnicott*, Cambridge, MA: Harvard University Press.

Rapaport, D.A. and Gill, M.M. (1959) The points of view and assumptions of metapsychology. *Int J Psychoanal* 40: 153–62.

Rayner, E. (1990) *The independent mind in British psychoanalysis*, London: Free Association Books.

Riviere, J. (1927) Symposium on child analysis. *Int J Psychoanal* 8, 320–377. In: Hughes, A. (ed.) (1991) *Joan Riviere: The inner world and Joan Riviere*, London: Karnac Books.

Roazen, P. (2001) *The historiography of psychoanalysis*, New Brunswick, NJ: Transaction.

Rodman, F.R. (ed.) (1987) *The spontaneous gesture: Selected letters of D. Winnicott*, Cambridge, MA: Harvard University Press.

Rodman, F.R. (2003) *Winnicott: Life and work*, Cambridge, MA: Perseus.

Roussillon, R. (1991) *Paradoxes et situations limites de la psychanalyse*, [Paradoxes and borderline situations in psychoanalysis] Paris: PUF.

Rudnytsky, P.L. (ed.) (1993) *Transitional objects and potential spaces literary uses of D.W. Winnicott*, Columbia University Press.

Sandler, J., Holder, A., Dare, C., and Dreher, A.U. (1997) *Freud's models of the mind: An introduction*, London: Karnac. (Psychoanalytic monographs, No 1.)

Tuckett, D. (1996) Editorial introduction for my experience of analysis with Fairbairn and Winnicott. *Int J Psychoanal*, 77: 739–740.

Wallbridge, D. and Davis, M. (1981) *Boundary and space: An introduction to the work of D.W. Winnicott*, New York: Brunner-Mazel.

Winnicott, C. (1978) DWW: A reflection. In: Grolnink, S.A. and Barkin, L. (eds) *Between reality and fantasy: Transitional objects and phenomena*, 17–33. New York: Aronson.

Winnicott, C. (1984) Introduction In: Winnicott, D.W. *Deprivation and delinquency*, 1–5 London: Tavistock Publications.

Winnicott, D.W. (1919) To Violet Winnicott [Letter, 15 November]. In: Rodman F.R. (ed.) (1987). *The spontaneous gesture: Selected letters of DW Winnicott*, Letter 1, 1–4 Cambridge, MA: Harvard University Press.

Winnicott, D.W. (1928) The only child. In: Erleigh E.V. (ed.) *The mind of the growing child*, 47–64 London: Faber & Gwyer.

Winnicott, D.W. (1930a) Pathological sleeping [case history]. *Proc R Soc Med* 23: 125–7.

Winnicott, D.W. (1930b) Enuresis [Short communication]. *St Bartholomew's Hosp J* 37: 125–7.

Winnicott, D.W. (1931a) *Clinical notes on disorders of childhood*, London: Heinemann. (Practitioner's aid series, No 1.)

Winnicott, D.W. (1931b) Arthritis associated with emotional disturbance. In: 1931a, 81–86.

Winnicott, D.W. (1931c) Fidgetiness. In: 1931a, 87–97.

Winnicott, D.W. (1931d) A note on normality and anxiety. In: 1931a, 98–123.

Winnicott D.W. (1931e) The rheumatic clinic. In: 1931a, 64–68.

Winnicott, D.W. (1934a) The difficult child. *Journal of State Medicine*, November, 1934, 42: 628–631.

Winnicott, D.W. (1934b) Papular urticaria and the dynamics of skin sensation. *British Journal of Children's Diseases*, 31: 5–16.

Winnicott, D.W. (1941) The observation of infants in a set situation. *Int J Psychoanal* 22: 229–49.

Winnicott, D.W. (1942) Child department consultations. *Int J Psychoanal*, 23: 139–146.

Winnicott, D.W. (1944) Ocular psychoneuroses of childhood. *Transactions of the Opthalmological Society*, 64: 46–52. "General Discussion".

Winnicott, D.W. (1945a) *Getting to know your baby*, London: Heinemann.

Winnicott, D.W.(1945b) Primitive emotional development. *Int J Psychoanal* 26: 137–43.

Winnicott, D.W. (1945c) Towards an objective study of human nature. *The New Era in Home and School*, "Postscript" 179–182.

Winnicott, D.W. (1945d) Thinking and the unconscious. *Liberal Magazine*, March, 1945: 125–126.

Winnicott, D.W. (1947) Babies are persons. *The New Era in Home and School*, 28: 199–202.

Winnicott, D.W. (1948) Children's hostels in war and peace. *British Journal of Medical Psychology*, 21: 175–180.

Winnicott, D.W. (1949a) *The ordinary devoted mother and her baby*, London: C. Brock & Co.

Winnicott, D.W. (1949b) The innate morality of the baby. In: 1949a: 38–42.

Winnicott, D.W. (1949c) Hate in the countertransference. *Int J PsychoAnal.* 30: 69–74.

Winnicott, D.W. (1953a) Transitional objects and transitional phenomena: A study of the first not-me possession. *Int J Psychoanal* 34: 89–97.

Winnicott, D.W. (1953b) Psychoses and child care. *British Journal of Medical Psychology*, 26: 68–74.

Winnicott, D.W. (1954) Mind and its relation to the psyche-soma. *British Journal of Medical Psychology*, 27: 201–209.

Winnicott, D.W. (1955a) Metapsychological and clinical aspects of regression within the psychoanalytical set-up. *Int J Psychoanal* 36: 16–26.

Winnicott, D.W. (1955b) The depressive position in normal emotional development. *British Journal of Medical Psychology*, 28: 89–100.

Winnicott, D.W. (1955c) Withdrawal and regression. *Revue Francais de Psychanalyse*, 19: "Regression et repli." 323–330.

Winnicott, D.W. (1957a) *The child and the family*, London: Tavistock.

Winnicott, D.W. (1957b) *The child and the outside world: Studies in developing relationships*, London: Tavistock

Winnicott, D.W. (1957c) Aggression [1939] In: 1957b, 167–175.

Winnicott, D.W. (1958a) *Collected papers: Through paediatrics to psycho-analysis*, 1st edition. London: Tavistock.

Winnicott, D.W. (1958b) The manic defence [1935] In: 1958a, 129–144.

Winnicott, D.W. (1958c) Anxiety associated with insecurity [1952] In: 1958a, 97–100.

Winnicott, D.W. (1958d) The anti-social tendency [1956] In: 1958a, 306–315.

Winnicott, D.W. (1958e) Appetite and emotional disorder [1936]. In: 1958a, 33–51.

Winnicott, D.W. (1958f) Reparation in respect of mother's organised defence against depression. [1948] In: 1958a, 91–96.

Winnicott, D.W. (1958g) Aggression in relation to emotional development. [1950–55] In: 1958a, 204–218.

Winnicott, D.W. (1958h) Primary maternal preoccupation [1956] In: 1958a, 300–305.

Winnicott, D.W. (1958i) The capacity to be alone. [1957] *Int J Psychoanal* 39: 416–420.

Winnicott, D.W. (1958j) Birth memories, birth trauma, and anxiety [1949–54] In: 1958a, 174–193.

Winnicott, D.W. (1960) The theory of the parent infant relationship. *Int J Psychoanal* 41: 585–595.

Winnicott, D.W. (1962) Adolescence [1961] *The New Era in Home and School*, October, 43: 145–161.

Winnicott, D.W. (1963a) The development of the capacity for concern. [1960] *Bulletin of the Menninger Clinic*, 27: 167–176.

Winnicott, D.W. (1963b) Morals and education. [1962] In: Niblett, W.R. (ed.) *Moral education in a changing society*, 96–111. London: Faber.

Winnicott, D.W. (1964) *The child, the family and the outside world*, London: Harmondsworth: Penguin Books.

Winnicott, D.W. (1965a) *The family and individual development*, London, Tavistock.

Winnicott, D.W. (1965b) *The maturational processes and the facilitating environment: Studies in the theory of emotional development*, London: Hogarth. (International Psycho-analytical Library, No 64.)

Winnicott, D.W. (1965c) A personal view of the Kleinian contribution. In: 1965b, 171–8.

Winnicott, D.W. (1965d) The family affected by depressive illness in one or both parents. [1958] In: 1965a, 50–60.

Winnicott, D.W. (1965e) Ego distortion in terms of true and false self. [1960] In: 1965b, 140–152.

Winnicott, D.W. (1965f) Providing for the child in health and crisis [1962] In: 1965b, 64–72.

Winnicott, D.W. (1965g) Communicating and not communicating leading to a study of certain opposites. [1963] In: 1965b, 179–192.

Winnicott, D.W. (1965h) From dependence towards independence in the development of the individual. [1963] In: 1965b, 83–92.

Winnicott, D.W. (1966) Psycho-somatic illness in its positive and negative aspects. *Int J Psychoanal* 47: 510–516.

Winnicott, D.W. (1967a) The location of cultural experience. *Int J PsychoAnal* 48: 368–372.

Winnicott, D.W. (1967b) Mirror-role of mother and family in child development. In: Lomas, P. (ed.) *The predicament of the family: A psychoanalytical symposium*. London: Hogarth Press, 1967: 26–33.

Winnicott, D.W. (1968a) Communication between infant and mother, and mother and infant, compared and contrasted. In: *What is Psychoanalysis?* 15–25. London: Balliere, Tindall & Cassel Ltd.

Winnicott, D.W. (1968b) The aetiology of infantile schizophrenia in terms of adaptive failure. [1967] *Recherches* (special issue 'Enfance alienee', II): 'La schizophrenie infantile en termes d'echec d'adaption': 27–31.

Winnicott, D.W. (1968c) Environmental health in infancy. *Maternal and Child Care*, 4: 7–9 'Infant feeding and emotional development'.

Winnicott, D.W. (1968d) Playing: Its theoretical status in the clinical situation *Int J Psychoanal* 49: 591–597.

Winnicott, D.W. (1969) The use of an object and relating through identifications. *Int J Psychoanal* 50: 711–6.

Winnicott, D.W. (1971a) *Playing and reality*. London: Tavistock.

Winnicott, D.W. (1971b) *Therapeutic consultations in child psychiatry*. London: Hogarth.

Winnicott, D.W. (1971c) Creativity and its origins. [1970] In: 1971a, 65–85.

Winnicott, D.W. (1971d) The split-off male and female elements to be found in men and women. [1966] In: 1971a, 72–85.

Winnicott, D.W. (1971e) Dreaming, fantasying and living: A case history describing a primary dissociation. [1970] In: 1971a, 26–37.

Winnicott, D.W. (1971f) Playing: Creative activity and the search for the self. [1970] In: 1971a, 53–64.

Winnicott, D.W. (1971g) The place where we live. [1970] In: 1971a, 104–110.

Winnicott, D.W. (1971h) Le corps et le self, translated by Victor N. Smirnoff, [Body and self] *Nouvelle Revue de Psychanalyse* 3, Printemps: 15–51.

Winnicott, D.W. (1974) Fear of breakdown [1963?] *Int Rev PsychoAnal* 1: 103–107.

Winnicott, D.W. (1977) *The Piggle: An account of the psychoanalytic treatment of a little girl* [1963], London, Hogarth.

Winnicott, D.W. (1984a) *Deprivation and delinquency*, Winnicott, C. Shepherd, R. Davis, M. (eds), London, Tavistock.

Winnicott, D.W. (1984b) Aggression, guilt and reparation. [1960] In: 1984a, 136–144.

Winnicott, D.W. (1986a) *Holding and Interpretation: Fragment of an analysis*, London: Hogarth.

Winnicott, D.W. (1986b) *Home is where we start from: Essays by a psycho-analyst*, Winnicott, C. Shepherd, R. Davis, M. Reading (eds), MA: Addison-Wesley.

Winnicott, D.W. (1986c) Living creatively. [1970] In: 1986b, 39–54.

Winnicott, D.W. (1987a) *Babies and their mothers*, Winnicott, C. Davis, M. Shepherd, R. (eds), Reading, MA: Addison-Wesley.

Winnicott, D.W. (1987b) *The spontaneous gesture: Selected letters*, Rodman, F.R. (ed.) Cambridge, MA: Harvard University Press 1987.

Winnicott, D.W. (1988) *Human nature*, Bollas, C. Davis, M. Shepherd, R. (eds), London: Free Association Books.

Winnicott, D.W. (1989a) *Psycho-analytic explorations*, Winnicott, C., Shepherd, R., Davis, M. (eds), Cambridge, MA: Harvard University Press.

Winnicott, D.W. (1989b) Postscript: D.W.W. on D.W.W. in *Psychoanalytic explorations*, 569–582. [1967] Winnicott, C., Shepherd, R., Davis, M. (eds), Cambridge, MA: Harvard University Press.

Winnicott, D.W. (1989c) The fate of the transitional object. [1959] In: 1989a, 53–58.

Winnicott, D.W. (1989d) The use of an object in the context of Moses and Monotheis. [1969] In: 1989a, 240–246.

Winnicott, D.W. (1989e) The beginnings of a formulation of an appreciation and criticism of Klein's envy statement. [1962] In: 1989a, 447–457.

Winnicott, D.W. (1989f) Contribution to a symposium on envy and jealousy. [1969] In: 1989a, 462–464.

Winnicott, D.W. (1989g) Early disillusion. [1939] In: 1989a, 21–23.

Winnicott, D.W. (1993a) *Talking to parents*, Winnicott, C., Bollas, C., Davis, M., Shepherd, R. (eds), Reading, MA: Addison-Wesley.

Winnicott, D.W. (1993b) What do we know about babies as cloth suckers? [1956] In: 1993a, 15–20.

Winnicott, D.W. (1993c) What irks? [1960] In: 1993a, 65–86.

Winnicott, D.W. (1996a) *Thinking about children*, Shepherd, R., Johns, J., Taylor-Robinson, H. (eds), London: Karnac Books.

Winnicott, D.W. (1996b) Environmental needs: The early stages: total dependence and essential independence [1948] In: 1996a, 29–36.

Winnicott, D.W. (2002) *Winnicott on the child*, New York: Perseus Publishing.

Winnicott, D.W. and Gibbs, N. (1926) Varicella encephalitis and vaccinia encephalitis. *Br J Child Dis* 23: 107–22.

Wright, K. (1991) *Vision and separation: between mother and baby*, London: Free Association Books.

Young-Bruehl, E. (2003) Rodman, F.R. *Winnicott: Life and work*, [Review]. *Int J Psychoanal* 84: 1661–5.

4

From Freud to Winnicott

Aspects of a paradigm change[1]

Zeljko Loparic

The main purpose of this paper is to present a unified view on Winnicott's contribution to psychoanalysis. Although Winnicott is presently recognized as one of the great figures in the history of psychoanalysis it is evident that a systematic philological, historical and conceptual study of his writings is rare, in spite of some notable exceptions (see Abram 2007, 2008; Davis and Walbridge 1981; Ogden 1986; Phillips 1988). Moreover, we are still waiting for the publication of Winnicott´s Collected Works,[2] and generally speaking, Winnicott research can hardly be compared with current Freudian scholarship. This situation is changing, particularly in Latin America, where Winnicott has become the most quoted psychoanalytic author after Freud (cf. Abadi and Outeiral 1997). Unfortunately, citation does not necessarily mean that the work is truly studied and understood.

My emphasis in this paper is on the nature of Winnicott's contribution rather than a focus on one or another of his many contributions to psychoanalysis. I aim to achieve this by conceptual analysis largely based on a study of the historical development of Winnicott's ideas. Winnicott himself recommended a historical approach to the understanding of his views on emotional development. In his posthumously published book *Human Nature*, after explaining some of his ideas on the imaginative elaboration of body functioning, he added:

> The reader must form a personal opinion of these matters, after learning what is thought as far as possible in the historical manner,

which is the only way that the theory of any one moment [in personal development] becomes intelligible and interesting.

(Winnicott 1988: 42)

Here I suggest that 'interesting' means both personally appealing and theoretically important. Clearly this applies to any attempt to understand other parts of Winnicott's theory and indeed psychoanalysis in general:

Readers of analytic literature may easily become impatient if they take some statement of analytic theory and treat it as if it were a final pronouncement, never to be modified. Psychoanalytic theory is all the time developing, and it must develop by natural process rather like the emotional condition of the human being that is under study.

(Ibid.: 46)

It would be very tempting to try to develop this Winnicottian 'natural process' view of the origin of the scientific attitude and of the growth of scientific knowledge as Winnicott begins to do in the first chapter of *Human Nature*, but instead, I shall limit myself to applying an already existing model of natural growth of science expounded by Thomas S. Kuhn.[3]

There is one straightforward reason to appeal to Kuhn's theory in the present context: both Winnicott and Kuhn were strongly influenced by Darwin. Winnicott is indebted to Darwin for his view that '. . . living things could be studied scientifically, with the corollary that gaps in knowledge need not scare me' (Winnicott 1996: 7). Kuhn, in turn, learned from the British biologist that the growth of science is a struggle between rival paradigms for survival in scientific communities. The aim of that struggle is not towards something like the final truth, but the temporarily greater problem-solving efficiency of scientific knowledge.[4] This shaky goal is achieved by dramatic changes in established scientific world-views or, more technically, by Gestalt switches in scientific paradigms commonly called 'scientific revolutions.'

Following Kuhn, I shall therefore be discussing the paradigm switch introduced by Winnicott into the psychoanalytic discipline. To present this with clarity I shall start with an outline of Freud's paradigm that resulted from 'normal research,' and show how it was the emergence of anomalies that subsequently brought about a crisis that triggered Winnicott's revolutionary research. My main thesis here is that Winnicott's research concluded by Winnicott introducing a new paradigm for psychoanalysis, i.e. new guiding problems and a new conceptual framework that would enable him to solve the anomalies he discovered. My conclusion is that Winnicott was a revolutionary thinker and that he paved a new way for scientific research and practice in psychoanalysis. Furthermore, I aim to show how he achieved a great deal of such research, without ever intending that his alternative framework or his results were 'final pronouncements.'[5]

I am not the first one to speak of Winnicott's paradigm and several authors have used Kuhn to study the history of psychoanalytic thought (Modell 1968; Levenson 1972; Lifton 1976). Greenberg and Mitchell view the history of psychoanalysis as

> the dialectic between the original Freudian model,[6] which takes as its starting point the instinctual drives, and an alternative comprehensive model initiated in the work of Fairbairn and Sullivan, which evolves structure solely from the individual's relationships with other people.
>
> (Greenberg and Mitchell 1983: 2)

The results reached by the latter two authors are, however, severely limited by the fact that they only considered the metaphysical component of psychoanalytic theory, which completely leaves aside concrete problem-solutions, i.e., the so-called 'exemplars' which are the main components of Kuhn's model of analysis.

Kuhn's concept of the exemplar is applied by Judith Hughes whose attempt is to depict 'the paradigms which constitute psychoanalytic theory' by describing the 'Freudian paradigms' and scrutinizing their 'transformation' in the work of Klein, Fairbairn and Winnicott (Hughes 1989). To that end, she not only analyzes specific theoretical difficulties in paradigm formation, but also pays attention to clinical issues and clinical practice, which forced the re-shaping of the psychoanalytic domain within the British Psychoanalytical Society. With Klein, she concentrates on the case of 'Richard,' and with Winnicott, the case history entitled The Piggle. 'The consulting room,' writes Hughes, 'has, after all, provided the empirical base for the psychoanalytic enterprise, and nowhere has it been more apparent than in Britain' (Hughes 1989: 176). More recently, a view congenial to applying Kuhn's approach to the history of psychoanalysis has been adopted by

Joyce McDougall (McDougall 1996: 226) and Jan Abram has referred to the Kuhn-based paradigm switch thesis as an arguable alternative interpretation of Winnicott's contribution to psychoanalysis (Abram 2008: 1205).[7]

In 1988, Adam Phillips approached Winnicott in a way which, although not presented in Kuhn's terms, uses a very similar language. Phillips admitted, without the ambiguities which spoil so many other accounts, that Winnicott introduced 'important innovations' in psychoanalytic practice and technique which represent, despite Winnicott's 'disingenuous' disguises, 'radical departures from Freud.' The main departure selected by Phillips consists in the observation that Winnicott 'would derive everything in his work, including a theory of the origins of scientific objectivity and a revision of psychoanalysis, from the paradigm of the developing mother–infant relationship' (Phillips 1988: 5). For Winnicott, says Phillips, the mother–infant relationship was becoming 'the primary model for the psychoanalytic situation' and the main 'source of analogy in his work' (ibid.: 87). Let me provide an example among many given by Phillips:

> But whereas for Freud psychoanalysis was essentially a 'talking cure', for Winnicott, the mother–infant relationship, in which communication was relatively non-verbal, had become the paradigm for the analytic process, and this changed the role of interpretation in psychoanalytic treatment.
>
> (Ibid.: 138)

Guided by the mother–baby paradigm, Winnicott was led to new questions and thus to new results. Examples of such questions 'rarely addressed in psychoanalytic theory' are the following: What do we depend on to make us feel alive or real? And: Where does our sense come from, when we have it, that our lives are worth living? Winnicott approached these issues, continues Phillips, by linking the 'observation of mothers and infants' with 'insights derived from psychoanalysis' (ibid.: 5–6). But it was not simply that Winnicott also enriched psychoanalysis with essential new insights which turned out to be incompatible with those of Freud, since they were 'rarely linked by him [Winnicott] with the place of the erotic in adult life.' For Winnicott, the 'crux of psychoanalysis' was the 'infant's early dependent vulnerability' in a two-person relationship with the mother, not 'the Oedipus complex – a three-person relationship.' Whereas Freud, starting from the Oedipus situation, was interested 'in the adult's struggle with incompatible and unacceptable desires,' which put in danger their 'possibilities for satisfaction,' Winnicott, starting with the relationship of total dependence, treated these possibilities as 'part of a larger issue of the individual's possibilities for personal authenticity, what he [Winnicott] will call 'feeling real' (ibid.: 7). Working in that manner, and 'neglecting Freud's metapsychology' (Phillips 1993: 43), Winnicott evolved, during the 1940s, 'a powerful rival developmental theory to those of both Freud and Klein' (Phillips 1988: 97).

What have I to add to the above results? Firstly, a more systematic and precise account of the essential constitutive elements of Winnicott's paradigm and, secondly, a more detailed analysis of the process Winnicott went through in searching for these elements. To that end, I shall use, as previously stated, the word 'paradigm' not just in the common sense meaning of a model, but in the more technical sense defined by Thomas Kuhn in the Postscript of the second edition of his book *The Structure of Scientific Revolutions* (Kuhn 1970a). I shall also borrow Kuhn's general view on scientific research and on the growth of science.[8] In substance, I aim to produce a more accurate picture of Winnicott's procedures and contributions, which may serve as a blueprint for further research on his contribution as well as helping to avoid some not infrequent misunderstandings.[9]

Kuhn's view of empirical science

According to Kuhn, normal, everyday science is a problem-solving activity guided by a paradigm. Scientific problems resemble puzzles in so far as they are thought of as having an assured solution within the adopted theoretical framework (Kuhn 1970a: 37). Socially important problems become scientific only after they have been reduced to puzzles, their solution depending exclusively on the ingenuity of practitioners trained in a paradigm. Scientists do not intend, and even refuse, to cope with every problem. 'Scientism' – the idea that science can solve all questions that are important for human kind – is a peculiar philosophical stance on science and not at all part of what scientists actually are aiming at.

Paradigms, presupposed in scientific puzzle solving, are of two kinds. Firstly, there are accepted examples of actual scientific practice which provide 'models from which spring particular coherent traditions of scientific research' (ibid.: 10). In the Postscript to the second edition of his book, Kuhn calls these accepted models 'exemplars,' by which he means 'the concrete problem-solutions that students encounter from the start in their scientific education' (ibid.: 187). Secondly, paradigms are 'conceptual, theoretical, instrumental and methodological commitments that guide the scientific research' (ibid.: 42). In the Postscript Kuhn offered a more detailed analysis of this second concept of paradigm and specified that its main components are guiding empirical generalizations,[10] ontological models of the subject matter, authorized heuristic procedures (preferred or permissible analogies and metaphors) and finally, values or norms which define scientific practice by specific groups and provide their members with a sense of community (ibid.: 182–5). Exemplars and constellations of commitments, taken together, constitute the 'disciplinary matrix' of a scientific discipline.

Exemplars are the more important of the two. To start with, a science is not learned by becoming acquainted with verbal statements of laws or rules, but by being taught how to see new problems in the light of exemplars: 'That [scientific] sort of learning is not acquired by exclusively verbal means. Rather it comes as one is given words together with concrete examples of how they function in use, nature and words, learned together' (ibid.: 191). By saying that we learn 'nature and words' together, Kuhn implies that scientific groups with different paradigms live, in some sense, in different worlds and that they use language in essentially different ways. This in turn accounts for the incommensurability of theoretical statements and the absence of supra-paradigmatic criteria of truth and interpretation. Indeed, in order to be able to interpret a statement we must first be able to see a case of it, and this requires a paradigm for observing the case. The verbal interpretation, (being 'a deliberative process by which we choose among alternatives as we do not in perception itself') always comes second (ibid.: 194). The knowledge that is learned from paradigmatic examples is not 'explicit', but rather 'tacit.'

The change of paradigms for seeing the world is initially also a tacit, unintentional and even unconscious process. It resembles Gestalt switches, which happen 'suddenly' and 'involuntarily', and 'over which we have no control' (ibid.: 111, 194). The central aspect of Gestalt switches which are at the 'heart of the revolutionary process' (ibid.: 202) is 'that some of the similarity relations change' (ibid.: 200), which again implies the changes in the use of language. Kuhn writes:

Objects that were grouped in the same set before are grouped in different ones afterward and vice versa. [. . .] Since most objects within even the altered sets continue to be grouped together, the names of the sets are usually preserved. Nevertheless, even the transfer of a subset is ordinarily part of a critical change in the network relations among them. [. . .] Not surprisingly, therefore, when such re-distributions occur two men whose discourse had previously proceeded with apparently full understanding may suddenly find themselves responding to the same stimulus with incompatible descriptions and generalizations.

(Kuhn 1970a: 200–1)

Differences in responses to the same stimuli do not only mean that our world-view has modified, they also reveal that the world itself has suffered a change. These disagreements cannot be eliminated 'simply by stipulating definitions for troublesome terms,' nor can we resort to a 'neutral language,' for no paradigm independent of language exists. A paradigm change is, therefore, necessarily followed by a 'communication breakdown.' In such cases, translation from one scientific idiom to the other is a resource of dialogue, but not of consensus; moreover 'it is threatening and is entirely foreign to normal science' (ibid.: 203). It is clear that holding different paradigms scientists usually disagree on at least three points: (1) the list of problems that any candidate must be able to resolve in order to enter a paradigm; (2) the list of criteria for acceptable solutions; (3) the list of criteria for what exists, since, when a paradigm changes some things simply cease to exist and others start to exist. For instance, what was previously seen as a duck, was called, and has been a duck is now seen as, is called, and has become a rabbit. Under such circumstances, the procedure of translating does not lead us very far, because, according to the context, being a duck might indeed have a very different meaning from being a rabbit.[11]

The other important point is that science does not make progress in solving problems by applying theories and rules, but by seeing new problem situations in the light of exemplars: 'Scientists solve puzzles,' writes Kuhn, 'by modelling them on previous puzzle situations, often with minimal recourses to symbolic generalizations' (ibid.: 190). That brings us back to the thesis that scientific knowledge is embedded in shared exemplars rather than in rules, laws, or criteria of identification.

119

Guided by a specific way of seeing the world, scientists attempt 'to force nature into the pre-formed and relatively inflexible box which the paradigm supplies' (ibid.: 24). Kuhn adds:

> No part of the aim of normal science is to call forth new sorts of phenomena; indeed those that will not fit the box are often not seen at all. Nor do scientists normally aim to invent new theories, and they are often intolerant of those invented by others. Instead, normal scientific research is directed to the articulation of those phenomena and theories that the paradigm already supplies.
>
> (Kuhn 1970a: 24)

To summarize: in normal science scientists restrict their efforts to solve three kinds of problem: to determine significant facts, to match facts with theory and to articulate existing theories (ibid.: 34).

Why then, do paradigmatic changes occur at all? The answer is: when a crisis occurs, that is, 'a pronounced failure' of the old theory 'in the problem-solving activity' (ibid.: 74–5). Now, every paradigm is constantly confronted with anomalies, recalcitrant problems which should have been solved but were not. Usually, scientists leave such problems provisionally to the side and do not reject the paradigm because of this kind of failure. However, it also happens that some persistent anomalies may oblige a scientist to interrupt their normal research and pause over them and reasons may vary. They may become concerned about the absence of guiding generalizations, or about the impossibility of solving a particularly important social problem or a problem felt to be significant for technical and technological reasons (ibid.: 82). When anything like this happens, 'an anomaly comes to seem like more than just another puzzle of normal science' and the transition to crisis and to extraordinary science or to revolutionary research has begun. Kuhn describes the emergence of a crisis in the following way:

> More and more of the field's most eminent men devote more and more attention to it. If it still continues to resist, as it usually does not, many of them may come to view its resolution as the subject matter of their discipline. For them the field does no longer look quite the same as it had earlier. [. . .] An [. . .] important source of change is the divergent nature of the numerous partial solutions that concerted attention to the problem has made available. [. . .]

Through this proliferation of divergent articulations (more and more frequently they will come to be described as ad hoc adjustments), the rules of normal science become increasingly blurred. Though there is still a paradigm, few practitioners prove to be entirely agreed about what it is. Even formerly standard solutions of solved questions are called in question.

(Kuhn 1970a: 82–3)

Finally, how are we to describe the progress achieved through scientific revolutions? The answer is that they will not be an approximation to the truth. Whereas normal science is cumulative, revolutions introduce new problem fields and incommensurable world-views. We have therefore to 'relinquish the notion, explicit or implicit, that changes in a paradigm carry scientists, and those who learn from them, closer and closer to the truth' (ibid.: 170). Scientific growth is not a process of evolution in the direction of an ultimate goal at all. In what terms then can we speak about the progress of science? Let's take an analogy inspired by Darwin: just as the evolution of species is a result of a natural selection of organisms 'more adapted' to the environment (and has no final goal set by God or by nature), so the evolution of scientific theories is a product of 'the selection by conflict, within scientific communities, of the fittest way to practice future science' (ibid.: 172). This evolution also has no final goal.

Not all sciences are mature enough to be able 'to work from a single paradigm or from a closely related set' (ibid.: 162). This kind of maturity is rather rare. Even in highly developed sciences we encounter competing paradigms at any given time (ibid.: 209). Moreover, one has to distinguish scientific communities that have achieved the mature paradigm stage from schools that are still in the 'pre-paradigm' period. During such a period individuals may be said to practise science, but 'the results of their enterprise do not add up to science as we know it' (ibid.: 163). Fact gathering, for instance, may occur, 'but it is far more nearly at random than the one subsequent scientific development makes familiar . . .' (ibid.: 15). Some data may be obtained from observation, others from experiments and still others 'from established crafts like medicine,' which is 'one readily accessible source of facts that could not have been casually discovered' (ibid.: 15). When the 'fundamental tenets of a field are once more at issue' and 'doubts are continually expressed about the very possibility of continued progress if one or another of the opposed paradigms are adopted,' that is, during periods of revolution, scientific fact gathering usually regresses to a situation very similar to the pre-paradigmatic one. Cumulative scientific progress seems both obvious and assured only during periods of normal science (ibid.: 163).

Objections against the application of Kuhn's theory to review the history and structure of psychoanalysis

Before applying Kuhn's view of science and scientific progress to Winnicott's contribution to psychoanalysis, I shall briefly address two possible objections to a Kuhnian reading of psychoanalysis in general. In the first place, it might be said that Kuhn's view only applies to natural sciences and therefore not to psychoanalysis, which is a science of man. This way of reading Kuhn is not without difficulties. It is true that for Kuhn it remains an open question 'what parts of social science have yet acquired such fully-fledged paradigms at all' (ibid.: 15). However, by saying this, Kuhn does not imply that there are no paradigm-like elements in social sciences. In fact, Kuhn observes:

. . . members of all scientific communities, including the schools of the 'pre-paradigm' period, share the sorts of elements which I have collectively labeled 'a paradigm'. What changes with the transition to maturity is not the presence of a paradigm but rather its nature. Only after that change is normal puzzle solving research possible.

(Kuhn 1970a: 179)

Nor are we prohibited to speak of progress in disciplines different from natural sciences, or even in areas very remote from empirical research, such as theology and philosophy: 'The theologian who articulates dogma or the philosopher who refines Kantian imperatives contributes to progress, if only that of the group that shares his premises' (ibid.: 162). The real issue for Kuhn in discussing psychoanalysis and social sciences in general is the problem of transition from pre-scientific or pre-paradigmatic kinds of questions answering to the specifically scientific or paradigmatic way of problem-solving. This process can be studied in its own right, since it is constantly going on in several fields of Western culture. Current research 'in parts of philosophy, psychology, linguistics, and even art history' suggest, according to Kuhn, that these disciplines are looking for new paradigms (ibid.: 121 and 162).

In the Postscript of the second edition Kuhn stresses once again that his main theses about the structure of science and of scientific revolutions are applicable to many other fields as well: 'To the extent that the book portrays scientific development as a succession of tradition-bound periods punctuated by non-cumulative breaks, its theses are undoubtedly of wide applicability' (ibid.: 208). And he explains why it is so:

But they should be [applicable], for they are borrowed from other fields. Historians of literature, of music, of the arts, of political development, and of many other human activities have long described their subjects in the same way. Periodization, in terms of revolutionary breaks in style, taste, and institutional structure, has been among their standard tools. If I have been original with respect to concepts like these, it has mainly been by applying them to the sciences, fields which had been widely thought to develop in a different way.

(Ibid.)

As Kuhn says earlier in the text (ibid.: 92), it was indeed politics which provided him with the initial idea of revolution. What Kuhn did is nothing other than isolate features of problem-solving activity 'none necessarily unique to science' (ibid.: 209). This is why he cannot but agree with those who feel the need 'for comparative study of the corresponding communities in other fields.' The questions to be asked are:

How does one select and how is one elected to membership in a particular community, scientific or not? What is the process and what are the stages of socialization to the group? What does the group collectively see as its goals; what deviations, individual or collective, will it tolerate; and how does it control the impermissible aberration? A fuller understanding of science will depend on answers to other sorts of questions as well, but there is no area in which more work is so badly needed.

(Ibid.: 209–10)

Against my application of Kuhn's theory of scientific problem-solving to psychoanalysis it might be objected, in the second place, that Kuhn did not consider that psychoanalysis was a scientific activity at all, since, in an article written in 1970, he agreed with Karl Popper who wrote that psychoanalysis 'cannot now properly be labelled a "science"' (Kuhn 1970b: 7).

A careful reading of Kuhn's article allows for several caveats to argue against this objection. To start with, the very phrasing of Kuhn's agreement with Popper indicates that it is restricted to the present, the implication being that though psychoanalysis is not a science now there is no reason for thinking that it could not become a science in the future. There is thus nothing intrinsically non-scientific in the project of psychoanalytic research.

This reading is confirmed by Kuhn's comparison of 'contemporary [sic] psychoanalysis' with 'older medicine' and with crafts and practical arts in general, such as astrology as it was practised in the more remote past by famous astronomers, including Ptolemy, Kepler and Tycho Brahe, and even with engineering and meteorology, as they were 'practised a little more than a century ago.' Kuhn writes:

> In all these fields shared theory was adequate only to establish the plausibility of the discipline and to provide a rationale for the various craft-rules which governed practice. These rules had provided their use in the past, but no practitioner supposed they were sufficient to prevent recurrent failure.
>
> (Kuhn 1970b: 8)

All the crafts mentioned were constantly searching for a more stable and effective paradigm. Indeed, writes Kuhn:

> . . . a more articulated theory and more powerful rules were desired, but it would have been absurd to abandon a plausible and badly needed discipline with a tradition of limited success because these desiderata were not yet at hand. In their absence, however, neither the astrologer nor the doctor could do research. Though they had rules to apply, they have no puzzles to solve and therefore no science to practice.
>
> (Ibid.: 9)

From this historical sketch, Kuhn extracts that the main consequence for psychoanalysis is that it is still unable to formulate puzzles of the kind which are currently being solved by normal science during normal research. The problem-situation of psychoanalysis is similar to that of medicine (engineering and meteorology in the recent past), and to that of astrology, in earlier periods of Western culture. If, for that reason, it may be said that psychoanalysis resembles astrology, this does not imply that it must have the same destiny or that it cannot possibly come to formulate its own fully fledged paradigms to solve puzzles.

Kuhn's article contains an important remark about the similarity between the behaviour of scientists in pre-paradigmatic and revolutionary periods and that of philosophers in general. Kuhn understands that 'the reasons for the choice between metaphysical systems,' as described for instance by Popper, 'closely resemble' his own 'description of the reasons for choosing between scientific theories.' In other words, the main resemblance between paradigms consists in the fact that, in neither choice '. . . can testing play a quite decisive role' (ibid.:7): just as there are no second level criteria for choosing between rival metaphysical systems, there are no meta-scientific criteria for choosing between sets of scientific test-criteria.[12] The difference between science and philosophy is thus not a matter of decision-procedures for networks of commitments. Rather, it is due to the capacity of science to produce exemplars, that is, commonly accepted solutions of shared empirical or factual problems. Whereas philosophers remain always, so to speak, in a pre-scientific stage and never 'come down' to 'normal science,' scientists only go through this same kind of process in early phases of their disciplines or in periods of crisis. Since psychoanalysis is a new science, which is still trying to produce its full paradigmatic frame, it is only natural – and this seems to be the position of Kuhn – that it goes on making choices which are more like those which are currently practised by philosophers than like those which characterize mature sciences, and that therefore, it still lacks shared exemplars.

Now, Kuhn seems to be right as to the first point, but he is apparently wrong as to the second. It is simply not true that psychoanalysis does not have puzzles to solve. Psychoanalysis actually started (I shall come back to this point later on), by Freud's formulation of specific puzzles and by his solving them in a way that he himself and the psychoanalytic community in general considered extraordinarily fruitful in current psychoanalytic research and practice. My difference with Kuhn here is not conceptual but factual, the implication being that Kuhn was simply not familiar enough with what was and what is going on in psychoanalysis.

I trust that the way is now free to start a description of the (natural) process by which Winnicott found his paradigm related to Kuhn's thesis. I shall proceed historically in the first place, by reconstructing the Freudian Oedipal, triangular, 'three-body' paradigm from which Winnicott started.[13] I shall then go on to examine the crisis that Winnicott fell into soon after he began his study of psychoanalysis. I shall suggest that this crisis was initially motivated by the result of Winnicott's observations of very early infantile psychic disturbances which seemed to go against the Freudian theory of sexuality (i.e. against the leading generalization of the Freudian paradigm). Secondly, Winnicott came to recognize that the problems of maladjusted children were not thought to be sexual and were, therefore, excluded from treatment by psychoanalysts; instead children were sent to institutions. Thirdly, related to the first two problems, the original Freudian setting showed up technical insufficiencies. In short, Winnicott's crisis was founded on all of the three main grounds stated and explained by Kuhn as the existence of a crisis.

Following the above suggestion I go on to show how Winnicott tried to find his way out of the crisis by making an alliance with Melanie Klein, but that he gradually came to the conclusion that Klein, and others (including Fairbairn), offered no solution to the observed problem areas. Subsequently, I shall re-construct the main steps of Winnicott's own revolutionary research that led him to propose a new non-Oedipal, dual or 'two-body'[14] paradigm, based on the infant-mother dual relationship. According to my perspective, Winnicott's main contribution to psychoanalytic theory and practice is seen as an attempt to overcome his particular crisis with psychoanalytic theory by developing a new theoretical matrix for psychoanalysis as a whole that would be capable of solving the problems which had led him and others into a cul-de-sac. It should be added that his achievement did not lose anything of his predecessors' and contemporaries' achievements that he saw as important.

Freud's Oedipal paradigm

What are the main exemplars that classical psychoanalysts encounter in their formation and apply in their clinical practice? In a paper delivered in 1913 to a broad scientific audience, Freud characterized psychoanalysis by showing how it proceeds in explaining slips and dreams. Dreams, in particular, are regarded 'as normal prototypes of all psychopathological structures.' Anyone who understands dreams 'can also grasp the psychical mechanism of the neuroses and psychoses' (SE 13: 172). In this statement, there is no special significance attributed to sexuality. Freud comes to that topic later on in the same paper, by saying that:

> . . . at an early stage of its researches psychoanalysis was driven to the conclusion that nervous illnesses are an expression of disturbance of the sexual function and it was thus led to devote its attention to an investigation of that function – one which had been far too long neglected.
>
> (SE 13: 180)

To that effect, it was necessary, in the first place, to develop the 'unduly restricted concept of sexuality, a development that was justified by reference to the behaviour of children.' Freud's final formula on the nature of neuroses was: 'The primary conflict which leads to neuroses is the one between the sexual instincts and those which maintain the ego' (ibid.: 181).

The important question is: what was the clinical material regarding the primary conflict that this formula was related to? In Kuhn's terms, what were the concrete clinical problems that the theory of sexuality was supposed to make intelligible and to solve? The unequivocal answer is not just slips or dreams, but all problems that arise for the child from what Freud called the Oedipus complex. This is the meaning of Freud's later statement, found in a footnote added in 1920 to the fourth edition of *Three Essays on the Theory of Sexuality*:

> . . . it has justly been said that the Oedipus complex is the nuclear complex of neuroses, and constitutes the essential part of their content. It represents the peak of infantile sexuality, which, through its after-effects, exercises a decisive influence on the sexuality of adults.
>
> (SE V11: 226, footnote)

A close study of Freud's research on sexual development leads to the conclusion, firstly, that Freud's theory of sexuality started simultaneously with discoveries in the clinical material of work with hysterics alongside Freud's self-analysis. These discoveries led and illustrated the existence of the Oedipal constellation and the theory of infantile sexuality. Secondly, the theory developed mainly by recognizing, to an ever-increasing extent, the importance of the Oedipus complex 'as the central phenomenon of the sexual period of early childhood.' In the same footnote that I have just quoted, Freud says: 'With the progress of psychoanalytic studies the importance of the Oedipus complex has become more and more clearly evident.' And he adds: 'Its recognition has become the shibboleth that distinguishes the adherents of psychoanalysis from its opponents.' (SE V11: 226, footnote).

By making a 'shibboleth of the Oedipus complex,' i.e. an 'identification sign,' Freud was specifying what Kuhn named the 'exemplar' that serves to establish the community of psychoanalysts. Freud's identity criterion for psychoanalysis is a problem-situation that, in his opinion, has been solved in an exemplary manner by the constellation of psychoanalytic theoretical commitments. Thus, the psychoanalytic theory of sexuality reinforced Freud's metapsychology. It was not long before Freudians started to use the Oedipus complex as a concrete rule for expelling dissident members. The example was provided by Freud's theoretical separation from Jung. It is important to observe in the specifics of that argument that Freud's only text in which he makes an attempt to prove the historical and material existence of the primal scene (i.e. the Oedipal situation) is 'The Wolf Man' which is a text directed explicitly to refuting Jung's position.[15]

We have thus identified the main exemplar and the most important guiding generalization that constitutes a central part of the new 'constellation of commitments' by which Freud produced his revolution in the scientific research on sexuality and psycho-neuroses and created psychoanalysis i.e. the Oedipal conflict and its solution by means of the theory of sexuality.[16] In the constellation of commitments that constitute Freud's disciplinary matrix there are three further elements that I wish to account for: his ontological model of man, his heuristic rules and his values. Very briefly, Freud's ontology includes a number of suppositions, more precisely, 'speculations' about psychic forces and energies as well as those of the innate constitution of the mental apparatus.[17] As to Freud's methodology and heuristics, they are based on the transference relationship, specific to psychoanalysis, combined with methods common to all scientific research: fact-gathering, formulation and testing of hypotheses (empirical generalizations). Freud also believed, as did all other members of the Helmholz School of natural sciences, in some methodological tenets which, in essence, go back to Kant. Namely, that no empirical science can be complete without 'auxiliary constructions,' and that all explanations have to be dynamic explanations based on quantifiable forces. Furthermore, in the case of human individuals, the interplay of forces takes place in an apparatus that is inherited and further developed. This methodological stance allowed for bold speculations which, for Freud, were based on a vast range of metaphors, taken mainly from biology and from both psychological and philosophical theories of consciousness.[18]

Finally, there is a set of values contained explicitly or implicitly in the Freudian paradigm. Just as any other inquiry that is guided by the scientific method, psychoanalysis is a never-ending search for empirical truth about clinical phenomena. And, as in all other sciences, the results achieved by psychoanalysis are essentially revisable in the sense that there is no final truth, no absolute true belief, since in science we can have only provisional beliefs, subject to correction.[19] Although he assumes a positivistic view of science,[20] Freud is obliged to work with heuristic speculations which are metaphysical in character, and he proceeds thus as a Kantian. Nevertheless, psychoanalysis, as a science, remains different from philosophy – in so far as it does not offer a general and final world-view but rather a way of attempting, step by step, to enlarge objective knowledge – as distinct from the arts and, particularly, from religion. As to the social utility of psychoanalysis, it is concerned with relieving unpleasure and pain caused by an excessive repression of desire, i.e. by the censured libido.[21]

It was within this disciplinary matrix that Freud produced a clinical psychology and a metapsychology. The first one is an empirical science that studies four main areas: sexuality, neuroses, psychic structures and social order. The second is a 'speculative superstructure' of the first. Whereas the theory of sexuality and other parts of clinical psychology may lay claims to empirical truth, metapsychological parts of psychoanalysis are introduced as mere conventions. For instance, instincts (*Triebe*) are conventions. Accordingly, metapsychology cannot be used as a foundation of clinical psychology: the only possible foundation of this kind of knowledge is clinical experience itself. Nevertheless, metapsychology was viewed by Freud as having great heuristic value through providing guide-lines for empirical (clinical) research and schemes for organizing results already obtained. To that effect, metapsychological hypotheses and speculations must be coherent with clinical experience and with conscious experience in general, as well with each other.[22]

Freud's metapsychology is a vast and sophisticated speculation about an unconscious scene of mental life that is seen to be inhabited by entities analogous to conscious mental entities, for instance representations, impulses and desires. Mental processes that govern these entities (although they do not obey the same laws as those that govern conscious mental processes) are conceived as resulting from psychic forces that act in agreement with the principle of universal determinism. In that way, Freud transferred to the unconscious domain the general empirical, as well as metaphysical, properties of conscious states. Most of these elements, well known to the empirical psychology of his time,[23] are taken from the Kantian theory of subjectivity, which, as is well known to philosophers, was founded on a dynamic view of nature, and included the two basic forces of attraction and repulsion, and a theory of psychic structure. The Freudian dualism of forces appears to be an adaptation of the Kantian metaphysical dualism, and the main elements of his psychic apparatus are the Kantian faculties, now called agencies or instances for the purpose of psychoanalytic research.[24] Influenced by his medical training, Freud naturalized all these ingredients of the unconscious and even tried to construct a machine capable of producing the same effects as those observed in clinical practice and everyday life. In the initial version of Freud's metapsychology the machine was a biological one (cf. the Project of a Scientific Psychology). In the later version, formulated around 1915, the prevailing metapsychological model of the human being is a psychological machine, which appears to be inherited from Leibniz, Kant and others. At that period, Freud was speaking exclusively of psychic forces and of the 'psychic apparatus'.

There are several reasons why Freud's metapsychological speculations have to be carefully distinguished from his exemplar (the Oedipus complex) and his guiding generalizations (that belong to the theory of sexuality and its extensions). Firstly, exemplars are different from other commitments and, furthermore, are by far the most important elements of a disciplinary matrix. Secondly, empirical commitments should not be mixed up with ontological ones. Thirdly, these differences are important for the understanding of the history of psychoanalysis. As we shall see later, Winnicott's crisis was not triggered, in the first place, by problems related to Freudian metapsychology, but rather because the Oedipus exemplar (and theory of sexuality) did not always assist with the clinical problems that he happened to find important in his paediatric and psychoanalytic practice.

Winnicott's crisis

The Oedipal paradigm proved itself extremely successful in dealing with a number of new problems, and the theory of sexuality served as the starting point for various extensions and applications of psychoanalysis. Firstly, and most significantly for psychoanalysis itself, it served to develop the theory of neuroses and of psychic disturbances in general (paranoia, homosexuality, fetishism.) Secondly, it helped in elaborating the theory of psychic development and of the structure of the psychic apparatus. Thirdly, it served as a starting point in the theory of society, religion and morals. Let me note that Freud ventured a very bold assertion about morals, namely, that 'Kant's categorical imperative is the direct heir of the Oedipus complex' (SE XIX: 167), which implies that the very essence of traditional morality was a derivative of human sexual life.

But the Oedipal paradigm was also confronted very soon with serious anomalies. Freud himself found one of them: the early pre-Oedipal relation of female children with their mothers. Melanie Klein followed this up and made the case for the existence of anxieties earlier than the fully developed phallic or genital Oedipus complex.[25] In the 1940s, Fairbairn added a new criticism to the Oedipal paradigm and indeed to the whole of Freud's libido theory (Fairbairn 1952).

However, according to my research, the first real challenge to Freud's Oedipal paradigm within psychoanalysis came from Winnicott. While still undergoing psychoanalytic training, Winnicott became 'astounded both by the insight psychoanalysis gave to the lives of children and by a certain deficiency in psychoanalytic theory' (Winnicott 1965: 172). He describes this deficiency in the following way:

> At that time, in the 1920s, everything had the Oedipus complex at its core. The analysis of the psycho-neuroses led the analyst over and over again to the anxieties belonging to the instinctual life at the 4–5-year period in the child's relationship to the two parents. Earlier difficulties that came to light were treated in analyses as regressions to pre-genital fixation points, but the dynamics came from the conflict at the full-blown genital Oedipus complex of the toddler or late toddler age [. . .].
>
> (Ibid.)

Winnicott makes the same point in a later autobiographical report about his learning process of psychoanalysis, phrased almost directly in Kuhnian terms:

> When I came to try and learn what here was to be learned about psychoanalysis, I found that in those days we were being taught about everything in terms of the 2-, 3-, and 4-years-old Oedipus complex and regression from it.
>
> (Winnicott 1989: 574–5)

While learning to see every psychic disturbance in the light of the Oedipus complex, Winnicott, who at the same time was a practising paediatrician, found himself in the following difficulty:

> Now, innumerable case histories showed me that the children who became disturbed, whether psycho-neurotic, psychotic, psycho-somatic or anti-social, showed difficulties in their emotional development in infancy, even as babies. [. . .] Something was wrong somewhere.
>
> (Winnicott 1965: 172)

What is described here are the clinical problems that triggered Winnicott's revolutionary research, namely the disturbances which belong to the intended field of the Oedipal paradigm but which do not fit it. The Oedipal paradigm was not entirely wrong, it was even constantly confirmed, but it was insufficient; more precisely, it could not do all that Freud hoped it could do. Winnicott's first, and by far his most important, difficulty with Freudian psychoanalysis was thus about its shibboleth, not about metapsychology. In Kuhn's terms, what happened to Winnicott during his learning process is that he found a serious anomaly in the framework of the paradigm he was trained in. What is more, he found an entire field of problems that resisted the 'classical' psychoanalytic understanding and treatment.

After having made this discovery, although maybe not as a direct consequence of it, Winnicott was alone and found himself in between both the Anna Freudians and the Kleinian group post Controversial Discussions. In the 1920s and 1930s, he writes in 'D.W.W. on D.W.W' (Winnicott 1989) (Chapter 1), that the very existence of something like obsessional neurosis in a 16-month baby was simply denied as a fact. It was rebuffed with the objection: 'But this can't happen.' Winnicott comments:

> There wasn't an audience for that, because of the fact that to have an obsessional neurosis one would have to have had a regression from the difficulties of the Oedipal stage at 3. I know that I overdo the point but that was something that gave me a line. I thought to myself, I'm going to show that infants are very ill early, and if the theory does not fit it, it's just got to adjust itself. So that was that.
> (Winnicott 1989: 575) (see Chapter 1)

We have thus identified the exact point at which Winnicott started to depart from Freud and initiated his revolutionary research which, as I argue here, concluded by the substitution of Winnicott's new mother-baby or two-body paradigm instead of the original Freudian Oedipal or three-body paradigm.

The attempt to find a solution in the 'learning area' of Melanie Klein

Winnicott's first move, however, was to try to save the Oedipal paradigm. From the mid-1920s onward he gave 'many tentative and frightened papers to his colleagues,' in which he described samples of cases histories of emotionally ill babies 'that had to be reconciled somehow with the theory of the Oedipus complex as the point of origin of individual conflicts' (Winnicott 1965: 172). Yet Winnicott soon came to the conclusion that what he needed was a psychology of the newborn infant which would not try to reduce all problems just to 'castration anxiety and the Oedipus complex' (Winnicott 1958: 34). He felt 'that the psychology of the small child and of the infant is not so simple as it would at first seem to be, and that a quite complex mental structure may be allowed even in the new born infant' (Winnicott 1958: 34). But Winnicott did not know where to look for such a psychology. He stood quite alone, and without a guiding paradigm.

It was an important moment in Winnicott's life when James Strachey, his analyst at that time, sent him to Melanie Klein, who was also trying to apply psychoanalysis to small children (Winnicott 1965: 173). Winnicott took her a paper which presented an example of 'pre-Kleinian' child analysis which he realized on the basis of his own analysis with Strachey. 'This was difficult for me,' remembers Winnicott, 'because overnight I had changed from being a pioneer into being a student with a pioneer teacher' (Winnicott 1965: 173).

Winnicott discovered very soon, however, that the psychology of the newborn infant he was looking for could not be of the Kleinian type. In different writings, Winnicott spelled out his main reasons for rejecting the Kleinian line of approach (e.g. Winnicott 1965: 177). According to Klein, the relevant clinical material 'either has to do with the child's object relationships or with mechanisms of introjection and projection' (ibid.: 174). These were 'deep' mechanisms, but, Winnicott argued, not 'early' mechanisms. As he puts it in 1962, much of what Klein wrote in the last two decades of her fruitful work may have been 'spoiled' by her tendency to push unwarrantedly the age at which deeper mental mechanisms appear further and further back. According to Winnicott, Klein made mistakes because 'deeper in psychology does not always mean earlier.' Winnicott was convinced that 'when you are going back to the deepest things you won't get to the beginning' (Winnicott 1989: 581). For instance, the talion dread and splitting the object into 'good' and 'bad' are truly deep mechanisms. Yet, the capacity to use them is not established before the capacity of using projection and introjection mechanisms, and these capacities, in turn, are dependent upon previous good mothering which, by the way, is neither a mental mechanism nor a mental phenomenon at all. Moreover, Winnicott never accepted Klein's theory of the nature and aetiology of psychosis, formulated in terms of hereditary mental mechanisms and conflicting instincts.

Winnicott and Fairbairn

One might think that Winnicott should have felt himself closer to Fairbairn, who was also critical of the Oedipus paradigm. Indeed, in 1941, Fairbairn complained about the misconception of regarding 'the Oedipus situation as a psychological, in contrast to a sociological, phenomenon' (Fairbairn 1952: 36–7). In 1944, he declared that the Oedipus situation is not 'an explanatory concept,' but rather a 'phenomenon to be explained' (ibid.: 121).

These remarks seem to be compatible with Winnicott's findings. However, a closer examination of Fairbairn's position shows that this is not so. Fairbairn looked for causes of all pathological psychic conditions in disturbances of object relations (ibid.: 82), in particular of relations with internalized objects. Schizoid disturbances, specifically, were thought of as results of introjections. As such they were viewed not as primary processes but as a defence mechanism (Winnicott 1989: 418). The question is: defence against what? Against ambiguity in object relations, that calls for the repression of the libido. The rationale for repression is not to be found in the (late) Freudian Oedipus situation, because the initial oedipal situation 'is not really an external situation at all, but an internal situation.' The fundamental difference from Klein is that the situation is not built around the symbolic mental equation 'breast = penis' and the conflict between death and libido instincts, but '. . . around the figures of an internal exciting mother and an internal rejecting mother' (Fairbairn 1952: 123–4). Fairbairn sums up his position in the following way:

> Thus, in my view, the triangular situation which provides the original conflict of the child is not the one constituted by three persons (the child, his mother and his father), but the one constituted essentially by the central ego, the exciting object and the rejecting object.
>
> (Fairbairn 1994 vol. I: 28)

Fairbairn's aetiology of pathological conditions is thus still Oedipal, triangular, although the triangle is defined differently from Freud and Klein. It is no more the actually lived objective Oedipal situation, as it was originally in Freud, but an 'internalized' condition. Internalization implies the existence and the functioning of mental operations and mechanisms that Winnicott came to reject, as I said above, on the basis of his clinical observations.

In 1953, Winnicott wrote a devastating review of Fairbairn's 1952 book of articles. What were his main critical points? Firstly, that Fairbairn '. . . starts off with an infant that is a whole human being, one experiencing the relation to the breast as a separate object, an object that he has experienced and about which he has complicated ideas' (Winnicott 1989: 416). Secondly, Winnicott criticizes Fairbairn's explanation of the disturbances found in individuals displaying schizoid features as a regressive phenomenon determined by unsatisfactory emotional relations with parents, without making clear whether '. . . the mother only "provokes the regression" to this early state or is the creator of it.' In other words, Fairbairn does not decide '. . . whether deprivation is the result of a deficiency in the mother's care or inevitable in childcare.' It is therefore very difficult '. . . to work out whether Fairbairn considers this maternal failure to be truly the mother's failure or the child's projection on her of his own fate' (Winnicott 1989: 417–18). If the two are held to be the same on account of the imperfect maturity of all persons (including mothers), then it must be said that Fairbairn did not '. . . find the language that covers both the normal and the abnormal' (ibid.: 417). This faulty 'theoretical structure' spoils what can be learned from Fairbairn's valuable 'flashes of clinical insight.'

This is essentially the same objection Winnicott addressed to Klein, regarding the treating of early disturbances as internal mental problems without taking enough account of the actual mother-baby relationship dynamic. This difference is all-important because, in the second case, one is confronted with the additional task of defining the good enough maternal care whereas, in the first case, no such question arises.[26]

Winnicott's revolutionary research

Winnicott did not want to abandon the efficient problem-solving procedures of classical psychoanalysis, even though they were embedded in metapsychological postulates (psychic forces and mental mechanisms) which he rejected. We have seen him saying that the existence of the Oedipus complex was confirmed. He also recognized the Kleinian theory of the depressive position as important and empirically founded, in which he saw a dual and not, as Klein saw, a triangular situation.[27] On the other hand, he needed, as I have indicated, a new and more powerful procedure to solve clinical problems that have their origin in the very early actual mother-baby relationship. So, how did he get out of this predicament?

One important element of Winnicott's solution came from his study of the 'environment.' Beginning in 1923 he became increasingly aware of the fact that there is a relationship between the environment and psychic disease, and, he says, this '. . . led to something in me' (Winnicott 1989: 576). In the 1920s and the 1930s no analyst was interested in this problem. Winnicott was even deterred from doing this sort of research by his first analyst James Strachey (1923–33), who was a classical Freudian, and later on by Joan Riviere, his second analyst (1933–8[?]).[28] Riviere bluntly refused even to consider a planned paper of Winnicott's on the classification of environments. At that time, psychoanalysts, writes Winnicott, '. . . were the only people [. . .] who knew there was anything but the environment' (Winnicott 1989: 577) (see Chapter 1). Yet, Winnicott could not help but agree with those who were screaming out that a child might become ill by his father being drunk. Thus he was confronted with the following: 'How to get back to the environment without losing all that was gained by studying inner factors' (ibid. :577).

How did Winnicott solve this? He was helped very much by an accidental factor: the war, and probably also by Clare Britton, his future wife. By being involved in the evacuation operations of small children in the London area, Winnicott was obliged, 'at last', he writes, to treat abandoned and maladjusted children.[29] Until then, he avoided treating such cases, remaining in line with the official position that psychoanalysis has nothing to do with 'real' situations. This is how Winnicott came to the 'original idea' of the links between the 'anti-social tendency' and 'hope' which is one of the essential discoveries of his child psychology and 'extremely important' for his clinical practice. The idea was that 'the thing behind the anti-social tendency in any family, normal or not, is deprivation,' and that hope has the unconscious meaning of 'trying to reach back over the deprivation area to the lost object' (ibid.: 577).

Having discovered the connection between maturational processes and the facilitating environment, between nature and nurture, Winnicott found himself confronted with a new task, i.e. of formulating 'a sort of theoretical basis of environmental provision starting at the beginning with 100 percent adaptation and quickly lessening according to the ability of the child to make use of failure of adaptation' (ibid.: 579). This task, in turn, required elaboration of 'dependence and adaptation theories' in a developmental and historical perspective (ibid.: 579).

Winnicott's exemplar: the baby on the mother's lap

While working on the theory of the infant's relationship to what he named the 'environment', Winnicott came to two decisive results. Firstly, that it is 'impossible to talk about the individual without talking about the mother,' because, speaking the language of late Winnicott, the mother 'is a subjective object [. . .] and therefore how the mother

137

behaves is really part of the infant' (ibid.: 580).[30] Secondly, that the initial mother-baby relationship is not a triangular internal (mental) relationship, but a very special kind of dual external (not mental) relationship. In 1958, Winnicott put this point in the following terms:

> Any attempt to describe the Oedipus complex in terms of two people must fail. Nevertheless two-body relationships do exist, and they belong to relatively earlier stages in the history of the individual. The original two-body relationship is that of the infant and the mother or mother-substitute, before any property of the mother has been sorted out and moulded into the idea of a father.
>
> (Winnicott 1965: 29–30)

In the beginning the father, from the baby's point of view, may or may not have been a mother-substitute. If he has, he was not there as father, i.e. as somebody endowed with properties or roles different from that of the mother. In the initial two-body relationship, the mother can be said to start off 'as a part object or as a conglomeration of part objects.' The same is true of her surrogates and thus of the father as the mother-substitute. Yet, 'at some time,' the father does begin 'to be felt to be there in a different role.' The time comes at which the individual is likely to use the father for a very specific purpose, namely:

> . . . as a blueprint for his or her own integration when just becoming at times a unit. If the father is not there the baby must make the same development but more arduously, or using other fairly stable relationships, to a whole person.
>
> (Winnicott 1989: 243)

This being so, the main initial role of the father with respect to the developing child who is no more a baby is not at all that of a partial object, but rather to '. . . be the first glimpse [. . .] of integration and of personal wholeness. In favourable cases, the father '. . . as father, not as a mother surrogate' starts off '. . . as a whole person,' '. . . as an integrate in the ego's organization and in the mental conceptualization of the baby' (ibid.: 243).

It is only later that he '. . . becomes endowed with a significant part object,' (the penis) which then plays a very important role in the child's three-body relationships.

This conception of the initial dual mother-baby relationship allowed Winnicott to come to a clear-cut formulation of his paradigmatic problem. This is the point from which he started, i.e. that babies suffer from anxieties which are not to be conceived as products of putative innate mental forces and mechanisms, but, as a consequence of an external factor, albeit psychic, the early maternal failure to provide a good enough environment.[31] In a late text, Winnicott wrote:

> To make progress towards a workable theory of psychosis, analysts must abandon the whole idea of schizophrenia and paranoia as seen in terms of regression from the Oedipus complex. The aetiology of these disorders takes us inevitably to stages that precede the three-body relationship. The strange corollary is that there is at the root of psychosis an external factor.
>
> (Ibid.: 246)

Winnicott ends this passage, with a remark probably aimed at the Kleinians, by noticing that it is '. . . difficult for psychoanalysts to admit this after all the work they have done drawing attention to the internal factors in examining the aetiology of psycho-neurosis.'

By turning to 'external factors' as the cause of psychotic illness, Winnicott reversed the then prevalent tendency in psychoanalytic theory to formulate clinical problems in terms of mental mechanisms and still more radically in terms of innate symbolic equations, e.g. breast = penis, or of Lacanian symbolic castration.[32] Psychosis became a 'natural' process, having its causes in actual external human relations, not in inner, or still less symbolic, relations and processes. In opposition to Freud, Winnicott did not define external relations as sexual, social nor even as psychological, but rather as 'personal,' based on special forms of mutuality and intimacy between mothers and their babies. Thus, he switched to his new dual paradigm, or, as I propose to call it, 'baby-on-the-mother's-lap' paradigm.[33] From that new perspective of clinical experience, situations causing schizophrenia cannot be seen as triangular:

> Just as a study of psycho-neurosis leads the student to the Oedipus complex and to the triangular situations that reach their height in the child at the toddler age and again in adolescence, so the study of psychosis leads the research worker to the earliest stages of infant life. This implies the infant-mother relationship since no

infant develops outside such a relationship. (It involves the idea of dependence prior to the establishment of the operation of mental mechanisms of projection and introjection).

(Winnicott 1965: 131)

What Winnicott is rejecting, in this and many other texts, is the very idea that early infantile schizophrenia and paranoia can have anything to do with triangular or three-body relationships. The only facts that can possibly be potential causes of psychic disturbances of the kind mentioned are related to the not good enough early mother–infant relationship at a time when, for the baby, there is no awareness of father, and therefore, there cannot be any third. This is why Winnicott states that schizophrenia is '. . . a sort of environmental deficiency disease' (Winnicott 1958: 162).[34]

Here we come to the crux of the matter: the psychology of a newborn is essentially different from the psychology of adults and even from that of young children. Not only does the theory of sexuality not apply, but also the Freudian metapsychological approach cannot be incorporated. A baby's life and his 'unconsciousness,' if there is something like that at all in a baby, cannot be described in terms of mental forces and processes. In particular, his needs have to be distinguished from desires, which are mental states, as well as from drives or instincts, which are putative or actual biological entities, with or without a mental, 'psychological' or conscious-like counterpart. Such mental states and processes are not there at the beginning. An individual's life develops out of something else, namely, out of an early psycho-somatic partnership established by the imaginative elaboration of body functions, instincts, sensations and feelings, which requires maternal care in order to succeed. In Winnicott, the binomial nature and nurture has taken the place of the classical polarity between an instinct-driven subject and its objects.

Yet, in a way, Winnicott was going back to Freud, since he saw no meaning in talking about Oedipus in terms of partial and internal objects. In *Human Nature*, Winnicott treats Freud's Oedipus complex as part of the problem of '. . . management of the first triangular relationship, with the child power-driven by newly established instincts of genital quality characteristics of the 2-5 year period' (Winnicott 1988: 49). Thus there is no substance in the frequently repeated statements that Winnicott is fleeing from the erotic into infancy (cf. Phillips 1988: 152). Winnicott is not fleeing from anything, on the contrary, he is confronting the problem traditional psychoanalysis is trying to escape, namely the fact that Freud's theory of sexuality implied in the Oedipal situation does not account for disturbances which arise in the dyadic relationship between mothers and their babies. None of the later efforts to extend the Oedipal situation and sexual theory related to it (theories rejected by Freud himself, Otto Fenichel and Anna Freud, among others) produced the desired results. These extensions were theoretically degenerative, if not meaningless:

> I think something is lost if the term 'Oedipus complex' is applied to the earlier stages, in which there are only two persons involved and the third person or part object is internalized, a phenomenon of inner reality. I cannot see any value in the use of the term 'Oedipus complex' where one or more of the trio is a part object. In the Oedipus complex, for me at least, each of the three of the triangle is a whole person, not only for the observer but also and especially for the child.
>
> (Winnicott 1988: 49)

Winnicott did not just retain Freud's late Oedipus complex, he even developed it further, by introducing, for instance, a new explanation of the origin of the fear of castration. This fear, says Winnicott, '. . . becomes welcome as an alternative to the agony of impotence' which characterizes the genital phase of sexual development where '. . . the child's performance is deficient, and the child must wait (till puberty as we know) for the ability to act out the dream' of genital relation with the mother (ibid.: 44). I want to emphasise that it is a serious, though widespread, error to think that Winnicott flees from sexuality to early infancy. What he demonstrably does is to place each of these developmental moments into the appropriate stage in the process of personal growth. Thus he makes it clear and precise how the environment impacts on the individual at each stage of early development (Winnicott 1958: Chapter 13).

Winnicott's main guiding generalization: the theory of maturational processes

The guideline for Winnicott's treatment of psychosis is his theory of emotional or personal development:

To examine the theory of schizophrenia one must have a working theory of the emotional growth of the personality. [. . .] What I must do is to assume the general theory of continuity, of an inborn tendency towards growth and personal evolution, and to the theory of mental illness as a hold up in development.

(Winnicott 1989: 194)

Here Winnicott is describing two things: his main scientific problem – infantile schizophrenia – and the theoretical tool he uses to solve it – his theory of maturational processes or personal growth. In the study of schizophrenia, this theory has the same paradigmatic role as that held by the theory of sexuality in the study and treatment of psycho-neuroses within Freud's three-body paradigm:

Also, I can say that the statement of infantile and child development in terms of a progression of the erotogenic zone, that has served us well in our treatment of psycho-neurosis, is not useful in the context of schizophrenia as is the idea of a progression from dependence (at first near-absolute) towards independence [. . .].

(Ibid.: 194)

Like Freud's theory of sexuality, Winnicott's theory of dependency (from dependence towards independence) is an empirical generalization and not a metapsychological speculation (Abram 2007: 130–47). It was initially constituted from clinical material in relation to deprived children and developed by application to the study of two-body relationships.

The theory of emotional growth stands at the very centre of Winnicott's theoretical matrix and represents one of his main contributions to psychoanalysis. In almost every article Winnicott consistently returns to the main problem of the '. . . treatment of psychiatrically ill children, and the construction of a better, more accurate and more serviceable theory of emotional development of the individual human being' (Winnicott 1986: 84).[35] Curiously enough, in the secondary literature, this theory as such has received little attention, being simply forgotten or viewed as trivial and reducible to psychoanalytic common sense.

Other components of Winnicott's paradigm

In order to complete this schematic re-construction of Winnicott's paradigm, I will now examine his ontological model of man, his heuristics and the values he stressed: items which, according to Kuhn, must be present in the disciplinary matrix of any science.

Firstly his ontology – Winnicott's theory of personal growth is based on a new view of the human being. Winnicott defines psychoanalysis (perhaps in an unexpected and seemingly old-fashioned way) as 'the study of human nature' (Winnicott 1988: 1). What Winnicott has in mind is the assumption that '. . . fundamentally all individuals are essentially alike, and this in spite of the hereditary factors which make us what we are and make us individually distinct' (Winnicott 1964: 232–3). At face value, this assumption seems to be more philosophical in kind than biological. This impression is strengthened by Winnicott's subsequent commentary:

> I mean, there are some features in human nature that can be found in all infants, and in all children, and in all people of whatever age, and a comprehensive statement of the development of the human personality from earliest infancy to adult independence would be applicable to all human beings whatever their sex, race, colour of skin, creed, or social setting. Appearances may vary, but there are common denominators in human affairs.
>
> (Ibid.: 233)

The common denominators identified are of two kinds - structural and developmental. The structural are that 'The needs of infants and small children are not variable; they are inherent and unalterable' (ibid.: 179). This same thesis is expressed in the following way:

> The essential needs of the under-fives belong to the individuals concerned, and the basic principles do not change. This truth is applicable to human beings of the past, present, and future, anywhere in the world, and in any culture.
>
> (Ibid.: 184)

As to developmental common denominators, they are obviously the invariant features of human personal growth. There is a straight connection between the two kinds of denominators, since needs are essentially related to the tendency towards integration, that is, to growth.

It is no surprise that some commentators interpret Winnicott's concept of human nature as a return to essentialism.[36] But this point should not be overdone. Human nature is something which, in spite of being invariable, has a beginning. 'The only certain date of which is that of conception' (Winnicott 1988: 29). It is not easy to ascertain the correct meaning of what Winnicott is saying here. One possible interpretation is that human nature is not a Platonic essence, but the invariant structure of a particular kind of temporalization which manifests itself as a human being, who, as Winnicott puts it, '. . . is a time sample of human nature,' just that. Where does this process of being start from? The answer is that it starts from 'not being', 'from nowhere', 'from aloneness' (ibid 131).[37] Next we may ask where does the process go? The answer is the same – to 'not being', to 'nowhere', to 'aloneness.' Winnicott states that 'The life of an individual is an interval between two states of unaliveness' (ibid.: 132). The important thing to notice here is that these two states of unaliveness, which are the extreme points of the human life interval, belong to human nature and can even be experienced. 'The experience of the first awakening gives the human individual the idea that there is a peaceful state of unaliveness that can be peacefully reached by an extreme of regression' (ibid.: 132). If this is so, then human nature is, in itself, the negation of any fixed essence. The only thing a human being can have, as a time sample of human nature, is his history, that occurs due to the tendency '. . . to begin to exist, to have experiences, to build a personal ego, to ride instincts, and [. . .] to have a self that can eventually even afford to sacrifice spontaneity, even to die' (Winnicott 1958: 304). ' . . . Natural death follows as the "final seal of health"' (Winnicott 1988: 12).

This is the main ontological hypothesis presented by Winnicott. Elsewhere, I have tried to show that Winnicott's argument is in close agreement with Heidegger's concept of the human being as happening-in-the-world of a being-to-death (Loparic 1995 and 1999b). Be that as it may, one thing is certain: there is a great difference between Winnicott's concept of human nature and Freud's naturalistic concept of the mental apparatus driven by instinctual forces. The latter concept, as I have said, is taken from modern empirical psychology and, in the last resort, from the modern philosophical concept of a naturalized subjectivity.

As to heuristics – Winnicott continues to accept the Freudian method of research, i.e. the clinical setting and work in the transference. However, he modifies its meaning, by allowing for the occurrence, in the clinical setting, of regression to dependence. Moreover, Winnicott does not allow for any kind of metapsychological speculation and prohibits going 'behind' phenomena by means of metaphors. His view of human nature is based on a very general hypothesis concerning the development of the human capacity to live an experience, rather than a metapsychological structure and functioning of something like a 'psychic apparatus.'

As to his values – they can be divided into the theoretically and practically significant. Theoretically, Winnicott sees psychoanalysis as a science, which has to test its hypotheses and to obey the verdict of observed facts.[38] As any science, psychoanalysis must be formulated so that it can be submitted to public discussion by psychoanalysts, by other scientists in the related fields, such as child psychiatry and paediatrics, and by the public in general. In so far as practical values are concerned, Winnicott takes into account unduly censured sexuality (Freud) and intrapsychic pain caused by internal conflicts (Klein, Fairbairn). Yet he thinks that by far the most severe suffering is that which arises from unmet needs that originate from the infant's predicament at the beginning of his life, i.e. the need for the continuity of being. Paradigmatic examples of this kind of pain are described as 'unthinkable agonies,' unthinkable, because they precede the time the baby is able to have any mental representation, and agonies, because they imply a lack of a good enough holding environment in which there is a struggle for the continuity-of-being. These troubles are 'early' but not 'deep,' because they originate in the two-body relationship, before the existence of any representation structure in the human baby (Winnicott 1989: 581).

A comparison between the paradigms of Freud and Winnicott

Both Freud and Winnicott agree that psychoanalysis is a science, not a craft, art, philosophy or religion.[39] Neither classifies it together with 'mixed disciplines' like astrology or alchemy. Both conceive psychoanalysis as a problem-solving activity, guided by concrete clinical problem-situations and their solutions, completed by an additional theoretical framework. Whereas exemplary problem–solutions are considered to be beyond question in normal research, they are not viewed as having an unlimited heuristic power. Both thinkers concede that new exemplars might be needed to complete the psychoanalytic picture of psychic diseases and to promote further research.

However, Freud and Winnicott disagree as to which problems are exemplary for psychoanalytic research and as to what empirical generalizations are to be taken as guiding lines. Freud made normal psychoanalytical research possible by demonstrating, through his work with the hysteric, that all psychopathological situations relate to Oedipal conflicts and by interpreting this situation in terms of his theory of sexuality. Winnicott, beginning his study of psychoanalysis in the 1920s, found that he could not see things exclusively in that way. He concluded his work by viewing the mother–baby situation as exemplary, a result which in turn forced him to develop a theory of emotional growth, that is, of nature and nurture. This is, in essence, the paradigm change which accounts for the difference between the Freudian Oedipal, triangular or three-body psychoanalysis and Winnicott's mother–baby, dual or two-body psychoanalysis.

There are also radical differences with regard to theoretical commitments. Whereas Freud, following the Kantian tradition, admitted a number of speculative auxiliary suppositions that he used to formulate his metapsychology, Winnicott decidedly rejected such a mode of theorizing and limited his explanatory hypotheses to the experiences of persons in treatment, in particular babies and young children. Winnicott does not allow for the reduction of personal 'subjective' phenomena to apply to the point of view of the patients' consciousness nor, even less, to that of an observer. He wants it the other way round: to make sure that these points of view, though external to the phenomena themselves, capture the patient's way of being and experiencing, even if this patient is a newborn baby. This is not always possible. In such cases, the analyst must stop trying to know what is happening 'behind the scene,' he must refrain from making metapsychology and from theorizing, which in clinical terms means that he must give up interpreting and even saying anything whatsoever.

Thus, both Freud and Winnicott set limits on our possibility of actually knowing 'unconscious phenomena.' But they deal with this fact differently. Freud permits himself to speculate, that is, to project to the unconscious the properties, the dynamics and the structures of conscious subjectivity. And on the contrary, Winnicott, based on his experience with mothers and their babies, understands that such a procedure is not legitimate, because it makes us think of babies as being adults and forget what happened during the process of emotional growth. Winnicott's baby is a human being, yes, but not the one who can be thought of in terms of conscious mental phenomena. Seen from the vantage point of Winnicott's theory of emotional growth, Freud's theoretical errors come from the incorrect view that what is beyond consciousness may be conceived of as being similar to consciousness, as 'un-conscious.' What, in babies, is beyond consciousness is not just primary processes, which have nothing to do with anything like conscious forces and mechanisms. The baby's experience of the continuity-of-being is something very different from any state of consciousness. Thus, the true philosophical difference between Freud and Winnicott is that whereas Freud still thinks in terms of the theory of subjectivity, initiated by the seventeenth century's philosophers and represented paradigmatically by Kant, Winnicott in contrast thinks of human beings in an entirely different theoretical key, which has much affinity to Heidegger's fundamental ontology, as presented in *Being and Time* (Heidegger 1962).[40]

Winnicott's heritage

Although the evidence is clear that Winnicott has introduced a new paradigm, the question remains as to whether he also instigated a revolution? Kuhn distinguishes between 'major revolutions' and 'small scale' revolutions. A scientific revolution being '. . . a special sort of change involving a certain sort of reconstruction of group commitments' it need not be 'a large change, nor need it seem revolutionary to those outside the single community, consisting perhaps of fewer than twenty-five people' (Kuhn 1970a: 181). It seems to me that there are more than just twenty-five psychoanalysts in the world who would be willing to declare themselves ready to do 'normal science' within the two-body paradigm proposed by Winnicott and these could appropriately be called Winnicottians. We are thus in a position to declare that a truly Winnicottian international community is beginning to arise, which could very well prove to make real contributions to present day psychoanalytic research and practice as a whole.[41]

There are some standard objections, frequently repeated but never really argued, against the possibility of creating a Winnicottian Research Community or a Winnicottian School in psychoanalysis. One such argument is that Winnicott was not a man of institutions. This is simply not true, as can be seen from Winnicott's many engagements in institutional matters (see Chapter 3 and Chronology). Winnicott's protest was not against psychoanalytic societies but, rather, against societies and theories that were turned into propaganda machines and instruments of indoctrination. What he fought for was open scientific research and discussion within and between psychoanalytic societies.

The second argument, defended for instance by Charles Rycroft, states that Winnicott was '. . . too idiosyncratic to be readily assimilated into the general body of any scientific theory' (Rycroft 1985: 114). Phillips in a sense echoes Rycroft when he says that, 'Winnicott did not become systematically coherent at the cost of his own inventiveness' (Phillips 1988: 99). However, if we seriously consider the reconstruction of Winnicott's paradigm offered here, this objection is far from doing justice to Winnicott's oeuvre and reveals not so much Winnicott's theoretical laziness as that of his objectors. Winnicott certainly did value his own inventiveness, nevertheless his main task as a psychoanalyst and paediatrician was not to cultivate and develop his originality but to help psychotics and deprived children. In order to do that he had to proceed in a methodical, coherent way. In other words, scientifically, and therefore he could not afford simply to be creative. That would mean being intrusive. Indeed in many situations he simply had to wait, that is, to sacrifice his own creativity in order to facilitate the patient to be creative. Winnicott needed, of course, to use much of his inventiveness in order to give a scientific format to this simple conclusion, but after that, he had to apply it and help his patients invent their lives. Like so many others, Phillips is confusing different aspects of Winnicott's work and personality, to the damage of an understanding of both.

Thirdly, it is said that Winnicott did not want to become a 'master.' He certainly did not want to master-mind people by telling them what to do and what to think. Nevertheless he developed an extraordinary capacity to make his own ideas public by writing, lecturing and teaching. In *Therapeutic Consultations*, for instance, he explicitly addresses the problem of training psychoanalysts in his technique of squiggle games. The basis for this training is 'a long term psychotherapy of individuals' (Winnicott 1971: 270). If this condition is not available, the teacher has to consider whether the candidate possesses a certain number of 'desirable qualities,' specified either by orthodox or Winnicott's own psychoanalytic theory and practice. Once the choice of a good candidate is made, the teaching of the technique of therapeutic consultations can begin. For this purpose, the case histories described by Winnicott in considerable detail '. . . may prove to be good teaching material' (ibid.: 9). Winnicott thus assumes the teaching role, with, however, the following caveat:

> It would be from my point of view a satisfactory outcome if the material could be used for criticism and I would much prefer this to the alternative whereby what I have described here might simply be imitated. As I have already stated, the work cannot be copied because the therapist is involved in every case as a person, and therefore no two interviews could be alike as they would be carried through by two psychiatrists.
>
> (Winnicott 1971: 9)

In the same vein, Winnicott points out that his case descriptions reflect his own personality, without forgetting to point out that his personality is not the only 'constant factor' in this kind of research, since in doing it he has had one constant companion:

> The only companion that I have in exploring the unknown territory of the new case is the theory that I carry around with me and that has become part of me and that I do not even have to think about in a deliberate way. This is the theory of emotional development of the individual which includes for me the total history of the individual child's relationship to the child's specific environment.
>
> (Ibid.: 6)

The cases presented in *Therapeutic Consultations* are, therefore, neither 'fruits of chance' nor 'genial insights of a creative psychoanalyst', but rather they are essentially illustrations of theoretical perspectives developed by Winnicott during years of dedicated scientific work and of a personal technique based on this perspective (ibid.: 215, 218, 220).

Winnicott compares his positions as a teacher of therapeutic consultations to that of the 'cellist who first slogs away at technique and then actually becomes able to play music, taking technique for granted,' and who is moved by the wish 'to communicate with those who are still slogging at technique, at the same time giving them the hope that will one day come from playing music' (ibid.: 6). Winnicott hates the idea of being 'simply copied,' but he does want to teach what he knows in order that other people might create their own capacity to acquire knowledge and to do psychotherapeutic work by themselves. It would be better, admits Winnicott, '. . . if the student could gather the material for himself or herself from personal contact with children instead of reading my descriptions.' But he knows very well that this is not always possible, especially for students who are starting to learn (ibid.: 11).

What we have here is a very subtle presentation of the learning process involved in the squiggle game (derived from the spatula game) that takes the personal dimension into account, while nevertheless recognizing that teaching is founded on a pre-existing theory, i.e. the theory of emotional development of the individual, which is the 'backbone of all the work described here.' Winnicott has essentially written a textbook on the technique of therapeutic consultations, based on his theory of emotional development. Not only can Winnicott's theory and technique be taught, it also seems to me that he wants it to be taught to the beginner analysts. In essence, Winnicott subscribes to the general view that there is no other way to become a scientist other than within a scientific tradition.[42]

I have tried to show that in Winnicott's work there is a constant, long range and carefully conducted scientific effort to solve a clinical problem: that of nature and the aetiology of psychotic disturbances. I am quite ready to admit that his solution to this problem has left many unanswered questions. However, I understand that there can be no reasonable doubt about Winnicott's commitment to scientific research conducted in agreement with methods of psychoanalysis and, to a lesser degree, of ordinary paediatrics and psychiatry. I would suggest that neither of the latter two disciplines are in much better shape than psychoanalysis. In all of them rival theories are struggling for survival and all continue to remain in, what Kuhn would term, a 'pre-paradigmatic phase.' In other words, they are all undergoing, more or less, frequently smaller or greater revolutions – the kind of activity that is generally known as normal 'scientific research.'

Notes

1 This is a revised version of 'Winnicott's paradigm outlined' published in 2000, which was based on my 'Madeleine Davis Lecture' for the Squiggle Foundation, delivered by kind invitation of Jan Abram who was in her final year as Director of the Foundation.

2 See D.W.Winnicott Publications 1931–2002 in the Appendix, which indicates where to find the complete bibliography of Winnicott's papers and books.

3 As is well known, Kuhn himself leaned heavily on psychology and sociology (especially on L. Fleck's theory of scientific communities [1935]) as well as on some philosophical sources (Wittgenstein's philosophy of language) in framing his view of science and scientific research. It could be a rewarding exercise to re-examine and eventually to complete Kuhn's theory of science by taking into account Winnicott's views on the genesis and the function of intellectual and other mental processes in human life.

4 In 1990 Kuhn characterized his position as a 'sort of post-Darwinian Kantianism' (Kuhn 1990: 12). For comments on the resemblance between Darwin's history of life and Kuhn's history of science, see Hodge and Radick (eds) 2009: 165–6 and 172.

5 Winnicott strongly criticized a similar claim of Riviere's as regards the Kleinian development of psychoanalysis (Winnicott 1987: 35, 97).

6 In this passage and elsewhere, Greenberg and Mitchell prefer, for reasons which are not quite clear to me, to use the later Kuhnian term 'model' instead of the original term 'paradigm.'

7 For other accounts of the development of Winnicott's ideas cf. Greenberg and Mitchell (1983) and Jacobs (1995).

8 In 1989, Holton and his collaborators introduced the concept of the 'solace paradigm' in an attempt to solve the problem of human need for 'consolation', particularly urgent in our epoch which is 'overwhelmingly nihilistic'. In this context, Winnicott's concept of the transitional object is treated as a 'very important sub-class of solacing objects' (Holton et al. (eds) 1988: 62), the elements of 'transitional relatedness' being 'no less ubiquitous in life than are elements of the Oedipus complex' (ibid.: 88). Though I agree that Winnicott's transitional objects are an important component of his new paradigm and that this paradigm is no longer based on the Oedipus complex, I cannot follow Holton and his group in the attempt to embed this concept in the solace paradigm of their own, presented as an 'enlargement' of the scientific world-view by a 'multi perspective' strategy, which combines scientific, philosophical and even theological backgrounds. There is little doubt that philosophy and theology have been and continue to be influential in framing scientific world-views, but I cannot see any value, just as Freud and Winnicott did not, in mixing up science with these two disciplines. Holton's concept of paradigm does not square with what we know about paradigms in

scientific disciplines, but rather portrays what happens in philosophical and theological disputes about fundamentals.

9 Let me give an example. Dodi Goldman (1993) puts much emphasis, as many other commentators do, on the personal factors in Winnicott's procedures. For example he writes: 'By temperament, Winnicott was more an innovator than a curator. He needed to seemingly destroy certain facets of psychoanalytic theory so as to re-create them in his own image: Only then could theory feel real to him' (Goldman 1993: 132–3). And: 'Winnicott's original contributions to psychoanalytic theory are best understood, therefore, as efforts to re-create for himself, in a personal way, aspects of theory that he has imaginatively destroyed.' (p. 133). As I see it, Winnicott did not 'destroy' psychoanalytic theory and practice driven by needs flowing from his temperament. He rather developed and modified it, in such a way, however, that 'bridges that lead from older theory to newer theory' are kept 'open' (Winnicott 1989: 256). In some cases, this was done in order to increase the problem-solving capacity of psychoanalysis, in others to correct errors ('blunders') of Freud's. One of the reasons for my use of Kuhn's theory of paradigms is that it illustrates more accurately that the kind of move practised by Winnicott is part of the common scientific practice and that Winnicott took Freud as approving and welcoming 'revolutionary' procedures in psychoanalysis.

10 Kuhn's term for this component is 'symbolic generalizations', which covers empirical laws and definitions of empirical phenomena.

11 Cf., for instance, the very special personal significance of the duck figure in the squiggle game of Winnicott with Iiro, as specified in Winnicott 1971, Chapter 1, which would get completely lost if this figure were seen as a rabbit.

12 At this point Kuhn agrees entirely with Heidegger who denies that there are independent criteria for choosing between competing metaphysical systems (cf. Heidegger 1961, vol. 2: 258, 264 and 290).

13 This is an expression which Winnicott takes from J. Rickman, who introduced the distinction between 'two-body' and 'three-body' relationships' (see Winnicott 1965: 29). I wonder whether Rickman's usage was not inspired by distinction made in classical mechanics between two- and three-particle problems.

14 See the previous note.

15 Freud's coolness towards Melanie Klein can be explained in the same way. Moreover, the essential points of the debate between Anna Freud and Melanie Klein can be summed up as turning around the question of how far back are we allowed to displace the Oedipal elements of the mental apparatus? (see Phillips 1988: 43).

16 Freud's theory of sexuality is a result of a continuous, both empirical and metapsychological research, which extended over decades. At the beginning, it paid much attention to the problem of perversions– since Freud was standing still under the influence of Krafft-Ebbing – and to the differences

between adult and infantile sexuality, including puberty. Yet, with time, questions related directly and specifically to infantile sexuality became predominant. Some of this work appears in additions to later publications of *Three Essays*. Particularly noteworthy are sections 5 and 6 of the Second Essay, which deal with infantile sexual theories and phases of development of sexual organization (the erotogenic zones), as well as section 3 of the Third Essay, which deals with the libido theory. Among significant developments in sexual theory present in other writings of Freud's we can mention the theory of libidinal types and of female sexuality.

17 See Loparic 1999a.

18 The term 'speculation' is my translation of Freud's 'Spekulation', which is taken from Kantian philosophy and characterizes Freud's way of constructing his metapsychology. Metapsychology is the speculative part of his new science, parallel to the speculative part of physics, which includes expressions and terms like 'gravitational force,' 'particle of matter,' 'absolute space,' 'infinitesimal' etc. One main trait of Freud's speculative concepts is that they are 'conventions' ('Konventionen'), to be used not for making statements about matters of fact, conscious or unconscious, but exclusively for heuristic (problem-solving) and merely expository purposes, being 'heuristic fictions' in the Kantian sense. I guess that on this point many British Contemporary Freudians differ sharply from Freud (perhaps due to the British empiricist tradition and Winnicott's influence).

19 Winnicott thinks the same way since he praises Freud's openness to criticism and his readiness to abandon his ideas, whereas he criticizes the dogmatism of Klein and the Kleinians as not scientific (cf. Winnicott 1989: 460).

20 In 1911, Freud signed, together with Einstein and several other first rate scientists of the epoch, a manifesto in favour of the foundation of a 'Society for Positivistic Philosophy.' This document is now published in *Natureza humana,* vol. 2, no. 2, 2000.

21 Klein was concerned about 'psychic pain.' Winnicott, as we shall see, is concerned about real failures in human relations (which are not just 'social,' but personal, at any stage of development).

22 A non-coherent theory is a false theory. Since *ex falso sequitur quodlibet,* inconsistency has to be avoided.

23 As we know, one of the sources used by Freud in elaborating his metapsychology was the article by Theodor Lipps, a philosopher of psychology, entitled: 'The Concept of the Unconscious in Psychology', from 1897.

24 As Heidegger noticed (1987: 220), Freud's id is a new scientific name for unconscious *sensibility* and passions, ego for unconscious *understanding,* and super-ego for unconscious *reason,* in particular, practical reason.

25 As we know, Freud was not very happy about the proposal made by Klein.

26 In 1953, Winnicott still thought that Fairbairn was trying to take his distance from Klein. In his autobiographical report of 1967 (1989, Postscript),

he admitted however that Klein and Fairbairn had several important things in common, but that he 'could not see that for years and years' (Winnicott 1989: 579).

27 On Winnicott's interpretation of the depressive position as a two-body situation see Winnicott 1965: 22, 30 and 176.

28 Cf.: Chronology – It is not clear what were the exact years when Winnicott was in analysis with Joan Riviere but it's likely to be these years.

29 It is interesting to note that WWI triggered a similar need for further articulation in classical psychoanalysis. The discovery of the 'war neuroses' opened the way to a series of clinical developments and to Freud's new addition to his metapsychology of the death instinct (Freud 1920).

30 The same is true of transitional phenomena and has, according to Winnicott, 'quite a lot of philosophical importance.' I have tried to spell out a possible philosophical meaning of the environment as a part of the individual by approximating this idea to Heidegger's concept of man as having the structure of 'being-in-the-world' (cf. Loparic 1995).

31 It may not be beyond the point to notice that Peter Sloterdijk, a German philosopher influenced by Heidegger and interested in psychoanalytic theory, also defends in his recent writings (cf. Sloterdijk 1998) the thesis that our original relationship to the external world is dual, not triangular. However, he does not conceive this relationship as the one between the baby and his mother, obtaining in the 'subjective' world, but as a pattern which is realized in couples found in very different fields of study, such as theology (relation between soul and God or the soul and the Guardian Angel) or adult sexuality.

32 This tendency started with Freud's rejection of his first seduction theory.

33 This image, obvious in itself, is based in particular on a particular remark of Winnicott's that the relation of a child to his mother must be such that he can feel comfortable 'on her lap' (Winnicott 1964: 133).

34 This argument is parallel to the one used by Winnicott in criticizing Klein's theory of envy. Envy cannot be attributed to a newborn baby because the word 'envy' refers to an attitude, something maintained over a period of time, and to several other mental states which imply 'a degree of ego organization in the subject which is not present at the beginning of life' (Winnicott 1989: 444).

35 A brief account of this theory can be found in Winnicott 1988: 8 and 101–2.

36 Phillips, for instance, says that Winnicott was a 'pragmatist with an essentialist theory' (Phillips 1988: 97).

37 Thus, not as in Freud who states that the individual emerges from an inorganic state.

38 See Winnicott 1996: Chapter 1.

39 This stance is taken by Winnicott in many texts, cf. Winnicott 1986: 13ff. and 1996: Chapters 1 and 29.

40 This idea is developed in Loparic 1996 and 2001.

41 There are several psychoanalysts who took the same direction as Winnicott, for example Ogden (1986) and Mitchell (2000).

42 The same is true, for instance, of his papers on the psychoanalytic technique itself.

References

Abadi, Sonia and Outeiral, José (eds) (1997) *Donald Winnicott na América Latina.* Rio de Janeiro, Revinter.

Abram, J. (2007) *The Language of Winnicott: A Dictionary of Winnicott's Use of Words.* 2nd Ed. London, Karnac Books.

Abram, J. (2008) Donald Woods Winnicott (1896-1971): a brief introduction. *Int J Psychoanal,* 89: 1189–1217.

Fairbairn, W.R.D. (1952) *Psychoanalytic Studies of Personality.* London, Routledge. Fairbairn, W.R.D. (1994) *From Instinct to Self. Selected Papers of W. R. D. Fairbairn,* 2 vols. London, J. Aronson.

Fleck, Ludvik ([1935] 1980) *Entstehung and Entwicklung einer wissenschaftlichen Tatsache.* Frankfurt a. M., Suhrkamp.

Freud, Sigmund: 1953–74: *The Standard Edition of the Complete Psychological Works.* 24 vols. London, The Hogarth Press.

Goldman, Dodi (1993) *In the Search of the Real. The Origins and Originality of D. W. Winnicott.* London, J. Aronson.

Greenberg, Jay R. and Mitchell, Stephen A. (1983) *Object Relations in Psychoanalytic Theory.* Harvard, Harvard University Press.

Heidegger, Martin (1961) *Nietzsche,* 2 vols. Pfullingen, Neske.

Heidegger, Martin (1962) *Being and Time.* New York, Harper & Row.

Heidegger, Martin (1987) *Zollikoner Seminare.* Frankfurt a. M., Klostermann.

Hodge, Jonathan and Radick, Gregory (eds) (2009) *The Cambridge Companion to Darwin.* Cambridge, Cambridge University Press.

Holton, Paul C., Gewirtz, Herbert and Kreutter, Karole J. (eds) (1988) *The Solace Paradigm: An Eclectic Search for Psychological Immunity.* Madison, Conn., International University Press.

Hughes, Judith M. (1989) *Reshaping the Psychoanalytic Domain. The Work of Melanie Klein, W.R.D. Fairbairn, and D.W. Winnicott.* Berkeley, University of California Press.

Jacobs, Michael (1995) *D. W. Winnicott.* London, Sage Publications.

Kuhn, Thomas S. (1970a) *The Structure of Scientific Revolutions.* Chicago, University of Chicago Press.

Kuhn, Thomas S. (1970b) Logic of discovery or psychology of research? In Lakatos and Musgrave (eds): 1–23.

Kuhn, Thomas S. (1990) The road since structure. In *PSA 1990,* 2: 3–13.

Lakatos, Imre and Musgrave, Alan (eds) (1970) *Criticism and the Growth of Knowledge.* London and New York, Cambridge University Press.

Loparic, Z. (1995) Winnicott e o pensamento pós-metafísico. *Psicologia USP*, 6, 2: 39–61.

Loparic, Z. (1996) Winnicott: uma psicanálise não-edipiana. *Percurso*, 9, 17: 41–7.

Loparic, Z. (1999a) O conceito de *Trieb* na psicanálise e na filosofia alemã. In *Filosofia e psicanálise – um diálogo* (ed. Jorge Machado). Porto Alegre, EDI-PUCRS: 97–157.

Loparic, Z. (1999b) Heidegger and Winnicott. *Natureza Humana*, I, 1: 103–35.

Loparic, Z. (2000) Winnicott's paradigm outlined. *Revista latinoamericana de psicopatologia fundamental*, V, 1: 61–98.

Loparic, Z. (2001) Além do inconsciete – sobre a desconstrução heideggeriana da psicanálise. *Natureza Humana*, 3, 1: 91–120.

McDougall, Joyce (1996) *Éros aux mille et un visages*. Paris, Gallimard.

Mitchell, Stephen A. (2000) *Relationality: From Attachment to Intersubjectivity* London, The Analytic Press

Ogden, T.H. (1986) *The Matrix of the Mind: Object Relations and the Psychoanalytic Dialogue*. Northvale, N.J.: J. Aronson.

Phillips, A. (1988) *Winnicott*. London, Fontana Press.

Phillips, A. (1993) *On Kissing, Tickling and Being Bored*. London, Faber and Faber.

Rycroft, Charles (1985) *Psycho-Analysis and Beyond*. London, Chatto & Windus.

Sloterdijk, Peter (1998) *Sphären I*. Frankfurt a. M., Suhrkamp.

Winnicott, D.W. (1958) *Collected Papers: Through Paediatrics to Psycho-analysis,* 1st edition. London: Tavistock. Reprinted 1975 as *Through Paediatrics to Psychoanalysis. Collected Papers*. London: Karnac Books.

Winnicott, D.W. (1964) *The Child, the Family and the Outside World*. London, Penguin.

Winnicott, D.W. (1965) *Maturational Processes and the Facilitating Environment*. London, The Hogarth Press.

Winnicott, D.W. (1971) *Therapeutic Consultations in Child Psychiatry*. London, The Hogarth Press.

Winnicott, D.W. (1986) *Home Is Where We Start From*. London, Penguin.

Winnicott, D.W. (1987) *The Spontaneous Gesture*. London, Harvard University Press.

Winnicott, D.W. (1988) *Human Nature*. London, Free Association Books.

Winnicott, D.W. (1989) *Psycho-Analytic Explorations*. London, Karnac Books.

Winnicott, D.W. (1996) *Thinking about Children*. London, Karnac Books.

PART TWO

Personal perspectives

5

A personal view of the Kleinian contribution[1]

D.W. Winnicott

In the course of your explorations outside Freud's own writings you will already have come across other important names, and you will have met analysts who have contributed in an original way, and whose contributions have been found generally acceptable. For instance, you will have met Anna Freud, who had a unique position in her father's life during the last two decades, and who cared for him with fortitude when he was ill, and you will be familiar at least with her classic summary of psychoanalytic theory in her *Ego and the Mechanisms of Defence* (1936). In any case, Anna Freud has had an immense influence on the way psycho-analysis has developed in the United States, and her stimulating interest in what others are doing has been responsible for much research that is published under other names.

Now Anna Freud was not so important in England as she has been in the United States, simply because of the very great developments that took place in London in the twenty years after the end of World War I, before Miss Freud came over with her father, refugees from Nazi persecution. It was during this period that my own psycho-analytic growth was making root and stem, and it might interest you therefore to hear from me something of the soil in which I had become planted.

You see, there developed a Melanie Klein–Anna Freud controversy, and this has not yet resolved itself. But this was not important for me in my early and formative years, and it is only important to me now in so far as it hampers free thought. In fact Melanie Klein and Anna Freud had a relationship in the Vienna days but this had no meaning for me.

From my point of view psychoanalysis in England was an edifice whose foundation was Ernest Jones. If any man earned my gratitude it was Ernest Jones, and it was Jones to whom I went when I found I needed help in 1923. He put me in touch with James Strachey, to whom I went for analysis for ten years, but I always knew that it was because of Jones that there was a Strachey and a British Psychoanalytical Society for me to use.

So I came to psycho-analysis ignorant of personality clashes between the various analysts, and only too pleased to get effective help for the difficulties that were mine.

I was starting up as consultant paediatrician at that time, and you can imagine how exciting it was to be taking innumerable case histories and to be getting from uninstructed hospital-class parents all the confirmation that anyone could need for the psychoanalytic theories that were beginning to have meaning for me through my own analysis. At that time no other analyst was also a paediatrician, and so for two or three decades I was an isolated phenomenon.

I mention these facts because by being a paediatrician with a knack for getting mothers to tell me about their children and about the early history of their children's disorders, I was soon in the position of being astounded both by the insight psycho-analysis gave into the lives of children and by a certain deficiency in psycho-analytic theory which I will describe. At that time, in the 1920s, everything had the Oedipus complex at its core. The analysis of the psycho-neuroses led the analyst over and over again to the anxieties belonging to the instinctual life at the 4–5 year period in the child's relationship to the two parents. Earlier difficulties that came to light were treated in analyses as regressions to pregenital fixation points, but the dynamics came from conflict at the full-blown genital Oedipus complex of the toddler or late toddler age, that is just before the passing of the Oedipus complex and the onset of the latency period. Now, innumerable case histories showed me that the children who became disturbed, whether psycho-neurotic, psychotic, psycho-somatic or antisocial, showed difficulties in their emotional development in infancy, even as babies. Paranoid hypersensitive children could even have started to be in that pattern in the first weeks or even days of life. Something was wrong somewhere. When I came to treat children by psycho-analysis I was able to confirm the origin of psycho-neurosis in the Oedipus complex, and yet I knew that troubles started earlier.

I gave many tentative and frightened papers to colleagues from the mid-twenties onwards pointing out these facts, and eventually my point of view boiled up into a paper (1936) which I called 'Appetite and Emotional Disorder'. In this I gave samples of the case histories that had to be reconciled somehow with the theory of the Oedipus complex as the point of origin of individual conflicts. Babies could be emotionally ill.

It was an important moment in my life when my analyst broke into his analysis of me and told me about Melanie Klein. He had heard about my careful history-taking and about my trying to apply what I got in my own analysis to the cases of children brought to me for every kind of paediatric disorder. I especially investigated the cases of children brought for nightmares. Strachey said: 'If you are applying psycho-analytic theory to children you should meet Melanie Klein. She has been enticed over to England by Jones to do the analysis of someone special to Jones; she is saying some things that may or may not be true, and you must find out for yourself for you will not get what Melanie Klein teaches in my analysis of you.'

So I went to hear and then to see Melanie Klein, and I found an analyst who had a great deal to say about the anxieties that belong to infancy, and I settled down to working with the benefit of her help. I took her a case written up in great detail, and she had the goodness to read it right through, and on the basis of this one pre-Klein analysis that I did on the basis of my own Strachey analysis I went on to try to learn some of the immense amount that I found she knew already.

This was difficult for me, because overnight I had changed from being a pioneer into being a student with a pioneer teacher. Melanie Klein was a generous teacher, and I counted myself lucky. I remember on one occasion going to her for a supervision, and of a whole week's work I could remember nothing at all. She simply responded by telling me of a case of her own.

I now learned psychoanalysis from Melanie Klein, and I found other teachers comparatively rigid. For one thing, she had an amazing memory. On Saturday evening, if she so wished, she could go over every detail of the week's work with each patient, without reference to notes. She remembered my cases and my analytic material better than I did myself. Later she entrusted me with the analysis of someone near and dear to her, but it should be made clear that I never had analysis by her, or by any of her analysands, so that I did not qualify to be one of her group of chosen Kleinians.[2]

Now I must try to specify what I did get from Melanie Klein. This is difficult because at the time I simply worked on the material of my cases, and on cases she told me about, and I had no idea that what was being taught me was highly original. The thing was that it made sense, and joined up my case-history details with psychoanalytic theory.[3]

For Melanie Klein child analysis was exactly like adult analysis.[4] This was never a trouble from my point of view as I started with the same view, and I hold this view now. The idea of a preparatory period belongs to the type of case, not to a set technique belonging to child analysis.

Then Melanie Klein used sets of very small toys. These I found truly valuable, as they are easily manipulated and they join up with the child's imagination in a special way. It was an advance on talking and also on the drawing which I always used because of the convenience of one's having the drawings to keep to remind one of the nightmare or sample of playing.

Melanie Klein had a way of making inner psychic reality very real. For her a specific play with the toys was a projection from the child's psychic reality which is localized by the child, localized inside the self and the body.

In this way I grew up thinking of the child's manipulation of the little toys, and other special and circumscribed playing as glimpses into the child's inner world, and one saw that psychic reality can be referred to as 'inner' because it does belong to the child's concept of himself (or herself) as having an inside that is part of the self and an outside that is not-me and that is repudiated.

So in this way there was a close connexion between the mental mechanisms of introjection and the function of eating. Also projection had a relation to the bodily functions that are excretory – saliva, sweat, faeces, urine, screaming, kicking, etc.

In this way the material of an analysis either had to do with the child's object relationship or with the mechanisms of introjection and projection. Also the term object relationship could mean relationship to inner or to external objects. The child thus grew in a world, both the child and the world all the time being enriched by projection and introjection. The material for projection and introjection had a pre-history, however, for at basis what is in and of the child was at first taken in relation to the bodily function of eating. In this way, while one could analyse for ever in terms of projection and introjection, the changes came about in relation to the eating, that is the oral erotism and sadism.

Following this, angry biting in the transference in relation to a week-end or a holiday would lead to an increase in the strength of the internal objects that had a persecutory quality. In consequence of this the child had a pain, or felt threatened within, or was sick, or else by the mechanisms of projection the child felt threatened from outside, developed phobias or had threatening fantasies either awake or asleep, or became suspicious. And so on.

Thus a very rich analytic world opened up for me, and the material of my cases confirmed the theories and did so repeatedly. In the end I came to take it all for granted. In any case these ideas are adumbrated in Freud's 'Mourning and Melancholia' (1917); and Abraham (1916) (Klein's teacher in Berlin) opened up the new territory which Melanie Klein so much enjoyed pegging out.

The important thing for me was that while none of the impact of the Oedipus complex was lost, work was now being done on the basis of anxieties related to pregenital drives. One could see that in the more or less pure psycho-neurotic case the pregenital material was regressive and the dynamics belonged to the four-year-old period, but on the other hand, in many cases, there was illness and an organization of defences belonging to the earlier times in the infant's life, and many infants never in fact arrived at so healthy a thing as an Oedipus complex at toddler age.

In my second child training case in the early thirties I was lucky in that I had a girl of three who had started her illness (anorexia) on her first birthday. The material of the analysis was Oedipal, with reactions to the primal scene, and the child was in no way psychotic. Moreover she got well and she is now married happily and rearing her own family. But her Oedipus conflict started on her first birthday when she for the first time sat at table with her two parents. The child, who had shown no symptoms previously, reached out for food, solemnly looked at her two parents, and withdrew her hand. Thus started a severe anorexia, at exactly one year. In the material of the analysis the primal scene appeared as a meal, and sometimes the parents ate the child, whereas at other times the child upset the table (bed) and destroyed the whole set-up. Her analysis was finished in time for her to have a genital Oedipus complex before the onset of the latency period.

But this was an old-fashioned case. Melanie Klein's approach enabled me to work on the infantile conflicts and anxieties and primitive defences whether the patient was child or adult, and gradually threw light on the theory of reactive depression (started by Freud) and

163

the theory of some states characterized by persecutory expectation, and made sense of such things as the clinical alternations to and fro between hypochondria and delusions of persecution, and between depression and the obsessional defence.

All the time working with Klein I found that there was no variation on the strict application of Freudian principles of technique. There was a careful avoidance of stepping outside the analyst's role, and the main interpretations were transference interpretations. This was natural for me because my own analyst was strictly orthodox. [Later I had a second analyst: Mrs Joan Riviere.]

What I did find was a much enriched understanding of the material presented, and in particular I found it to be valuable to be in a position to localize the item of psychic reality, inside or outside, and to get free of the use of the phrase 'weaker fantasy', even spelt with a 'ph.'[5]

Working along Klein lines one came to an understanding of the complex stage of development that Klein called the 'depressive position.' I think this is a bad name, but it is true that clinically, in psychoanalytic treatments, arrival at this position involves the patient in being depressed. Here being depressed is an achievement, and implies a high degree of personal integration, and an acceptance of responsibility for all the destructiveness that is bound up with living, with the instinctual life, and with anger at frustration.

Klein was able to make it clear to me from the material my patients presented, how the capacity for concern and to feel guilty is an achievement, and it is this rather than depression that characterizes arrival at the depressive position in the case of the growing baby and child.

Arrival at this stage is associated with ideas of restitution and reparation, and indeed the human individual cannot accept the destructive and aggressive ideas in his or her own nature without experience of reparation, and for this reason the continued presence of the love object is necessary at this stage since only in this way is there opportunity for reparation.

This is Klein's most important contribution, in my opinion, and I think it ranks with Freud's concept of the Oedipus complex. The latter concerns a three-body relationship and Klein's depressive position concerns a two-body relationship – that between the infant and the mother. The main ingredient is a degree of ego-organization and strength in the baby or young child, and for this reason it is difficult to place the beginnings of the depressive position earlier than 8–9 months, or a year. But what does it matter?

All this belongs to the era between the wars, when there was rapid growth in the British Society and when Klein was the fertilizing agent. Paula Heimann and Susan Isaacs were in support, and also Joan Riviere, my second analyst.

Since those days a great deal has happened, and I do not claim to be able to hand out the Klein view in a way that she would herself approve of. I believe my views began to separate out from hers, and in any case I found she had not included me in as a Kleinian. This did not matter to me because I have never been able to follow anyone else, not even Freud. But Freud was easy to criticize because he was always critical of himself. For instance, I simply cannot find value in his idea of a Death Instinct.[6]

Well, Klein has done a great deal more that we cannot afford to ignore. She has gone deeper and deeper into the mental mechanisms of her patients and then has applied her concepts to the growing baby. I think it is here that she has made mistakes because deeper in psychology does not always mean earlier.[7]

It has become an important part of the Klein theory to postulate a paranoid-schizoid position which dates from the very beginning. This term paranoid-schizoid is certainly a bad one, but we nevertheless cannot ignore the fact that we meet, in a vitally important way, the two mechanisms (1) talion dread (2) splitting of the object into 'good' and 'bad.'

Klein seemed to think at the end that infants start in this way, but this seems to ignore the fact that with good-enough mothering the two mechanisms may be relatively unimportant until the ego-organization has made the baby capable of using projection and introjection mechanisms in gaining control over objects. If there is not good-enough mothering, then the result is chaos rather than talion dread and a splitting of the object into 'good' and 'bad.'

In regard to good and bad, I think it doubtful whether these words can be used before the infant has become able to sort out benign from persecutory internal objects.

So much of what Klein wrote in the last two decades of her fruitful life may have been spoilt by her tendency to push the age at which mental mechanisms appear further and further back, so that she even found the depressive position in early weeks; also she paid lip-service to environmental provision, but would never fully acknowledge that along with the dependence of early infancy is truly a period in which it is not possible to describe an infant without describing the mother whom the infant has not yet become able to separate from a self. Klein claimed to have paid full attention to the environmental factor, but it is my opinion that she was temperamentally incapable of this. Perhaps there was a gain in this, for certainly she had a powerful drive to go further and further back into the personal individual mental mechanisms that constitute the new human being who is at the bottom rung of the ladder of emotional development.

The main point is that whatever criticism we may want to make of Klein's standpoint in her last two decades, we cannot ignore the very great impact her work had in England, and will have everywhere, on orthodox psychoanalysis.

As for the controversy between Klein and Anna Freud, and between the followers of each, this has no importance to me, nor will it have to you, because it is a local matter, and a strong wind will blow it away. The only important thing is that psychoanalysis, firmly based on Freud, shall not miss Klein's contribution which I shall now attempt to summarize:

Strict orthodox technique in psychoanalysis of children.

Technique facilitated by use of tiny toys in initial stages.

Technique for analysis of two-and-a-half-year-old children and all ages older.

Recognition of fantasy as localized by the child (or adult), i.e. inside or outside the self.

Understanding of internal benign and persecutory forces or 'objects' and their origin in satisfactory or unsatisfactory instinctual experiences (originally oral and oral sadistic).

Importance of projection and introjection as mental mechanisms developed in relation to the child's experience of the bodily functions of incorporation and excretion.

Emphasis on the importance of destructive elements in object relationships, i.e. apart from anger at frustration.

Development of a theory of the individual's attainment of a capacity for concern (depressive position).

Relationship of constructive play
      work
      potency and child-bearing
   to the depressive position.

Understanding of denial of depression (manic defence).

Understanding of threatened chaos in inner psychic reality and defences related to this chaos (obsessional neurosis or depressive mood).

Postulation of infantile impulses, talion fears and the splitting of the object prior to attainment of ambivalence.

Always an attempt to state the infant's psychology without reference to the quality of the environmental provision.

Then come certain more *doubtful* contributions:

Retaining a use of the theory of the Life and Death Instincts.

An attempt to state infantile destructiveness in terms of

(a) heredity
(b) envy

Notes

1 This paper was a talk given to the candidates of the Los Angeles Psychoanalytic Society, 3rd October 1962. It was first published in 1965 in *The Maturational Processes and the Facilitating Environment* London: The Hogarth Press.
2 According to Pearl King (King and Steiner 1991) Winnicott was indeed designated one of Klein's supporters at the very beginning of the Controversial Discussions. But as it was only at the beginning one wonders if Winnicott had forgotten this or felt it was easier not to go into any detail (Editor's Note).
3 This tradition of focusing on clinical work is still prevalent in the British P-A Society (Editor's Note).
4 This is one of the main differences between Melanie Klein and Anna Freud. The latter believed that child analysis should be different from adult analysis (Editor's Note).
5 Winnicott does not elaborate here but it is striking that across his work he does not use the 'ph' when he uses the word 'fantasy' (Editor's Note).
6 See Chapter 13.
7 See Chapter 1.

References

Abraham, K. (1916) 'The first pregenital stage of the libido', in *Selected Papers of Karl Abraham* (1927); trans. D. Bryan and A. Strachey, London: Hogarth.
Freud, A. (1936) *The Ego and the Mechanisms of Defence* (1937), London: Hogarth.
Freud, S. (1917) 'Mourning and Melancholia', in J. Strachey (ed) (1957) *The Standard Edition of the Complete Psychological Works of Sigmund Freud*, vol 14, London: Hogarth/Institute of Psychoanalysis.
King, P., Steiner, R. (1991) *The Freud–Klein Controversies 1941–45*, London and New York: Tavistock/Routledge.
Winnicott, D. W. (1936) 'Appetite and Emotional Disorder', in *Collected Papers: Through Paediatrics to Psycho-Analysis* (1958), London: Tavistock/ New York: Basic Books.

Winnicott

Overlapping circles and the two way journey[1]

Marion Milner

Winnicott and the two-way journey

This paper was my contribution to the memorial meeting for D.W. Winnicott, given to the British Psycho-Analytical Society in 1972. Often, when I talked to people about D.W. Winnicott they would say, 'Oh, but of course, he was a genius.' I do not know what makes a genius. All I know is that I must take as my text for this paper something he once said to his students just before a lecture: 'What you get out of me, you will have to pick out of chaos.'

I want to describe the highlights of my contacts with him in matters of theory. I find this particularly hard to do, because I am one of those people who Freud reminded us exist, people who think in pictures. So what I want to say about Winnicott must centre around certain visual images.

One night in 1957, driving through France, I saw a crowd in the market-place of a little town, all gathered around an arc lamp where a trapeze had been set up by travelling acrobats. The star performers were there, in spotless white, doing wonderful turns and handstands on the bar. Below them was a little clown in a grey floppy coat too big for him, just fooling around while the others did their displays. Occasionally he made a fruitless attempt to jump up and reach the bar. Then, suddenly, he made a great leap and there he was, whirling around on the bar, all his clothes flying out, like a huge Catherine wheel, to roars of delight from the crowd.

This is my image of Winnicott. Often over the years when we had a gap of time and arranged to meet to discuss some theoretical problem, he would open the door, and there he would be, all over the place, whistling, forgetting something, running upstairs, making a general clatter, so that I would become impatient for him to settle down. Gradually, I came to see this as a necessary preliminary to those fiery flashes of his intuition that would always follow. He has actually written about the logic of this in one of his papers, where he talks of the necessity, when doing an analysis, of recognizing and allowing for phases of nonsense, when no thread ought to be searched for in the patient's material because what is going on is preliminary chaos, the first phase of the creative process.[2]

After the whirling clown on the bar comes another image, an actual Catherine wheel firework, nailed to a tree and lit by a small boy, in the still dark of the countryside. The wheel at first splutters and misfires, then gets going as a fizzing, fiery ring of light, sending off sparks into the darkness around. I always have an image of the dark disc at the centre whenever I read in his writings about the unknowable core of the self.

My third image, woven into my thoughts for this paper, is part of a shared joke we had. During the war I had shown him a cartoon from the New Yorker. It was of two hippopotamuses, their heads emerging from the water, and one saying to the other, 'I keep thinking it's Tuesday.' It was typical of him that he never forgot this joke. After all these years, I see how it fits in with a dominant preoccupation of mine – the threshhold of consciousness, the surface of the water as the place of submergence or emergence.

And from this picture of the water's surface I come to one of his images, that is, the quotation from Tagore[3] that he put at the head of his paper 'The Location of Cultural Experience',[4] 'On the sea-shore of endless worlds children play'. I too have had this line at the back of my mind, ever since I first read it in 1915. Winnicott said that, for him, the aphorism aided speculation upon the question, if play is neither inside nor outside, where is it? For me it stirred thoughts of the coming and going of the tides, the rhythmic daily submergence and smoothing out of this place where children play.

Later in this paper about the place of cultural experience he uses another image that we both had in common – only I had completely forgotten about it. He is talking about how the baby comes to be able to make use of the symbol of union and can begin to allow for and benefit from separation, a separation that is not separation, but a form of union; and here he refers to a drawing that I made, long ago in the 1930s, showing the interplay of the edges of two jugs. He says the drawing conveyed to him the tremendous significance there can be in the interplay of edges.

I too found myself using this same drawing as a visual symbol for his concept of potential space. And it still has many overtones for me, since a patient of mine used it constantly, in the more abstract form of overlapping circles which become two faces and then oscillate between being two and being one.

So much for the images. Now for the actuality.

I first saw Winnicott when he was giving a public lecture in the late 1930s, talking about his work with mothers and babies and the famous spatula game. He told how he would leave a spatula on the table in front of the mother and baby, well within the baby's reach. Then he simply watched what the baby did with the spatula, watched for variations in the normal pattern of reaching for it, grabbing it, giving it a good suck and then chucking it away. He told how, out of this very simple experimental situation, he could work out, according to the observed blocks in the various stages, a diagnosis of the problems between the mother and the baby. As he talked, I was captivated by the mixture in him of deep seriousness and his love of little jokes, that is, the play aspect of his character, if one thinks of true play as transcending the opposites of serious and non-serious.

It was after this lecture that I began to attend his clinic as an observer, and I well remember the pleasure he took in this spatula game. I feel it was the neatness that satisfied both the artist and the scientist in the man, the formal qualities so simple and clear, providing a structure within which he made his observations. And this same feeling for aesthetic form continued in his therapeutic use with children of what he called the squiggle game. In fact, as described in his book on the subject, he used these games to structure the therapeutic consultations.[5] Each account of those drawing sessions with the child exemplifies as well his beautiful concept of potential space – an essentially pictorial concept, although he defines it as 'what happens between two people when there is trust and reliability'. Thus there is also the way the account of each session organizes time. Time stretches back, not only through the child's lifetime, but also through Winnicott's own years of psychoanalytic practice, so that he has at his fingertips the tools of psychoanalytic concepts, though using them here in a different setting.

Then there is what I have gained from his concept of the holding environment. I will not say much about this, for I have already given it extensive form in my book about a patient's drawings, having even embodied the idea in my title: *The Hands of the Living God*.[6] The phrase is in fact taken from a poem by D. H. Lawrence, a poem in which Lawrence describes the ghastly feelings of terror at falling forever when contact with the inner holding environment is lost.[7]

I would in addition like to say something about Winnicott's comment, in his paper on play,[8] on my 1952 paper on the play of a boy patient.[9] Near the beginning of his paper Winnicott points out that I have related playing to concentration in adults, and that he has done the same thing. A little later he quotes my remark about 'moments when the original poet in us created the world for us perhaps forgotten. . . because they were too much like visitations of the gods'. His quoting this reminded me that one of the jumping-off places for my paper had been a growing preoccupation with certain moments in the boy's play, moments which seemed both to express and to be accompanied by a special kind of concentration, moments actually symbolized, it seemed to me, by his continual play with lighted candles and fires in the dark, as well as by explicit play concerning visitations of the gods. All this seems to me now to link up with what Winnicott came to call 'creative apperception', the colouring of external reality in a new way, a way that can give a feeling of great significance and can in fact, as he claims, make life feel worth living, even in the face of much instinct deprivation.

I realized too that this starting-point for that paper of mine had also been the starting-point for the first book I ever wrote, a book based on a diary I kept in 1926, about the sudden moments when one's whole perception of the world changes – changes that happen, sometimes apparently out of the blue, but sometimes as the result of a deliberate shift of attention, one that makes the whole world seem newly created.[10] Although when I became an analyst I tried to fit these experiences into such psychoanalytic concepts as manic defences against depression and so on, these ideas did not seem quite adequate to account for the phenomena. But then I found Winnicott making the distinction between the vicissitudes of instinct and what happens in creativity, which for him was the same as creative playing. This seemed to offer a more useful approach. Not that I found his way of putting his ideas about creativity entirely easy: sometimes he seemed to be talking about a way of looking at the world, sometimes about a way of doing something deliberately, and sometimes about simply enjoying a bodily activity, breathing, for instance, that just happens. I asked myself, in what sense are these all creative? Certainly they are different, as he says, from the making of anything, such as a house or a meal or a picture, though all these may include what he is talking about. Then I happened upon a statement that helped me clarify the problem. It was Martin Buber's remark about 'productivity versus immediacy of the lived life'.[11] He was referring to what he called the dominant delusion of our time, that creativity (meaning, I supposed, *artistic* creativity) is the criterion of human worth. Buber went on to say that 'the potentiality of form also accompanies every experience that befalls the nonartistic man and is given an issue as often as he lifts an image out of the stream of perception and inserts it into his memory as something single, definite and meaningful in itself'. This phrase – lifting an image out of the stream of perception – clearly related to Winnicott's comment, 'What you get out of me you must pick out of chaos.' Thus one gets the idea of creativeness as not simply perceiving, but as deliberately relating ourselves to our perceiving. It is a perceiving that has an 'I AM' element in it. And this brings me to Winnicott's use of the word *self*.

First, what does he say about the way self comes into being? He claims that the sense of self comes only from desultory formless activity or rudimentary play, and then only if reflected back; he adds that it is only in being creative that one discovers oneself. I have a difficulty here. I can understand him when he claims that the sense of self comes on the basis of the unintegrated state, but when he adds that this state is by definition not observable or communicable, I begin to wonder. Not communicable, yes. Not observable, I am not so sure. I think of the dark still centre of the whirling Catherine wheel and feel fairly certain that it can, in the right setting, be related to by the conscious ego discovering that it can turn in upon itself, make contact with the core of its own being, and find there a renewal, a rebirth. In fact isn't Winnicott himself referring to this when he speaks of 'quietude linked with stillness?' This reminds me of T. S. Eliot's 'still point of the turning world' or 'words after speech reach into silence'.[12]

Linked to this question of the discovery of the self is surely the discovery of one's own body. So the question arises: what is the relation of the sense of being, which Winnicott says must precede the finding of the self, to the awareness of one's own body? I think there is a hint about this when he speaks of the 'summation or reverberation of experiences of relaxation in conditions of trust based on experience'. For me this phrase stirs echoes throughout years of observation of how deliberate bodily relaxation brings with it, if one can wait for it, a reverberation from inside, something spreading waves, something that brings an intense feeling of response from that bit of the outer world that is at the same time also oneself: one's own body. Here is what I think he means when he speaks of enjoying one's own breathing as an example of creativity.

As for his statements concerning the first toy, which he says we do not challenge as to its coming from inside or from outside, these serve as a bridge for me, particularly to the special cultural field of religion.[13] When I encounter, in a book entitled *The God I Want,* the idea that to discover God as myself is also to discover Him as other than myself, when I read that receiving implies otherness and that at the same time what we receive is our own, I am reminded of the creative paradox so dear to Winnicott.[14] And when he speaks of the transitional object as the symbol of a journey, it seems really to be a two-way journey: both to the finding of the objective reality of the subject – the I AM.

There was, as well as this word creativity and all its implications, another term that, since the late 1940s, had given me a lot of uneasiness, like a shoe beginning to feel too tight. The term was *primary process.* I had been taught that this was a form of archaic thinking that had to be outgrown. But slowly, over the years, primary process seems to have changed its meaning, so that it is now seen, certainly by some writers, as part of the integrating function of the ego, in order to preserve the ego's wholeness. As such it is not something to be grown out of, but, rather, is complementary to secondary process functioning, and as necessary to it as male and female are to each other. It is this primary process that enables one to accept paradox and contradiction, something that secondary process does not like at all, being itself bound by logic, which rejects contradiction. Although Winnicott hardly ever uses the term, I feel that given this new meaning, the concept of primary process is implicit in all of his work and integral to his idea of what it means to be healthy.

So what the hippopotamus joke means to me now is this: One must not try to make the hippo live only on land, because it is, by nature, incurably amphibious. And whatever it means to say that someone is a genius, I do wish to make clear that I believe Winnicott was on excellent terms with his primary process; it was an inner marriage to which there was very little impediment.

173

Overlapping circles

In this paper I have decided to limit myself to certain ideas of D.W. Winnicott's that seem to have been most fertilizing for my own thinking. To do this I will take as my starting-point a reference of his to the drawing of the two jugs that I made in the 1930s. I have also chosen this drawing because it foreshadowed, for me, the image of overlapping circles made many years later by my patient, Susan, an image which had, still later, become a kind of flag or model for my own thinking about my work with patients and with myself.

Winnicott's reference to my drawing was in his paper about the place for cultural experience (Winnicott 1971). It occurs when he is talking about how the baby comes to be able to make use of the symbol of union and becomes more able to allow for and benefit from separation and a separation that is not a separation, but a form of union. As I have said, my drawing had been made from nature years before I ever knew of Winnicott or his work. The two jugs were placed side by side, one slightly in front of the other so that they could, in fact, be seen as two circles overlapping.[15] As I have said my concern in making the drawing had been with observing how shadows cut across or bring about a merging of boundaries; his response to it was to say that I had drawn his attention to the tremendous significance that there can be in the interplay of edges. My concern now in using the image is with the area of overlap in the circles just because it is impossible to say which circle the area belongs to since it belongs to both. Because of this it seemed to me an apt symbol for Winnicott's concept of the transitional area that he says is the place where all culture belongs.

The second place of overlap occurs in his paper on play,[16] where he refers to the paper I wrote about the play of the boy, Simon, moments particularly concerned with lighted candles and fires in the dark.[17] Now I realized that this starting-point of moments in the boy's play had also been the starting-point for the first book I ever wrote, those sudden moments when one's whole perception of the world changed, or as Winnicott has put it, became coloured in a new way.

There is the further overlap in his paper on playing when he says that I related playing to concentration in adults and that he has done the same thing, but he then goes on to talk of a difference between us. He says that, while I was talking about the prelogical fusion of

174

subject and object, he was trying to distinguish between this fusion and the fusion or defusion between the subjective object and the object objectively perceived. But he adds that he thinks this theme is inherent in the material I presented.

I therefore tried to see more clearly what this difference between us might imply. For instance, as I have said, my paper had also been an attempt to work through some misgivings I had felt about what seemed to me to be the too – narrow aspects of the classical Freudian concept of symbol formation. It was as a result of this attempt that I had tried out wording Freud's 'two principles of mental functioning' in terms of this fusion or defusion between subject and object; that is in terms of two ways of being which differ according to whether one feels joined up, merged with what one looks at, or separate from it. It had only slowly become apparent to me that we know a lot about the separated state of mind, since our very speech depends on it (subject, verb, object), but that the unseparated phase, that of merged boundaries, is quite a different matter and is defended against, partly out of fear, fear that it means some kind of loss of definition, loss of identity, even loss of sanity.

What had followed had been this idea that the illusion of no–separateness between either the subject and the object, or between what Winnicott came to talk about as the subjective object and the objective object, could possibly be a necessary phase in all creativity, even in the process of coming to perceive the reality of the external world at all. In fact it had seemed that perception itself is a creative process. So it was here that I had had to think of Santayana's way of putting it:

> Perception is no primary phase of consciousness; it is an ulterior function acquired by a dream which has become symbolic of its own external conditions, and therefore relevant to its own destiny.[18]

In fact this is the statement which had become so important to me when writing *On Not Being Able to Paint*, from 1940 onwards.

'Symbolic of its own external conditions', surely this was another way, though a more academic one, of describing what Winnicott talks about of how the mother's breast becomes felt by the baby to be what he needs; or as Winnicott puts it, the baby comes imaginatively to 'create' the breast? In short, by now I was nearly coming

175

to believe that this recurrent phase of feeling one with what one sees is part of the rhythm of oneness – twoness, unity – separation that the creator in all of us has used, from earliest infancy, to make the world significant to us, a capacity which is perhaps what William Blake meant by his phrase 'each man's poetic genius'.

(Blake 1788?)

Having struggled to reach this point it was no surprise to me to read Winnicott's statement that creativity belongs to being alive, that it belongs to the whole approach of a person (if not ill) to external reality.[19] Yet when I settled down to consider the various other ways in which he uses this word creativity I had to draw on further experiences on my own. In the first place, I thought about how he says that anything that happens to one is creative, unless stultified by the environment. I asked myself just exactly what does he mean by this? Sometimes he seems to be talking about a way of looking at the world, sometimes about a way of doing something deliberately and sometimes about simply enjoying a bodily activity that just happens, such as, he says, enjoying breathing.

Certainly I did have to ask myself, in what sense are all these creative? I could agree when he says they are different from the making of any thing, such as a house or a meal or a picture, though, as he says, all of these may include what he means by creative. And when he talks of just enjoying breathing, I found it linked up with the whole collection of observations about different kinds of concentration that I have already written about in the Athens and the mysticism papers (see Chapters 14 and 18 in Milner 1987).

While trying to link up these statements of Winnicott's with my own enquiries I even remembered an example of how I had, long before becoming an analyst, observed the effects of simple non-purposive looking. For example, I had noticed how, through staring at an outside object that one especially liked (or even an object that one did not like, for instance, an ugly white tin mug), staring at it in a contemplative way, without any ideas about making use of it, there had gradually emerged a feeling of change in one's whole body perception as well as a move towards a feeling of intense interest in the sheer 'thusness', the separate and unique identity, of the thing I was staring at.[20]

This effect of the changing awareness of one's own body on one's perception of the object and also the opposite set of phenomena, the effect of certain kinds of concentrating on the object on one's own body awareness naturally took me back to my Athens paper[21] and Ruskin's experience with the tree.[22] It also took me to my own attempts to describe what happened in terms of change to proprioceptive sensations, a change from a body image, or images, to body perceptions, that is from body re-presentation to body presentation. In fact, to a perception that is concerned with the actual coenaesthetic awareness of one's existence in space and time, including the sense of one's own weight and natural speed of moving and awareness of one's breathing. In addition, there was the fact that this deliberately directing one's attention to the body presentation requires a wide focus of attention; it cannot be done with the narrow focus which is a characteristic aspect of discursive argumentative thought. Also, when it did happen there was, as I have said, not the narcissistic impoverishment of one's relation to the external world that one might have expected, but an actual enrichment of it. Not only this but also I had found that it resulted in a sense of well-being that is a different kind from that which results from lack of tension between the ego and the super-ego, as when feeling one has lived up to one's standards.

Something else that I had to consider in all this was the fact that the direct body presentation has no clear boundary. This now reminded me of the child's first 'not-me' possession, what Winnicott called the transitional object, the bit of blanket or its equivalent, and later the teddy bear or woolly animal and how they are nearly always fluffy, perhaps partly suggesting, I thought, the fuzziness of the sense of the body boundary in direct sensation.[23] Further, it seemed that this kind of direct body awareness must be, developmentally, a capacity intimately bound up with the mother's, or her substitute's, loving care of the infant's body and so can be an important aspect of what Winnicott calls 'the facilitating environment' that is necessary for the infant if fullest maturation is to occur. I suspected too that Winnicott himself knew a lot about this kind of relation to the body and that it could have entered into his so astonishing awareness of what was going on in all those child-therapeutic consultations where he used what he called the squiggle game, that is when he and the child in turn drew a squiggle and the other made it into whatever caught his or her fancy.[24]

As for what Winnicott calls the 'holding' aspect of the facilitating environment I have already given extensive form to my debt to this concept in the book about my patient, Susan, and even embodied it in the title of the book, *The Hands Of The Living God*, with its association to falling in D. H. Lawrence's poem.[25] Significantly Winnicott himself talks about the feeling of falling forever, as an aspect of what he calls 'unthinkable anxiety'.

There was another and related area of overlap which was connected with what Winnicott says about relaxation. He talks of 'the summation or reverberation of experiences of relaxation in conditions of trust based on experience.'[26] This sentence had echoes for me throughout years of observations of how deliberate bodily relaxation brings with it, if one can wait for it, deep reverberation from within, something spreading in waves, something that brings an intense feeling of response from that bit of the outer world that is yet also one's self, one's own body.

This theme now brought me once more to consider something of what he has to say about the sense of self in relation to creativity. As I have said, up to now I had found that I could go a long way with him in his ideas about creativity, that is with the idea of it as not just perceiving, but as deliberately relating ourselves to our own perceiving, which has an 'I am' element in it. I therefore continued to consider what he has to say about the sense of 'I am' – or lack of it – in relation to creativity and the difficulty I had had here. Thus, although he says that it is only in being creative that one discovers one's self, he also says that the actual work of art, the finished creation, never heals an underlying lack of sense of self. I thought I could agree here with what he says about the finished creation but I felt a need to consider further just what his use of the phrase 'sense of self' implies. For instance, I still thought I could agree when he says that the sense of self comes into being on the basis of a rudimentary kind of play that reflects back. But I still could not agree wholeheartedly that it is also unobservable. However, it could be that observable is the wrong word and that one should say 'contactable'. Certainly I had found that there is a contact that can result in a renewal, a rebirth; provided, that is, that one is prepared to stop the inner chatter of introspective arguments and face the inner silence, the basic formlessness from which all form comes, and which at first can feel like total emptiness, annihilation even, and be defended against at almost any cost. And especially so when this inner silence is liable to get mixed up with the phantasy of the destruction of the inner needed object. In fact, for some patients this is a crucial issue, especially those who are afraid of, intolerant of, being alone. Often it seems they cannot find renewal by relating themselves to the formless core of their own being, and it may be that they cannot do this partly because of fears of the results of their own destructive phantasies against their good inner objects. Thus inner silence can mean that everybody is dead.

It was after I had just read for the first time Winnicott's paper on the destruction of the good object that I rang him up and said, 'Yes, but just why does the good object have to be destroyed?'[27] He thought for a little and then said, 'Because it is necessary.' This idea led to a welding process in me, it joined up his idea of the need to destroy the satisfying object with all that I had thought about primary omnipotence and the intensity of the shock of disillusionment, the sheer incredulity and abysmal depth of dread that can come at the discovery that one is not omnipotent, if it comes, through environmental failure, at a moment when the ego is not strong enough to bear it, when it has even been feeling, not only that it was king of the castle but also that it was both king and castle itself.

Such ideas naturally led me on to the theme of nothingness, or zero, and the thought that one of the advantages of the overlapping circles model was that it can be adapted by bringing the two circles closer and closer together till they coincide as a single circle; in fact, a unity which can be seen as either everything or nothing, as a total eclipse of the sun, a dark night of the soul, or a blissful consummation.

Since Winnicott died in 1971 it is unlikely that he knew about a saying of Freud's which was not published till 1975. In a short paper Bruno Goetz tells of how he, as a young poet fascinated by the Bhagavadgita, had had talks with Freud (during 1905 and 1906) in which Freud said:[28]

> Do you know what it means to be confronted by nothingness? the Hindu Nirvana is not nothingness, it is that which transcends all contradictions. It is . . . the ultimate in superhuman understanding, an ice-cold, all-comprehending yet scarcely com-prehensible insight. Or, if misunderstood it is madness.

Could Winnicott's concept of 'unthinkable anxiety' fit in somewhere here?

Re-reading this paper at the end of 1986 and nearly ten years after it was written, I felt the need to add to my flag another visual model; I remembered once hearing Wilfred Bion say that one should not have too many theories but could have as many models as one liked. The added model that I now found myself enjoying was a diagram said to

179

have been used by Wittgenstein with his students. He asked them to say what they thought the diagram represented.

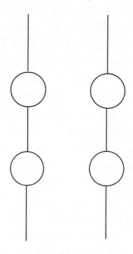

His answer was 'A koala bear climbing a tree'. In practice I have found that this answer usually brings a gasp of surprised laughter, following the imaginative leap of filling the emptiness, the nothingness between the two lines and the four circles, filling this no-thing with a some-thing and that something very much alive.

For myself, I found the experience of the four small circles suddenly coming together to form the unseen image of a living wholeness useful in clinical work. It provided me with a symbol for thinking about those patients with a precarious sense of self who can suddenly come together, even though maybe only momentarily, instead of existing in isolated fragments. It also provided me with a condensed symbol for the infant's achievement of coming to recognize that all the different contacts with the mother, both 'bad' and 'good' do come together and add up to a whole living person.

In fact, here was the imaginative leap which can be looked upon as ushering in what Melanie Klein called the 'depressive position'[29] and what Winnicott, on the whole, prefers to call 'the phase of concern'.[30]

I also found myself using the diagram with its empty space between the two lines as a way of reminding myself how emptiness, formlessness, must be the basis of new forms, almost perhaps that one has to be willing to feel oneself becoming nothing in order to become something.

As for the area of overlap in the two circles model, I found myself using it, amongst many other ways, as standing for the overlap between, on the one hand, whatever it is that we call mind, psyche, consciousness, and on the other hand, what we call body, a model for what can happen when consciousness does deliberately suffuse the whole body, when 'soul' and 'body' do meet again.

It is also, for me, a convenient way of thinking about what could perhaps be seen as the aim of all therapy, the bringing together of both the accepted and the rejected part of the personality; in fact, to allow the interpenetration of opposites to form a new whole.

References and notes (as in original publication)

1 Editor's Note: This paper is a combination of two papers. 'Winnicott and the two-way journey' was Milner's contribution to the memorial meeting for D.W. Winnicott, given to the British Psychoanalytical Society in 1972 and first published in 1978 in S. Grolnick (ed.) *Between Reality and Phantasy: Transitional Objects Phenomena.* London and New York: J. Aronson. It was published for a second time in 1987 in Marion Milner's collection of papers for the New Library *The Suppressed Madness of Sane Men.* Later, in 1977, Milner was commissioned to write an article for *L'Arc*, a French journal, that dedicated one issue to the work of D.W. Winnicott. That essay was published in 1977 under the title 'Winnicott and Overlapping Circles'.

2 Winnicott, D.W. (1971) Playing: Creative Activity and the Search for the Self. In *Playing and Reality.* London: Tavistock.

3 Tagore, R. (1986) *Collected Poems and Plays.* London: Macmillan.

4 Winnicott, D.W. (1971) The Location of Cultural Experience. In *Playing and Reality.* London: Tavistock.

5 Winnicott, D.W. (1971) *Therapeutic Consultations in Child Psychiatry.* New York: Basic Books.

6 Milner, M. (1969) *The Hands of the Living God.* London: Hogarth.

7 Lawrence, D. H. (1929) *Pansies.* London: Secker.

8 Winnicott, D.W. (1971) Playing: A Theoretical Statement. In *Playing and Reality.* London: Tavistock.

9 Aspects of Symbolism in Comprehension of the Not-Self. *International Journal of Psychoanalysis* 33: 181–95.

10 Milner, M. (1952) The Role of Illusion in Symbol Formation. In M. Klein, P. Heimann, S. Isaacs, and J. Riviere (eds.) *New Directions in Psychoanalysis.* London: Tavistock.

11 Buber, M. (1969) *The Healthy Personality.* Reading edited by Hung-min Chiang and A. Maslow. London: Van Nostrand Reinhold.

12 Eliot, T.S. (1959) Burnt Norton. In *Four Quartets.* London: Faber & Faber.

13 Winnicott, D.W. (1953) Transitional Objects and Transitional Phenomena. In *Collected Papers.* New York: Basic Books.

14 Williams, I.H.A. (1967) (ed. J. Mitchell) *The God I Want*. London: Constable.

15 Milner, M. (1950) *On Not Being Able to Paint*. London: Heinemann.

16 Winnicott, D.W. (1971) Playing: A Theoretical Statement. In *Playing and Reality*. London: Tavistock.

17 Milner, M. (1952) Aspects of Symbolism in Comprehension of the Not-Self. *International Journal of Psychoanalysis* 33(2): 181–95.

18 Santayana, G. (1920) The Suppressed Madness of Sane Men. In *Little Essays*. London: Constable.

19 Winnicott, D.W. (1971) Creativity and its Origins. In *Playing and Reality*. London: Tavistock.

20 Milner, M. (1934) *A Life of One's Own*. London: Chatto & Windus.

21 Milner, M. (1956) The Communication of Primary Sensual Experience (The Yell of Joy). *Int J Psychoanal*. 37: 278–81.

22 Milner, M. (1960) The concentration of the body: 236. In (1989) *The Suppressed Madness of Sane Men*. The New Library of Psychoanalysis and The Institute of Psychoanalysis.

23 Winnicott, D.W. (1951) Transitional Objects and Transitional Phenomena. In (1958) *Collected Papers*. London: Tavistock.

24 Winnicott, D.W. (1971) *Therapeutic Consultations in Child Psychiatry*. London: Hogarth and the Institute of Psychoanalysis.

25 'It's a fearful thing to fall into the hands of the living God. But it is a much more fearful thing to fall out of them.' Milner, M. (1969) *The Hands of the Living God*. London: Hogarth.

26 Winnicott, D.W. (1971) Playing: Creative Activity and the Search for the Self. In *Playing and Reality*. London: Tavistock.

27 Winnicott, D.W. (1971) The Use of an Object and Relating Through Identification. *International Journal of Psychoanalysis* 50: 711–16.

28 Goetz, B. (1975) That Is All I Have to Say about Freud. *International Review of Psychoanalysis* 2(2): 139–43.

29 Klein, M. (1935) A Contribution to the Psychogenesis of Manic-depressive States. In (1948) *Contributions to Psychoanalysis*. London: Hogarth & Institute of Psychoanalysis.

30 Winnicott, D.W. (1954–5) The Depressive Position in Normal Emotional Development. In (1958) *Collected Papers*. London: Tavistock.

Potential space in psychoanalysis[1]

The object in the setting

André Green

The object in analysis – the analysis of the object – the object of analysis

On several occasions, Freud was led to assert that psychoanalytic concepts have chiefly an heuristic value and that only secondarily can they be defined more rigorously or replaced by others. No concept since the founding of psychoanalysis has been more broadly utilized than that of the object. According to Littré, the French Academy Dictionary gives the same illustration in defining the word 'subject' as it does in defining the word 'object': natural bodies are the *subject* of physics; natural bodies are the *object* of physics. Rather than deplore the confusion that arises here, or protest against philosophies which would divide subject and object absolutely, I wish instead to emphasize that their relationship is one of symmetry or of complementarity: no object without a subject, no subject without an object. From Freud's time to ours psychoanalytic theory has not been able to avoid facing up to the truth of this.

Freud completely disrupted the old relation between subject and object. Instead of opposing to the object the subject as it was defined by philosophical tradition, he coupled the object to the drive – the *anti-subject*. For it is quite clear that the drive cannot assume a subjective function. In his theory, drive – and the agency which connotes it, the id – represents for Freud that which is the most impersonal, the least capable of an individual will: both because it is rooted in the body and because it is associated with the radical characteristics of the species as such.

Although the drive of Freudian theory is sharply distinguished from the classical notion of instinct, the two remain related by their fundamentally improper 'nature' – that is, in their departure from the propriety of self sameness of the subject. However, with the development of object relations theory, Freud's concept of the ego could no longer provide an adequate theoretical complement to newly emergent formulations of the object. Attempts to supply this deficiency led to the elaboration of such ego-related concepts as the 'self' and the 'I'. Thus the subjectivity of the subject (which Freud had managed, as it were, to bracket off) makes its reappearance in contemporary analytic theory. It returns explicitly in Pasche who gives it an existential dimension, and in Lacan, who, following the structuralist movement, insists on its impersonal character and relates its effects to those of a non-representable set of combinations which he calls the order of the Symbolic. Elsewhere, and from different cultural perspectives, Hartmann, Jacobson, Spitz, Winnicott, Kohut, and Lichtenstein have distinguished, for varying reasons, the ego of Freudian theory from the concept of the self. But the self, which approximates the academic notion of the subject, is unrelated to the function of the subject as viewed from a structuralist perspective.[2]

Freud's conception of the object

The question of the object must therefore be posed in terms of its historical evolution, since the object in psychoanalysis, the analysis of the psychoanalytic object, and the object of psychoanalysis itself are closely interrelated issues. In Freud (1915) the object is part of a setting, a montage, to which it is simultaneously internal and external. It is internal insofar as it forms a constitutive element of this montage, as one of the components of the drive apparatus. For if there is a psychic apparatus, it is because there is a drive apparatus. The source, the pressure, the aim, and the object of the drive comprise this apparatus. However, the source and the pressure have a physical origin and as such are not displaceable; the displacement or the replacement of one source by another does not eliminate the problem of pressure at the original source. For example, one can try to cheat hunger by masturbating, or sexual desire by eating, but the hunger like the sexual desire will remain unappeased and the illusion can only briefly be sustained. Above all it is crucial to observe that such a displacement of source and such a displacement of pressure can be achieved only through the artifice of a change of aim (e.g., fellatio in the place of coitus) which may also be accompanied by a change of object (e.g., choosing a homoerotic or autoerotic object in the place of a heterosexual one). Autoeroticism is an obligatory solution, a replacement dictated by the discontinuity of the object's presence and, in the end, by the more or less belated awareness of its loss. The drive components are sharply separated into two polarities: the source as a somatic, internal element and the object as a non–somatic and external one.

Thus the conceptual framework of the object in Freudian theory includes the following characteristics:

1. The object is part of the drive apparatus: the *included* object.
2. The object is external to the drive: the *excluded* object. At first the object of need, it becomes, by *leaning on* the need, the object of the desire (anaclisis).[3]
3. Of all the components of the drive apparatus, the object is that for which *substitutes* are most easily found. Thus it is eminently an object of transference.
4. The *absent* object can be replaced by another external object or by a part object taken either from the external object (e.g., the breast) or from one's own body (e.g., the thumb).
5. The object can be *incorporated* (as a familiar or as an alien, uncanny thing); it can be *introjected* (as a psychic process); it can be the object of *identification* (as the object which is both identified and identified-with in incorporation or introjection); it can be *internalized* (taken from the outside to the inside).
6. The object is initially *confused* with that which objectifies it and presents it *as* an object, i.e., with that which puts it forth (*ob-ject*). The result may be either a formless chaos where there is neither object nor *anti-object*; or, more often, a state of reversibility pertaining to both the object and the anti-object. (In this context, *anti-object* means *counter-object*, antagonistic yet at the same time close to the object.) Here we have the object of projection.
7. The distinction between object and non-object is made by way of the integration of *object loss*.[4] Its consequence is the creation of an *internal object* distinct from the *external object*. This evolution parallels the distinction between *part object* and *whole object*.

8. Corollary to the formation of the internal object is that of the *fantasied object*. Inversely, the fantasy is itself taken, in its turn, as object. Its opposite is the *real object*. The first is governed by the pleasure principle, the second by the reality principle. The fantasied object is located in an extraterritorial position within a psychic apparatus ruled by the reality principle.

9. The choice of object depends on multiple criteria. One of the basic distinctions governing object-choice is that between the *narcissistic object*, formed on the model of the narcissism of the non-object, and the *anaclitic object*, based on the model of the objectal object. This difference is redoubled by the notion of *investment:* the narcissistic investment of the object, the objectal investment of the object – which suggests the importance of the economic transformation.

10. The play of differences which characterize the object may be situated, as we have just seen, along various axes. But two of them have a dominant role: on the one hand, separation of the *good* and the *bad* and, on the other, separation according to the *difference between the sexes* – the phallic versus the castrated object, the masculine versus the feminine object (penis/vagina), and the paternal versus the maternal object (in the Oedipus complex).

11. The object is bound both to *desire* and to *identification* – identification being the primary mode of relationship with the object, leading then to a secondary identification with the object of desire after its renunciation.

12. The object is in a *mediating position* with respect to narcissism: at once its agonist and antagonist.

13. The object can be a product of the *constructiveness or the destructiveness of the drives*. It can be either constructive or destructive for the non-object (i.e., for the ego or the self).

14. The *erotic object* (i.e., the object as invested by the constructive qualities of Eros in Freud's final theory of the drives) evolves toward sublimation; whereas the object of destructiveness evolves, not toward objectal chaos, but toward *objectal nothingness* (i.e., the zero point of excitation) because the object is always a source of excitation, whether external or internal, pleasurable or unpleasurable.

15. The study of object relations concerns the relationship to the object or *between* objects. The nature of the link is more important than the action which unites object to non-object or objects amongst themselves. This link is one of conjunction or of disjunction.

Thus the object according to Freud, is by nature polymorphous and polysemous. Here it is vital to point out that in Freud's work the object never depends exclusively on its existence or its essence, its perception or its conception. It should be defined as neither form nor essence but rather as *a network of relationships with shifting boundaries and with variable investments which keeps the anti-object for the anti-subject awake and alive, i.e., in a state of desire.*[5]

The coherence of Freudian theory

The aim and object of psychoanalysis is, in short, the construction of the *analytic object*, which the analysand can carry away with him from the analysis and can make use of in the absence of the analyst, who is no longer the object of transference. Inversely, the detachment from the analyst of the analysand-as-object implies that the countertransference can be displaced onto another analysand and that the analysand is now capable of becoming another kind of object for the analyst, an *other*.

The avatars of the object in the work of Freud's disciples

Freud's disciples went on to tamper with this remarkable theoretical construction, adding on to or else whittling away the main edifice so as to impair, more often than not, the harmony of the whole. The empirical/theoretical gap, i.e., the disparity between facts encountered in practice and the theory which accounts for them, led to an overvaluation of one or another partial aspects of the theory. Thus, with Reich, the problems of character analysis gave rise to an emphasis on the relation to the external object. Then, with Abraham, the true pioneer of object relations theory, the genetic debate led to the specification of the subphases of development, going from the differentiation of the pre-ambivalent part object through to that of the post-ambivalent genital whole object.

One of the consequences was a 'genetic' psychoanalysis whose reduction of the structural dimensions of analytic thought to the merely genetic has seriously impoverished the complex temporal mechanisms of Freudian theory, suppressing, for instance, the crucial

concept of deferred action. Psychoanalytic time became psychobio-
logical time, distinguished by mere successiveness, evolutionary and
normative (the genital relationship as the Ideal). Linear 'development'
replaced temporal dialectic. To be sure, Freud's scheme of libidinal development contributed a good deal to this situation. In consequence, analytic theory began to grow rather less psychoanalytic,
rather more psychological. Attention shifted from libidinal development to the development of the ego, whose relationship to reality
became (ideally) equivalent to the post-ambivalent genital relationship. (But it is certainly not among psychoanalysts that we will find
this ideal illustrated.) Later on, a further step was taken when, with
Hartmann, the ego gained a measure of autonomy, allowing the id
to become autonomous in its turn (M. Schur). All that remained to
complete the process was the introduction into analytic theory of
Piaget, whose thought had formerly been entirely antithetical to it.

Given that Freud's work is open to multiple interpretation and thus
is susceptible to divergent modes of development, it cannot be said
that the orientation adopted by Hartmann and most of North American psychoanalysis is unjustifiable. And, after all, it tallies in many
respects with that of Anna Freud. It would seem that psychoanalysis
has yielded in large part to the fascinating ascendancy of child analysis.
It has been inclined to rely not only on what has been learned from
the *psychoanalysis of children*, but also on the *psychoanalytic understanding
of the child* (Lebovici and Soulé 1970), that is, on information gleaned
from psychoanalytic applications in fields external to it: direct observation (Spitz); the genetic study of development (Mahler); and the
study of the ego through its sensorial or cognitive tools, or through
the observation of children brought up under unusual circumstances
(D. Burlingham and A. Freud on infants without families). Melanie
Klein took an altogether different approach, which has ended in the
dissension we are all aware of. But here we must go back again, the
better to understand this theoretical lineage.

Groddeck undermined Freud's radical dualism: the object was no
longer 'psychic'. It became psychosomatic, and the id was made into
a natural divinity. Rank and Ferenczi gave the object, in their turn,
quite a different shape. The former emphasized the original separation – birth, which establishes the separation of mother and child and
hence that of the object and the non–object. Freud rightly reminded
him that this original separation is, at the time, only relative (biological), that it is repaired by the subsequent fusion of mother and

child, and that only with the metaphorical loss of the breast does the difference between ego and object get properly established. As for Ferenczi, while calling back into question the split between psyche and soma, his essential contribution was to change the meaning of the transference by understanding it as a process of introjection (as well as of projection), and above all by stressing, in his final years, the significance of the analyst as object, thereby implicitly shifting the emphasis onto the role of the countertransference.

Abraham and Ferenczi were to influence various independent currents of thought. Balint, the spiritual heir of Ferenczi, emphasized *primary object love*, denying all autonomy to primary narcissism. Later on he gave much importance to the fact that Freud's work dealt essentially with clinical structures which had already achieved a more or less successful internalization of the object, whereas non-neurotic structures are characterized by a failure, more or less, of internalization. *Failure*, in this context, is no more than an approximate term, since what is at stake is rather a *fault*. The basic failure is actually a *basic fault*, a primordial defect giving rise to the fault which then devolves upon the primary love object and which the analyst must, in the course of treatment, replace by a 'new beginning'.

But Melanie Klein (who had undergone analyses with both Ferenczi and Abraham) was already in the process of developing a quite opposed theory of object relations, insofar as she focused on *internal* objects, *fantasied* objects (part or whole), relegating entirely to the background the role of the external object and appealing (like Freud) to the role of constitutional and innate factors, especially the destructive drives. However, she was not able to avoid a misunderstanding. The destructive drives – one should rather say the *instincts* of destruction – are directed onto the object first and foremost by projection. Although she recognized that this projection is not total (in other words, that some internal destructiveness remains in spite of projection), *she behaved as if only this projected part should be taken into consideration*. Note that it matters little whether the object is, in the present case, internal or external, since what counts in Melanie Klein's theory is the *centrifugal* orientation of projection; at all events, a centripetal orientation is never more than the consequence of the return upon himself of the subject's destructive projection (projective identification).

Ferenczi had his disciples, and Klein has hers as well, whether analyzed by her or not. Fairbairn resumes her approach when he deflects the aim of the object. For Freud, the drive sought satisfaction through the object; for Klein, the drive seeks chiefly to cope with destructiveness. For Fairbairn, the drive (but is there still such a thing as drive for Fairbairn?) seeks the object itself (object seeking). Finally Winnicott arrives on the scene. His contribution, derived from the analysis of borderline states, has a number of facets:

a. The baby all by himself does not exist; he is *coupled* with the object of maternal care.
b. Before the inauguration of the paranoid-schizoid phase, we must take into consideration the role of holding – i.e., the change involved in the transition from the intra-uterine to the extra-uterine condition. Nestling within the womb is replaced by nestling in the mother's arms. The phase of *holding* is followed by *handling* and finally by *object-presenting*.
c. The object is at first subjective (or the object subjectively conceived), and then becomes the objective object (or the object objectively perceived). *It is essential that the subjective object precede the objective object.*
d. The object is answered to by the *self.* The self is silent and secret, in a state of permanent non~communication. It shelters the subjective objects and may experience states either of *disintegration* under the influence of anxiety (Winnicott called it 'agony'), or of return to *non-integration* (diffused states going from fusion all the way to non-existence).
e. The mother/object's intolerance of the baby's spontaneity can bring about in the baby a dissociation between psyche and soma, or between the two components of bisexuality, or between one aspect of the drives (e.g., the destructive drives) as against the other. The creation of a *false self*, conforming to the image of the mother's desire, allows protection to the *true self*, which is kept in secrecy. Let us remember that we can communicate only indirectly with the true self.
f. The problem with these states is the problem of dependency. The analyst's attitude in the face of the patient's regression, especially his complicity in preventing regression, may lead to his collusion with the false self an interminable analysis or a psychotic breakdown is likely to result.
g. The analyst's work consists in a *metaphorical* replacement of the deficiencies of maternal care, either through accepting the

analysand's dependence or through accepting his need for fusion within the symbolic interplay — for the analyst does not represent the mother, he is the mother. The *analytic setting* represents maternal care. The analyst must also be able to accept his periodic destruction (along with the resultant hatred in the countertransference) as a condition of his periodic resurrection, so that the analysand may be able to *use* the analyst.

h. The *transitional object*, which is neither internal nor external but located in the intermediate area of *potential space*, comes to life and comes into use 'in the beginning' of the separation between mother and baby. The transitional object invokes the idea of *transitional space*, which is extended into the cultural experience of sublimation.

i. The transitional object is coextensive with the category of *playing* and with the *capacity to be alone* (in the presence of the mother or of the analyst).

j. Analytic technique is directed toward bringing about the capacity for play with transitional objects. The essential feature is no longer interpreting, but enabling the subject to live out creative experiences of a new category of objects.

k. If the transitional object is a not-me possession, two other possibilities are involved:

1. The non-creation of this object, through being excessively bound to experiences of either fusion or separation.
2. The inversion of the sense of possession by the démarche: 'All I have got is what I have not got.' This suggests a somewhat different concept, which I have formulated as *negative satisfaction*.

It is easy to see that Winnicott has in fact described not so much an object as a space lending itself to the creation of objects. Here the line itself becomes a space; the metaphorical boundary dividing internal from external, that either/or in which the object has traditionally been entrapped, expands into the intermediate area and playground of transitional phenomena. In *Playing and Reality* (1971) Winnicott gives us glimpses into the private elaboration of this line of thinking: from his early fascination with the image of the seashore where children are playing, to his discovery in talks with Marion Milner of the 'tremendous significance there can be in the interplay of the edges of two curtains', through to an even more personal, and yet thoroughly practical, extension and amplification of the line in his use of the squiggle game.

French analysts have long held themselves aloof from this development, meanwhile splitting up into two main factions. Bouvet's work on object relations grows out of a theoretical blend in which a concept of defensive activity inspired by A. Freud, Reich, Federn, and Fenichel is augmented by Bouvet's own contributions, most significantly his concept of *distance from the object* as illustrated in the variations of the *rapprocher*. The economic dimension, always present in Bouvet, is salient as well in the work of the French psychosomatic school (Marty, Fain, de M'Uzan, David) and in those who stress the role of affect in technique, clinical description, and theory (Green). In opposition to these trends, Lacan has adopted a formalistic approach and has built up theoretical models in which the object (which he calls 'the object (a)') is of great importance, especially in relation to the mirror-image. But it would be impossible, within the limits of the present chapter, to give a full account of all the functions of the object (a), as this would require an exposition of the whole Lacanian theory, which differs considerably from all those previously discussed (see, however, Green 1966).

Another, although quite different, formalistic approach is that of Bion, who addresses the problem of the object from a perspective unusual to modern psychoanalysis. Adapting to his own ends the Kantian concept of the thing-in-itself, he inserts it into the symbol '0' standing for that unknowable state of being forever and always inaccessible to being known in itself, and yet at the source of all knowledge, which will never constitute more than an approximation of '0'. In this he rejoins the formulations of Freud's 'Project for a Scientific Psychology' (Freud 1895). Note that, just as in Winnicott, it is once again the *space* of thinking that takes precedence over the object. However, it is regrettable that in the work of both Winnicott and Bion the concept of analytic time is less well developed than that of analytic space. We may register our dissatisfaction with the constructions of genetically minded analysts, but we have as yet no theory to offer in their place.

Analytic experience has convinced me that the only way out of the impasse of empiricism versus intellectualism, or 'realism' versus 'abstraction', is through exploiting the technical and theoretical possibilities suggested by Winnicott's work, making all necessary modifications. And so I want now to examine more closely certain of Winnicott's propositions, of interest for the following reasons:

1. They emerge from the study of the analytic setting taken as reference point, which means that theory stays in direct touch with practice.
2. Practice here has to do with borderline patients who, more than classical neurotics, have become the paradigm cases for current analytic practice and theory.
3. The theory deriving from such work is the fruit of an imaginative elaboration deeply rooted in the countertransference feelings of the analyst. Thus the transference gives way to the countertransference as the centre of attention.
4. Winnicott's thought may be open to criticism in many respects, but it reflects, above all, a richly alive experiencing rather than an erudite schematizing.
5. Winnicott's work poses, with remarkable acuteness, the question of the future of psychoanalysis. Rigidly maintaining its classical stance, psychoanalysis could on the one hand attach itself to an embalmed and stiffened corpse, failing to pursue a critical evaluation of its theories as challenged by present practice. In this case it would be pledged to the mere safeguarding of its acquisitions, without ever calling into question the theory sustaining them. The alternative is a psychoanalysis which, periodically renewing itself, strives to extend its range, to subject its concepts to radical rethinking, to commit itself to self-criticism. In which case it must run the risks entailed by such self-examination, from which the best as well as the worst may emerge.

Analytic play and its relationship to the object

A great creative thinker – and such Winnicott undoubtedly was, perhaps the greatest of the contemporary analytic epoch – provides endless proof of his gifts, I ought to say even of his genius, throughout his life's work. But often it is during the final stage of his career, struggling it may be against the threat of a fast-approaching death, that he rises to his full stature. I was deeply impressed by feelings of this kind while reading *Playing and Reality* (1971). I should like here to pay tribute to this book, elaborating in my own way what I brought away from it.

Winnicott's name will always be associated with the idea of the transitional object and transitional phenomena, of potential space, of playing and illusion. What has progressively emerged from his initial description of the transitional object – which was constantly being enriched as the years went by – is that Winnicott, in a series of observations which seemed harmless and unassuming enough, had in fact delineated a conceptual field of the highest importance, whose definition was based at one and the same time on child observation and the analytic situation. We must get one thing straight: in his case the observation of the child did not, as one might think, take priority over the observation of the analytic situation. On the contrary: it was because Winnicott was first analyzed, and then went on to become an analyst himself, that he was able, in looking at children, to notice what had been escaping everyone's attention. For we cannot say that the discovery of the transitional object brought to light some recondite and obscure reality. Freud once said that he had done nothing but discover the obvious. The same could be said of Winnicott. The least observant of mothers has always known that her child likes to fall asleep with his teddy bear, or while fondling a bit of cloth or a corner of his blanket. But before Winnicott no one had understood the importance of this, just as no one before Freud had ever been struck by the significance there might be in an eighteen-month-old's game, played during his mother's absence, of throwing away from him and then pulling back again a reel of cotton. Here too it had to be a psychoanalyst, the very first one, who could observe this spectacle with new eyes.

Thus, analytic experience seems to have been the determining factor in the formation of Winnicott's concepts, as it was in those of Freud. Nor is it by accident that it should be Winnicott and his students Khan, Milner, and Little who have provided us with the most fertile reflections on the analytic setting.

In 'The analyst, symbolization and absence in the analytic setting' (Green 1986) I proposed the hypothesis that the analytic situation is characterized by the fact that each of its two partners produces a double of himself. What the analysand communicates is an analogue, a double of his affective and bodily experience; what the analyst communicates is a double of the effect produced on his own bodily, affective, and intellectual experience by the patient's communication. Thus the communication *between* analysand and analyst is an object made up of two parts, one constituted by the double of the analysand, the other by the double of the analyst. What is called the 'therapeutic alliance' or 'working alliance', which I prefer to call the *analytic association*, is, in my belief, founded on the possibility of creating an *analytic object* formed by these two halves. This corresponds precisely to the etymological definition, in Robert's *Dictionary*, of a symbol: 'an object cut in two, constituting a sign of recognition when its bearers can put together the two separate pieces'. In my opinion this is what occurs in the analytic setting. The analytic object is neither internal (to the analysand or to the analyst), nor external (to either the one or the other), but is situated *between* the two. So it corresponds exactly to Winnicott's definition of the transitional object and to its location in the intermediate area of *potential space*, the space of 'overlap' demarcated by the analytic setting. When a patient terminates his analysis, it is not only that he has 'internalized' the analytic interplay, but also that he can take away with him the potential space in order to reconstitute it in the outside world, through cultural experience, through sublimation and, more generally, through the possibility of pairings or (let us rather say) of coupling.

The analytic situation differs from the game of chess (to which Freud was fond of comparing it) in that it is *the analyst who determines the rules of the game*, as Viderman (1970) has rightly observed. In case of disagreement, arbitration is possible only if (in a juridical sense) the rules of law are contravened; but the law governing analysis remains in the hands of the analyst, who exercises both legislative and executive power. These rules which are laid down before the game begins confer a considerable advantage upon the analyst (1) because he has already been analyzed and (2) because usually he has already conducted other analyses. All equality between the two parties is abolished.

But this spatial account of the game needs to be complemented by a temporal one. In analysis it is always the analysand who makes the first move. No analysis is conceivable in which, after the statement of the fundamental rule, the analyst speaks first. The analyst can only respond to the first move, which is always played by the patient and only when he decides on it. Similarly, it is always the analysand who makes the last move in the final farewell, the analyst taking leave of his patient only in answer to this farewell (although it may be only temporary).

This structure, which invokes the notion of the double, must also make room for the absent. The absent one in analysis is none other than the analyst's own analyst[6] – which goes to show that analysis always proceeds across generations. As I said before, even if it is his first analysis, the analyst has already been analyzed. In the analytic interplay, the absent metaphorically represented by the analyst's analyst is connected with two other modes of absence: that of past reality, inaccessible as such both to analyst and to analysand, and that of an equally inaccessible present reality. The analyst cannot get to know his patient's real life; he can only imagine it. And likewise the analysand can never know the analyst's life; he too can only imagine it. Both are reduced to approximations. Even as the analytic process unfolds, each partner communicates, through verbalization, only a part of his life experience. Here we get back to Winnicott's concept of the silent self, and a memorable sentence comes to mind: 'each individual is an isolate, permanently non-communicating, permanently unknown, in fact unfound' (1963). From this springs the importance of the capacity to be alone (in the presence of the mother or of the analyst) and its consequence: the analyst is always having to navigate between the risk of separation anxiety and that of anxiety concerning his intrusiveness.

Winnicott has formulated an essential paradox for us, one that, as he says, we must accept as it is and that is not for resolution. If the baby is in health, he 'creates the object', but the object was there waiting to be created and to become a cathected object. I tried to draw attention to this aspect of transitional phenomena by claiming that in the rules of the game we all know we will never challenge the baby to elicit an answer to the question: did you create that or did you find it?' (1971: 89). This paradox joins up with another: the transitional object is and is not the self.[7]

The qualities peculiar to the transitional object confront us with an unimpeachable double truth. *The analyst is not a real object; the analyst is not an imaginary object.* The analytic discourse is not the patient's discourse, nor is it that of the analyst, nor is it the sum of these two. The analytic discourse is the *relation* between two discourses which belong neither to the realm of the real nor to that of the imaginary. This may be described as a *potential relationship*, or, more precisely, as a *discourse of potential relationships*, in itself potential. Accordingly, the analytic discourse has, in regard to past and present alike, only a potential relationship to the truth. But this does not mean that the analytic discourse may consist in simply anything at all. It must bear an *homologous* relationship to imaginary (or psychic) reality; it forms its counterpart. This implies an approximate correspondence, but an affective approximation, *without which its effect would be nil.* The homology is one we are obliged to construct, for lack of positive evidence. Nevertheless, this construction is not arbitrary, since we cannot help but construct the real, even when it pleases us to think we are doing no more than perceiving it.

In one of his most fundamental papers, inspired by Lacan's work on the mirror phase, Winnicott (1966) analyzes the function of the mother's face as the precursor of the mirror. Here he stresses the importance of the baby's initial communication not only with the breast but also with the mother's face. We know that the baby at the breast (or bottle) sucks while looking not at the breast but at his mother's face. Winnicott rightly points out that while this is going on the baby may see in the mother's gaze either himself or herself. If, too precociously, it is the face of the mother/object that he perceives, he cannot form the subjective object, but will prematurely evolve the object objectively perceived. The result is that he must organize a false self, as an image conforming to the mother's desire. He must then hide away, in secret, his true self, which cannot and indeed must not be allowed expression. With his false self, he can achieve only an external identity. But this is a pathological solution. In the normal progress of events, a compromise is obtained through the creation of the transitional area of experience.

'If the baby is in health . . .' said Winnicott. Some babies, we know, are not. And among these some will later impress us with the intensity of their negative therapeutic reaction. It is striking that Winnicott found it necessary to add, in *Playing and Reality*, a supplement to his original paper on the transitional object. The difference between these two pieces of work is considerable, the fruit of twenty years' experience. In the later version Winnicott discusses what he calls the *negative side of relationships*. In certain borderline cases, the absence of the mother is felt as equivalent to her death. Here the time factor must be duly weighed, since it is in terms of temporal accretion ($x + y + z$ quantity of deprivation, expressed as the accumulated moments of the mother's absence) that Winnicott imagines how the baby can move from distress to 'unthinkable anxiety' by way of a traumatic break in life's continuity ('The location of cultural experience'). For such infants '*the only real thing is the gap*; that is to say, the death or the absence [in the sense of non-existence] or the amnesia' (1971: 22 [italics Green's]. While analyzing a patient of this kind, Winnicott arrived at the conclusion that from the point of view of the child *the mother was dead*, regardless of her absence or presence. It occurred to him that in the transference 'the important communication for me to get was that there could be a blotting out, and that this blank could be the only fact and the only thing that was real' (ibid). This remark bears out precisely my own observations about the importance in psychosis of the negative hallucination of the subject. For Winnicott's patient, who had had previous analysis, the negation of the first analyst was more important than the fact of the existence of the second analyst. 'The negative of him is more real than the positive of you.' Such vengefulness is particularly severe with respect to an object which has failed. Here retaliation is a negative response to a negative trauma; in other words, the trauma is not only something which has occurred – in the classical sense of a traumatization (through sexual seduction or an aggressive act) – but that which *did not occur, owing to an absence of response on the part of the mother/object.* 'The real thing is the thing that is not there.' A very true statement, revealing how the thing that is not there, the symbol, is taken as reality; which recalls Hanna Segal's idea of symbolic equation, but in an exactly contrary sense. In Segal's example, violin=penis. But in Winnicott's example, and here he meets up with Bion, the *non-object is the object.* The non-object, in this context, means not the representation of the object but the non-existence of the object.

Winnicott speaks of symbols which disappear. Patients in whom structures of this type are found can seem mentally disabled, and in my own initial encounters with such analysands I have come away with a strong impression of their psychic and intellectual poverty. Their motto is: 'All I have got is what I have not got.'

This line of speculation, which Winnicott adds in 1971 to his original hypothesis about transitional objects and not-me possessions, is crucial, as it opens the way to a new conceptual theme, *negative investment.* I have postulated (1967, 1969) the existence of a negative narcissistic structure characterized by the valorization of a state of non-being. Striving for that state of quietude which follows satisfaction with an object, but finding himself in a state where satisfaction has not occurred within limits tolerable for his psychic apparatus, the subject seeks to attain the same state as if satisfaction had been achieved, through the strategy of renouncing all hope of satisfaction, through inducing in himself a state of psychic death not unrelated to Jones's idea of *aphanisis.*

In his paper on the mirror-role of the mother's face, Winnicott uses the illustration of the patient who said to him, 'Wouldn't it be awful if the child looked into the mirror and saw nothing?' The anxiety of the negative hallucination is truly unthinkable. In my opinion, all the defensive manoeuvres described by Melanie Klein's advocates amount to nothing but an awesome strategy for avoiding this fundamental and primordial anxiety.

If 'negative symbolization' can provide an extreme (and very costly) solution, another kind of solution is adopted in borderline cases. In my own experience, what I have most often observed is a need to hold on to and to preserve at all costs a bad internal object. It is as if, when the analyst succeeds in reducing the power of the bad object, the subject has no other recourse than to make it reappear, in fact to resurrect it, in its original or in an analogous form, as if the thing most dreaded were the *interval between the loss of the bad object and its replacement by a good object. This interval is experienced as a dead time, which the subject cannot survive. Hence the value for the patient of the negative therapeutic reaction, which ensures that the analyst will never be replaced, since the object which would succeed him might never appear or might only appear too late.*

In another section of *Playing and Reality*, 'The use of an object and relating through identifications', Winnicott discusses the patient's ability to *use* the analyst. For this to be possible, the analyst must allow himself to be destroyed as frequently as the subject wishes, so that the latter may be reassured that the object has the capacity to survive his destruction of it. Winnicott makes the interesting comment that destructiveness of this kind is not related to aggressiveness. This states yet another paradoxical truth. It must be understood that what is here in question is not the fantasied activity of an experience of mentally acted-out destruction; rather it is a radical decathexis. Hence what we are concerned with is a succession of libidinal or aggressive cathexes and of decathexes which abolish the preceding cathexes and the objects linked to them. When carried to an extreme, such decathexes lead to psychic death, just as anarchic cathexes deeply pervaded by aggressiveness lead to delusion. Thus the fundamental dilemma becomes: delusion or death (physical or psychic). The work of the analyst is aimed at transforming these alternatives into something less extreme, so that delusion may become playing, and death absence. In this context absence does not mean loss, but potential presence. For absence, paradoxically, may signify either an imaginary presence, or else an unimaginable non-existence. It is absence in this first sense which leads to the capacity to be alone (in the presence of the object) and to the activity of representation and of creating the imaginary: the transitional object, constructed within that space of illusion never violated by the question. Was the object created or was it found?

Freud, as I remarked above, sometimes compared the analytic situation to chess. If Winnicott is the master-player of psychoanalysis, it is surely not chess that he plays with his patient. It is a game with a cotton reel, with a piece of string, with a doll or teddy bear. Finally, with children Winnicott plays the squiggle game, in which each partner takes a turn drawing a scribble, which is then modified by the other (Winnicott 1971). The spontaneous movement of a hand which allows itself to be guided by the drive, a hand which does not act but rather expresses itself, traces a more or less insignificant and formless line, submitting it to the scrutiny of the other, who, deliberately, transforms it into a meaningful shape. What else do we do in the analysis of difficult cases? The beautiful clarity of the chess game, unfurling itself under the open light of day, is absent there. Instead we find ourselves in a murky night pierced by flashes of lightning and sudden storms. Meaning does not emerge complete as Aphrodite rising from the waves. It is for us to construct it. Viderman believes that, prior to the analytic situation, the meaning that we seek has never existed; it is the analytic process which constitutes it as such for the first time. Meaning is not discovered, it is created. I prefer to describe it as an absent meaning, a virtual sense which awaits its realization through the cuttings and shapings offered by analytic space (and time). It is a potential meaning. It would be wrong to think that like Sleeping Beauty it merely waits there to be aroused. It is constituted in and by the analytic situation; but if the analytic situation reveals it, it does not create it. It brings it from absence to potentiality, and then makes it actual. To actualize it means to call it into existence, not out of nothing (for there is no spontaneous generation), but out of the meeting of two discourses, and by way of that object which is the analyst, in order to construct the *analytic object*.

This theory implies that mental functioning has to be taken into consideration. In chess, there is only one kind of material at stake; the pieces have different *values* and an unchangeable mode of progression. The analytic situation, on the contrary, brings varying materials to light: drives, affects, representations (of things or of words), thoughts, actions. Their specific modes of functioning – to be the plaything of a drive (directed toward the body or toward the world), to feel, to imagine, to say, to think, to act – all these modes are capable of an ultimate exchange of function. The vectorization of drive into language is placed in check here. For speaking could become tantamount to acting, acting to evacuating, imagining to filling up a hole, and thinking could, at the extreme verge, become impossible (cf. 'blank psychosis', Donnet and Green 1973).

Here we have evidently reached the limits of Freudian practice and theory. There is urgent and growing need for another system of reference which gives pride of place to the countertransference and clarifies its elaborative potentialities. The analyst ought either to use his imagination, or resign, for the unconscious creates its own structure only by way of the Imaginary.

The importance of the analytic setting arises from the fact that it allows the development of a metaphoric regression which is a double, an analogue of infantile regression. In the same way, the response of the analyst, comparable to holding, is itself only a double of maternal care. It is as if, out of the totality of physical and psychic maternal care, only the psychic aspect were to be admitted into the analytic situation. The part which is not given play in analysis is the one that is missing when the analytic object is constituted. This object, which takes shape through the communication of psychic maternal care, leaves in abeyance any actual regression to the past on the part of the patient, and any physical care on the part of the analyst.

But we must go yet further. And here my agreement with Winnicott reaches its limit. When Winnicott pointed out that there is no such thing as a baby, reminding us of the couple that it forms together with its cradle or with its mother in the holding situation, his observation, as we know, caused quite a stir.

I would maintain, for my part, that there is no such entity as a baby with his mother. No mother-child couple exists without a father somewhere. For even if the father is hated or banished by the mother, erased from her mind in favour of somebody else, of her own mother or father, the child nevertheless is the product of the union of the father and mother. Of this union he is the *material, living, irrefutable* proof. There are mothers who want to wipe out any trace of the father in the child. And we know the result: a psychotic structure. Thus we can assert that ultimately *there is no dual relationship*. There can be no dual exchanges, but there is always some link establishing the possibility of duality, in the form of areas of reunion and separation within the dual relationships.

In the analytic situation, this third element is supplied by the analytic setting. *The work of the analytic setting is comparable to the mirror-work, without which it is impossible to form an image from an object.* This induces the thought that reflection is a fundamental human property. Probably this attribute is innate, but we do now know that an object is indispensable in order to transform this *innate potentiality into its actual realization, failing which, the potentiality dies out and is lost. The analyst is the object necessary to such a transformation, but he can bring it about only with the help of the work of the not-me, which is the analytic setting defined spatially and temporally. What answers for the setting is the combined discourse of the analysand and the analyst, doubles of their respective experience.* Without affect there is no effective language. Without language there is no effective affect. The unconscious is not structured like a language (Lacan); *it is structured like an affective language, or like an affectivity having the properties of language.*

Winnicott was much blamed, and is still being blamed, for his delight in distorting the classical analytic setting. Since I am not prepared to endorse any and every deformation of the analytic setting, I must distinguish between those I would find acceptable and those I would have to reject. It seems to me that the only acceptable variations of classical analysis are *those whose aim is to facilitate the creation of optimal conditions for symbolization.* For classical neurosis, classical analysis serves this function. With borderline patients (taking this term in its broadest sense), the analyst must preserve in each case the minimum conditions requisite to the maximum development of symbolization. Today the analyst's major difficulty lies in this area. No one can decide for him the modalities or the extent of the variations required by such cases. This predicament has several possible results:

1. The cynicism of the analyst who, exploiting for personal ends his patient's need for dependence, gains a pseudo-independence through such shameless manipulation.
2. The collusion involved in a mutual dependency.
3. Guilt connected with the feeling of having transgressed the implicit analytic law.
4. Freedom in analysis based upon the principle that analysis is the construction of the analytic object.

A protective device is necessary here: the analyst's constant awareness of his countertransference and his full employment of it by way of the transference of the analysand. By the term *countertransference* I mean to take into account not only the affective effects, positive or negative, of the analysand's transference, not only the analyst's capacities for antipathy or for sympathy, but also his total mental functioning, including his reading and his exchanges with colleagues. Having said this, I would still agree with the restrictions that Winnicott imposed upon the countertransference in limiting it to the professional attitude. However far we may wish to extend our identification with the patient, this human identification is still a professional one. Hypocrisy is quite out of place here. We terminate the session and do not yield to the patient who wishes it would go on indefinitely. We leave for vacation without him and are paid for our work. We do our best to listen to him, but we see and hear only what we are prepared to see and hear, just as the patient can only understand what he was already on the verge of understanding, although he could not arrive at it all by himself.

In our activity as analysts, our real work does not lie in a mere receptivity to what the patient is communicating, nor on the other hand is it wholly determined by those preconceptions and presuppositions which are necessarily prior to all communication. The analyst's creativity takes shape within the time and space of the communicative exchange where the analytic object is formed by continuously and discontinuously constructing itself.

Analysts listen more easily to their patients than they can to each other. Doubtless because – and this is the final paradox – a colleague is more an-other than he is an a-like, and a patient is more an a-like than he is an-other. Alter ego.

Notes

1 This chapter, which is translated by Anita Kermode and Michele Sirègar, first appeared in *Between Reality and Fantasy: Transitional Objects and Phenomena*, ed. Simon Grolnick and Leonard Barkin, in collaboration with Werner Muensterberger (New York, Jason Aronson, 1978). An earlier version, 'La psychanalyse, son objet, son avenir', was published in French in *Revue Française de Psychanalyse* (1975), 39.

   It was subsequently published in André Green's first collection of papers translated into English and published in 1986 – *On Private Madness* The Hogarth Press Ltd. London (Editor's Note).

2 As used here, the term structuralist belongs not to the perspective of Hartmann, Kris, and Loewenstein, but rather to that of F. de Saussure, R. Jakobson, C. Lévi-Strauss, and J. Lacan. [Green's footnote in *On Private Madness*]

3 The German term is *Anlehnung*, which suggests the idea of a supporting function – the sexual instincts as being supported by the instincts of self-preservation. For example, oral pleasure at first *leans upon* hunger (i.e., oral need) and later develops independently from it in the form of pleasure [Green's footnote in *On Private Madness*].

4 This implies that the object exists before it is lost, but that its very loss is what determines its existence as such.

5 This mobility of boundaries is discernible throughout the history of psychoanalysis. After Freud, Melanie Klein curtailed the territory of the external object while extending proportionately that of the internal object. But after Klein, Winnicott in his turn encroached on the domain of internal objects by putting back into the maternal environment – i.e., the external object – what Klein had taken away from it. Nevertheless, this process has not been circular, since the result was to create a third object: the transitional object.

6 Hence the inequality and the heterogeneity of the double analytic discourse. The analyst relies upon a discourse with the absent, namely his own analyst, author of his difference from the analysand.

7 What Winnicott in fact said was that the transitional object is and is not the breast, but the same formulation may be applied to the self [Green's footnote in *On Private Madness*].

References

Donnet, J. L. & Green, A. (1973) *L'enfant de ça. La psychose blanche* (Paris, Editions de Minuit).

Freud, S. (1915) Instincts and their vicissitudes S.E.14.

Green, A. (1966) 'L'objet (*a*) de J. Lacan, sa logique et la théorie freudienne' *Cahiers pour l'analyse 3;* translated as 'The logic of Lacan's *objet a* and Freudian theory: convergences and questions', in *Intepreting Lacan*, ed. J.H. Smith and W. Kerrigan, *Psychiatry and the Humanities* 6 (Yale Univ. Press).

Green, A. (1986) The analyst, symbolization and absence in the analytic setting. In *On Private Madness* (London, Karnac).

Viderman, S. (1970) *La construction de l'espace analytique* (Paris, Denoel).

8

Nachträglichkeit and Winnicott's 'Fear of Breakdown' (1998)[1]

Haydée Faimberg

Introduction

Curiosity and surprise: this is a good state of mind in which to come together and explore the creative power of dialogue. I expect this Conference[2] to have the refreshing effect instilled in me by the work of the pioneers, at a time when everything was to be done. Throughout this Conference, we have been seeking to discover the implicit basic assumptions that underlie the positions that each of us takes in our psychoanalytical dialogue. Our purpose is to grasp what we hear when a colleague speaks, paying special attention to the context of the culture to which he belongs, respecting as much as we can the specific issues, without immediately translating his problems into our own terms. We wish to avoid any temptation to propose a synthesis, or anything that could be taken for a unified conception of psychoanalytical thought. We are trying to understand differences, and to respect them for what they are. My aim is to meet these requirements in my own presentation.

The heart of the matter

Since the concept of *Nachträglichkeit* (*après-coup*) is lacking in some psychoanalytical cultures, I thought it interesting to take another look at it. I should like to do so from a personal perspective and then to elicit your view in a dialogue.

Up to now (1998) Winnicott's 'Fear of Breakdown' and the Freudian concept of *Nachträglichkeit* had never been put together by way of a conceptual link. Actually Winnicott never explicitly spoke of *Nachträglichkeit*.

I propose, to my knowledge for the first time, that Winnicott in 'Fear of Breakdown' offers us an excellent illustration of the concept of Nachträglichkeit. I deeply believe that such is the case.

I consider that Winnicott proposes a construction (at a certain moment in the transference) to the patient who fears a breakdown. I shall therefore refer to a previous paper in which the concept of construction is studied from a Freudian perspective (Faimberg and Corel 1989).[3]

Let us first recall what Jean Laplanche said, in his paper discussed in this Conference, on *Nachträglichkeit* (concept translated in English [by Strachey in the Standard Edition] as 'deferred action' and in French as *après-coup*).[4] In the operation of *Nachträglichkeit* there are always two steps: the first one is constituted by an event that leaves a trace that Laplanche refers to (with Pontalis [1967]) as an 'already there' and a phase of retroactive meaning. I prefer to designate this 'already there' (as they call it) as a phase of *anticipation* (as I have in previous papers) (Faimberg 1981, 1993, 1995).

From my side, reading through earlier works of mine in which I coined the concept of 'listening to [the patient's] listening' (Faimberg 1981, 1993) and articulated it with historicization (Faimberg 1981/1985) and *après-coup*, I discovered retrospectively that I had used the concept of *après-coup* in a much broader sense than Freud.[5] This I realized came from my own clinical experience. The two phases of anticipation and retroactive meaning are of course necessarily present in the broader concept of *Nachträglichkeit*.[6]

I invite you to join me in thinking about this extension of the concept and thus give fresh thought to the concept of *Nachträglichkeit*. This shall enable us to better understand why I link the concept of *Nachträglichkeit* with Winnicott's conception of temporality – as shown in 'Fear of Breakdown'.

The concept of *Nachträglichkeit* must be integrated with other psychoanalytical concepts[7] in order to understand how it operates in the psychoanalytical process. So we shall also examine other Winnicottian concepts I have identified in Winnicott's 'Fear of Breakdown' that allow us to do this.

Winnicott writes that there is a possibility that the breakdown –

that the patient fears will inexorably occur in the future – has already happened, near the beginning of the individual's life.

> The patient needs to 'remember' this but it is not possible to remember something that has not yet happened, and this thing of the past has not happened yet because the patient was not there for it to happen to. The only way to 'remember' in this case is for the patient to experience this past thing for the first time in the present, that is to say, in the transference. This past and future thing then becomes a matter of the here and now, and is experienced by the patient for the first time. This is the equivalent of remembering, and this outcome is the equivalent of the lifting of repression that occurs in the analysis of the psycho-neurotic patient (classical Freudian analysis).
>
> (Winnicott 1963: 92)[8]

In this passage, Winnicott refers, first, to the repetition in the transference that allows the analyst to acknowledge and voice for the first time this experience of breakdown. And second, he also says that the breakdown that the patient fears will inexorably occur in the future already took place at a time when there was, properly speaking, nobody yet there to register it.

As I understand his text, what he designates here as breakdown is equivalent to his concept of primitive agony and implicitly he is referring to the Freudian concept of *Hilflosigkeit* (the helplessness due to prematurity).

Why am I saying that I shall link the concept of *Nachträglichkeit* with 'Fear of Breakdown'? As I said, Winnicott never spoke of this concept. Would not the idea of repetition compulsion suffice to explain this? I hope that this presentation may help us to reformulate this question posed by analysts, I think, in particular those belonging to an Anglo-Saxon tradition.

Winnicott makes it possible to give – from the present moment of the experience of helplessness in the transference – *a retroactive meaning (to the patient's fear of breakdown in the future) by means of a construction:*

The breakdown he is now experiencing for the *first* time, already took place at a moment when the patient was not yet there to have the experience.

From the standpoint I wish to discuss with you, this operation merits the name of an operation of *Nachträglichkeit* for the following reasons:

1 It is characterized by a *twofold* movement: one of anticipation (primitive agony) and another of retrospection (given by the analyst's words).
2 It takes place in the present time of the analytical relationship and gives *retroactive meaning to the movement of anticipation*.
3 Lastly, the two points in time are linked by a relationship of meaning.

Winnicott establishes this unprecedented link of meaning by way of a construction. He names, for the first time, the primitive agony (the breakdown) and – what in my reading is essential – he also gives for the first time a sense of temporality. The reasoning runs thus: this thing that is happening now, has already occurred but in fact, paradoxically, has 'not happened yet because the patient was not there for it to happen to'. The movement of anticipation is crystallized in the words 'not happened yet', and 'for it to happen to'.

In Winnicott's construction the status of remembering has great importance: 'The only way to "remember" in this case is for the patient to experience this past thing for the first time in the present . . .'.

With the aim of exploring the relationship between construction, remembering and *Nachträglichkeit* let us now revisit a previous paper on the subject centred on Freud's works (Faimberg and Corel 1989).

Remembering, construction, Nachträglichkeit

Construction consists in exposing to the patient 'a piece of his early history that he has forgotten'.

(Freud 1937: 261)

The concept of construction in its very structure, implies a very fertile paradox: being by definition *retroactive*, it is at the same time *anticipatory*, in the sense that it establishes a precondition for access to psychical truths. We refer to the concept of *Nachträglichkeit* . . .

(Faimberg and Corel 1989)

I said that Winnicott establishes an unprecedented link of meaning by way of a construction, with nothing to remember.

This link is a *logical* one in the construction, similar to the logical link that Freud constructed in the second phase of the girl's fantasy in 'A child is being beaten'[9] ('it has never had a real existence. It is never remembered . . . It is a construction of analysis, but it is no less a necessity . . .') (Freud 1919: 185).

Freud wrote in 1914: 'The patient repeats instead of remembering . . .' (Freud 1914: 151) '. . . and in the end we understand that [repeating] is his way of remembering' (ibid.: 150).

> Freud's two papers read in conjunction help us to understand that, if the patient repeats instead of remembering, it is because there is *nothing to remember:* The analyst's construction provides *a missing link.* . . .
>
> (Faimberg and Corel 1989)

We developed in the same paper the hypothesis that the past is not a given but is constituted as such:

> According with what we are saying when Freud wrote that 'construction consists in exposing to the patient a piece of his early history that he has forgotten', he meant that construction provides a new and unprecedented link whereby *the past is constituted as such and the patient acquires a history, his history.*
>
> (Faimberg and Corel 1989)

The Freudian concept of construction (according to our reading) articulated with the broader concept of *Nachträglichkeit* refers not only to the lifting of infantile amnesia. It applies to cases – as I am proposing for Winnicott – in which there is 'not, properly speaking, a memory content to recover because there is nothing to remember'.

In this sense let us recall that Winnicott writes: 'the patient needs to "remember" this but it is not possible to remember something that has not yet happened' . . . 'The only way to "remember" in this case is for the patient to experience this past thing for the first time in the present . . . ' and then he adds: 'This is the equivalent of remembering . . .'.

Moreover, Freud writes about the 'assured conviction of the truth of the construction which achieves the same therapeutic result as a recaptured memory' (Freud 1937: 265–6).

'A piece of the early history that the patient has forgotten' (as Freud writes) may be the equivalent to the '. . . disaster that already took place when there was not a subject to register it . . .' as Winnicott says.

Winnicott provides a new link between repetition of the primitive agony in the present, in the transference, and interpreting (as a construction for the first time) that this primitive agony (with non-accessible traces) has already taken place. *By this construction the primitive agony is constituted as past.*

It is my hope that, through this joint approach to the operation of *Nachträglichkeit* and construction in Winnicott and Freud (with the construction of the patient's past), the dilemma so often posed between interpreting in the present or interpreting in the past will appear in a new perspective:

In the clinical situation the second phase of the operation of *Nachträglichkeit* occurs in the present time of the session (Winnicott's construction) and gives retroactive meaning to the first one – the anticipatory phase ('the not happened *yet*').

Let us say it once again: Winnicott's construction gives a sense of temporality; through the operation of *Nachträglichkeit*, the fear of breakdown is constituted as past.

Notes

1 This was a paper read on Wednesday 29 July 1998 in the final plenary session chaired by Glen Gabbard at the Standing Conference on Psychoanalytical Intra-cultural and Inter-cultural Dialogue of the International Psychoanalytical Association (IPA).

2 This Conference consisted of a new experimental forum proposed by the author of this paper (formerly vice-president of IPA) and chaired by her, with the aim of extending dialogue among analysts belonging to different psychoanalytical cultures beyond what was possible through the usual international exchanges. Its distinctive feature was to incorporate the intra-cultural psychoanalytical dialogue *before* the inter-cultural dialogue took place.

The aim of this Conference was to study the various ways of conceptualizing and practising psychoanalysis that exist among colleagues belonging to different psychoanalytical cultures. The Conference, held in Paris, focused on French theoretico-clinical approaches to temporality and its construction in the psychoanalytical process. The task was not to seek homogeneity, but rather to study real differences and similarities (known and unknown) among psychoanalytical cultures, and to facilitate communication among these cultures.

Prior study of the French texts was crucial for the unfolding of the meeting, because they were not read in the plenary sessions (with the exception of the present paper which was discussed with the floor). Each plenary session was opened by a French discussant focusing on one of the papers in French. The aim of this first phase was to respect the intra-cultural modalities of dialogue and to detect the explicit and implicit issues at stake within that specific concept. At this intra-cultural moment, simultaneous translation ensured respect for the characteristics of French discourse, including language. The author would answer and then, at a third stage, two different intercultural discussants would address comments and questions to the author who would then answer. The participants then split into small groups and the moderators centred the discussion mostly on not-knowing, helping to overcome the difficulties that arise in the understanding of a different point of view and to acknowledge and respect differences. The idea was that a context had to be created to facilitate understanding of different approaches.

3 Faimberg and Corel (1989) 'Repetition and Surprise: clinical validation of constructions'; read at the IPA Congress, Rome.

4 '*Après-coup*' is the title of Laplanche's paper. Let me add that it was Lacan who first drew attention to this Freudian concept in the Wolf Man.

5 In 1895 Freud wrote to Fliess as follows: '. . . As you know, I am working on the assumption that our psychical mechanism has come into being by a process of stratification: the material present in the form of memory traces is being subjected from time to time to a *re-arrangement* in accordance with fresh circumstances – to a *re-transcription*. Thus what is essentially new about my theory is the thesis that memory is present not once but several times over, that it is laid down in various species of indications. I postulated a similar kind of re-arrangement some time ago (*Aphasia*) [. . .]' (Freud 1895 [1950]: 235).

6 For further developments of this concept see Faimberg (2006).

7 For further ways I have done this see Faimberg (2005).

8 This fragment will serve as our guide, for Winnicott's concept, throughout the present paper.

9 'This second phase is the most important and the most momentous of all. But we may say of it in a certain sense that it *has never had a real existence. It is never remembered*, it has never succeeded in being conscious. It is a *construction of analysis, but it is no less a necessity* on that account.' (Freud 1919: 185) (italics added).

References (pre-1998)

Faimberg, H. and Corel, A. (1989) 'Repetition and Surprise: Construction and its Validation', presented at the Congress of the International Psychoanalytical Association.

Freud, S. (1895) Letter 52 (6 December 1895), in *Extracts from the Fliess Papers, The Standard Edition of the Complete Psychological Works of Sigmund Freud* (1950–74), Vol. 1, London: Hogarth Press and the Institute of Psychoanalysis.

Freud, S. (1914) 'Remembering, Repeating and Working-through', *The Standard Edition of the Complete Psychological Works of Sigmund Freud* (1950–

74), Vol. 12, London: Hogarth Press and the Institute of Psychoanalysis.

Freud, S. (1919) 'A Child Is Being Beaten', *The Standard Edition of the Complete Psychological Works of Sigmund Freud* (1950–74), Vol. 17, London: Hogarth Press and the Institute of Psychoanalysis.

Freud, S. (1937) 'Constructions in Analysis', *The Standard Edition of the Complete Psychological Works of Sigmund Freud* (1950–74), Vol. 23, London: Hogarth Press and the Institute of Psychoanalysis.

Laplanche, J. and Pontalis, J.-B. (1967) *Vocabulaire de la Psychanalyse*, Paris: Presses Universitaires de France; trans. D. Nicholson Smith (1983), *The Language of Psycho-Analysis*, London: Hogarth Press.

Winnicott. D.W. 'Fear of Breakdown' (1963?) in *Psycho-Analytic Explorations*, London: Karnac 1989.

Further bibliography since 1998

Faimberg, H. (1981/1985) 'The Telescoping of Generations: A Genealogy of Alienated Identifications', in Chapter 1, *The Telescoping of Generations: Listening to the Narcissistic Links Between Generations*, London and New York: Routledge 2005.

Faimberg, H. (1981) '"Listening to Listening": An Approach to the Study of Narcissistic Resistances', in Chapter 2, *The Telescoping of Generations: Listening to the Narcissistic Links Between Generations*, London and New York: Routledge 2005.

Faimberg, H. (1993) '"Listening to Listening" and *Après-coup*', in Chapter 7, *The Telescoping of Generations: Listening to the Narcissistic Links Between Generations*, London and New York: Routledge 2005.

Faimberg, H. (1995) 'Misunderstanding and Psychic Truths', in Chapter 8, *The Telescoping of Generations: Listening to the Narcissistic Links Between Generations*, London and New York: Routledge 2005.

Faimberg, H. (2005) *The Telescoping of Generations: Listening to the Narcissistic Links Between Generations*, London and New York: Routledge 2005.

Faimberg, H. (2006) 'Plea for a Broader Concept of *Nachträglichkeit*', *The Psychoanalytic Quarterly,* 76: 4, 1221–40, 2007 (One of the two French papers published in the Joint Anniversary issue of the *Quarterly* and the *Revue Française*).

Faimberg, H. and Corel, A. (1989) 'Repetition and Surprise: Construction and its Validation', in Chapter 3, *The Telescoping of Generations: Listening to the Narcissistic Links Between Generations*, London and New York: Routledge 2005.

Laplanche, J. (1998) 'Notes sur l'*après-coup*', paper presented at the IPA Standing Conference on Psychoanalytical Intracultural and Intercultural dialogue, Paris, 27--29, July 1998; in John Fletcher and Martin Stanton (eds) (1992), *Seduction, Translation and the Drives*, London: Institute of Contemporary Arts; and also in *Essays on Otherness* (1998), London: Routledge.

9

Reading Winnicott

Thomas H. Ogden

In its first century, psychoanalysis has had several great thinkers, but to my mind, only one great English-speaking writer: Donald Winnicott. Because style and content are so interdependent in Winnicott's writing, his papers are not well served by a thematic reading aimed exclusively at gleaning 'what the paper is about.' Such efforts often result in trivial aphorisms. Winnicott, for the most part, does not use language to arrive at conclusions; rather, he uses language to create experiences in reading that are inseparable from the ideas he is presenting, or more accurately, the ideas he is playing with.

I offer here a reading of Winnicott's (1945) 'Primitive Emotional Development,' a work containing the seeds of virtually all the major contributions to psychoanalysis that Winnicott would make over the course of the succeeding twenty-six years of his life. I hope to demonstrate the interdependence of the life of the ideas being developed and the life of the writing in this seminal paper of Winnicott's. What 'Primitive Emotional Development' has to offer to a psychoanalytic reader cannot be said in any other way (which is to say that the writing is extraordinarily resistant to paraphrase). It has been my experience – which I hope to convey to the reader – that an awareness of the way the language is working in Winnicott's writings significantly enhances what can be learned from reading them.

Style and content are inseparable in writing. The better the writing, the more this interdependence is utilized in the service of creating meaning. In recent years, I have found that the only way I can do justice to studying and teaching Winnicott is to read his papers aloud, line by line, as I would a poem, exploring what the language is doing in addition to what it is saying. It is not an overstatement to say that a great many passages from Winnicott's papers well deserve to be called prose poems. In these passages, Winnicott's writing meets Tom Stoppard's (1999) definition of poetry as 'the simultaneous compression of language and expansion of meaning' (p. 10).

In this paper, I will focus on Winnicott's 1945 paper, 'Primitive Emotional Development,' which I view as his earliest major contribution to psychoanalysis. I will not be limiting myself to an explication of Winnicott's paper, though a good many of the ideas developed there will be discussed. My principal interest is in looking at this paper as a piece of nonfiction literature in which the meeting of reader and writing generates an imaginative experience in the medium of language. To speak of Winnicott's writing as literature is not to minimize its value as a way of conveying ideas that have proved to be of enormous importance to the development of psychoanalytic theory and practice; on the contrary, my effort will be to demonstrate the ways in which the life of the writing is critical to, and inseparable from, the life of the ideas.[1]

Before looking closely at 'Primitive Emotional Development,' I will offer a few observations about matters of writing that run through virtually the entirety of Winnicott's opus. The first quality of his writing to strike the reader is its form. Unlike the papers of any other psychoanalyst I can think of, Winnicott's papers are brief (usually six to ten pages in length), often containing a moment in the middle when he takes the reader aside and says, in a single sentence, 'the essential feature of my communication is this . . .' (Winnicott 1971a: 50). But the most distinctive signature of Winnicott's writing is the voice. It is casual and conversational, yet always profoundly respectful of both the reader and the subject matter under discussion. The speaking voice gives itself permission to wander, and yet has the compactness of poetry; there is an extraordinary intelligence to the voice that is at the same time genuinely humble and well aware of its limitations; there is a disarming intimacy that at times takes cover in wit and charm; the voice is playful and imaginative, but never folksy or sentimental.

Any effort to convey a sense of the voice in Winnicott's writing must locate at its core the quality of playfulness. The types of playfulness encountered in Winnicott's writing have an enormous range. To name only a few: There are the un-self-conscious feats of imaginative, compassionate understanding in his accounts of 'squiggle games' (1971b) with his child patients. There is serious playfulness (or playful seriousness) when Winnicott is involved in an effort to generate a form of thinking/theorizing that is adequate to the paradoxical nature of human experience as he understands it. He takes delight in subtle word play, such as in the repetition of a familiar phrase in slightly different forms to refer to the patient's need to begin and to end analysis: 'I do analysis because that is what the patient needs to have done and to have done with' (1962: 166).

While his writing is personal, there is also a certain English reserve to Winnicott that befits the paradoxical combination of formality and intimacy that is a hallmark of psychoanalysis (Ogden 1989). In terms of all these matters of form and voice, Winnicott's work holds strong resemblances to the compact, intelligent, playful, at times charming, at times ironic, always irreducible writing of Borges's Fictions (1944) and of Robert Frost's prose and poetry.

Winnicott's inimitable voice can be heard almost immediately in 'Primitive Emotional Development' as he explains his 'methodology':

> I shall not first give an historical survey and show the development of my ideas from the theories of others, because my mind does not work that way. What happens is that I gather this and that, here and there, settle down to clinical experience, form my own theories and then, last of all, interest myself in looking to see where I stole what. Perhaps this is as good a method as any.
>
> (1945: 145)

There is playful wit to the words 'Perhaps this is as good a method as any.' This seemingly tacked-on afterthought expresses what is perhaps the central theme of the paper as a whole: To create a 'method,' a way of being alive that suits the individual and becomes his unique 'watermarking' (Heaney 1980: 47), is perhaps the single most important outcome of primitive emotional development. In the process of coming into being as an individual, the infant (and mother) 'gathers this and that, here and there.' Early experience of self is fragmented, and at the same time, it is (with the help of the mother) 'gather[ed]' in a way that allows the infant's experience of self, now and again, to come together in one place. Moreover, for the infant, the bits of others (introjects) – or for the writer, the ideas of other writers – must not be allowed to take over the process of creating meaning. 'My mind does not work that way,' nor does that of the healthy infant in the care of a healthy mother. The individual's own lived experience must be the basis for creating coherence for one's self and the integrity of oneself. Only after a sense of self has begun to come into being (for the infant and for the writer) can one acknowledge the contributions of others to the creation of oneself (and one's ideas): '. . . last of all I interest myself in where I stole what.'

Winnicott then briefly discusses several aspects of the analytic relationship, with particular emphasis on the transference-countertransference. It is this body of experience that he believes is a major source of his conception of primitive emotional development. I will examine only one brief passage (two sentences, to be precise) of Winnicott's discussion of the transference-countertransference in 'Primitive Emotional Development.' I have selected these sentences because I find them to be of enormous importance, both from the standpoint of understanding his conception of the workings of the analytic relationship, and from the standpoint of the powerful interdependence of language and ideas in Winnicott's work:

> The depressed patient requires of his analyst the understanding that the analyst's work is to some extent his effort to cope with his own (the analyst's) depression, or shall I say guilt and grief resultant from the destructive elements in his own (the analyst's) love. To progress further along these lines, the patient who is asking for help in regard to his primitive, pre-depressive relationship to objects needs his analyst to be able to see the analyst's undisplaced and coincident love and hate of him.
>
> (Ibid.: 146–7)

In the opening clause of the first of these two sentences, Winnicott not only offers a theory of depression radically different from those of Freud and Klein, but he also proposes a new conception of the role of countertransference in the analytic process. He suggests here that depression is not, most fundamentally, a pathological internationalization of a narcissistically loved (and lost) object (in an effort to evade experiencing the loss of the object) (Freud 1917). Nor does Winnicott understand depression as centered around the unconscious fantasy that one's anger has injured, driven away, or killed the loved object (Klein 1952).

In the space of a single sentence, Winnicott suggests (by means of his *use of the idea*, rather than through his explication of it) that depression is a manifestation of the patient's taking on as his own (in fantasy, taking into himself) the mother's depression (or that of other loved objects), with the unconscious aim of relieving her of her depression. What is astounding is that this conception of the patient's depression is presented not through a direct statement, but by means of a sentence that is virtually incomprehensible unless the reader takes the initiative of doing the work of creating/discovering the conception of the intergenerational origins and dynamic structure of depression. Only after the reader has accomplished this task does it begin to make sense why 'The depressed patient requires of his analyst the understanding that the analyst's work is to some extent his effort to cope with his own (the analyst's) depression.'[2] In other words, if the analyst is unable to cope with his own feelings of depression (both normative and pathological), arising from past and current life experience, the analyst will not be able to recognize (to feel in the moment) the ways in which the patient is unconsciously attempting to, and to some degree succeeding in, taking on the depression of the analyst-as-transference-mother.

Those aspects of the analyst's depression that arise from sources independent of the analyst's unconscious identification with the patient's depressed internal object mother are far less available to the patient's ministerings. This is because the patient cannot find in the analyst the depression of his mother, which for nearly the entirety of his life, the patient has intimately known and attended to. The patient is single-mindedly concerned with the depression that is unique to the internal object mother. (Each person's depression is his or her own unique creation, rooted in the particular circumstances of life experience and personality organization.)

Winnicott is suggesting that the analyst must cope with his own depression in order that he might experience the patient's (internal object) mother's depression (which is being projected into the analyst). Only if the analyst is able to contain/live with the experience of the (internal object) mother's depression (as distinct from his own depression) will the analyst be able to experience the patient's pathological effort to relieve the mother's psychological pain (now felt to be located in the analyst) by introjecting it into the patient's self as a noxious foreign body.

The second clause of the sentence under discussion, while introduced by Winnicott as if it were simply another way of saying what he has already said in the first clause ('or shall I say') is in fact something altogether new: '[The analyst of a depressed patient must cope with his own] . . . guilt and grief resultant from the destructive elements in his own (the analyst's) love.' Thus, the analyst of the depressed patient must also be able to live with the inevitable destructiveness of love, in the sense that love involves a demand on the loved object, which may (in fantasy, and at times, in reality) be too much of a strain for the person one loves. In other words, the analyst, in the course of personal analysis and by means of ongoing self-analysis, must sufficiently come to terms with his own fears of the draining effects of love to be able to love the patient without fear that such feelings will harm the patient, thereby causing the analyst 'guilt and grief.'[3]

Winnicott does not stop here. In the sentence that follows the quoted passage, he revolutionizes (and I use the word advisedly) the psychoanalytic conception of 'the analytic frame' by viewing it as a medium for the expression of the analyst's hatred of the patient: '. . . the end of the hour, the end of the analysis, the rules and regulations, these all come in as expressions of [the analyst's] hate' (p. 147). These words derive a good deal of their power from the fact that the truth of the idea that the analyst expresses his hate in these actions (which are so ordinary as to frequently go unnoticed) is immediately recognizable by the analytic reader as part of his experience with virtually every patient. Winnicott is recognizing/interpreting the unspoken expressions of hate that the analyst/reader unconsciously and preconsciously experiences (often accompanied by a feeling of relief) in 'throwing the patient out' (by punctually ending each meeting), and by establishing the limits of what he will provide for the patient (in maintaining the other aspects of the analytic frame). Implicit here is the notion that the analyst's fear of the destructiveness of his hatred of the patient can lead to treatment destructive breaches of the analytic frame, such as the analyst's extending the session for more than a few minutes in order 'not to cut the patient off,' or the analyst's setting the fee at a level below what the patient is able to afford 'because the patient was consistently exploited by his parents in childhood,' or reflexively telephoning the patient when the patient has missed a session 'to be sure he is all right,' and so on.

Only by looking closely at these sentences can one discern and appreciate what is going on in the very living relationship between the writing and the reader, which constitutes so much of the life of the ideas being developed. As we have seen, the writing demands that the reader become an active partner in the creation of meaning.

The writing (like the communications of an analysand) suggests, and only suggests, possibilities of meaning. The reader/analyst must be willing and able not to know in order to make room inside himself for a number of possible meanings to be experienced/created, and to allow one meaning or another, or several meanings concurrently, to achieve ascendance (for a time).

Moreover, it is important to note that the writing 'works' (to borrow a word from Winnicott's statement of his 'method') in large measure by means of its power to understand (to correctly interpret the unconscious of) the reader. Perhaps all good writing (whether it be in poems, plays, novels, or essays), to a significant degree, 'works' in this way.

Winnicott's writing in the paper under discussion (and in almost all the works included in his three major volumes of collected papers [1958, 1965, 1971c]) is surprisingly short on clinical material. This, I believe, is a consequence of the fact that the clinical experience is to such a large degree located in the reader's experience of 'being read' (that is, of being interpreted, understood) by the writing. When Winnicott does offer clinical material, he often refers not to a specific intervention with a particular patient, but to a 'very common experience' (1945: 150) in analysis. In this way, he implicitly asks the reader to draw on his own lived experience with patients for the purpose not of 'taking in' Winnicott's ideas, but of inviting from the reader an 'original response' (Frost 1942: 307).

Still other forms of the generative interplay of style and content, of writing and reader, take on central importance in a passage a bit later in 'Primitive Emotional Development,' one that addresses experiences of unintegration and integration in early development:

An example of unintegration phenomena is provided by the very common experience of the patient who proceeds to give every detail of the week-end and feels contented at the end if everything has been said, though the analyst feels that no analytic work has been done. Sometimes we must interpret this as the patient's need to be known in all his bits and pieces by one person, the analyst. To be known means to feel integrated at least in the person of the analyst. This is the ordinary stuff of infant life, and an infant who has had no one person to gather his bits together starts with a handicap in his own self-integrating task, and perhaps he cannot succeed, or at any rate cannot maintain integration with confidence. . . . There are long stretches of time in a normal infant's life in which a baby does not mind whether he is many bits or one whole being, or whether he lives in his mother's face or in his own body, provided that from time to time he comes together and feels something.

(1945: 150)

Implicit in this passage is the recognition of the analyst's anger at patients who 'give every detail of the week-end,' leaving the analyst with the feeling 'that no analytic work has been done.' Winnicott leaves it entirely to the reader to imagine the analyst's impulse to dump anger and feelings of failure back into the patient in the form of a resistance interpretation ('You seem to be filling the hour with details that serve to defeat any possibility of analytic work getting done' [my example]).

Winnicott then provides the reader with a major revision of analytic technique. He accomplishes this so subtly that the reader is apt not to notice it if he is not attending carefully to what is going on in the writing. Nothing short of a new way of being with and talking to patients is being offered to the reader, without preaching or fanfare: 'Sometimes we must interpret[4] this [the patient's giving every detail of his week-end] as the patient's need to be known in all his bits and pieces by one person, the analyst.' The phrase 'sometimes we must' addresses the reader as a colleague who is familiar with the clinical situation being described, and who has very likely felt it necessary to intervene in the way Winnicott describes. Perhaps the reader/analyst has not fully named for himself what he has been experiencing and doing with his patient. The language does not debunk the angry resistance interpretation that the reader/analyst has either made or has been inclined to make in response to feelings of frustration and sense of failure. Winnicott, by means of the language with which he addresses the reader, provides an experience in reading, one that helps the reader undefensively gather together his own unarticulated experiences from his own analysis and from his analytic work with patients.

Moreover, the simple phrase 'very common experience' conveys an important theoretical concept (again without calling attention to itself): primitive states of unintegration are not restricted to the analysis of severely disturbed patients; such states regularly occur in the analysis of all our patients, including the healthiest ones. This writing 'technique' does not have the feel of manipulation of the reader;

rather, it feels like a good interpretation – a statement that puts into words what the reader/analyst has known all along from personal experience, but has not known that he has known it, and has not known it in the verbally symbolized, integrated way that he is coming to know it.

The second paragraph of the passage being discussed is remarkable:

There are long stretches of time in a normal infant's life in which a baby does not mind whether he is in many bits or one whole being, or whether he lives in his mother's face or in his own body, provided that from time to time he comes together and feels something.

(Ibid.: 150)

This sentence is distinctive, not only for the originality of the ideas it develops, but also for the way in which its syntax contributes in a sensory way to the creation of those ideas. The sentence is constructed of many groups of words (I count ten) that are read with very brief pauses between them (for instance, after the words 'time', 'life', 'mind', and so on). The sentence not only refers to, but brings to life in its own audible structure, the experience of living in bits ('from time to time'), in a meandering sort of way, before coming together – for a moment – in its final two bits: 'he comes together,' 'and feels something.' The voice, syntax, rhythm, and carefully chosen words and expressions that constitute this sentence – working together as they do with the ideas being developed – create an experience in reading that is as distinctively Winnicott as the opening paragraph of *The Sound and the Fury* is distinctively William Faulkner, or as the opening sentence of *The Portrait of a Lady* is uniquely Henry James.

The reader of the sentence being discussed is not moved to question how Winnicott can possibly know what an infant feels, or to point out that regressions in the analyses of children and adults (whether psychotic, depressed, or quite healthy) bear a very uncertain correlation with infantile experience. Rather, the reader is inclined to suspend disbelief for a time, and to enter into the experience of reading (with Winnicott), allowing himself to be carried by the music of the language and ideas. The reader lives an experience in the act of reading that is something like that of the imagined infant who does not mind whether he is in many bits (experiencing a floating feeling that accompanies nonlinear thinking) or one whole being (experiencing a 'momentary stay against confusion' [Frost 1939: 777]). Winnicott's writing, like a guide 'who only has at heart your getting lost' (Frost 1947: 341), ensures that we will never get it right in any final way, and we do not mind.

Subliminally, the pun on mind allows the clause 'a baby does not mind whether he is in many bits or one whole being' to concentrate into itself different overlapping meanings. The baby 'does not mind' because the mother is there 'minding' him (taking care of him). And he 'does not mind' in that he feels no pressure to be 'minded,' that is, to create premature, defensive mindedness that is disconnected from bodily experience. The writing itself, in punning, deftly and un-self-consciously, creates just such an experience of the pleasure of not minding, of not having to know, of not having to pin down meaning, and instead simply enjoying the liveliness of a fine experience in the medium of language and ideas.

The language that Winnicott uses in describing the infant's coming together in one place is surprising, in that the 'place' where coming together occurs is not a place at all, but an action (the act of feeling something). Moreover, the infant, in 'coming together,' does not simply feel, he 'feels something.' The word something has a delightful ambiguity to it: 'something' is a concrete thing, the object that is felt; and, at the same time, 'something' is the most indefinite of words, suggesting only that some feeling is being experienced. This delicate ambiguity creates in the experience of reading the flickering of the feeling-world of the infant, a world loosely bound to objects, loosely localized, experienced now in the body as objectless sensation, now in the more defined and localized sensation of feeling an object, now in the mother's face.[5]

The unexpected turns, the quiet revolutions occurring in this early Winnicott paper, are too numerous to address. I cannot resist, however, taking a moment simply to marvel at the way in which Winnicott, the pediatrician, the child analyst, nonchalantly jettisons the accrued technical language of fifty years of psychoanalytic writing in favor of language that is alive with the experiences being described:

> . . . There are the quiet and the excited states. I think an infant cannot be said to be aware at the start that while feeling this and that in his cot or enjoying the skin stimulations of bathing, he is the same as himself screaming for immediate satisfaction, possessed by an urge to get at and destroy something unless satisfied by milk. This

means that he does not know at first that the mother he is building up through his quiet experiences is the same as the power behind the breasts that he has in his mind to destroy.

(Ibid.: 151)

The infant has both quiet and excited states – everyone who has spent time with a baby knows this, but why had no one thought to put it this way? The baby feels 'this and that' [there is ease in the language, just as there is ease in the baby's state of mind-body], and enjoys the 'skin stimulations of bathing' and 'cannot be said to be aware . . . that [in the quiet states] . . . he is the same as himself screaming for immediate satisfaction . . .' How better to describe the feeling of continuity of identity over different feeling/meaning states than with unobtrusive alliteration of S sounds – sixteen times in one sentence – in words carrying a very wide range of meaning, including: states, start, skin, stimulation, same, screaming, satisfaction, something, and satisfied?[6]

Winnicott continues:

Also I think there is not necessarily an integration between a child asleep and a child awake. . . . Once dreams are remembered and even conveyed somehow to a third person, the dissociation is broken down a little; but some people never clearly remember their dreams, and children depend very much on adults for getting to know their dreams. It is normal for small children to have anxiety dreams and terrors. At these times children need someone to help them to remember what they dreamed. It is a valuable experience whenever a dream is both dreamed *and* remembered, precisely because of the breakdown of dissociation that this represents.

(Ibid.: 151, italics in original)

In this part of the paper, Winnicott speaks of the importance of the experience of the child's dream being conveyed 'somehow to a third person.' Every time I read this sentence, I find it jarring and confusing. I attempt to account for a third person in the apparently two-person experience of a dream (not yet the child's creation or possession) being 'conveyed somehow' to a third person. Is the third person the experience of the father's symbolic presence even in his absence? Perhaps, but such an idea seems too much an experience of the mind disconnected from the bodily feel, the sense of aliveness that one experiences when engaging with a child in spoken or unspoken conversation. A dream can be unobtrusively inserted into a conversation or into playing, sometimes wordlessly, because the child is the dream before the dream is the child's.

Thus, from this perspective, the three people are the dreaming child, the waking child, and the adult. This interpretation is suggested by Winnicott's language, but the reader, once again, must do the work of imaginatively entering into the experience of reading. The language quietly creates (as opposed to discusses) the confusion that the reader/child experiences about how many people are present in the act of conveying a dream to an adult. The reader experiences what it feels like for a child to be two people and not to notice that experience until an adult gives him help in 'getting to know . . . [what are becoming *his*] dreams.' 'Getting to know' his dreams – the expression is uniquely Winnicott; no one else could have written these words. The phrase is implicitly a metaphor in which an adult 'makes the introductions' in the first meeting of a waking child and the child's dreams. In this imaginary social event, not only is the child learning that he has a dream life, but also the child's unconscious is learning that 'it' (who, in health, is forever in the process of becoming 'I') has a 'waking life'.

The metaphorical language of this passage, without the slightest evidence of strain, is carrying a heavy theoretical load. First of all, there is the matter that as Freud (1915) put it, the unconscious 'is alive' (p. 190), and consequently, 'getting to know' one's dreams constitutes no less than the beginnings of healthy communication at the 'frontier' (p. 193) of the unconscious and preconscious mind. As the waking child and the dreaming child become acquainted with one another (i.e., as the child comes to experience himself as the same person who has both a waking life and a dream life), the experience of dreaming feels less strange (other to oneself) and hence less frightening.

It might be said that when a dream is both dreamed and remembered, the conversation between the conscious-preconscious and the unconscious aspects of mind across the repression barrier is enhanced. But having put it in these terms, the reasons for the enjoyment to be taken in Winnicott's writing become all the more apparent. In contrast to the noun-laden language of the preconscious, conscious, unconscious, repression, and so on, Winnicott's language seems to be all verb: 'feeling something,' 'getting to know their dreams,' 'screaming,' 'possessed,' and so on.

Having discussed the infant's early experience of coming together (in health) from his experience of living in bits and pieces (unintegration) and from a variety of forms of dissociation (e.g., the dissociation of dreaming and waking states), Winnicott turns his attention in 'Primitive Emotional Development' to the infant's experience of his earliest relations with external reality:

> In terms of baby and mother's breast (I am not claiming that the breast is essential as a vehicle of mother-love), the baby has instinctual urges and predatory ideas. The mother has a breast and the power to produce milk, and the idea that she would like to be attacked by a hungry baby. These two phenomena do not come into relation with each other till the mother and child *live an experience together.* The mother being mature and physically able has to be the one with tolerance and understanding, so that it is she who produces a situation that may with luck result in the first tie the infant makes with an external object, an object that is external to the self from the infant's point of view.
>
> (Ibid.: 152, italics in original)

In this passage, the language is doing far more than is apparent. '. . . The baby [at this juncture] has instinctual urges and predatory ideas. The mother [with an internal life quite separate from that of the infant] has a breast and the power to produce milk, and the idea that she would like to be attacked by a hungry baby.' The deadly seriousness (and violence) of these words – instinctual urges, predatory feelings, power, attack – plays off against the whimsy and humor of the intentionally overdrawn images. The notion of a baby with 'predatory ideas' conjures up images of a scheming, mastermind criminal in diapers. And in a similar way, the notion of a mother who would like to be 'attacked by a hungry baby' stirs up images of a woman (with large breasts engorged with milk) walking through dimly lit alleys at night, hoping to be violently assaulted by a hoodlum baby with a terrible craving for milk. The language, at once serious and playful (at times even ridiculous), creates a sense of the complementarity of the internal states of mother and infant, a complementarity that is going on only in parallel, and not yet in relation to one another.

In the sentence that immediately follows, we find one of Winnicott's most important theoretical contributions to psychoanalysis, an idea that has significantly shaped the second fifty years of the history of psychoanalytic thought. As the idea is rendered here, it is to my mind even more richly suggestive than it is in later, more familiar forms: 'These two phenomena [the infant with predatory urges and ideas, and the mother with instinctual urges and the wish to be attacked by a hungry baby] do not come into relation with each other till the mother and child *live an experience together.*'

'*Live an experience together*' – what makes this phrase remarkable is the unexpected word live. The mother and child do not 'take part in,' 'share,' 'participate in,' or 'enter into' an experience together; they live an experience together. In this single phrase, Winnicott is suggesting (though I think he was not fully aware of this as he wrote it) that he is in the process of transforming psychoanalysis, both as a theory and as a therapeutic relationship, in a way that involves altering the notion of what is most fundamental to human psychology. No longer will desiring and regulating desire (Freud), loving, hating, and making reparations (Klein), or object-seeking and object-relating (Fairbairn) constitute what is of greatest importance in the development of the psyche-soma from its beginnings and continuing throughout life. Instead, what Winnicott starts to lay out here for the first time is the idea that the central organizing thread of psychological development, from its inception, is the experience of being alive and the consequences of disruptions to that continuity of being.

The specific way in which Winnicott uses language in this passage is critical to the nature of the meanings being generated. In the phrase '*live an experience together,*' live is a transitive verb, taking experience as its object. Living an experience is an act of doing something to someone or something (as much as the act of hitting a ball is an act of doing something to the ball); it is an act of infusing experience with life. Human 'experience' does not have life until we live it (as opposed to simply having it in an operational way). Mother and child do not come into relation to one another until they each *do something* to experience – that is, they live it *together*, not simply at the same time, but while experiencing and responding to one another's separate acts of being alive in living the experience.

The paragraph concludes: 'The mother being mature and physically able has to be the one with tolerance and understanding, so that it is she who produces a situation that may with luck result in the first tie the infant makes with an external object, an object that is external to the self from the infant's point of view' (ibid.: 152). The unstated paradox that emerges here involves the idea that living an experience *together* serves to separate the mother and infant (to bring them 'into relation with each other' as *separate* entities, from the infant's perspective). This paradox lies at the heart of the experience of illusion: 'I think of the process as if two lines came from opposite directions, liable to come near each other. If they overlap, there is a moment of *illusion* – a bit of experience which the infant can take as *either* his hallucination *or* a thing belonging to external reality' (Ibid.: 152, italics in original).

Of course, what is being introduced is the concept that Winnicott (1951) later termed 'transitional phenomena' (p. 2). The 'moment of illusion' is a moment of psychological 'overlap' of the mother and infant: a moment in which the mother lives an experience with the infant in which she actively/unconsciously/naturally provides herself as an object that can be experienced by the infant as the infant's creation (an unnoticed experience because there is nothing that is not what is expected) or as the infant's discovery (an event with a quality of otherness in a world external to the infant's sense of self).

> In other language, the infant comes to the breast when excited, and ready to hallucinate something fit to be attacked. At that moment the actual nipple appears and he is able to feel it was that nipple that he hallucinated. So his ideas are enriched by actual details of sight, feel, smell, and next time this material is used in the hallucination. In this way he starts to build a capacity to conjure up what is actually available. The mother has to go on giving the infant this type of experience.
>
> [pp. 152–153]

What Winnicott is attempting to describe (and succeeds in capturing through his use of language) is not simply an experience, but a way of experiencing that is lighter, more full of darting energy than other ways of experiencing. The initial metaphor with which he introduces this way of experiencing involves the image of mother and infant as two lines (or is it lives?) coming from opposite directions (from the world of magic and from the world of grounded consensual reality), which are 'liable to come near each other.' The word liable is unexpected, with its connotation of chance events (of an unwelcome nature?). Is there a hint of irony about accidents serving as a port of entry into the 'real world'?

For Winnicott, the maternal provision is even more complex than that of creating a psychological-interpersonal field in which the infant gains entry at the same moment into external reality, internal reality, and the experience of illusion. In 'Primitive Emotional Development,' he states that the mother's task at this stage involves protecting 'her infant from complications that cannot yet be understood by the infant' (p. 153). 'Complications' is a word newly made in this sentence. In Winnicott's hands, complications takes on a rather specific set of meanings having to do with a convergence of internal and external stimuli that have a relationship to one another, one that is beyond the capacity of the infant to understand. A few years later, in speaking of the mother's efforts 'not to introduce complications beyond what the infant can understand and allow for,' Winnicott (1949) added that 'in particular she tries to insulate her baby from coincidences' (p. 245). 'Coincidences' is a word even more richly enigmatic than complications. It is a word with a long and troubling history in Western myth and literature. (Sophocles' version of the Oedipus myth represents only one instance of the ruin that 'coincidence' can leave in its wake.)

Winnicott does not explain what he means by 'coincidences' or 'complications', much less how one goes about insulating babies from them. His indefinite, enigmatic language does not fill a space with knowledge; it opens up a space for thinking, imagining, and freshly experiencing. One possible reading of the words 'complications' and 'coincidences' (as Winnicott is using/creating them) that I sometimes find useful goes as follows: Coincidences or complications from which a baby needs to be insulated involve chance simultaneities of events taking place in the infant's internal and external realities at a time when the two are only beginning to be differentiated from one another. For instance, an infant who is hungry may become both fearful and rageful while waiting longer for the mother than the infant can tolerate. The mother may be feeling preoccupied and distraught for reasons that have nothing to do with the infant, perhaps as a consequence of a recent argument with her husband, or a physical pain that she fears is a symptom of a serious illness. The simultaneity of the internal event (the infant's hunger, fear, rage) and the external event (the mother's emotional absence) is a coincidence that the infant cannot understand. He makes sense of it by imagining that it is his anger and predatory urges that have killed the mother. The mother who earlier wished to be attacked by a hungry baby is gone, and in her place is a lifeless mother, passively allowing herself to be attacked by the hungry baby, like carrion available to be consumed by vultures.

Coincidence leads the infant to defensively bring a degree of order and control to his experience by drawing what was becoming the external world back into the internal world by means of omnipotent fantasy: 'I killed her.' In contrast, when a mother and child are able to 'live an experience together,' the vitality of the child's internal world is recognized and met by the external world (the mother's act of living the experience together with the child). Winnicott does not present these ideas explicitly, but they are there to be found/created by the reader.

A note of caution is needed here with regard to the license a reader may take in creating a text, and that caveat is provided by Winnicott himself. It is implicit in all Winnicott's writing that creativity must not be valorized above all else. Creativity is not only worthless – it is lethal in a literal sense in the case of an infant when disconnected from objectivity, that is, when disconnected from acceptance of external reality. An infant forever hallucinating what he needs will starve to death; a reader who loses touch with the writing will not be able to learn from it.

Winnicott's conception of the infant's earliest experience of accepting external reality is as beautifully rendered as it is subtle in content:

> One thing that follows the acceptance of external reality is the advantage to be gained from it. We often hear of the very real frustrations imposed by external reality, but less often hear of the relief and satisfaction it affords. Real milk is satisfying as compared with imaginary milk, but this is not the point. The point is that in fantasy things work by magic: there are no brakes on fantasy, and love and hate cause alarming effects. External reality has brakes on it, and can be studied and known, and, in fact, fantasy is only tolerable at full blast when objective reality is appreciated well. The subjective has tremendous value but is so alarming and magical that it cannot be enjoyed except as a parallel to the objective.
>
> (Ibid.: 153)

This passage has muscularity to it. After acknowledging what is already self-evident ('Real milk is satisfying as compared with imaginary milk'), the passage seems to break open mid-sentence: '. . . but this is not the point. The point is that in fantasy things work by magic: there are no brakes on fantasy, and love and hate cause alarming effects.' External reality is not simply an abstraction in these sentences; it is alive in the language. External reality is a felt presence in the sounds of the words – for instance, in the dense, cold, metallic sound of brakes (which evokes for me the image of a locomotive with wheels locked, screeching to a halt over smooth iron tracks). The metaphor of a vehicle without the means to be stopped (a metaphor implicit in the expression without brakes) is elaborated as the sentence proceeds: '. . . love and hate cause alarming effects.' Love and hate are without a subject, thus rendering the metaphorical vehicle not only without brakes, but also without a driver (or engineer).

The modulating effects of external reality can be felt in the restraint and frequent pauses in the first half of the sentence that immediately follows: 'External reality has brakes on it -, and can be studied and known -, and -, in fact . . .' Having been slowed, the sentence – and the experience of internal and external reality – unfolds in a more flowing (which is not to say bland or lifeless) way: '. . . Fantasy is only tolerable at full blast when objective reality is appreciated well.'

Winnicott returns to the subject of illusion again and again in 'Primitive Emotional Development,' each time viewing it from a somewhat different perspective. He is without peer in his ability to capture in words what illusion might feel like to a baby. For instance, on returning to this subject late in the paper, he says that, in order for illusion to be generated, . . . a simple contact with external or shared reality has to be made, by the infant's hallucinating and the world's presenting, with moments of illusion for the infant in which the two are taken by him to be identical, which they never in fact are' (p. 154). For this to happen, someone '. . . has to be taking the trouble [a wonderfully simple way to allude to the fact that being a mother to an infant is a lot of work and a lot of trouble] all the time [even when she longs for even an hour of sleep] to bring the world to the baby in understandable form [without too many complications and coincidences], and in a limited way, suitable to the baby's needs' (p. 154). The rhythm of the series of clauses making up this sentence heaps requirement upon requirement that the mother must meet in creating illusion for the baby. These efforts on the part of the mother constitute the intense backstage labor that is necessary for the infant's enjoyment of his orchestra seat in the performance of illusion. The performance reveals not a hint of the dirty grunt work that creates and safeguards the life of the illusion.

The humor of the contrast between illusion as seen from backstage and from an orchestra seat is, I think, not at all lost to Winnicott. The juxtaposition of the passage just quoted (something of a job description for the mother of a baby) and the paragraph that follows (which captures all of the sense of wonder and amazement a child feels on seeing a magic show) can hardly be a coincidence: 'The subject of illusion . . . will be found to provide the clue to a child's interest in bubbles and clouds and rainbows and all mysterious phenomena, and also to his interest in fluff. . . . Somewhere here, too, is the interest in breath, which never decides whether it comes primarily from within or without . . .' (p. 154). I am not aware of a comparable expression anywhere in the psychoanalytic literature of the almost translucent, mystifying quality of imaginative experience that becomes possible when the full blast of fantasy is made safe by the child's sturdy grasp of external reality.

Concluding comments

Winnicott, in this, the first of his major papers, quietly, unassumingly defies the conventional wisdom, which holds that writing is primarily a means to an end, a means by which analytic data and ideas are conveyed to readers, much as telephones and telephone lines transport the voice in the form of electrical impulses and sound waves. The notion that our experiences as analysts and the ideas with which we make sense of them are inseparable from the language we use to create/convey them, for some analysts, is an idea that is strenuously resisted. For them, it is disappointing to acknowledge that the discourse among analysts, whether written or spoken, will forever remain limited by our imprecise, impressionistic – and consequently confusing and misleading – accounts of what we observe and how we think about what we do as analysts. For others, an appreciation of the inseparability of our observations and ideas, on the one hand, and the language we use to express them, on the other, is exciting, in that it embraces the indissoluble interpenetration of life and art, neither preceding the other, neither holding dominion over the other. To be alive (in more than an operational sense) is to be forever in the process of making things of one's own, whether they be thoughts, feelings, bodily movements, perceptions, conversations, poems, or psychoanalytic papers. The writing of no psychoanalyst better bears witness than that of Winnicott to the mutually dependent, mutually enlivening relationship of life and art.

231

Notes

1 In previous contributions (Ogden 1997a, 1997b, 1997c, 1997d, 1998, 1999, 2000), I have discussed the challenge to psychoanalysts of developing an ear for the way we and our patients use words. In the course of these discussions, I have frequently turned to poets and writers of fiction in an effort to attend to and learn from the ways they succeed – when their writing is good – in bringing language to life and life to language.

2 The term depression, as it is used in this sentence, seems to refer to a wide spectrum of psychological states, ranging from clinical depression to the universal depression associated with the achievement of the depressive position (Klein 1952). The latter is a normative stage of development and mode of generating experience (Ogden 1986), involving whole object relatedness, ambivalence, and a deep sense of loss in recognizing one's separateness from one's mother.

3 I am aware of the awkwardness of my language in discussing this passage. These ideas are difficult to convey, in part because of the extreme compactness of Winnicott's language, and in part because Winnicott had not yet fully worked out the ideas he was presenting at this point. Moreover, the ideas under development here involve irresolvable emotional contradictions and paradoxes: the analyst must be sufficiently familiar and conversant with his own depression to experience the depression that the depressed patient projects into him. The analyst must also be able to love without fear of the toll that this love takes – for if the analyst is frightened of the destructive effects of his or her love, there is little chance of analyzing the patient's fears of the taxing effects of the patient's love on the analyst.

4 It seems that Winnicott is referring here to silent interpretations that the analyst formulates for himself in words in the moment, and may at a later time present to the patient.

5 The role played by the word *something* in this sentence is reminiscent of Frost's use of nouns to simultaneously invoke the mysterious and the utterly concrete and mundane – for example, in lines such as 'Something there is that doesn't love a wall' (1914: 39), or 'One had to be versed in country things/Not to believe the phoebes wept' (1923a: 223) or 'What was that whiteness? Truth? A pebble of quartz? For once, then, something (1923b; 208).

6 Of course, I am not suggesting that Winnicott planned, or was even aware of, the way in which he was using alliteration, syntax, rhythm, punning, and so on to create specific effects in his use of language – any more than a talented poet plans ahead of time which metaphors, images, rhymes, rhythms, meters, syntactical structures, diction, allusions, line lengths, and so on that he will use. The act of writing seems to have a life of its own. It is one of the 'rights and privileges' as well as one of the pleasures, of critical reading to attempt to discern what is going on in a piece of writing, regardless of whether the writer intended it or was even aware of it.

References

Borges, J. L. (1944) *Ficciones* [Fictions]. Buenos Aires, Argentina: Editorial Sud.

Freud, S. (1914) Mourning and melancholia. S.E., 14.

Freud, S. (1915) The unconscious. S.E., 14.

Frost, R. (1914) Mending wall. In *Robert Frost: Collected Poems, Prose, and Plays*, ed. R. Poirier & M. Richardson. New York: Library of America, 1995, p. 39.

Frost, R. (1923a) The need of being versed in country things. In *Robert Frost: Collected Poems, Prose, and Plays*, ed. R. Poirier & M. Richardson. New York: Library of America, 1995, p. 223.

Frost, R. (1923b) For once, then, something. In *Robert Frost: Collected Poems, Prose, and Plays,* ed. R. Poirier & M. Richardson. New York: Library of America, 1995, pp. 208.

Frost, R. (1939) The figure a poem makes. In *Robert Frost: Collected Poems, Prose, and Plays*, ed. R. Poirier & M. Richardson. New York: Library of America, 1995, pp. 776–778.

Frost, R. (1942) The most of it. In *Robert Frost: Collected Poems, Prose, and Plays*, ed. R. Poirier & M. Richardson. New York: Library of America, 1995, p. 307.

Frost, R. (1947) Directive. In *Robert Frost: Collected Poems, Prose, and Plays*, ed. R. Poirier & M. Richardson. New York: Library of America, 1995, pp. 341–342.

Heaney, S. (1980) Feeling into words. In *Preoccupations: Selected Prose, 1968–1978*. New York: Noonday, pp. 41–60.

Klein, M. (1952) Some theoretical conclusions regarding the emotional life of the infant. In *Envy and Gratitude and Other Works, 1946–1963*. New York: Delacorte, 1975, pp. 61–93.

Ogden, T. (1986) *The Matrix of the Mind: Object Relations and the Psychoanalytic Dialogue*. Northvale, NJ: Aronson; London: Karnac.

Ogden, T. (1989) *The Primitive Edge of Experience*. Northvale, NJ: Aronson; London: Karnac.

Ogden, T. (1997a) Some thoughts on the use of language in psychoanalysis. *Psychoanal. Dial.*, 7:1–22.

Ogden, T. (1997b) Listening: three Frost poems. *Psychoanal. Dial.*, 7:619–639.

Ogden, T. (1997c) Reverie and metaphor: some thoughts on how I work as a psychoanalyst. *Int. J. Psycho-Anal.*, 78:719–732

Ogden, T. (1997d) *Reverie and Interpretation: Sensing Something Human*. Northvale, NJ: Aronson; London: Karnac.

Ogden, T. (1998) A question of voice in poetry and psychoanalysis. *Psychoanal. Q.*, 67:426–448.

Ogden, T. (1999) 'The music of what happens' in poetry and psychoanalysis. *Int. J. Psycho-Anal.*, 80:979–984.

Ogden, T. (2000) Borges and the art of mourning. *Psychoanal. Dial.*, 10:65–88.

Stoppard, T. (1999) Pragmatic theater. *The New York Review of Books*, 46(14): 8–10, Sept. 23.

Winnicott, D. W. (1945) Primitive emotional development. In *Through Paediatrics to Psychoanalysis*. New York: Basic Books, 1958, pp. 145–156.

Winnicott, D. W. (1949) Mind and its relation to the psyche-soma. In *Through Paediatrics to Psychoanalysis*. New York: Basic Books, 1958, pp. 243–254.

Winnicott, D. W. (1951) Transitional objects and transitional phenomena. In *Playing and Reality*. New York: Basic Books, 1971, pp. 1–25.

Winnicott, D. W. (1958) *Through Paediatrics to Psychoanalysis*. New York: Basic Books.

Winnicott, D. W. (1962) The aims of psycho-analytical treatment. In *The Maturational Processes and the Facilitating Environment*. New York: Basic Books, 1965, pp. 166–170.

Winnicott, D. W. (1965) *The Maturational Processes and the Facilitating Environment*. New York: Basic Books.

Winnicott, D. W. (1971a) Playing: a theoretical statement. In *Playing and Reality*. New York: Basic Books, pp. 38–52.

Winnicott, D. W. (1971b) *Therapeutic Consultations in Child Psychiatry*. New York: Basic Books.

Winnicott, D. W. (1971c) *Playing and Reality*. New York: Basic Books.

10

Winnicott and the acquisition of a freedom of thought

Daniel Widlöcher

One of the most interesting periods in the history of psychoanalysis in France was undoubtedly the time in the mid-1960s when the influence of D. W. Winnicott – the man as well as his work – was at its height. It was all the more surprising since the psychoanalytic world, at that time, was in a turmoil because of the very sharp doctrinal controversies and splits among the different institutions. Winnicott was immediately acknowledged and adopted by all those groups, those who remained faithful to Lacan's teaching as well as those who kept their distance or even moved on to other ideas.

In an issue published in 1977 of the literary review *L'Arc* containing articles from psychoanalysts from very different horizons, one of the contributors, O. Mannoni, a follower of Lacan, wrote, 'To analytic circles as such, what Winnicott brought more than anything else was freedom; it was only to be expected that that freedom led him to push back the limits of those circles and even to go beyond them.'

It would of course be interesting to examine in detail what each person found particularly refreshing in his or her theoretical and practical work; what was shared by all, however, was the feeling of freedom, its impact on the principles of psychoanalytic treatment, and Winnicott's focus on clinical empiricism and the value of creativity.

Thus set free, in the midst of theoretical deviations and the search for the 'real' Freud, from the burden of doubt and anathema, the French found in Winnicott a concrete developmental model that was simple and evocative, one whose reference was the individual, one which acknowledged the importance of the relationship dimension – there was truly something refreshing about all of this.

That message about freedom and creativity, the anti-conformism that became a way of thinking, could be seen not only in all of Winnicott's writings as they were diligently translated in the 1960s and 1970s, but also in encounters with the man himself and the unforgettable way he had of manifesting his own freedom of expression and of thought.

Invited by Masud Khan to review *The Maturational Processes and the Facilitating Environment* for the *International Journal* in 1970, I wrote:

> Winnicott's particular style is felt in all these papers, his ease in addressing different types of audience, speaking in his capacity as analyst to experienced psychoanalysts as well as to psychiatrists and social workers; his deep feeling for the analytical processes. We observe even more clearly his close attention to facts, his capacity to hold to a few clues without trying immediately to build them into a system, his reluctance to view the development of the psychic apparatus dialectically and his taste for empiricism.
>
> (Widlöcher 1970)

What we discovered there was implicitly denied by those who preceded us, since they were still very much under the influence of what could be described as the Puritanism of the earlier generation.

But style is not everything. We have to say in what precise domain of practice and theory this freedom of thought was manifested. For my part, there are four different levels that I would like to discuss: freedom of thought in the way analysts listen to their analysands' material, as regards the various metapsychological systems, as to the role of paradox, and with respect to the aims of psychoanalytic treatment.

Freedom of thought in psychoanalytic communication

Freedom of thought is an essential element of the way in which the analyst's mind and that of the analysand communicate with each other, 'Psychotherapy takes place in the overlap of two areas of playing, that of the patient and that of the therapist' (Winnicott 1971a: 38).

It was in the 1960s that Winnicott made his ideas clear on this topic in a series of articles that would form the basis of two chapters in *Playing and Reality* (ibid.) and *Therapeutic Consultations in Child Psychiatry* (1971b). The significance of such concepts as shared reverie and play, together with their expression in working with children through the Squiggle technique, highlights in a particularly sensitive way this sharing of associations, which becomes the source of a kind of conversation that is specific to psychoanalysis – we could think of it as shared creativity.

The idea of freedom of thought was present from the very beginnings of psychoanalysis through what is called the fundamental rule of that technique, i.e. the free associations that the analysand is asked to share with the analyst. However, as has often been pointed out, that rule, said to be the necessary condition for psychic work to take place in any psychoanalytic treatment, also highlights the difficulties that may be encountered in its implementation.

As for the second fundamental rule, that of evenly-suspended attention, it only indirectly involves the idea of freedom to associate in the analyst and, importantly, it is not explicitly linked to the analyst's power of free association – quite the opposite in fact: it gives the analyst a freedom of thought that is protected as much as possible from any countertransference influence so that he or she can observe with complete neutrality whatever the analysand's mind produces.

The importance of the theoretical turning-point of the 1950s as regards the countertransference cannot be over-emphasized: that was when it stopped being seen as an obstacle to the objectivity of the psychoanalysts's investigation and began to be treated as the driving force behind the intersubjective communication between the activity of the analysand's mind and that of his or her analyst. Winnicott played a highly significant role in that shift of emphasis, as Margaret Little and Harry Guntrip have shown.

But Winnicott went further than countertransference theorists, pointing out that it is not simply in response to the analysand's transference that an empathic understanding of his or her unconscious can develop – the origins of that kind of mutual communication lie in the interaction between mother and baby. Co-associativeness or co-creativity makes for shared reverie, the infant's capacity to be alone in the mother's presence. She helps her child to play, just as the analyst helps his or her patient to play – in other words, and somewhat paradoxically, to work at the combinatorial associations between representations and affects. In working with children, the Squiggle has this two-fold impact:the manifestation of a combined system of signs and the shared working-through of a composite image that expresses how thinking together can operate. It facilitates a working partnership between adult and child that also involves the mother–infant matrix. The freedom of thought that therapist and patient claim for each other in their work together guarantees that there will be at least some degree of interplay between traces of external reality and the way in which the internal reality of the unconscious has taken these on board. Thanks to the shared work of free association, the self can become aware of a two-fold kind of transformation: that of the primary interpersonal experiences which participate in fantasy construction, and the development of these fantasies in the service of the ego's attempts at constructive working-through.

In order to avoid confusion through the use of the word intersubjectivity, I suggest that the term co-thinking could be used to describe the impact on the analysand's associative process and representations. It should not be seen as some new device but as a description of the process of mutual enrichment of the activity of free association. The words uttered, together with their interrelated meanings, their associations, words which are omitted or struck down by censorship – these various elements coming from one of the protagonists enter into the other's thinking and become objects of that person's thoughts too. Any meaningful outcome will depend on the associative context in which they originated and on the one they create in the other person.

Co-thinking can be seen as the means whereby one unconscious communicates with another. From a dynamic point of view, the interplay of transference and countertransference has to do with the content and associative dynamics of co-thinking.

Interpretations should therefore be seen as a direct effect of co-thinking. The network of free associations set up in the psychoanalyst should be thought of as an expression of the analysand's psychic reality. In part, this is because the analysand's psychic reality contributes to the empathy of their interaction; and, since there are elements in operation which are missing from the pre-conscious associative network, the work the analyst has to do in his or her mind enables the analysand's unconscious representations or associations to be identified. In this manner, hypothetical representations and provisional interpretations are built up; when the time is right they make their way into the analyst's mind as words that can be communicated to the analysand in order to open up new pathways in his or her network of free associations. Co-thinking creates a repertoire of potential interpretations, 'key representations' that may well 'unlock' a pre-conscious system that resists the pressures coming from the unconscious (the 'portions of the id' of which Freud writes in 'Analysis Terminable and Interminable').

If drive-related transference and transference of thinking are usually linked, there are clinical situations in which they are found to be disjoined. The psychoanalyst's thought-associations may be induced by certain things the patient says or certain events linked to him or her without it being possible to identify any underlying drive-related theme. Further, transference and countertransference movements can be directly brought about by the situation itself, without any mobilization of free associations having occurred ('paralyzing' affects or enactments).

The model does, however, leave some matters in need of clarification – in particular the forces of control and regulation that oversee the transformation process and deal with its economic aspects. A strictly topographical perspective can account for transforming operations; we may well, however, want to include the mechanisms that regulate these processes, bringing them more quickly to a close or deferring their implementation – this requires a shift from a topographical to a structural model.

Freedom of thought and metapsychological constraints

From the outset, Freud acknowledged the fact that the topographical processes of transformation between the Id, Preconscious (Pcs) and Conscious (Cs) systems could never be entirely free of the need for facilitation or inhibition. Initially these processes were no more than simple mechanisms linked to the fulfilment or the prevention of drive functioning. It was only when Freud developed what has unfortunately sometimes come to be called the second topographical model – it is, in fact, a structural model – that a proper theoretical design was constructed in order to define the processes that provide not only for the implementation but also for the creation of this regulation.

Strangely enough, Winnicott did not give much thought to redefining these. Even more strangely, he hardly bothered about how regulatory models could be applied to those involving transformation. In the 1960s and 1970s, it was often said that there was no metapsychology in Winnicott's theory. It was as though his idea was to let others make up their own minds as regards resistance to or availability for change, untrammeled by any metapsychological model; this was a new, non-conformist kind of freedom of thought or epistemological approach.

What interested Winnicott above all was the cycle which begins with the human being's early relationship with someone else and which provides the mind with food for thought in a whole series of patterns that range from unconscious fantasy (or even primary non-representability) to conscious subjectivity. The final link in the chain that runs from conscious subjectivity to the surrounding world depends on the ability to hold in one's mind everything that prepares the individual for living in that environment. Freud not only provided us with the basic model of this cycle in *The Interpretation of Dreams*, but also, in his studies on the psychopathology of the neuroses, described the mechanisms which modify or re-organize them.

Winnicott took up this topic and pushed back the frontiers of pathology in order to include deprivation and trauma alongside intrapsychic neurotic conflicts. He focused exclusively, however, on a genetic point of view in order to describe their origins and distortions. For him, therapeutic technique has to do with reparation and a countertransference focus on the patient's material. The internal world to which Winnicott refers is the space in which forms of thought unfold. Whenever he felt himself closer to Kleinian thinking than to Freud's ideas, he would describe the gap between them by differentiating fantasy and internal reality. The fundamental issue for him was not the contrast between fantasy and external reality but between internal and external reality, insofar as internal reality is based on a hallucinatory idea as opposed to an apprehension of external reality.

Freud began to develop the concept of psychic reality in *Totem and Taboo* as a trace in the individual unconscious of primitive magical thinking and of a belief in the omnipotence of thought. Freud made use of the term in all of his discussions on the origins of neurotic thinking. He puts it quite emphatically in his 23rd Introductory Lecture, 'The phantasies possess *psychical* as contrasted with *material* reality, and we gradually learn to understand that *in the world of the neuroses it is psychical reality which is the decisive kind*' (Freud 1916: 368 [Freud's italics]). The idea and the term itself would be employed in the 1919 edition of *The Interpretation of Dreams* and later developed on numerous occasions throughout the 1920s. Strangely enough, after this, the term itself never appeared in any of his writings, including the *New Introductory Lectures* and *An Outline of Psychoanalysis*, with the sole exception of *Moses and Monotheism* (Freud 1933, 1939, 1940). I have the impression that this has to do with the development of Freud's thinking about the id. The concept of psychic reality is closely linked to the idea of historical truth, i.e. to past events, especially excitatory ones such as seduction or trauma, whereas thinking in terms of the id gives pride of place to the drives. Freud left the idea of trauma to one side and returned to that of drive-related processes.

In other words, from the moment he opened up the topographical model to a system-oriented perspective, as he demonstrated so brilliantly in his *New Introductory Lectures*, Freud no longer used the idea of psychic reality to explain the compulsive force of the unconscious. The id is not only a space in which the unconscious in the strict sense of the word is thought about, but it is also a functional system that produces unconscious fantasy. Kleinian theory, on the other hand, has always remained attached to the concept of psychic reality, even if, at times, it tends to blur into that of internal reality. In her essay on the nature and function of fantasy, the initial aim of which was to contribute to the controversial discussions that were taking place in the British Psycho-Analytical Society in 1948, Susan Isaacs wrote, 'Freud's discovery of dynamic psychical reality initiated a new epoch in psychological understanding' ('The Nature and Function of Phantasy'. *Int. J. Psycho-Anal.*, 29: 73–97). Jones himself referred to that statement in opening the discussions. We could suggest that, when Winnicott signalled his adoption of Kleinian theory in 1935 by referring to the importance of internal reality, he was struck by the role that had to be accorded to the hallucinatory aspect of the unconscious.

There is, however, one difference. When he introduced the structural dimension, Freud did not restrict himself to a purely descriptive point of view or to a new 'topographical' model. He was henceforth talking about systems, about the functional dimensions of mental life, not about forms of thought. I would like to emphasize that point, and differentiate between transformation processes (which act on the Cs-Pcs-Id forms of thinking) and the regulatory processes which govern these.

From that point on, the various schools of psychoanalytic theory developed different system-oriented or regulatory models (ego-psychology, the Kleinians and, more recently, the Lacanians, the self-psychology of those who think in terms of inter-subjectivity, etc). The distinction between transformation and regulation reflects what I have always maintained as the contrast between the first (topographical) model and the second (structural) one; this is well illustrated when we compare that of *The Interpretation of Dreams* with the one in the *New Introductory Lectures*. The former is linear in structure and expresses a to-and-fro movement between what is perceived and what is dreamed of unconsciously; the second is a model of functional organization which identifies systems that are interrelated. These functions gave rise to the various explanatory models specific to each school of thought.

When, in the *New Introductory Lectures*, Freud gave a detailed definition of the different types of unconscious, he provided us with a clear descriptive model of the forms of thought with which clinical practice in psychoanalysis makes us familiar. However, when he went on to state that the unconscious in the strict sense of the term is the id, he moved from a descriptive model to one that is explanatory. The id is a concept which is meant to describe that 'compartment of the mind' which constitutes a permanent source of excitation (the 'cauldron full of seething excitations' [Freud 1933; (1932)]); we can see that this is a reference to the original state of the unconscious, the excitatory quality of a form of thinking which is implemented in terms of something achieved (it / id is, it / id does, it / id says, etc). When it comes to explaining the origin of the id (the discussion about the nature of the drives), its relationship to external reality (the discussion about otherness), its origins, etc, we see that the way is open for all kinds of uncertainty, speculation and explanations that are part of every metapsychological approach.

When Winnicott was close to the Kleinian point of view, it was with reference to the status of internal reality (psychic reality?) that he adopted that standpoint. In all of Kleinian metapsychology, what really interested him was the depressive position; he never paid much attention to the paranoid-schizoid position nor to what its implications were for the workings of the mind.

How are we to understand his evincing so little interest in regulatory mechanisms? Quite simply, they had nothing to do with what he was putting forward – or, more precisely, he was interested mainly in the metaphors he required in order to understand the psychic work that defines the relationship between analyst and analysand and not in explanatory theories about resistance and facilitation with respect to processes of change.

Winnicott's thinking is implicitly concerned with freedom as regards explanatory systems that account for the way in which the mind controls this transformation process from External reality to Unconscious to Pre-conscious. We could just about use the term 'ego' to describe this final stage in the transformation process. This does not mean that we have to put aside the explanatory /structural point of view, or the models and clinical applications that the various schools of thought have worked out in order to account for the regulatory processes. Winnicott distanced himself from the Kleinian model more because he looked at these issues from a different perspective than because of any fundamental disagreement as to theory.

The same goes for the opposite point of view. System theorists have criticized Winnicott's 'non-system-oriented' approach; they have usually maintained a distinction between the way in which thoughts are transformed in moving from one topographical compartment to another and the manner in which the functional systems of the mind emerge, the 'provinces' of the mind which govern such transformations. This kind of freedom of thought is very different from the earlier one I discussed, which implies above all a certain flexibility in the way the analyst listens to the analysand's material, a pattern of intersubjective understanding. Here the emphasis is on a theoretical a priori, a theory of the personality. There is all the same a link between the two, since associative co-thinking will easily find its place in an evenly-suspended attention that is ready to take on board all kinds of paradox and opposites without attempting to explain them or break them down into their component mechanisms. What then is to be done with these opposites and paradoxes? Ignore them? Of course not. Evade them by simply acknowledging the conflicts to which they give rise then letting the matter drop? That neither. This is where we have to go deeper into what lies behind Winnicott's freedom of thought, where we have to accept paradoxes and dialectical principles.

Freedom of thought and paradox

If Winnicott did not feel particularly concerned by metapsychological discussions and if, when all is said and done, he made do with their diversity, it was because the perspective he adopted had little to do with the traditional concepts of conflict and conflict resolution. For

Freud, the conflictual nature of mental patterns in the unconscious is an inherent part of drive-related phenomena. The dualistic opposites he gradually discovered – starting with that between the libido and the self-preservation drives all the way through to that between Eros and Thanatos – enabled him to elucidate the conflictual nature of the drives. The later discoveries of the schools of thought which continued in this vein – ego-psychology just as much as Kleinian theory – complemented Freud's perspectives. The constraints inherent in the drives laid the foundations for metapsychological models.

The concept of paradox reverses the situation and is at the very heart of Winnicott's thinking. As André Green has pointed out, 'Since Freud, no other psychoanalyst has thought more deeply about experiencing limits and dealing with paradoxes' (Green 1977: 12). Opposites are no longer thought of as a series of antagonistic constraints but as forming a dialectical structure that lies at the very foundations of the mental apparatus. There are many examples in Winnicott's writings of this kind of dialectical thinking. We could start with the transitional object, with its position somewhere between external and internal reality. Ogden (1992) has shown quite remarkably how Winnicott's theory of subjectivity is based on a dialectically-constructed pattern, unity or duality in the primary maternal preoccupation, I-me dialectics of mirroring relationships, transitional object-relatedness, and dialectics of the creative destruction of the object. These dialectical phenomena could also be described as paradoxical propositions. We could also reverse the terms: if paradoxical propositions are so important, it is because Winnicott substituted the principle of conflict situations with that of a dialectical perspective. It is not a matter of resolving or going beyond conflict but of taking on board a dialectical conception, 'The paradox must be accepted, not resolved' (Winnicott 1989: 205).

Here we must give due consideration to the use Winnicott made of antithetical words. In 'The Use of an Object' (Winnicott 1971a: 86–94), 'using' the object is to be understood in both senses: make use of and waste or destroy. In other cases, it is not a matter of opposite meanings but of two possible meanings – 'capacity', for example, means both the ability to do something and what can be contained.

Acknowledging paradox from a dialectical perspective has to do with cultural factors. The cultural experience that underlies its implementation is not an individual dream but an inheritance of humankind such as we find in the arts, historical myths, slow development of philosophical thinking and the mysteries of mathematics, social institutions and religion. It should not surprise us, therefore, that, for Winnicott, psychoanalytic thinking was the most significant feature of the twentieth century as a representation of the cultural domain.

Acknowledging paradox, bringing it to life through play, encouraging in the analysand his or her capacity to contain this structured world within a dialectical perspective meant that Winnicott's logic had all the intensity of the fundamental freedom to take on board antithetical opposites instead of trying to make them submit to the constraints of conflict. Illusion is truly part of psychic reality, the proper role of which has to be accepted.

Magical thinking of the kind that we may have inherited in our unconscious is not an irrational belief of which we must rid ourselves; it is a form of thought in its own right. Like God, the unconscious creates what it is thinking about. We must emphasize the connection between the hallucinatory fulfilment of an unconscious fantasy and magic; magic claims to change external reality through pretence, through simulating change.

In my own work I have on several occasions attempted to show how the interpretation of 'Wunscherfüllung' (wishfulfilment), not simply as 'satisfaction' but as 'fulfilment of a desire' (the interpretation suggested by Lacan in 'The direction of treatment and the principles of its power'), has the advantage of situating drive-related phenomena alongside the act of representation, as long as the act of representation is not simply a representation of itself.

It is quite definitely the theory of dreams that evokes in us this property of unconscious fantasy. A dream is not a thing-presentation. In spite of the aphorism according to which pigs should dream of acorns, or little Anna's dream in which she talks out loud about strawberries and pudding, dreams are never simple images. They are representations of actions. The manifest content can always be described as a scene in which some action is taking place or as a series of scenes. This can always be seen to be the case if we consider the dreamer him or herself to be an active or passive participant in, or witness to, what is going on. The dream setting, together with the objects and persons that are part of it, are there to make these actions meaningful. When they appear to have no connection with the manifest meaning, are incongruous or simply pointless, this implies that we have to look for a scene of which they are a significant feature and to suppose that that scene (the latent content) is one of the ingredients of the manifest content.

245

From this point of view, the unconscious is less of a messenger of truth than an agent of some illusory power. The omnipotence of thought has no difficulty in finding its place in such a situation. The unconscious is less of an oracle to be decoded than a continuous creator of scenes. In my *Métapsychologie du sens* [Metapsychology of meaning] (1986), I attempted to show that the primary process has to do with mental acts that have no mediation whatsoever. The unconscious fantasy accomplishes an action that, for it to be carried out, requires nothing else. If we go back to Danto's theory about basic actions and the image he suggests according to which, although an individual (in actions that conform to the secondary process, one should add) may act in such a way that whatever he or she does is linked together, God alone acts exclusively through basic actions. (He carries out the act, fully intending to do so.) In that paper, I suggested that the same image could be applied to the unconscious: like God, the unconscious thinks only in terms of what is fulfilled.

The fact that this act of creation can be expressed in words does not change its nature. The words used are not a description of the action undertaken; they themselves constitute the action as such. This is similar to the performative function of language described by Austin and to what Lacan brilliantly described as the characteristic feature of the unconscious. Words bind the person who utters them; they bring into existence the event they designate: 'God said . . . and it was so,' says the Bible.

The statement that the unconscious is structured like a language seems to me in fact to be in contradiction with the powerful intuitive idea according to which utterances have a performative function. It would be better to say that, through words and images, the unconscious brings into existence whatever tries to exist. Should we then say that it operates as God does or, better, that God (or the gods, or the deity) was made in the image of the unconscious? Voltaire's words come to mind at this point, 'If God created us in his image, we have more than returned the compliment.'

Perhaps, then, we could say, as Ogden does:

Winnicott is perhaps the principal architect of a modern conception of psychoanalysis in which the central focus of the analytic process has been broadened from the task of making the unconscious conscious (in the language of the topographic model) or of transforming id into ego (in the language of the structural model). The analytic process for Winnicott (1971) has as its central concern the expansion of the capacity of analyst and analysand to create 'a place to live' in an area of experiencing that lies between reality and fantasy.

(Ogden 1997: 120–1)

This bridges the gap between freedom of thought as the basis for a dialectical theory of the mind and as a therapeutic goal.

Freedom of thought and therapeutic goals

Freedom of thought comes quite naturally to be seen as one of the goals of analysis. Expected of the analyst as he or she listens to the analysand's material, an open-minded attitude as regards the analyst's metapsychological references encourages in him or her a dialectical perspective that can integrate paradoxes as an element of the interaction and of the analyst's own states of mind; it is expected also of the analysand as a guarantee for the work of the analysis. 'What is then involved is the patient's ability to use the analyst,' wrote Winnicott (1971a: 87). We could perhaps say that every analytic treatment is nearing its end when the analyst has the experience that his or her thinking is echoing that of the analysand. Given that the analyst should be able to associate as freely as possible, echoing the analysand's own free associations, it could be said to be self-evident that the one's freedom of thought must be co-extensive with that of the other.

Although this feature may be taken to be one of the goals of analysis a little too easily, it sometimes becomes over-idealized or, on the contrary, trivialized. Ogden's idea that it is the third-party subject produced by intersubjectivity which constitutes a new subjectivity, a dialectical tension between the individual subjectivities of analyst and analysand, is an interesting one, but it describes the aim of analysis in terms of the final process in the treatment: 'The sense of aliveness and deadness are generated and experienced in and through the intersubjective analytic third' (Ogden 1997: 31–5). What becomes of this when applied to the 'post-treatment' phase? The risk is that we make do with generalizations about health (as Winnicott himself was often tempted to do) or with the ethical dimension of liberal thinking. 'The analytic task more fundamentally involves the effort of the analytic pair to help the analysand become human in a fuller sense than he has been able to achieve to this point.' What could we say in more

247

specific psychoanalytic terms about this 'human way' and this 'ability'? In my view, two concepts are necessary if we are to make any headway in this specific domain: that of creativity and that of mental space, both of which are directly related to a freedom of thought.

It is hardly conceivable to dissociate creativity from a freedom of thought. The reports we have of analyses with Winnicott make it clear that his associative thinking was made up of imaginative hypotheses (Guntrip 1975: 155). Martin James spoke of improvised tinkering (quoted in Posner et al. 2004, p. 94). Indeed, the analyst does strive to develop the analysand's creativity. Winnicott himself stated that the infant lives in a subjective world and that the mother adapts in such a way as to offer her child the experience of a necessary dose of omnipotence. The analyst could be thought of as being in a similar position to that of a mother. By giving life to the power of illusion in psychic reality, he or she may well be encouraging the creative use of omnipotence in psychic reality.

We are sometimes reluctant to accept this creative quality of unconscious illusion because, once reintegrated within subjectivity, it may well appear as an alienating delusion. It becomes acceptable only once we combine the idea of subjectivity with that of mental space. Subjective appropriation in this case does not consist in considering oneself to be the agent of a thought act as such – this would mean being the agent of an illusory belief – or of omnipotence; experiencing oneself as a subject in this case means acknowledging oneself as a space in which thinking takes place inside the self. What we do appropriate in terms of a subjective experience is the space in which illusion and creative omnipotence can be experienced as internal reality.

Freedom of thought, then, would seem to be part of the potential space of subjectivity. It is at work within us and makes us think. It is not a return to the illusion of being an agent with complete freedom as regards our thinking and our actions. It implies acknowledging that inside each of us there is a creative function the significance of which must be duly recognized; it is a road that remains open in our subjective space.

References

Freud, S. (1916) *Introductory Lectures*. Standard Edition 16, lecture 23: 358–77.
Freud, S. (1933) *New Introductory Lectures*. Standard Edition 22, lecture 21: 57–80.

Guntrip, H. (1975) My Experience of Analysis with Fairbairn and Winnicott. *Int. Rev. Psychoanal.*, 2: 145–56.

Isaacs, S. (1948) The Nature and Function of Phantasy. *Int. J. Psychoanal.*, 29 : 73–97.

Mannoni, O. (1977) La part du jeu in D.W. Winnicott. *L'Arc*, 69: 39–45.

Ogden, T. (1992) The Dialectically Constituted/decentred Subject of Psycho-analysis. II. The Contributions of Klein and Winnicott. *Int. J. Psychoanal.*, 73: 613–626.

Ogden, T. (1997) *Reverie and Interpretation*. London, Jason Aronson.

Posner, B. Melmed, Wolfe-Glickman, R., Coyle-Taylor, E., Canfield, J. and Cye, F. (2004) Agressivité et créativité. In *Winnicott insolite* [An unexpected facet of Winnicott]. Monographies de Psychanalyse, Paris, Presses Universitaires de France.

Widlöcher, D. (1970) On Winnicott's 'The Maturational Processes and the Facilitating Environment'. *Int. J. Psychoanal.*, 51: 526–30.

Widlöcher, D. (1986) *Métapsychologie du sens*. Paris, Presses Universitaires de France.

Winnicott, D.W. (1971a) *Playing and Reality*. London, Tavistock Publications.

Winnicott, D.W. (1971b) *Therapeutic Consultations in Child Psychiatry*. London, Hogarth.

Winnicott, D.W. (1989) Playing and culture. In *Psychoanalytic Explorations*. Cambridge, Harvard University Press.

The search for form

A Winnicottian theory of artistic creation[1]

Kenneth Wright

Introduction

In spite of possessing marked aesthetic sensibility and writing with a poet's feeling for words (Ogden 2001), Winnicott never developed a comprehensive theory of artistic creation. He was more interested in what he called the creativity of everyday life and how this related back to early experience. Nevertheless, a theory of art is implicit in his writings and it cries out for fuller development. In this paper I build on previous papers (Wright 1998, 2000) and make a further attempt to draw such a theory from his work.

Winnicott's ideas were rooted in clinical experience and he seldom developed their full theoretical potential. They were only as abstract as the clinical need demanded and like rich metaphors they continue to invite exploration. There are hints, for example, of a more aesthetic way of thinking in his statement that 'cultural experiences are in direct continuity with play, the play of those who have not yet heard of games . . .' (Winnicott 1967b/1971: 100), and likewise in his reference to 'a third area, that of play, which expands into creative living and into the whole cultural life of man' (ibid: 102).

More cogently, perhaps, he writes of the infant's *innate potential for creativity*, its roots lying at the very beginning of life in the feeding situation but only realized within and through the mother's provision. As Winnicott puts it, the infant has the experience of 'creating the breast' ('primary creativity') but only when the mother is attuned enough to give it in a way that corresponds to the baby's anticipation (Winnicott 1953). It is important to note that this way of thinking subtly transforms the classical concept of wish-fulfillment by stressing its object-relational aspect: primary creativity is more than libidinal satisfaction – *it involves the finding by the baby, and provision by the mother, of an external form (the breast) that corresponds to the baby's inner, subjective state.*

This kind of relation between inner and outer is critically important in Winnicott's account of infant development and suggestively prefigures those theories of art which stress the relation of outer form to experiential pattern within the art work. One such theory is that of the philosopher, Susanne Langer, who described the art object as a structure of non-verbal symbols that *portray the forms of emotional life* (Langer 1942; 1953). Her basic definition of art was quite simple: 'Art is the creation of forms symbolic of human feeling' (Langer 1953: 40); in other words, we could say that in creating his work, *the artist, like the baby, creates (or finds) external forms for inner feeling states.* Seen in this way, artistic creation echoes the transaction of 'primary creativity' in which an inner 'something' is realized through the mother's provision of a matching form.

In what follows, I attempt to develop this bridge between the *self-created* forms of the artist and the answering forms provided by the mother in infancy. I shall start by considering Winnicott's theory of transitional phenomena.

Transitional phenomena, mirroring and creativity

The transitional object (Winnicott 1953) is the infant's first 'not-me' possession (a part of the external world that lies beyond the infant), but it also constitutes a discovery – something the infant has *found.* From yet another perspective, the infant has *created* the object by transforming an ordinary bit of blanket into *something more than* an ordinary bit of blanket. So we might ask: What is this 'something more' that the bit of blanket now contains? It is, says Winnicott, *a subjective part of the infant*, the memory of earlier experiences with the mother. He likens the transformed object to the transubstantiated Host that for the Catholic *becomes* the body and blood of Christ; in a similar way, he says, the bit of blanket *becomes* for the baby (an experience of) the mother's body.

251

In Winnicott's model, the transitional process has a history: it is made possible by the mother having given the baby an experience of 'primary creativity' – of finding the imagined breast in the actual feeding situation. The earlier experience initiates a line of development in which the baby can create his own external objects; because of the mother's original adaptation, his external objects are not simply 'there' but available for investment with personal significance. From this point of view, the transitional object is not a one off occurrence but prototypical of a creative relation to the world. Winnicott writes:

> . . . [If the mother can supply the right conditions], every detail of the baby's life is an example of creative living. Every object is a 'found' object [in the way that the breast was a found object in the feeding situation]. *Given the chance*, the baby begins to live creatively, and *to use actual objects to be creative into and with*.
>
> (Winnicott 1967a/1971: 101 [my italics])

Winnicott extrapolates from this and suggests that creative living always involves a transaction with the object of this kind. First we put ourselves *into* the object, then realize ourselves *through* this object which has become significant for us.[2] A 'found object' is significant because of its subjective investment, and this applies not only to the baby's transitional object, but to any object that in later life arrests our attention through its having a special aura. Pebbles, pieces of driftwood, images provided by the natural world, even people can be thought of in this way.[3] All are 'found objects' in which we 'find' parts of ourselves (the element of personal significance). Artists are particularly likely to collect 'found objects' that resonate in this way, and the wider notion of *finding oneself in, and through, an objective medium* is central to understanding the artistic enterprise from a Winnicottian perspective.

However, in order to develop this way of thinking, I need to mention a further piece of Winnicott's theory, namely *maternal mirroring*. Mirroring is also a form of *transitional* functioning but it marks an evolution in infant development from the concrete level of tactile exchange (infant and breast, infant and transitional object) to a more distanced, visual form of interaction. Although retaining features of the pre-separation state, it entices the infant into a less embodied, quasi-symbolic arena of social exchange. Thus, while the image of the self reflected in the mother's face (a non–verbal signal) can no longer be apprehended physically by the infant, it is not yet experienced as separate from the infant and 'belonging' to the mother but occupies a *transitional space* in which the infant feels supported and contained within her animated response.[4] In Balint's phrase, there is a 'harmonious mix-up' between mother and infant (Balint 1959) in which the maternal reflection is merely an external phase, from the observer's point of view, of the infant's sense of being.

In mirroring, the mother's face, like the baby's bit of blanket, functions as a responsive *medium* for the infant.[5] In other words, we can think of this maternal 'medium' as an extension of the infant from which he draws out the *significant forms* of the mother's responsive expressions. These expressions are significant for the infant, not simply because they are an aspect of the caring figure, *but because they constitute the responses he has anticipated*.[6] Each maternal expression provides an image of the corresponding feeling state, and thus gives the infant the possibility of *finding himself* within it. Once the link between expression and feeling has been made,[7] the infant can use the mother's face as a medium from which to draw out the external forms of his own experience.

To rephrase Winnicott's insights in this way is to make the link with art more apparent: for both baby and artist there is an emotional reaching out towards an object with perhaps the expectation of response; a medium that allows itself to be transformed by the subjective image; and a 'finding' or creating within the medium of significant forms with at least the potential to reveal the subject to himself. Winnicott's model thus readily transposes into the language of art and my use of the phrase *significant form* is deliberate, for as with the term *found object* it moves easily between the languages of infant development and aesthetics.

Picture surface as maternal face

Connections of this kind between art and infancy have been noted before. The art critic Peter Fuller perceived the relevance of Winnicott's work to an understanding of art and discussed the work of the American painter, Robert Natkin from this perspective (Fuller 1980). He suggested that the picture surface could be thought of as a face-like structure and he saw the artist as communicating with it in ways that reached back to earlier experiences with the mother's face. Significantly, he pointed out that while the *maternal* response is largely beyond the infant's control, the artist can modify his picture surface until it gives back to him the 'responses' that he 'needs'. These are the colours, forms, shapes, and relationships that constitute the elements of his painting – the forms that resonate with the *inner* structures which intuitively he is trying to realize in his work. 'The canvas surface,' wrote Fuller, '[becomes] a surrogate for the good mother's face' (ibid: 211) and a more reliable provider of responsive forms than the mother of infancy. Natkin's own account of a chronically disconfirming childhood supported this idea: his mother was erratic, emotional, and punitive, and slapped him whenever he showed emotion.

Natkin was preoccupied with faces throughout his career. Starting as a portrait painter (a painter of faces), he later turned to more abstract painting in which colour and texture were paramount – he could not stand the 'limitations and fixity which the physiognomy of facial features imposed on his (portrait) work' (ibid: 210). Fuller took this to mean that portraits replicated for the artist the rigidity of his mother's face, so that in painting them, he felt prevented from freely interacting (communicating) with his canvas. It was as though the constraints of portraiture recreated the rigid and un-confirming dialogues of childhood, and to get beyond these he needed a less prescriptive medium. Experimenting with new ideas, he moved increasingly towards abstraction and as he did so his paintings became more alive. Through use of brilliant colours and varied textures his picture surfaces began to give back an increasingly rich display of resonant feeling; at long last he had discovered a medium that responded to his emotional gestures.

Fuller sometimes watched Natkin painting and noted how intensely he was focused as he made his marks on the canvas:

> He dabs the pigment on in layer after layer using indented cloths wrapped around a sponge . . . The rhythms of his body inform the way in which he gradually builds up the image . . . controlled and seemingly instinctive . . . There is . . . a real sense in which every painting he makes is imprinted with his touch and movement: it cannot but stand in an intimate close relation with his body, and be expressive of the emotions and sensations he uses in his body.
>
> (Ibid: 233)

It seems then that abstract painting offered Natkin a new responsiveness that the portraits (and the mother's face) were unable to provide. Through experiment and struggle, he had found a way of producing for himself the expressive surface ('face') that he needed, the materials he used, and ultimately the canvas itself, being drawn into the service of this need. He told Fuller that 'everything he had ever painted from the early portraits on was, in fact, a face' (ibid: 210), and he 'found' himself as an artist at the point when these 'faces' began to give back to him the shapes and rhythms of his own being.

The significance of this example transcends the particular case and raises the possibility of a more general statement: The artist, we could say, operates in dialogue with his canvas, and creates an illusory and expressive surface through his technique. With all the varied elements of that technique, he learns to draw from his medium an array of forms that reflect and recreate the pulse and rhythm of his inner life. According to this view, the new relation between artist and medium parallels, but also improves on, an earlier preverbal relation with the mother, whose facial expressions mirrored, or failed to mirror, the emotional gestures of the artist as infant.

If this is so, we could say that artistic creation has a therapeutic function for the artist. Winnicott believed that when the mother's face fails as responsive 'mirror', the infant 'look[s] around for other ways of getting something of [himself] back from the environment (ibid: 112).' Artistic creativity can be seen as a later means of achieving these ends: the artist's medium becomes a new version of the maternal face, and like the face for the infant, serves as responsive extension of the artist – an external medium within and through which he attempts to resume an earlier but unfinished dialogue. In these terms, *creating forms for human feeling* (Langer's definition of art) is a 'new beginning' (Balint 1952) on a more sophisticated level and revives a process of self-creation (and transformation) that was insufficiently established in the medium of the first relationship.

Maternal attunement

Winnicott's work has been seminal for psychoanalysis: in emphasizing the communicative dimension of early experience, and in placing the maternal face at the centre of early relatedness, he made a new kind of vision possible. I think, however, that one reaches a limit in using this insight to explore creative activity. For while the principle of mirroring offers a new conception of self-development, the tools it provides seem insufficient. The shortfall lies in the limitations of the face as expressive object, for while it provides a limited range of reflective expressions for emotional states and a number of 'qualifiers' in the shape of discreet 'looks' and facial gestures, it is not versatile enough to reflect the expanding variety of infant vitality. This is where Stern's work on attunement is so important (Rose 1996; Stern 1985).[8]

According to Stern, 'attunement is a recasting . . . of a subjective state (ibid: 161).' But so too, in a slightly different way, is maternal mirroring and so too is art: each 'recasts' subjective feeling states into more or less objective form. Mirroring 'recasts' the infant's spontaneous affect into the visible form of the mother's facial expression; art 'recasts' human feeling and experience into the objective forms of the art object.

So what is attunement and why is it such a relevant concept? The term is used by Stern for the many different ways in which the mother recasts her infant's experience. Peaking in the late preverbal period, its expressive forms are varied and make use of both sight and hearing. Eventually, as verbal comprehension develops, it gives way to language. How then does it work, and what does the mother do? What kinds of infant states provide the material for her recasting?

As I have described, the essence of attunement lies in the mother's ability to identify with the 'shape' of the baby's experience as revealed in the baby's manifest behaviour. She 'reads' the changing rhythm of its interest – its way of being-in-the world – in the contour of its bodily tensions, the speed and variation of its activity, the patterning of its vocalizations. Stern calls these the infant's *vitality affects*. Without conscious deliberation, the mother internalizes these contours and transforms them into expressive patterns of her own. These she spontaneously shares with the baby, giving back a stream of 'performances', or mini-enactments that reflect the baby's 'experience' as she has perceived it. These enactments may transform the baby's expressive behaviour into *different* sensory modalities and they modulate and vary it, much as a musical theme on one instrument is taken up and repeated, with subtle differences, by another. Such recasting distinguishes the mother's response from mimicry: in other words, she does not copy the baby's *behaviour* but grasps its *experience*, replaying it in a way that bears her stamp. Stern believes these variations and transformations are important because they give the enactment an aura of otherness.[9] Looking towards the later transformations of art, it could be said that in passing through the *medium* of the mother, the baby's lived emotional pattern is creatively changed and begins to confront him as an objective form within the gestures the mother has 'shaped'.

Attunement thus envelops the baby in a fabric of images (maternal responses) which recast its quirky vitality into (potentially) objective forms. The baby thrives within this imagined space and feels enhanced by feelings of resonance.[10] But the process goes further than mirroring, for while mirroring reflects the major patterns of affective arousal in a limited range of expressive forms (the mother's facial expressions), attunement has the potential to capture the essence of the baby's living in all its developing richness and diversity . The variety of forms (visual, vocal and kinetic) that attunement furnishes are more suited to match the increasing complexity of infant expression and arguably pave the way for language which will soon become the overriding form of exchange.

What is the relevance of this for artistic creativity? It is surely the possibility that the richness of the artist's imagination and his skill in finding forms for inner feeling states is a later development of the mother's intuitive skills – or perhaps a compensation for her relative lack of them. In mastering the techniques of his art, the artist has taken over the mother's form-making capacity, and brought it to fruition in his work. Not only does he now make the spontaneous and vital gestures that express his individuality; he also finds in his chosen medium the answering forms that bring them to reality in the objective world (Wright 1998; 2000).[11]

Aesthetic experience

In exploring the artist's involvement in the objects he creates, it becomes clear that the creative process is a kind of dialogue in which he struggles with his medium until it gives back to him the resonating forms for which he is searching. I have assumed (following Langer) that these are the elusive shapes of his own subjective life, which only achieve realization in the aesthetic objects he creates.[12]

For the viewer of art, the situation is different because the work confronts us as a finished product, and the making dimension, so

257

important to the artist, recedes into the background. As spectators we have no say in the creation of the object's forms; it confronts us as finished and given. Yet in spite of this, the work remains a responsive object that lends itself to the viewer. Whenever anyone connects with it in a meaningful way, there is dialogue between its forms and the viewer's emotional being; in spite of the constraints, its finished shapes allow themselves to be inhabited by the viewer's sentience and it then gives resonant form to these emotional intuitions, just as it did for the artist.

This is the territory of the much discussed *aesthetic* response – the feeling of often unspecified *significance* that a work of art engenders in the sensitive viewer. We must therefore examine this significance and see how it can be illuminated by psychoanalytic ideas.

Freud himself was deeply interested in art but tended to focus on the specifics of its *content*. He approached the work of art as though it was a dream or neurotic symptom, asking what it was 'about', what unconscious fantasies it expressed and what it revealed about the psychological make up of the artist. He thought the meaning of art lay in its unconscious symbolism and failed to grasp the more elusive issues to do with its form. In short, he never sufficiently addressed the all important question: 'What kind of thing is a painting?' but assumed it was similar to other psychic productions that had yielded to his method of investigation (Freud 1908; 1910; 1914).

From an aesthetic point of view, this was a fateful decision and psychoanalytic investigations based on Freud's model have generally failed to illuminate aesthetic experience. This is because it was assumed that the work of art was essentially a vehicle for repressed or forbidden wishes, and from this point of view, the impact of Shakespeare's *Hamlet*, or the *Oedipus Rex* of Sophocles, for example, lay in the fact that they expressed forbidden oedipal fantasies. Strictly speaking, however, such considerations lie outside the aesthetic question which relates to formal characteristics of the work of art; while the content of the art object may affect us deeply, it remains distinct from the question of artistic value. This at least is the formalist assumption.

I shall now discuss how an understanding of *formal structure* (as opposed to content) can begin to illuminate the aesthetic question. The literature is vast but I draw on just three non-analytic sources (Bell 1914; Fry 1924; Langer 1942, 1953) and two recent psychoanalytic contributions of particular relevance (Segal 1991; Bollas 1987).

I begin with the formal approach of Clive Bell and Roger Fry, which centres on the idea of 'significant form'. These writers were both concerned with *significance* in art, and they asked: 'What is it that makes art significant, and is there something unique in our response to it that is different from our response to ordinary objects?' Bell was the first to say there was:

That there is a particular kind of emotion provoked by works of visual art, and that this . . . is provoked by every kind of visual art . . . is not disputed, I think, by anyone capable of feeling it. This emotion is called the aesthetic emotion; and if we can discover some quality common and peculiar to all the objects that provoke it, we shall have solved what I take to be the central problem of aesthetics. [He asks what this 'essential quality' might be and replies that] . . . Only one answer seems possible – significant form. *In each [instance], lines and colours combined in a particular way, certain forms and relations of forms, stir our aesthetic emotions.* These . . . aesthetically moving forms, I call 'Significant Form'; and 'Significant Form' is the one quality common to all works of visual art.

(Bell 1914, in Harrison and Wood
1992: 113 [my italics])

Bell's analysis referred only to the visual arts but Fry extended his theory more widely and attempted to define the *aesthetic emotion*. The concept, however, proved difficult to pin down. The aesthetic emotion was not, he said, like ordinary emotions that are linked to particular objects or situations, but is stirred in us when we recognize *significant form*. This concept too was hard to define but seemed to depend on the 'the recognition of inevitable sequences' in the art object: in other words, on a certain perception of pattern and form that felt 'right' to the viewer, and in that sense 'had to be' the way it was. Fry's argument was self-enclosed and circular, and in some ways lacking in substance: We experience the aesthetic emotion when confronted with significant form; we deem a form significant when it arouses our aesthetic emotion.

Within this approach, aesthetic experience is not linked to any particular motif – to what is depicted – but to some more general characteristic of the art object. Our *aesthetic* response to *Hamlet*, for example, does not depend on the *content* of the story but on other elusive aspects of the play that we struggle to define. To approach their nature, we have to turn to some overall *quality* of the depiction.

In this context, the work of Bollas (1987) is helpful. Discussing the aesthetic emotion from a broadly Winnicottian perspective, he suggests that objects triggering such a response are connected in our minds with early 'transformational experiences' in which the mother's care was felt to transform the infant's being in a profound way. Such ministrations would not have been special events but part of the baby's normal experience of the mother in the early stages: 'Whenever we desired, despaired, reached towards, played, or were in rage, love pain or need, we were met by [the] mother and handled according to her idiom of care (ibid: 36)'. Thus she transformed our experience – for example from hunger to satiation – but in her own unique way, with her own particular style. This style he called her 'idiom of care' and suggested it was inscribed in our being in a pre-symbolic way that we can recognize but not remember. In his terms, it constituted part of 'the un-thought known' (Stern calls it the 'structural unconscious'), and he referred to it as a 'maternal aesthetic'.

From this perspective, aesthetic experience depends on the revival of such early feelings:

> The uncanny pleasure of being held by a poem, a composition, a painting, or for that matter, any object, rests on those moments when the infant's world is given form by the mother, since he cannot shape them or link them together without her coverage. . . . The transformational object [from our point of view, the art object] seems to promise the beseeching subject *an experience where self-fragmentations will be integrated through a processing form.*
>
> (Ibid: 32–3 [my italics])

This comes close to the idea of the art object as a source of containing and resonating forms, but for Bollas, the revival of early memory – the sense of being *in the presence of* a transformational object – seems more important than the value of the forms themselves as integrating agents in the contemporary life of the subject. This slant on aesthetic experience seems to make the work of art a nostalgic object, inducing recollection and hope of transformation but downplaying its contemporary therapeutic possibilities as a repository of needed forms. In this sense, Bollas' views differ significantly from my own.

I shall next consider the work of Hannah Segal, a Kleinian psychoanalyst who has written cogently and sensitively on aesthetic issues

(Segal 1991). Taking the criticisms of Freud's 'content' approach seriously, she believes aesthetic experience is linked to wider issues than the depiction of specific content. Foremost is what she calls the 'truthfulness' of a representation: a form is 'significant' when it 'truthfully' portrays an emotional structure or situation. Thus, while we might respond to *Hamlet* emotionally because of *what* it depicts (e.g. aspects of the oedipal conflict with which we identify), the *aesthetic power* of the play – its capacity to arouse the aesthetic emotion – would depend on the 'truthfulness' with which that content was portrayed. This is a formal consideration which refers to the adequacy of symbolic means, and indirectly, the skill of the creator, so in *Hamlet*, or indeed any other play, this would take us into the area of language and the power of imagery and metaphor, timbre and cadence, to reflect the pattern and coherence of emotional life.

With the notion of 'truthfulness', Segal directs attention to the *construction* of the art object – the way it is made and put together, and how this reflects or fails to reflect the structure of our emotional being. However, on a vastly simplified scale, similar questions confront us when we turn to mirroring and attunement: how truthfully does the mother's facial expression mirror the baby's affective state; and how truthfully does her mini-enactment portray the 'vitality affect' which has just unfolded before her eyes.[13]

This way of thinking links aesthetic significance to wider emotional issues. It is no longer a self-enclosed process depending on formal relations *within* the art object (Fry's definition of 'significant form') but now concerns the relation *between* these and dynamic forms of emotional life. The aesthetic emotion thus becomes *an indicator of personal significance*, telling us that the forms and organization of a particular work of art correspond truthfully to a felt inner pattern of experience. In this sense, every object with aesthetic import is potentially in tune with *some* elements of human feeling, and while any *particular* work of art will be limited by its creator's range of sensibility, every 'truthful' work will have its supporters because it resonates and speaks to them. Finally, this approach enables bridges to be made with early experience (Bollas' 'maternal aesthetic' and Fuller's link to the maternal face), for if *in infancy* the very means to selfhood depend on the truthfulness of representation – in other words, on the accuracy of maternal reflection/attunement (Winnicott 1967a; Stern 1985) – we can understand how art, its distant successor, is able to evoke such powerful reactions.

Integration, wholeness and aesthetic impact

The concept of truthful representation has considerable value. As Segal notes, however, the complexity of artistic creation and our response to its products cannot be fully accounted for in this way because it fails to take account of something we intuitively feel – namely that the art object has an *integrative* capacity, an ability to draw together disparate elements into more complex wholes. To explain this, she falls back on a 'content' type of explanation and thereby gives the aesthetic emotion a Kleinian twist. Arguing that destruction and re-creation (re-integration) lie at the heart of artistic endeavour, she suggests that significance in art is inseparably linked with the core depressive conflict of destruction and reparation. In my view, this seriously narrows her definition of art and closes the door to alternative explanations of its integrative effect.

One example of this is the way her Kleinian view focuses on the *object*, internally damaged by the artist's attacks, then restored and made whole in the creative act. A Winnicottian perspective raises different possibilities: if the work of art functions in a transitional way as extension of the artist's self, might not artistic creation aim to establish and restore the *self*, rather than perform reparative work on the *object*? This would place the artist's most urgent need at a narcissistic rather than a depressive level and suggest that the sense of integration we get from a work of art might reflect a new found wholeness of the *self* rather than the wholeness of a previously damaged and now repaired *object*.[14]

I have already discussed in relation to Natkin's work how the artist's skill in making resonant forms may result from an original deficiency; how through internalizing and developing the deficient maternal function, the artist learns to provide significant forms for himself; and how by treating his canvas as a surrogate maternal extension, he coaxes, cajoles and extorts the responses he needs from a more or less resistant medium. I have sketched how in normal development, a similar process completes the baby's experience, marking and containing it within a maternal form, and how this stands at the threshold of symbolization, offering a first means of drawing experience into objective (perceivable) form, and paving the way for language. Following Winnicott, I have argued that the sense of 'being me' *depends* on the experience of being 'held' in this way and that we first become selves through this process.

Within this framework, attunement and mirroring are core processes that bring the self into being, and un-mirrored, non-attuned elements are like creatures that have yet to be recognized. Without any resonant sensory representation, and lacking objective form, they cannot be organized into larger patterns of experience and remain unavailable for self-enrichment. *It is not until an emotional element is marked and symbolized that it enters the realm of real experience, for only within such a structure of containment is it possible to 'hold' it and contemplate it.*

From this perspective, the artist's most pressing need is to bring his unrealized self into being through his creative work. By providing his own forms for latent elements of his affective life, he is able himself to bring them into fuller existence and gather them into his own purview and jurisdiction.[15] According to this view, the unmarked elements awaiting discovery are those that have been ignored – through either the imperviousness of an un-empathic mother or perhaps through a kind of selective inattention that is arguably more normal.[16] Stern (1985: 160), for example, has suggested that there may be an *inherent* difficulty in attuning to certain negative affects, and if this were indeed the case, the shortfall the artist is driven to address would be universal.

The present perspective displaces reparation of the object from its central role in artistic creation and replaces it with self-creation and discovery. From this point of view, the first task of the artist is not so much to repair the *object* but to capture the *self* in a fabric of resonating forms. Only when corralled in this way within the art work can the secondary task begin – namely to integrate these forms of feeling into more complex structures and thus the self into a more coherent whole.[17]

For the viewer of the work of art the creative, *making* phases are inevitably curtailed; he can only *seek,* and find through *looking creatively.* The viewer is drawn to works of art with which he feels a particular resonance – in other words, he engages with their forms in a meaningful way, as transitional extensions of himself and as medium for self-transformation. Like the artist, the viewer too needs such forms to draw his experience into being, and because his needs overlap with those of the artist, he is a kind of artist by default. We can thus see that the art object functions in a similar way for creator *and* viewer – as a surrogate maternal object, made or chosen as the case may be, providing resonant forms for his sentient core.

Conclusion

In approaching artistic creativity, in particular the process of painting, I have built on Winnicott's seminal ideas. His astonishing understanding of early processes allows one to grasp in an almost concrete fashion the dialogical, relational core of the self. He enables us to see that latent or *potential* elements of the self require completion by a resonant maternal response (mirroring, and later attunement) and the sense of falseness and emptiness that results from failure in this process.

I have argued that *art* in its deeper purpose is genetically linked to this preverbal arena, and *significant form*, in the aesthetic sense, is objective (perceivable) form that truthfully (i.e. accurately) resonates with subjective elements, thereby giving them the possibility of being. Significant form enables a person to 'exist and feel real', as Winnicott puts it (ibid: 117) and the artist is someone with the skill and capacity to create such forms. He uses his *medium* as a transitional extension of himself in a way that is similar to the infant's early use of the mother. I have suggested that the development of such skills stems from the need to make good an early deficit by drawing into the purview of symbolic containment those aspects of self that were hitherto unrecognized. I regard such symbolic retrieval as a necessary precursor of integrative tasks, but I take issue with Segal that artistic creation *inevitably* involves restoration (integration) of a damaged object. In my view, the striving of art towards wholeness and integration is better understood as an attempt to realize the wholeness of the *self*, a task that is never complete because of the vagaries of early mothering and the vicissitudes of ordinary life.

I have focused on the visual arts but regard the model I have proposed as relevant to creation in other media. I have emphasized non-verbal dialogue but would argue that similar processes operate in the verbal arts, where the poet, for example, infuses language with his own being and remakes it in the service of his expressive need.

Finally, I would suggest that the interaction between patient and analyst has important similarities to that between the artist and his medium. Whether we think of the medium as the *affective matrix* of the analytic relationship, or the *language* in which this is progressively articulated, analysis too makes 'forms for human feeling' (Langer), and like the artist's forms these must resonate with experience if they are to serve a containing function. This view differs significantly from insight approaches which use explanatory language and which too often make 'clever and apt interpretations' (Winnicott 1967a: 117). In this more receptive and aesthetic mode, the analyst seeks *resonating* forms for the patient's experience and in Winnicott's words, will regard his activity as 'a complex derivative of the face that reflects what is there to be seen' (ibid: 117).

Notes

1 This paper was first published in Kenneth Wright's recent book *Mirroring and Attunement* (Wright 2009) [Editor's Note].

2 It would be possible and more usual to discuss this kind of exchange in terms of projective processes. Projection, however, has never completely lost its original sense of getting rid of something unwanted, and projective identification implies a sense of boundary that is lacking in Winnicott's formulation. In his account of mirroring, for example, the infant just gets on with things and the mother identifies, responds and reflects in an equally spontaneous way. Neither mother nor infant tries to get rid of anything and neither 'puts anything into' the other, at least in this sense. My intention here is to develop a more communicational framework in which the gap between subjects is bridged by non-verbal communication (i.e. through non-verbal signals). This renders less necessary the use of a projective model which sees projection by one person into the other as the primary means of bridging the gap. The non-verbal communication model is based on the idea that a potential for communication is a primary given in the human being's equipment, so that when the baby cries or smiles, for example, such action carries with it a built in expectation of response from the environment/mother.

3 I would argue that transference objects can also be thought of in this transitional way as examples of 'found' objects – a person 'finds' their father, mother, sibling or some aspect of these original figures in the analyst, or other figure in their present day life.

4 As Diamond and Marrone (2003) pointed out, this way of thinking was anticipated by the phenomenologist Merleau-Ponty (1962: 146) who wrote: 'I *live* in the facial expressions of the other.'

5 I developed the idea of the mother as responsive *medium* in a previous paper (Wright 1998) and to think in this way not only captures the sense of the baby acting on the mother and playing on her sensibilities – it also makes a link to the artistic process and the medium out of which the artist creates his forms.

6 The same considerations apply here as in note 2. To conceptualize events in terms of 'anticipated response' invokes a communicational frame of reference ('two body') rather than a projection/introjection frame ('one body').

7 Since the pioneering work of Ekman (1983) and Zajonc (1985), it is increasingly believed that innate connections exist between the motor acts of facial expression and corresponding states of autonomic arousal. This appears to be a two way process: on the one hand, each emotional arousal is linked to a specific facial expression; on the other, the making of a facial expression specific to an emotional state fires off, at least in some degree, the corresponding autonomic arousal. It is argued that this forms the basis of the universality of emotional expressions – the fact that they can be read cross culturally. Such hard wiring would mean that if I see your facial expression (of joy, for example) it will trigger in me, perhaps via my subliminal automatic adoption of your facial expression, autonomic elements of the same emotion. In other words, as in so called *projective identification*, I will tend to experience 'your' emotion, even if you yourself are unaware of being in such a state of emotional arousal. Recent work proposes that mirror neurons may play a part in this subliminal process (Gallese et al. 1996, 2007) but Winnicott's and Stern's work (Winnicott 1967a; Stern 1985) suggests that further development of such a propensity would depend on symbolic mediation of a non-verbal kind and sufficient early experiences of such non-verbal reflection. The relevance of this to my argument should be clear.

8 Gilbert Rose, in a number of different publications, has explored the relevance of Stern's ideas for a psychoanalytic perspective on aesthetics. He has also made extensive use of Langer's theory of art in his synthesis. His work is couched within the framework of classical American psychoanalysis with its own idiom of expression, but in so far as I can understand his position, there is much with which I would agree. A recent publication is Rose (1996).

9 In this nascent phase of symbol-formation, the *difference* between the mother's response and the infant's expression is probably important, helping to differentiate the maternal pattern from the experience itself. A difference might help the infant to grasp the notion, which at some point has to be grasped, that the pattern *stands for* the object (symbolic function) rather than indicating *the presence of* the object itself (signal function). In the transitional stage, such separateness is not an issue: patterns are important here as a means of *re-evoking* experience and providing containers for it (cf. the bit of blanket). If, however, recasting and mirroring prefigure language, it is possible that a growing separateness of pattern and experience might nudge the infant towards more symbolic modes of relating.

10 Maternal enactments present the baby with a portrayal, which in effect is the baby that the mother has imagined. If her imagining is reasonably accurate, we can suppose that the baby happily inhabits the form provided, and as with mirroring, feels enhanced by the feeling of resonance. If the imagined baby is skewed by the mother's own phantasies, the outcome will be different, for the mother's portrayal will then *dis*confirm the actual baby. This was probably the situation with which the poet Rilke had to contend

(Wright 2000), his mother calling him by a girl's name (Maria) and dressing him like a girl in his early years. In such circumstances, the struggle to escape entrapment by the mother's image and find new ways of affirming one's true nature becomes a major life task, though conceivably one in which the creative arts can help. I have argued in the above paper that for Rilke, transformation (confirmation) through his own poetic forms was a central part of his struggle as both man and artist.

11 Stern (1985: 158) has one paragraph where he mentions the work of Langer and the possible relevance of attunement to artistic creativity. I am not aware that he has elaborated on this further.

12 Langer coined the term 'presentational symbol' for a type of non-verbal symbol that 'presents' or portrays that to which it refers in iconic form. Such symbols are quite different from 'discursive symbols' such as words which merely *refer* to what they represent in an arbitrary but conventional way. Discursive symbols can be formed into languages because they have fixed, conventional referents; presentational symbols cannot be so deployed because the reference is entirely personal and arbitrary, being based on analogical similarity. It makes no sense, therefore, to argue that artistic forms constitute a *language* of feeling. A presentational form will portray the 'shape' of a feeling, but there can be no lexicon of presentational forms.

13 Perhaps even more pertinent is the accuracy of the mother's labeling when language becomes the predominant form of communication.

14 I have discussed this idea more fully in relation to the poet Rilke (Wright 2000). Rilke believed it was the poet's task to give life and voice to all the 'dumb' creatures of the world, animate and inanimate; these creatures had no voice of their own and depended on the poet to proclaim (present) their living essence in his verse. For Rilke, the poetic medium as transitional extension of the poet was equivalent to the artist's canvas, and the forms through which he sings the dumb creatures into existence are the self-same forms that he himself needs in order to realize his own self.

15 In discussing the poet's attempt to get the feel of experience into words, Seamus Heaney uses the expression 'the jurisdiction of form'. 'Technique', he says, '. . . is that whole creative effort of the mind's and body's resources to bring the meaning of experience within the jurisdiction of form.' (Heaney 2002: 19). This sentence perfectly captures the way in which an emergent meaning is brought into a new kind of existence (symbolic, apprehensible) through creative utterance and would apply equally to other artistic endeavours.

16 Bion's theory of containment (Bion 1962a, 1962b, 1965) overlaps with Winnicott's (1967a) mirroring and also provides an approach to the transformation of infant experience. However, Bion's concept is subtly different from Winnicott's and fails to capture elements which are central to the mirroring process. To give just one example: Bion's notion of the mother 'processing' her infant's feelings within her 'reverie' and giving them back to the infant in manageable form, undoubtedly draws attention to the dialogic

relation between mother and infant. What it lacks, however, is the sense of *making experience feel real through recognition* which was Winnicott's primary concern. To capture the sense of this requires a more interactive or dialogical language – e.g. something out there *resonates with* and *confirms* something in here – and such words are part of a different semantic landscape. Bion's ideas are interwoven with the concept of projective identification, and the idea that the infant communicates primarily through this means. References to such processes are absent from Winnicott's account – indeed, it could be argued that Winnicott's baby has an embryonic communicative potential from the beginning which already anticipates a responsive other. This would place Winnicott closer to Suttie (the infant has a 'primary need for the mother') and Trevarthen (a need for 'companionship' and 'proto-conversation') than to Klein (Suttie 1935; Trevarthen 1979).

17 I do not want to suggest that the Kleinian concept of reparation is unimportant in a theory of mind, but I do want to challenge its supremacy as an explanatory concept, both in general, and more specifically in relation to the creative process. It seems quite probable that *some* creative acts are driven by guilt and remorse and directed towards the restitution of the object; it is highly improbable that *all* creative acts are so driven, and even possible that they constitute a minority.

References

Balint, M. (1959) *Thrills and Regressions*, London: Hogarth.
Balint, M. (1952) *Primary Love and Psychoanalytic Technique*, London: Hogarth.
Bell, C. (1914) *Art*, Oxford: Oxford University Press.
Bion, W. R. (1962a) *Learning from Experience*, London: Heinemann; reprinted London: Karnac, 1984.
Bion, W. R. (1962b) 'The psychoanalytic study of thinking', *International Journal of Psychoanalysis* 43: 306–10; reprinted in Spillius (ed.) (1988), vol 1, London: Routledge.
Bion, W. R. (1965) *Transformations*, London: Heinemann Medical Books.
Bollas, C. (1987) *The Shadow of the Object – Psychoanalysis of the Unthought Known*, London: Free Association Books.
Diamond, N. and Marrone, M. (2003) *Attachment and Intersubjectivity*, London: Whurr.
Ekman, P. (1983) 'Autonomic nervous system activity distinguishes among emotions', *Science* 221: 1208–1210,
Freud, S. (1908) 'Creative writers and day-dreaming', S.E. 9.
Freud, S. (1910) 'Leonardo Da Vinci and a memory of his childhood', S.E. 11.
Freud, S. (1914) 'The Moses of Michelangelo', S.E. 13.
Fry, R. (1924) *The Artist and Psychoanalysis*, London: Hogarth.
Fuller, P. (1980) *Art and Psychoanalysis*, London: Writers and Readers Cooperative.

Gallese, V., Fadiga, L., Fogassi, L. and Rizzolati, G. (1996) 'Action recognition in the premotor cortex', *Brain* 119: 593–609.

Gallese, V., Eagle, M. N. and Migone, P. (2007) 'Intentional attunement: mirror neurons and the neural underpinnings of interpersonal relations', *Journal of the American Psychiatric Association* 55: 131–176.

Harrison, C. & Wood, P. Eds. (1992) *Art in Theory 1900–1990. An Anthology of Changing Ideas*, Oxford: Blackwell.

Heaney, S. (2002) *Finder's Keepers. Selected Prose 1971–2001*, London: Faber and Faber.

Langer, S. (1942) *Philosophy in a New Key*, Cambridge, MA: Harvard University Press.

Langer, S. (1953) *Feeling and Form*, London: Routledge and Kegan Paul.

Merleau-Ponty, M. (1962) *The Phenomenology of Perception*, trans. C. Smith, London: Routledge and Kegan Paul.

Ogden, T. H. (2001) 'Reading Winnicott', *Psychoanalytic Dialogues* 70: 299–323.

Rose, G. J. (1996) *Necessary Illusion: Art as Witness*, Madison CT: International Universities Press.

Segal, H. (1991) *Dream, Phantasy, Art*, London: Routledge.

Stern, D. (1985) *The Interpersonal World of the Infant*, New York: Basic Books.

Suttie, I. (1935) *The Origins of Love and Hate*, London: Kegan Paul; reprinted Pelican Books 1960 and Peregrine Books 1963.

Trevarthen, C. (1979) 'Communication and cooperation in early infancy: A description of primary intersubjectivity', in M. Bullowa (ed.) (1979) *Before Speech*, pp. 321–49, Cambridge: Cambridge University Press.

Winnicott, D. W. (1953) 'Transitional objects and transitional phenomena – a study of the first not-me possession', *International Journal of Psychoanalysis*, 34: 89–97; reprinted in *Collected Papers – Through Paediatrics to Psychoanalysis* (1958), London: Tavistock; and also in *Playing and Reality* (1971), London: Tavistock.

Stern, D. (1985) *The Interpersonal World of the Infant*, New York: Basic Books.

Winnicott, D. W. (1967a) 'Mirror role of mother and family in child development,' in *Playing and Reality,* pp. 111–118, London: Tavistock.

Winnicott, D. W. (1967b) 'The location of cultural experience', in *Playing and Reality,* pp. 95–103, London: Tavistock, 1971.

Winnicott D. W. (1971). Winnicott, D. W. (1971) *Playing and Reality*, London: Tavistock.

Wright, K. (1998) 'Deep calling unto deep: Artistic creativity and the maternal object', *British Journal of Psychotherapy* 14: 453–67.

Wright, K. (2000) 'To make experience sing', in: *Art, Creativity, Living,* Ed. L. Caldwell, London: Karnac.

Wright, K. (2009) *Mirroring and Attunement: Self Realisation in Psychoanalysis and Art*, London: Routledge.

Zajonc, R. B. (1985) 'Emotion and facial efference: a theory reclaimed', *Science* 228: 15–22.

Winnicott's deconstruction of primary narcissism[1]

René Roussillon

Dissecting primary narcissism

Freud's contribution focused particularly on the analysis of different mental states (neurotic, narcissistic, psychotic). This was based on his exploration of the effect on the vagaries of identity related to how the difference between the sexes and generations is structured in the mind, as well as the changes in the organization of the differences that both unites and separates infantile sexuality from the sexual sphere within their adult counterparts. Winnicott invites us to extend Freud's ideas by thinking about the impact of the primary construction of the me /not-me distinction in narcissistic states and their adjustments. His contribution is crucial to the analysis of narcissistic states of mind and of pathological forms of the ego's defence processes when the self has to contend with the risk of trauma in early childhood.

For Winnicott, primary narcissism cannot be conceived of in any solipsistic way. How it develops should be thought of within the context of the primary psychic relationship that is set up with the specific features of any given environment. A kind of primitive illusion, however, tends to obliterate that particular aspect of its construction. Analysing primary narcissism thus implies reintroducing what the primary narcissistic illusion has erased, i.e. the role played by the primary object in its foundation because narcissism involves two and perhaps three people.

In cases where narcissistic and self-identity issues are uppermost, the individual remains a prisoner of that primary illusion. The subject deludes herself that she is exclusively formed. That is the impasse: the individual forgets that she is not self-generated, whether as a flesh-and-blood creature or as far as her mental apparatus is concerned. That is what Winnicott meant where he states that narcissism cannot be thought of exclusively in terms of the self (Winnicott 1972: 191). The self cannot be thought of without taking into account the object considered as 'another-self', i.e. a distinct self that has its own mental life and wishes. That other self who may be present has now become an important element since there has been a definite attempt to acknowledge that the countertransference reveals hidden aspects of the transference. Historically it is the 'other' with which the individual constructed herself in the past. To understand fully the implications of Winnicott's ideas, we must first of all remind ourselves of Freud's original position.

In 'Mourning and Melancholia', Freud wrote that 'the shadow of the object fell upon the ego' (Freud [1915]1917: 249). This is an essential element in thinking about the blending of ego and object, and it suggests a fundamental direction for analysing narcissism. If suffering involves the shadow of the object that has fallen on the ego, the analyst will have to help the patient give that shadow back to the object, break free of the blend brought about by her narcissistic defences and deconstruct the basic narcissistic postulate of the self-generation of the mind.

Freud went on to emphasize the fact that one of the characteristic features of narcissism is not simply that it brings everything back to the self – all cathexes are aimed at the ego – but also that it erases or attempts to erase anything that comes from another individual. In 'The Ego and the Id' (1923) – and even more so in 'Inhibitions, Symptoms and Anxiety' (1926) – Freud showed how the ego assimilates and takes as its own what it cannot remove. Narcissism assimilates the object and takes in the shadow of the object that has fallen on the ego. At the same time, it erases the fact that there is a shadow that has fallen on the ego and is henceforth mixed up with it. The 'lost' object does not have to be mourned by the ego. In bringing the cathexis of the lost object back onto itself, the ego incorporates the traces left by that object. Later I shall come back to the meaning of the idea of 'the shadow of the object' that has also become much clearer thanks to Winnicott.

The narcissistic process does not simply erase all trace of the object, it wipes out the process by which that erasing occurs; it erases for the individual that by which she developed and what she owes to the object thanks to which the self came into being. Moreover, it erases the process by which the self assimilated what came from the other person in its own organization. These processes go to make up the primary narcissistic illusion.

The primary mirror-object

We can now examine in more detail the ideas that Winnicott contributed to the above concepts. How do his hypotheses help us in the practice of psychoanalysis to locate and identify retroactively those traces that have since become mute, silenced, assimilated, i.e. the traces of the object's primary responses, the first human mirror reflecting the self's drive-related impulses and primary needs?

When the clinical presentation seems to involve only the relationship between the individual and her own self, Winnicott recommends that we try to reintroduce the historical aspect of the primary object and reconstruct what must have occurred between the individual and the object that gives rise to the narcissistic pattern we see before us.

Winnicott's main hypothesis is that the individual expects the primary object to be an emotional mirror that offers a representation of the self. In the relationship between the individual and her self, Winnicott reintroduces the gap, the fork in the road as it were, generated by the primary mirror of the object. He restores the paradox of an identity that is constructed through internalizing the reflection sent out by another person. Identity is the precipitate of primary narcissistic identifications, those that incorporate an object that is a mirror and the self's double. Later, the theoretical model that this implies will be explored but for the moment the focus is on clinical matters.

One concrete clinical consequence of Winnicott's hypothesis is that, when the individual is defined inherently as identical to her self, that identification and the identification of her internal states of mind include something of the other person, i.e. some degree of otherness brought about by the 'reflection' carried out by the other person, through identification with what those primary objects reflected.

Any attempt at psychoanalytically restoring that 'otherness' aspect and deconstructing the solipsistic narcissistic postulate of self-identity means that the objectification function of the drives is made possible or perhaps restored. This implies the possibility of rediscovering traces of the lost object in the ego. These traces represent the shadow that has been assimilated.

The following clinical sequence, from the standard form of treatment with a female patient who had suffered from severe anorexia nervosa, will serve as an illustration of this problem and the kind of analytic clinical work that is required.

Echo[2] was a woman patient of mine whose clinical anorexia nervosa gradually diminished as the analysis proceeded. Her social life, however, was still extremely limited in scope. She was saving her strength, as it were, convinced that she could slow down the passing of time or even bring it to a complete halt. She limited her social contacts to what was strictly necessary. She herself toned down whatever faint drive-related impulses she did have and repressed her affects. In her sessions, she was often immobile and silent. It was only very sparingly that she talked of some aspects of her inner thoughts and feelings. I had the impression that she was treating the work of the analysis as she did food in her anorexic states, as well as the rest of her life, including her mental functioning: she neutralized everything. My impression was not particularly useful on a practical level – the idea that, in a kind of transference reversal which was an attempt to share her internal world, she evoked in me an experience – and therefore was communicating to me – what she herself had gone through. This was useful only insofar as it helped me to tolerate the specific features of the transference without retaliating too much.

It was in another aspect of the transference that we had to find the wherewithal to revive her drive-related processes. When Echo became able to break free of her 'from self to self' defences – in other words her narcissistic defences – she brought those issues into the transference, so that the analytical process could start to become meaningful. I helped her to externalize the shadow of the object by drawing attention to the fact that she seemed to be treating herself and treating me in much the same way as her primary environment had treated her.

As the work of the analysis progressed, the following intersubjective pattern began to emerge in the transference. Echo gradually began to express in words what was going on inside her when she came to her sessions. Initially she would feel pleased and want to explain something that she had been able to formulate and understand between sessions. But as soon as we were both together, as soon as she came into my consulting-room, the source of that pleasure and the wish to share something dried up immediately. She remained cold, with no vital spark to her. What she had intended to say suddenly seemed insipid to her, devoid of any interest whatsoever – and she felt this before she even opened her mouth. The vigour she had felt before finding herself in my presence just melted away. That transformation sometimes occurred as soon as I entered the waiting room to welcome her – as soon as I opened the door, in fact, as soon as she caught sight of me.

Gradually the incidental thought that came into her mind at that point could begin to be put into words. When she looked at my consulting-room full of books and files, she thought that I must be a very busy person, and probably not particularly available, whereas she herself was just a tiny little thing of hardly any importance to me, the 'great professor'. Gradually, these transference elements could be linked to certain specific features of the patient's relationship with her mother. When her sister was born, Echo suddenly felt de-cathected, because her mother gave all her attention to the new baby. Mother's mind was elsewhere, and she was unable to think simultaneously about both of her children.[3] As we worked through that time in her past, there was some warming-up of her drives, but basically her relationship to the outside world remained much as before.

It was necessary to work through the everyday aspects of her life as a child, over and beyond the specific event that was the birth of her sister, because what then appeared could be seen as running through the whole of her relationship with her mother. Day by day, in the ordinary life of the family, Echo's mother gradually showed herself to be a hyperactive woman, always running around; there was no way to make contact with her. At meal-times, for example, she would rush around, serving one person then another, eating while she was still on her feet or at the edge of the table without sitting down, without ever stopping for a rest. She would serve someone and then start to clear everything away before the meal was over; she was a kind of 'household tornado'. Whenever Echo tried to get close to her mother in an upsurge of emotion, it would all fall flat because her mother was already elsewhere – she had turned away, busying herself with something else. Echo would simply slide off a smooth-surfaced object that could never be reached, and whose attention could never be captured. The upsurge of emotion fell flat, disappeared; the drive broke down, withdrew, retracted. At the same time, life itself became more restricted. No 'use' could be made of the object and Echo's drives could not keep up their momentum; she had to neutralize everything as much as she could. She had to repeat that kind of sequence very many times in her sessions – and I had to formulate, just as often, my transference interpretations in terms of the 'nullifying' effect of her mother's responses on her drive-related and emotional impulses – before any significant change in the way she related to her drives and her affects could be integrated.

No such clinical pattern can be understood in terms of solipsistic thinking because it implies an intersubjective conception of the life of the drives, as well as an intersubjective conception of their organization. The idea of a 'messenger' drive – one that is addressed to another person and is dependent for its development on the response of that other person – is one that all clinicians must come to acknowledge as a key concept. It widens the scope of what the psychoanalyst can take in and expands clinical thinking in psychoanalysis.

In my work with Echo, I was initially confronted with a 'from herself to herself' kind of behaviour as the focus of the clinical picture at that time. That behaviour was solipsistic in nature, it was purely self-related. It participated in her narcissistic economy, and did not appear to be aimed at anyone in particular. Even when she was not in her sessions, Echo behaved in much the same way. The shadow of the object had fallen on her ego, which had assimilated its impact and the problem then became an internal one, one that was self-related. However, since it was after all brought into the psychoanalytic sessions, it began to take on an interactive dimension and had an impact on the analyst within the analysing space. Thus it became a kind of enacted message, a transference communication. In the end, I acknowledged it to be (or endorsed it as) a particular form of the *Agieren* transference.[4] Insofar as it affects the analyst, insofar as another person feels involved and can think about such a behaviour pattern in terms of an enacted message addressed to the other, then the idea that there is an intersubjective dimension to that behaviour which has an impact on the other person can be explored.

By taking melancholia as the fundamental model of narcissistic impasse, Freud gave a certain direction to psychoanalysis. The vector he thus introduced was taken up and put to extremely good use by Winnicott. Thanks to the latter's hypothesis of the object as the self's emotional mirror, Freud's intuition was made operational for the analysis of the psychopathological aspects of narcissistic and identity-related states of mind. This question will be discussed more fully later. Before doing so, another aspect of Winnicott's hypotheses should be pointed out concerning the various complementary features that he introduced which makes it possible to deconstruct the theory of narcissism itself.

The narcissistic theory of the drives simply involves the tendency to discharge; the object is looked upon merely as being the instrument through which drive-related discharge can take place. The object in this position is not experienced as another person. If the object is present, the drive can be discharged, released. If the object is absent, the self is threatened with loss of some kind, and has to set up palliative auto-erotic measures in order to deal with that threat and await the beneficial return of the object. Putting the emphasis on the object's function in the construction of the self and on the object's responses to the self's libidinal impulses introduces a new dimension into the life of the drives, one which implicitly contains the idea that drives also carry a message addressed to the object, a message that is waiting for some kind of response. Drives are constructed through the interplay that is set up between self and object. A brief example will help us to understand the issues that this kind of hypothesis raises in our clinical work.

In one of his sessions, a male patient said that he felt 'empty' and that his mind had 'gone blank'. The classic interpretation of that state, the one that I was taught when, in supervision, I was learning my craft as a psychoanalyst, was to link that inner emptiness to the feeling that, given the drive-related avidity of the patient, something was experienced as missing. The analysis would then attempt to explore the all-or-nothing processes that are typical of primary avidity. Later, I learned that this feeling of inner emptiness could be linked also, in a complementary manner, to thought processes such as negative hallucination. The empty feeling could then perhaps be seen also as a hollow space, an awaiting, a potential space for receiving something. Thanks to Winnicott, another complementary interpretation became available, one which, without in any way nullifying the previous two, points them in a new direction. The feeling of emptiness can be looked upon as the effect on the ego of the shadow of an unresponsive object that remained silent in the face of the self's entreaties, indifferent to the self's urges, perhaps even turning away in hostility. As Albert Camus put it in his *Myth of Sisyphus*: 'The absurd is born

of this confrontation between the human need and the unreason-
able silence of the world' (2006: 21). The emptiness of the object's
response is then incorporated, leaving in the ego a trace of the echo
of that silence and of the way in which it may have shattered the self's
drive-related urges. The previous patient Echo is a good example of
that process.

When Winnicott said to his patient Margaret Little,[5] that her
mother was chaotic, he was not attempting to designate the mother
as 'the bad object' (Little 1985): that would have been neither appo-
site nor psychoanalytically helpful. The notions of 'good' and 'bad'
objects have to do with infantile definitions of the object and do not
correspond to the kind of categories that are useful to psychoanalysts
in their attempt to think about the patient's past. In describing the
mother as 'chaotic', Winnicott helped the patient to move away from
the idea that her inner chaos was simply the outcome of an anarchic
and disorganizing drive or the result of an avid and limitless libido.
The patient was able to grasp the intelligibility of an inner impulse
that came up against a chaotic and disorganizing response from the
environment. The analytic space illuminates the relationship with the
self, and revives the impact and the form of the response made by the
primary mirror-object in the past. This means that the initial impulse
can also be rediscovered in the present analytic relationship, and the
message addressed to the object via that drive-related impulse might
have a better chance of meeting with a different kind of response.
The following clinical example will serve as an illustration of these
ideas.

This patient from time to time had breakdowns that were melancholic in nature – loss of all liveliness and probably a disintegration of his immunological defences. His overall condition improved
significantly during an initial period of analysis with a female analyst. However, when he asked me to help him carry on exploring
psychoanalytically his inner mental states, he was still suffering from
a generalized depressive state and major inhibition of his potential.
He had attended some of my lectures on narcissistic states and felt
that I might be able to help him in a different manner from that of his
previous analyst.

I shall skip the initial part of the analytical process, devoted to his
working through in the transference the relationship with his father
who was a man showing little emotion, unyielding and not very often
present. Processing his intense hostility towards a paternal figure who

disappointed the love that his son had for him and who showed little interest in his son did indeed impact on the patient's depressiveness, but not in any really decisive way. The transference relationship began to show signs of how the patient and his mother related. She suffered from manic–depressive psychosis with delusional aspects, and this had a significant effect on the patient. When the analysis of that relationship came to the fore, the patient had two severe depressive breakdowns with major melancholic features. On each occasion, a psychosomatic disorganization ensued, with the patient 'falling apart' as his immunological defences collapsed. The decisive phase in his processing of these depressive breakdowns occurred when it became possible to link the collapse of all liveliness in the patient, when he was falling apart, with the response made by the maternal object to the impulses of the child he had then been. Very slowly we had to reconstruct the characteristic features of the primitive conversation between the baby, i.e. the infant the patient was at that time and a mother who oscillated between melancholic and manic phases.

From the perspective opened up by Winnicott extending Freud's comment on the shadow of the object, the work of analysis enables the reconstitution and processing of the effects of the chaotic and erratic aspects of the mother's emotional responses. From time to time the patient's mother would accept her son's affection towards her, exaggerating it until it became too powerful to keep in check, then her attitude would suddenly change and she would reject it. Most of the time the mother's sole response to any affect-based impulse was to turn her face away, close in on herself or even reject it as though she felt she was under attack. Her son was left in complete confusion – confusion between love and hate, between affectionate and aggressive impulses. At that point, all forward movement came to a halt; his liveliness weakened and collapsed and at that point he fell apart. His affectionate impulses towards the object were experienced by the child he then was as highly destructive. The paradoxical position in which he found himself, that had been created by the confusion between his affectionate impulses and his experience of being destructive, tended to paralyse all mental activity on his part. If, in the baby, the good (love) and the bad (destructiveness, according to the mother's interpretation of the impulse) are no longer opposable – with each creating the other – the pleasure- unpleasure principle and its transformation into the reality principle are paralysed, to such an extent that all mental activity tends to stop.

In the various clinical situations that are described here, the really crucial part of the clinical work was to facilitate a return of the patients' mental dynamics through highlighting the specific nature of the primary object's responses and reactions to the infant's drive-related impulses and urges. When the clinical picture gave the impression that the patient was in an impasse and that her mental processes were repetitively going round in circles, I reintroduced the specific element that had been the object's response. I tried to reconstruct that response on the basis of the transference indications that the patient evoked in each session.

There are two phases to that process. The first has to do with the present and it takes place in the transference. It is initially perceived and worked on at that level. Since the process is insistent by nature, historical reconstruction becomes possible in the second phase which enables the process to be stabilized and means that change is sustainable.

Naturally enough, this leads us to delve deeper into Winnicott's ideas concerning the process of subjectifying identification on the one hand and, on the other, the hypothesis that he put forward concerning what he called the use of the object.

The process of subjectification: subjectifying identification

The reading of Winnicott with Freud that describes the context in which mother and baby first come into contact with each other, leads to the suggestion of the concept of a primary homosensual relationship that is 'double' in nature (Roussillon 2004). This context brings about the process of subjectification that lies at the heart of the organization of the primary narcissistic / self-identity pattern.

French-speaking psychoanalysts differentiate between the sexual sphere and sexuality as such (Roussillon 2006). The term 'sexuality' is used to designate behaviour, while the 'sexual sphere' refers to the pleasure-unpleasure issues that infiltrate all mental processes. From that point of view, the 'sensual dimension' has to do with the sexual sphere. French-speaking psychoanalysts would therefore argue that, although everything is not sexual, there is a sexual element in everything, insofar as drive-related cathexes always accompany mental processes or intersubjective encounters. To describe that relationship as 'primary homosensuality' or 'primary homosexuality' emphasizes the fact that pleasure and unpleasure have to do with the movement in which the other person is either encountered or lost as a 'double' of oneself (Roussillon 2004).

Three of Winnicott's ideas could be seen as making this point more explicit: the found-created object,[6] the mother's mirror function and the experience of interaction in the early feeding situation (Winnicott 1953; 1967; 1969; 1971).

The idea of the found-created object is that the maternal environment which presents the breast at the proper time and in a manner suited to the infant enables the latter to have the productive illusion of being able to 'create', via hallucination, the breast that he or she actually 'finds' through perception. Contrary to the usual metapsychological description of mental functioning, which emphasizes the contrast between hallucination and perception, Winnicott describes a paradoxical – 'transitional' – metapsychological dimension in which that contrast no longer holds. The perceived breast meets up with the hallucinated one, and is superimposed on it as a real substantive double. This process lies at the heart of the infant's invention of the subjective illusion of being able to create the satisfaction that he or she finds. Maternal adequacy transforms that primitive hallucination into a positive illusion that supports the infant's belief in her capacity to produce a satisfactory world. Object-cathexis and narcissism are therefore not necessarily opposed to each other; they combine their effects and produce a specific kind of subjective state – one that is 'transitional' – in which the hallucinated representation of the object and the 'objective' object come together in such a way that pleasure is obtained. Self-preservation and drive-related cathexes thus go hand in hand and auto-eroticism and object-cathexis converge. Pleasure comes about from that merging together and is a signal of that encounter and blending.

This conception of Winnicott's takes us beyond the metapsychological impasse that is caused by the opposition between drive theory and object-relations theory. Here, due to space limitation, it is not possible to discuss everything that follows on from a conception of the mental apparatus which sees it as capable, under certain specific circumstances, of simultaneously hallucinating and perceiving, without becoming confused in the process.[7] Rather, I shall focus on describing the kinds of double relationship to which Winnicott drew our attention.

A further aspect of Winnicott's theory concerns his conception of the mother's face as 'mirroring' her infant's internal states. Winnicott argued that his hypothesis was a development of Lacan's intuition about the function of the mirror stage. It involves the point at which issues concerning identification are uppermost, and when narcissistic identification and the sense of self are joined together. The main thrust of Winnicott's hypothesis is that what infants see when they look at their mother's face is a reflection of their own internal and emotional state. Some comments and complementary ideas would be useful here.

The first point is that the idea of the 'good-enough' mother is implicit in this hypothesis. The mother, together with her surrounding environment, which in particular includes the father, adapts her movements, facial expressions and physical posture to those of her infant. She attunes emotionally to her infant, with whom she identifies and whose internal states she shares in her own way (Winnicott 1958). The infant sees in the mother's face a reflection of this supportiveness as a double, which is aesthetic, sensory and emotional (Winnicott 1967). I would nevertheless argue that we have to go beyond Winnicott's hypothesis and see this first 'mirror' as being not only the mother's face but also her entire body and her behaviour.

This mirror, personified by the mother's body when she is sufficiently adapted to her infant's needs, sufficiently malleable and sensitive towards her infant's internal states, has the effect of producing a narcissistic double (Roussillon 1991). A 'double' is something that is both 'the same' – similar to the self – and also 'an other'. No double can ever be simply the same because that situation would create confusion, rather than a reflection of the self. The mother must therefore show that she is different, an other, through the way in which she reflects to her infant her sharing of emotions. The emotions and internal states that she reflects are similar, but not identical, to those of her infant. They have the same basic components, the same matrix, but not the same form. The maternal reflections are identical to those of her infant, except as to their mode: they are homomorphic but not isomorphic. Maternal adjustment is intermodal. Gergeli has pointed out that, beside this intermodal accompanying 'double', the mother indicates also that the emotional states she reflects back to her infant are not her own emotional states but rather those of the infant (Gergeli 2003). The message or meta-communication that the mother receives means that she is able to take on the role of a simple 'mirror' of her infant's internal states. She can think of herself as a reflecting mirror. It is obvious that, if one is to be able to mirror the internal states of another person, one must be able to empathize with that person's emotional states and identify, acknowledge and therefore share them, at least to some extent.

The concept of the mother as the infant's primary mirror implies that a primary relationship is set up and cathected as a movement reaching out towards the other person in an attempt to construct a relationship with that person as a potential double of the self. Here too satisfaction and pleasure depend on the capacity of the two partners to come together and see the other as a double – as a separate person, yet the same as the self. It is that movement, that ballet as it were, which governs pleasure and unpleasure. That interplay between mother and infant initiates the construction of a rudimentary form of symbol, i.e. what represents their initial encounter and what is shared between them and the union for which it strives. If a manifestation of the infant's mind-set can be echoed by the mother, it is no longer simply a discharge: it begins to take its place in a primitive system of communication, taking the form of a 'shared sign,' i.e. of a message that can be addressed to the object. Sharing is the first prerequisite for the emergence of symbols, conceived of as a sign that meeting and coming together is taking place. Both infant and mother acknowledge and recognize themselves in such symbols, and the symbols carry traces of their encounter and their coming together.

These comments on Winnicott's hypothesis must, if they are to be complete, mention another implicit element of that conception. If we say that the mother's face is her infant's mirror, this implies not only that the mother must behave in such a way that she offers herself as her infant's mirror, but also that, whatever transpires, the infant treats what is expressed in the mother's face and body as a reflection of herself. In other words the infant identifies with what reverberates through the manner in which the mother and other significant persons in the environment are present for him. 'Whatever transpires' means that the infant treats the substance of what the mother expresses as a message that, in effect, concerns her, as a kind of response to the infant's own impulses directed towards the mother. Whether the mother's response is an accurate reflection of the infant's emotions, the effect of her own internal state, or the way in which she feels and interprets the signals addressed to her, her infant will receive these messages as reflections. This point is of particular relevance for our understanding of the pathology of narcissism, which can then be seen to involve the specific features of the way in which the primary mirror has carried out the role potentially allotted to it. Either the primary parental mirror may have reflected only very little material for the infant to be able to identify her internal states, which then may become blanked out in the absence of any 'double' response, or the reflection may have distorted them to such an extent that they have become warped.

Thinking along these lines enables us to hypothesize how Freud's enigmatic formula, 'the shadow of the object', can be better understood. In 'Mourning and Melancholia', Freud argued that, in melancholia, the source of the feeling of loss of the object derives from a disappointment emanating from the object. The hypothesis suggested here is that the shadow of the object arises from that which the object did not reflect back to the self as regards the latter's emotions and internal states. In other words, the object failed to fulfil its role as a mirror, and the primary narcissistic expectations of the self were thus disappointed. To go beyond both Freud and Winnicott, I would say that the self then tries to incorporate the object and the part of the self felt to be confiscated by the object when nothing is reflected back. The self sticks to the object in what some post-Kleinian analysts have called 'adhesive identification,'[8] and it lies at the root of an area of non-differentiation between self and object. This is a shared area that, in fantasy, holds self and object stuck to each other as if they were Siamese twins. The process of mourning the loss of the object is thus paralysed from the outset and trapped within a paradox, because giving up the object implies giving up also the part of the self that is sequestered inside the object. Yet, letting go of the object, for example in the process of mourning, is carried out in the name of preserving the self or the self's wholeness and consistency (as in castration anxiety, for example).

The third point I wish to make concerns something that appeared later in Winnicott's writings. The most explicit indication of it that I have been able to find dates from a paper he wrote in 1969 (Winnicott 1970)[9] where he emphasizes the importance of the two-way movement, the mutuality that is typical of the early feeding situation and, over and beyond that, of the mother–infant relationship as a whole (cf. Chapter 3). He comments on the fact that infants try to put their fingers into their mother's mouth, and so 'feed' the mother. Here again is the idea of the 'double'. Winnicott emphasizes the importance of this reciprocity for a positive integration of the experience of being fed. The maternal mirror is no longer simply an effect of the illusion derived from the found-created dimension, it is not simply an effect of an emotional or sensory reflection, rather it implies also a two-way process of reciprocity, a mutual feeding, and perhaps, also a mutual transformation. Once again, the maternal mirror contributes to the emergence of a form of symbolic dialogue.

The process of objectification and the discovery of the object's otherness

The concept of a primary homosensual relationship that is 'double', which entails the gradual construction of an encounter with the object as a 'double' of the self, is tenable only if it comprises a theory of the discovery of the object's otherness and maintains a dialectical relationship with that theory (Winnicott 1969). The process is twofold: identify with the other person and through that other person; differentiate oneself from the other person and differentiate that other person from oneself. Differentiation is meaningful only insofar as it is based on the construction of the other person as the self's double. It is because the other person is initially conceived of as a double that the difference can be constructed in a manner that is not simply a form of splitting or repudiation. On that point, too, Winnicott was an innovator: he complemented Freud's hypotheses and in so doing compelled us to dig more deeply.

For Freud, reality is a primary 'given' of perception. There exists from the outset a reality-ego that is in a dialectical and conflicting relationship with the pleasure-ego. Reality-testing makes use of perception and the perception-motor pairing in doing its work and in maintaining active, during wakefulness, i.e. in consciousness. This is the difference between hallucination and perception. Nonetheless, at certain points in his theory, Freud did seem to hesitate as to where his ideas were leading him. The sense of reality is not just a matter of perception; it entails conception. Similarly, the relationship with the object is not just a matter of perception; it too entails conception. When Freud wrote in 1915 that, at the very beginning, 'The external world, objects, and what is hated are identical,' adding: 'If later on an object turns out to be a source of pleasure, it is loved, but it is also incorporated into the ego; so that for the purified pleasure-ego once again objects coincide with what is extraneous and hated' (1915: 136), this goes much further than a mere perception of the object. As we can imagine, what complicates the question is the fact that hallucinatory cathexis of the object becomes mixed with the simple perception of it. Hallucination and perception may be in a dialectical relationship, in conflict, one with the other, or threaten to merge together.

Winnicott suggested that hallucination and perception could be superimposed on each other, a hypothesis that Freud himself seemed about to accept in his paper, 'Constructions in Analysis' (Freud 1937) in order to solve the problem of psychosis. Although Winnicott opened up a new way of looking at this issue, he did add a further complication.

When perception is cathected and the hallucination of a previous trace becomes mixed in with it, the result is an experience of illusion that carries with it a potential threat of confusion. Freud emphasized that in Inhibitions, Symptoms and Anxiety (1926 [1925]) and discussed the topic again in his 'Constructions' paper (op. cit): there is no point in trying to 'prove' anything concerning the unreality of an illusion or a hallucination. An illusion does not contradict the reality principle; rather it is part of the relationship with reality and expresses the wish which structures that relationship. Reality-testing cannot have, as its basis, perception or muscular activity when these are libidinally cathected; experiences of pleasure cannot provide such a basis either, because from the outset they have their source in the superposing of hallucination and perception, and in the 'double' encounter between these.

Illusion may give rise to unpleasure and lead to a lack of satisfaction, but such an experience does not bring about a disillusion which offers the possibility for some differentiation between internal and external reality. That is the essence of Winnicott's position. The experience of unpleasure gives rise to what I have suggested should be called 'negative illusion' (Roussillon 1991). This is not disillusion[10] but a negative form of illusion based on the subjective impression that the individual has destroyed her capacity to produce satisfaction. It triggers wounds, anger and destructiveness which, eventually and in the face of the disorganizing character of these states, incites the individual to restrict her cathexis of the outside world, withdraw from all contact, shut everything down, move towards dis-objectification and away from any discovery of the otherness of the object.

Winnicott's hypothesis makes the problem more complex in that it introduces, between the experience of unpleasure and the discovery of the reality or of the otherness of the object, an additional phase, a structural level that includes the part played by the environment and its response to the individual's drive-related impulses.

The object is 'encountered' in an atmosphere of primitive rage, it is pre-conceived in the experience of unpleasure and in the individual's reaction to that unpleasure. The object is potentially perceived in an experience of unpleasure that triggers destructive impulses. Destructiveness does not bring about a disillusion directly; it gives rise to a negative illusion, the illusion that one is the source of all the evil that inhabits the world (Roussillon 1991). According to Winnicott, what then happens depends on the way in which the object responds to the infant's destructiveness. That is when the veil that surrounds the mirror of the object will darken, become cloudy, and burst; it will harden or harden its reflection.

If the object retaliates, mirroring or doubling the infant's drive-related impulses, if it counter-attacks, if it withdraws from the relationship, these responses will give substance to the negative illusion and anchor feelings of badness in the individual, a deep malaise, a nucleus of primary guilt that is pre-ambivalent because it is not in a dialectical relationship with love. Destruction takes place – it is no longer a message of unpleasure, an internal signal, a potentiality for differentiation; it has turned into a fact, and the destruction is real. The result is that narcissism remains locked in solipsism.

Conversely, if the object survives the destructive impulses and impotent anger, if it appears to be wounded but does not retaliate, if it does not withdraw either perceptively or emotionally from the relationship, if it keeps alive the link with the self, then destructiveness does not break anything; it remains potential. Reality-testing then becomes possible, and differentiation between internal and external objects may begin to take place. The object is 'discovered' in its externality; it is no longer simply 'perceived' as external – as we now know, this is achieved very early on in life – but 'conceived of' as being external, as an external object cathected libidinally, as another being, not simply as the self's double or reflection. The experience of differentiation between the internal object – the fantasy object destroyed by the self's destructiveness and impotent anger – and the external object, the other person, the object which survives, can then start to become meaningful. At that point, the topography of the mind can begin to organize itself. It is when there are two or three participants that it becomes possible to move beyond primary narcissistic solipsism; it is when we think about the object's responses, the questions these raise and the forms they take, that we can break free of the primary narcissistic negative illusion and its existential impasses.

The object cathected as the self's 'homosensual double', which is the present object in its function of reflecting the self, is cathected and loved. The absent object, i.e. the object that does not take on the role, the object that becomes different and is not present as the self's double, the non-narcissistic object, is hated because it is absent and because of the gap that it leaves in its wake. That gap constitutes a negative illusion, the opposite of the illusion of omnipotence.

There are thus two different trajectories. Either there is a negative illusion, without any conflict as to ambivalence – which cannot be organized in such a way as to govern the life of the drives; or there is an experience of something lacking, which, when accepted for what it is, leads to feelings of dependence. The object is loved for what it brings and at the same time hated because it offends narcissism by reminding the self that it is not all-powerful, that something is indeed missing. Hate results from the fact that love creates a certain degree of dependence and the feeling of missing the object.

The object's response seals the fate of destructiveness in the subject and its role in psychical economy. On the one hand, it can withdraw into itself and turn away or turn its effects against the mind and its cathexes; on the other, it can enable differentiation between the internal world – that of mental representation and fantasy – and the external world of perception, cathected but maintained, outside of the self's omnipotent creativeness.

Conclusion

In his exploration of the construction of primary narcissism and the ordeal that is its deconstruction, Winnicott argued that there is a gap between the individual and her self. He widened the gap that makes narcissism and breaking free of narcissism analysable and thus able to be symbolized. He introduced the element that demolishes self-identity and forces psychoanalysis into an impasse. By bringing in this additional phase – that of the object's reflection and its responses to the self's drive-related impulses and that of the specific role the object plays in the construction and deconstruction of narcissism – he 'de-narcissized' psychoanalytic theory. With the help of a theory in which solipsism is analysed and deconstructed, Winnicott explored – and made thinkable – how narcissism is organized or becomes disorganized, puts itself into an impasse or finds a way out through organizing what is lacking and through the discovery of the objects that go to make up narcissism.

Notes

1 This paper was first published in the *International Journal of Psychoanalysis* (*Int J Psychoanal* (2010) 91: 821–837) (Editor's Note).
2 I call her 'Echo' in memory of the way in which Narcissus treated Echo's love and affection, causing her to feel ashamed, to become anorectic and to wither away.
3 All of the children in that [large] family were in trouble of some kind or another: drug addiction, psychosis and antisocial behaviour were some of the 'solutions' that they had implemented.
4 Enactment/actualization/acting out.
5 For a fuller discussion of this particular example see Roussillon 2002.
6 The *trouvé-créé* is a term in French that is not a direct translation of Winnicott's terminology. However, it has recently been widely used in the French psychoanalytic literature and refers to Winnicott's conception of the process involved in 'creating the object' (Editor's Note).
7 For more details on this point see Roussillon 2001.
8 See Meltzer, 1975.
9 Although the beginnings of this formulation can be seen in his earlier work.
10 In my view, disillusion is a slow process which does not destroy the capacity to delude oneself (as happens in melancholia, for example). Here illusion is 'reversed' such that it is always its negative aspect that is seen. In French, we would say: 'Voir tout en noir' – to look on the black side of everything. This is the opposite of idealization: everything that can be expected of other people will turn out to be bad. This stems from very early disappointment with respect to one's expectations; thereafter it is better not to expect anything so as not to risk more pain. Negative illusion destroys expectations.

References

Camus, A. (1942) *Le Mythe de Sisyphe*. Paris: NRF. [trans. J. O'Brien, *The Myth of Sisyphus*. Harmondsworth: Penguin Classics, new edition 2006].

Freud, S. (1915) Instincts and their Vicissitudes. SE 14, 111–40.

Freud, S. (1917 [1915]) Mourning and Melancholia. SE 14, 243–59.

Freud, S. (1923) The Ego and the Id. SE 19, 3–63.

Freud, S. (1926) Inhibitions, Symptoms and Anxiety. SE 20, 87–174.

Freud, S. 1937) "Constructions in Analysis". SE 23, 257–69.

Gergeli, G. (2003) "Naissance de la capacité de régulation des affects" ["The Birth of the Capacity to Regulate Affects"]. *Prendre soin du jeune enfant [Looking After Infants]*. Érès.

Lacan, J. (1966) *Écrits*. Paris: Le Seuil. [*Ecrits* (trans. B. Fink). New York: Norton, 2006].

Little, M. (1985) Winnicott working in areas where psychotic anxieties predominate: a personal record. *Free Associations* 3: 9–42.

Meltzer, D. (1975) Adhesive Identification. *Contemp. Psychoanal.* 11: 289–310.

Roussillon, R. (1991) *Paradoxes et situations limites de la psychanalyse [Paradoxes and Borderline Situations in Psychoanalysis]*. Paris: Presses Universitaires de France.

Roussillon, R.(1999) *Agonie, clivage et symbolisation* [Agony, Splitting and Symbolization]. Paris: Presses Universitaires de France.

Roussillon, R. (2001) *Le plaisir et la répétition* [Pleasure and Repetition]. Paris: Dunod.

Roussillon, R. (2002) "Le transfert délirant" ["The Delusional Transference"], in P. Fédida (ed.), *Transfert: États-limites [Transference and Borderline States]*. Paris: Presses Universitaires de France.

Roussillon, R. (2004) La dépendence primitive et l'homosexualité primaire 'en double'. *Rev Fr Psychanal* 68: 421–39.

Roussillon, R. (2006) Processus de sexualisation et désexualisation en psychanalyse, Russian translation Pashova, E. 62–85 (English translation in *Anthology of French Psychoanalysis*, forthcoming).

Winnicott, D.W. (1945) Primitive Emotional Development. *Int J Psychoanal* 26: 137–43.

Winnicott, D.W. (1953 [1951]) Transitional objects and transitional phenomena: A study of the first not–me possession. *Int J Psychoanal* 34: 89–97.

Winnicott D.W. (1958) Primary maternal preoccupation [1956]. In: *Collected Papers. Through Paediatrics to Psycho-Analysis*. London: Tavistock Publications; New York: Basic Books. 300–5.

Winnicott, D.W. (1958) *Collected Papers. Through Paediatrics to Psycho-Analysis*. London: Tavistock Publications; New York: Basic Books.

Winnicott, D.W. (1965) *The Maturational Processes and the Facilitating Environment*. London: Maresfield.

Winnicott, D.W. (1967) Mirror-role of mother and family in child development. In: Peter Lomas (Ed.) *The Predicament of the Family: a psychoanalytical symposium*. London: Hogarth Press, 1967.

Winnicott, D.W. (1969) The use of an object. *Int J Psychoanal* 50: 711–716.

Winnicott, D.W. (1970) [1969] The mother-infant experience of mutuality. In: E. James Anthony & Therese Benedek (Eds), *Parenthood: Its psychology and psychopathology*. Boston: Little, Brown & Co.

Winnicott, D.W. (1971a) *Therapeutic Consulations in Child Psychiatry*. London: Hogarth; New York: Basic Books.

Winnicott, D.W. (1971b) *Playing and Reality*. London: Tavistock. (new edition, with C. Winnicott, New York: Methuen, 1982).

Winnicott, D.W. (1971c) [1970] Creativity and its origins. In: 1971b, 65–85.

Winnicott, D.W. (1972) [1968–69] Answers to my comments (on the split-off male and female elements) *Psychoanalytic Forum* 1972: 4.

PART THREE

Late Winnicott studies

The use of an object in the context of *Moses and Monotheism*[1]

D.W. Winnicott

Comments on my paper 'The Use of an Object'

Comment I

In my view the main idea incorporated in this paper necessitates a rewriting of an important area in psychoanalytic theory. I will state this in the following way. Dr Fine[2] referred to the libidinal theory, clearly stated in Hartmann Kris-Loewenstein terms and in Anna Freud's *Mechanisms of Defence,* etc. We go on teaching about libidinal stages and erotogenic zones because of the truth of this part of our theory. Also we teach that in health there comes about a *fusion* of libidinal and aggressive drives (though here we can get into trouble because at the start aggressive drives are associated with muscle erotism and not with anger or hate).

My careful research, using many long cases and a truly large amount of short child-psychiatry material, shows me that the fusion part of our theory is not only right but is also wrong. It is at the place where it is wrong that I am trying to make a contribution.

There is a phase prior to that which makes sense of the concept of fusion. In the individual's early development it is not a case of fusion, because what is there in the activity that characterizes the baby's aliveness starts off as a unit or unity. To get quickly to the idea that I have in mind one could profitably use the idea of the fire from the dragon's mouth. I quote from Pliny who (in paying tribute to fire) writes, 'Who can say whether in essence fire is constructive or destructive?' Indeed the physiological basis for what I am referring to is the first and subsequent breaths, out-breathing.

The paper I have presented gives psychoanalysis a chance to rethink this subject. In this vitally important early stage the 'destructive' (fire-air or other) aliveness of the individual is simply a symptom of being alive, and has nothing to do with an individual's anger at the frustrations that belong to meeting the reality principle.

As I have tried to state, the drive is destructive. Survival of the object leads on to object-use, and this leads on to the separation of two phenomena

1 fantasy and
2 actual placing of the object outside the area of projections.

Therefore this very early destructive urge has a vital positive function (when, by survival of the object, it works), namely the objectivisation of the object (the analyst in the transference). This task is bypassed in the schizoid personality or borderline case, and presumably in schizophrenic illness (see Comment II).

I see that all this may have some flaw in it, but if I am able to make my point clear then at any rate it can be discussed.

In practice the result could be of great importance, throwing light even on the adolescent characteristic by which the good is not that which is handed down by parental benignity but that which is forced into being by individual adolescent destructiveness. The parental task and society's task here is (as with mother and baby) one of survival, and this includes survival with the quality of non-retaliation, that is, a containment of what the individual adolescent brings without becoming provoked even under provocation. But this is an application of my new (as I believe) principle of the capacity to use an object arrived at by the subject through the experiences involving survival of the object.

Comment II

I realize that it is this idea of a destructive first impulse that is difficult to grasp. It is this that needs attention and discussion. To help I wish to point out that I am referring to such things as eagerness. I need to include such things as expiration, salivation, burning, and certain sensory experiences such as the extreme sensory sensitivity that belongs to the minutes immediately following birth, and special features of smell, phenomena that are intolerably real, or almost intolerably so, for the baby, even under good-enough conditions of holding and handling. Just here one must allow obscurity to have a value that is superior to false clarification.

It seems likely that Rilke, by using Raum and Welt, gives this same idea in environmental terms. Raum is an infinite space in which the individual can operate without passing through the risky experience of destruction and survival of the object; Welt is by contrast the world in so far as it has, by survival, become objectified by the individual, and to be used.

The use of an object in the context of Moses and Monotheism

In 'Analysis Terminable and Interminable,' a late masterpiece of clear and undogmatic statement, Freud seems to me to be struggling to use what he knows to be true, because of his analytic experiences, to cover what he does not know. I almost wrote, what he does not yet know, since it is so difficult for us to believe that he has left us to carry on with the researches that his invention of psychoanalysis makes possible, and yet he cannot participate when we make a step forward.

The first part of '*Moses and Monotheism*' is a beautiful example of an idea put forward with strength, clarity and conviction, yet without propaganda and indeed with humility. In the last part, Freud can be seen to be reaffirming the belief in repression and (as it would seem to me) overreaching himself in his formulation of monotheism as important because of the universal truth of the loved father and the repression of this in its original and stark (id) form. But the reader knows that the argument does not bear close examination. It is not that Freud is wrong about the father and the libidinal tie that becomes repressed. But it has to be noted that a proportion of persons in the world do not reach to the Oedipus complex. They never get so far in their emotional development, and therefore for them repression of the libidinized father figure has but little relevance. If one looks at religious people it is certainly not true to say that monotheistic tenets only belong to those who reached the Oedipus complex. A great deal of religion is tied up with near-psychosis and with the personal problems that stem from the big area of baby life that is important before the attainment of a three-body relationship as between whole persons.

Freud was labouring under a disadvantage. He could only use psychoanalysis as far as it had gone at the time when he was writing. No-one would blame him for this especially as Freud was always prepared to let a poet or a philosopher or his own intuition open up the way for phenomena that had not been covered by the metapsychology of the time.

Freud came to an expression of his own dissatisfactions near the end of 'Analysis Terminable and Interminable' while expressing satisfaction in a generous way with the writings of Empedocles. This remarkable man (born ca. 495 B.C.) of a remarkable period in the birth and growth of science in Greece formulated a 'love-strife' state both for man and for the universe, and this is as near as may be to Freud's life-death instinct formulation. Freud is pleased.

It is my purpose to put forward the idea that Empedocles the Greek may have got just one step ahead of Freud, at least in one important respect. (To warn the reader I should say that I have never been in love with the death instinct and it would give me happiness if I could relieve Freud of the burden of carrying it forever on his Atlas shoulders. To start with, the development of the theory from a statement of the fact that organic matter tends to return to the inorganic carries very small weight in terms of logic. There is no clear relationship between the two sets of ideas. Also, biology has never been happy about this part of metapsychology while on the whole there is room for mutuality between biology and psychoanalysis all along the line, up to the point of the death instinct.)

It is always possible that the death instinct formulation was one of the places where Freud was near to a comprehensive statement but could not make it because, while he knew all we know about human psychology back to repression of the id in relation to cathected objects, he did not know what borderline cases and schizophrenics were going to teach us in the three decades after his death. Psychoanalysis was to learn that a great deal happens in babies associated with need, and apart from wish, and apart from (pregenital) id-representatives clamouring for satisfaction.

In other words he did not know in the framework of his own well-disciplined mental functioning that we now have to deal with such a problem as this: what is there in the actual presence of the father, and the part he plays in the experience of the relationship between him and the child, and between the child and him? What does this do for the baby? For there is a difference according to whether the father is there or not, is able to make a relationship or not, is sane or insane, is free or rigid in personality. If the father dies this is significant, and when exactly in the baby's life he dies, and there is a great deal too to be taken into account that has to do with the imago of the father in the mother's inner reality and its fate there. We now find all these matters coming along for revival and correction in the transference relationship, matters which are not so much for interpretation as for experiencing.

Now, one thing, in all this has very special relevance. This has to do with the immature ego – rendered strong by the mother's adapting well enough to the baby's *needs*. (This is not to be lost in the concept of her satisfaction of the baby's instinctual drives.)

As the baby moves from ego strengthening due to its being reinforced by mother's ego to having an identity of his or her own – that is, as the inherited tendency to integration carries the baby forward in the good-enough or average expectable environment – the third person plays or seems to me to play a big part. The father may or may not have been a mother-substitute, but at some time he begins to be felt to be there in a different role, and it is here I suggest that the baby is likely to make use of the father as a blue-print for his or her own integration when just becoming at times a unit. If the father is not there the baby must make the same development but more arduously, or using some other fairly stable relationship to a whole person.

In this way one can see that the father can be the first glimpse for the child of integration and of personal wholeness. It is easy to go from this interplay between introjection and projection to the important concept in the world's history of a one god, a monotheism, not a one god for me and another one god for you.[3]

It is easy to make the assumption that because the mother starts as a part object or as a conglomeration of part objects the father comes into ego-grasp in the same way. But I suggest that in a favourable case the father starts off whole (i.e. as father, not as mother surrogate) and later becomes endowed with a significant part object, that he starts off as an integrate in the ego's organisation and in the mental conceptualisation of the baby.

Could it not be said that 'poetically' Freud was ready for this idea, not that monotheism had its root in the repressed idea of the father but that the two ideas of having a father and of monotheism represented the world's first attempts to recognize the individuality of man, of woman, of every individual? (Remember, the Greeks had slaves, which diminishes our regard for the amazing insights of their great thinkers, especially of the centuries around the birth date of Empedocles. Science had to wait some centuries before restarting on the basis of the universal right to be a free or an integrated autonomous individual.)[4]

I can support my thesis by quoting from Freud who wrote that, according to Empedocles, the love power '*strives to agglomerate the primal particles of the elements*' (of universe and man), '*of the four elements into a single unity*'; while the strife power 'seeks to undo, etc. etc.' Here then is the idea of the ego activity *agglomerating,* which is not object-relating. Presently I shall try to carry my argument further by a contribution that I feel needs to be made in regard to this dualism, philia (love) and neikos (strife). I believe a step further could now be made.

Before I describe this new detail I wish to refer to a footnote of Freud's. I am somewhat addicted to his footnotes and quotations which he perhaps allows to go further than he can go in terms of theory as it obtains at the time of his writing.

I refer to: Breasted (1906) calls him (Amenophis) the first individual in human history. Here, for me, is Freud stating the thesis that I am striving to present in my own laboured way. Freud was not, one feels, able to bring this up into the text because he could not deal with it in terms of repression and the mechanisms of defence and of the interplay of id, ego and superego. I feel Freud would welcome new work that makes sense of Breasted's comment in terms of a universal in the emotional development of the individual, namely, the integrative tendency that can bring the individual to unit status.

I am now free to make the contribution that I feel does possibly go in advance of Freud's position. This that I wish to put forward is a culmination of a trend in my thinking, and I can now see evidence of this trend in my papers of a decade ago. (See, for instance, 'Roots of Aggression', in *The Child, the Family and the Outside World*. This is the only new chapter in the book. It is also implied in the cumbersome title of my book *The Maturational Processes and the Facilitating Environment*.)[5]

I have recently tried to give my ideas life in a paper read to the New York Psychoanalytic Society (12th November 1968), but from the papers of the discussants (Jacobsen, Ritvo and Fine) I learned that I had by no means made myself clear, so that the idea as presented there and then was unacceptable at the time. I have revised this paper.[6] I gave the paper the name 'The Use of an Object,' and I wanted to state that in the emotional development of any baby there is a time of dependence when the behaviour of the environment is part and parcel of the child's development, and that this cannot be omitted. That is to say, there is no statement of the development of a baby, dependent on ego support from a mother figure or parent figure, that leaves out of account the environmental factors. This is simply saying that it is *true* that at the beginning the baby has not himself or herself achieved a perception, recognition and repudiation of the NOT-ME. This is something I must believe because of my clinical work.

To illustrate my meaning I looked at the early stage of drives in the individual baby. I drew a sharp distinction between the fate (in terms of personality pattern) of a baby whose first strivings were accepted and of a baby whose first strivings were reacted to. This is a statement reminiscent of Klein's paranoid position, but with this difference, that it is given in terms of environment running *pari passu* with individual life pulses. Retaliation takes the place of talion fears.

It is necessary here to rethink something that we have come to accept (to accept because in analysis of 'analysable' cases it is so true), namely that one of the integrating phenomena in development is the fusion of what I will here allow myself to call life and death instincts (love and strife: Empedocles). The crux of my argument is that the first drive is itself *one* thing, something that I call 'destruction,' but I could have called it a combined love-strife drive. This unity is primary. This is what turns up in the baby by natural maturational process.

The fate of this unity of drive cannot be stated without reference to the environment. The drive is potentially 'destructive' but whether it is destructive or not depends on what the object is like; does the object *survive*, that is, does it retain its character, or does it *react*? If the former, then there is no destruction, or not much, and there is a next moment when the baby can become and does gradually become aware of a cathected object plus the *fantasy* of having destroyed, hurt, damaged, or provoked the object. The baby in this extreme of environmental provision goes on in a pattern of developing personal aggressiveness that provides the backcloth of a continuous (unconscious) fantasy of destruction. Here we may use Klein's reparation concept, which links constructive play and work with this (conscious) *fantasy backcloth* of destruction or provocation (perhaps the right word has not been found). But destruction of an object that survives, has not reacted or disappeared, leads on to use.

The baby at the other extreme that meets a pattern of environmental reaction or retaliation goes forward in quite a different way. This baby finds the reaction from the environment to be the reality of what should be his or her own provocative (or aggressive or destructive) impulse. This kind of baby can never experience or own or be moved by this personal root for aggression or destructive fantasy, and can therefore never convert it into the unconscious fantasy destruction of the libidinized object.

It will be seen that I am trying to rewrite one limited part of our theory. This

> provocative
> destructive
> aggressive
> envious (Klein)

urge is not a pleasure–pain principle phenomenon. *It has nothing to do with anger at the inevitable frustrations associated with the reality principle.* It precedes this set of phenomena that are true of neurotics but that are not true of psychotics.[7]

To make progress towards a workable theory of psychosis, analysts must abandon the whole idea of schizophrenia and paranoia as seen in terms of regression from the Oedipus Complex. The aetiology of these disorders takes us *inevitably* to stages that precede the three-body relationship. The strange corollary is that there is at the root of psychosis an *external factor*.[8] It is difficult for psychoanalysts to admit this after all the work they have done drawing attention to the internal factors in examining the aetiology of psycho-neurosis.

Notes

1 This chapter combines two papers that were written in response to Winnicott's experience of giving his paper, 'The Use of an Object' to the New York Psychoanalytic Institute on November 28th 1968. The first

part, 'Comments on my paper "The use of an object"' was written on 5th December 1968 and the second part, 'The use of an object in the Context of "Moses and Monotheism"', was written on January 16th 1969. They were first published in 1989 in *Psychoanalytic Explorations* (eds. Clare Winnicott, Ray Shepherd, Madeleine Davis) Karnac Books: London. (For a discussion of the background to these papers and themes see Chapter 14). [Editor's Note]

2 See Introduction p. 16 and Chapter 14 Note 2 pp. 305–306 [Editor's Note]

3 See *Moses and Monotheism*, S.E. vol. 22, pp. 305–306 [D.W.W.'s Note]

4 Farrington, *Greek Science*. [D.W.W.'s Note]

5 See the Complete Winnicott Bibliography in Abram 2007. [Editor's Note]

6 See the Winnicott Trust Editors' Notes in Winnicott 1989: pp. 217–218) [Editor's Note]

7 Here I can turn to Bettelheim for support. I find him difficult to read simply because he says everything and there is nothing to be said that one could be certain has not been said by him. But one must read him because he can be exactly right, or more nearly right that other writers. This applies especially to his opening chapters in *The Empty Fortress* (New York: Free Press, 1967; London: Collier-Macmillan Ltd., 1967). [D.W.W.'s Note]

8 See Winnicott, 'Psychoses and Child Care' (1952), in *Collected Papers: Through Paediatrics To Psychoanalysis* (London: Tavistock, 1958; New York: Basic Books, 1975; London: Hogarth Press, 1975) [Winnicott Trust Editors' Notes in original publication 1989].

DWW's notes for the Vienna Congress 1971

A consideration of Winnicott's theory of aggression and an interpretation of the clinical implications

Jan Abram

Prelude

In the Winnicott archives a set of unpublished notes stands as Winnicott's final statement on his theory of aggression. Stimulated by this archive discovery Part One of this paper examines the notes associated with Winnicott's theoretical advances in his late writings 1968–70. I suggest that Winnicott's emphasis in the 'survival of the object' constitutes a clinical concept of aggression rooted in psychoanalytic methodology that contrasts with Freud's speculative concept of the death instinct with its roots in biology. My conclusions in Part One set the foundations for Part Two.

The main aim in Part Two is to re-present my interpretation and attempt to extend Winnicott's thesis as presented in Part One. I propose that the clinical implications in Winnicott's formulations suggest the notion of an intra-psychic surviving and non-surviving object. These intra-psychic objects arise through an admixture of the primary object's oscillations between psychic survival and non-survival of the newborn's needs. I conclude that this specific inter-psychic dynamic between object and subject is at the heart of human development which is naturally revivified in the transference-countertransference matrix. Consequently, the notion of psychic survival constitutes the specificity of clinical psychoanalysis as a therapeutic treatment.

Part One

Vienna 2008: The 21st European Psychoanalytic Federation (EPF) Congress[1]

The shadow of heritage

... it is not possible to be original except on a basis of tradition
(Winnicott 1967)

The theme of the 21st EPF Congress in 2008 invited reflection on how the shadow of Freud's heritage – 'the shadow of the object' – falls on the practice and theory of psychoanalysis today. That the congress was to take place in Vienna added considerable significance to this theme and instigated my re-examination of the notes in the Winnicott archives. As far as can be ascertained these notes had been written weeks or even days before Winnicott died on January 25, 1971. A close study of the notes linked to his late writings shows a continuation of his theoretical advance on aggression that had first been developed in his paper 'The use of an object.' Therefore, before an examination of the notes, I propose to track the relevant aspects of Winnicott's thought that led up to the formulations related to 'The use of an object.' My intention is to examine Winnicott's argument for rejecting Freud's formulation of the death instinct on the basis that it was not rooted in clinical psychoanalysis (Freud 1921).

Although here it will be seen that Winnicott focuses on his disagreement with Freud's concept of the death instinct, it is well known that the contemporaneous Kleinian development stimulated and sharpened Winnicott's explorations and led to a combination of agreement and divergence (cf. Winnicott 1965c) (Ogden 1985). The explicit disagreements focused on two main points: the environment and the Kleinian development of the death instinct – both being interconnected with Winnicott's alternative theory of psychic survival.

My interpretation of Winnicott's concept of the 'environment' is that it refers to the *psychic* environment; how the m/other feels in relation to her infant; her primary maternal preoccupation (Winnicott [1956] 1958a: 300–5). While Winnicott acknowledged his debt to Melanie Klein he had gradually felt that their theoretical divergences emerged because she and her followers did not take *enough* account of the mother's psychic impact on the baby's inner world (Winnicott 1989a: 576).

The second main difference stemmed from Klein's interpretation and development of Freud's concept of the death instinct.[2] For Klein the death instinct is innate in the newborn and manifested by the affects of hate, sadism and envy (Bronstein 2001; Laplanche and Pontalis 1973). In contrast, Winnicott's view was that these affects emerged as a result of the infant's development. In other words the infant had to develop a *capacity* to hate, to be sadistic and to envy. To postulate an innate envy was, for Winnicott, equivalent to a theory of original sin (Winnicott 1971b: 82).[3] Rather, he saw innate aggression as a 'symptom of being alive' (Winnicott 1989a: 239). The newborn's kicks and movements are aimed at *discovering* the reality of the object. While this could be described as a 'benign' aggression, there is no implication here in Winnicott's work, or in my interpretation of it, that the infant's kicks and moves towards the environment are not intense and mobilized by an instinctual force. Indeed, Winnicott referred to the newborn's needs as ruthless (Abram 2007a: 21). This point will be elaborated later linked with Winnicott's decision in his later work to use the word 'destruction' instead of 'aggression' as a way of qualifying the meaning of early aggression i.e. that it is object-related in as much as the object has to survive.

In the third and final phase of his work (1960–71) (Abram 2008: 1205; Chapter 3: 94–104), Winnicott examined the specifics of the psychic environment that facilitated the infant's sequential movement from 'creatively apperceiving' to 'objectively perceiving.' By the beginning of 1968, two years before he died, his formulations concerning the infant's journey from Me to Not-me took shape in his paper 'The use of an object' – a paper especially written and prepared for the New York Psychoanalytic Society. As we shall see, it was to be his final formulation and constitutes his alternative theory to that of the death instinct – both Freudian and Kleinian.

New York 1968

The use of an object

To use an object the subject must have developed a *capacity* to use objects . . . This capacity cannot be said to be inborn, nor can its development in an individual be taken for granted. The development of a capacity to use an object is another example of the maturational process as something that depends on a facilitating environment.

(Winnicott 1969: 713)

In the early part of 1968 Winnicott was invited to give a paper to the New York Psychoanalytical Society for the autumn. This would be an opportunity for him to develop his ideas about 'the way in which the infant develops the capacity to see beyond the world he has created through the projection of his internal objects' (Ogden 1985). There have been several accounts of what happened on that evening and the event has taken on a mythology of its own (Goldman 1993; Samuels 1996; Rodman 2003). This 'mythology' has occurred for two main reasons: firstly, the paper is a radical challenge to instinct theory (although this was not explicit in the original paper); and secondly, shortly after the presentation Winnicott had to be hospitalized and for several weeks was on the brink of death (Goldman 1993; Rodman 2003).

The reasons why Winnicott wanted to present this particular paper to the Freudians of one of the oldest Psychoanalytic Societies in the world has raised many questions.[4] I suggest that he was searching for an audience whom he expected to be receptive to his new formulations – namely his rejection of the death instinct – as well as his attempt to revise the psychoanalytic theory of aggression (Davis and Wallbridge 1981: 66–72). After all he had already come into contact with several American analysts who were also theorizing on the earliest stages of emotional development, e.g. Greenacre, Hartmann and Kris (see Thompson 2008; 2012: Chapter 17). Moreover, Winnicott was aware that there were many ego psychology/classical Freudians (including Anna Freud herself), who were not in agreement with Freud's theory of the death instinct.[5] But he later recorded that he was disappointed that there had been no time for any such discussion due to the three substantial discussion papers. Even so,

305

in a letter to Anna Freud several weeks later, Winnicott claims that he '. . . got considerable personal benefit from the reaction of the three discussants, so that I am now in the process of rewriting it in a quite different language' (Rodman 1987: 185). In the same letter he explains that he was already ill before giving the paper, which seems to show that his serious illness *after* the presentation had nothing to do with the discussants' criticisms (Rodman 2000: 330). It has often been speculated that he became ill[6] as a reaction to the criticism. This may have been assumed because after hearing the three discussants Winnicott was reported to have said that his '. . . concept was torn to pieces and that he would be happy to give it up' (Milrod 1968). I suggest however, that this comment indicates, given what he later wrote to Anna Freud, that Winnicott realized a complementary paper was required that would address his thinking on Freud's concept of the death instinct (see below; Winnicott 1989a).

The problem of a culture clash, especially between America and Europe, has its own history since Freud first lectured in America in 1908. The parallel developments between ego psychology, with its emphasis on ego development at each stage of libidinal development, in contrast to object relations theory, with its emphasis on the baby's need for the m/other and the environment, can inevitably cause confusion (Rycroft 1972: vii–xxvi). A close reading of the discussion papers illustrates that there was indeed confusion related to these two different psychoanalytic cultures, however, it also raises the question as to why Winnicott did not take this into account when preparing his paper. I suggest that having been determined to develop his own ideas in 1945, as a response to the end of the 'controversial discussions,' 23 years later he was conceptualizing from a different paradigm, without being fully aware of how far he had moved away from the classical Freudian model (cf. Loparic 2002; Chapter 4 this volume). Moreover it is important to recognize that 'The use of an object' was a work in progress and given to be read alongside several other papers (see Winnicott's 'Summary' below). In addition he had sent two substantial clinical examples that there was no time to discuss.[7] Nevertheless, the American discussants did stimulate Winnicott to sharpen his argument which fortuitously took him to a new advance in his formulation of the father's role in the early parent–infant relationship (cf. Chapters 4 and 15).

It is not entirely accurate to say that Winnicott had ignored the role of the father in his theoretical developments up to that point.

For instance, in 1957, in a postscript to his first collection of broadcast talks entitled (in a later publication) 'The Mother's Contribution to Society,' he states:

> Fathers, I know, are just as important, and indeed an interest in mothering includes an interest in fathers, and in the vital part they play in child care. But for me it has been to mothers that I have so deeply needed to speak.
>
> (Winnicott 1957a: 123)

So, although the father had been a 'vital part' of Winnicott's formulations, it wasn't until the postscripts of 'The use of an object' (Winnicott 1989b: 217–40) that the father found a place in his theoretical matrix as a 'vital part' in the mother's mind (cf. Green [1996] 2000). As I hope to show, it is this 'vital part' in mother's mind that expands the concept of survival of the object.

Before going into more detail concerning the main argument in 'The use of an object' let us first of all examine Winnicott's original summary of his paper sent in advance of the planned talk along with the lengthy clinical examples.

★ ★ ★

The New York Psychoanalytic Society

Summary of paper to be presented on Tuesday, November 12, 1968, The use of an object by Dr. D. W. Winnicott (London)

Object relating can be described in terms of the experience of the subject. Description of object-usage involves consideration of the nature of the object. I am offering for discussion the reasons why, in my opinion, a capacity to use an object is more sophisticated than a capacity to relate to objects; and relating may be to a subjective object, but usage implies that the object is part of external reality.

This sequence can be observed:

1. Subject *relates* to object.
2. Object is in process of being found instead of placed by the subject in the world.

3. Subject *destroys* object.
4. Object survives destruction.
5. Subject can *use* object.

The object is always being destroyed. This destruction becomes the unconscious backcloth for love of a real object, that is, an object outside the area of the subject's omnipotent control.

Study of this problem involves a statement of the positive value of destructiveness. The destructiveness plus the object's survival of the destruction places the object outside the area in which projective mental mechanisms operate, so that a world of shared reality is created which the subject can use and which can feed back into the subject. How this usage develops naturally out of play with the object is the theme of this talk.

It would help in my exposition if a reading of the following papers could be taken for granted:

1. (1966) The Location of Cultural Experience. Int. J. Psa. 48: 3, 368–72
2. (1962) Hogarth Press, London, 1965. Ego Integration in Child Development, (Chapter 4 in: The Maturational Processes and the Facilitating Environment) N.Y. I.U.P. – 1965, pp. 56–63
3. The Capacity to be Alone. Int. J. Psa. 39: 5, 416–20, 1958
4. Playing: Its Theoretical Status in the Clinical Situation. Int. J. Psa. V. 49, 1968 – still in press

10/29/68

★ ★ ★

The added footnote: a clue

In 1970, Winnicott added a footnote to the manuscript of his book *Human Nature,* to the effect that the issue of 'recognition of the destructive[8] element in the crude primitive excited idea' was resolved when he wrote 'The use of an object.' This footnote, I suggest, indicates that it was the notion of the object's psychic survival that had answered his question related to how the infant could move from apperception to perception; from pre-ruth to ruth (Winnicott 1988: 79). From the 'Summary' reproduced above it is clear that Winnicott hoped his audience would have already accepted, or at least understood, many of his previous arguments that set the stage for his new formulation because he felt he had resolved the problem of defining the fate of the primitive love impulse.

Winnicott's formulations preceding 1968

The papers Winnicott recommends are not listed in chronological order, which suggests that he wished to emphasize an order of importance. In the following I highlight the salient concepts of each paper in an attempt to track Winnicott's trajectory up to that point in 1968. All these concepts are intrinsically related to his theory of psychic survival.

1. In the 'Location of Cultural Experience' (1966), Winnicott posits a 'potential space' which, for the baby, is located *in between* the subjective object and the object objectively perceived.[9] 'From the beginning the baby has maximally intense experiences *in the potential space between the subjective object and the object objectively perceived*, between me-extensions and the not-me' (Winnicott 1971a: 100) [italics in original].

2. Earlier, in 1962, Winnicott had offered a departure from Freud by stating that the newborn's ego, distinct from the self, was provided by the mother in her state of primary maternal preoccupation – ego-relatedness. This is why he states, 'There is no id before ego.' Therefore, at the very beginning '. . . instinctual life can be ignored, because the infant is not yet an entity having experiences' (Winnicott 1962: 56). A self has to be in place before the infant is able to 'experience' otherwise s/he can only 'react,' which constitutes trauma.

3. Winnicott had introduced the term ego-relatedness in 1956 to describe the phase of absolute dependence when, in his terminology, the baby is merged with the mother and benefits from ego-coverage that emanates from the mother's primary maternal preoccupation. In his paper on 'The capacity to be alone' (1958b) he had stated that this capacity was based on the introjection of an 'ego-supportive environment' – a consequence of the early good enough mother's attention and adaptation i.e. ego-coverage. In Klein's theory this indicated the existence of a good internal object and in Freud's theory it indicated an ability to tolerate the

'. . . feelings aroused by the primal scene.' Winnicott's emphasis is that the introjection of the good internal object and the resolution of the Oedipus complex could not occur without the 'introjection of an ego-supportive environment' at the very beginning. The capacity to be alone is based on the paradox of being alone in the 'presence of mother' (Winnicott 1958b: 30).

4. The theory of playing was present in Winnicott's early paediatric work when he discovered in the 1930s that the 'spatula game' could be used as a way of assessing the infant's emotional difficulties in first consultations (Winnicott 1941: 229–49). Later, the 'squiggle game' became a natural successor to the earlier game for toddlers, as well as a helpful diagnostic tool for children and adolescents. In 1942, Winnicott had already observed that the '. . . child values finding that hate or aggressive urges can be expressed in a known environment, without the return of hate and violence from the environment to the child' (Winnicott 1942: 43). Here we find the very theme of the subject's attack and the object's tolerance that would begin to crystallize in the papers of 1968. The critique of psychoanalytic technique is also raised (as it is in 'The use of an object'), and Winnicott is unequivocal that '. . . interpretation outside the ripeness of the material is indoctrination . . . a corollary is that resistance arises out of interpretation given outside the area of overlap of the patient's and analyst's playing together' (Winnicott, [1967] 1968: 597).

The above four papers show how Winnicott's re-formulations were moving towards a 'paradigm shift' in psychoanalysis (Chapter 4). It does not imply that instinct theory is irrelevant in Winnicott's formulations but rather that, from the infant's point of view, the instinctual/biological impulse might just as well be an external clap of thunder *before* the sense of self could develop; and a sense of self will only come about through a psychic environment capable of meeting the infant's biological and emotional needs (Winnicott 1965d: 141).

Winnicott clearly thought that something was missing in psychoanalytic theory: 'There is a phase prior to that which makes sense of the concept of fusion' (ibid.: 239). In his original thesis in 1939, aggression in the infant was primary and simply 'muscle erotism,' and a 'symptom of being alive,' '. . . and had nothing to do with anger,' let alone hate, sadism and envy. By this last decade of his work he used the term 'destructive,' but both words – 'aggression' and 'destruction'

– in Winnicott's language signify a benign force in the infant at the beginning (although the word 'destruction,' as we shall see, takes on a supplementary meaning in his final formulation).

In 'Metapsychological and clinical aspects aspects of regression within the psychoanalytic set up' (1955a), Winnicott argued that Freud took for granted the early good enough environment, and his work with neurotics, therefore, meant that he did not have the clinical data that analysts with borderline patients discover (cf. Raphael-Leff 2007a). In 'The use of an object in the context of Moses and Monotheism,' Winnicott reiterates this point, stating that this is the reason that Freud did not theorize about the pre-fusion stage and the question of how the infant develops a capacity to think symbolically (Winnicott 1989a: 240–6). As already stated above, it is in this very late paper that Winnicott introduces a new thought when he suggests that the father has an important role at this pre-fusion stage of the subject's psychic life (Abram 2007a: 38).

The father's imago, he suggests, starts off as a whole object in the infant's psyche as a presence in mother's mind, i.e. the fact of the parental intercourse (ibid.: 39). I suggest that this notion advances the concept of primary maternal preoccupation because Winnicott states that the '*father as a whole object at the beginning*' constitutes an integrative force in the infant – a clear suggestion that the father (in mother's mind during her state of primary maternal preoccupation) is transmitted and internalized by the infant, which will lead to an ego capacity [my italics]. Indeed, it seems clear that without the father in mother's mind there is no such thing as survival of the object in Winnicott's theory (cf. Green [1996] 2000).

Vienna 1971: The 27th IPA Congress

The psychoanalytical concept of aggression: theoretical, clinical and applied aspects[10]

The reader should know that I am a product of the Freudian . . . school. This does not mean that I take for granted everything Freud said or wrote, and in any case that would be absurd since Freud was developing, that is to say changing, his views . . . right up to his death in 1939.

(Winnicott [1950] 1965a: 21)

311

In the early days of 1971 Winnicott booked a room at the Hotel Sacher, Vienna, from July 23 until July 31. He was planning to attend the IPA Congress to be held that year in Vienna, to speak on a panel entitled 'The Role of Aggression in Child Analysis.' But, it was a Congress that he was destined not to attend – he died on January 25.

In the Winnicott archives, in a file written in Clare Winnicott's hand – 'DWW's Notes for the Vienna Congress never given' – there are a set of unpublished notes that were written by Winnicott in preparation for that panel. The notes consist of hand-written sheets in Winnicott's hand with instructions (in the top left-hand corner) for his secretary. The typed pages correlate exactly with his instructions and offer a clear sequence of statements that were presumably to serve as his plan for the paper. Stimulated by the announcement of the 2008 EPF conference to be held in Vienna on the theme – 'the shadow of Freud's heritage' – I returned to the file. Closer examination led me to surmise that the first four pages (out of seven) of the planned paper, compared and contrasted with key papers of the previous two years, show further clarification on Winnicott's formulations. Therefore, the notes of this unwritten paper stand as Winnicott's 'last word' on 'the use of an object' theory and offer a consolidatory advance to his final theoretical conclusions on the psychoanalytic concept of aggression.

The notes show a trajectory that passes through several of Winnicott's major themes in his work: dissociation, hate, male and female elements, the use of an object and regression. Since this present study aims to address a consideration of Winnicott's theory of aggression I will focus on the first four pages.

The unpublished archival notes

Page 1

> I am asking for a kind of revolution in our work. Let us re-examine what we do. It may be that in dealing with the repressed unconscious we are colluding with the patient and the established defences. What is needed of us, because the patient cannot do the work by self-analysis; someone must see and witness the parts that go to make the whole, a whole that does not exist except as viewed from outside.

In time we may have to come to the conclusion that the common failure of many excellent analyses has to do with the patient's dissociation hidden in material that is clearly related to repression taking place as a defence in a seemingly whole person.

Perhaps by now, so near to death, Winnicott was able to articulate something that he had been in the process of since 1945 – a psychoanalytic revolution. Thomas Kuhn had only just published his book *The structure of scientific revolutions* (1962), and although Winnicott never refers to this book, his use of this word at the beginning of these notes suggests that he intuited his formulations were moving psychoanalysis towards something new. There is a sense that Winnicott wants to be clear this time – as if to correct the misunderstanding in New York – and as is evident in the postscript papers. Winnicott speaks directly to Freud – no coincidence then that this was the paper to be presented in Vienna. But his concepts should not to be construed as an attack on Freud's psychoanalysis, rather they show the wish to have a dialogue with the aim of continuing Freud's work.

When he writes '. . . *what is needed of us is to witness the parts* . . .' it reminds us of a paper he had just written on his view of the 'self' that is made up of a huge number of parts/identifications. In 1970, months before these notes were written, he wrote 'On the basis for self in body' in which he stated:

> For me the self, which is not the ego, is the person who is me, who is only me, who has a totality based on the operation of the maturational process. At the same time the self has parts, and in fact is constituted of these parts. These parts agglutinate from a direction interior-exterior in the course of the operation of the maturational process, aided as it must be (maximally at the beginning) by the human environment which holds and handles and in a live way facilitates.
>
> (Winnicott 1971c)

As has already been examined above, in Winnicott's theory a [sense of] self can only grow in a *facilitating* environment: without that *essential,* an imitation self will develop on the basis of compliance leading to degrees of false self as described in 'Ego distortion in terms of true and false self' ([1960] 1965d). This is the kind of conceptualizing that 'advances the psychoanalytic conception of the subject' (Ogden 1992: 619), and it involves the creation of a new psychoanalytic language that invokes the nature of human relations, in contrast to a language that tends to distance and estrange (Bettelheim 1983; Ogden 2001; Fulgenzio 2007: 455).

The reference to the 'common failure of analysis' presumably refers to Winnicott's experience and observation that there were many analyses that appeared to succeed but which never really reached the patient's dissociated parts – a false self analysis. This crucial issue of a 'failed analysis' is one rarely referred to in the literature although all analysts are aware of its existence. So that when he writes on Page 2

> My own analysis was being done by my colleagues who at this time (1947) accepted my paper: 'Hate in the countertransference.'

there is a strong allusion that not only does Winnicott witness many patients who do not get better despite an excellent analysis, but that he too has experienced this. His own analysis with Strachey lasted ten years (1923–33). Subsequently he was in analysis with Joan Riviere for five years (which suggests that he did not feel he'd completed his first analysis). He qualified as an analyst in 1934 and by 1947 when he wrote 'Hate in the countertransference,' he had not been in analysis for several years. From his writings (see Winnicott 1989a: 569–84) we can glean that, despite feeling 'enormously helped,' he was also disappointed at the end of his second analysis. The manifest reason, he states, was because his analyst refused to accept his idea to classify the environment and its impact on the newborn's psyche (see Winnicott 1989a; Abram 2008). We know that it '. . . took a long time to recover . . .' from this experience (ibid.: 576) and presumably it was followed by on-going self-analysis. The result, as seen in 'Hate in the countertransference' ([1947] 1949), illustrates how Winnicott arrives at his conception of hate. Like all his theories, the concept of hate was crystallized through clinical work alongside self-analysis. In clarifying the difference between the psychotic and neurotic he focuses on the psychic environment and writes:

> There is a vast difference between those patients who have had satisfactory early experiences which can be discovered in the trans-ference, and those whose very early experiences have been so defi-

cient or distorted that the analyst has to be the first in the patient's life to supply certain environmental essentials.

(Winnicott 1949: 198)

When Winnicott says that his colleagues helped his self-analysis, we wonder whether he means that through the acceptance of his argument in 'Hate in the countertransference' they help. The thrust of his argument focuses on early deficiency. He compares the mother's hatred for her newborn with the analyst's hate for the psychotic patient whose emotional demands are equal to that of the newborn. The ability to hate comes about as a result of ambivalence having been reached during the time of 'relative dependence' and the 'stage of concern' (Abram 2007a: 182).

Page 3

It was here that my clinical experiences were able to drive me to complete the analysis of the man who had carried a girl self round with him all his life, but who did not know this, and none of his dozen analyses had been able to recognize the vital fact.

In 1966 Winnicott had presented his paper, 'The split-off male and female elements to be found in men and women' to the BPaS (Winnicott 1971d: 72–85). He reports work with a patient where ordinary psychoanalytic work was going well but he (Winnicott) felt something was missing. In one session Winnicott finds himself saying to the patient that although he is aware that the person on his couch is a man he seems to be talking about penis envy. The patient responds, 'If I were to tell someone about this girl I would be called mad.' Winnicott's interpretation is that it is he (in the transference) who is mad. Winnicott sees that the patient had introjected his mother's madness because she had related to him as (if he were) a baby girl when he was first born. Winnicott's point in this paper, and relevant to the unwritten paper, is that no previous analysis, including the analysis conducted by Winnicott himself up to that point, had recognized this dissociated part of this man's self; and that fundamentally the aetiology of the dissociated part had its roots in the m/other's madness. Once this 'madness' came to the fore in the transference it could then be identified and thus interpreted. Later, in 1969, Winnicott wrote a paper he entitled, 'Mother's madness appearing in the clinical material as an ego–alien factor,' which is an account of a therapeutic consultation with a six year old who showed how he also carried within him an aspect of the madness of his mother; described in this paper as 'the traumatic agent' (Winnicott, [1969] 1989a: 375). These examples offer clinical evidence for survival and non-survival of the original object (see Part Two).

Page 4

> Eventually these matters became lost to me in my conscious daily life, and yet the idea evolved and made me go to New York to give 'The Use of an Object.' This paper takes me as far as I can get, and its new feature is that it recognizes the survival of the object – i.e. the world's separate existence – as a vital fact in personal emotional growth. It involves the theory of the beginning of fantasy, and it also introduces the idea that aggression is not <u>generated</u> by the externality of the object, so the place and moment of origin of the object's externality is not at origin destructive.[11]

It seems to me that the last sentence on Page 4 of the notes is what he has not said previously (although it is implicit in 'The use of an object'): i.e. that the survival of the object '. . . introduces the idea that aggression is not <u>generated</u> (underlined by Winnicott) by the externality of the object, so the place and moment of origin of the object's externality is not at origin destructive.'

And this is precisely Winnicott's point of departure from both Freud and Klein. He posited that at the beginning (the summation of beginnings) something had to occur that *preceded* the moment of fusion. This stage of development had not been accounted for in Freudian theory and that lack had led him to seek assistance from Melanie Klein whose own work focused on the earliest stages of emotional development (Abram 2008: 1197; Chapter 3). Although he concurred with much of what Klein was developing in the 1930s, as we have seen (Winnicott 1962, 1989a), he was in complete disagreement about her interpretation and development of Freud's death instinct, i.e. that envy, hate and sadism were components of the death instinct and innate in the infant from the start. For him these emotions belonged to a later stage of development and were contingent on the environment – the mother's capacity to respond to the newborn's needs.

The striking phrase is the 'new feature' – the 'survival of the object' – which constitutes the *non retaliation* of the external object and is the vital component that will provide the subject a chance to develop. Although Winnicott has observed this fact and has written about it extensively from 1937 until 1968, it is only in the conceptualizing of 'the use of an object' that he can clearly state that the survival of the object is a new feature in his formulations. In other words, the capacity to think symbolically and to reach a position in which the 'Other' is perceived as truly separate, not just a 'bundle of projections,' is entirely contingent on the survival of the object from the very beginning when the baby is not able to differentiate between Me and Not-me. Indeed, the capacity to discern this differentiation is contingent on the original survival of the object – the 'theoretical beginning.' Winnicott refers to the 'summation of beginnings' which he describes as an 'accumulation of beginnings' that go to make up a 'theoretical beginning' (Winnicott [1954] 1955a: 283). Perhaps the pinnacle of development, at the point of death, if still psychically alive, we could think of as the 'summation of endings.'

Illusion (of omnipotence)

Primary creativity, the theoretical first feed, and creating the object

Here, in order to elaborate further on Winnicott's formulations related to what he names the 'stage of pre-fusion,' let us briefly discuss three of the key related concepts that he had already outlined before 1968 – *primary creativity, the theoretical first feed, and creating the object* (Abram 2007a: 114 and 209). This discussion is aimed at an illumination of the core concept in 'The use of an object' and will hopefully lead on to an understanding of how and why it offers an alternative theory to the death instinct.

As we saw above, for Winnicott, the Freudian theory of fusion of the instincts could only occur *after* the establishment of 'unit status' or a 'unit self' (Winnicott 1955b and 1962). This stage cannot occur in the infant before the age of three or four months. And, as we have seen, the establishment of a self was contingent on the mother's survival of her infant's ruthless, destructive love. Winnicott emphasizes that it is the biological need in the baby that has to be attended to by the emotionality of the m/other/psychic-environment; and it is this attending to the infant's biological need (which at the very early stage of life is not separable from emotional need), through the mother's emotional response, that will constitute what Winnicott describes as the 'theoretical first feed.'

> The theoretical first feed is represented in real life by the summa-tion of the early experiences of many feeds. After the theoretical first feed the baby begins to have material with which to create.
>
> (Winnicott [1953] 1988: 106)

Following Freud, Winnicott sees that the baby is born into the world equipped with a creative potential. This 'inherited tendency,' described as a predisposition to grow, is bound up with the sensations in the body and the baby's absolute dependence. The mother's ability to recognize her baby's predicament enables her to adapt to his needs, e.g. offering her breast when he cries. Winnicott stresses that the mother's adaptation has to involve the mother's desire and enjoyment in order to provide what the baby needs through her deep 'primary maternal preoccupation' – an intense and unconscious identification with her baby's predicament of absolute dependence (1956). This very first contact between mother and infant is the beginning of a gradual building up of the baby's 'illusion of omnipotence' which means that, from the baby's point of view, his need (hunger) creates the breast (food). Winnicott sees this as a crucial moment that con-stitutes the foundations for all further development. The mother's ability to adapt to her baby's needs facilitates in the baby/subject the 'illusion of omnipotence.' This experience is a necessary aspect of what he describes as 'the theoretical first feed.'

> At least until we know more I must assume that there is creative potential, and that at the theoretical first feed the baby has a per-sonal contribution to make. If the mother adapts well enough the baby assumes the nipple and the milk are the results of a gesture that arose out of need, the result of an idea that rode in on a crest of a wave of instinctual tension.
>
> (Winnicott [1953] 1988: 110)

The wave of instinctual tension is, for example, the sensation of hun-ger (or any other biological impulse). Hunger that is met, through the mother's 'adaptation to her baby's need,' does not necessarily mean that she is able to provide the theoretical first feed. There are many more essential ingredients involved in the good enough mother's ability to feed her baby (Abram 2007a: 235). In Winnicott's final formulations of the mother–infant relationship he focuses on the process of mother's adaptation to the infant's needs, and suggests that these ingredients culminate and constitute her 'survival' of the newborn's ruthless need for her. As we have seen, in 1968 he explores how the good enough external object survives the baby's primitive need. This is another aspect of what occurs at the theoretical first feed and is associated with the baby's excited states and the mother's capacity to identify and respond to her baby's communications. The 'good enough mother' *survives* due to her state of primary maternal preoccupation. The fact of the mother's survival facilitates the baby's ability to 'create the object.' In contrast, the mother who is not able to tolerate the baby's ordinary demands, but instead tends to feel attacked by the baby and even persecuted (as we saw in the mother of the 1939 paper on aggression), is the mother who does not survive (Winnicott 1984). The 'survival of the object' is central – a crucial fact in the early life of the human being – that either enables or disables the subject to move from object relating to object usage. Here is Winnicott's famous sequence:

> After subject relates to object comes subject destroys object (as it becomes external); and then may come 'object survives destruction by the subject . . . A new feature thus arrives in the theory of object relating. The subject says to the object: 'I destroyed you,' and the object is there to receive the communication. From now on the subject says: 'Hullo object!' 'I destroyed you.' 'I love you'. 'You have value for me because of your survival of my destruction of you'. 'While I am loving you I am all the time destroying you' . . . in unconscious fantasy.
>
> (Winnicott [1968] 1969)

A dissection of the sequence

The reader will note that in his outline summary for the audience in New York (as shown above), Winnicott lists four stages to the sequence just quoted and underlines the words 'relates' 'destroys' and 'use.' Let us dissect the sequence and pay attention to the word emphasis.

1. Subject <u>relates</u> to object.
   This is the baby at the beginning of life who is unaware of the care he receives and is merged with the m/other during the phase

of absolute dependence. The baby is ruthless during this stage – a state of pre-ruth – and he cannot know about the demands he puts on the environment; indeed it is paramount that the baby is *not* made aware of what he is doing. The environment mother must protect him from this fact so that he can get on with the tasks involved in being out of the womb.

2. Object is in process of being found instead of placed by the subject in the world.

    The baby's needs are met and this leads to the object being experienced although not yet consciously. The baby cannot yet be aware that the mother/object is a separate Other. The process of finding out and moving towards more conscious awareness has to be given space and time. The baby is not yet ready to be aware because further crucial processes need to take place before he will be able to 'place the object in the world.'

3. Subject <u>destroys</u> object.

    The repeated and uninhibited ruthless demand for the environment's adaptation amounts to a continual destruction of the object. The ongoing destruction is not intentional but rather a necessary process of 'discovering' the externality of the object.

4. Object survives destruction.

    The mother's sustained capacity to tolerate the baby's endless demands because of her state of primary maternal preoccupation offers the infant a sense of continuity and reliability. Survival involves primary identification, mirroring, ego protection, processing and, crucially, non-retaliation. The myriad aspects of the good enough m/other's survival enables the baby to move from apperception to perception in the potential space between relating to subjective objects to perceiving objects objectively perceived. This phase of the baby's life takes him from absolute to relative dependence as he moves from total unawareness to a gradual awareness of the environment.

5. Subject can <u>use</u> object.

    The previous merger of the 'environment mother' and 'object mother' in the phase of absolute dependence gave the baby the impression that he had two different mothers. Due to the consistent survival of the object, this perspective has gradually changed and by now the baby is able to see that both mothers are actually one (Winnicott 1963).

This sequence depicts the step-by-step process of the baby's aggression (biological urge/need) being survived (received and digested) by the external object which simultaneously leads to the baby's internalization, as Winnicott said, of the 'ego supportive environment' (Winnicott 1962: 63). The infant's primary aggression, i.e. a benign instinctual impulse – forces the object to adapt (or not) to the baby's instinctual needs. At the very beginning the subject cannot differentiate between instinctual bodily need and the object's separateness. Good enough adaptation to the newborn's needs means there is also no differentiation for the infant between psyche and soma. This harmonious mix between psyche and soma, mother and infant, is incrementally internalized culminating in the baby's intrapsychic 'imaginative elaboration' about what is happening to and in his body. Winnicott's thesis is that there is *no duality* in the biological/instinctual demand, because at the beginning it is a movement concerning being alive and has no intention other than to relate, i.e. to feel the extent of the boundary and to find the object for needs to be met.

The crucial moment in Winnicott's sequence of object relating to object use, is that the object is there to *receive the communication* – i.e. the object is able to *receive* the subject's loving destruction. It is this *reception* (which inevitably includes *reflection*) that constitutes the object's *survival*. Because of the object's ability to receive, and thus survive, the subject will experience that his ruthless love has been survived by the object, because she – the object – continues to receive and reflect; respond and adapt. This is the essential experience of mutuality that will lead on to the establishment of an internalized 'ego supportive environment' without which the subject is not able to distinguish between their projections and the integrity of the m/other.

Part Two

The surviving and non-surviving objects

My interpretation of the clinical implications in Winnicott's theory of aggression

My observation of the specific nature of psychic survival in the consulting room has led me to formulate a personal interpretation of the way in which I understand Winnicott's conceptualizations as I have set out in Part One. Here, with reference to my previously published clinical papers, I present a summarized retrospective of my attempt to extend Winnicott's concept of 'survival of the object.' Although it is mostly with the borderline patient (to use a broad diagnostic term) that the need for the analyst's psychic survival is paramount, I suggest that in all analyses there is a primitive layer of experience revivified in the transference in which needs have not been met by the original object. Therefore, the analyst's fine attunement to the analysand's communications constitutes the meeting of emotional needs – a 'failure mended.' Thus the analytic attitude involves different qualitative aspects of survival that in a variety of ways emulate the stages of emotional development from birth to death. I argue that survival of the object is relevant to each developmental stage of life but that it is the failure of the object (both environment and object mother) to survive in infanthood that has the potential to be ameliorated through a good enough psychoanalysis.

In 1996, in a paper written for Winnicott's centenary year, I began to formulate the notion of an internalized surviving object. This is not an object that Winnicott referred to per se but it seemed to me that Winnicott's notion of the internalization of an 'ego supportive environment' emerging out of the mother's intense identification with her baby – primary maternal preoccupation – meant that the newborn would also have internalized the experience of the object mother having survived his excited states. The combined experience of both the object mother and environment mother surviving suggested to me the notion of an intrapsychic surviving object (Abram 2003). This concept is of course similar to Klein's concept of good and bad internal objects (Bronstein 2001: 108–24), but its distinctive features are intrinsically part of the object mother's ability to survive the newborn's intense instinctual needs (as opposed to wishes) (see Abram 2007a: 84). The surviving object is therefore *inseparable* from what has occurred in the mother–infant relationship and evolves as a *consequence* of the mutuality between the mother's good enough response to the infant's demands. Whereas in Kleinian theory the mother mitigates the baby's innate aggression (designated the manifestation of the death instinct), in Winnicott's theory the mother becomes an integrated part of the fabric of the baby's internal world whose [sense of] self emerges through her ego-coverage and her inter-psychic unconscious identifications.

Later in 2000 (Abram 2005), with reference to the traumatic moments in a different patient's early life, I expanded on the earlier paper by applying the notion of psychic survival to each stage of development up until maturity. This idea occurred to me because it was clear that my patient's childhood screen memories illustrated a consistent non-survival of the object, repeated in the transference, so that her stunted development became more and more fixed. Subsequently, by the time she reached adolescence she had not had a sufficient amount of experiences of survival of the object to facilitate the transition into adulthood. This led me to propose that the surviving object cannot be fully established until the emotional tasks of adolescence have been completed. Thus a 'whole surviving object' is the result of a developmental process that is ongoing from before the beginning of birth, throughout childhood and reaches a particular peak of growth at the onset of adulthood (which simultaneously marks the [theoretical] end of childhood). From then on, I suggested that the continued consolidation, enrichment and growth of the surviving object will come about through ongoing interpersonal/interpsychic relationships, as it were, feeding the intrapsychic surviving object in the internal world. Consequently the individual is able to 'live creatively' (Winnicott 1986b) and fulfil potential.

Following on from that paper in the context of working with a violent borderline patient, I focused on the corollary of the surviving object, i.e. the non-surviving object (Abram 2007b). During a phase of the treatment when the maternal transference was on the brink of becoming a delusional transference I understood from my countertransference experience of terror that the patient was in fact terrified himself. This made me postulate that terror is at the root of a non-surviving object since the non-survival of the object had been internalized because of the mother's early failures of the object that inevitably left the newborn in a state of unthinkable anxiety and primitive agony. This experience, following Winnicott's formulations, does not come about because of the internal death instinct but rather through a lack of ego coverage from the psychic environment that constitutes the process of holding and containing (Abram 2007a). As a consequence of no protective ego support the benign/destructive/creative impulse becomes thwarted and the infant has no other option than to withdraw or attack the self – having catalogued the culmination of non-survivals of the object that carries the history of a *lack of reception and reflection* from the object. This constitutes psychic

323

trauma. The cumulative effect of the non-survival of the environment means that the non-surviving object begins to grow and is liable to dominate the internal picture of the analysand. It overwhelms the internal world i.e. eclipses the undeveloped surviving object. Everyone alive will have introjected a good enough experience, however brief, that will give birth to a surviving object. But, through a consistent lack of nourishment from an object that survives, (externally and internally) the intrapsychic surviving object remains stunted.

With Winnicott's notion of the 'first theoretical feed' in mind, I suggested that the surviving object is the result of the first theoretical feed, that in turn facilitates the infant to create the object. The notion of Winnicott's first theoretical feed is clinically useful as it refers to the initiation of symbolic thinking. I postulated that accepting this idea means we could think of subsequent theoretical feeds at each stage of development. In other words the interpsychic environment continues to be crucial for the intrapsychic surviving object to grow and take shape. Late adolescence is the final stage of this journey and I posited the notion of a whole surviving object that comes into being once the specific tasks of that phase are completed. It is true that the parents' role for each developmental stage is qualitatively different and if the early stages have been successful the infant's healthy development augers well. Nevertheless, as we see in countless clinical examples every child continues to need the object to continue to survive, because for a whole surviving object to come into being, the interpsychic environment must survive at each stage to reach the 'final theoretical feed' (Abram 2005).

The notion of a 'whole surviving object' means that the subject is able to 'live creatively' and 'feel real.' Moreover, it continues to grow and develop through each stage of adult life until death, through the nourishment that emanates from the intrapsychic, inter-psychic and interpersonal relationships of individuals, families and groups. The failure of the growth of a surviving object results in the consolidation of a non-surviving object, which impoverishes and depletes the sense of self. In severe cases there is only psychic deadness while in the less severe case the subject has to live through a false self (Winnicott 1960).

Recently (Abram 2010), again emerging out of clinical work with a female patient whose fear of analysis revealed a fear of her own desire, I explored the concepts of desire and transference-resistance linked to non-survival of the object. In that paper I suggested that desire dominated by an intrapsychic non-surviving object inhibits growth and lies at the root of transference-resistance. In contrast, desire in the context of a surviving object unfolds a *capacity to love*. This paper concludes that the development of an intrapsychic surviving object in analysis relies on the analyst's psychic survival which facilitates the *working through* in the transference and the *work of mourning*. While fulfilling desire liberates and strengthens the self to mature, the reality principle demands that it be accompanied by disappointment because the m/other is ultimately unattainable. The point at which the subject is able to realize her desire and simultaneously recognize her disillusionment heralds the capacity for discernment of the Other that leads to the capacity for concern and mature love (Winnicott 1963).

It will be noticed that, following Winnicott, I suggest a linear development of both a surviving and non-surviving objects that grow in relation to the primary object's survival and non-survival throughout childhood. But I want to emphasize that in the sequence from object relating to object usage, a continuous dynamic process gradually builds up in the psyche and, at each stage of development, the surviving and non-surviving objects contain particular configurations of memories at each phase along a developmental line (A. Freud, 1974). These multilayered configurations and constellations are sets of dynamic object relationships related to a continuous relationship to time and space; repression and the unconscious.

Clinical examples throughout the literature illustrate how the analytic setting offers an opportunity for an undeveloped surviving object to grow through the specialized analytic relationship within the transference-countertransference. It is the analyst's psychic survival that potentially facilitates the subject's (stunted) surviving object to grow which in turn, strengthens and facilitates the development of the [sense of] self. The incremental build-up of an object that survives in the analytic encounter, in a way that the object did not survive hitherto, offers the patient a reinforcement for the undeveloped intrapsychic surviving object. In a good enough analysis, the surviving object can overcome and eclipse the non-surviving object. This does not infer that the analyst is internalized as a new object for the patient but rather, it is the new experience of object survival in the transference that reinforces the original experience of the primary object that had once survived. The surviving object gains power within the matrix of the après coup that potentially leads to the working through. Thus traumata can subsequently be relegated to the past and a different level of psychic work will subsequently lead to a deeper and more authentic mourning of the lost object.

Conclusions

> At the beginning . . . I found Freud and the method he gave us for investigating and for treatment . . . if there's anything I do that isn't Freudian, this is what I want to know. I don't mind if it isn't but I just feel that Freud gave us this method which we can use.
>
> (Winnicott 1989b: 574)

Winnicott's theoretical matrix constitutes a deficiency model in which psychosis is an 'environment-deficiency disease.' In his last year, as a consequence of the responses to his paper in New York, he wrote 'The use of an object in the context of Moses and Monotheism' in which he proposed an important theoretical extension, i.e. that the father is there from the beginning as a whole object in the mother's mind while she is in her state of primary maternal preoccupation. Thus the father – real and symbolic – is an integrative force in the baby's psyche (in health) at the very beginning of life.

By the end of his life Winnicott was unequivocal about his view of Freud's 'Todestrieb,' particularly as seen in Freud's later writings (Freud 1937), and he formulated an alternative that had derived from his clinical work. Therefore, instead of understanding psychosis as an indication of particular qualities and/or quantities of a 'death instinct,' Winnicott's 'use of an object' theory in my view suggests that pathological sadism, masochism, contempt, envy, jealousy and perversion arise as a result of reactions to cumulative non-survivals of the object. Winnicott's clinical thinking and focus is what ultimately confirms Green's view that 'he did not break off with Freud but rather completed his work' (Green [1996] 2000).

Following Winnicott's thesis in 'The use of an object,' i.e. that the m/other must survive the subject's ruthless destruction, I have suggested the notion of an intrapsychic surviving object and non-surviving object. I made the link between Winnicott's conceptualizations of primary creativity and the theoretical first feed to show how the analytic setting and the analyst's interpretations, in the context of the après coup within the transference-countertransference matrix, offer an opportunity for the patient to internalize subsequent theoretical feeds, *for the first time.* I suggest that the final theoretical feed constitutes the final tasks of the adolescent in order to reach a theoretical whole surviving object. I think that most patients, whatever age they are, usually have a stunted surviving object that requires the analyst's psychic survival, i.e. analytic technique for the analysand to achieve a whole surviving object.

Here I have suggested that Winnicott's late concept of survival of the object offers psychoanalysis an alternative to the notion of the death instinct. My attempt to extend this late concept led me to suggest that the non-survival of the object results in an intrapsychic non-surviving object. The capacity to use the object signifies growth of the intrapsychic surviving object that leads to an increasing capacity to discern the other as separate and 'not just a bundle of projections.'

Notes

1 An earlier version of this paper was originally presented at the EPF Congress in 2008.

2 It is beyond the scope of this essay to explore the differences between the Freudian and Kleinian death instinct (See Glossary; cf. Akhtar and O'Neil 2011).

3 There is a suggestion that the concept is equivalent to a religious notion instead of a scientific concept.

4 This question has recently been raised by Nellie Thompson (forthcoming) and discussions with Dr. Thompson as well as the relevance of her recent work on American psychoanalysts and émigré analysts have stimulated my suggestions here (Thompson 2008; 2010) (See Chapter 17).

5 See Donald Campbell's review of the 1986 publication 'The essentials of psychoanalysis' *Int J Psychoanal* 1987 68: 425–30.

6 In several publications it has been mistakenly reported that Winnicott had a heart attack after his presentation in New York but in fact he had caught an Asian influenza which led to a pulmonary edema. This is a condition that is sometimes related to chronic heart failure which Winnicott had suffered from for many years (Rodman 2003: 330).

7 Only one of the clinical examples is published (1989a). The more lengthy one can be found in the archives of the New York Psychoanalytic Society.

8 As previously stated, in his late work Winnicott often replaced the word 'aggression' with 'destruction' (Abram 2007a).

9 See Abram 2007a: 221.

10 Five main papers were commissioned for this historic conference. It is interesting to note that three out of the five papers argued against the theory of the 'death instinct.' Rosenfeld argued in favour of the death instinct

whilst at the same time stating that he did not find it a clinically useful concept (see *Int J of Psychoanal* 1971: 52).

11 Presumably this 'destructive' refers to the death instinct, rather than Winnicott's alternative use of 'destructive' as benign motility – otherwise the notes make no sense.

References

Abram, J. ([1996] 2003) Squiggles, clowns and Catherine wheels: reflexions sur le concept winnicottien de 'violation du self' *Le Coq Heron* 173.

Abram, J. (ed.) (2000) *André Green at the Squiggle Foundation* London: Karnac Books.

Abram, J. (2005) L'objet qui survit, D. Alcorn trans. *J Psychanal l'enfant* 36: 139–74. Paris: Bayard.

Abram, J. (2007a) *The Language of Winnicott: A dictionary of Winnicott's use of words* 2nd edition London: Karnac Books.

Abram, J. (2007b) L'objet qui ne survit pas. Quelques réflexions sur les racines de la terreur D. Houzel trans. *J Psychanal l'enfant* 39: 247–70.

Abram, J. (2008) Donald Woods Winnicott: a brief introduction *Int J Psychoanal* 89: 1189–1217.

Abram, J. (2010) On desire and female sexuality: some tentative reflections *Bulletin 64* European Psychoanalytical Federation.

Akhtar, S. and O'Neil, M.K. (2011) *On Freud's 'Beyond the pleasure principle'* Contemporary Freud Turning Points and Critical Issues London: Karnac Books.

Bettelheim, B. (1983) *Freud and Man's Soul* London: Chatto & Windus.

Bronstein, C. (2001) *Kleinian Theory: A contemporary perspective* London: Whurr Publishers.

Davis, M. and Wallbridge, D. (1981) *Boundary and Space: An introduction to the work of DW Winnicott* New York: Brunner/Mazel.

Freud, A. (1974) A psychoanalytical view of developmental psychopathology *Journal of the Philadelphia Association for Psychoanalysis* 1: 7–17.

Freud, S. (1921) Beyond the pleasure principle SE 18, 7–64.

Freud, S. (1937) Analysis terminable and interminable *Int J Psychoanal* 18: 373–405.

Fulgenzio, L. (2007) Winnicott's rejection of the basic concepts of Freud's metapsychology *Int J of Psychoanal* 88 Part 2: 443–61.

Goldman, D. (1993) *In Search of the Real: The origins and originality of D.W. Winnicott* Northvale, NJ: Aronson.

Green, A. (1996) On thirdness. In *André Green at the Squiggle Foundation* 2000 ed. J. Abram London: Karnac Books.

Kuhn, T. (1962) *The Structure of Scientific Revolutions* Chicago, IL: University of Chicago Press.

Laplanche, J. and Pontalis, J.-B. (1973) *The Language of Psycho-Analysis* D. Nicholson-Smith trans. New York: W.W. Norton.

Loparic, Z. (2002) Winnicott's paradigm outlined. *Rev Latinoam Psicopat Fund* 5(1): 61–98. Available from:http://www.centrowinnicott.com.br/

Milrod, B. (1968) Account of Donald Winnicott's visit to the New York PASociety unpublished manuscript Archives of the New York Psychoanalytical Society.

Ogden, T.H. (1985) The mother, the infant and the matrix: interpretations of aspects of the work of Donald Winnicott *Contemp Psychoanal* 21: 346–71.

Ogden, T.H. (1992) The dialectically constituted / decentred subject of psychoanalysis. II. The contributions of Klein and Winnicott *Int J Psychoanal* 73: 613–26.

Ogden, T.H. (2001) Reading Winnicott *Psychoanal Q* 70: 299–323.

Raphael-Leff, J. (2007) Freud's prehistoric matrix: owing 'Nature' a death *Int J Psychoanal* 88: 1345–73.

Reeves, C. (2012) On the margins: the role of the father in Winnicott's writings. In *Donald Winnicott Today* ed. J. Abram, Chapter 16 London: Routledge.

Rodman, F.R. (ed.) (1987) *The Spontaneous Gesture: Selected letters of DW Winnicott* Cambridge, MA: Harvard UP.

Rodman, F.R. (2003) *Winnicott: Life and work* Cambridge, MA: Perseus.

Roussillon, R. (2010) The deconstruction of primary narcissism *Int J of Psychoanal* 821–37.

Rycroft, C. (1972) *A Critical Dictionary of Psychoanalysis* London: Penguin Books.

Samuels, L. (1996) A historical analysis of Winnicott's 'The use of an object' *Winnicott Studies: The Journal of the Squiggle Foundation* 11 Spring: 41–50.

Thompson, N.L. (2008) A measure of agreement: an exploration of the relationship of D.W. Winnicott and Phyllis Greenacre *Psychoanal Q* 77: 251–81.

Thompson, N.L. (2010) The transformation of psychoanalysis in America: émigré analysts and the NYPSI, 1935–1961 unpublished 58th A.A. Brill Lecture New York

Thompson, N.L. (2012) Winnicott and American analysts In: *Donald Winnicott Today* Chapter 17 New Library of Psychoanalysis and The Institute of Psychoanalysis London: Routledge.

Winnicott, D.W. (1941) The observation of infants in a set situation *Int J Psychoanal* 22: 229–49.

Winnicott, D.W. (1942) Why children play In: Winnicott 1964.

Winnicott, D.W. (1949) Hate in the countertransference *Int J Psychoanal* 30: 69–74.

Winnicott, D.W. (1953) Transitional objects and transitional phenomena: a study of the first not-me possession *Int J Psychoanal* 34: 89–97.

Winnicott, D.W. (1955a) Metapsychological and clinical aspects of regression within the psychoanalytical set-up *Int J Psychoanal* 36: 16–26.

Winnicott, D.W. (1955b) The depressive position in normal emotional development *Br J Med Psychol* 28: 89–100.

Winnicott, D.W. (1957a) The mother's contribution to society In: 1986a.

Winnicott, D.W. (1957b) Aggression [1939] In: 1964, 167–75.

Winnicott, D.W. (1958a) Primary maternal preoccupation [1956] In: 1958a, 300–5.

Winnicott, D.W. (1958b) The capacity to be alone [1957] *Int J Psychoanal* 39: 416–20.

Winnicott, D.W. (1962) Ego integration in child development In: 1965, 56–63.

Winnicott, D.W. (1963) The development of the capacity for concern [1960] *Bull Menninger Clin* 27: 167–76.

Winnicott, D.W. (1964) *The Child, the Family and the Outside World* Harmondsworth: Penguin.

Winnicott, D.W. (1965a) *The Family and Individual Development* London: Tavistock.

Winnicott, D.W. (1965b) *The Maturational Processes and the Facilitating Environment: Studies in the theory of emotional development*. London: Hogarth (International Psycho-analytical Library No. 64).

Winnicott, D.W. (1965c) A personal view of the Kleinian contribution In: 1965b, 171–8.

Winnicott, D.W. (1965d) Ego distortion in terms of true and false self [1960] In: 1965b, 140–52.

Winnicott, D.W. (1967) The location of cultural experience *Int J Psychoanal* 48: 368–72.

Winnicott, D.W. (1968) Playing: its theoretical status in the clinical situation *Int J Psychoanal* 49: 591–7.

Winnicott, D.W. (1969) The use of an object and relating through identifications *Int J Psychoanal* 50: 711–16.

Winnicott, D.W. (1971a) *Playing and Reality* London: Tavistock.

Winnicott, D.W. (1971b) Creativity and its origins [1970] In: 1971a, 65–85.

Winnicott, D.W. (1971c) Le corps et le self, V.N. Smirnoff trans. [Body and self] *Nouv Rev Psychanal* 3: 15–51.

Winnicott, D.W. (1971d) The split-off male and female elements to be found in men and women [1966] In: 1971a, 72–85.

Winnicott, D.W. (1984) *Deprivation and Delinquency* ed. C. Winnicott, R. Shepherd R and M. Davis London: Tavistock.

Winnicott, D.W. (1986a) *Home Is Where We Start From: Essays by a psychoanalyst* ed. C. Winnicott, R. Shepherd R and M. Davis Reading, MA: Addison-Wesley.

Winnicott, D.W. (1986b) Living creatively [1970] In: 1986a, 39–54.

Winnicott, D.W. (1988) *Human Nature* ed. C. Bollas, M. Davis and R. Shepherd London: Free Association Books.

Winnicott, D.W. (1989a) *Psychoanalytic Explorations*, ed. C. Winnicott, R. Shepherd R and M. Davis Cambridge, MA: Harvard UP.

Winnicott, D.W. (1989b) Postscript: DWW on DWW [1967] In: 1989a.

15

Vital sparks and the form of things unknown

Dodi Goldman

Towards the end of his life, Winnicott kept a notebook for jotting down fragments of personal memory. The first page opens with a prayer: 'Oh God! May I be alive when I die.' The supplication is followed by a graphic description of what he looks like to himself after dying: how 'the hearse was cold and unfriendly,' and 'the lung heavy with water that the heart could not negotiate . . .' But at least his prayer had been answered: he was alive when he died.

It is easy to hear in Winnicott's supplication the desire to be an omnipotent self-preserver. Like the baby who needs the illusion of creating the breast, Winnicott wishes to be protected from awareness of limit. Despite death, he can continue going-on-being. It would be a mistake, however, to confine our understanding of Winnicott's prayer solely to the realm of omnipotence. From a different point of view, what is striking about the prayer is how Winnicott yearns for a psychic space in which he can simultaneously hold both life and death. His desire, in other words, is not simply to survive omnipotently but to find a way to bridge the ultimate dissociation *between* life and death. Winnicott is recognizing that aliveness and death have meaning only to the extent that a link can be retained between the two.

Yet what if we allow ourselves the latitude of hearing Winnicott as *asking a question* rather than uttering a prayer? May a part of me live, Winnicott may be asking, while another part dies? Is there, perhaps, an uncanny psychic capacity to die a partial death so as to salvage another part of the self?[1] Or, in another language: What need be done to preserve continuity of being in the face of traumatic disruption?

331

The opening passage of Winnicott's autobiographical fragments, in other words, offers a window into two central currents of his sensibility: the precariousness of aliveness and the bridging of dissociative gaps. The statement I wish to make in this paper is that Winnicott was deeply attuned to the *relationship* between these two currents: the extent to which 'aliveness' is accessible and sustainable, at any given moment, is related to *how one uses* dissociation.

A vital spark

Winnicott draws our attention to how psychological aliveness cannot be taken for granted. While naturally given, it is at the same time contingent. Indeed, his work is a virtual cartography of the precarious relationship between the environment and the psychosomatic equipment necessary to sustain aliveness.

For Winnicott, aliveness originates in an undifferentiated field which, *only from an external point of view,* appears as a newborn needing to be met by a responsive environment. Rather than a quality located *within* a distinct individual, aliveness has its roots in a *psychic field* as mother shields infant from premature awareness of 'complications' and 'coincidences' beyond its ken. Many of Winnicott's seminal formulations – spontaneous gesture, True Self, potential space, object use – are variations on the theme of how aliveness either grows and flourishes or is hidden or dampened as the developing child negotiates a personal way of finding a meaningful connection to the environment from which it is also differentiating itself. They are all ways of charting the gradual shift in the center of gravity of aliveness from an undifferentiated field to the child's growing capacity to become an integrated unit able to keep inner and outer separate but interrelated. Winnicott's preoccupation with the field of play between inner and outer suggests that even as the center of gravity shifts, aliveness itself is never fully localizable.

The notion of psychological aliveness enters psychoanalysis through the back door. It was only after Freud introduced his speculation about a death instinct that aliveness *as something distinct from either sexuality or self-preservation* became something that needed to be accounted for. While the feasibility of a presumed death instinct generated much heat in psychoanalytic debate, it was actually Freud's introduction of the concept of Eros that was truly innovative. 'The death instinct,' writes Loewald 'is really nothing new. . . . What is new, and this does not seem to fit with the inertia principle . . . is the concept of Eros, the life or love instinct.' It remained, Loewald argued, an 'insoluable problem' for Freud to integrate Eros into his theory of instinct (Loewald 1971: 62).

Indeed, one of the implications of Freud's way of thinking about the death instinct is that 'aliveness' is merely a disruption of the inorganic that the death instinct strives to reconstitute. Aliveness is nothing but a diversion on the way to death. In Freud's words:

> The attributes of life were at some time evoked in inanimate matter by the action of a force of whose nature we can form no conception . . . The tension that arose in the previously inanimate matter, strives towards its own dissolution, the first instinct had become a reality, the instinct to return to the inanimate.
>
> (Freud 1920: 38)

And while from a clinical point of view, the 'death instinct' could at least be recognized as a biologizing of the compulsion to repeat, when it came to Eros, Freud never quite figured out what to do with it (Lear 1996).

When looked at this way, Winnicott's oft repeated rejection of the notion of the death instinct is really less significant than his implicit endorsement of a force constituting life. What Freud summarily dismissed as 'the action of a force of whose nature we can form no conception' became, for Winnicott, an organic energy worthy of near reverence. 'In each baby,' he once remarked,

> . . . is *a vital spark*, and this urge towards life and growth and development is a part of the baby, something the child is born with and which is carried forward in a way that we do not have to understand.
>
> (Winnicott 1964: 27)

At the heart of Winnicott's work lies an abiding concern for the *urge toward life* and with the deadness that results from failures to create and discover a world that can tolerate one's own aliveness. 'Bringing in the death instinct,' he once wrote, 'muddles everything up . . . it is a concept which Freud introduced because he had no notion whatever about the primitive love impulse' (Rodman (ed.) 1987: 40).

One way of thinking about Winnicott's focus on aliveness is as an extension of Ernest Jones's idea of aphanisis, or fear of psychic annihilation. Jones suggests the possibility that there is a common denominator in the sexuality of boys and girls *more fundamental* than castration anxiety:

> . . . in both sexes castration is only a partial threat, however important a one, against sexual capacity and enjoyment as a whole. For the main blow of total extinction we might do well to use a separate term, such as the Greek word 'aphanisis.'
>
> (Jones 1927: 460)

With the concept of aphanisis, Jones opens the door for a shift of emphasis from a fear of loss of sexual capacity and pleasure to a dread that all desire or aliveness itself might be extinguished. Paula Heimann, recognizing the implication, concluded that the concept of aphanisis

> . . . seems to me to constitute a step forward in our understanding of the fear of castration; for it shows that the experience is not simply that of losing an organ which produces gratification, but that *a totality of experience* is in question, a threat of the loss of all capacities for ever experiencing any gratification of the libido and thus of all capacity for establishing a 'good' relation to an object . . .
>
> (Heimann 1942: 14)

Winnicott, too, believed that 'the value of [Jones's] term aphanisis has not yet been fully explored' (Winnicott 1958: 298). Linking his own ideas about the state of affairs before the ego is able to experience anxiety derived from either instinct tension or object loss to Jones' original contribution, Winnicott states:

> Anxiety at this early stage is not castration anxiety or separation anxiety; it relates to quite other things, and is, in fact, anxiety about annihilation (cf. the aphanisis of Jones).
>
> (Winnicott 1960: 587)

For Winnicott, it is the threat to one's aliveness, not one's sexuality, that is bedrock. Aliveness – which Winnicott also refers to as 'being' so as to distinguish it from physical self-preservation – is the animating idea behind many of his imaginative hypotheses. He transforms, for example, the concrete image of mother holding an infant in her arms into a profound metaphor for the ontological foundation of life, a virtual 'blue-print for existentialism' (Winnicott 1963: 86). The earliest quality of aliveness generated in the context of holding is aptly captured by the rhythmic verb 'going-on-being' – Winnicott's way of communicating what it means to be alive at a time before the infant becomes a subject capable of knowing anything about what time means (Ogden 2004). In earliest development, Winnicott suggests, if awareness of the structure of time prematurely pre-empts the infant's experience of his own rhythms, a warp occurs in the continuity-of-being. Mother's primary maternal preoccupation allows her to live briefly outside of time herself, surrendering to the infant's rhythms of sleep and wakefulness, vitality and lassitude, crankiness and agreeableness, hunger and satiation, alertness and distraction, engagement and aloneness. Her 'live, human holding,' (Winnicott 1955: 147) says Winnicott,

> . . . provides a setting for the infant's constitution to begin to make itself evident, for the developmental tendencies to start to unfold, and for the infant to experience spontaneous movement and become the owner of the sensations that are appropriate to this early phase of life.
>
> (Winnicott 1956: 303)

If mother does this well enough, and she usually does, then 'the infant's own *line of life* is disturbed very little by reactions to impingement.' Maternal failures of holding, in contrast, . . . 'produce phases of reaction to impingement and these reactions interrupt the "going on being" of the infant.' An excess of this reacting generates horrific agony, a 'very real primitive anxiety, long antedating any anxiety that includes the word death in its description.' (ibid.: 303).

If the pattern of relating between the child and environment is a good enough fit – which includes 'alive neglect' when that is what is called for – the child 'discovers the world by impulse, movement, gesture, salivation, sight, etc.' and external reality itself becomes '*part of the life of the individual.*' (Rodman (ed.) 1987: 42). If the fit, however, is not good enough – if the child collides with the world rather than finds himself in it – he will be forced to react by '. . . withdrawal from contact for the *re-establishment of the sense of being.*' (ibid.: 42).

To be clear: for Winnicott, the 'withdrawal from contact' might even include a preference to die. He believed that at the core of each individual is what he once referred to as a precious 'chosen area' where 'there is no room for compromise' (Winnicott 1986: 70). Physical death might be preferable to the profound deadness that arises from violation of the integrity of one's aliveness.

If temporary withdrawal is insufficient, and a need to react to impingements becomes *the pattern* of an infant's life, the result, says Winnicott , is 'a serious interference with the natural tendency that exists in the infant to become an integrated unit, able to continue to have a self with a past, present, and future' (Winnicott 1963: 86). Winnicott has in mind here far more than a simple conscious acknowledgement of the linear flow of time. 'Continuing to have a self,' or psychosomatic unity, Winnicott suggests, is related to one's capacity to simultaneously hold potentially incompatible aspects of memory, perception, and desire. Memory points to the past, perception to the present, desire to the future. Any or all of these can be compromised or forfeited in the processing of experience.

'It is an essential part of my theory,' Winnicott (1960a: 148) writes elsewhere, that the True Self that 'comes from the *aliveness of the body tissues* . . . including the heart's action and breathing' only '*begins to have a life* . . . as a result of the mother's repeated success in meeting the infant's spontaneous gesture.' (ibid.: 145). Development, for Winnicott, proceeds through the negotiation of increasingly more object- related ways of being alive. Clinically, what interests him is the distinction between moments of generative animation as opposed to empty lifeless accommodation: how a person creates a space between the 'thingness' of the world and his own subjectivity so that brute reality may be gradually brought to life with meaning.

Winnicott speaks little of agencies or structures of mind, focusing instead on *movements in relationship* that make aliveness sustainable. That is why he preferred the word 'transition' to the word 'intermediate' when introducing his third area of experiencing. 'The word intermediate is certainly useful,' he wrote once in a private letter,

> but the word transition implies movement and I must not lose sight of it otherwise we shall find some sort of static phenomenon being given an association with my name . . . Experience is a constant trafficking in illusion, a repeated reaching to the interplay between creativity and that which the world has to offer. Experience is an

achievement of ego maturity to which the environment supplies
an essential ingredient. It is not by any means always achieved.

(Rodman (ed.) 1987: 42–3)

For Winnicott, one root of the vital capacity to 'traffic in illusion'
can be found in how the infant invents its own transitional object.
One way of understanding the transitional object is that it contains in
condensed form the intensity and aliveness of the baby–mother dyad.
It is a way to maintain continuity of being through creative substitution of a special object for the mothering person. But to serve as a
substitute for mother's aliveness, the object must be imbued with its
own sense of aliveness by the infant. Put differently: the infant finds
his own way of *letting go* of the 'not-yet-fully-differentiated' mother
while *holding on* to the 'mother-who-is-part of me.' The transitional
object – baby's first not-me possession – is an object that is no longer
part of himself but nevertheless belongs to him. In health, baby's
own devices help mother remain good enough! Winnicott's theory
of development is not simply one of how mother's attunement enables baby to thrive. Rather, baby's healthy competence to make use
of his own inventiveness and imbue the transitional object with significance is part and parcel of what it means to be alive.

What makes aliveness particularly precarious, however, is that so
very much hinges upon the *quality of response to the inherent destructiveness* that is also part of being alive. Calling into question Freud's
and Klein's clinical anthropology whereby the vital helplessness of
childhood is thought to be universal, inevitable, non-contingent, and
derived from the power of instinctual life, Winnicott contrasts two
dramatically distinct worlds awaiting a newborn, emphasizing that 'it
makes all the difference which you and I were born into' (Winnicott
1970: 287). The first possible world is one in which 'a baby kicks
the mother's breast. She is pleased that her baby is *alive and kicking*
though perhaps it hurt and she does not let herself get hurt for fun'
(ibid.: 287). In the alternative world, however, '. . . a baby kicks the
mother's breast, but this mother has a fixed idea that a blow on the
breast produces cancer. She reacts because she does not approve of
the kick. This overrides whatever the kick may mean for the baby'
(ibid.: 287).

So much is contingent, in other words, upon mother's capacity
to accept that '. . . destructive aliveness of the individual is simply a
symptom of being alive' (Winnicott 1968: 239). The environment's

response to the destructiveness inherent in aliveness determines whether or not the individual can create/discover an external world in which he can be fully alive. It is mother's capacity to experience and contain the full alive stream of feelings within herself – love, hate, annoyance, tenderness, joy, jealousy, exhilaration, fatigue – that affords the infant adequate space for a form of undefensive omnipotence that underpins vitality. She must, in another language, survive her own emotional reactions – remaining herself without losing connection to what the infant needs her to be. Only then can the child be enriched rather than shocked by her difference. The healthy transformation of destructive aliveness – Winnicott's 'use of an object' – allows what is internal to be felt to have substance and what is external to be recognized as significant. Winnicott sees the mothering function, in other words, as what enables and supports the child's capacity to have a rich emotional life. Whereas Klein assumes that disturbance in the feeling life is the end result of active defense against the destructive force within, Winnicott entertains the possibility that the early individual-environmental set-up might fail to facilitate the growth of a capacity to generate, sustain, abide, or make use of one's emotions.

The form of things unknown

'If one wished to read the contemporary psychoanalytic literature as a serialized Gothic romance,' writes Philip Bromberg , 'it is not hard to envision the restless ghost of Pierre Janet, banished from the castle by Sigmund Freud a century ago, returning for an overdue haunting of Freud's current descendants' (Bromberg 1995: 511). What Janet's restless ghost clamors to have acknowledged, Bromberg argues, is the significance of dissociative processes – both normal and pathological – in the psyche.

Psychoanalysis, after all, was to some extent, and for good reason, *founded* on the presumed superior explanatory power of repression and the defeat of dissociation. Bromberg, however, is part of a growing chorus of American thinkers (Bromberg 1995, 1998, 2006; Davies 1996; Goldberg 1995; Howell 2005; Mitchell 1993; Pizer 1996; Slochower 1996, 2006; Stern 1997; Stoeri 2005) who hope to rescue dissociation from obscurity without sacrificing hard won insights into the *dynamic* nature of mental life. While differing as to whether or not they believe the unconscious structure of mind is *fundamentally dissociative*, they share the project of formulating *a distinctly psychoanalytic theory* of dissociation as a type of psychic organization. They are reinvigorating and meaningfully extending the earlier insights of Winnicott and others (Ferenczi 1980; Fairbairn 1952) as to the importance of dissociative phenomena.[2]

Understood in its simplest form, dissociation means that two or more mental processes or contents are not associated or integrated in awareness, memory, or identity. A sequestered feature of mental life – a form unknown to consciousness – operates almost autonomously as the mind adaptationally limits its own self-reflective capacity. While *both* a natural human capacity as well as a distinct response to trauma, *it makes a vast difference how and in what context dissociation is used.*

As a natural capacity, dissociation may be employed more or less voluntarily to allow playful or artistic absorption. Absorption is the ability to be so immersed in a central experience that context loses its frame. Subjectively, it is experienced in retrospect as a being 'carried away' or 'lost' in a narrowed, concentrated focus of attention that necessarily excludes other contents from the phenomenal field. It may take the form of playing, reverie, contemplation, meditative states, or automatic dual tasking. Such a healthy loosening of integrative bonds generates a tolerable experience of 'flow' or 'creative disorder.' *A relative freedom from needing to prematurely integrate allows a readiness to create experiences of greater aliveness.*

As a response to trauma, however, dissociative processes are liable to be activated unconsciously as a defense against unmanageable arousal with deadening effect. They may be triggered fleetingly or become hardened into a structured disposition. For some people, dissociation becomes a preferred means of sustaining self continuity through a dramatic severing of valuable psychic connections. It remains an open question whether at its first appearance dissociation is brought about by the overpowering *effect* of emotions occasioned by a traumatic event or as a *defense against* those emotions. There is also a range of views as to whether dissociation is best understood as the end result of an active severing of connections or as a primary failure to integrate. Whichever the case, unlike defenses against internal conflict, dissociation does not simply restrict access to potentially threatening feelings, thoughts, and memories. Instead, it is akin to a 'quasi-death,' an obliteration of the self to whom trauma might reoccur. As Masud Khan noted:

There is more to human experience and psychic functioning than conflict, defence, and repression. It is here that I believe the concept of dissociation can help us recognize certain types of clinical material and subjective experiences of the patient more fruitfully. What is repressed is always sensible to us through its absence and the countercathexis against it (i.e., defence mechanisms). In the case of dissociations no such evidence is available to us clinically. The person *is* all the elements of his dissociated states and lives them as such.

(Khan 1974: 245)

Winnicott's theory and clinical work demonstrate a keen awareness of how the use of dissociation – both natural and in response to trauma – impacts experiences of aliveness. Although he operated within an *espoused* theoretical context that made little explicit reference to dissociative processes, *in practice*, attention to them is a recurring feature of his sensibility. A distinction drawn by Argyris and Schon (1980) between an 'espoused theory' of action and a 'theory-in-use' is valuable in this respect. Winnicott's contribution is replete with formulations suggesting both an explicit awareness and a silent background 'theory-in-use' of dissociative processes.

Quite early on, Winnicott introduced the notion that unlinked dissociated states are not a complex defense but, instead, at the root of all self experience. 'Dissociation,' he writes, 'can usefully be studied in its initial or natural forms' (Winnicott 1945: 151). For example,

. . . there are the quiet and the excited states. I think an infant cannot be said to be aware at the start that while feeling this and that in his cot or enjoying the skin stimulations of bathing, he is the same as himself screaming for immediate satisfaction, possessed by an urge to get at and destroy something unless satisfied by milk.

(Ibid.:151)

Rather than focusing on the active separation of conflictual repressed mental contents, Winnicott's description of a normal dissociative process places in the foreground how the infant cannot yet be aware of how *'he is the same'* across disparate states of mind. The excited self is not yet linked to the quiet self. Similarly, in describing a child dreaming, Winnicott contends that:

. . . there is not necessarily an integration between a child asleep and a child awake. This integration comes in the course of time. Once dreams are remembered and even conveyed somehow to a third person, the dissociation is broken down a little . . . It is a valuable experience whenever a dream is both dreamed and remembered, precisely because of the breakdown of dissociation that this represents. However complex such a dissociation may be in child or adult, the fact remains that it can start in the natural alternation of the sleeping and awake states, dating from birth.

(Winnicott 1945: 151)

Notice that according to Winnicott what holds the potential for bridging the dissociative gap – in both the child and adult – is the telling of the dream to a *third* person. There are, in other words, three 'people' involved: the sleeping dreamer, the waking one who remembers, and the person to whom the dream is told. It is the affectively safe relationship with an engaged other that facilitates the linking of naturally unlinked dissociated selves and with it – as dream and awake states enrich each other – the possibility of being more fully alive.

Earlier in the same article, Winnicott makes the point that

. . . there are long stretches of time in a normal infant's life in which a baby does not mind whether he is many bits or one whole being, or whether he lives in his mother's face or in his own body, provided that from time to time he comes together and feels something.

(Ibid.: 150)

At the root of earliest self-experience, Winnicott suggests, is an unintegrated state that periodically gels into dissociated self-states or partial integrations. The infant is free to drift about as there is not yet any built-up version of a self or hardened way of representing 'me' and 'not-me.' What makes the pulses of drifting and gelling life enhancing as opposed to terrorizing is, again, the tether of maternal holding. *It is the early maternal holding function and good-enough maternal object experience that allow dissociated states to be entered and tolerated because they enhance aliveness without threatening the child's connection to mother.* In the absence of maternal holding, however, the child's affect states themselves become so discontinuous that the experience of going-on-being is seriously disrupted. (Slochower 1996) An alive drifting and gelling is replaced by arousal, alarm and abyss. *The breakdown of holding and early object relating means that the child cannot move seamlessly between dissociated states without a disruptive loss in the continuity of being.*

Winnicott calls our attention to how – given adequate maternal care – raw formless sensory arousal periodically congeals into potentially meaningful psychic formations – 'coming together to feel something.' A force is at work – a type of imagination he later will call 'primary creativity' – that spontaneously generates form out of formlessness. Winnicott echoes Shakespeare's idea that as imagination ushers forth 'the form of things unknown', a creative force 'turns them to shapes and gives airy nothing a local habitation and a name' (Shakespeare 1969: 125).

For Winnicott, the self is recurrently formed and found in a creative process. But for this to occur, a particular kind of environment is necessary. Searching for the self, writes Winnicott:

> . . . can come only from *desultory formless functioning* . . . It is only here, in this unintegrated state of the personality, that that which we describe as creative can appear. This if reflected back, *but only if reflected back*, becomes part of the organized individual personality, and eventually this in summation makes the individual to be, to be found; and eventually enables himself or herself to postulate the existence of the self.
>
> (Winnicott 1971: 64)

What eventually may become the inclusive symbolization of one's own being has its start in desultory formless functioning. The shape the self assumes – 'a local habitation and a name' – follows from the meeting up of the freedom of the mind's own processes with an environment safe enough to allow the individual to be surprised without being shocked by what comes unbidden from within.

Winnicott's evocation of subjectivity has something in common with the version of dissociation put forth by contemporary analysts such as Donnel Stern. Stern (1997) coined the term 'unformulated experience' to describe a form of mentation characterized by lack of clarity and differentiation that may or may not be brought into articulate form. Although all articulate experience begins as unformulated experience, much of what is unformulated is never fully sculpted into a distinct object of reflective consciousness. Echoing Winnicott's (1971) emphasis on 'apperception' and the blurring of edges in transitional space, Stern likens the phenomenon of 'unformulated experience' to what people often feel at twilight, when the light is dim and familiar shapes hard to recognize. 'Just as well-formed percepts do not exist "in" or "behind" the indistinct, unrecognizable experiences of twilight shapes,' writes Stern, 'well-formed cognitions do not exist in or behind the unformulated states that precede them. Rather, the well-formed version remains to be shaped' (Stern 1997: 37). Or, as Winnicott once put it: 'I take care not to see what is not there to be seen' (Winnicott 1971: 114).

For Stern, most experience remains unformulated, either '. . . because circumstances do not make the formulation relevant or because the unformulated experience has not yet "percolated" enough to have become something more than it is' (Stern 1997: 86). Still, according to Stern, there is also a form of *active defense* that is sometimes employed to prevent well or more fully formed versions of experience from being shaped. That defense is dissociation, which differs from other forms of defense that assume an active pushing of unwanted content out of consciousness. Stern compares the formulation of experience to hauling up a rock from the bottom of the ocean. For a consciousness constituted by active interpretation rather than passive registration, the basic defensive process is the *prevention of interpretation* in reflective awareness and not the *exclusion from awareness* of elements already fully formed (Stern 1997: 87). Dissociation is the term Stern gives to the active avoidance of certain formulations of experience. 'To dissociate,' he writes, 'is simply to restrict the interpretations one makes of experience. Or perhaps better stated, because the interpretation is hard to separate from the experience itself, dissociation is a restriction on the experiences we allow ourselves to have' (ibid.: 88).

Dissociation, in other words, needs to be understood not only as the mere defensive avoidance of cognitive clarity but, rather, as an unconscious refusal to allow the possibility that full-bodied meaning be created. It is a strategy designed to ensure that nothing new, unpredictable, and alive ever happens. In another language, it is essentially a failure to allow the free play of one's imagination. 'Dissociated meaning,' writes Stern, 'is style without substance, the story that accounts for what it addresses but tells us nothing we don't already know, the conversation we can fill in without having to listen. Dissociation is the deletion of imagination' (ibid.: 98).

For Winnicott, too, pathology is, to a large extent, a failure of imagination. The psyche itself, is understood by Winnicott as the

'. . . *imaginative elaboration* of somatic parts, feelings, and functions, that is, of physical aliveness' (Winnicott 1949: 244). As mother reliably shields her baby from undue 'complications beyond those which the infant can understand and allow for,' (ibid.: 245) – which may be just another language for trauma – the outcome is a smooth '*interrelating* of the psyche with the soma' (ibid.: 244). In contrast, certain failures of the environment produce an 'over-activity of the mental function-ing' (ibid., 246). In such a case, there can develop what Winnicott calls '. . . an opposition between the mind and the psyche-soma' such that the '. . . thinking of the individual *begins to take over* and organize the caring for the psyche-soma' (ibid.: 246).[3]

To be clear: the 'opposition' between the mind and psyche-soma is not to be mistaken for 'splitting' or internal conflict. Rather, it is a dissociative split whereby the 'mind' ends up functioning some-what autonomously from the center of self to protect the illusion of unitary selfhood from potential traumatization. Winnicott's focus is not on repressed symbolized content but on a dissociative disconnect between a person's imaginative and adaptive capacities.

In a similar vein, Winnicott's description of 'ego distortion' in terms of 'True' and 'False' Self is a way of theorizing about the dis-sociative process in which the 'center of gravity of being' transfers from 'the kernel' to the 'shell' (Winnicott 1952: 99). He is quite clear that the origins of false self functioning are to be found in the 'infant-to-mother living' and *not* in the 'early mechanisms of ego defence organized against id-impulse' (Winnicott 1960a: 144). Indeed, for Winnicott, instinct life itself might be experienced more dissocia-tively than through the derivatives of repression. As he puts it: 'The instincts can be as much external as can a clap of thunder or a hit' (ibid.: 141). The question that concerns him is how the True Self, or 'sensori-motor aliveness' is at risk for becoming dissociatively split off for adaptational purposes. A close reading of the text suggests three potentially distinguishable 'False Selves': a 'shielding false self' whose function is to act as a stimulus barrier, a 'defence against that which is unthinkable, the exploitation of the True Self, which would result in its annihilation' (ibid.: 147); a 'split-off compliant false self' charged with gaining the awards of compliance at the expense of personal expression or growth (ibid.: 150); and a 'compensatory false self' that takes the form of a 'caretaker self' compensating for deficiencies in environmental care (ibid.: 142). Whether one prefers to conceptu-alize these varied constellations as structural entities or as transient processes, what they hold in common is their deadening effect upon the individual. Their hallmark is a depleted presence, a thinness or shallowness of being, best captured by the idea of dissociation.

But it is not only toward the experiential outcomes of dissociation that Winnicott displays an acute sensitivity. He also monitors the effects of failed efforts to master dissociative experiences. Repeatedly, he notes how some patients' lives can become little more than a medium through which dissociated past trauma may be actively sought out in the here-and-now with the unconscious hope of bringing about some form of integration. Meaningful existence is foreclosed by the repetitive present search for an experience that could not be processed in the past. Why does the patient go on compulsively worried by something that belongs to the past? 'The answer must be,' writes Winnicott:

> . . . that the original experience of primitive agony cannot get into the past tense unless the ego can first gather it into its own present time experience . . . In other words the patient must go on looking for the past detail which is *not yet experienced*. This search takes the form of a looking for this detail in the future . . . On the other hand, if the patient is ready for some kind of acceptance of this queer kind of truth, that what is not yet experienced did nevertheless happen in the past, then the way is open for the agony to be experienced in the transference . . .
>
> (Winnicott 1963a: 91)

What Winnicott refers to as 'a queer kind of truth' is the mind's capacity to sequester an event that *occurred* but was never *experienced*. The event cannot be remembered as something real to the traumatized person because '*the patient was not there* for it to happen to.' (ibid.: 92). At the same time, however, the patient unconsciously searches for opportunities to engineer the re-emergence in the transference of the original trauma situation (Stoeri 2005). For the 'agony to be experienced in the transference' the patient will have to be 'ready for some kind of acceptance of this queer truth.' In the language of dissociation, Winnicott implies that if a good enough holding environment has been created the patient will both actively seek out aspects of the analyst that permit experiencing the trauma while temporarily dissociating other aspects of the relationship involving goodness and trust.

The original unexperienced trauma and the search for an opportunity to relive it are, Winnicott writes, '. . . a fact that is carried round hidden away in the unconscious.' But, the 'unconscious' that Winnicott has in mind is not 'the unconscious of psycho-neurosis, nor is it the unconscious of Freud's formulation of the part of the psyche that is very close to neuro-physiological functioning . . . nor the unconscious of Jung . . .' Instead, in this '. . . special context the unconscious means that the ego integration is not able to encompass something' (Winnicott 1963a: 91–2). Winnicott leads us to a 'queer kind of truth' recognizable in 'a special context' namely: dissociation.

Let there be meaning

The distinction Winnicott draws between *something merely happening* and *living an experience* permeates his therapeutic work. An event can become an experience only if it alters the structure of feeling. Otherwise, it remains a dissociated circumstance. The writer Denis Donoghue (1981) captures this well when he notes that events become experience, '. . . only with time, distance, memory, and imagination. At that point they are incorporated for the first time in the person who, surviving them, has been changed by the reception of their force. Not by the force itself, but by its reception' (Donoghue 1981: 18).

The relational context, according to Winnicott, has significant bearing on how the force of an event is received. The reliability of the relationship allows the patient to diminish use of certain kinds of dissociative processes and surrender to the uncertainty and contingencies of life.

What Winnicott first described in terms of mother-infant feeding would eventually become a metaphor for the therapeutic encounter. 'The baby has instinctual urges and predatory ideas,' and 'the mother has a breast and the power to produce milk,' he once wrote. But, 'these two phenomena do not come into relation with each other till the mother and child *live an experience together* . . . I think of the process as if two lines came from opposite directions, *liable* to come near each other' (Winnicott 1945: 152). What concerns Winnicott is not that the feed happens but how the contact between two people *may or may not* be infused with life.

From a therapeutic point of view, what are most fundamental for Winnicott are not the patterns of regulating desire but the experiences of aliveness and the consequences of disruptions to the continuity of being. The patient needs to be afforded the opportunity to follow his own rhythm of drifting, gelling, dissociating and integrating. He passionately pleads with analysts not to inadvertently foreclose spontaneous communication among dissociated states through excessive interpretive activity. 'The person we are trying to help,' says Winnicott (1971), 'needs a new experience in a specialized setting. The experience is one of a non-purposive state, as one might say a sort of ticking over of the unintegrated personality. I refer to this as formlessness . . .' (Winnicott 1971: 55).

The value of such a non-purposive state is that it allows the patient to achieve '. . . the resting place out of which creative reaching-out can take place' (ibid.: 55). In this highly specialized setting, the individual '. . . can *come together* and exist as a unit, not as a defence against anxiety but as an expression of I AM, I am alive, I am myself. From this position everything is creative' (ibid.: 56). Premature articulation of coherence can be a deadening form of dissociation. 'Integration' should not be equated with health. Free association that reveals a coherent theme, argues Winnicott, '. . . is already affected by anxiety, and the cohesion of ideas is a defence organization.' What the patient needs, he concludes, is for the analyst to accept 'nonsense' without being forced to *prematurely* integrate. 'Nonsense,' for Winnicott, is not to be interpreted as resistance, but appreciated as the formlessness out of which aliveness might emerge. 'The therapist who cannot take this communication,' he writes,

> . . . becomes engaged in a futile attempt to find some organization in the nonsense, as a result of which the patient leaves the nonsense area because of hopelessness about communicating nonsense. An opportunity for rest has been missed because of the therapist's need to find sense where nonsense is.
>
> (Winnicott 1971: 56)

By introducing the idea of a 'resting place out of which creative reaching-out can take place,' Winnicott points to the potentially healthy use of normal dissociative processes. One reason Winnicott tended to valorize both artistic endeavors and playing is because he appreciated how they provide opportunities for a creative 'voluntary' use of dissociation. As Stoeri (2005) notes, we are all the beneficiaries of the artist's risk taking. 'The artist,' he writes:

. . . must risk entering and sustaining dissociated states; the artist's dread is the dread of failing *or* succeeding in the endeavor. Failure means being 'haunted' forever by voices or presences needing to be pressed into existence. Succeeding means risking not finding a way back to the rest of who one is, and being stuck interminably in a changed state.

(Stoeri 2005: 185)

Similarly, the capacity for playing, which for Winnicott is a virtual hallmark of health, rests upon the innate capacity to become dissociatively absorbed. While playing, one *need not be fully integrated* and there is room to be safely surprised by the unexpected so long as there is no premature disruption of the double bookkeeping by which playing is contained within its own illusory space.

The ease with which the quality of illusion can be disrupted is captured by the Dutch historian Huizinga's (1955) description of a father finding his four year old son sitting in front of a row of chairs playing 'trains.' When the father kissed his son the boy said: 'Don't kiss the engine daddy, or the carriages won't think its real!' The child imagining himself to be an engine can be safely absorbed in play so long as he is not *forced to choose* whether he is or is not an engine. The form of illusion filling potential space allows something to be itself and something else at the same time. Paradoxically, one finds oneself by not needing to be some hardened built-up version of the self. One is lost, however, when creative use of dissociation is replaced by a built-up dissociative structure (Bromberg 1998).

Deeply influenced by Milner's (1952) work on illusion, Winnicott came to envision therapy more as a protosymbolic performative activity that *generates meaning* than as one focused on information exchange and insight that *uncovers hidden meaning*. Two clinical examples illustrate Winnicott's particular sensitivity to the evidence of dissociation that often appears in the encounter as dead spots, gaps, stereotypes, absences, repetitions, or what is enacted but unsayable in words. With luck and patience, Winnicott hopes that the delicate play between therapist and patient will allow access to imagination to bridge unhealthy dissociative gaps.

In the paper, 'Dreaming, Fantasying, and Living' Winnicott describes a middle-aged woman who, in her analysis gradually discovers '. . . the extent to which fantasying or something of the nature of daydreaming has disturbed her whole life' (Winnicott 1971:

348

26–37). He makes the claim that dreaming and real living are 'of the same order' while fantasying is of 'another order.' Dreams '. . . fit into object-relating in the real world and living in the real world fits into the dream world.' By contrast, '. . . fantasying remains an isolated phenomenon, absorbing energy but not contributing-in either to dreaming or to living.' That is why dreams and living can contribute to growth while fantasying can '. . . remain static over the whole of [a patient's] life.' These two orders of mental life are further distinguished by the fact that whereas '. . . a great deal of dream and of feelings belonging to life are liable to be under repression,' the inaccessibility of fantasying is '. . . associated with dissociation rather than with repression.'

As the youngest of several siblings, this patient would fit in to other children's games but never really enjoyed or was enriched by them. The games were unsatisfactory because '. . . she was simply struggling to play whatever role was assigned to her and the others felt that something was lacking in the sense that she was not actively contributing-in.' What the older children probably were unaware of, however, was that their sister was essentially absent. 'From the point of view of my patient,' he writes,

> . . .while she was playing the other people's games she was all the time engaged in fantasying. She really lived in this fantasying on the basis of a dissociated mental activity . . . and over long periods her defence was to live here in this fantasying activity and to watch herself playing the other children's games as if watching someone else in the nursery group.

As this patient grew older, she managed to construct a life in which '. . . nothing that was really happening was fully significant to her.' Her life, Winnicott concludes, '. . . was dissociated from the main part of her, which was living in what became an organized sequence of fantasying.' Her activities '. . . brought no joy. All they did was to fill the gap, and this gap was an essential state of doing nothing while she was doing everything.'

Through collaborative work on a series of dreams, the patient is able to recognize that in her choice of wardrobe, she is dressing for a child as well as for her middle-aged self. She also begins to experience '. . . a wave of hate of her mother which had a new quality to it. It was much nearer to murder than to hate and also it felt to her that the hate was

349

much nearer than it had previously been to a specific thing.' Together they are able to understand how '. . . material that had formerly been locked in the fixity of fantasying was now becoming released for both dreaming and living . . .' Yet even as they explore how the dissociative activity of fantasying is damaging and makes her feel ill, the very notion under discussion becomes enacted between them. As Winnicott speaks, the patient notices that she is distracting herself by fiddling with the zip of her bag: '. . . why was it this end? How awkward it was to do up!' The patient could feel, Winnicott reports:

> . . . that this dissociated activity was more important to her sitting there than listening to what I was saying. We both tried to make an attack on the subject in hand and to relate fantasying to dreaming. Suddenly she had a little insight and said that the meaning of this fantasying was: 'So that's what *you* think.' She had taken my interpretation of the dream and she had tried to make it foolish . . . At this moment she reported that she had already 'gone off to her job and to things that happened at work' and so here again while talking to me she had left me, and she felt dissociated as if she could not be in her skin. She remembered how she read the words of a poem but the words meant nothing.
>
> (Winnicott 1971: 32)

The clinical material captures the distinction between the unlived life of fantasying and the lived life of dreaming. She had allowed a part of herself to die so that what remained could survive. *As long as dissociation is used to safeguard survival, there is a collapse of the potential space necessary for aliveness.* As the dissociative gaps are actually experienced in the new context of Winnicott's holding, the woman gradually becomes aware of how vitally she has relied upon them. A space opens and the patient is able to reflect upon how in early life she enjoyed the cocoon existence of psychic web-spinning but that eventually she became entombed in it. *The relational bridging of the dissociative gap loosens the rigidity of the dissociated structure and allows greater access to self-reflexivity.* In the session, she is able to be aware of 'making Winnicott's interpretation foolish' while simultaneously retaining her connection to him. *A new experience of bearing the conflict in mind replaces the old strategy of absenting herself through dissociation.* At the same time, Winnicott concludes, the fantasying '[changes] into imagination related to dream and reality.'

As Philip Bromberg (2006) puts it:

> A patient's transition from a dissociative mental structure to increased affective tolerance for intrapsychic conflict is a complex process in which realities that have been kept apart by discontinuous states of consciousness are gradually able to be held within a single transitional state of mind.
>
> (Bromberg 2006: 196)

Put differently: the new use of imagination allows what is inside to be felt as having substance and what is outside as having significance.

A second example of Winnicott's work in the dissociative domain involves the treatment of a middle-aged married man who felt, despite years of beneficial analysis, that '. . . what he came for, he has not reached.' He went through life convinced that his analysis was doomed to interminability. On one particular occasion Winnicott found himself saying:

> I am listening to a girl. I know perfectly well that you are a man but I am listening to a girl, and I am talking to a girl. I am telling this girl: 'You are talking about penis envy.'
>
> (Winnicott 1971: 73)

The remark had '. . . an immediate effect in the form of intellectual acceptance, and relief, and then there were more remote effects. After a pause the patient remarked: 'If I were to tell someone about this girl I would be called mad.' *Winnicott was quite surprised to hear what he then said in response*:

> It was not that *you* told this to anyone; it is *I* who see the girl and hear a girl talking, when actually there is a man on my couch. The mad person is *myself*.
>
> (Ibid.: 73–4)

The patient experienced enormous relief because he finally felt sane in a mad environment. He was released from a dilemma that had plagued him most of his life. As he subsequently said to Winnicott: 'I myself could never say (knowing myself to be a man) "I am a girl." I am not mad that way. But you said it, and you have spoken to both parts of me.' Winnicott writes:

351

This madness which was mine enabled him to see himself as a girl from my position. He knows himself to be a man, and never doubts that he is a man. Is it obvious what was happening here? For my part, *I have needed to live through a deep personal experience* in order to arrive at the understanding I feel I now have reached.

(Ibid: 74)

The understanding that Winnicott reached with this man was that '. . . his mother . . . saw a girl baby when she saw him as a baby before she came round to thinking of him as a boy.' This man, in other words, '. . . had to fit into her idea that her baby would be and was a girl.' It was the mother's 'madness' that was 'brought right into the present by my having said "It is I who am mad."'

While this constructed meaning appeared to resonate deeply with the patient, he arrives at the following session and reports that although he had '. . . had a satisfactory sexual intercourse with his wife,' now he is ill. What is more, he invites Winnicott to '. . . *interpret* this illness . . . as if it were psychosomatic.' Winnicott says to the patient:

You feel as if you ought to be pleased that here was an interpretation of mine that had released masculine behavior. *The girl that I was talking to, however, does not want the man released*, and indeed she is not interested in him. What she wants is full acknowledgement of herself and of her own rights over your body.

(Ibid: 75)

What is striking about this vignette is how *the analytic exchange allows a channel of communication to eventually open between the previously dissociated male and female elements*. Winnicott is quite clear in his account that the experience has nothing to do with either homosexuality or the predisposition towards bisexuality. Instead, it is recognized as a 'complete dissociation' between the 'split-off male and female elements.' An implication of Winnicott's formulation is that the childhood experience of being a boy seen as a girl was an awful one that needed to be avoided. *What is avoided is not simply the memory of the trauma, but the entire experience of being that person who went through it.* The 'complete dissociation' is the means adopted by the patient to guarantee that he will never again be the person who suffered what he suffered. At the same time, however, the sequestered experience of being a little girl from the mother's point of view and the little girl's demand for control over the man's body are dissociated elements hollering to be heard. And no less important: *both Winnicott and the patient come alive through the shifts in mutual dissociative processes.* The unexpected and surprising appearance of the unbidden in the encounter – both Winnicott's and the patient's – indicates relational bridging of mutually dissociated aspects of their experience.

Winnicott's account suggests a striking and courageous clinical innovation: by acknowledging that he was startled to discover that *he had become the mad person seeing the girl* he is locating the dissociation intersubjectively. He is neither just an interpreter of a patient's unconscious nor an absorber of the patient's projections. Instead, he becomes a subject who deeply identifies with the patient's projection and owns it as his own. By *living through together* an experience, previously dissociated elements are symbolized in thought and language. What had been unsayable in words is now contained within the self without loss of continuity of being.

Witnessing the parts that go to make the whole

In Chapter 14 Abram reports on her work in the Winnicott Archives in London, where she recently found a set of notes for Winnicott's last paper:

> In the early days of 1971 Winnicott booked a room at the Hotel Sacher, Vienna, from July 23rd until July 31st. He was planning to attend the IPA Congress to be held that year in Vienna, to speak on a panel entitled 'The Role of Aggression in Child Analysis.' But, it was a Congress that he was destined not to attend – he died on January 25th.
>
> In the Winnicott archives, in a file written in Clare Winnicott's hand – 'DWW's Notes for the Vienna Congress never given' – there are a set of unpublished notes that were written by Winnicott in preparation for that panel. The notes comprise of hand written sheets in Winnicott's hand with instructions (in the top left hand corner) for his secretary. The typed pages correlate exactly with his instructions and offer a clear sequence of statements that were presumably to serve as his plan for the paper.
>
> (Chapter 14: 312)

The significance of these notes is that they literally constitute Winnicott's final word on therapeutic matters close to his heart, placing his ideas about dissociation front and center. The notes open with the words: 'I am asking for a kind of revolution in our work. Let us re-examine what we do' (Quoted in Abram Chapter 14: 312). Winnicott's choice of the word 'revolution' is quite uncharacteristic. While he had spent his life creatively innovating and extending existing theory, he tended to emphasize how originality is only possible on the basis of tradition. 'Any theories that I may have which are original,' he once wrote to Harry Guntrip, '. . . are only valuable as a growth of ordinary Freudian psycho-analytic theory' (Rodman [ed.] 1987: 75). But at the same time, Winnicott believed that '. . . mature adults bring vitality to that which is ancient, old and orthodox by re-creating it after destroying it' (Winnicott 1960b: 94).

At the very end of his life, Winnicott is poised once again to *destroy, re-create and thereby bring to life* the psychoanalytic world in which he flourished. The Notes for the Vienna Congress continue:

> It may be that in dealing with the repressed unconscious we are colluding with the patient and the established defences. What is needed of us, because the patient cannot do the work by self-analysis; someone must see and witness the parts that go to make the whole, a whole that does not exist except as viewed from outside. In time we may have to come to the conclusion that the common failure of many excellent analyses has to do with the patient's dissociation hidden in material that is clearly related to repression taking place as a defence in a seemingly whole person.
>
> (Winnicott quoted in Chapter 14: 312–313)

By giving prominence to dissociation, Winnicott was well aware of entering troubled waters. He was, in a sense, returning psychoanalysis to the very crossroad that led Freud away from Janet. But, as he noted in a different context:

> No advance in psycho-analytic theory is made without nightmares. The question is: who is to have the nightmare? . . . In our Society here, although we serve science, we need to make an effort every time we attempt to re-open matters which seem to have been settled. It is not only the inertia which belongs to the fear of doubt; it is also that we have loyalties.
>
> (Winnicott 1968: 58)

The theoretical loyalty that Winnicott was challenging had enormous clinical implications. A singular focus on the repressed unconscious, he suggests, is at the root of 'common failures' of analysis. What is required in its place, he says, is to '. . . *witness the parts that go to make the whole, a whole that does not exist except as viewed from outside.*' As engaged witness to dissociated experience rather than as knowing interpreter of the patient's unconscious, the analyst may help open a space for the form of things unknown to meet a vital spark of life.

Notes

1 A wonderful rendering of this process is provided by the Nobel prize winning Polish poet Wislawa Szymborska in her poem 'Autotomy'. Szymborska describes how the holothurian, a sea slug, when attacked, divides itself into unlinked parts. In the middle of the holothurian's body, writes, Szymborska, 'a chasm opens and its edges immediately become alien to each other'. The holothurian manages 'to die as much as necessary' so as 'to grow again from a salvaged remnant' (Szymborska 1983: 115–16).
2 The poet Yeats in his 'Prayer for Old Age' similarly distinguishes between two forms of thinking. He asks God to protect him from those '*thoughts that men think in the mind alone*' and those thoughts *in a marrow-bone* (Yeats 1983: 282).
3 It is beyond the scope of this paper to discuss the ways in which the emerging Interpersonal/Relational tradition diverges from Winnicott's formulations.

References

Abram, J. ([2008] 2012) D.W.W.'s Notes for the Vienna Congress 1971: A Consideration of Winnicott's Theory of Aggression and an Interpretation of Its Clinical Implications In: *Donald Winnicott Today* (2012) New Library of Psychoanalysis. London: Routledge.

Argyris, C. and Schon, D. (1980) *Theory in Practice: Increasing Professional Effectiveness*. San Francisco: Jossey-Bass Publishers.

Bromberg, P. (1995) Psychoanalysis, Dissociation, and Personality Organization: reflections on Peter Goldberg's essay. *Psychoanalytic Dialogues*, 5: 511–28.

Bromberg, P. (1998) *Standing in the Spaces: Essays on Clinical Process, Trauma and Dissociation*. Hillsdale, NJ: The Analytic Press.

Bromberg, P. (2006) *Awakening the Dreamer: Clinical Journeys*. Hillsdale, NJ: The Analytic Press.

Davies, J. (1996) Linking the 'Pre-Analytic' with the Postclassical: Integration, Dissociation, and the Multiplicity of Unconscious Process. *Contemp. Psychoanal.*, 32: 553–76.

Donoghue, D. (1981) *Ferocious Alphabets*. Boston and Toronto: Little, Brown and Company.

Fairbairn, W.R.D. (1952) *Psychoanalytic Studies of the Personality*. Boston: Routledge & Kegan Paul.

Ferenczi, S. (1980) *Final Contributions to the Problems and Methods of Psycho-Analysis* ed. M. Balint (trans. E. Mosbacher). London: Karnac Books.

Freud, S. (1920) *Beyond the Pleasure Principle*. SE, 18: 1–64.

Goldberg, P. (1995) 'Successful' Dissociation, Pseudovitality, and Inauthentic Use of the Senses. *Psychoanalytic Dialogues*, 5: 493–510.

Heimann, P. (1942) A Contribution to the Problem of Sublimation and Its Relation to Processes of Internalization. *Int. J. Psychoanal.*, 23: 8–17.

Howell, Elizabeth F. (2005) *The Dissociative Mind*. Hillsdale, NJ: The Analytic Press.

Huizinga, J. (1955) *Homo Ludens*. Boston: Beacon Press.

Jones, E. (1927) The Early Development of Female Sexuality. *Int. J. Psychoanal.*, 8: 459–72.

Khan, M. (1974) *The Privacy of the Self*. New York: International University Press.

Lear, J. (1996) The Introduction of Eros: Reflections on the Work of Hans Loewald. *JAPA*, 44: 673–98.

Loewald, H. (1971) The Id and the Regulatory Principles of Mental Functioning: Discussion. In: *Papers on Psychoanalysis*. New Haven: Yale University Press, 1980, pp. 58–68.

Milner, M. (1952) Aspects of Symbolism in Comprehension of the Not-Self. *Int. J. Psychoanal.*, 33: 181–94.

Mitchell, S.A. (1993) *Hope and Dread in Psychoanalysis*. New York: Basic Books.

Ogden, T. (2004) On Holding and Containing, Being and Dreaming. *Int. J. Psychoanal.*, 85: 1349–64.

Pizer, S. (1996) Negotiating Potential Space: Illusion, Play, Metaphor and the Subjunctive. *Psychoanal. Dial.*, 6: 689–712.

Rodman, F.R. (1987) *The Spontaneous Gesture: Selected Letters of D.W. Winnicott*. Cambridge, MA: Harvard University Press.

Shakespeare, W. (1969) A Midsummer Night's Dream. In: *The Complete Pelican Shakespeare: Comedies and Romances*. London: Penguin Books.

Slochower, J. (1996) *Holding and Psychoanalysis: A Relational Approach*. Hillsdale, NJ: The Analytic Press.

Slochower, J. (2006) *Psychoanalytic Collisions*. Hillsdale, NJ: The Analytic Press.

Stern, D.B. (1997) *Unformulated Experience: From Dissociation to Imagination in Psychoanalysis*. Hillsdale, NJ: The Analytic Press.

Stoeri, J. (2005) Surprise, Shock, and Dread, and the Nature of Therapeutic Action. *Contemp. Psychoanal.*, 41, 2, April.

Szymborska, W. (1983) Autotomy. In: *Postwar Polish Poetry*, 3rd ed., ed. and trans. C. Milosz. Berkeley: University of California Press, pp. 115–16.

Winnicott, D.W. (1945) Primitive Emotional Development. In: *Through Paediatrics to Psycho-Analysis* pp. 145–56, New York: Basic Books, 1975.

Winnicott, D.W. (1949) Mind and Its Relation to the Psyche-Soma. In: *Through Paediatrics to Psycho-Analysis* pp. 243–54, New York: Basic Books, 1975.

Winnicott, D.W. (1952) Anxiety Associated with Insecurity. In: *Through Paediatrics to Psycho-Analysis* pp. 97–100, New York: Basic Books, 1975.

Winnicott, D.W. (1955) Group Influences and the Maladjusted Child: The School Aspect. In: *The Family and Individual Development* pp. 146–55, London: Tavistock, 1965.

Winnicott, D.W. (1956) Primary Maternal Preoccupation. In: *Through Paediatrics to Psycho-Analysis* pp. 300–5, New York: Basic Books, 1975.

Winnicott, D.W. (1958) Ernest Jones. *Int. J. Psychoanal.*, 39: 298–304.

Winnicott, D.W. (1960) The Theory of the Parent-Infant Relationship. *Int. J. Psychoanal.*, 41: 585–95.

Winnicott, D.W. (1960a) Ego Distortion in Terms of True and False Self. In: *The Maturational Processes and the Facilitating Environment* pp. 140–52, London: Hogarth Press, 1979.

Winnicott, D.W. (1960b) The Family and Emotional Maturity. In: *The Family and Individual Development* pp. 88–96, London: Routledge, 1989.

Winnicott, D.W. (1963) From Dependence towards Independence in the Development of the Individual. In: *The Maturational Processes and the Facilitating Environment,* pp. 83–92, London: Hogarth Press, 1979.

Winnicott, D.W. (1963a) Fear of Breakdown. In: *Psychoanalytic Explorations* pp. 87–95, Cambridge, MA: Harvard University Press, 1989.

Winnicott, D.W. (1964) The Baby as a Going Concern. In: *The Child, the Family, and the Outside World.* Harmondsworth: Penguin Books.

Winnicott, D.W. (1968) Comments on My Paper 'The Use of an Object.'. In: *Psychoanalytic Explorations* pp. 238–40, Cambridge, MA: Harvard University Press, 1989.

Winnicott, D.W. (1970) Individuation. In: *Psychoanalytic Explorations* pp. 284–8, Cambridge, MA: Harvard University Press, 1989.

Winnicott, D.W. (1971) *Playing and Reality.* London and New York: Routledge.

Winnicott, D.W. (1986) *Home Is Where We Start From: Essays by a Psychoanalyst.* New York: W.W. Norton.

Yeats, W.B. (1983) *The Collected Poems of W.B. Yeats* (paperback edition). New York: Simon and Schuster, Inc.

On the margins

The role of the father in Winnicott's writings

Christopher Reeves

I like 'edges'. They show where I stop and you start.
(Words of a child at the Mulberry Bush School
c.1955, quoted by Dockar-Drysdale 1993)

Introduction

The proposition that Winnicott largely ignored the father's role is taken as almost axiomatic by present day commentators and critics of his work, and likewise its corollary, that this neglect represents a serious limitation in respect of his developmental theory. This has not always been the prevalent view. Following Winnicott's death in 1971, his first exponents (Davis and Wallbridge 1981; Clancier and Kalmanovitch 1987) confined themselves to alluding without further comment to his predisposition towards the mother-infant perspective. Yet the omission had been remarked on. Thereafter most commentators, sympathetic or otherwise, followed Rycroft (1985) in lamenting the virtual absence of the paternal dimension in his writings, while offering various conjectures for this neglect (Chodorow 1989; Sayers 1991; Jacobs 1995; Rodman 2003). A small volume edited by Richards and Wilce (1997) contains a thoughtful series of essays on the topic of the elusive Winnicottian father, acknowledging and attempting to redress the perceived deficiency. Yet the presumption has remained as entrenched as ever. Armellini (2001) is to my knowledge the only writer so far to have seriously challenged the received view. Like him I shall be arguing that a balanced reading of Winnicott's written legacy shows that this claim of neglect remains at best a partial truth, and the consequent criticism misconceived, at least in part.

My standpoint is this: Winnicott (1957: 123) readily admitted that he felt especially drawn to the intricacies of the evolving mother-child relationship. Moreover, he regarded the mother's role at the start of the infant's life as primary, even exclusive. Naturally therefore, his contributions to psychoanalytic theory focus principally on this early period with all its potential vicissitudes and impact on the individual's future psychological well-being. As a consequence the father's role is thematically marginal in the context of his work as a whole. Winnicott nevertheless attached considerable importance to the paternal factor in practice and would have vigorously challenged the suggestion that his concentration on the maternal role in his writings meant that he had little to offer concerning the psychological dimension of the father's role. For him it was more a matter of choosing a focus than of expressing a conviction about relative importance that led him to concentrate primarily on the role and function of the mother in the child's upbringing.

To substantiate this argument I propose to undertake a survey of Winnicott's treatment of the father's role in his writings. I shall show that throughout his career Winnicott maintained a fairly developed, though not altogether uniform view about it. This found expression in his popular works, as well as running like a hidden thread through many of his theoretical contributions to psychoanalysis proper. True, even there the father tends to receive only passing mention. Nevertheless, it can be clearly demonstrated that his role is integral to Winnicott's understanding of how families properly function as social units, and how infants develop into psychologically healthy children and adolescents.

My first task, therefore, will be to demonstrate how the role of the father was at once *important, intrinsic* and *implicit* for Winnicott. Given that his primary focus was on the evolving nature of the early infant-mother relationship, I aim to show where the father fits in with this primary frame of reference, and why the topic of fathers was treated so parsimoniously. From there I shall go on to examine Winnicott's conception of the father's role that derives not so much from child care as from his understanding and development of psychoanalytic theory in what he called '. . . a line of development that is peculiarly mine' (Winnicott 1971: 86), and then consider to what extent these twin facets overlap. There remains a third issue relevant to a fully comprehensive account of his treatment of the father, namely how and to what extent Winnicott actually understood, interpreted and embodied the paternal transference in his clinical practice. However, this large topic falls outside the ambit of the present chapter, requiring a separate study of its own.

There from the start: 'the co-nurturant father'

In 'The Theory of the Parent–Infant Relationship' (1960: 39) Winnicott quotes a footnote that occurs in Freud's 'Formulations on the Two Principles of Mental Functioning'. Here the latter was arguing in favour of the proposition that at birth the infant can be thought of in biological terms as a self-sufficient closed system (at least 'as a fiction'), before adding in parenthesis, 'provided one includes with it the care it receives from its mother' (Freud 1911: 220). Seizing on this last phrase, Winnicott goes on:

> Here Freud paid full tribute to the function of maternal care, and it must be assumed that he left this subject alone only because he was not ready to discuss its implications.
>
> (Winnicott 1960: 39)

Winnicott's comment on Freud's parenthetical reference to 'the mother's care' in this passage can be taken as a cue to the reader, not to equate lack of coverage with lack of regard of the paternal factor in respect of his own writings. Evidence crops up repeatedly that when talking about mothers in relation to their children he took for granted the important background function of fathers. For example, when the mother is being referred to as the infant's earliest 'environment' there routinely occur interpolations of the kind 'I include father' (Winnicott 1962: 69), or 'This of course applies to fathers too' (1963a: 88). Again, when talking about the mother's special state of 'primary maternal preoccupation' at the start of the infant's life, he insists that the maintenance of this naturally occurring adaptation depends on the continuing support of 'her man' whose job is to provide for and protect the 'nursing couple' (Winnicot 1962a : 71; 1963a: 85). He sums up his position – 'An interest in mothering includes an interest in fathers, and in the vital part they play in child care.' (Winnicott 1964: 141)

However, the fact that these and similar references occur quite frequently in his writings is perhaps less noteworthy than that when they do, it is nearly always in the form of an aside. He gives the impression of mentioning something so 'terribly obvious' (Winnicott 1963a: 85) as hardly to require drawing the reader's attention to it, somewhat as Freud had in passing invoked 'the mother's care'. Yet fathers were much more integral to Winnicott's account of the child's psychological development than mothers were in Freud's, despite the similarly casual treatment accorded the partners each deemed secondary in the parenting process. In practice, Winnicott had quite a lot to say about the father's role. It was just that his thoughts on the subject were often scattered and piecemeal. More damagingly, they suffered from a degree of internal inconsistency that Winnicott never seems quite to have dispelled, or, more charitably, from an element of paradox that he chose not to resolve. The resultant conceptual ambiguity, I believe, contributed significantly to his authorial marginalization of the father.

Superficially, the theoretical role attributed to the father seems clear enough. His primary purpose is initially to provide a service for the mother and baby, that of acting in the role Winnicott variously described as a 'protection' ([1950]1986: 248) 'cover' (1955: 151) or 'shield' (1962a: 71). Such protective cover does not exhaust the father's usefulness, or the extent of his involvement in the birth of the baby. Winnicott was ready to countenance the possibility of a father sharing some degree of the primary maternal preoccupation (1963b: 251), of being, or becoming for a time, a necessary maternal substitute for the emotionally unavailable mother (1959: 73); even, in certain cases, of being in unconscious competition with the mother for the primary maternal role (1986b: 69–70). However, this 'covering' for, rather than direct participation in, the maternal function is what the father is ideally there to provide, a service both necessary in itself, and not readily performable without detriment by the mother either in the phase of primary maternal preoccupation, or its aftermath, when her primary task is to facilitate the infant's first strivings after personal autonomy.

Winnicott's paediatric practice afforded ample evidence about the desirability of the father supplying protective covering to the 'nursing couple' in this fashion. So did the insights gained from his psychoanalytic practice about the psychological consequences for the child of the absence or unavailability of the father and its effect on the mother's emotional state (Winnicott 1960b: 15–20). However, the conceptual basis for his claim about the importance of the father's protective function had its roots elsewhere. It derived from Winnicott's (1960c: 147) particular way of understanding and applying Freud's concept of the stimulus barrier ('*Reizschutz*'), with its function of protecting the fledgling 'psychic apparatus' from excessive external excitation (Freud 1920: 28). Change the term 'psychic apparatus' into Winnicott's preferred 'unit status', and one has the rudiments of his theory about how the new–born infant progresses through determinate stages from initially being a 'not-yet-I' to becoming an integrated unit, an individual, able to experience, and hence to utter, an I AM (Winnicott 1968: 56).

Foremost in facilitating this development was the part played by the mother as she interacted with, and impinged upon, the budding psyche of the child. Around the time of the birth the 'ordinary devoted mother' was identified with the baby in a particularly intimate way (Winnicott 1956: 300–1). Though physically a unit, the baby was psychically still a foetus, requiring the mother to provide a womb-like cover, without which the infant could not begin the process of developing his own psychic 'skin'.

> [E]xternal impingements require the baby to adapt to them, whereas at the birth age the baby requires an active adaptation from the environment. There comes a state in the labour in which, in health, a mother has to be able to resign herself to a process almost exactly comparable to the infant's experience at the same time. Belonging to this feeling of helplessness is the intolerable nature of experiencing something without any knowledge of when it will end.
>
> (Winnicott 1949: 184)

This initial state of 'primary maternal preoccupation' continues 'the physiological provision that characterizes the prenatal state' (Winnicott 1967: 60). Although he has not been part of this earlier physiological process the father fits into this scheme of things by supplying the missing cover for the mother, as the mother had to do for her baby:

It is important that when the mother is in the state [of primary maternal preoccupation] she is highly vulnerable. This is not always noticed because of the fact that there is usually some sort of provision around the mother, perhaps organized by her man. These secondary phenomena can arrange themselves naturally around a pregnancy just like the mother's special state around the infant.

(Winnicott 1960b: 16)

Here one can quite clearly see Winnicott speaking about the father's function as an outgrowth and extension of the maternal one. His argument is that if the baby at birth is effectively a foetus from a psychological point of view, then the mother must be womb for that foetus; and if the mother is the womb, the father must fill the equivalent role for the nursing mother.

Perhaps the clearest statement of this position occurs not in Winnicott's own writings, but from the pen of a close colleague – Dockar-Drysdale[1]:

The unintegrated mother-baby unit must be protected by what Freud called 'the barrier against stimuli'. This . . . means protection by the father and by the whole secure containing home environment. During the unintegrated phase the mother is in an extremely sensitive and vulnerable state: she is undefended, in the sense that for the duration of the unity she has abandoned her own defences and is completely dependent on the barrier which surrounds herself and the part-of-herself which is the baby.

(Dockar-Drysdale 1960: 15)

Here a quite explicit association is made between the mother's attunement to the baby, and the father's special attentiveness to the mother and baby. It is not so much the baby as the mother-baby dyad that is 'unintegrated'. The latter is spoken of as the 'unit' before the stage has been reached when the baby itself has achieved 'unit status'. As for the father, he provides a type of pro-maternal function in virtue of *not* being the mother.

The attribution to the father of a function analogous to Freud's 'limiting membrane' ties in with the claim that in the later stages of pregnancy and shortly after the baby's birth the father may go through a state of heightened sensitivity comparable to the mother's state of 'primary maternal preoccupation' (Winnicott 1950: 155–169; 1963b:

251). And this is of a piece with a yet further claim – that failure on the father's part to provide adequate cover for the mother at this point through physical or psychological absence may have the effect of causing the infant to grow up 'inhibited' (Winnicott 1988: 70). All of which justifies him being called, at least at this time and under this aspect, the *co-nurturant father*. In this capacity the father acts as mother's auxiliary, providing a maternal function by proxy, in virtue of his being at once distinct and different from the mother, at the same time as being intimately associated with her in her investment in the baby.

The beginnings of differentiation: father as foil and displacement object

Everything so far has indicated how intrinsic and indispensible what I have just termed the co-nurturant father was to the emotional management of the baby. Not for nothing, however, is Winnicott noted for his entertainment of paradox. The foregoing description is far from exhausting what he has to say about the father, his role and its limits at the earliest stages of a baby's life. In seeming contrast to these remarks about his centrality there occur several others that downplay the father's role, even going so far as to make it appear supplementary or even supernumerary to that of the mother. For instance, Winnicott states that the father (*qua* father) is initially an unknown entity for the baby, both as a person and a factor or 'idea'.

> The original two-body relationship is that of infant and mother . . . before any property of the mother has been sorted out and moulded into the idea of a father.
>
> (Winnicott 1958: 29–30)

Elsewhere, he writes of the infant being 'independent' of the father (Winnicott 1988: 70), and of not yet being 'old enough to recognize that father as a man.' (Winnicott 1959: 73).

Furthermore, even when he asserts that the father's availability is indirectly important (because of the support afforded to the mother), it is not vital in the way that the mother's is. The father can readily be substituted by other providers of the requisite 'social security' for the mother (Winnicott 1964: 114) since his use rests on the function he serves, whereas the mother's rests on being the person she is.

It seems as if the infant is really designed to be cared for from birth by his own mother.

(Winnicott 1945: 153)

The tension between the father as an indispensable adjunct of successful maternal care at the earliest stages of the infant's life, and as peripheral when viewed from the baby's standpoint, carries over into the description of the next developmental phase of childhood. The baby, sustained by the intimate moment-by-moment adaptation provided by the mother, begins to develop a 'surface', 'skin,' 'limiting membrane' of its own – becomes a 'unit'. As this happens, the mother gradually changes from being the immediate shell for the infant's as yet undifferentiated psyche–soma, to become the provider of an (outer) enclosing shield. She becomes the 'environment mother', the mediator of the external world, protecting her child from undesirable impingements, but gradually causing 'disillusionment' for him by her less than perfect adaptations (Winnicott 1958a: 240).

As his account unfolds, Winnicott concentrates almost exclusively on this emerging role of the mother. She now comes to represent the outer resourcefulness that was mediated through the father at an earlier stage and the various epithets denoting protective screening that had previously characterized the paternal function become attributed to her. She is regarded as the locus of the child's feelings of distress, anger, hate, fears of annihilation and abandonment, at the same time as continuing to be his centre and source of well-being. In short, she is at once the 'object-mother' and the 'environment-mother' (Winnicott 1963a: 75).

Insofar as the father continues to have a role through this transitional stage, it is as a foil, receptacle or displacement object for the infant's frustrations, as it becomes troublingly aware of the non-continuity between its own existence and that of the mother, and conscious for the first time of smallness and vulnerability. Foremost amongst these new anxieties is the infant's growing realization of mother's intermittent unavailability, inflexibility or intransigence, all of which engender rage and aggression. What happens then is that:

Certain qualities in the mother that are not essentially part of her gradually group together in the infant's mind, and these qualities draw to themselves the feelings which the infant at length becomes willing to have towards the father.

(Winnicott 1964: 114)

Winnicott does not explain why predominantly mother's negative attributes become displaced onto the father. Whereas with grandparents he readily concedes that one of their useful functions in the emotional life of the child is to be the repository of idealized properties originally attributed to the parents, in the case of the father a different set of internal imperatives seemingly applies. His statement here that the negative attributes in question 'are not essentially part of [the mother]' seems to conflict with his previous assertion about the inevitability of disillusionment vis à vis the mother as the child actually experiences her as less than ideally adaptive.

Putting this consideration to one side for the moment, let us observe the supposed consequence as regards the child's emerging view of the father. The end term of this process of negative displacement is that the father becomes:

> . . . an aspect of the mother which is hard, strict, intransigent and indestructible and . . . gradually turns out to be a human being, someone who can be hated and feared and loved and respected.
>
> (Winnicott [1966]1986: 131)

This depiction is somewhat removed from the earlier one of the co-nurturant father adaptively facilitating the mother and not otherwise impinging on the baby's consciousness. Instead the father becomes actual, in the baby's eyes, through being a useful target for negative or distressing feelings.

> The infant is not able to bear . . . the fact that aggressive ideas in primitive ruthless instinctual love are directed towards the mother . . . Moreover the child is not yet advanced enough to make use of the idea of a father intervening, and by intervening make instinctual ideas safe.
>
> (Winnicott 1988: 70)

Here Winnicott directs attention towards the adaptive function of maternal impingements, as if to suggest that this is the channel by which external reality, including the presence of the father, can eventually impress itself upon the child. His argument is that the 'ordinary devoted mother' will inevitably impinge upon the young child through failures of adaptation. These are unsought, from one aspect undesirable, but nevertheless necessary (as long as not too great or frequent) in order to spur the small child onto some degree of auton-omy and awareness of objects as 'real', including awareness of the father (Winnicott 1958a: 235).

This, however, does not really dispose of the difficulty of under-standing *how* the infant becomes aware of the father, and of what sort of father, or in what guise, it becomes aware of him. After all, the father supposedly makes his presence felt by 'intervening', thereby rendering instinctual ideas 'safe' for the young child. The mother too renders instinctual ideas safe, but this she does by containing them. Winnicott argues that, differently from the mother, it is an asset rather than a liability in terms of subjective experience that the father impinges. Otherwise, the infant is unable to recognize, and hence to make use of him. Yet this proposition is difficult to reconcile with the father's facilitating role as the co-nurturer, with the stress that is there laid on the continuity between mother's and father's role.

A problem has arisen in harmonizing these divergences in Win-nicott's depiction of the father, whether or not he was aware of, or exercised by, the paradox. Underlying the problem is Winnicott's desire to retain both options, to insist on the father's distinctiveness of role and differentiation from mother where the family unit is being viewed as a threesome, while laying stress on the essential continuity of the father's role with that of the mother, when the focus is on the dyadic 'core' of the family – the mother and the baby. It is a charac-teristic of Winnicott's theorizing not to seek to resolve paradoxes by precise conceptual differentiation. Consequently, in the interests of sketching a unitary and evolving theory of child development, Win-nicott was inclined to play down these divergences in the depiction of the father. The paternal function was more important than the person of the father. The implication seemed therefore to be that just as the father could assume a maternal role, as need arose, so could the mother assume a paternal role when circumstances required it. If challenged, Winnicott could point to the different explanatory ways Freud himself had invoked and used the 'stimulus barrier' or 'limit-ing membrane' models (see Laplanche and Pontalis 1973: 357–8). Still, it became apparent to Winnicott, at least in the case of the child who was no longer an infant, that the father's 'objectivity' (more precisely perhaps his 'exteriority') was critical, even if subjectively apprehended. The child needed to experience the reality of the father as a person, not just as an adjunct or a foil to the mother. For this circumstance a different model had to be invoked.

I, you, she: the 'sire-father'

At this point what might almost appear a sleight of hand on Winnicott's part needs to be uncovered, or the paradox dissolved, whereby these twin aspects of the father, as both coterminous with the mother and as different from her, seem to be allowed to converge or co-exist. Earlier I claimed that Winnicott had a developed, but not altogether coherent view of the role of the father. In fact, it is truer to say that even from the outset he actually held two views, or templates, depending on whether he was talking about the father in relation to infants or to older, and in particular antisocial children. In the former it was the co-nurturant template that applied. In the case of the latter, what was needed of the father, according to Winnicott, and what the delinquent youngster too often lacked, was for him to be 'strict and strong'. This view he stated very clearly in an early paper, long before he had begun to articulate his ideas about the importance for the baby of the maternal holding environment and the father as a facilitator of that provision:

> [The child] is also looking for his father, one might say, who will protect the mother when she is found. The strict father that the child evokes may also be loving, but he must first be strict and strong. Only when the strict and strong father figure is in evidence can the child regain his primitive love impulses, his sense of guilt, and his wish to mend.
>
> (Winnicott [1946]1984 : 117)

This other template I propose calling the 'sire-father'. The father in this guise is what Winnicott elsewhere refers to as 'the third person . . . the begetter, the mother's husband' (Winnicott 1988: 54). Here the idea of differentiation from the mother is uppermost. And as for the child, the father intrudes not primarily as an accessory to the primary infant-mother relationship but on account of his sexual union with his wife. Thus, the father's gender now becomes a critical factor. Instead of the mother-child dyad being paramount in defining the family unit, it is the pre-existing union of the parents that is salient. The sexual union of the parents is the enduring element around which the transitional, and transitory, relationships of the growing child cascade like waves over a rock (Winnicott [1957]1964: 115).

Of course, there are common features, and a degree of continuity between the two templates. It was precisely this overlap that allowed the element of paradox to thrive in Winnicott's account of fathers in relation to children. Each template in different ways reflects Winnicott's conviction about the father's importance as a *boundary figure* for the child's psychological and social growth. Each invokes the factor of *triangularity*, that is to say, the sharing of input of mother and father, male and female, and the tensions arising therefrom, as crucial to the psychological engendering of the child. Each presupposes the presence of the child as necessary for the family to exist, and for sexual partners to become parents. And each, though in different ways, attributes to the father a protective function.

Yet their conceptual antecedents are different. What I have termed the 'sire-father' has its thematic origins in the classical theory of the Oedipus complex, rather than in ideas about the 'limiting membrane' or the 'shield against stimuli' that lie at the root of the 'co-nurturant father' template. Although Winnicott invoked the persona of the Oedipal father far less frequently than either Freud or Klein in his writings, he nevertheless integrated key elements of the traditional Freudian theory into his overall account of child and adolescent development. There remains, though, a discernible difference of emphasis in Winnicott's psychogenetic application of the Oedipus myth, as we shall see.

Freud, as is well known, had situated the origins of the Oedipus complex in the conflicts engendered by the child's instincts of loving and hating, conflicts that reached their peak in the roughly five year-old child's unconscious wish to possess as partner the parent of the opposite sex and the corresponding destructive wish for the death of the same sexed parent, followed by their resolution through the child's temporary instinctual renunciation and subsequent identification with the same sexed parent. For Freud the wellsprings of the complex lay in the interplay of love and hate, which, as pervasive drives, were regarded as expressions of the ubiquitous life and death instincts.

This hypothesis accorded well with Freud's underlying belief in the principle of inertia as the explanatory formula best suited for making sense of behaviour and development, animal and human, at the level of maximum generality. Freud set out this principle in works such as *The Two Principles of Mental Functioning* (1911) and *Beyond the Pleasure Principle* (1920) as a meta-prescription regarding the ultimate

369

sameness-through-change of all biological and psychological processes. The Oedipus complex represented a significant instance of a
transformation of this principle operating both in the life of the individual, and in the destiny of the species. Viewed from this perspective
the onset and resolution of the Oedipus complex in the case of the
individual boy served a developmental function only in the sense that
the onset of the crisis enabled, indeed impelled him, to devise other,
better adapted survival strategies at a critical time in development,
firstly through fear of retribution, then through instinctual renunciation and finally through repression. Although negotiating the
Oedipus complex according to the traditional account represented a
'learning experience' for the child in one respect (because it brought
about the harnessing and redirection of instinctual energies towards
socially appropriate goals), in another respect it simply signalled a
compromise in the perennial dialectic between opposing and untam-
able instinctual forces: the child's instinctual propensities simply came
up against an obstacle. As a growing human being he encountered
an interdict.

Winnicott, for his part, chose to situate the Oedipus complex
squarely within an account of the typical child's developmental history, stressing its continuity with what had gone before, not its character of conflict and disruption:

> The Oedipus Complex is a description of an achievement of
> health. Ill-health belongs not to the Oedipus Complex, but to the
> repression of ideas and inhibitions of functions that follow from
> the painful conflict that is expressed in terms of ambivalence, as
> . . . when a boy finds he hates and wants to kill and fears the father
> that he loves and trusts, because he is in love with his father's wife.
> Happy and healthy is the boy who reaches just exactly this in his
> emotional and physical development when the family is intact.
>
> (Winnicott 1988: 50)

For him, as for Klein, the confluence of childish love and hate directed
towards the same sexed parent had its original source, and had established a dynamic, well before the onset of the classical Oedipus complex. Love and hate were partly instinctual, arising from developmental drives, and partly the experiential correlates of the continuous
separating-out process going on between child and mother. These
naturally entailed the deployment of destructive impulses in the

child, the consequences of which were the gamut of infantile feel-ings and anxieties that were set in train – fear of loss of the mother, sorrow, anger, love and guilt. Yet always for Winnicott, and perhaps to a lesser extent for Klein – although he disputed the latter's claim to have taken proper account of environmental factors (1962b: 454) – such phenomena were primarily to be regarded as by-products of a forward moving process, not as evidence of the omnipresence of instinct duality, as they were for Freud.

> The [infant's] impulsive gesture reaches out and becomes aggres-sive when opposition is reached. . . . *[I]t is this impulsiveness, and the aggression that develops out of it that makes the infant need an external object*, and not merely a satisfying object.
>
> (Winnicott [1954]1958a: 217 [my italics])

Thus, Winnicott attributes the main dynamism for change and growth as lying with the ambivalent feelings engendered in the infant by the inevitable separating-out process on the way to establishing 'unit status'. This process generates and determines the course of its development from dependence to independence with all its accom-panying eddies. In respect of the parents, the emphasis is not placed on the idea of the interruption of the young child's relationship to the mother as such (because for him the instincts which bind them are natural and not misdirected), but on the idea of the mother's survival of the child's aggression.

The father's role in this is vital but secondary, deriving from the primary mother–child relationship:

> It is much easier for the child to have two parents; one parent can be felt to remain loving while the other is being hated, and this in itself has a stabilizing influence.
>
> (Winnicott 1964: 115)

Here Winnicott does not imply that the father has to be 'created' by the child as a repository of angry feelings, but that he exists as a fact, the child comes to recognize him, and he serves a vital role in the sharing and deflection of the child's feelings. The *raison d'être* of the father is not primarily as a cover for the mother's care, but as the countenancer and mitigator of the child's instincts.

> In the first triangular relationship between persons . . . the child is overtaken by instinct and loves . . . The child hates the third person . . . Here at last, in the triangular relationship, hate can appear freely, since what is hated is a person, one who can defend himself, and one who is already loved, the father. Love of the mother is released . . . by the father's becoming the hated object, the father who can survive and punish and forgive.
>
> (Winnicott 1988: 54)

The suggestion now seems to be less the earlier one, that the (co-nurturant) father is the natural target of the child's hate, like a foil, but instead that the child's hate is qualitatively different, 'freer,' because of being directed towards the (sire) father rather than the mother. This not only reinforces the sense of the initial separateness of the father as a defining factor in the baby's experience of him, in contrast to what Balint, in a phrase that might well have been coined by Winnicott himself, called the 'interpenetrating mix-up of mother and baby'(Balint 1968: 66). It also emphasizes the notion of the father being someone *external*, a 'stranger', consequent on his not having been a presence within that subjective world from the first. It is as if their mutual independence both licenses and liberates the child's expression of hate.

Winnicott wrote in stark terms about the enmity directed by the child at the sire-father. The parents' sexual union provided 'a hard fact' to which 'he can cling and against which he can kick' (1964: 115). The infant's destructive impulses towards the mother may have been forceful, but they were initially 'pre-ruth' in character ([1955a]1958a: 265), and even at a later stage were typically laced with a strong measure of ambivalence and guilt. Towards the father, on the other hand, they appear to be more straightforwardly ruthless, albeit depending on the existence of a prior bond of love so as to serve the purpose of channelling the child's ambivalence. Already, in a very early paper we find the following passage:

> In our inner reality the internalized father is all the time being killed, robbed, and burnt and cut up.
>
> (Winnicott [1935]1958a: 131)

And from one of his last writings, again talking about the child's unconscious fantasy, he states:

372

If the child is to become adult, then this move is achieved over the dead body of an adult.

(Winnicott 1971: 145)

A subtle shift can be seen to have taken place in the way that hate and the 'stern' qualities become progressively associated by Winnicott with the figure of the father. Originally the father was seen as being the target for them through displacement from the mother. Now they are treated as intrinsically associated with the realization of him by the child. It is not that Winnicott deflected from his view of the mother as the initial object of the young child's anger and destructiveness. Rather, the type and provenance of the feelings of hate were different. Towards the mother, feelings of hatred were fraught with ambivalence long before the male child, in Winnicott's eyes, could begin to contemplate himself as a potential rival to father as sexual partner of mother. They were associated with adaptation failures by the mother, failures that were both inevitable and necessary. With the father, on the other hand, the realization of his separateness – of his being 'the first glimpse of integration and of personal wholeness' ([1969]1989: 243) – seems to be a condition, not a consequence, of the child's capacity to experience feelings of hate as well as love towards him.

The same applies to the other more positive aspects of the father's potential relationship with the child:

The father is needed by the child because of his positive qualities and the things that distinguish him from other men, and the liveliness of his personality.

(Winnicott 1964: 115)

When Winnicott writes directly about the stage of the Oedipus complex, and its aftermath, he emphasizes the link between the father's stabilizing influence through his interposing limits in the mother-son relationship, and the natural development of internal prohibitions typical of latency. Thus:

The father is used by the boy as the prototype of conscience. The boy takes in the father he knows and comes to terms with him . . . By identification with the father . . . the boy gets a potency by proxy, and a postponed potency of his own, which can be recovered at puberty.

(Winnicott 1988: 55)

The theme of the father's beneficial role as a figure who, ideally at least, can be both loving and firm, reappears elsewhere in his writings about the antisocial tendency, in particular when dealing with the causes of delinquency and talking about the sort of provision the young delinquent needs:

> This may be a kind of loving but often it has to look like a kind of hating, and the key word is not treatment or cure but rather it is survival.
>
> (Winnicott [1970]1984: 228)

In Freud's original depiction the 'precipitating cause' of the Oedipus complex was the child's attempted usurpation of the father's place and role as mother's partner. An immediate result of the resolution of the complex, therefore, was frustration of the child's unconsciously determined ambition. Subsequent effects – the development of the superego, identification with the father, the onset of latency – were secondary consequences of a necessary instinctual renunciation. In other words, the Freudian father did not impose his paternal interdict in order to teach the son through a process of graduated disillusionment about the nature of external reality, about fatherhood and sonship. Rather, it was a matter of the son having to experience unaided the blow to his narcissism that accompanies instinctual renunciation consequent on the realization of the father's prohibition. Winnicott's 'sire-template' of the father, in contrast, delineates the father who intervenes, and imposes himself in the evolving child-to-mother relationship in a protective, parental fashion. So, when Winnicott speaks of the Oedipus Complex as an 'achievement of health' he is treating it as a process of learning-through-interaction with the father, a process of gradual 'disillusionment' comparable to that which the child had earlier experienced in regard to the mother during the separating out phase. Thus the father, through his 'intransigence' – his inhibitory function – is acting as the child's mentor in a much more active way than the Freudian father.

In this way Winnicott reframes a vital part of the classical theory of the neuroses within the panorama of learning and disillusionment that 'good enough parents' visit on their children. In practice, the father is always seen as being there to fulfil a facilitating function, distinct from, but in partnership with, the mother. Yet the language of the basic instincts of love and hate that Winnicott habitually uses to describe the process does not always succeed in conveying the sense of an enabling function being discharged, but rather one of confrontation or opposition.

I shall now summarize some of the differences in the twin templates of the 'co-nurturant-father' and 'sire-father' that have so far emerged. The co-nurturant father in terms of Winnicott's later customary terminology is a 'subjective object' for the child before becoming an object 'objectively perceived' (1971). In becoming the latter in the child's eyes the actual co-nurturant aspect becomes discarded in favour of the father being seen as differentiated from, and in some degree antithetical to, the nurturing mother. The objective recognition of the father as external ('found') is a consequence of the child's wider recognition of the existence of an external world independent of himself. Here 'thirdness', differentiation, are products of developmental need.[2]

The sire-father, on the other hand, is externally presented from the start, a prototypical 'ob-ject' – lexically, an obstacle encountered on the path – in this instance, the path of development. A condition of the child's recognition of the father's independent existence and presence, or what I have called his 'exteriority', is that he can be experienced as at once a foil and a rival. In this respect the child does not so much 'create', as 'find' the father; more precisely, he first finds him as an object in order to create him as a 'subjective object'. 'Thirdness' is here a fact of life that the child must confront. This I take to have been the crucial insight gained from Winnicott's reflecting on the text of Freud's *Moses and Monotheism* late in life (Reeves 2007) (see Chapter 13).

Reconciling the two templates and the besetting problem of instincts

For the most part, however, Winnicott was content to keep these two representations of the father separate. On one occasion he referred to them respectively as 'the paternal father' and 'the standing-in-for-the-mother father' (Winnicott [1967]1989: 578). In line with this, he was in the habit of drawing a precise distinction between the treatment proper to psycho-neurosis and psychosis respectively (Winnicott [1959]1965b: 69–78). The former required the 'standard technique'; that is to say, the verbalization of unconscious content, with the analyst working in, through and beyond the transference neurosis. The latter required the management of regression to pre-Oedipal levels of failure and breakdown rather than interpretation of unconscious content. In this differential classification a very close link is made between the child's capacity to negotiate the Oedipus complex and the ability of the patient in analysis to accept the parameters and processes of the standard technique (these being premised on the realization of an actual separateness between the two parties). Conversely, psychosis was bound up with the small child's original failure, due to impingement, to negotiate successfully the crossover from subject-dominated apprehension of the infantile world to objective awareness. Thus we observe two parallel clinical entities in play, and two corresponding techniques to meet them.

Similarly, in setting out his longitudinal picture of childhood emotional development in the programme of lectures for students he gave over many years (Winnicott 1988) he introduced a two-fold depiction of its stages and hazards, one based on traditional instinct theory, the other on his account of the establishment of 'unit-status', 'integration', and the achievement of 'relationship with the outside world'. In the former, the role of the father is presented as a given, in the latter as having been generated in response to need.

It is evident that although Winnicott tolerated this rather artificial explanatory division, he was never entirely at ease with it. In his final year of life he seems to have made a sustained effort to bring the two into closer correspondence. The immediate focus of this attempt turned out to be not a fresh look at the role of the father vis-à-vis the mother in the mental economy of the child, but more fundamentally, an assault on Freud's deterministic theory of instinct duality by means of a fresh statement of his own about how a unitary basic human life-force ('motility') encountered and progressively adapted to the exigencies of its environment.

The link between these two sets of concerns is not immediately obvious, and in all probability was not altogether apparent to Winnicott himself when he embarked on this revisionary exercise. To see the connection it will be necessary to examine how he first attempted to deal with reconciling the duality of instincts into a single explanatory framework. Its equivocal outcome and the need to confront the question of how 'the external' meets the 'internal' and vice versa, meant that the urgency of reconciling his twin father templates eventually came to a head.

Winnicott's attitude to instincts was always thoroughly ambiguous. He wanted to hold on to a sense of the imperiousness of instincts, and felt that any qualification of their basic, unconditioned nature could seem to detract from their role, power and pervasiveness in human life. At the same time he wanted to emphasize their progressive controllability and modifiability, either healthily (as in creativity) or pathologically (as in neurosis and the development of a 'false self'). In this context the roots and causes of aggression, in particular, were a major and continuing preoccupation for him.

A revealing footnote occurs in the course of his résumé of the theory of child development, *Human Nature* (the text that furnished his lectures to teachers referred to earlier). It serves to indicate one source of Winnicott's dilemma.

It is thought by many that the primary excited impulse is not destructive, but that destructiveness enters into the imaginative elaboration through anger at frustration. . . . I consider that this theory, although correct, is not basic, since anger at frustration does not go early enough. At the present time I find I need to assume that there is a primary aggressive and destructive impulse that is indistinguishable from instinctual love appropriate to the very early stage of development.

(Winnicott 1988: 79)

In a much later postscript to the footnote Winnicott went on to state that his dilemma over the roots of aggression was eventually 'resolved' through his writing 'The Use of an Object' (Winnicott [1968]1971: 86–94). The solution, as he there saw it, lay in recognizing that the child's destructiveness did not actually succeed in destroying the object of his attack (provided it (she) stood up to him). Rather, at a certain stage in the child's development, the fantasy of successfully destroying the object came up against the reality of the object's non-destruction. This realization in turn enabled the child to relate in a new way to the object as something actual and existing independently of himself. In other words, this fresh experience of the conjunction of attack and survival made possible a developmental process that was the converse of the one that had first ushered in the child's awareness of an outside world. Originally, the infant had created as a subjective reality what was actually there to be found in objective reality in order to protect itself from the threat of gross impingement. Now, further on in development, the child could recognize the object as objectively presented by being spurred to 'uncreate' the subjective experience through seeing the subjective object's actual survival of his destructive attacks. So the need to (attempt to) destroy the object was basic, and the aggressive impulse its expression, yet the urge was born out of an equal need for the object's survival, resilience and non-retaliation in the face of this infantile attack. Aggression, in other words, was not just self-preservative but ultimately other-preservative as well. It formed the basis of the child's experience of the 'real'.

The issue of aggression, and his treatment of it, was to have an important bearing on his deepening understanding of the father's role. There is a discernible similarity between this account of the roots of aggression, via the gradual emergence of 'object use' from 'object relating,' and Winnicott's description elsewhere of how the boy at the Oedipal stage is able to make a developmental jump into latency as a result of the sire-father's interdict confronting his fantasy of supplanting him. Each instance presupposes a dialectical process involving an initially overmastering internal drive coming up against an equal but opposing external force or factor, resulting in a resolution through their transformation. The boy at the Oedipal stage, first 'hates' the father-rival, who retaliates with the threat of castration. This leads to the turning of the boy's hate into positive identification. In the case of the object:

> The subject says: 'I destroyed you', and the object is there to receive the communication. From now on the subject says: 'Hullo object!' 'I destroyed you.' 'I love you.'
>
> (Winnicott [1968]1971: 90)

Yet significantly and crucially, Winnicott did not attempt at this point to link his thoughts about object relating and object use to the classical theory of the Oedipus complex, or indeed to his own revised version of it that I considered above. One can discern a possible confluence of reasons for this restricted focus. The first was his paramount interest in what ordinary mothers contribute to their children's psychological well-being. The second was his immediate concern to unravel the puzzle of the roots of aggression and its relationship with this critical phase of early development. For Freud, the destructive impulse had been treated as a given to be worked with, not as a problem to be solved. This meant that individual psychological development, insofar as it involved conflict and the evolving of mental structures, presented itself as an issue not so much of 'how', as of 'why' aggression came about. Winnicott's starting point, on the other hand, was more nuanced. He sought to treat destructiveness as a concomitant of living and growing, rather than as an unconditioned instinctual force, whose vicissitudes remained to be explained within a developmental framework, and the living and growing he had in mind was that of the infant in relation to his primary 'subjective object', the mother.

Thus it was that in developing his new thinking about the phenomena of play, transference and culture, those areas where paradigmatically, the primitive destructive impulse was tamed and creativity supervened, Winnicott's first inclination was to leave the problematic father role to one side, in line with his abiding primary focus, and to concentrate on the mother's enabling part in relation to the child. The negative outcome from our present viewpoint is that in his 'Use of an Object' paper he not only disregarded the father, but in so doing he countenanced just one acceptation of that slippery term 'the subjective object', the one appertaining to the mother, wherein it denotes the object as subjectively *created* by the child through being objectively presented. Yet, an object may surely also be a subjective object in the sense of being experienced subjectively as something objectively *presented*. As such it can serve as precursor and prototype of the outside world as experienced by the infant.

It is with this second way of understanding the term 'subjective object', I believe, that Winnicott's concept of the distinctive role of the father properly belongs; or rather, where it is possible to account in his chosen developmental terms for the father's entry into the child's experiential world. (As already indicated, this realization dawned on him subsequently, in the course of reading afresh Freud's *Moses and Monotheism*). Whereas the mother, through initially providing the facilitating environment, and later sponsoring her child through the phase of transitional objects and phenomena, eventually enables him to *find* a world that is objectively there, the father starts from the position of being subjectively *findable* (because external) and serves as the exemplar of the child's *finding out* (1964: 116).

The father's fate: from ambiguity to marginality

The extent to which Winnicott was eventually able to distinguish the different senses implicit in the terms 'subjective object', and 'the object objectively perceived', or to recognize a need to distinguish them, are matters of continuing debate.[3] However, what is not in doubt is that in the aftermath of what Winnicott perceived as the hostile reception of 'The Use of the Object' paper in New York in November 1968, he embarked on an attempted clarification of the term 'use', in the course of which the externality and perceptibility of the object as given were accorded greater prominence. At the same time, more was made of the role of the father. In his posthumously published notes on 'The Use of an Object in the Context of Moses and Monotheism' ([1969]1989: 240–246) (Chapter 12), written soon after this lecture, Winnicott even attempted to integrate those elements traditionally associated with the father-son relationship of the Oedipus Complex in Freud's account – rivalry, interdict, death, destruction – with those primarily associated with the figure of the co-nurturant father, in particular that of being a reliable protective shield. This Winnicott did by situating the Oedipus complex securely within the developmental paradigm from which he started, instead of keeping it tied to its traditional context, where it represented a moment in the never-ending play of dualistic instinctual forces. In practice, it was these life-enhancing, liberating aspects of the Oedipal conflict that Winnicott had always sought to stress, both in his writings and in his therapeutic interventions. Previously he had failed to bring out in his theoretical work this quality of fatherhood intermediate between the two polarities of co-nurturant father on the one hand and traditional sire-father on the other, one where the father simply embodies the boundary function of *externality*, the figure the child comes up against as real, a discovery rather than a challenge. Here the father shows the way ahead, and thwarts only in order to redirect energies and impulses in more productive directions. Above all, he is an enabler of integration.

This role designation coincides closely with much that he had already ascribed to the second parent, namely, that of being the person whom the child has to 'find out' and who directs the child's 'finding out' towards the external world (Winnicott 1964: 116). Understood thus we can also see the father's original role as cover for the mother-infant dyad not altering drastically, but evolving gradually in parallel with the mother's. As she becomes the 'environment mother', experienced subjectively by the infant, so the father becomes invested with the subjective experience of objectivity. And as, a little later, the mother herself becomes an object objectively perceived, so the father becomes the prototype of the 'object presented', and hence the gateway to the child's discovery of the objective world. The aggressive impulses prompting the infant's first self-assertive endeavours are, on this view of things, simply the precursors of all the child's later efforts at mastering his environment.

I said that this designation of the subjective object in a secondary sense fits in neatly with the role ascribed to the father. However, in claiming that this was the thrust of Winnicott's final writing about the father, I have to admit that it represents my own understanding of his position, rather than being Winnicott's own unequivocally stated conclusion. His own focus always remained on how the infant 'realized' the objectivity or the outside world, rather on the nature of the outside world that the child came to realize, in particular, the fact and the implications of its 'externality'. So while it is probable that Winnicott was finally on the point of harmonizing his twin templates of the father, the exercise was never quite concluded, the paradox left unresolved. To the very end, the father remained a shadowy figure in many of his formulations about the early life processes involving mother and child. He does not feature prominently in Winnicott's late flowering ideas about the stages of integration, personalization and realization that the child goes through in the course of discovering himself and the object world he inhabits, as developed in his posthumously published *Playing and Reality* (1971). Had Winnicott lived some years longer, perhaps his formulations about these would also have undergone further revision and amplification with the father coming to feature more prominently in his own right. About this we can only conjecture.

Writing anecdotally about his own father Winnicott once regretted:

> It is probably true that in the early years he left me to all my mothers. Things never quite righted themselves.
>
> (Quoted in Winnicott C. [1978]1990: 8)

A similar observation might perhaps be made about the father figure as presented in and through Winnicott's writings: situated 'on the edges', present, available when needed, yet always as a background figure. This 'authorial marginality', as I earlier called it, undoubtedly restricts the explanatory reach of his theory. However, another perspective on this issue is permissible. In a further recollection, Winnicott wrote approvingly of his father's response when asked about how to interpret a certain passage from the Bible. Came the reply: the text was there to be read, not taught, so 'what you find there will be true for you' (ibid.). Viewed in this light, precisely those 'marginal' aspects of Winnicott's thinking about the father can serve us in the present both as an invitation to creative thought and as a spur to further elaboration.

Notes

1 Winnicott and Dockar-Drysdale first met in 1955. For a detailed account of their subsequent professional relationship and mutual influence see my article on the subject (Reeves 2002).
2 See Green [2000: 45]) for an alternative view of how, and to what extent, the notion of 'thirdness' applies to the infant's experience to the father. Green, more influenced by Bion than I, regards what Winnicott calls 'the imago of the father in the mother's inner reality' (Winnicott [1969]1989: 242]) as primary in the infant's experience of him, whereas I interpret Winnicott as meaning here that what is primary is the part the father plays in the actual experience of the child (the father as 'environment') – and whether the father is present at all – with 'the imago of the father in the mother's inner reality' as secondary, though important. The passage in question is susceptible to either interpretation.
3 Elsewhere I have argued (Reeves 2007) that in the last analysis the search for a grounding of 'objectivity' and 'perceptibility' was Winnicott's paramount quest in all this concern with differentiating subjective and objective, that is to say, it was at root a philosophical issue. Abram, covering much the same ground in Chapter 14 (2012), has focused rather on the developmental importance here of the aspect of the child's crucial establishment of 'feeling real' and 'feeling perception as real' through the experience of the survivability of the object, that is to say, she regards it as primarily a developmental issue. I do not think that there is an intrinsic conflict between our two positions. I would say that Abram's 'take' is closer to what Winnicott himself would have regarded as the fundamental point at issue, whereas I, for reasons given in the paper already referred to, incline to believe that his ultimate 'solution' to the problem of aggression was wanting epistemologically.

References

Abram, J. (2012) D.W.W. Notes on the Vienna Congress 1971: a consideration of Winnicott's theory of aggression and an interpretation of its clinical implications. In: *Donald Winnicott Today* Chapter 14.

Armellini, M. (2001) The Father as Function, Environment, Object. In: *Squiggles and Spaces* Vol. 2 ed. Bertolini, M. et al. London: Whurr Publishers.

Balint, M. (1968) *The Basic Fault* London: TavistockW

Chodorow, N. (1989) *Feminism and Psychoanalytic Theory* Berkeley: University of California Press.

Clancier, A. and Kalmanovitch, J. (1987) *Winnicott and Paradox* (tr. Sheridan, A.) London: Tavistock.

Davis, M. and Wallbridge, D. (1981) *Boundary and Space: An Introduction to the Work of D.W. Winnicott* New York: Brunner Mazel.

Dockar-Drysdale, B. (1960) Contact, Impact and Impingement. In: *The Provision of Primary Experience* 1990 London: Free Association Press.

Dockar-Drysdale, B. (1990) *The Provision of Primary Experience* London: Free Association Press.

Dockar-Drysdale, B. (1993) *Therapy and Consultation in Child Care* London: Free Association Press.

Freud, S. (1911) *Formulations on the Two Principles of Mental Functioning* S.E. 12 London: Hogarth.

Freud, S. (1920) *Beyond the Pleasure Principle.* S.E.18 London: Hogarth.

Giovacchini, P. (ed) (1990) *Tactics and Techniques in Psychoanalytic Therapy Vol. 3: The Implications of Winnicott's Contributions* Northvale, NJ: Jason Aronson.

Green, A. (2000) On Thirdness. In: *André Green at the Squiggle Foundation* ed. Abram, J. London: Karnac.

Jacobs, M. (1965) *D. W. Winnicott* London: Sage Publications.

Laplanche, J. and Pontalis, J.-B. (1973) *The Language of Psycho-Analysis* London: Hogarth.

Reeves, A. C. (2002) A Necessary Conjunction: Dockar-Drysdale and Winnicott *Journal of Child Psychotherapy* 28(1): 3–28.

Reeves, A. C. (2007) The Mantle of Freud: Was 'the Use of an Object' Winnicott's *Todestrieb*? *British Journal of Psychotherapy* 23(3) 365–382.

Richards, V. and Wilce, G. (eds) (1997) *Fathers, Families, and the Outside World* London: Karnac.

Rodman, F. R. (2003) *Winnicott: Life and Work* Cambridge MA: Perseus Publishing.

Rycroft, C. (1985) *Psychoanalysis and Beyond* London: Chatto & Windus.

Sayers, J. (1991) *Mothering Psychoanalysis* London: Penguin Books.

Winnicott, C. (1978) D.W.W.: A Reflection In: *Tactics and Techniques in Psychoanalytic Therapy* Vol. 3. ed. Giovacchini, P. 1990 Northvale, NJ: Jason Aronson.

Winnicott, D. W. (1935) The Manic Defence. In: *Collected Papers: Through Paediatrics to Psychoanalysis* 1958a London: Tavistock.

Winnicott, D. W. (1945) Primitive Emotional Development. In: *Collected Papers: Through Paediatrics to Psychoanalysis* 1958a London: Tavistock.

Winnicott, D. W. (1946) Some Psychological Aspects of Juvenile Delinquency. In: *Deprivation and Delinquency* (ed. Winnicott, C., Shepherd, R. and Davis, M.) 1984 London: Tavistock.

Winnicott, D. W. (1949) Birth Memories, Birth Trauma, and Anxiety. In: *Collected Papers: Through Paediatrics to Psychoanalysis* 1958a London: Tavistock.

Winnicott, D. W. (1950) Some Thoughts on the Meaning of the Word 'Democracy'. In: *The Family and Individual Development* 1965b London: Tavistock.

Winnicott, D. W. (1954) Aggression in Relation to Emotional Development. In: *Collected Papers: Through Paediatrics to Psychoanalysis* 1958a London: Tavistock.

Winnicott, D. W. (1955a) The Depressive Position in Normal Development. In: *Collected Papers: Through Paediatrics to Psychoanalysis* 1958a London: Tavistock.

Winnicott, D. W. (1955b) Group Influences and the Maladjusted Child. In: *The Family and Individual Development* 1965b London: Tavistock.

Winnicott, D. W. (1957) The Mother's Contribution to Society. In: 1986b: 123–127.

Winnicott, D. W. (1958a) *Collected Papers: Through Paediatrics to Psychoanalysis* London: Tavistock.

Winnicott, D. W. (1958b) The Capacity to Be Alone. In: *The Maturational Processes and the Facilitating Environment* 1965a London: Hogarth.

Winnicott, D. W. (1959) The Effect of Psychotic Parents on the Emotional Development of the Child. In: *The Family and Individual Development* 1965b London: Hogarth .

Winnicott, D. W. (1960c) The Theory of the Parent Infant Relationship. In: 1965b 37–55.

Winnicott, D. W. (1960b) The Relationship of the Mother to her Baby at the Beginning. In: *The Family and Individual Development* 1965b London: Hogarth.

Winnicott, D. W. (1960c) Ego Distortion in Terms of True and False Self. In: *The Maturational Processes and the Facilitating Environment* 1965a London: Hogarth.

Winnicott, D. W. (1962a) Providing for the Child in Health and in Crisis. I *Maturational Processes and the Facilitating Environment* 1965a London: Hogarth.

Winnicott, D. W. (1962b) The Beginnings of a Formulation of an Appreciation and Criticism of Klein's Envy Statement. In: *Psycho-analytic Explorations* (ed. Winnicott, C., Shepherd, R. and Davis, M.) 1989 London: Karnac.

Winnicott, D. W. (1963a) The Development of the Capacity for Concern. In: *The Maturational Processes and the Facilitating Environment* 1965a London: Hogarth.

Winnicott, D. W. (1963b) Dependence in Infant-Care, Child-Care and the Psychoanalytic Setting. In: *Maturational Processes and the Facilitating Environment* 1965a London: Hogarth.

Winnicott, D. W. (1964) *The Child, the Family and the Outside World*. London: Tavistock.

Winnicott, D. W. (1965a) *The Maturational Processes and the Facilitating Environment* London: Hogarth.

Winnicott, D. W. (1965b) *The Family and Individual Development* London: Hogarth.

Winnicott, D. W. (1966) The Child in the Family Group. In: *Home Is Where We Start From* 1986b London: Penguin Books.

Winnicott, D. W. (1967a) Environmental Health in Infancy. In: *Babies and Their Mothers* (ed. Winnicott, C., Shepherd, R. and Davis, M.) 1987 London: Free Association Press.

Winnicott, D. W. (1967b) D.W.W. on D.W.W. In: *Psycho-Analytic Explorations* (ed. Winnicott, C., Shepherd, R. and Davis, M.) 1989 London: Karnac.

Winnicott, D. W. (1968a) The Use of an Object and Relating through Identifications. In: *Playing and Reality* 1971 London: Tavistock.

Winnicott, D. W. (1968b) *Sum, I Am.* In: *Home Is Where We Start From* (ed. Winnicott, C., Shepherd, R. and Davis, M.) 1986b London: Penguin Books.

Winnicott, D. W. (1969) The Use of an Object in the Context of Moses and Monotheism. In: *Psycho-Analytic Explorations* 1989 (ed. Winnicott, C., Shepherd, R. and Davis, M.) London: Karnac.

Winnicott, D. W. (1970) Residential Care as Therapy. In: *Deprivation and Delinquency.* (ed. Winnicott, C., Shepherd, R. and Davis, M.) 1984 London: Tavistock.

Winnicott, D. W. (1971a) *Playing and Reality* London: Tavistock.

Winnicott, D. W. (1986a) *Holding and Interpretation* London: Hogarth.

Winnicott, D. W. (1986b) *Home Is Where We Start From* (ed. Winnicott, C., Shepherd, R. and Davis, M.) London: Penguin Books.

Winnicott, D. W. (1988) *Human Nature* London: Free Association Press.

17

Winnicott and American analysts[1]

Nellie L. Thompson

. . . I feel we are all trying to express the same things . . .
(Winnicott's letter to Anna Freud (Freud 1954) 1987: 58)

Since the publication in 1953 of Winnicott's paper, 'Transitional Objects and Transitional Phenomena,' his writings have exercised a profound impact on how American psychoanalysts think about the mother-infant relationship, the vicissitudes of development, and creativity. The impact of the work of American psychoanalysts on Winnicott is less well appreciated, however. A close reading of his writings and correspondence reveals, in fact, that he had many personal and professional contacts with Americans, both analysts and non-analysts, and was deeply impressed, and influenced, by their work. Through his reading, reviewing, and encounters at professional gatherings, Winnicott was familiar with the theoretical and clinical contributions of both child and adult American analysts. This includes the writings of Heinz Hartmann (1894–1970), Ernst Kris (1900–1957), and Phyllis Greenacre (1894–1989), leading exponents of American ego psychology, whose impact on his work he himself pointed out (Winnicott 1967b). Winnicott wrote to Greenacre as early as May 1949.

I have just read to the British Psychoanalytical Society the preliminary stage of a lecture on birth experience, birth trauma, and anxiety. Your work on this subject had escaped me, and I have now read your recent writings and I find that my point of view is very much indeed the same as yours . . . I am extremely impressed with your three articles, and hope that in the course of time we may be in personal contact. In case you want to know what sort of a person I am, I am enclosing a reprint, and a pamphlet for mothers which is about to be published . . . also you would see an article by me in the so-called International Journal of Psychoanalysis, Volume XXVI, Parts 3 & 4. 1945 ['Primitive Emotional Development']. If ever I am in the States I shall make a bee-line for your Clinic

(Winnicott 1949a)

In this letter Winnicott is referring his paper, 'Birth Memories, Birth Trauma' (1949b) which was not published until 1958. The Greenacre writings he finds himself in agreement with are: 'The Predisposition to Anxiety, Parts I and II' (1941a, b) and 'The Biological Economy of Birth' (1945). In an earlier paper, 'A Measure of Agreement: An Exploration of the Relationship of D.W. Winnicott and Phyllis Greenacre' (Thompson 2008), I explored in detail their relationship, which I first became aware of while reading 'The Use of an Object.' The infant's capacity to use an object, writes Winnicott:

. . . cannot be said to be inborn, nor can its development in an individual be taken for granted. The development of a capacity to use an object is another example the maturational process as something that depends on a facilitating environment.

(Winnicott 1969: 713)

In a footnote to this passage he notes that:

In choosing *The Maturational Processes and the Facilitating Environment* as the title of my book . . . I was showing how much I was influenced by Dr. Phyllis Greenacre at the Edinburgh Congress [of 1961]. Unfortunately, I failed to put into the book an acknowledgment of this fact.

(Ibid: 713)[2]

Given Winnicott's explicit acknowledgement of the influence of American analysts on his work, illustrated by his relationship with Greenacre, it is intriguing that the literature on Winnicott is almost silent on this influence on his work.[3] Two reasons for this are, first, the traditional location of Winnicott within the British Society, and second, his well known tendency not to cite the work of analysts who influenced him (see Chapter 1: 33).

The goals of this paper are to trace in some detail the history of Winnicott's contacts with American analysts, and to assess how their writings facilitated the creative evolution of his thinking. A prologue suggests that Winnicott's paper, 'Metapsychological and Clinical Aspects of Regression Within the Psycho-Analytical Set-Up,' was his response to hearing a paper in 1953 by the Hungarian-American analytic author David Rapaport (1911–1960). I then demonstrate Winnicott's familiarity with the work of Heinz Hartmann and Ernst Kris with two types of materials: (1) references to their work in his correspondence and papers; (2) writings where it is plausible to infer he was influenced by papers which he is known to have heard at professional meetings or which were presented at meetings he is known to have attended, but which he does not cite. Given Winnicott's insufficient referencing of the work of other analysts, the latter approach, while speculative, is potentially useful for widening our understanding of the intellectual milieu within which he worked out his ideas.

A paper Winnicott wrote in Hartmann's honour and some striking affinities between Winnicott's clinical writings and those of Kris and Greenacre illustrate that Winnicott was conversant with their work. The similarity of all three analysts' views on the mother–infant relationship, child development, the nature of the transference, and the role of regression in the psychoanalytic setting is highlighted. I argue that in these types of papers Winnicott's assimilation of the theoretical and clinical precepts of ego psychology provided a 'transitional space' that supported his creativity.

Encountering David Rapaport

After arriving in the United States in 1938, David Rapaport (1911–1960) spent 8 years at the Menninger Clinic in Topeka, Kansas before moving to Austen Riggs, a private psychiatric clinic in Massachusetts.[4] Although he was not a clinician, his voluminous, erudite writings, notably his treatise *Organization and Pathology of Thought* (1950), which was devoted to explicating the development of psychoanalytic theory, especially ego psychology, made him an influential and respected figure in American psychoanalysis. In 1953, on the evening of 7 October, at the beginning of a lecture tour of Europe and Israel, he gave a paper to the British Society.

In a letter dated 9 October, Winnicott wrote to Rapaport to say how much he had enjoyed this paper:

> . . . I felt that you really began to enable me to start giving my own ideas more in terms of psychoanalytic theory of an *accepted kind*. I am one of those people who feel compelled to work in my own way and to express myself in my own language first; by a struggle I sometimes come around to rewording what I am saying to bring it in line with other work, in which case I usually find that my own 'original' ideas were not so original as I had to think they were when they were emerging . . .
>
> (Rodman 1987: 53 [my italics])

Winnicott closes by voicing the hope that Rapaport and Masud Khan would soon have an opportunity to meet because he 'shall benefit in an indirect way.' Two observations are invariably made when this letter is cited. First, Winnicott's description of himself as 'compelled' to use his own language when expressing his ideas is noted. Second, the comment that he will indirectly benefit from a meeting between Rapaport and Khan is viewed as an example of his using Khan as an emissary to enrich himself (Rodman 2003: 53–4; Willoughby 2005: 53).

Khan did meet with Rapaport, and several days after his paper at the British Society, Rapaport met Winnicott at the latter's seminar 'Reconstruction and Direct Observation of Infancy' at the Cassel Hospital.[5] In a note to Rapaport about the arrangements for the seminar, Khan wrote:

> About the seminar I should like to make it clear that the important thing for us will be your presence. Please don't think that you are being called upon to make any weighty contributions. We wish you to come & just be among us & then should the spirit move you, naturally your discussion & comments will be our delight and gain. I am saying this because I know that Dr. Winnicott will feel very unhappy if he thought that you had been imposed upon to strain yourself.
>
> (Rapaport Papers 1953)

Khan and Rapaport maintained an intermittent exchange of letters and papers until the latter's death in 1960. After Rapaport had returned to the United States, in a letter, dated 20 May 1954, he wrote to Khan that he is grateful

> . . . for your having brought me in contact with Dr. Winnicott. I read his papers and have thought a lot about them. I found them very stimulating but again I am very uncertain about many points. I hope I will be able to write to him within a few weeks and will be curious to know both his and your reactions.
>
> (Rapaport Papers 1954)

To date this projected letter has not been discovered. It may of course, never have been written.

In light of Winnicott's declaration that he felt that Rapaport's talk would enable him to express his ideas 'more in terms of psychoanalytic theory of an accepted kind', it is surprising that neither the title of Rapaport's paper, 'The Theoretical Structure of Present-day Ego Psychology,' nor its content have been thought worthy of mention by commentators, such as Rodman and Willoughby. All that survives of Rapaport's talk in his papers, however, is a fragmentary outline divided into three sections. The first is an account of the historical roots of ego psychology; Freud's systematic description of the ego in *The Ego and the Id,* i.e., the ego is a cohesive organization of mental processes, a sediment of the identifications sequel to abandoned object cathexes, and primarily a body ego organized around the system Perception-Conscious, with defensive functions. In a third section labeled 'New Problems' Rapaport (apparently) focused on the 'ontogenic continuity of subjective experience: the self or the identity . . .' and noted that the self cannot be equated with the ego (Rapaport Papers).[6]

Winnicott's anticipation that Rapaport's discussion of ego psychology would help him express his ideas in a more *accepted kind of* theoretical language, raises the question of whether he did in fact later use such language. Evidence that he did is found in Winnicott's paper, 'Metapsychological and Clinical Aspects of Regression within the Psycho-analytical Set-up' read at a meeting of the British Psychoanalytic Society a little over five months later, on 17 March 1954. He emphasizes two points: first, the case he is discussing has led him to re-examine his technique; and second, this is a *theoretical* rather than a clinical paper (Winnicott 1955: 18). The theoretical point of departure for his new account of regression, and its therapeutic potential, is the 'existence of an ego-organization,' with a highly organized ego-defence mechanism, characterized by the existence of a false self and a true self. The development of the false self is one of the *most successful defence organizations*, designed for the protection of the true self (ibid: 25). Although the ego-organization permits regression to be a healing mechanism, it remains only a potential unless the psychoanalytical set-up provides a new and reliable environmental adaptation which can be used by the patient in correction of the original adaptive failure (Winnicott 1955: 16). Regression may be of two kinds: one originating in an early failure situation and the other related to an early success situation. In the case of environmental failure 'what we see is evidence of *personal defences* organized by the individual and requiring analysis.' In the more normal situation we see a memory of *dependence* and we therefore encounter an *environmental situation* rather than a personal defence organization' (ibid: 19, italics in original).

Thus the false self, which develops to protect the true self, originates in an environmental failure at an early stage of the individual's emotional development, and is characterized by feelings of unreality and futility. For these cases the setting of psychoanalysis, the environment of the analytic work, is paramount. The setting reproduces the 'early and earliest mothering techniques. It invites regression by reason of its reliability' (Winnicott 1955: 21). The patient returns to early dependence and is able to meet the original environmental failure without the organization of defences that produce a false self, protecting a true self. An important component of Winnicott's theory is the 'observing ego', which enables the patient to regress during the analytic hour and then emerge from the regression at the end of session (Abram 2008: 291; Chapter 3: 89–90).

The morning following his paper, Winnicott wrote a note to Anna Freud, who had been unable to attend:

> My aim will be now to try to correlate my ideas with those of Kris and Hartmann, as I feel [from] what they have recently written that we are all trying to express the same things, only I have an irritating way of saying things in my own language instead of learning how to use the terms of psycho-analytic metapsychology.
>
> (Rodman 1987: 58)[7]

Upon first reading this letter (and for a long time thereafter) I assumed that Winnicott was offering a description of a future aim and, further, one he did not follow through on. But further reflection on Winnicott's response to Rapaport's papers, the theoretical nature of his lecture, and his reference to the recent writings of Hartmann and Kris suggested a different way to view this paper. That is, it represents an initial effort, albeit in Winnicott's own language, to marshal the theoretical framework of psychoanalytic ego psychology to support and advance his own position on the paramount role of the environment, the mother–infant relationship, in early development. Winnicott's new understanding of the role of regression in treating psychotic patients is narrated in terms of the ego's defensive functions and its capacity to observe itself, i.e. 'the observing ego.'[8] Consistent with this, in describing his thinking on the clinical usefulness, and potential, of regression in the psychoanalytic setting Winnicott clearly states that regression only has the potential to be healing because of the ego's organization and its defensive functions. Further, he distinguishes the self from the ego in language very similar to that used by the ego psychologists. That is, the self is characterized by affects, e.g. unreality and futility, whereas the ego is an organization of functions, that is, defences, and apparatuses, for example, perception.

But which writings of Hartmann and Kris was Winnicott alluding to in his letter to Anna Freud? His practice of not referencing the work of other analysts in his papers is a problem here. But since Winnicott's paper is a theoretical statement of the usefulness of regression in the clinical situation that highlights the role of the ego in regression, and he himself linked Kris with his views on regression (1967b), the conclusion seems inescapable that he had in mind Kris's formulation 'regression in the service of the ego' which the latter first described in 'The Psychology of Caricature' (1936):

> We have now to elucidate in greater detail the relations of wit and caricature to dreams: in dreams, the ego abandons its supremacy and the primary process obtains control, whereas in wit and in caricature this process remains in the service of the ego. This formulation alone suffices to show that the problem involved is a more general one; the contrast between an ego overwhelmed by regression and a 'regression in the service of the ego' – *si licet venia verbo* – covers a vast and imposing range of mental experience.
>
> (Kris 1936: 290)

Winnicott may also have had in mind Kris's 1950 paper, 'On Pre-conscious Mental Processes,' which emphasized that the 'integrative functions of the ego include self-regulated regression' (Kris 1950b: 558). This concept of 'regression in the service of the ego' also appears in papers written by Hartmann, Kris and Loewenstein and in the British edition of Kris's *Psychoanalytic Explorations in Art* (1952), which appeared a year before Winnicott wrote his paper. It is also of interest that Winnicott was present when Kris gave his paper, 'Ego Development and the Comic,' to the British Society on 24 May 1937.[9] Winnicott was present in October 1949 when James Strachey read Kris's paper, 'Freud's Earliest Discoveries' to the British Society. In his capacity as Scientific Secretary he wrote to Kris thanking him for letting the paper be read to the Society, and described what he personally derived from hearing the paper:

> . . . I have no doubt that the most important thing that came out of it was the clear view which people got of Freud's personal growth and the development of his ideas and the feeling that he really was a person.
>
> (Kris, Papers 1949)

Winnicott may also have felt vindicated in his conviction of the importance of the mother–infant relationship in shaping the infant's psychological development by Kris's observation that in 1895 when Freud was endeavoring to establish the relationship between the age at which trauma occurred and the later neurosis, he emphasized:

> . . . the uniqueness of the mother in the life of the child, the dependence of the newborn being on his environment, the crucial importance of the relief of tension in the situation at the breast . . .
>
> (Kris 1950a: 5)

Another possibility is that Winnicott had in mind Hartmann, Kris, and Loewenstein's 1946 paper, 'Comments on the Formation of Psychic Structure.' Their depiction of the mother–infant relationship deeply resonated with Winnicott's view of the importance of the maternal environment in the infant's life. Their writings emphasize that the ego and id are undifferentiated at birth, that the ego's inborn apparatuses, e.g., motility, perception, memory, insure its relationship to reality (the environment), and the newborn's readiness for environmental adaptation. The infant, in other words, has inborn apparatuses which create a state of adaptedness preparatory to the adaptation that begins after birth.[10]

> The most essential part of the new environment [outside the womb] is the infant's mother . . . The nature of the biological equipment of the infant and the nature of his environment account for the fact that the infant's first reactions are related to indulgence and deprivation experienced at the hands of his mother . . . the infant tends to experience the source of satisfaction as part of the self; partial deprivation thus is probably an essential condition of the infant's ability to distinguish between the self and the object . . . he develops understanding for [the mother's] communications . . . reactions to the actual handling of the child by the mother, to touch and bodily pressure . . . the understanding of the child for the mother's facial expressions grows . . . The mother, as the first love object, is the object most highly cathected in the child's world, and the child's earliest learning proceeds partly by identifying with this object.
>
> (Hartmann, Kris, and Loewenstein 1946: 37, 39)

Symposium on infantile neurosis, New York Psychoanalytic Society, 1954:

Winnicott's response

In May of 1954, shortly after Winnicott gave his March paper, the New York Psychoanalytic Society held a symposium, chaired by Ernst Kris, on Infantile Neurosis, whose proceedings were published later that year in *Psychoanalytic Study of the Child* (Kris 1954). The main speakers were Phyllis Greenacre and Heinz Hartmann. Anna Freud was the primary discussant with contributions from members of the audience, among them, Bertram Lewin, Sibylle Escalona, Edith Jacobson, Rene Spitz, and Margaret Mahler. Although Winnicott was not present, in effect, he participated in the symposium via his subsequent paper, 'Primary Maternal Preoccupation,' (1957 [1958d]) written largely in response to Anna Freud's remarks.[11] In this paper Winnicott wrote that although he found himself in agreement with much of what Anna Freud said, he was nonetheless unhappy with some of her language when discussing early infancy. He noted her comment that the relationship to the mother, '. . . although the first to another human being, is not the infant's first relationship to the environment. What precedes it is an earlier phase in which not the object world but the body's needs and their satisfactions or frustration play the decisive part.' He wished she had not used the terms 'satisfaction' or 'frustration' here since 'a need is either met or not met, and the effect is not the same as that of satisfaction and frustration of id impulse.' Winnicott presents his contribution as an overdue examination of the mother *at the earliest phase* of the infant's life. His thesis is that at the earliest phase we are concerned with the mother's state of mind, a psychological state which deserves the name *Primary Maternal Preoccupation*. This paper, his favorable reference to Greenacre's symposium presentation, which depicted the role of rhythm in the infant's life, and his 1954 paper, clearly demonstrate both his need and wish to participate in the larger psychoanalytic dialogue about theoretical and clinical issues that were of fundamental importance to him.

British Psychoanalytical Society meeting, May, 1956

On 6 May when Winnicott was President of the British Psychoanalytical Society, Heinz Hartmann, Ernst Kris, Phyllis Greenacre, and Winnicott were all brought together at a day-long meeting held by the Society to celebrate the centenary of Freud's birth. The topic of the morning gathering was 'The Theory of Technique,' which featured Greenacre's paper, 'Re-evaluation of the Process of Working Through' (1956), and Kris's 'On Some Vicissitudes of Insight in Psychoanalysis' (1956). The afternoon session was devoted to Heinz Hartmann's paper, 'The Development of the Ego Concept in Freud's Work' (Hartmann 1956).

Winnicott may have especially welcomed the papers by Greenacre and Kris for two reasons. The first was related to the recent rupture in his relationship with Joan Riviere and Melanie Klein which may be traced to their position that he had no positive contribution to make to Klein's efforts to depict the psychology of earliest infancy. In a letter to Joan Riviere written earlier that February, Winnicott vehemently contested their dismissal of his work and, in turn, was critical of Klein's paper, 'A Study of Envy and Gratitude,' and reiterated his view that it is impossible to describe early infancy without considering ego development (Rodman 1987: 94–7). The second reason is that he may have heard resonances in their papers of his statement on transference, 'Clinical Varieties of Transference,' delivered the summer before at the 1955 IPA Congress in Geneva. The panel on transference was chaired by Elizabeth Zetzel, whose incisive opening statement on current views of the transference noted that the significance of the analytic relationship as a repetition of the early mother–child relationship had increasingly been emphasized, albeit from different points of view (Zetzel 1956: 369).

Zetzel's observation was borne out by Winnicott's paper which argued that the transference was shaped by the care that the infant received from the mother. Further, when this care is accompanied by an environmental failure a 'false self' takes hold of the individual. For these patients the setting of the analysis is more important than the interpretations offered by the analyst.

Greenacre's paper 'Re-evaluation of the process of working through' discussed a small but significant group of patients for whom she believed the process of 'working through' is crucial. In her earlier 1954 paper she had drawn a distinction between the basic transference, a 'matrix' originating in the early mother–infant union, and the full transference, where the patient experiences memories with 'their *full* emotional resonance' and not merely as something reported or partially relived (Greenacre 1954: 674 [italics in the original]). I believe that Winnicott was familiar with Greenacre's 1954 paper, published in *JAPA,* because it follows Douglas Orr's paper 'Transference and Countertransference: A Historical Survey' (1954) which he cited in an early draft of his Congress paper.

In Greenacre's paper to the British Society she built on these themes to argue that without the reconstruction of the original trauma these patients will not benefit from analysis. While she underscored the analyst's interpretive role, the emphasis she placed on the need for the patient to experience memories with their full emotional resonance parallels Winnicott's prescription for what needs to transpire for the patient to feel real: 'One characteristic of the transference at this stage is the way in which we must allow the patient's past to *be* the present . . . the present goes back into the past, and *is* the past' (Winnicott 1956: 387).

Ernst Kris framed his paper 'On Some Vicissitudes of Insight in Psychoanalysis' by considering the antecedents of the 'good analytic hour,' which reflect or build on 'the integrative functions of the ego.' There are notable affinities between his clinical experiences and observations and Winnicott's on the question of how and why changes occur in analysis. Kris argues that analytic insight, and its various forms, is rooted in infantile prototypes, which, in turn, determine the state of the transference. Thus, insight may be utilized in order to compete with or gain independence from the analyst. Or intellectualization may take the place of insight allowing the patient's illness to become detached from the rest of the personality. The 'good analytic hour' occurs when patients experience an especially meaningful comprehension of their material.[12] Kris postulates that the insight realized during these hours, and its infantile prototype, draws on some infantile unconscious fantasy. But in every case 'the function of insight was differently embedded in . . . the personality.'

By contrast, the (insidious) 'deceptively good hour' originates in the patient's compliant wish to please or merge with the analyst. Kris's observations resemble Winnicott's in several ways. The latter's insistence that change only occurs when the trauma comes under the omnipotent control of the patient is compatible with but not identical to Kris's description of the integrative work of the ego responsible for analytic insight. In Winnicott's writings the false self shields and even isolates the true self, while Kris argues that one deleterious consequence of intellectualization, a distortion of insight, is that it enables illness to grow and even become detached from the rest of the personality. Even insight itself must always be scrutinized for its potential as a form of gratification or defence. In every case analytic work will not be complete until there is 'an analysis of the infantile prototypes which give full meaning to the experience of insight during the analytic process, (and) are sometimes also responsible for it' (Kris 1956b: 449). Again, this resonates with Winnicott's argument that the original situation which gave rise to the false self must be experienced for its hold on the self to be dissipated.[13]

Less than a year after this meeting of the British Psychoanalytical Society, Ernst Kris died on 27 February 1957. After his death Winnicott wrote that his death 'has robbed psycho–analysis of one of its clearest thinkers' (Winnicott 1958a). In describing what Kris's death meant for psychoanalysis, Winnicott may have had in mind, beyond his writings on regression, Kris's papers on infants and young children written as a result of his observational studies at the Yale Child Study Center (Kris 1951a,b, 1954, 1956a,b,c), which are cited by Winnicott.

Travels to America: the 1960s

Winnicott undertook four trips to the United States in 1962, 1963, 1967, and 1968,[14] which brought him into personal contact with many individuals from a range of backgrounds captivated by his thinking. The publication of Winnicott's books in the United States, beginning in 1958 with *Mother and Child* and followed the next year by *Collected Papers: Through Paediatrics to Psychoanalysis* contributed to intense interest in his work before his visits to the United States. His writings on infancy and development, his approach to child therapy (the squiggle game), and his delineation of the role of transitional objects and transitional phenomena in development had generated, and continue to do so, an outpouring of books and papers devoted to his theoretical and clinical contributions.[15] But he also possessed a wide and deep knowledge of developments in psychoanalysis in the United States through his attendance at international psycho-analytic meetings where he had met and heard American analysts, his correspondence with Americans, and his extensive activities as a reviewer.

As early as 1949 Winnicott had reviewed the proceedings of the second conference on Infancy and Early Childhood sponsored by the Josiah Macy, Jr. Foundation in New York, and in the end he reviewed three of the six conference reports (Winnicott 1949c, 1951a, 1953b). He praised them for bringing together a range of experts and noted that it would be useful for the British to hold similar gatherings. Of special note is his review (1952) of the sixth conference which fea-tured a long report by the psychologist and infant researcher Sibylle Escalona (1915–1995).[16] Winnicott wrote in praise of her work:

> . . . she gives the results of highly sensitive observations on the infant-mother relationship at its initiation. There is a full apprecia-tion not only of the qualitative detail but also of the importance of all the details in the establishment of the mental health of the individual infant who is to grow into an adult.
>
> (Winnicott 1953b: 664)

In applauding Escalona's close and acute rendering of the mother-infant relationship, Winnicott may also have identified with her acknowledgement of the personal sources that accompanied her systematic efforts to study infant behavior which she described as a 'peculiar conglomeration of impressions, thoughts and fantasies' (Escalona 1952: 11).

Winnicott's eight reviews of *Psychoanalytic Study of the Child* (Winnicott 1948, 1951b, 1958a,b, 1962b, 1963, 1966a, 1968) further exposed him to the latest developments in psychoanalytic research on infant and child development, clinical reports, and theoretical papers on a broad range of analytic topics by American analysts. (It should be noted that Winnicott's British colleagues also published in *Psychoanalytic Study of the Child*.) He customarily commented that it was impossible to do justice to the content of each volume, nonetheless it is useful to note the papers and authors he singled out. For example, in Winnicott's review of volume 2 (1946), he lauded the 'excellent the material' in Rene Spitz's paper, 'Anaclitic Depression,' but also found his references to Melanie Klein's work 'uninformed' and urged her critics to more closely study her ideas (Winnicott 1948: 389). In Winnicott's review of volume 11 (1956) the papers by Phyllis Greenacre on awe in childhood, Elizabeth Zetzel's discussion of the work of Melanie Klein, Ernst Kris on childhood memories, and Heinz Hartmann's essay on the 'reality principle' were singled out (Winnicott 1958a). Papers by Bertram Lewin, Margaret Mahler, and Edith Jacobson on depression, grief, and sadness in infancy and adolescent moods are noted in his review of volume 16 (Winnicott 1963). One is driven to speculate that Winnicott may actually have found more support and stimulus for his thinking on infancy and the mother–child relationship among American analysts than from his British colleagues.

Winnicott's contacts and exchanges with Americans are also documented in his published and unpublished letters. In general his letters show him to have been forthright in expressing his appreciation and praise for papers he learned from, direct in answering questions, and testy and aggressive when he believed his theoretical contributions and clinical findings were being ignored; his letters to a wide range of American correspondents display all of these characteristics. They also testify to the impact of his writings on a diverse range of American correspondents and record the personal visits he made during trips to the United States. For example, Katherine Read, an educator of young children, sent Winnicott a copy of her book, *The Nursery School A Human Relationships Laboratory*, and they later met when she visited England. Eva Meyer, the librarian of the A.A. Brill Library of the New York Psychoanalytic Society and Institute in the 1950s, who had a scholar's devotion to building up the library's collections, wrote to Winnicott in January 1958, and requested some reprints both for the library and herself. She noted that she

> . . . had the great pleasure and privilege of attending the extraordinary summer meeting of the British Psycho-Analytical Society at which you gave your brilliant and fascinating paper. It was the highlight of my trip to Europe, and I would be most grateful if you could spare a copy for my personal use.
>
> (Meyer 1958)

She ended by noting that his books find an honoured place in 'our library and enjoy brisk sales in our little bookshop.' The paper Meyer referred to in her letter was 'The Capacity to be Alone' (Winnicott 1958c), given in 1957 at a summer meeting of the British Psychoanalytic Society. Benjamin Spock, the pediatrician, received a long and detailed letter from Winnicott commenting on his paper 'Observations on the Striving for Autonomy and Some Regressive Object Relationships after Six Months of Age' (Spock 1963). Winnicott also sent reprints to Lili Peller, an émigré child analyst who published extensively on language development and play.

Winnicott's correspondence also offers glimpses of personal visits he and his wife Clare made during their 1963 trip to the United States when they stayed with Elizabeth Zetzel and her husband in Boston, and in New York spent an evening with Kurt and Ruth Eissler. Afterwards, the Eisslers sent the Winnicotts prints of New York scenes, which they had enjoyed on their visit, especially the Brooklyn Bridge. They also visited with Lawrence Kubie, a member of the New York Psychoanalytic Society, who was then the director of the Shepard and Pratt psychiatric hospital, outside Baltimore.[17] In 1968 Winnicott wrote a charming note to Kubie about his 1955 paper, 'Say You're Sorry,' which recounts the treatment of a little girl's psychotic episode.

> My dear Kubie, I have just read your 1955 paper, 'Say You're Sorry.' It is so very good that I want to write in appreciation. 'I am very very sorry' that I have not read it before. Every good wish, Yours, D.W. Winnicott
>
> (Winnicott 1968)

In his reply Kubie described the treatment as an extraordinary clinical experience and noted the girl had undergone a further ten years of therapy.

Winnicott's paper in honour of Heinz Hartmann

Winnicott's 1965 paper 'A Clinical Study of the Effect of a Failure of the Average Expectable Environment on a Child's Mental Functioning' was written in honour of Heinz Hartmann. While he was a cerebral theorist, Winnicott demonstrably felt a strong affinity with the description of the early mother–infant relationship in Hartmann's *Ego Psychology and the Problem of Adaptation* (1939 [1958]), which he would cite to support his position that the infant's dependence on the mother was of unparallelled importance, and in his papers written with Ernst Kris and Rudolph Loewenstein. It also appears that Winnicott, renowned for his intensely personal voice, did not equate Hartmann's austere writing with a lack of a personal voice. It was, moreover, one to which he responded as evidenced by his remarks about Hartmann in 1967 to the 1952 Club when he sketched out links between his work and that of his fellow analysts. Winnicott prefaced his remarks by saying, 'I thought that if you had a pencil you might feel like writing down Hartmann and (Willi) Hoffer, you know, in the corner at the edge' (Winnicott 1989: 571–3), suggesting that his listeners should view their writings as a backdrop or screen against which (or within which) he locates his own ideas. In the chart depicting these links Hartmann's name is written next to 'Conflict-free sphere I Ego' and 'Good-Enough Mother.'

> Here we have to bring in Hartmann's 'conflict-free sphere' which really, I think I'm right in saying (he didn't mind when I said it to him), has to do with the inherited tendencies. Then I found I had to formulate a sort of theoretical basis of environmental provision starting at the beginning with 100 percent adaptation and quickly lessening according to the ability of the child to make use of failure of adaptation
>
> (Winnicott 1967b: 579)

Winnicott's paper describes a diagnostic interview with a six-year-old boy, accompanied by drawings by the child and Winnicott, that he characterized as a 'piece of deep therapy.' According to Winnicott, the aim of the treatment was to 'unhitch' a developmental catch, so that the environmental influences might resume their function of facilitating the process of maturation in the child (Winnicott 1965: 81). He endeavors to show 'the effect on a child of a specific example of failure in the area of what Hartmann (1939) has called "the average expectable environment"' (ibid: 87). The little boy had earlier been thought to be 'simple', probably because he had a learning difficulty and did not speak until 3 years of age; even then his words were hard to follow. Winnicott observes that 'it is interesting to note that schizophrenia, or the psychotic condition that resulted here in a learning difficulty, is in fact a highly sophisticated defence organization' (ibid: 86). The defence is against unbearable, archaic anxiety produced by environmental failure in the stage of the child's near-absolute dependence. In other words, the child's ego has known a certain limited type of disaster, has experienced breakdown, has reorganized against being traumatized anew, and at the same time cannot be induced to regain vulnerability and dependence.

> All details of the experience have been retained and have been subjected to classification, categorization, and collation, and to primitive forms of thinking.
>
> (Ibid: 86)

It is striking how here Winnicott conceptualized the very young child's response to the mother's depression, when he was 14 months old, in terms of classification and primitive forms of thinking he brought to dealing with this experience. Thinking was an ego function that had long preoccupied Hartmann and here Winnicott paid him the compliment of using it clinically to understand this young child. Winnicott concluded that the child can now forget this disastrous experience '. . . because it has been remembered. That is, it has become available for a sophisticated thinking process that is relatively detached from psychosomatic functioning' (ibid: 87).

Hartmann responded to Winnicott's paper in a note, dated 19 November 1965, whose content indicates that Winnicott had written to him about the case.

> It was very kind of you to let me hear about the boy you introduced to me in the January issue of the Journal and about some of

the thinking that led to your Psychotherapeutic Interview technique. I am very far from understanding what this means in terms of ego-psychology, though you hint at some possible connections. I trust, it will become clearer to me, once I had the opportunity of studying the work along the same lines you are planning now. Thank you once more for your letter. With regards to you and your wife. Sincerely yours, Heinz Hartmann

(Hartmann 1965)

1968: 'The Use of an Object'

The enormous impact that Winnicott's paper 'Transitional Objects and Transitional Phenomena' had on American analysts was noted at the beginning of this paper. Indeed, shortly after its 1953 publication it was discussed at a meeting, led by Margaret Mahler, of the Kris Study Group in October of 1954. The group also read his paper 'Paediatrics and Psychiatry' (1948) for this meeting.[18] However, Winnicott's paper 'The Use of an Object' which he presented to the New York Psychoanalytic Society on the evening of 12 November 1968, on his last trip to the United States, did not meet with the enthusiastic reception that followed the publication of the paper on transitional objects and phenomena or his other writings. Today, however, Winnicott scholars view his paper as a seminal development in his thinking on the role of destruction or aggression in establishing the infant's relationship to an external object beyond its omnipotent control (Abram 2012: Chapter 14 (this volume); Goldman 1998; Reeves 2007; Samuels 1996, 2001).

Baudry's recent paper (2009) reviewed the events of that evening, and summarized the thesis advanced by Winnicott and the responses of his three discussants: Edith Jacobson, Samuel Ritvo, and Bernard Fine. While acknowledging that the discussants were respectful of Winnicott, Baudry argued that their comprehension of the paper was compromised because they read it from a 'classical' point of view. He also noted, however, that Winnicott's presentation of his thesis was at times difficult to follow and that the two clinical examples he sent the discussants did not effectively support his thesis (Baudry 2009: 1061). It is not generally known that the discussants of Winnicott's paper read it accompanied by these two clinical examples, only one of which was published many years after his death (Winnicott

1968d), whereas the audience only heard the paper. The letter that Winnicott wrote to Merrill H. Whitney, executive secretary of the NYPSI, enclosing the clinical material, hints at the difficulties that he was encountering in writing the paper, and also provides a glimpse of how he wished the evening to proceed:

> I am enclosing a rather heavy piece of clinical material. As I came to illustrate the point that I am trying to make . . . I found myself in great difficulties and I decided not to try to deal with this difficulty by reading a long case description . . . It might be possible, for instance, for the discussants to claim that the material does not illustrate my theme. My hope is that the point that I am making may remind hearers of clinical material of their own . . . It is important for me that I do not allow myself to occupy much of the evening. I want to put my thesis forward and then give time for its discussion . . . I may say that I greatly look forward to the prospect of a discussion in your Society and I am honoured to see that Dr. Edith Jacobson, Dr. Samuel Ritvo and Dr. Bernard Fine have agreed to discuss the paper.
>
> (Winnicott 1968)[19]

The following Summary statement of the paper's thesis was also sent to the discussants by Winnicott:

> Object-relating can be described in terms of the subject. Description of object-usage involves consideration of the nature of the object. I am offering for discussion the reasons why, in my opinion, a capacity to use an object is more sophisticated than a capacity to relate to objects; and relating may be to a subjective object, but usage implies that the object is part of external reality. . . Study of this problem involves a statement of the positive value of destructiveness. The destructiveness plus the object's survival of the destruction places the object outside the area in which projective mental mechanisms operate, so that a world of shared reality is created which the subject can use and which can feed back into the subject. How this usage develops naturally out of play with the object is the theme of this talk.
>
> (Winnicott 1968c; cf. Chapter 14)

Following the Summary Winnicott listed four papers, written in the previous decade, which he described as the current paper's antecedents, and noted that it would be helpful to his exposition if their reading could be taken for granted.[20] The most recent paper had been published earlier that year: 'Playing: Its Theoretical Status in the Clinical Situation' (1968b), and this had been preceded by 'The Location of Cultural Experience' (1967a), 'Ego Integration in Child Development' (1965), and 'The Capacity to be Alone' (1958c).

Read in sequence, from 1958 to 1968, these four papers advance a series of interrelated ideas about the foundational importance of object relating whose *dénouement* is the capacity to use an object. The first three papers propose maturational descriptions of the infant's psychic development in terms of experiences that Winnicott characterized as 'object relating'. In 'The Capacity to be Alone' (1958c) he argued that the requisite experience for the capacity to be alone is the '. . . *experience . . . of being alone, as an infant and small child, in the presence of the mother*' (Winnicott 1958c: [italics in original]). During this early period when mother and infant are for all intents and purposes merged, made possible by the mother's near perfect adaptation to her infant's needs, their relationship is best described as one of 'ego-relatedness.' Winnicott had introduced the term 'ego-relatedness' a year earlier in 'Primary Maternal Preoccupation' (1957 [1958d]), but later replaced it with 'object-relating.' (Abram 2007: 42). This later change in Winnicott's theoretical vocabulary may explain why he recommended this paper to the discussants. The 'capacity to be alone' depends on a mother–infant relationship of 'ego-relatedness' or 'object relating', which may be thought of as the touchstone of the infant's future emotional health.

In 'Ego Integration in Child Development' (1965) the role of the ego, which is based in the body, is described by Winnicott as initiating object relating which then takes hold 'within the framework of a baby's experience and growth' (Winnicott 1962: 62). This is a complex process, which can only take place within the 'environmental provision of object-presenting, done in such a way that the baby creates the object.' The good–enough mother makes this possible and 'the baby comes to feel confident in being able to create objects and to create the actual world' (ibid).

Winnicott described 'The Location of Cultural Experience' as doing little more than extending the ideas found in 'Transitional Objects and Transitional Phenomena' (1951 [1953a]). Nonetheless, in this paper he wanted to provide a positive statement about where in the mind cultural experience resides: '. . . *play is in fact neither a matter of inner psychic reality nor a matter of external reality*' (Winnicott 1967a: 368

[italics in original]). So where then is play? When an infant employs a transitional object it represents the first use of a symbol and the first experience of play. Symbol and play can be located in space and time when the mother, in the baby's mind, is no longer merged with it but is 'being experienced as an object to be perceived rather than conceived of.' 'The use of a [transitional] object symbolizes the union of two now separate things, baby and mother, *at the point of the initiation of their state of separateness'* (ibid: 369). But these phenomena, transitional objects and play, belong to *'the experience of relating to objects'* (ibid). Cultural experience is located in the *potential space* between the individual and the environment (originally the object). Moreover, 'this potential space is at the interplay between there being nothing but me and there being objects and phenomena outside omnipotent control' (ibid: 371). These experiences belong to object relating or to what can be called ego-relatedness, at the place where it can be said that *continuity* ceases and gives place to *contiguity*.

Published before Winnicott's visit to the New York Psychoanalytic Society, his paper 'Playing' advanced the thesis that playing has a place and a time and is a thing in itself and not an expression of instinctual urges. Playing is neither inside nor outside, but related to the 'not-me' which the infant has recognized as truly external and beyond its magical control. Thus, the paper on playing and 'the use of an object paper' are companion pieces because essential to both is the infant's recognition of an external reality, and object, beyond its magical, omnipotent control.

In his Summary statement Winnicott confirmed this linkage when he declared that the capacity to use an object develops naturally out of play with the object. Further, study of the problem of object relating versus object usage 'involves a statement of the positive value of destructiveness.' Although Winnicott and the discussants agreed on the importance of the mother–infant relationship for the psychological health of the infant, they did not accept his position on the necessity for and positive value of the continual destruction, and survival, of the object in the unconscious. In their view Winnicott's thesis ignored the libidinal tie between mother and infant that protected the former against the latter's destructiveness. Fine also observed that his thesis was a move away from previous work where Winnicott emphasized this tie (Fine 1968).[21]

Winnicott's reasons for choosing the New York Psychoanalytic Society as the venue for presenting this important paper are unclear, although previous visits to the United States had also provided him with the occasion to deliver significant papers (see note 14). The contention that the discussants' comprehension of Winnicott's thesis was compromised by their 'classical' orientation is arguable (Baudry 2009: 1061). As I have sought to show in this paper and elsewhere, there are striking affinities between Winnicott's thinking and that of American 'classical' analysts which he himself acknowledged (Thompson 2008). Winnicott went to great lengths to locate his thesis within a maturational matrix of infantile development associated with the developmental thinking of these analysts.

> This capacity cannot be said to be inborn, nor can its development in an individual be taken for granted. The development of a capacity to use an object is another example of the maturational process as something that depends on a facilitating environment.
>
> (Winnicott 1968: 89)

Winnicott further reinforced this link with American analysis in the footnote that accompanied this sentence where he acknowledged that Greenacre's 1960 Edinburgh paper influenced his decision to title his book *Maturational Processes and the Facilitating Environment* (Winnicott 1965).

After giving the paper, Winnicott fell seriously ill during the night and was hospitalized. His wry and poignant reactions to the evening and his illness are described in two letters written, in a very shaky hand, to Lawrence Kubie. The first is dated 29 November 1968.

> Dear Lawrence Kubie, I saw you at the Tuesday . . . P-A Soc meeting but did not have the chance to greet you. I hope you are well. It happened that I was already ill that evening, and that night had acute pulmonary oedema. Both Clare and I had got a terrible Asian flu virus, and she was already very ill in bed in the hotel. All this spoilt the evening for me. ? did get some help from the discussion. I can now formulate my idea better on <u>use</u> of object in infancy and in transference. So I got taken to the cardiac care unit because I've had 2 or 3 coronaries, so I am still in Lennox Hill Hospital. My one aim is to get out well or ill. I have had every care and attention as you would expect, but it feels trapped to be in a hospital in another country. I am in the hands of Dr. Rosenblatt, who give me confidence in myself which must needs remain the

central factor, until one dies. One day, let me know if you see any value in this exploration of the word use– you have probably written on this theme somewhere. I had a visit both from Phyllis Greenacre (bless her!) and Milton Malev, chair of the Program Committee [who had invited Winnicott to give a paper]. Fortunately I have the continuous calm support of my wife Clare who has now nearly recovered from her own Asian flu visit which made her very ill indeed. Well – much ado about nearly meeting! Good wishes, Yours Donald W. Winnicott

(Kubie Papers 1968)

Kubie had written to Winnicott two days earlier, on 27 November, to say how sorry he was about Winnicott's illness which he had just learnt of from a colleague, and asked Winnicott to let him know how he was doing. Winnicott wrote again on 4 December to say that he was on the mend, and now knew it was not Kubie he had seen the evening of his paper.

I've have had visits from all the GREAT and I can't really believe it.[22] I'm not sure yet about this Soc meeting on 'The Use of an Object', but some tell me that it was OK. Certainly I got something from it, although I was already ill, and living on my enthusiasm. Well it was very good to get your letter, good wishes, Donald W. Winnicott

(Kubie Papers 1968)

Conclusions

Winnicott's intellectual relationship with American analysts was wide-ranging and complex. Some key aspects have been described above, although this is not a comprehensive account. Throughout the late 1940s, 1950s and 1960s his writings and reviews show familiarity with the work of many American colleagues beyond those I have discussed in this paper. These include Virginia Axline, Berta Bornstein, Erik Erikson, Margaret Mahler, Elizabeth Zetzel, and Margaret Ribble. Winnicott's relations with these many individuals and his ways of absorbing, presenting, and describing what he drew from them and their influences on him were anything but straightforward. He offered a whimsical description of his mind and his way of working when he wrote:

I shall not give an historical survey and show the development of my ideas from the theories of others . . . what happens is that I gather this and that, here and there, settle down to clinical experience, form my own theories and then, last of all, interest myself in looking to see where I stole what.

(Winnicott 1945: 145)

This is highly disingenuous. In fact, Winnicott was a serious reader and listener, deeply engaged with the ideas of colleagues. He respected their work and ideas and also had a compelling need to communicate with and be heard by them. Given this, it is poignant that his relationship with American analysts should end with his serious illness following his presentation of 'The Use of an Object', accompanied by a palpable sense of disappointment that his ideas had not been understood.

Famously, Winnicott's language was not that of his colleagues. He insisted on using his own language. His poetic, vernacular abstractions, such as the 'good enough mother' and 'transitional object', powerfully convey the importance of object relations in human development and health. They were also immeasurably enriched by his linking of them to accounts of the ego's origins, nature, functions, and defences found in the writings of Hartmann, Kris, and Greenacre. As I have shown, Winnicott drew heavily on their theoretical and clinical work to strengthen his own positions and arguments. He recognized that their writings delineating the infantile origins and development of the ego, the self, and object relationships, and their associated clinical work, supported and enriched the thinking which he expressed in terms of the 'good enough mother' and the 'transitional object.' In a letter to Greenacre Winnicott also expressed the pleasure he found in encountering his thinking in the work of others:

I have read [your paper] and enjoyed the experiencing the sort of things which I am trying to think out my way in your terms and language . . . I always feel I learn something from reading your way of expressing things.

(Winnicott quoted in Thompson 2008: 271)

In these ways, Winnicott's theory of object relations was influenced by the writings of American psychoanalysts on the origins and developmental vicissitudes of the ego and object relations. Although this conclusion is at some points inferential, it seems well founded. It rests partly on a reconstruction of meetings and papers where ideas and clinical findings were discussed, and partly on the demonstration that in some of his papers he assimilated their thinking on the ego's defensive functions and its role in precipitating change in the psycho-analytic setting.

Winnicott had a driving need to communicate and be heard. This is attested to by his correspondence, his prolific output of papers and his talks before a wide and diverse range of audiences. It was vitally important to him that he participate in and contribute to the debate among analysts on the nature and vicissitudes of infancy and devel-opment, the consequences of an adaptive failure for the self, and the nature of the transference and treatment in the psychoanalytic setting. He pursued this need with his American as well as his British col-leagues, even though the latter channel is more widely recognized. Winnicott, Hartmann, Kris, and Greenacre were all gifted psycho-analysts with distinctive voices whose clinical and theoretical ideas were expressed in different vocabularies. Winnicott's writings serve as a much-needed and indeed striking reminder that creative ana-lysts are especially responsive to the discovery of themselves and their thoughts in the language of others.

Notes

1 This paper is based on a lecture given to the Squiggle Foundation, London June 13th, 2009.
2 Winnicott and Greenacre were invited to present papers on 'The theory of the parent-infant relationship' for a plenary session of the 1961 Edinburgh Congress. Their papers were published prior to the Congress (Winnicott 1960; Greenacre 1960). Anna Freud's discussion, contributions from the audience, and the authors' responses were also published (Winnicott 1962a; Greenacre 1962).
3 See, however, Fromm 1989.
4 For a sketch of Rapaport's life and work, see Gill 1967.
5 The itinerary of Rapaport's trip to Europe indicates that he and Winnicott met again in October in Paris at a party given in Rapaport's honour by Daniel Lagache. Also present were Jeanne Lampl-de Groot and Hedwig Hoffer because they and Winnicott were in Paris, having been appointed by Heinz Hartmann, President of the IPA, to investigate and write a report on the split in the Société Psychanalytique de Paris caused by the resignations of Jacques Lacan and Daniel Lagache. Phyllis Greenacre, although not

present in Paris, was also a member of this committee (Unpublished Papers of David Rapaport, Library of Congress).

6 Rapaport's paper 'Present-day Ego Psychology' (1956) contains wordings very similar to those found in his 1953 outline.

7 He continues: 'I am trying to find out why it is that I am so deeply suspicious of these terms. Is it because they can give the appearance of a common understanding when such understanding does not exist? Or is it because of something in myself? It can, of course, be both.'

8 In notes on the false self and the true self, probably written in the early 1950s, Winnicott comments that these terms are used to describe a defensive organization in which the infant adapts to an environmental failure. Without identifying them, he notes that other writers have used the term observing ego to describe what he is describing. (This term is found in the writings of Fenichel (1938), Fairbairn (1944), and Kris (1950b).)

9 Among members of the British Society who also attended the lecture were E. Jones, E. Glover, P. Heiman, J. Strachey, S. Payne, J. Riviere, M. Klein, M. Brierley, E. Sharpe, and J. Rickman (Minutes, Scientific Meeting, British Psychoanalytical Society). After leaving Vienna Ernst and Marianne Kris were members of the British Society during the years 1938–43, although they left London in the fall of 1940 for the United States. The nature and extent of Winnicott's personal contact with Kris during these years is unknown.

10 Winnicott's 'Ego Integration in Child Development' (1965) offers a similar account of the ego.

11 Winnicott wrote to her about the symposium in November of 1955, noting that while he thought many important things had been said, a more definite statement about the emotional state of the mother at the very beginning of the infant's existence was needed. He wanted to write a short paper about this and asked if she would respond. She replied that she looked forward very much to receiving the paper: 'and further I should like to do it in the way which appeals most to you, that is to supply you either with an audience of one (me) or an audience of 10 or 12, or 3 or 4. There will be no difficulty in arranging for it.' (A. Freud, November, 1955).

12 In Kris's clinical example he observes that when all seemed to click and material came flowing, the mood of the patient, the atmosphere in the room was heavy. The transference was a negative one, as if even 'spontaneously' offered productions had ultimately been forced out of him (Kris 1956b).

13 A letter written by Martin James to Kris indicates that Winnicott commented on the latter's paper. James wrote: 'What seemed especially timely is the combination of your very broad and scientific approach with the close observation of actual clinical examples . . . These seem to me to parallel the clinically and observationally grounded comments of Dr. Winnicott . . .' Whether James's notes on these comments survive is unknown at present. (Unpublished, Martin James to Ernst Kris, 1956, Ernst Kris Papers, Library of Congress.)

14 On his first trip to the United States in October of 1962 he gave papers in San Francisco (On Communicating and Not Communicating), Los Angeles (A Personal View of the Kleinian Contribution), at the Menninger Clinic in Topeka, Kansas (The Development of the Capacity for Concern), and Boston (Dependence in Infant-Care, Child-Care and the Psychoanalytic Setting). He returned the following October and presented lectures in Atlanta (From Dependence towards Independence in the Development of the Individual), Philadelphia (Psychiatric Disorder in Terms of Infantile Maturational Processes), and Boston (Hospital Care in Supplementing Intensive Psychotherapy in Adolescence). He returned to Boston in 1967 where he gave a paper at McLean Hospital (The Concept of Clinical Regression Compared with that of Defence Organisation). The occasion for his last trip in 1968 was to present his paper The Use of an Object at the New York Psychoanalytic Society.

15 See for example, Grolnick and Barkin 1978; Modell 1985; Fromm and Smith 1989; Fogel 1992; Posner et al. 2001.

16 Sibylle Escalona, born in Berlin, Germany, came to the United States in 1935 with Kurt Lewin, who was a close friend of her family. She spent eight years doing research and clinical work with infants and young children at the Menninger Foundation where David Rapaport was the Director of Research, a position Escalona eventually assumed. In 1951 she accepted a research position at the Yale Child Study Center, and then in 1956 she moved to the Albert Einstein College of Medicine in New York. In a 1982 interview she recounted (Escalona 1983) the breadth of infant research in the 1940s and 1950s, and described in detail the research that culminated in two books: *Prediction and Outcome* (1959, with Heider) and *The Roots of Individuality* (1968).

17 Kubie and Winnicott first met in 1937 when Winnicott and his first wife, Alice, were sailing on Malcolm Forbes's yacht off Cape Cod. Twenty years later, in 1957, Kubie wrote to say he was coming to London to give a paper to the Royal Society and hoped they could meet. This meeting did not take place because Kubie cancelled his trip due to the death of his son-in-law. In 1963 Winnicott stayed with Kubie during a visit to Baltimore and the latter later sent him a copy of his book, *Neurotic Distortion in the Creative Process* (1958). In response Winnicott wrote and asked him for two more copies as he wanted to donate them to the library that belonged to a university extension course (The Visual Image) connected with London University (Kubie Papers 1966).

18 Unfortunately no record of this meeting survives. There was, however, a correspondence with Winnicott requesting reprints of his paper 'Pediatrics and Psychiatry' which he sent to the group with a request that they be returned after the meeting.

19 Handwritten notations on the letter indicate that copies were sent to Drs. Malev, Jacobson, Ritvo, Fine, and Milrod.

20 Baudry mentions these papers without listing them (2009: 1067). Abram (Chapter 13 of this volume) also offers a discussion of these papers as antecedents to the paper 'The Use of the Object'.

21 In notes dated 5 December 1968 Winnicott responded to Fine's comment by noting that: 'We go on teaching about libidinal stages and erotogenic zones because of the truth of this part of our theory. Also we teach that in health there comes about a *fusion* of libidinal and aggressive drives (though here we can get into trouble because at the start aggressive drives are associated with muscle erotism and not with anger or hate).' In Winnicott's view he is trying to make a contribution related to the phase prior to fusion (Winnicott 1968e).

22 Among those who visited Winnicott were Heinz and Dora Hartmann, Elizabeth Zetzel and her husband, and Bernard Fine and his wife.

References

Abram, J. (2007) *The Language of Winnicott: A Dictionary of Winnicott's Use of words*. 2nd Ed. London: Karnac Books.

Abram, J. (2008) 'Donald Woods Winnicott (1896–1971): A Brief Introduction', *International Journal of Psychoanalysis* 89: 1189–1217.

Baudry, F. (2009) 'Winnicott's 1968 Visit to the New York Psychoanalytic Society and Institute: A Contextual View', *Psychoanalytic Quarterly* LXX-VIII: 1059–1090.

Escalona, S. (1952) 'Emotional Development in the First Year of Life', *Problems of Infancy and Childhood. Transactions of the Sixth Conference, March 17–18, 1952*, New York, Josiah Macy Jr. Foundation.

Escalona, S. (1968) *The Roots of Individuality: Normal Patterns of Development in Infancy*. Chicago: Aldine Publishing Company.

Escalona, S. (1983) 'The Reminiscences of Sibylle Escalona', Oral History Interviews April 1st and 15th, 1982. Infant Development Project, Columbia Oral History Office, Columbia University, New York.

Escalona, S. and Heider, G.M. (1959) *Prediction and Outcome: A Study of Child Development*. New York: Basic Books.

Fairbairn, W.R.D. (1944) 'Endopsychic Structure Considered in Terms of Object-Relationships', *International Journal of Psychoanalysis* 25: 70–93.

Fenichel, O. (1938) 'Ego-Disturbances and their Treatment.' *International Journal of Psychoanalysis* 19: 416–38.

Fine, B. (1968) Discussion 'The Use of an Object.' Archives, A.A. Brill Library, New York Psychoanalytic Society and Institute.

Fogel, Gerald L. (1992) 'Winnicott's Antitheory and Winnicott's Art: His Significance for Adult Analysis', in *Psychoanalytic Study of the Child* 47: 205–222.

Freud, A. (1955) Unpublished. The Papers of Anna Freud, Library of Congress, Manuscript Division, Washington, DC.

Fromm, M. Gerard (1989) 'Winnicott's Work in Relation to Classical Psychoanalysis and Ego Psychology', in *The Facilitating Environment: Clinical Applications of Winnicott's Theory*. Eds. M. Gerard Fromm and Bruce L. Smith. Madison, CT: IUP.

Fromm, M. Gerard and Smith, Bruce L. (Eds.) (1989) *The Facilitating Environment: Clinical Applications of Winnicott's Theory*. Madison, CT: IUP.

Gill, Merton M. (Ed.) (1967) 'In Memoriam – David Rapaport, 1911–1960' *The Collected Papers of David Rapaport*. New York: Basic Books.

Goldman, D. (1998) 'Surviving as Scientist and Dreamer: Winnicott and The Use of an Object', *Contemporary Psychoanalysis* 34: 359–367.

Greenacre, P. (1941a) 'The Predisposition to Anxiety', *The Psychoanalytic Quarterly* 10: 66–96.

Greenacre, P. (1941b) 'The Predisposition to Anxiety', *The Psychoanalytic Quarterly* 10: 610–637.

Greenacre, P. (1945) 'The Biological Economy of Birth', *Psychoanalytic Study of the Child* 1: 31–51.

Greenacre, P. (1954) 'The Role of Transference', *Journal of the American Psychoanalytic Association* 2: 671–684.

Greenacre, P. (1956) 'Re-evaluation of the Process of Working Through', *International Journal of Psychoanalysis* 37: 439–444.

Greenacre, P. (1960) 'Considerations Regarding the Parent-Infant Relationship', *International Journal of Psychoanalysis* 41: 571–584.

Greenacre, P. (1962) 'The Theory of the Parent-Infant Relationship; Further Remarks', *International Journal of Psychoanalysis* 43: 235–237.

Grolnick, S. and Barkin, L. (Eds.) (1978) *Between Reality and Fantasy: Transitional Objects and Phenomena*. New York and London: Jason Aronson.

Hartmann, H. (1939 [1958]) *Ego Psychology and the Problem of Adaptation*. Trans. David Rapaport 1958. Madison, CT: International Universities Press.

Hartmann, H. (1956) 'The Development of the Ego Concept in Freud's Work', *International Journal of Psychoanalysis* 37: 425–437.

Hartmann, H. (1965) Unpublished. The Papers of Heinz Hartman, Library of Congress, Manuscript Division, Washington, DC.

James, M. (1956) Letter to Ernst Kris. Papers of Ernst Kris, Manuscript Division, Library of Congress, Washington, DC.

Klein, M. (1957) *Envy and Gratitude*. London: Tavistock.

Kris, E. (1936) 'The Psychology of Caricature', *International Journal of Psychoanalysis* 17: 285–303.

Kris, E. (1938) 'Ego Development and the Comic', *International Journal of Psychoanalysis* 19: 77–90.

Kris, E. (1949) Unpublished. The Papers of Ernst Kris. Library of Congress, Washington, DC.

Kris, E. (1950a) 'The Significance of Freud's Earliest Discoveries', *International Journal of Psychoanalysis* 31: 108–116.

Kris, E. (1950b) 'On Preconscious Mental Processes', *Psychoanalytic Quarterly* 19: 540–560.

Kris, E. (1951a) 'Some Comments and Observations on Early Autoerotic Activities', *Psychoanalytic Study of the Child* 6: 95–116.

Kris, E. (1951b) 'Opening Remarks on Psychoanalytic Child Psychology', *Psychoanalytic Study of the Child* 6: 9–17.

Kris, E. (1952) *Psychoanalytic Explorations in Art.* New York: International Universities Press.

Kris, E. (1954) 'Problems of Infantile Neurosis: A Discussion', *Psychoanalytic Study of the Child* 9: 16–71.

Kris, E. (1956a) 'The Personal Myth: A Problem in Psychoanalytic Technique', *Journal of the American Psychoanalytic Association* 4: 653–681.

Kris, E. (1956b) 'On Some Vicissitudes of Insight in Psychoanalysis', *International Journal of Psychoanalysis* 37: 445–455.

Kris, E. (1956c) 'The Recovery of Childhood Memories in Psychoanalysis', *Psychoanalytic Study of the Child* 11: 54–88.

Kubie, L. (1955) 'Say You're Sorry', *Psychoanalytic Study of the Child* 10: 289–299.

Kubie, L. (1958) *Neurotic Distortion in the Creative Process.* Lawrence: University of Kansas Press.

Kubie, L. (1968 Unpublished) The Papers of Lawrence Kubie, Library of Congress, Manuscript Division, Washington, DC.

Meyer, E. (1958 Unpublished) Papers of D.W. Winnicott. Oskar Diethelm Library, Weill Cornell Medical College, New York.

Modell, A. (1985) 'The Works of Winnicott and the Evolution of His Thought', *Journal of the American Association: Supplement* 13: 113–137.

Orr, D. (1954) 'Transference and Countertransference: A Historical Survey', *Journal of the American Psychoanalytic Association* 2: 621–684.

Posner, B. Melmed, Glickman, R.W., Taylor, E.C., Canfield, J., and Cyr, F. (2001) 'In Search of Winnicott's Aggression', *Psychoanalytic Study of the Child* 56: 171–190.

Rapaport, D. (1953–54 Unpublished) The Papers of David Rapaport. Library of Congress, Manuscript Division, Washington, DC.

Rapaport, D. (1956) 'Present-Day Ego Psychology', in *The Collected Papers of David Rapaport.* Ed. Merton M. Gill. New York: Basic Books.

Reeves, C. (2007) 'The Mantle of Freud: Was 'The Use of an Object' Winnicott's *Todestrieb?*', *British Journal of Psychotherapy* 23: 365–382.

Rodman, R. (1987) *The Spontaneous Gesture: Selected Letters of D.W. Winnicott.* Cambridge, MA: Harvard University Press.

Rodman, R. (2003) *Winnicott: Life and Work.* Cambridge, MA: Perseus Books.

Samuels, L. (1996) 'A Historical Analysis of Winnicott's The Use of an Object', *Winnicott Studies* 11: 41–50.

Samuels, L. (2001) 'The Paradox of Destruction and Survival in D.W. Winnicott's The Use of the Object', *Fort Da* 7: 38–53.

Spock, B. (1963) 'Observations on the Striving for Autonomy and Some Regressive Object Relationships after Six Months of Age', *Psychoanalytic Study of the Child*, 18: 361–364.

Thompson, N. (2008) 'A Measure of Agreement: An Exploration of the Relationship of D.W. Winnicott and Phyllis Greenacre', *Psychoanalytic Quarterly* LXXVII: 251–281.

Willoughby, R. (2005) *Masud Khan: the Myth and the Reality*. London: Free Association Books.

Winnicott, D.W. (1945) 'Primitive Emotional Development', *International Journal of Psychoanalysis* 26: 137–143.

Winnicott, D.W. (1948) Review *The Psychoanalytic Study of the Child* 2. *British Medical Journal* August 21, 1948: 389.

Winnicott, D.W. (1949a) Letter to Phyllis Greenacre. Papers of D.W. Winnicott. Wellcome Collection, London.

Winnicott, D.W. (1949b) 'Birth Memories, Birth Trauma, and Anxiety', *Collected Papers: Through Paediatrics to Psycho-Analysis*. New York: Basic Books, 1958, pp.174–193.

Winnicott, D.W. (1949c) Review *Problems of Early Infancy. Transactions of the Second Conference, March 1–2, 1948*. New York: Josiah Macy, Jr. Foundation. 1949, *British Journal of Medical Psychology* 22: 217.

Winnicott, D.W. (1951a) Review *Problems of Infancy and Childhood. Transactions of the Third Conference, March 7–8, 1949*. New York: Josiah Macy, Jr. Foundation. 1949, *British Journal of Medical Psychology* 24: 145.

Winnicott, D.W. (1951b) Review *The Psychoanalytic Study of the Child* 3/4. *British Medical Journal* 13 October 1951: 894.

Winnicott, D.W. (1953a) 'Transitional Objects and Transitional Phenomena', *International Journal of Psychoanalysis* 34: 89–97.

Winnicott, D.W. (1953b) Review *Problems of Infancy and Childhood. Transactions of the Sixth Conference, March 17 and 18, 1952*. New York: Josiah Macy Jr. Foundation. 1953, *British Medical Journal* September 19, 1953: 664.

Winnicott, D.W. (1955) 'Metapsychological and Clinical Aspects of Regression within the Psycho-analytical Set-up', *International Journal of Psychoanalysis* 36: 16–26.

Winnicott, D.W. (1956) 'On Transference' *International Journal of Psychoanalysis* 37: 386–388.

Winnicott, D.W. (1958a) Review *The Psychoanalytic Study of the Child* 11. *British Medical Journal* 22 March 1958: 692.

Winnicott, D.W. (1958b) Review *The Psychoanalytic Study of the Child* 12. *British Medical Journal* 4 October 1958: 838.

Winnicott, D.W. (1958c) 'The Capacity to Be Alone', *International Journal of Psychoanalysis* 39: 416–420.

Winnicott, D.W. (1958d) 'Primary Maternal Preoccupation.' *Collected Papers: Through Paediatrics to Psycho-Analysis*. New York: Basic Books, 1958: 300–305.

Winnicott, D.W. (1960) 'The Theory of the Parent-Infant Relationship', *International Journal of Psychoanalysis* 41: 585–595.

Winnicott, D.W. (1962a) 'The Theory of the Parent-Infant Relationship – Further Remarks' *International Journal of Psychoanalysis* 43: 238–239.

Winnicott, D.W. (1962b) Review *The Psychoanalytic Study of the Child* 15. *British Medical Journal* 3 February 1962: 305.

Winnicott, D.W. (1963) Review *The Psychoanalytic Study of the Child* 16. *British Medical Journal* 26 January 1963: 253.

Winnicott, D.W. (1965) 'Ego Integration in Child Development', in *The Maturational Processes and the Facilitating Environment*. New York: IUP.

Winnicott, D.W. (1965) 'Clinical Study of the Effect of a Failure of the Average Expectable Environment on a Child's Mental Functioning', *International Journal of Psychoanalysis* 46: 81.

Winnicott, D.W. (1966) Review *The Psychoanalytic Study of the Child* 20. *British Medical Journal* 17 December 1966: 1510–11.

Winnicott, D.W. (1967a) 'The Location of Cultural Experience', *International Journal of Psychoanalysis* 48: 368–372.

Winnicott, D.W. (1967b) 'Postscript: D.W.W. on D.W.W.', in *Psychoanalytic Explorations*. Eds. C. Winnicott, R. Shepherd, and M. Davis. Cambridge, MA: Harvard University Press, 1989: 569–582.

Winnicott, D.W. (1968a) Review *The Psychoanalytic Study of the Child* 22. *New Society* 16: 5.

Winnicott, D.W. (1968b) 'Playing: Its Theoretical Status in the Clinical Situation', *International Journal of Psychoanalysis* 49: 591–599.

Winnicott, D.W. (1968c) 'Summary', Archives, A.A. Brill Library, New York Psychoanalytic Society and Institute.

Winnicott, D.W. (1968d) 'Clinical Illustration of The Use of an Object', in *Psychoanalytic Explorations*. Eds. C. Winnicott, R. Shepherd, and M. Davis. Cambridge, MA: Harvard University Press, 1989: 235–238.

Winnicott, D.W. (1968e) 'Comments on My Paper The Use of an Object', in *Psychoanalytic Explorations*. Eds. C. Winnicott, R. Shepherd, and M. Davis. Cambridge, MA: Harvard University Press, 1989: 238–240.

Winnicott, D.W. (1969) 'The Use of an Object', *International Journal of Psychoanalysis*, 50: 711–716.

Zetzel, E. (1956) 'Current Concepts of Transference', *International Journal of Psychoanalysis* 37: 369–375.

Squiggle evidence

The child, the canvas, and the 'negative labour' of history

Lisa Farley

This chapter reads D. W. Winnicott's 'squiggle game' as evidence that unearths the negative labor of witnessing that lies at the heart of the analytic situation, offering a glimpse into the processes by which unremembered events become psychologically significant. Two kinds of data are explored: the first is a set of drawings that Winnicott slipped into his notebook during World War II; the second is a published series of images created two decades later in a therapeutic consultation with a patient named Eliza. Both sets of evidence remind us of the impossibility of witnessing historical rupture, even as they also document 'creative struggles' to engage this impossibility through visual representation. It is argued that Winnicott's wartime work set the stage for his later formulation of the squiggle game, and an analysis of this relation sheds light on the significance of the visual realm as a site of memory.

'This game that I like playing has no rules' (Winnicott 1968: 301–302). The game would later be described as D. W. Winnicott's 'most famous technical invention' (Phillips 1988: 15). Winnicott himself gave it a more humble name: 'the squiggle game' (1968: 302). In this game with no rules, the analyst would sketch a rudimentary doodle onto a torn sheet of paper and then hand it over to his young patient with an invitation to 'make it into anything.' Then the roles were reversed and it was the child's turn to make a doodle to hand over to Winnicott for elaboration. All the way along, Winnicott invited his patients to talk about the meaning of these constructions. The purpose of this game, in Winnicott's words, was to allow for the child's 'communication of significance' of early life relationships captured in visual form (Winnicott 1968: 302). Because this was a game with 'no rules,' the history scripted onto its pages does not return us to an untrammeled origin. Quite the opposite: the squiggle etches onto the historical record forces over which a child has no direct memory and which take a detour through the unconscious on the way to becoming significant. While Winnicott's game is most often read for its practical significance (Günter 2007), here I read the squiggle as evidence of some of the paradoxes of representing and attending histories that at the same time elude our conscious efforts to recall them to memory.

Sigmund Freud had something similar in mind when he mused about dreams as documents of the unconscious past. 'Dreams produce memories,' Freud supposed, 'that the dreamer has forgotten, which would be inaccessible to him while awake' (1940: 21). Not unlike the squiggle, dreaming is, in Freud's view, a form of remembering events of which there is no conscious memory. Even more, the dream is a peculiar form of evidence insofar as its images portray not a factual account, but a jumble of wishes that accompany real and imagined events. With this claim alone, it is perhaps no wonder that the relation between psychoanalysis and the field of history is somewhat uneasy: after all, Freud's attention to the internal events of the psychical past have little to do with the material, social and political realities that concern the historian. Whereas history draws its data from concrete events and takes consciousness as the rule, psychoanalysis attends to the chaotic, irrational and libidinal drives that organize subjectivity. And while history does seek to narrate the goals and desires of its subject, it does not begin with the psychoanalytic principle of the unconscious, which seeks to describe the unknown recesses of the mind. In this sense, psychoanalysis may be said to represent the unconscious of history, and dreams a trace of this underside.

Despite this uneasy relation, Robert Jay Lifton (1974) suggests that psychoanalysis nonetheless shapes in important ways how we understand the work of writing history. He considers what happens to the dialogue between the fields of history and psychoanalysis when we let go of, and work against, the idea of 'psychoanalyzing' people of the past – a concept crucial to 1970s critiques (see also Gay 1985). Rather than apply psychoanalysis to history, Lifton begins with an assumption that works the other way around: while we cannot explain history solely in terms of psychology, the histories we undergo do have psychical effects. For Lifton, psychoanalysis offers a key lens through which to consider the ways 'particular experiences people have undergone' affect the psyche, and in turn, how the psyche affects what gets recorded as history (1974: 31). Lifton's use of psychoanalysis emerges from his work with the testimony of survivors of historical trauma – the Holocaust, Hiroshima and Vietnam. In each of these contexts, Lifton is interested in the psychical conflicts history leaves behind, together with the 'creative struggles' (1974: 31) survivors use to 'act upon and affect' the very events they have already undergone (ibid: 33). Psychoanalysis is here an interpretative frame that looks to silences, repetitions and symptoms – what Lifton calls 'shared psychohistorical themes' – as evocative memories that bypass conscious awareness (ibid: 36). The memory work at stake here is, of course, more than a recollection of what happened. It also entails the 'creative struggle' to transform the rawness of history's repeated irruptions into the symbolic realm, needed to make meaning of absence. Psychoanalytically, history is creative.

It might therefore be no coincidence that Deborah Britzman links history's 'working through' with the work of the artist: 'Artists,' she writes, 'cultivate aesthetic distance, even discordance, between the raw events that become experience and its afterlife in symbolization; they make from the ruins of what feels utterly wrecked a new beginning' (Britzman 2009: 104). While the question of whether children can be artists must be held open, I think Winnicott's squiggle game may be read as an invitation to 'cultivate aesthetic distance' and so as fertile ground for the mind's 'creative struggles' to transform the force of 'raw events' into the symbolic realm of representation. And yet, this story of 'struggle' is not simply a royal road back in time that settles a truth of the past; rather, the term 'creative struggle' is meant to denote encountering history itself as always already a conflict between internal and external reality, and of narrating this uncertain relation. There are two aspects to my argument that engage precisely this struggle. On the one hand, I investigate the unconscious as a visual site of memory and consider why it matters that Winnicott turned to drawing as a means to symbolize a relation to this internal realm: what André Green (1999) later described as 'negative labour' and Christopher Bollas (1987) as 'the unthought known.' On the other hand, I read the squiggle as an effect of an external context in which Winnicott became increasingly convinced of the child's need for a witness to the affective force of experiences that defied literal or immediate representation. Significant here is the historical detail that Winnicott began to gather children's drawings during World War II, a context that I believe shaped his later formulation of the squiggle game and his attention to the impossibility of witnessing as the grounds of analytic interpretation.

My approach in this chapter is rather like a squiggle in itself: a give and take between Winnicott's unique flair and his Freudian inheritance, between the visual and the verbal, between experience and representation, and between the historical and the theoretical, in an attempt to animate lines of communication between them, and with awareness of how contingent and playful these connections must always be. In the vein of Winnicott's game 'without rules,' then, I find myself wondering: How might the squiggle illustrate a visual quality of unconscious memory? In what ways might this game record the 'creative struggles' we use both to 'act upon and affect' events already undergone? What kind of history is a squiggle? In the following pages, these questions are explored through a single case of a young girl named Eliza, but first, I turn to consider Winnicott's concept of the 'subjective object' of history, which he built out of his reflections on the collaborative part he played in the context of this game. As we will see, Winnicott's theory of the subjective object mirrors contemporary discussions of trauma that posit witnessing as an attentiveness to what cannot be said, to the 'impossible saying' of testimony (Caruth 1995: 10). A related plot haunts Winnicott's work with youth during World War II, for it is here that Winnicott began to collect images of a history that was yet to be seen.

The 'subjective object' of history

In the last ten years of his life, Winnicott became increasingly preoccupied with the visual creations produced through his squiggle game. Looking back across almost a decade of sessions, the analyst reflected on how he was being used by children in this context:

> In language which I use now but which I had no equipment for using at that time I found myself in the role of subjective object. What I now feel is that in this role as subjective object . . . the doctor has a great opportunity for being in touch with a child.
>
> (Winnicott 1971a: 4)

Winnicott ordinarily reserved the term 'subjective object' to describe the earliest role of the mother. This is a position that, under 'good enough' circumstances, involved the mother's capacity to tolerate 'a discrepancy in what is being observed and what is experienced by the baby' (Winnicott 1971b: 130). What the mother observed of the baby – such as a cry or a smile – offered a clue about the baby's insides, never directly reflective of them. The discrepancy to which Winnicott refers posits the impossibility of knowing as the grounds of communication. In this gap of discrepancy, experience is not simply a thing in itself, but something one constructs through interpretation.

Implied here is an analytic shift from 'lifting' repression to 'holding' conflict (which Melanie Klein and later Wilfred Bion and Hanna Segal would describe as 'containment'). Winnicott came to the concept of 'holding' through his clinical work with mothers and infants. It required of the 'good enough' mother the capacity to contain the baby's projections of intolerable aspects of early life experiences, without herself becoming overly rigid (in the presumption to know too soon) or fragile to the point of going to pieces. Winnicott found the return of these infantile projections in the adult patient, which were felt as 'the tendency . . . to disintegrate, to cease to exist, to fall forever' (1963: 241). As 'subjective object,' the analyst's role in this context was to 'hold' projections and to return them to the patient in a form that did not carry the same pitch of anxiety that first constituted them. For the good enough mother, the capacity to 'hold' the baby's projections could create a potential space of communication. For the good enough analyst, it was the grounds of a useful interpretation.

Another way to think about Winnicott's space of discrepancy is through André Green's concept, 'the work of the negative.' While negativity itself refers to the unconscious, the work of the negative refers to the potential to symbolize its guises and effects, a work engendered by the analytic relationship. The 'negative' is a psychical labour, then, when it entails 'holding' in mind unconscious material and tolerating uncertainty as the fragile condition of knowledge. In Green's words, this work confronts one with what 'exist[s] even when the senses can no longer perceive it' (1999: 16). Winnicott's theory of the 'subjective object' may well foreshadow Green's negative labour, as well as cast the work as primarily maternal. The mother, as 'subjective object,' is the baby's first witness, and in that capacity she is called on to engage the negative labour of attending to experiences that cannot be known or seen directly, even as their unconscious force requires a response. Thus while at first glance Winnicott's attention to the 'discrepancy' between experience and representation conjures up notions of error, lack and miscommunication, it also designates a particular quality of communication that regards absence as heavy with potential meaning.

It is precisely this impossibility of witnessing, then, that is the condition for communication. This may be why Winnicott described the 'subjective object' in terms of another impossibility, or paradox:

> What I have called the 'subjective object' becomes gradually related to objects that are objectively perceived, but this happens only when a good enough environmental provision or 'average expectable environment' . . . enables the baby to be mad in one particular way that is conceded to babies. This madness only becomes true madness if it appears in later life. At the stage of infancy it is the same subject as that to which I referred when I talked about the acceptance of the paradox, as when a baby creates an object but the object would not have been created as such if it had not already been there.
>
> (Winnicott 1971c: 16)

Winnicott's statement here reaches into debates over how to interpret mental illness, on the one hand, as something to be cured or controlled and, on the other hand, as a kernel of negativity we all share (Phillips 2005). But he is also trying again to articulate the position of 'subjective object,' which, in this formulation, requires the mother's acceptance of a paradox: the baby creates the world that is already there. The mother, as baby's subjective object, accepts this early paradox as 'real.' There is another layer of paradox to consider here: the mother's acceptance of the baby's fantasy projections as 'real' is needed for the baby to enter into a reality of representation outside of those projections ('objects that are objectively perceived'). For Winnicott, this paradox is not the opposite of reality, but the condition needed to enter into it.

It is through the idea of the 'subjective object' that Winnicott would redefine the common medical practice of 'history taking' during his therapeutic consultations with children. More than a straightforward collection of facts, 'history taking' was, for Winnicott, a negative labour of archiving projections that were not yet thinkable, not yet known. 'History taking,' writes Winnicott, 'does not mean the collecting of facts; it means that the psychiatrist makes contact with the child in such a way that the process in the child leads the psychiatrist toward a significant area of distress' (1971a: 125). The analyst's 'distress' returns us to the condition and crisis of witnessing: it is made from a willingness to attend as significant 'the process in the child' without the consolation that one's observations directly correspond to inner experience. Put another way, history taking depended for Winnicott on the capacity of a witness who could tolerate the absences, displacements and deferrals of meaning that exceed what the 'facts' can tell. Through the lens of the 'subjective object,' the notion of witnessing is thus less about gaining access to an immediacy of the past (as in the eyewitness), and more about encountering the negativity of representation as offering important clues about what matters in what cannot be remembered.

As Winnicott wrote the case studies that were later compiled in *Therapeutic Consultations* (published shortly after his death in 1971), he came to understand his analytic position as 'subjective object.' The key point to underscore is this: as 'subjective object,' witnessing was for Winnicott a paradoxical event. It depended on the capacity to attend to experiences that had not, for all intents and purposes, happened insofar as they reside outside the realm of conscious understanding. Even more, Winnicott came to view the visual realm as a potent site in which to engender the work of the negative, a site that plunged him into the anxious – 'distressing' – conditions of witnessing itself. Despite his late formulation of the subjective object, it matters that Winnicott began to gather samples of visual testimony in a much earlier context of war, for it was in this context that he and his young patients sketched into existence experiences of breakdown and terror that scribbled over the smooth lines of representation.

Wartime images

During World War II, Winnicott oversaw the placement of approximately 285 youth who had been separated from their families in anticipation of German air raids.[1] In this ominous context, Winnicott had become anxious about the effects of a child's premature separation from home.[2] With two other psychiatrists, John Bowlby and Emanuel Miller, Winnicott penned a letter to the *British Medical Journal* on December 16, 1939. All three psychiatrists were sure that forced separation would cause an 'emotional black-out' that they believed could manifest later in a 'psychohistorical theme' (to return to Lifton's language) (1974: 36), which, at the time was called 'juvenile delinquency' (Bowlby, Miller and Winnicott 1939: 14). Winnicott saw it as his task – and the task of foster parents – to provide a reliable environment in which evacuated youth could risk a relationship to the fact of separation (and accompanying feelings of absence) that would otherwise be lost to the 'emotional black-out' of repression. In this context, Winnicott increasingly turned his attention to the child's defensive projections of aggression associated with the separation. Adam Phillips notes the effects of the evacuation not only on Winnicott but also on psychoanalysis itself, in the sense that 'the problems of evacuated children in Britain changed psychoanalytic thinking about childhood' (Phillips 1988: 62). The child that emerged in analysis in this time of war was one 'at war' with itself – in Winnicott's terms, 'a field play of destructive forces' – and who thus offered a close-up on the problem of human aggression (Winnicott 1939: 88). But the child also became a figure through which to understand the problem of how to enter into the social world as creatures born of that aggression.

What worried Winnicott was not, then, the bare fact of aggression: ruthlessness was, for him, a condition of being. In a talk for teachers given in 1940, Winnicott works against a wishful image of the child without aggression:

> It is sometimes imagined that children would not think of war if it were not put into their heads. But any one who takes the trouble to find out what goes on beneath the surface of a child's mind can discover for himself that the child already knows about greed, hate, and cruelty, as about love and remorse, and the urge to make good, and about sadness.
>
> (Winnicott 1949: 29–30)

To locate the cause of aggression in the outside world is to deny the child's mind. Winnicott even went so far as to say that the inability to express aggression – such as in an inhibited or compliant child – was a sign of greater difficulties than those experienced by one who could risk expressing feistier impulses. This was because Winnicott believed that there could be neither goodness nor sadness without first encountering an underside: 'greed, hate and cruelty.'

But if the psychoanalytic construction of the child at war with itself is too familiar to be immediately striking, what is significant to point out as well is Winnicott's growing emphasis on the outside environment – a reliable witness – who could acknowledge the child's 'instinctual urges, including aggressive ones' as the grounds for symbolization, imagination and creativity (1940: 89). In 1942 Winnicott brought these two terms together – aggression and symbolization – in a statement about why children play:

> It is commonly said that children 'work off hate and aggression' in play, as if aggression were some bad substance that could be got rid of. This is partly true, because pent-up resentment and the results of angry experience can feel to a child like bad stuff inside himself. But it is more important to state this same thing by saying that the child values finding that hate or aggressive urges can be expressed in a known environment, without the return of hate and violence from the environment to the child.
>
> (Winnicott 1942: 143)

For Winnicott (1939), it was an emotional achievement to tolerate the 'hate that . . . we know exists in the human bosom' without using it in the service of actual destruction (1939: 89).[3] Against the backdrop of war, Winnicott thus distinguished between 'instinctual aggressiveness . . . mobilised in the service of hate' and the destruction that 'is originally part of appetite' (1939: 87). Felt as a formless and at times ruthless state of wanting, appetite was for Winnicott the first glimpse of creativity, provided that the adult did not become overly anxious. In 1942, the precursor of Winnicott's squiggle game – and its theme of playful destruction – was already on the horizon.

Later, in a 1945 radio broadcast addressed to foster parents, Winnicott would elaborate the importance of a 'known environment.' His hope was to encourage caregivers to acknowledge the essential emotional task – and necessary tolls – of responding well to children of the evacuation. Winnicott was here leaning on experience, for we know that he cared for children who had 'reached the end of the line,' who had been bumped from place to place, too difficult to billet, and who finally found themselves on the doorstep of the hostel (C. Winnicott 1984: 2). Much more than providing 'food, clothes, and warmth,' Winnicott headlined this broadcast with the child's need for an adult who could respond well to the emotional fallout of ruptured bonds, such that for Winnicott, and foster parents, 'the real worry about bombs was not all' (1945: 42). The other 'real worry' was the child's reaction to loss and how, in the context of a new home, the foster parent managed to survive periods of distress associated with it. Foreshadowing his later formulation of the 'subjective object,' Winnicott aligned good-enough foster care with the foster parent's capacity to witness the emotional sediments that the separation stirred up – fears of abandonment, rage, loneliness, despair and guilt – and that were conveyed within a range of symptoms both rebellious (i.e. 'stealing in gangs' and 'burning of hay-ricks') and antisocial ('maniacal outbursts,' 'depressive phases' and 'sulky moods') (1947: 56). Reading between the lines of the symptom, the good-enough foster caregiver was able to create a reliable environment – a place of 'holding' – in which the difficult feelings could be 'lived through rather than reacted to' (C. Winnicott 1984: 3). The capacity of the child to integrate primal aggression depended on a witness who could contain, without correction or retaliation, the affective force of experiences seeking expression before they could be consciously understood. The 'real worry' about the evacuation was the child without a witness.

It is in this context that Winnicott began to collect drawings both by hostel youth and that he himself drew after work.[4] Something about drawing, it would seem, brought Winnicott and the youth in his charge nearer to experiences that words could not yet describe. Thus while Winnicott's first published mention of the squiggle game appeared in 1953, and the first full case study not until 1965,[5] there is evidence that Winnicott was drawing with children much earlier. And to this visual testimony, Winnicott was called to witness. Tucked between the pages of his hostel scheme notebook of 1945 are approximately a dozen drawings, etched onto the same square pages that he would later use to make squiggles. Some of these sketches resemble the spontaneous strokes of Winnicott's own hand (Figure 18.1), but all told, they depict a wide range of scenes: a guard in blue uniform (Figure 18.2), a figure of a witch with the barely legible caption, 'early dream' (Figure 18.3), colliding aircraft (Figure 18.4), a blazing hearth, as well as a number of figures in profile, some of which are missing hands.[6]

No significant commentary accompanies the drawings and just two are inscribed with a child's name and the date of its creation. For instance, 'early dream' is dated November 17, 1945, and the blazing hearth, December 14, 1945. Without any commentary, however, it is difficult to speculate about the significance of these visual renderings.

It is also unclear how many of these drawings were produced by children. Despite this ambiguity, the very presence of these square page images in Winnicott's notebook tells us that he was experimenting with visual testimony – and very likely children's visual testimony – as early as 1945. In an entry from March of that year, Winnicott catalogues his rounds with some of the children admitted to one of the family of five Oxfordshire hostels Winnicott oversaw with Clare Britton. One of these notes is a simple instruction to himself to 'see drawings' produced in his interview with a child named George.[7]

Winnicott's notebook from this period, with the stray images tucked between its pages, opens up significant questions about the pediatrician's

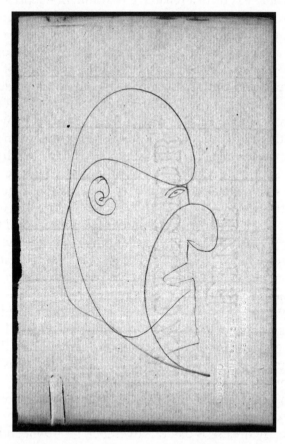

Figure 18.1 Drawing of a head in profile. Courtesy of Wellcome Library, London.

turn to drawing in the creative struggle to represent difficult history. The images pressed within its pages reveal not only a talent for drawing but also a propensity toward visuality as a mode of expression and communication where words might otherwise fall short. They thus give us pause to wonder about the visual quality of memory that Freud had proposed in his theory of dreams. We know already that Freud viewed the dream image as a collection of daily residues that had bypassed the realm of consciousness and were therefore prior to the verbal terms that typically organize historical narration. Much more than records of actual historical events (though they may be this too), for Winnicott, the work of image-making was akin to 'early dreaming' (what he would later call a 'dream screen') where impressions of the past could find expression, before they could be known. In his notebook images, we catch a glimpse of Winnicott's early efforts to document a visible quality of testimony of events that are difficult to know.

Figure 18.2 Crayon drawing of a guard. Courtesy of Wellcome Library, London.

Figure 18.3 Pencil drawing of a witch. Courtesy of Wellcome Library, London.

But these found images may also gesture toward the uncertain work of historical interpretation, which depends on the capacity to think about what is difficult to know with any degree of certainty: a labour of the negative. This uncertain quality of history is not very far away from Jacques Derrida's contemporary discussion of the 'Freudian impression' of the archive: where history is as much about what is intended for the official record as it is about the accidental traces it leaves behind, such as may be the case with these stray images (1996: 68). Sitting alone in the reading room of the Wellcome Library, I found myself wondering whether hostel youth or Winnicott himself had created the collection. I also wondered to what extent their visual cues registered the event of the evacuation.[8] The missing hands of the profile figures, for instance, reminded me of being dropped, or of the difficulty of holding. I wondered, too, about the status of the

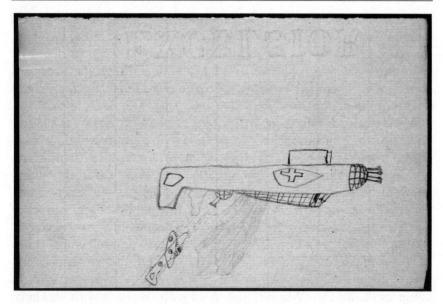

Figure 18.4 Drawing of colliding aircraft. Courtesy of Wellcome Library, London.

drawings as testimony to the Blitz. The larger of the two aircraft in Figure 18.4 bears the cross that marked German bombers of World War II. A closer look finds that the smaller aircraft bears the symbol stamped onto British planes of this era. Indeed, this little image documents air war.[9] Psychoanalytically, however, what this image makes visible is not only a reality of history, but also its collision in the life of the mind.

The point of curiosity is, then, how to read Winnicott's notebook collection as documenting a collision of external and internal realities. Questions swell in this potential space: if the air raids were largely invisible, detectible as flashes of light in clouds, from where did this artist draw his imagery? Is it possible that the safe distance of the hostel brought into clear view a horizon of bombers heading toward London? How might this image reveal a child's anticipation of the air raids? What is the relation between this image and the image of another flying danger – the witch – featured in one child's 'early dream'? Did Winnicott view drawing as a creative alternative to the 'psychohistorical theme' of delinquency that so concerned him (1964: 95)? To be sure, these queries bring us to the edges of what we can know for certain about the emotional life of the evacuation and about Winnicott's use of drawing in this context. At the same time, this very ambiguity would seem to fit the analyst who, in the years to come, located significance in the gap between representation and experience, where uncertainty, spontaneity and play are the central features of meaning-making.

My speculations on the evidentiary status of Winnicott's notebook collection may be sharpened by the fact that Marion Milner, a colleague since 1939, began an analysis with Winnicott in 1946.[10] The significance of this relationship is that Milner, who was deeply interested in the place of the visual in communication, very likely influenced Winnicott's own visual turn. In her published collection of diary entries and jottings, *A Life of One's Own*, Milner cites writer E. M. Forster to express her feelings on this: 'How can I tell what I think till I see what I say?' In this same text, Milner also recalled drawing, at the age of fifteen, an image of a dragon to express worries of being swallowed up. Milner, like Winnicott, worked with children: in 1933, she was commissioned through Susan Isaacs by the Girls' Public Day School Trust to assess students' well-being at the institution. Published in 1938, one aspect of the study sought to examine 'interest in intuitive experience' and involved asking adolescent girls to respond to a number of picture postcards, indicating their likes and dislikes and the reasons for these aesthetic judgments (Milner 1938: 114). Among them were two paintings: Frederick Walker's *The Harbour of Refuge* (1872) and John Pettie's *The Vigil* (1884) (both are housed in Tate Britain). Milner noted a difference in the girls' uses of *The Vigil* in particular: whereas Theodora and Nesta described the painting (respectively) as 'old-fashioned' (1938: 129) and a 'silly idea altogether' (1938: 131), another girl, Liz, expressed her appreciation of its depiction of emptiness: 'kneeling down in a lovely big place' (1938: 124). Combined with the girls' sketches of their daydreams, Milner came to define well-being as a capacity to 'use pictures' (both internal and external) to tolerate difficult, often intangible, aspects of human experience such as feelings of sadness or the vulnerability of living in a very old world – a 'big place,' as Liz put it.

It is significant, as well, that Milner did not limit her analysis to girls' education; it would seem that she followed her own 'interest in intuitive experience' by pursuing at this time a psychoanalytic education. In 1940, Milner became a training analyst and took cases during the evacuation working under the supervision of Melanie Klein, Joan

Riviere and Ella Sharpe. At this time, she also attended Winnicott's Saturday morning clinic for mothers and babies at Paddington Green (Sayers 2002). During the war, Milner continued to explore the uses of creativity in child analysis. She presented two papers at the British Psychoanalytical Society, one in 1943 and the other in 1945. Her emphasis was on the child's uses of symbols to bridge inner and outer worlds, and the defensive reaction of refusing relationships as a way to protect the self from premature separation from beloved others. Milner argued that the pain of these symptoms could be brought into relief by their visual representation, such as in tearing paper to bits or setting leaves on fire. Not only does Milner's attention to the use of aggression and the visual realm echo in Winnicott's squiggle game, these themes likely had something to do with his collection of images in the hostel scheme of 1945. As Milner recalls to Winnicott's biographer, F. Robert Rodman, Winnicott quite liked a particular set of pencil crayons she 'introduced him to' (2003: 140). Against this backdrop, the blue and yellow shading of the guard in Figure 18.2 animates questions about Milner's influence on Winnicott during the war years, when he began to gather visual testimony, and when he likely slipped those small square pages of drawings into his notes.

These things we cannot know for sure. But we do know that when Winnicott formalized the squiggle game about two decades later, the theme of visual expression – and its creative distortions of reality – was front and center once again. In fact, Winnicott read the tendency toward presence (or 'realistic' renderings) as a defense against encountering the unknown (or the 'negative'), an encounter needed to symbolize a relation between the outside world and the many affects it animated on the inside. Over the course of a series of drawings made during a session, Winnicott noticed a capacity for what Britzman has called 'aesthetic distance': children began to play in the gap – and so tolerate 'discordance' – between raw events and their representation. And they did so by embellishing aspects of an image or by making surprising additions that did not refer to – and sometimes did not resemble at all – external reality. These creative shifts indicated, to Winnicott, a capacity to symbolize internal fantasies and fears alongside actual events. It was here, in the face of an event's psychical modification or working over where Winnicott located both significance and creativity. For the witness, the effect was discomfort, or 'distress,' for it plunged one into a realm of uncertain meaning without the consolation of a pre-given narrative. As early as the war, it would seem, Winnicott was at work on his image technique and the reparative use of the aesthetic in the making of history: a child (squiggling or otherwise) required a witness who could hold open a space for the unknown – internal doubts, fantasies and anxieties – as the grounds of both memory and a 'loosening of the knot' of its unremembered repetition (Winnicott 1971a: 5).

By the time Winnicott started squiggling with children, he had made from his early concerns about the 'emotional black-out' of forced separation a theory of witnessing in visual form the more ubiquitous traumas of growing up.[11] Thus over twenty years after Winnicott slipped the images into his 1945 notebook, he would, in his *Therapeutic Consultations*, continue to use drawing to collect samples of difficult – and unknown – elements of history, and, perhaps unknowingly, as well, chronicle the difficulties of representing history at all. In the context of the squiggle game, Winnicott would continue to hold open the gap between representation and experience, between visible evidence and unseen psychical impressions, between immediate events and their belated signification, all tensions that might equally describe his wartime concerns about the evacuation, the 'first hours and days' of which, by 1945, 'had yet to be written'.

The case of Eliza

Eliza is seven and a half years old when her mother brings her to see Winnicott at Paddington Green. Winnicott describes Eliza as 'not ill enough to merit a psychiatric diagnosis' but nonetheless 'in need of a little help' (1971a: 42). This non-diagnosis is not unusual. Winnicott states, up front, that the intended aim of his therapeutic consultations was not to cure illness but, more simply and elusively, to respond to 'a need to report work done with children' (1971a: 8). This insight could be brought to bear on the literature of the history of childhood: that is, while adult influence is impossible to escape, there is nonetheless something of a need to examine representations produced by children themselves. The squiggle game is particularly interesting in this regard, for unlike the T.A.T. or the 'draw-a-person' test, Winnicott did not circumscribe the repertoire of what could be produced in a session.

On June 18, 1967, Winnicott illustrated this idea in his reply to L. Joseph Stone's inquiry about the nature of the game. 'Reluctant to put it down once and for all on paper,' Winnicott managed to describe the game's characteristic features in a way that reserved space for the unprecedented. 'Essential,' he wrote, 'is the absolute freedom so that any modification may be accepted if appropriate' (1967: 178). Significantly, Winnicott extended this right to both parties, noting that, 'the consultant contributes from his ingenuity as much as the child does' (1968: 301). To embrace the mutual construction of the squiggle, as Winnicott did, poses a challenge to the idea of an objective account of childhood history. And yet, much more than an obstacle to 'objectivity,' Winnicott's insistence on mutual ingenuity shifts what is meant by history. Before there can be an 'objective subject' of history (for instance, a plausible narrative account), there needs to be a 'subjective object' who can tolerate the unruliness of its earliest impressions.

Winnicott and Eliza's squiggles revolve around a number of issues, but what I wish to focus on here are two of the 'main themes' that Winnicott describes as significant (Winnicott 1971a: 44). The first involves 'the space between the front and back legs' and the second Winnicott names 'the hat complex,' which is evidenced in a number of figures wearing hats. This second theme begins with Eliza's mother's narrative, which she recounts to Winnicott as one of the events of Eliza's early life history. She recalls that she needed to be away from Eliza when the baby was ten months old. Upon return, she remembers rushing in to see her baby 'without taking off my hat first.' When Eliza saw her rush in with her hat on, the mother recalls that baby 'froze up.' For the remainder of the day, Eliza seemed listless or non-reactive, and the mother 'kept her in my arms' until she came around to a more lively, but relaxed state. Everything returned to normal, but it seemed that a residue of that event stayed with Eliza, now expressed as a phobia. As her mother puts it, 'For a long time, many months, the baby would not pass ladies with hats on' (Winnicott 1971a: 61). Psychoanalytically, the hats – and Eliza's complex around them – take the place of an earlier traumatic event that had to be forgotten. Or put differently, Eliza's fear of hats can be understood as a 'screen memory,' where a seemingly insignificant image bears the force of unnamable affect (Freud 1899). In this example, a residual anxiety of abandonment finds expression in Eliza's active avoidance of – and preoccupation with – hats.

Figure 18.5 'Something gone wrong.' Courtesy of The Marsh Agency on behalf of the Winnicott Trust.

As much as Winnicott agrees with the mother's interpretation, he is also committed to holding open a space for the unknown (that gap between experience and representation) and it is here that another theme begins to emerge. Beneath the hats, Winnicott sees in Eliza's squiggles themes about insides, origins and aggression. (Indeed, hat looks a lot like hate.) The very first squiggle (Figure 18.5) – 'something gone wrong' – gets us close to these themes (Winnicott 1971a: 43). Winnicott is the initiator of this first squiggle, which he invites Eliza to complete: 'She took my squiggle and put another leg on it, leaving a space between the legs' (1971a: 43). Winnicott makes no interpretation. Eight squiggles later, Eliza returns to this first image and makes a revision: where the space had been, she adds a line to make the shape of a tummy: '(The line of the tummy was added later)' (Winnicott 1971a: 43). And from here Eliza's squiggle sequence becomes increasingly populated by images related to a theme of empty spaces: pouches, tunnels and darkness. Negativity. The pinnacle of the squiggle series comes when Eliza uses darkness to illustrate 'a frightening dream' (Winnicott 1971a: 54). The first clue of the squiggle's significance comes when Eliza selects a larger sheet of paper on which to draw it. Yet another clue can be found in Eliza's urgent description of the dream's manifest content: 'a thing' that is 'as horrid as possible' (Figure 18.6) (Winnicott 1971a: 54).

Winnicott had from the beginning described the squiggle as a 'dream screen, a screen onto which a dream might be dreamed' (1968: 303). The squiggles are dream images that reach into the unconscious. Jan Abram's interpretation agrees: 'By "dream screen," Winnicott is referring to the unconscious nature of the squiggles, akin to a pencil drawing of a dream, replicating aspects of the early mother–infant relationship' (2007: 335). Viewing them as a canvas for the return of the repressed, Winnicott noticed the inherent risk in making squiggles. Unlike drawings at school, where images were more often prescribed and evaluated against reality, the squiggles brought children face-to-face with what was 'incontinent,' 'frightening' and 'naughty' within themselves (Winnicott 1968: 302). This idea returns us to Freud's theory of dreams as records of what is unthinkable about history. As Freud put it, dreaming is 'an abbreviated replay shaped by the accidents of

Figure 18.6 'A thing as horrid as possible.' Courtesy of The Marsh Agency on behalf of the Winnicott Trust.

life' (1900: 563) Akin to the squiggle, Freud underscored the power of visual imagery in the mind's reel of dreams: what he described as 'visually remembered scenes' of early forgotten experiences that return to us at night, when consciousness is sleeping (1900: 563–564).

Ernst Kris later picked up Freud's assumption in his comparison of the historical force of the image with that carried in words: 'The visual image has deeper roots, is more primitive' (1952: 200). This is to say, the visual image survives over time for much the same reason that Freud – and later Kris – surmised the survival of legends and fairy-tales. With reference to the persistence of dream symbols, Kris writes:

> We need not look far for evidence of this universal feeling with regard to the image. The lover who tears up the photograph of his faithless love, the revolutionary who pulls down the statue of the ruler, the angry crowd burning the straw dummy of a hostile leader.
>
> (1952: 201)

Each of these examples, for Kris, suggests a universal belief in the ability of the image to 'regain its power whenever our ego loses some part of its controlling function' (1952: 201). These images, in Kris's view, carry remnants of affect that are constants in history and humanity: despair, fury, outrage. Echoes of this history may reverberate in Eliza's squiggle sequence as well: the images produced through it convey not only the events themselves but, perhaps, a 'universal feeling' of anxiety that inscribes them in memory. After all, what could be more potent than the image of a formless terror of the night?

While it is precisely this 'epic' anxiety that underlies Eliza's dream squiggle, Winnicott is less interested in its universal appeal (as in Kris's image stock) and more interested in what, specifically, she needs her 'something horrid' for and to do. Significant as well is that Winnicott does not presume fantasy to be isolated from an actual violation ('a seduction of some kind'), though in the end, he considers it 'unlikely' (1971a: 55). But this does not mean the threat posed by the dream – and its seething sexuality – is safely written out of Eliza's history. Here is Winnicott's interpretation:

> I explored round with . . . the idea of some form of masturbation. I used words she could understand. I did not force this issue at all but let her know that I knew about it and she looked at me with wondering

eyes as if this was the first time that she had self-consciously thought about masturbation and guilt feelings related to masturbation.

(1971a: 55)

The idea of sexuality, that there could be a sexual dimension to a child's history, is not new in the history of child analysis. And in many ways, Winnicott's work may be understood as yet another instance where the child's 'independence of mind' disrupts adult constructions of childhood innocence (Freud 1909: 87). But what I find so compelling about Winnicott's discussion here is not the sexual content of the interpretation. It is rather Winnicott's implicit understanding of how the squiggle's work of distortion (akin to the dream) sets the terms for Eliza to think the 'unthought known' of the past, before its justification as external reality.

Eliza takes another risk when she sketches an image of a kangaroo (Figure 18.7). At first, Winnicott wonders whether the drawing may be a copy of the animals that fill the magazines of his clinic's waiting room. But for Winnicott, her rendering of this familiar enough image, like a dream, unmasks something other. Winnicott describes the otherness that he understands to be held deep inside its pouch:

> I gave Eliza some more of my own idea that this very awful thing that comes at her represents something that she has never properly accepted which is that she has feelings like that about the baby inside her mother's belly. The horrid thing would then be a return of something of her own that she could feel to be horrid but which she could not allow to be part of herself.

(Winnicott 1971a: 56)

Psychoanalytically, Winnicott's technique introduces significance to Eliza, which can be used in the service of making a relation to an inner aggression that is not yet thinkable, and not yet historical. Indeed, the squiggles sketch onto the historical record experiences that persist in residual – and visual – form before there exists the distance that narrative coherence affords. It would seem that the squiggling child came to illustrate a quality of the past that was ironically before the order of time, before knowledge and before history.

Winnicott's 'history taking' of Eliza thus reveals a 'close-up' snapshot of history's pre-linguistic force. In his essay of this title, 'Close-ups,' Adam Phillips makes precisely this argument. Phillips reminds us that when we get really close to things, they lose their exact position because they are without the usual cues that a context endows (2004: 146). Up close, objects lose their edges, their attachment to social meaning, and can be virtually unrecognizable. As readers will recall, Eliza was, in Winnicott's construction, too close to a childhood past to yet understand her squiggle images – something gone wrong, the horrid thing, the kangaroo – from the distance afforded by language. Through the squiggle, this game with 'no rules,' Winnicott constructed an archive of what it might look like to be totally and intolerably immersed in a past that is not yet historical, and which positions its witness in the realm of the unknown: that space between experience and representation. The child's squiggle came to record the uncanny time of history, a future history which, while forcibly felt, was 'yet to be written.'

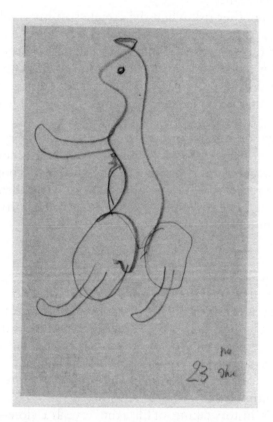

Figure 18.7 A kangaroo. Courtesy of The Marsh Agency on behalf of the Winnicott Trust.

André Green would further elaborate this unruly kind of history in the first lecture he presented to the Squiggle Foundation. Affectionately known as 'the French Winnicott' Green began his paper with a frank acknowledgment: 'As far as psychoanalysis is concerned,' he wrote, 'the historical is a very difficult notion to handle' (Green in Abram 2000: 2). This is because the history psychoanalysis does 'handle' is actually impossible to pin down. It could include any or all of the following: 'what has happened, what has not happened, what could have happened, what happened to someone else but not to me, what could not have happened, and . . . a statement that one would not have even dreamed of as a representation of what really happened' (Green in Abram 2000: 2–3). What makes history such a 'difficult notion to handle' in psychoanalysis is that it is experienced as any combination of the above-named variables, before they can be sorted out in time, such that first this happened, and then that happened to someone else. Green does not make reference to the squiggle itself, and yet this lecture's list nonetheless bears the playful marks of this game, where Green elaborates Winnicott's initial gesture toward empty space (or for Green 'negativity') as a site of potential significance. Thinking with Green's playful list of contradictions, I think we can rewrite Eliza's squiggle sequence in psychoanalytic terms of history: 'something one dreams without the defense of literal reality and yet that is nonetheless true.'[12] Such a portrait certainly disfigures that other historical fantasy of 'temporal succession' we more often use to iron out the contradictions of history (Scott 2001: 289). Winnicott's squiggle game similarly disfigures, engendering a space in which the unknown past, which can hardly be observed, may nonetheless be sketched into existence, and its paper trail of distorted images recognized as psychically true.

Already, I have sketched into existence a historical construction that links Winnicott's wartime work to his interest in the visual realm as a site of representation for difficult – unremembered – histories. To return to Phillips, we know that the war shifted the language of child analysis writ large:

bombs, and the real possibility of invasion, seem, in retrospect, to have been just what the child analysts needed to extend their account [of the mother–infant relationship]: the invasion by mothers; by their separateness or their intrusiveness; the invasion of the

441

mother by the child, the child invaded by his instinctual life and needing maternal protection.

(Phillips 2000: 49)

In the context of war, child analysts, among whom Winnicott ought to be counted, fought over the child, and the figure of the mother became a container for the anxiety produced in this context. But perhaps especially for Winnicott, those torn sheets of drawing paper became part of the reliable environment: a screen that could hold the experience of an unpredictable environment, in which bombs were literally dropped, and, perhaps to his mind, children metaphorically so.[13] Extending this idea, I think we can catch a glimpse of this history replayed in Winnicott's late formulation of his position as 'subjective object,' which, grounded in the discourse of mothering, refers to a witness who must contain all kinds of invasions – and who can hold in mind the idea of something whole in the midst of psychical attack.

The last image of Eliza's squiggles bears witness to this idea. The image is a rendering of 'a man's head' that Winnicott interprets as a portrait of himself (Figure 18.8). Its most prominent feature is a set of large eyes that might be seen, at first glance, as a literal representation (at this stage of his life, Winnicott wore dark framed glasses). On second glance, however, this collaborative image is more caricature than portrait. Read through the lens of the unconscious, the prominent feature of the eyes seems to communicate a deeper experience than realistic portrayal of Winnicott's appearance. Might this image not be evidence of the experience of having been seen?[14] Thinking with Eliza about this 'man's head,' Winnicott offers a more literal interpretation: He might be reading the newspaper. Eliza corrects him: 'No, he is crossing his arms.' At this point in the analysis, he decides that Eliza is 'ready to go,' for, as he puts it, she can 'now see' – and story – what she needed from her squiggles (Winnicott 1971: 59).

What Winnicott is calling here a matter of 'seeing' could be described as an effect of witnessing, which does not have direct access to Eliza's internal experience. There is that 'gap.' But what Winnicott does have is access to his own distress, which he reads as evidence of what the other – here Eliza – had to disclaim. Psychoanalytically, witnessing may be an uncertain work of attending to the affective force of events that had to be split off from the idea of them. But even more, witnessing may also involve returning the discarded content with the distance afforded by the symbolic realm and thus

442

Figure 18.8 A man's head. Courtesy of The Marsh Agency on behalf of the
   Winnicott Trust.

loosened up from the anxiety that accompanied its earliest impressions.
From the vantage of the squiggle, what Eliza 'now sees' in her portrait of the man 'crossing his arms' may be a tolerable version of her
aggressive – 'cross' – self. In turn, what Winnicott illustrates in his
discussion of the case is that this childhood history is not possible
without a witness. Indeed, because Eliza has been 'seen,' she can risk
seeing (for) herself, and begin a history of her own.

Squiggle evidence

The history recorded in the squiggle is one that reaches into an archive
of experience felt before understanding. As this chapter has suggested,

the visual realm may be a particularly potent site to represent these affective impressions that 'a set technique with rules and regulations' could not. Indeed, the history held within the spontaneous gesture of the squiggle is one that betrays the intentional effort to write it down. Reaching into the unknown, these little drawings archive a 'negative' quality of representation, and thus posit history itself as a crisis of witnessing the ways we are affected by what is unknown about the past, by that which 'exist[s] even when the senses can no longer perceive it' (Green 1999: 16). Winnicott may have forgotten about the images he tucked in his 1945 hostel scheme, almost like pressed leaves that remind you of a distant autumn walk. But these stray images, ambiguous as they are in their placement and context, nonetheless point to the negative labour of history making: not simply a matter of amassing 'facts' but a question of how to witness the ways memory itself works over and obscures the past.

As much as the squiggles plunge history into the unknown matters of memory, they also construct an image of the very child with whom Winnicott sat down to create them. As we have seen, this was a child in need of careful attention and who, in this sense, is an iteration of the twentieth-century construction of childhood in discourses of both medicine and literature. The child who emerged from Winnicott's clinic was one who embodied the ontological idea of subjectivity as a historical concept, while history itself became something a self can possess, develop and mark in time (Steedman 1995). But more tentatively and specifically, Winnicott's visual turn may be evidence, as well, of the 'creative struggle' of a subject, perhaps the child, and Winnicott himself, to work over and through the effects of being immersed in history before language, faced with events that are, initially at least, 'too close' to see or affect. Indeed, the child in Winnicott's clinic illustrated a quality of memory that could not be faithful to the past 'as it really was,' but to the fantasies it engendered. The squiggle may thus be evidence not only of the history of the child (as Winnicott believed) but also of the child that Winnicott constructed from history: against a backdrop of war, this was a child who could, with a reliable witness, put to use an innate aggression in the service of creativity, where a difficult past could be worked over anew.

At the end of Eliza's squiggle session, Winnicott makes a note that gestures in yet another direction, and which intrigues this reader: 'children very seldom want to take the squiggle game drawings home' (1971a: 60). More often, he admits, they leave them behind. Winnicott's squiggle collection thus begins with a reversed image of inheritance: the child who bequeaths something to the adult. One irony is that Winnicott understood that the best chance of receiving this endowment was to give up the idea of a coherent narrative account. A further irony is that Winnicott may have arrived at this insight – history taking as disrupting the past – because he was himself affected in significant ways by the historical context in which he lived and worked as a child analyst. Under an ominous sky, and in the midst of a city in ruins, Winnicott first turned to drawing as a recording device for traumatic experiences that had bypassed the linguistic realm, that were, to cite this analyst once again, 'yet to be written.' The child who squiggled in Winnicott's clinic two decades later seemed to embody for this analyst precisely that possibility of constructing a historical narrative from 'blacked-out' beginnings. The squiggling child was one who could put to creative use the difficulties of the past, and who could, if all went well, make something new from 'something gone wrong,' perhaps a kind of birth after bombs.

The squiggle is a history that eludes intentional or official representation; it is about the complicated relation between inner and outer realities, between wish and reality, and about a paradox: tracing the distortions of drawings and dreams offers powerful clues of the psychical truth of the past. The history at play here is not one objectively stamped onto the record, but a layered artifact born of social relationships, concrete events, desires and dreams, much like a squiggle itself. It is a history that cultivates imagination (Britzman's 'aesthetic distance') without doing away with reality. A squiggle is a reminder then, that history is as much a question of material events as it is, in Carolyn Steedman's words, 'a creation of the search itself' (2001: 77). A cast of characters constitute the creation of history in this chapter: there was Eliza and her mother, the hats, dreams 'horrid' and things 'gone wrong'; there was a kangaroo; and there was Winnicott, his Freudian inheritance, the air war and his work with hostel youth. And there remains, of course, the forgotten image collection.[15] The squiggle may be evidence of how we make from the stray fragments of the past a meaningful historical narrative. But this history in pictures may also testify to the labour of letting go, or leaving something behind so that the past may become, 'memorable rather than spellbinding' (Phillips 2004: 143) – which is, perhaps, the ultimate act of creativity, the art of history.

Acknowledgements

This paper is part of a three-year research project, 'Spaces of Memory: Between Internal Objects and Tangible Relics in Learning from the Past,' funded by the Social Sciences and Research Council of Canada, to which I am grateful for its support. Special thanks go to Jan Abram, Lesley Hall and Anna Smith.

Notes

1 Winnicott mentions the number 285 in a paper given at a meeting of the Medical Section of the British Psychological Society on February 27, 1946 (Winnicott 1948: 73). Winnicott's report conflicts with F. Robert Rodman's account that Winnicott oversaw the placement and progress of approximately 110 children, as cited in his historical biography, *Winnicott: Life and Work* (2003: 90).

2 While Winnicott had perhaps always had an interest in the mother-baby dyad, Winnicott's biographers Rodman and Phillips comment on the consolidation of this thinking in the decade of the 1940s, both during and after his wartime work with hostel youth. This context had given him ample opportunity to witness the effects of maternal bonding and separation in healthy environments and those of ill health. Perhaps the best evidence of this shift toward the maternal environment (rather than the child's internal state alone) can be found in an undated paper that is estimated to have been published in the early 1940s (Winnicott 1996: 51–53).

3 Winnicott begins to make this distinction in a bookend to his early paper on aggression, the second published in 1964 under the title, 'Roots of Aggression.' Here, Winnicott describes a 'mature alternative to aggressive behaviour' in the child's dreams, where destructive urges are experienced in fantasy and become the grounds for playing. The achievement of playing is its turn to the symbolic – rather than the actual – which protects both the world and the child from raw inner forces: 'It will readily be seen what an important part is played in healthy development by the child's acceptance of symbols. One thing 'stands for' another, and the consequence is that there is a great relief from the crude and awkward conflicts that belong to stark truth' (Winnicott 1964: 94–95).

Just one year later Winnicott added to his list of 'mature alternatives to aggressive behaviour' the use of art. Travelling home from Dartington Hall in 1965, Winnicott made the following note: 'The antisocial person who enters an art gallery and slashes a picture by an old master is not activated by love of the painting and in fact is not being as destructive as the art-lover is when preserving the picture and using it fully in unconscious fantasy destroying it over and over again' (232). There is for Winnicott a destructive element of object-use that is qualitatively different from the repressed aggression of antisocial tendencies. Winnicott may have intuited this qualitative distinction in gathering the visual testimonies of hostel youth. Then, and later, Winnicott seemed to use image-making as a destructive way to not wage war on/in the world – on the inside and the outside.

4 Winnicott did not undertake regular psychoanalysis with hostel children, 'owing to lack of time,' but he was called upon to interview particular children who expressed 'difficulties and who are giving special trouble' (Winnicott and Britton 1944: 104). Winnicott's interviews were thus conducted with particularly distressed children, a context in which drawing seemed an apt means of communication. In their co-authored paper, 'The Problem of Homeless Children,' Winnicott and Britton make precisely this observation. Here, they note the importance of 'drawing and painting, etc.' as 'doing important therapeutic work,' particularly in the case of 'introverted children' who had withdrawn into themselves as a means of coping with the evacuation (1944: 107).

Winnicott's paper 'Hate in the Counter-transference' provides more evidence of his wartime turn to drawing. In the context of his discussion of the child's searches for 'his guardians' ability to hate objectively,' Winnicott refers to a nine-year-old boy 'sent from London not because of bombs but because of truancy' (1947: 199). After this 'most loveable and maddening' child ran away from the hostel, Winnicott decided to take him into his home. It was only through drawing that any progress was made: 'I had established contact with him in one interview in which I could see and interpret through a drawing of his that in running away he was unconsciously saving the inside of his home and preserving his mother from assault, as well as trying to get away from his own inner world, which was full of persecutors' (Winnicott 1947: 199).

5 This is a tricky claim because Winnicott's paper, 'The Squiggle Game,' is actually an amalgamation of two papers: one, unpublished, written in 1964 and the other published in 1968. The published version of this paper features the case of Eliza, which is also the feature case of my own paper. The arrival of this paper at the publishing house in 1968 means that another case study, published in 1965, can be more suitably viewed as the first squiggle case. The paper I am referring to is Winnicott's (1965) 'A Clinical Study of the Effects of a Failure of the Average Expectable Environment on a Child's Mental Functioning,' *International Journal of Psychoanalysis*, 46: 81–87.

6 Wellcome Library, London, UK, file PP/DWW/L1/3.

7 Wellcome Library, London, UK, file PP/DWW/L1/3. George is a pseudonym, used here to maintain the legal protection extended to the child to whom Winnicott refers. We cannot know of what George's drawings consist or the nature (and existence at all) of Winnicott's notes on them until 2072 when the privacy law that is currently in place expires. The images of Winnicott's notebook collection, as well as a few other stray cases and squiggles, are available for public viewing because they do not provide

sustained commentary that would otherwise identify a child. Winnicott's notes in these cases are either scattered or nonexistent, creating a kind of in-built archival protection not unlike that of the censorship of a dream, where what is revealed is in disguise.

8 The evacuation actually occurred in waves, the first one in September 1939. A second evacuation, 'Operation Trickle' was set into motion the following year, in September 1940, and the third and final wave in July 1944 (Welshman 2010: 6).

9 The archive catalogue indicates that all three volumes of Winnicott's hostel schemes contained still other 'loose documents . . . inserted haphazardly,' and which have been re-filed to preserve the privacy of their creators. We are left to wonder about the content and form of these documents, and indeed, whether there are among them still more drawings. But the archival notation indicating their absence nonetheless reveals the negative labor of history that is the concern of this article. From the vantage of negativity, history is a matter of interpreting the absences, silences and uncertainties left behind in material traces.

10 In an interview with Winnicott's biographer F. Robert Rodman, Milner recalls that the analysis started in 1944 or 1945. And yet, in reference to her own discussion with Milner, Jan Abram (personal correspondence) confirms that the analysis was actually between 1946 and 1947 and that she was referred to Clifford Scott in 1950.

11 Four years after the war Winnicott first started to write about the everyday 'trauma' of being born, in his 1949 essay, 'Birth Memories, Birth Trauma and Anxiety.' The paper is itself silent on the question of war trauma, the 'emotional black-out' he worried about in his 1939 letter. Despite this apparent omission, Lyndsey Stonebridge (2000) reads between the lines of Winnicott's 1949 paper, arguing that the connection between 'bombs' and 'birth' might be closer than even Winnicott could admit. As she writes:

> The child being born is a child out of time and, Winnicott suggests, like a prisoner of war, suffers from an experience that appears to have no terminus. It is this type of impingement that makes birth feel like a form of persecution (Winnicott's word).
>
> (2000: 92)

Whether or not one agrees with Stonebridge's parallel between the child and war prisoner, I wish to underscore the importance of reading (as Stonebridge does) Winnicott's writing during the war as bearing traces of the psychical effects of having lived through its destructive context.

12 My construction here is inspired by Deborah Britzman's (2006) playful use of Green's list in her paper, 'Little Hans, Fritz and Ludo: On the Curious History of Gender in the Psychoanalytic Archive.' Britzman rewrites Green's last sentence ('a statement that one would not have even dreamed of as a representation of what really happened') to read: 'a statement we

dream and then forget, except that we do remember something found again in the unsolvable residue dreams leave behind' (2006: 139). In this stunning reformulation, Britzman is proposing a theory of history that involves constructing meaning from the remains of unresolved conflicts that both enable and exceed our narrative efforts. My own construction of history is derived from Britzman's: where history is made from the discontinuity that emerges from the space between what can be observed and what is experienced.

13 Phillips phrases this idea slightly differently in writing that, psychoanalytically, during the war, 'a dropped baby is a bomb' (2000: 58).

14 We can find a counter-example of this figure of the witness in the case of a six-year-old patient named Bob. Winnicott squiggles with Bob a range of images, one of which is a 'mother figure holding a baby' (1971a: 82). Winnicott uses the image to introduce the terrible 'danger of being dropped' by a depressed mother, at which point, Bob 'smudged' the woman's eyes (1971a: 82). According to Winnicott, Bob conveys in this visual cue 'the holding mother's withdrawal of cathexis,' or, using the language of the 'subjective object,' we could say, the mother's failure to hold the nameless dreads and terrors of Bob's becoming. 'The Case of Bob' was first published by Winnicott in 1965 under the title, 'A Clinical Study of the Effect of a Failure of the Average Expectable Environment on a Child's Mental Functioning,' *International Journal of Psychoanalysis*, 46: 81–87. Quotes here come from its reprinted iteration in Winnicott, *Therapeutic Consultations* (1971a).

15 Jan Abram gives a sense of just how apt this phrase, 'forgotten image collection,' may be. In 2003, as she compiled for transfer the documents of the collection that is currently housed at the Wellcome Library, she was endowed with another set of boxes after Ray Shepherd's death that same year. Abram recalls that she found dozens of squiggle images in boxes, 'piled on top of one another' and, until her discovery, 'literally forgotten' (personal correspondence, November 19, 2010).

References

Abram, J. (2007) *The Language of Winnicott: A Dictionary of Winnicott's Use of Words* 2nd Edition, London: Karnac.

Abram, J. (2008) 'Donald Woods Winnicott (1896–1971): A Brief Introduction', *International Journal of Psychoanalysis*, 89: 1189–1217.

Bollas, C. (1987) *The Shadow of the Object: Psychoanalysis of the Unthought Known*, New York: Columbia University Press.

Bowlby, J., Miller, E. and Winnicott, D. W. (1939) 'Evacuation of Small Children', in C. Winnicott, R. Shepherd and M. Davis (eds.) *Deprivation and Delinquency*, London: Tavistock.

Britton, C. (1984) 'Introduction', in C. Winnicott, R. Shepherd and M. Davis (eds.) *Deprivation and Delinquency*, London: Tavistock.

Britzman, D. (2006) 'Little Hans, Fritz and Ludo: On the Curious History of Gender in the Psychoanalytic Archive', *Studies in Gender and Sexuality*, 7(2):113–140.

Caruth, C. (1996) *Unclaimed Experience: Trauma, Narrative and History*, Baltimore: The Johns Hopkins University Press.

Derrida, J. (1995) *Archive Fever: A Freudian Impression*, trans. E. Prenowitz, Chicago: The Johns Hopkins University Press.

Figlio, K. (1988) 'Oral History and the Unconscious', *History Workshop,* 26: 120–132.

Freud, S. (1899) 'Screen Memories', in A. Phillips (ed.), *The Uncanny* (2003), trans. D. McClintock, London: Penguin.

Freud, S. (1900) *The Interpretation of Dreams*, trans. and ed. J. A. Underwood, London: Penguin, 2006.

Freud, S. (1909) 'Analysis of a Phobia in a Five-year-old Boy ['Little Hans'],' in A. Phillips, (ed.) *The Wolfman and Other Cases* (2002), trans. L. A. Huish, London: Hogarth Press.

Freud, S. (1938[1940]) 'An Outline of Psychoanalysis', in A. Phillips (ed.), *The Penguin Freud Reader*, trans. H. Ragg-Kirkby, London: Penguin.

Green, A. (1999) *The Work of the Negative*, trans. A. Weller, London: UK, Free Association Books.

Green, A. (2000)a 'Experience and Thinking in Analytic Practice', in J. Abram (ed.), *André Green at the Squiggle Foundation*, London: Karnac.

Green, A. (2000)b 'The Intuition of the Negative', in J. Abram (ed.), *André Green at the Squiggle Foundation*, London: Karnac.

Günter, M. (2007) *Playing the Unconscious: Psychoanalytic Interviews with Children Using Winnicott's Squiggle Technique,* London: Karnac.

Kris, E. (1952) *Psychoanalytic Explorations in Art*, Madison: International Universities Press.

Lifton, R. J. (1974) 'On Psychohistory' in R. J. Lifton and R. Olson (eds.), *Explorations in Psychohistory: The Wellfleet Papers*, New York: Simon & Schuster.

Milner, M. (1938) *The Human Problem in Schools: A Psychological Study Carried Out on Behalf of the Girls' Public School Trust*, London: Methuen.

Phillips, A. (1988) *Winnicott*, Cambridge, MA: Harvard University Press.

Phillips, A. (2000) 'Bombs Away', *Promises, Promises: Essays on Psychoanalysis and Literature*, New York: Basic Books.

Phillips, A. (2004) 'Close Ups', *History Workshop Journal*, 57: 142–149.

Phillips, A. (2005) *Going Sane: Maps of Happiness*, New York: Fourth Estate.

Rodman, F. R. (2003) *Winnicott: Life and Work,* Cambridge, MA: Perseus.

Scott, J. (2001) 'Fantasy Echo: History and the Construction of Identity', *Critical Inquiry,* 27(2): 284–304.

Steedman, C. (1995) *Strange Dislocations: Childhood and the Idea of Human Interiority 1780–1930*, Cambridge, MA: Harvard University Press.

Steedman, C. (2001) *Dust: In the Archive*, Oxford: Manchester University Press.

The Wellcome Library, images, 183 Euston Road. London, UK. NW1 2BE: File (PP/DWW/L1/3).

Welshman, J. (2010) *Churchill's Children: The Evacuee Experience in Wartime Britain*, Oxford: Oxford University Press.

Winnicott, D. W. (1939) 'Aggression and its Roots', in C. Winnicott, R. Shepherd and M. Davis (eds.) *Deprivation and Delinquency* (1984), London: Tavistock.

Winnicott, D. W. (1940) 'Children in the War', in C. Winnicott, R. Shepherd and M. Davis (eds.) *Deprivation and Delinquency* (1984), London: Tavistock.

Winnicott, D. W. (1941) 'Review of the *Cambridge Evacuation Survey*: A Wartime Study in Social Welfare and Education', in C. Winnicott, R. Shepherd and M. Davis (eds.) *Deprivation and Delinquency* (1984), London: Tavistock.

Winnicott, D. W. (1942) 'Why Children Play', *The Child and the Outside World* (1957), London: Tavistock.

Winnicott, D. W. (1945) 'The Evacuated Child', in C. Winnicott, R. Shepherd and M. Davis (eds.) *Deprivation and Delinquency* (1984), London: Tavistock.

Winnicott, D. W. (1947)a 'Hate in the Countertransference', *Through Paediatrics to Psycho-Analysis: Collected Papers* (1992), New York: Brunner-Routledge.

Winnicott, D. W. (1947)b 'Residential Management for Difficult Children', in C.

Winnicott, R. Shepherd and M. Davis (eds.) *Deprivation and Delinquency* (1984), London: Tavistock.

Winnicott, D. W. (1948) 'Children's Hostels in War and Peace', in C. Winnicott, R. Shepherd and M. Davis (eds.) *Deprivation and Delinquency* (1984), London: Tavistock.

Winnicott, D. W. (1953) 'Transitional Objects and Transitional Phenomena: A Study of the First Not-Me Possession', *International Journal of Psychoanalysis*, 24: 89–97.

Winnicott, D. W. (1963) 'Psychiatric Disorder in Terms of Infantile Maturational Processes', *The Maturational Processes and the Facilitating Environment: Studies in the Theory of Emotional Development* (1990), London: Karnac.

Winnicott, D. W. (1964)a 'Roots of Aggression', in C. Winnicott, R. Shepherd and M. Davis (eds.) *Deprivation and Delinquency* (1984), London: Tavistock.

Winnicott, D. W. (1964)b *The Child, the Family and the Outside World,* Cambridge: Perseus, 1987.

Winnicott, D. W. (1965) 'A Clinical Study of the Effects of a Failure of the Average Expectable Environment on a Child's Mental Functioning', *International Journal of Psychoanalysis,* 46: 81–87.

Winnicott, D. W. (1968) 'The Squiggle Game', in C. Winnicott, R. Shepherd and M. Davis (eds.), *Psycho-analytic Explorations* (1989), London: Karnac.

Winnicott, D. W. (1969) 'The Use of an Object and Relating through Identifications', *Playing and Reality* (1971), London: Tavistock.

Winnicott, D. W. (1971)a 'Creativity and its Origins', *Playing and Reality,* London: Tavistock.

Winnicott, D. W. (1971)b 'Interrelating apart from Instinctual Drive', *Playing and Reality*, London: Tavistock.

Winnicott, D. W. (1971)c *Therapeutic Consultations in Child Psychiatry*, New York: Basic Books.

Winnicott, D. W. (1992) 'Birth Memories, Birth Trauma and Anxiety', *Through Paediatrics to Psycho-analysis: Collected Papers,* New York: Brunner.

Winnicott, D. W. (1996) 'The Delinquent and the Habitual Offender', in R. Shepherd, J. Johns and H. Taylor (eds.) *Thinking about Children,* New York: DaCapo Press.

Winnicott, D. W. (1999) 'Letter to L. Joseph Stone', in F. R. Rodman (ed.), *The Spontaneous Gesture: Selected Letters of D.W. Winnicott,* London: Karnac.

Winnicott, D. W. (1965) 'The Concept of Trauma in Relation to the Development of the Individual within the Family', in C. Winnicott, R. Shepherd and M. Davis (eds.), *Psycho-analytic Explorations* (1989), London: Karnac.

Winnicott, D. W. (1965) 'Notes Made on a Train Part 2', in C. Winnicott, R. Shepherd and M. Davis (eds.), *Psycho-analytic Explorations* (1989), London: Karnac.

Winnicott, D. W and Britton, C. (1944) 'The Problem of Homeless Children', in J. Kanter (ed.), *Face to Face with Children: The Life and Work of Clare Winnicott* (2004), London: Karnac.

Appendix

The following brief notes on the Winnicott Publications, Archives and A Question of Biography are based on extracts taken from Part One of 'Donald Woods Winnicott: a brief introduction' (Abram 2008). Part Two of the paper is re-published as Chapter 3 in this volume.

D.W. Winnicott Publications: 1931–2002

Between 1931 and 2002, 23 collections of Winnicott's writings were published: 11 during his lifetime (five now out of print); 11 posthumously, plus a collection of selected letters (Rodman (ed.) 1987). The 23 books contain a combination of psychoanalytic papers, articles addressed to parents and professionals working with young families, notes, abstracts and reviews. With the exception of the two main volumes (Winnicott 1958a; 1965b), the Winnicott Publications Committee decided to organize the writings thematically (see Davis 1987).

Below the complete list of Winnicott's publications correlates to the 'Knud Hjulmand Bibliography' in *The Language of Winnicott* (2nd edition 2007: 361–450). Each book is dated according to Hjulmand's bibliography. Almost all the published papers of Winnicott will be found in one of the publications below.

1931 Clinical Notes on Disorders of Childhood [out of print]
1945 Getting to Know Your Baby [out of print]
1949 The Ordinary Devoted Mother and Her Baby (9 broadcast talks) [out of print]
1957 The Child and the Family [out of print]

1957	The Child and the Outside World [out of print]
1958	Through Paediatrics to Psychoanalysis
1964	The Child, the Family and the Outside World
1965	The Family and Individual Development
1965	Maturational Processes and the Facilitating Environment
1971	Playing and Reality
1971	Therapeutic Consultations
1977	The Piggle
1984	Deprivation and Delinquency
1986	Holding and Interpretation
1986	Home Is Where We Start From
1987	Babies and Their Mothers
1987	The Spontaneous Gesture
1988	Human Nature
1989	Psychoanalytic Explorations
1993	Talking to Parents
1996	Thinking about Children
2002	Winnicott on the Child

The Winnicott Archives

To date it is still unknown just how much Winnicott wrote. When he died on 25 January 1971, there was an enormous amount of material that had not yet been published. In 1974 his widow Clare Winnicott, who was also a psychoanalyst, formed the Winnicott Publications Committee (WPC), and invited Madeleine Davis, Ray Shepherd and David Wallbridge to assist as editors in the task of publishing all the unpublished work. Madeleine Davis was a philosopher who later trained as a psychoanalytic psychotherapist and had met Winnicott through her paediatrician husband, John Davis. Ray Shepherd and David Wallbridge were members of the BPaS. Shortly before Clare Winnicott died in 1984, the committee was formally constituted as the Winnicott Trust (WT).

The issue of where to house the archives became an urgent concern to Clare, especially after her diagnosis of cancer in the late 1970s, and she and the WPC searched for the most appropriate place. When it became clear that a suitable place could not be found in the UK Clare Winnicott approached several universities in the USA and eventually began negotiations with the Archives of Psychiatry of Cornell

University Medical College. In 1981 the first shipment of Winnicott material was sent to New York. The 'Donald Woods Winnicott
Papers' are presently housed in the Oskar Deithelm Medical Library
(a library and archive specializing in the history of psychiatry) on the
eleventh floor of The New York Presbyterian Hospital.

Due to the editing projects in progress at that time, a certain amount
of the material was retained and, when Clare Winnicott died in 1984,
the material was kept by the editors, Ray Shepherd and Madeleine
Davis. When Madeleine Davis died in 1992 the material she had
been working on was moved to the BpaS. Later, in 2003, when Ray
Shepherd died intestate, the rest of the material was listed by Polly
Rossdale, the Institute archivist at the time, and Jan Abram who was
Honorary Archivist of the Winnicott Trust. In 2008 the material was
moved to the Wellcome Library in London and catalogued by the
archives teams there. The archives can be viewed on line at the Wellcome Library website – PP/DWW is the search code.

Winnicott's appointment diaries

One significant finding relevant for Winnicott studies today is still in
the process of being prepared for publication as I wish to announce
here. In 2001 a patient who had been in analysis with Masud Khan
almost forty years previously published a disturbing article in a well-
known London literary magazine. This article described a complicated
analytic relationship which included a series of boundary violations on
the part of his analyst Masud Khan. During the years of being Khan's
patient (dates that the article does not cite but from my archival work
I estimate between 1959 and 1966), the patient claimed that Khan had
been in analysis with Winnicott during the same period. Moreover,
the article also claimed that Winnicott had been aware of Khan's analytic transgressions. The article seemed to correlate with several other
papers published in the 1990s, which maintained that Masud Khan had
been in analysis with Winnicott for 15 years (1951–1966). Naturally,
these articles reflected badly on Winnicott's reputation because of the
strong implication that Winnicott was accountable for Khan's behaviour. More publications followed that compounded and elaborated the
criticism of Winnicott's clinical practice. In my discussions with many
analysts at home and abroad, it seemed to be 'common knowledge' that
Khan had been in analysis with Winnicott for 15 years. However, as
far as I could assess, the publications that cited the length of the analysis

were solely based on the 'work books' (diaries) of Masud Khan. These work books are not generally available for research.

The Winnicott Collection at the Wellcome Institute includes Winnicott's appointment diaries 1949–1971. Examination of the relevant appointment diaries has ascertained that, according to the entries in the diaries of 'MK', the analysis of Masud Khan by Donald Winnicott (5x weekly) lasted for two and a half years (between 1951 and 1954) and not the assumed 15 years. The details of this finding is being prepared for publication by Jan Abram and Nellie Thompson and planned to be published in the near future.

A question of biography

Freud, in a letter to Arnold Zweig of 31 May 1936, in response to Zweig's letter in which he had proposed to write Freud's biography, wrote: 'Anyone who writes a biography is committed to lies, concealments, hypocrisy, flattery and even to hiding his own lack of understanding, for biographical truth does not exist, and if it did we could not use it' (Freud, E.L. 1970: 127). Presumably, Freud was referring to the biographer's transference that she is inevitably faced with by the task of writing about a person after their death. This would be exacerbated if the biographer had never met her subject. In his book *Footsteps*, Holmes (1985) illustrates the intricate layers of identification involved in the act of writing a biography. Later, in an Ernest Jones lecture, he outlined three components of the 'essential dynamic within allbiography': (a) the search for truth; (b) the narrative mode; and (c) objectivity (Holmes 1992: 1–3).

In the two decades after his death, there have been several biographical publications on Winnicott illustrating how he was as a husband, teacher, colleague, lecturer, and analyst. Gillespie (1971) wrote the official obituary for the *International Journal of Psychoanalysis* which conveys his affection and respect. Further publications were written by Pearl King (1972) and Marion Milner (1978: Chapter 6) which were included in the tributes of the *Bulletin* of the British Psychoanalytical Society in 1972. Later, Clare Winnicott (1978), his widow, wrote a reflection, and in 1983 was interviewed by Neve (1992). From France, Clancier and Kalmanovitch (1987) produced a short volume on Winnicott's work which includes interviews with André Green, Daniel Widlöcher and Jean-Bertrand Pontalis, who discuss their memories of Winnicott and reflect on his theories. The two condensed introductions to his work also include some biographical information (Davis and Wallbridge 1981; Phillips 1988). Paul Roazen published his 1965 interview with Winnicott (Roazen 2001: 173–82), and two of his analysands wrote about their experience of Winnicott as an analyst (Guntrip 1975; Little 1985). Recently, Issroff, Reeves and Hauptman have published a collection that includes biographical reflections (Issroff 2005). Two biographies have emerged so far: Kahr (1996) – reviewed in Layland (1996) and Rodman (2003) – reviewed in Young-Bruehl (2003) and Kermode (2004). While these biographies offer much useful information, there is an unfortunate tendency in both to 'analyze' Winnicott. This type of authorial intervention, throughout each biography, although in a different way, runs counter to the three components of Holmes's 'essential dynamics' and thus, overall, undermines the value of the accounts. While a chronological presentation of Winnicott's work has the potential to offer an intellectual biography of Winnicott's work, the research, particularly the archival work (as seen in Chapters 14, 17 and 18) increasingly show how much work is required to produce a balanced biography that would adhere to the Holmes's dynamics.

References

Abram, J. (2007) *The language of Winnicott: A dictionary of Winnicott's use of words*, 2nd edition. London: Kamac.

Abram, J. (2008) Donald Woods Winnicott: A brief introduction. *Int J Psychoanal* 89: 1189–1217.

Clancier, A. and Kalmanovitch, J. (1987) *Winnicott and paradox: From birth to creation*, Sheridan, A., translator. London: Tavistock [(1984) Le paradoxe de Winnicott: De la naissance à la création. Paris: Payot (Science de l'Homme series.)]

Davis, M. (1987) The writing of DW Winnicott. *Int Rev Psychoanal* 14: 491–502.

Davis, M. and Wallbridge, D. (1981) *Boundary and space: An introduction to the work of DW Winnicott*. New York: Brunner/Mazel.

Diatkine, G. (2005) Beyond the pleasure principle. In: Perelberg, R. *Freud: A modern reader*, 142–61. London: Whurr.

Freud, E.L. ed. (1970) *The letters of Sigmund Freud and Arnold Zweig*, Robson-Scott, E. and Robson-Scott, W., translators. New York: Harcourt, Brace & World.

Gillespie, W.H. (1971) Donald W Winnicott. *Int J Psychoanal* 52: 227–8.

Guntrip, H. (1975) My experience of analysis with Fairbairn and Winnicott. *Int Rev Psychoanal* 2: 145–56.

Green, A. (2000) The posthumous Winnicott: On human nature. In: Abram J, editor. *André Green at the Squiggle Foundation*. London: Karnac.

Hjulmand, K. (2007) D.W. Winnicott: Bibliography: Chronological and alphabetical lists. In: Abram, J. *The language of Winnicott: A dictionary of Winnicott's use of words* 363–435. 2nd edn. London: Karnac.

Holmes, R. (1985) *Footsteps: Adventures of a romantic biographer*. London: Hodder & Stoughton.

Holmes, R. (1992) Biographer's footsteps. *Int Rev Psychoanal* 19:1–8.

Hughes, A. ed. (1991) *Joan Riviere: The inner world and Joan Riviere*. London: Karnac.

Issroff, J. (2005) *Donald Winnicott and John Bowlby: Personal and professional perspectives*. London: Karnac.

James, M. (1962) Infantile narcissistic trauma: Observations on Winnicott's work in infant care and child development. *Int J Psychoanal* 43: 69–79.

Kahr, B. (1996) *DW Winnicott: A biographical portrait*. London: Karnac.

Kermode, F. (2004) Review: Clutching at insanity – Rodman F.R. *Winnicott: Life and work*. *London Rev Books* 26(5): 1–8.

Khan, M. (1975) Introduction. In: Winnicott D.W. *Through paediatrics to psycho-analysis*, xi–xviii. 2nd edn. London: Hogarth. (International Psychoanalytical Library, No. 100.)

King, P. (1972) Tribute to Donald Winnicott. *Bull Br Psychoanal Soc* 57: 26–8; 1214 *Int J Psychoanal* (2008) 89.

Layland, W.R. (1996) Review: Kahr B. D.W. Winnicott: A biographical portrait. *Int J Psychoanal* 77: 1269–71.

Little, M. (1985) Winnicott working in areas where psychotic anxieties predominate: A personal record. *Free Associations* 3: 9–42.

Neve, M. (1992) Clare Winnicott talks to Michael Neve. *Free Associations* 3: 167–84.

Ogden, T.H. (1985) The mother, the infant and the matrix: Interpretations of aspects of the work of Donald Winnicott. *Contemp Psychoanal* 21: 346–71.

Phillips, A. (1988) *Winnicott*. Cambridge, MA: Harvard UP.

Tuckett, D. (1996) Editorial introduction: My experience of analysis with Fairbairn and Winnicott. *Int J Psychoanal* 77: 739–40.

Wallbridge, D. and Davis, M. (1981) *Boundary and space: An introduction to the work of D.W. Winnicott*. New York: Brunner-Mazel.

Winnicott, C. (1978) D.W.W.: A reflection. In: Grolnink, S.A. and Barkin L., eds. *Between reality and fantasy: Transitional objects and phenomena*, 17–33. New York, NY: Aronson.

Young-Bruehl, E. (2003) Review: Winnicott: Life and work, Rodman F.R. *Int J Psychoanal* 84: 1661–5.

Further reading

Harry Karnac produced an invaluable compendium in 2007 – *After Winnicott: Compilation of works based on the life, writings, and ideas of D.W. Winnicott*.

Glossary

Most of the definitions for Winnicott's terminology can be found in Chapter 3 based on the second edition of *The Language of Winnicott: a dictionary of Winnicott's use of words* (Abram 2007). The following list includes concepts relevant to some of the chapters.

Anti-object
Aphanisis
Coenaesthesia
Death instinct
Fantasy/phantasy
Prelogical
Proprioceptive
Primary homosexuality
Primary process/secondary process
Surviving/non surviving objects

Anti-object (Chapter 7)

Green in Chapter 7 describes the anti-object in certain contexts as being the '. . . *counter-object*, antagonistic yet at the same time close to the object'. Denis (1988) expands this in pointing out that it is in the continuing interpretation of the transference in the session that the analyst becomes the anti-object. In other words the analyst attempts to reveal the various dimensions of the transference in his interpretations, showing himself to be the object of projection and not the object itself.

Reference

Denis, Paul (1988) 'L'avenir d'une désillusion: le contretransfert, destin du transfert' *Revue française de psychanalyse* 52(4), 829–842.

Aphanisis (Chapters 7 and 15)

Aphanisis is etymologically derived from the Greek word aphaneia meaning becoming invisible, particularly in an astronomical sense such as the disappearance of brilliance in a star. Laplanche and Pontalis (1973: 40) define it as the: 'disappearance of all sexual desire'.

The term was introduced by Ernest Jones in the context of his writings on female sexuality. Jones states that aphanisis is a common denominator in the sexuality of both sexes and constitutes a more profound fear than that of castration with which it is not identical.

In his 1927 paper 'Early Development of Female Sexuality' he writes: 'If we pursue to its roots the fundamental fear which lies at the basis of all neuroses we are driven, in my opinion, to the conclusion that what it really signifies is this aphanisis, the total, and of course permanent, extinction of the capacity (including opportunity) for sexual enjoyment.'

References

Jones, E. (1927) 'Early Development of Female Sexuality' in *Papers on Psycho-Analysis* (1950), London: Baillière, Tindall & Cox.
Laplanche, J. and Pontalis, J.B. (1973) *The Language of Psychoanalysis*; trans. Donald Nicholson-Smith, London: Hogarth; reprinted 1988, 2004, 2006, London: Karnac.

Coenaesthesia (Chapter 6)

The general feeling of inhabiting one's body that arises from multiple stimuli from various bodily organs.

Reference

www.encyclo.co.uk

Death instinct (Chapters 5, 12, 13, 14, 15)

Freud introduced the concept of the death instinct in 'Beyond the Pleasure Principle' in 1920, marking the final evolution in his formulation of a dual instinct theory. The earlier oppositions between ego instincts and sexual instincts, then between ego and object libido now gave way to this new dichotomy between life and death instincts. In part this theoretical development was prompted by his observations of clinical problems such as the compulsion to repeat, the negative therapeutic reaction and the problem of aggression and destructiveness.

According to Freud, the death instinct was concerned with the 'most universal endeavour of all living substance – namely to return to the quiescence of the inorganic world' (Freud: 1920). He further stated that the operation of the death instinct is usually silent and can only be rarely detected in its pure state when defusion from the life instinct has occurred, such as in melancholia. At the outset the death instincts are turned inwards, threatening self destruction and on being turned outwards they become evident, fused with the life instincts, as aggression and destructiveness.

Klein elaborated the concept of the death instinct in developing her ideas. She emphasized the presence of an innate destructive force in formulating her ideas regarding the early appearance of a harsh superego, the anxieties of the paranoid-schizoid position and the importance of envy.

The death instinct remains a controversial concept and many analysts, such as Winnicott, disagree with both Freud and Klein. Winnicott evolved his own theories of aggression, hatred and destructiveness.

References

Freud, S. (1920) *Beyond the Pleasure Principle*, SE 18: 3.

Hinshelwood, R.D. (1989) 'Death Instinct' in *A Dictionary of Kleinian Thought*, London: Free Association Books.

Laplanche, J. and Pontalis, J.B. (1973) *The Language of Psychoanalysis*; trans. Donald Nicholson-Smith, London: Hogarth; reprinted 1988, 2004, 2006, London: Karnac.

Fantasy/phantasy

According to the Oxford English Dictionary, the English word fantasy means: 'the faculty or activity of imagining impossible or improbable things', 'a fanciful mental image, typically one on which a person often dwells and which reflects their conscious or unconscious wishes' or 'an idea with no basis in reality'. It is a late Middle English word derived from the Old French 'fantasie', from the Latin 'phantasia' and is ultimately derived from the Greek 'imagination, appearance', later 'phantom', from phantazein. (Oxford English Dictionary on-line)

From a psychoanalytic perspective, Laplanche and Pontalis (1973: 314) offer the following definition:

> Imaginary scene in which the subject is a protagonist, representing the fulfilment of a wish (in the last analysis, an unconscious wish) in a manner that is distorted to a greater or lesser extent by defensive processes.

Susan Isaacs (1948), a close colleague of Melanie Klein, suggested that the distinction between conscious and unconscious modes of fantasy might be helpfully made by using the spelling 'fantasy' to designate the former, including daydreams, and the more archaic 'phantasy' to refer to the content of unconscious mental processes. A consensus has not been reached so that some confusion remains. Among psychoanalysts writing in English many British analysts employ this distinction but others, often from the US, do not. In the writings of Winnicott he does not make use of this distinction and always uses the spelling 'fantasy'. For example: see Chapter 1.

References

Isaacs, S. (1948) 'On the Nature and Function of Phantasy' *Int J of Psychoanal* 29: 73–97.
Laplanche, J. and Pontalis, J.B. (1973) *The Language of Psychoanalysis*; trans. Donald Nicholson-Smith, London: Hogarth; reprinted 1988, 2004, 2006, London: Karnac.

Prelogical (Chapter 6)

According to Maurice Green this is a term used by Charles Sanders Pierce to refer to the diffuse images and schemata emanating from the unconscious mind from which more logical thinking is later elaborated. Green (1961: 66) explains that he and co-author Edward Tauber adopted this concept in their book *Prelogical Experience. An Inquiry Into Dreams and Other Creative Processes* which was an inspiration to Marion Milner especially in her book *On Not Being Able to Paint* (1950).

References

Green, M. (1961) 'Prelogical experience in the thinking process' *Studies in Art Education* 3(1): 66–74.

Milner, M. (1950) *On Not Being Able to Paint*, London: Heinemann Educational Books.

Tauber, E. and Green, M. (1959) *Prelogical Experience. An Inquiry into Dreams and Other Creative Processes,* New York: Basic Books.

Proprioceptive (Chapter 6)

An adjective derived from the Latin proprius meaning 'own'. It is commonly used in scientific discourse to describe the reception of stimuli produced and perceived within the body especially those relating to the position and movement of the body. Milner considered that one could expand one's state of receptivity to the diverse sensations occurring within one's body linking this to an increased capacity for creative living and expression.

'It is the direct sensory (proprioceptive) internal awareness that I am concerned with; in fact, the actual 'now-ness' of the perception of one's body, and therefore of the perception of oneself.' Milner (1987: 263).

Reference

Milner, M. (1987) *The Suppressed Madness of Sane Men*, New Library of Psycho-analysis, London and New York: Tavistock Publications.

Primary homosexuality (Chapter 12)

Primary homosexuality is a concept introduced by Evelyne Kestemberg (1918–1989) who lived and worked in Paris. She was president of the Paris Psychoanlytical Society and editor of the *Revue Française de Psychanalyse*. While this term is well known in French psychoanalysis many exclusively English speaking and reading psychoanalysts may be less familiar with it. The Glossary of *Reading French Psychoanalysis* (781–2) tells us that the concept explains the passage from primary to secondary identification; that is: from '. . . being like the object to loving the object . . .'.

Thus a partial identification is made with the maternal object: '. . . in a first attempt at differentiation in terms of a "double" . . . .' The transition is thus between identification with an identical object and identification with an object that is similar but not identical. The 'double' is nevertheless, from the subject's point of view, also 'other'.

References

Birksted-Breen, D., Flanders, S. and Gibeault, A. (eds) 2010, *Reading French Psychoanalysis*, London: Routledge.

Denis, P. (2010) 'Primary homosexuality: A foundation of contradictions' in Birksted-Breen, D., Flanders, S. and Gibeault, A. (eds) 2010 *Reading French Psychoanalysis*, London: Routledge.

Kestemberg, E. (1984) '"Astrid" ou homosexualité, identité, adolescence. Quelques propositions hypothetiques' ['Astrid' or homosexuality, identity, adolescence. Some hypothetical propositions]. In *L'adolescence à vif* [Adolescence laid bare], Paris: Presses Universitaires de France, 1999.

Primary process/secondary process

The distinction between primary and secondary processes is one of the most fundamental concepts proposed by Freud and delineates two radically different modes of functioning of the psychic apparatus.

First, there is a topographical distinction. The primary process is characteristic of the system Unconscious (Ucs) whereas the secondary process is characteristic of the systems Pre-Conscious-Conscious (Pcs – Cs).

Second, there is an economic or dynamic distinction. In the primary process psychical energy is envisaged as freely mobile allowing for mechanisms such as displacement and condensation that are characteristic of both the dream work and symptom formation. The activity of the system is directed towards discharge of excitation that is experienced as satisfying. Primary processes are therefore associated with the Pleasure Principle.

The secondary process, in contrast, is associated with the Reality Principle. Psychical energy is bound and discharge is inhibited, diverted or delayed allowing for mental experiments, that is: rational thinking, to explore the best way to satisfaction.

Third, in the primary process the experience of satisfaction is found in the search for an 'identity of perception'. Using a 'hungry baby' as an illustration, Freud describes how satisfaction is obtained by the hallucination of an object perceptually identical to an object that is remembered as providing satisfaction before. Freud notes, however, that when hallucination fails to meet the persisting need it is necessary to find another solution by exploring other routes by which the perceptual identity is established in the external world. This requires the activity of the secondary process concerned with thought and reality testing. He adds, however, that: 'all this activity of thought merely constitutes a roundabout path to wish-fulfilment which has been made necessary by experience' (Freud 1900: 567).

References

Freud, S. (1900) *The Interpretation of Dreams*, in SE 5.
Laplanche, J. and Pontalis, J.B. (1973) *The Language of Psychoanalysis*; trans. Donald Nicholson-Smith, London: Hogarth; reprinted 1988, 2004, 2006, London: Karnac.

Surviving/non surviving objects (Chapter 14)

These terms are proposed extensions of Winnicott's theoretical advances in his late writings 1968–70 as seen especially in 'The use of an object'. Abram proposes that Winnicott's emphasis in the 'survival of the object' constitutes a clinical concept of aggression rooted in psychoanalytic methodology. This contrasts with Freud's 'speculative' concept of the death instinct with its roots in biology. She interprets that the clinical implications of 'survival of the object' indicate the notion of an intra-psychic surviving and non-surviving object. These intra-psychic objects arise through an admixture of the primary object's oscillations between psychic survival and non-survival of the newborn's needs/aggression. This leads her to conclude that the specific inter-psychic dynamic between object and subject at the heart of human development is naturally revivified in the transference-countertransference matrix. Consequently, the notion of psychic survival constitutes the specificity of clinical psychoanalysis as a therapeutic treatment.

Reference

Winnicott, D.W. (1969) 'The use of an object and relating through identifications' *Int J of Psychoanal* 50: 711–16.

Index